An Embassy to China

The Emperor Ch'ien-lung being carried in procession to the Imperial audience tent at Jehol on 14 September 1793

AN EMBASSY TO CHINA

*Being the journal kept by
Lord Macartney during his embassy
to the Emperor Ch'ien-lung
1793 - 1794*

Edited with an Introduction and Notes by
J. L. CRANMER-BYNG
Senior Lecturer in History at the University of Hong Kong

LONGMANS

Republished 1972
Scholarly Press, Inc., 22929 Industrial Drive East
St. Clair Shores, Michigan 48080

LONGMANS, GREEN AND CO LTD
48 Grosvenor Street, London W 1
Railway Crescent, Croydon, Victoria, Australia
Auckland, Kingston (Jamaica), Lahore, Nairobi

LONGMANS SOUTHERN AFRICA (PTY) LTD
Thibault House, Thibault Square, Cape Town
Johannesburg, Salisbury

LONGMANS OF NIGERIA LTD
W. R. Industrial Estate, Ikeja

LONGMANS OF GHANA LTD
Industrial Estate, Ring Road South, Accra

LONGMANS GREEN (FAR EAST) LTD
443 Lockhart Road, Hong Kong

LONGMANS OF MALAYA LTD
44 Jalan Ampang, Kuala Lumpur

ORIENT LONGMANS LTD
Calcutta, Bombay, Madras
Delhi, Hyderabad, Dacca

LONGMANS CANADA LTD
137 Bond Street, Toronto 2

© J. L. Cranmer-Byng 1962
First published 1962

Library of Congress Cataloging in Publication Data

Macartney, George Macartney, Earl, 1737-1806.
   An embassy to China.

   1. China--Description and travel. I. Title.
[DS708.M14 1972]   915.1   72-10117
ISBN 0-403-02250-9

Nothing could be more fallacious than to judge of China by any European standard.

Lord Macartney
(Journal, 15 January 1794)

CONTENTS

Preface	xi
Introduction	1
Lord Macartney's summary of the voyage from England to Cochin China	61
Lord Macartney's China Journal	63
Lord Macartney's Observations on China	221
Dr. Gillan's Observations on the state of Medicine, Surgery and Chemistry in China	279
Appendices:	
A Biographical Notes on some Personalities English and Chinese	307
B Note on the transmission of the manuscript of the Journal, with original table of contents	332
C An Edict from the Emperor Ch'ien-lung to King George the Third of England	336
D Annotated list of writings which contain first-hand material relating to the Macartney embassy	342
E List of embassies to China	353
Notes	355
Selected Chinese Characters	400
Index	401

ERRATA (Added in 1972) page 423

ILLUSTRATIONS

FRONTISPIECE

The frontispiece shows the Emperor Ch'ien-lung being carried in procession to the Imperial audience tent at Jehol on 14 September 1793.

From a colour-wash drawing by William Alexander made from a sketch taken on the spot by Lieut. Henry W. Parish. Alexander's drawing is preserved in the Department of Prints and Drawings in the British Museum. It measures approximately 16 × 24 inches.

IN THE TEXT

Elevation of a wheel used by the Chinese for raising water *page* 273

MAPS

Macartney's route from Tientsin to Jehol *page* 107

Macartney's route from Peking to Canton 157

NOTE ON DUST COVER

The picture on the cover is from a large Chinese tapestry-picture (*ko-ssu*) in the possession of the National Maritime Museum, and is on display at Flamsteed House in Greenwich Park. The tapestry shows a number of Europeans carrying heavy loads between bamboo poles. The poem inscribed at the top right-hand corner of the picture was written by the Emperor Ch'ien-lung to celebrate Lord Macartney's tribute embassy. The text can be found in the *Ta Ch'ing li-ch'ao shih-lu*, 1434, pp. 11a–b. Here follows a translation:

> 'The Emperor composed a poem recording the fact that the King of the red-haired English sent his envoy, Macartney, and others, who arrived bearing a state message and tribute.
> Formerly Portugal presented tribute;
> Now England is paying homage.
> They have out-travelled Shu-hai and Heng-chang;
> My Ancestors' merit and virtue must have reached their distant shores.
> Though their tribute is commonplace, my heart approves sincerely.
> Curios and the boasted ingenuity of their devices I prize not.
> Though what they bring is meagre, yet,
> In my kindness to men from afar I make generous return,
> Wanting to preserve my good health and power.'

The artist who composed the tapestry does not appear to have witnessed the actual scene at Jehol, because he has shown the Europeans wearing sixteenth-century dress. He may have copied illustrations of Europeans brought to China by the Jesuits early in the seventeenth century, or have seen impressions of Europeans made by Japanese artists at that time. As Dr. Joseph Needham has pointed out, the artist was ignorant of the nature of the astronomical instruments presented to the Emperor by Lord Macartney for he copied the celestial globe presented by the Jesuits to the Emperor K'ang-hsi in 1679 which can still be seen on the eastern wall of Peking where the old Observatory is situated. The presents were, in fact, carried by a large number of Chinese porters as described by Macartney in his Journal. The tapestry is approximately five feet long and three feet ten inches high. The colours are pale, the predominant ones being green, pink, brown, gold and blue.

PREFACE

ALTHOUGH Lord Macartney returned to England from his embassy to China in 1794, until now no full and satisfactory edition of his Journal has been available in print. Twice his biography has been attempted; in 1807 by John Barrow and in 1908 by Helen Robbins, and both authors reprinted inaccurately a substantial portion of his China Journal in their books. Thus, historians wishing to know what Macartney wrote in his Journal and unable to consult the original manuscript, had to rely on what Barrow or Mrs. Robbins gave them. The three manuscript volumes of the Journal were sold by the descendants of Lord Macartney in 1854, but remained in a private library in England until 1913 when they were sold to a private collector in Peking. Finally in 1917 they were again sold, and this time were taken to Tokyo where they eventually became part of a large Public Library. Even the whereabouts of these manuscript volumes has been known to only a very few scholars.*

My aim in editing Macartney's China Journal is to provide a full transcription of the text, together with adequate footnotes, and to identify, wherever possible, people and places mentioned in the text. The distinguished French sinologist, Henri Cordier, reviewing the life of Macartney by Helen Robbins in *T'oung Pao* took her to task for reproducing Chinese names as Macartney spelt them without attempting to identify them. He also showed that her footnotes left much to be desired and pointed out a number of elementary mistakes. It is clear that in order to help the reader to appreciate Macartney's Journal a considerable amount of editorial work is necessary. However, while keeping in mind the needs of the specialist, I have edited this Journal in such a way that I hope the general reader will be able to enjoy it. It would be a great pity if Macartney's lively narrative were to be so swamped by the apparatus of scholarship that the ordinary reader was repelled. However, the history of China under the Emperor Ch'ien-lung and the story of Anglo-Chinese relations during his long reign are subjects about which most people have only a hazy knowledge. Therefore the historical background to the embassy has been sketched in the Introduction. I should be very sorry, however, if the Introduction were to deter the reader

* For a detailed account of the transmission of the MSS of the Journal see pp. 332–4. For a note on the biographies of Lord Macartney by Barrow and by Helen Robbins see pp. 345–50.

PREFACE

from starting the actual Journal; it is meant to help and not to hinder.

The Tokyo manuscript of the Journal from which this book has been transcribed contains a number of appendices as well as the actual Journal. For the convenience of the reader the table of contents, as given in the Tokyo manuscript, has been printed on page 334, and those items reproduced in this book have been marked with an asterisk.

In transcribing Macartney's Journal I was tempted to retain the original spelling and punctuation in order to keep the proper eighteenth-century flavour. On the surface this seemed a good idea, but when I started to put it into practice the scheme became unworkable because the Journal is full of Chinese names, both of persons and places, which Macartney spells phonetically, as best he can, but some of his attempts to reproduce Chinese names are very queer. If these were all retained the editor would be forced to give a recognizable modern spelling in brackets, or to add a footnote each time which would clutter up the text. Moreover, Macartney does not keep to one spelling for each Chinese name; he varies them at whim. The effect of retaining his original spellings with continual explanations would be to make the text unreadable. Having decided to modernize the Chinese names and words it seemed illogical to retain the variations in Macartney's English spelling. People who kept journals and diaries in the eighteenth century, however educated they were, seldom adhered to any settled form of spelling. They spelt words by ear as fancy dictated at the moment. Macartney was no exception to this rule, and his orthography was haphazard and irregular. In such circumstances, unless the author is such a literary genius that it is important to preserve the exact details of his text down to the last variant spelling and the last comma, it is more merciful to the reader to reproduce the text in modern spelling and in a modernized punctuation. It may be objected that the author's punctuation, however peculiar, must be preferable to a modern editor's since it must give more closely the author's exact meaning. But punctuation, like spelling, was throughout the eighteenth century a highly personal matter and punctuation marks were scattered or omitted without any definite plan. In fact a reader today may often find eighteenth-century punctuation so irregular as to obscure the meaning. I have tried, therefore, to make the text read as easily as possible, and to make the meaning clear by a reasonable modernization of the punctuation. Also I have occasionally joined together paragraphs where Macartney seemed to have been over-liberal with their use in his Journal, in order to make it read less jerkily. Thus the text given here represents exactly what Macartney wrote; the words have not been altered, and a note has been made in the text of the few sentences omitted.* The only other liberty I have taken is to standardize the method of writing dates since Macartney uses several variations. The daily entries in the Journal are usually in the form of 'Saturday June 15th'; this I have amended to the form 'Saturday, June 15', as being easier to read at a glance.

When dealing with place names in the Journal I have given a recognizable modern spelling wherever there is no doubt as to which place Macartney is referring. Otherwise I have retained Macartney's spelling but have suggested in a footnote the place I think he is referring to. However, just to remind the reader that this is an eighteenth-century travel-book and not a modern one I have retained Macartney's spelling of 'Pekin' and 'Nankin'. For the benefit of specialists I have indicated in the Index Macartney's own spelling of most proper names by giving these in brackets after the modern version adopted. For reasons of convenience I have used the Wade-Giles system of romanizing Chinese characters throughout.

Immediately in front of the Index is printed a page of Chinese characters which I hope the sinologist will find sufficient for identifying the lesser-known Chinese names and works mentioned in the book. The numbers shown against these Chinese characters refer to the numbers printed immediately after the appropriate word in the Index. Thus in order to find the characters for Cheng-jui one only has to look for his name in the Index and find the key number after his name. However, where the characters of Chinese names can readily be found by reference to Hummel's *Eminent Chinese of the Ch'ing Period* I have not included them. Nor have I included the characters for Chinese titles which can be found in *Present Day Political Organization of China* by Brunnert and Hagelstrom. Diacritical marks have not normally been used in printing the romanized versions of Chinese names and words. The sinologist will refer to the Chinese characters themselves, while the ordinary reader would be none the wiser for their use.

The Index is fairly analytical, and I hope will be of use in bringing together scattered references to various people and topics. Thus, if the reader feels that the note on the missionary Grammont is too brief he may be able to find further information on Grammont by

* And see p. xvi.

PREFACE

using the Index, which will refer him to the Introduction, to several places in the Journal, and also to other notes.

One further word of explanation. Macartney's own footnotes have been reproduced throughout the Journal although they very often refer to material not included in this book, since it is felt that they may be of use to specialists who may wish to follow them up. The plans and drawings to which Macartney refers in the footnotes are probably those he sent to Sir George Staunton in December 1794 to be used by the latter in preparing the folio volume of illustrations which accompanied his 'authentic' account of the embassy, first published in 1797.* In my own notes, which are printed after the Observations, I have been at pains to take up topical references which would be familiar to Macartney's readers at the end of the eighteenth century but may be unfamiliar to the majority of present-day readers. Also I have given fairly full notes on most of Macartney's references to Chinese officials, institutions and places, since this information is not easily available. Thus the notes are designed for reference; to bring specific points into closer focus and to provide a fuller and richer background to Macartney's narrative. However, it would be a thousand pities if the notes were to distract attention from the Journal. May I suggest that it would be better to read the Journal as a whole before looking at the notes.

I wish to thank the Committee of the Tōyō Bunko, Tokyo, for permission to base the text of Macartney's Journal printed in this book on the manuscript Journal preserved in their Library. The Director of Libraries, Cornell University, for permission to quote from Macartney documents in the Wason Collection on China and the Chinese. The authorities of Duke University for permission to quote from the manuscript Journal of George Thomas Staunton. The Trustees of the British Museum for permission to quote from the manuscript Journal of William Alexander. The Editor of the *Journal of Oriental Studies* and the Hong Kong University Press for permission to quote from my own article on the Macartney embassy.

Also I wish to thank all those who have helped me in various ways by giving me the benefit of their special knowledge. In particular I wish to thank Mr. Akira Nagazumi, Librarian of the Tōyō Bunko, Tokyo; Miss G. E. Gaskill, Curator of the Wason Collection of books and manuscripts on China, Cornell University; Mr. Kenneth Darwin, Deputy Keeper, Public Record Office of Northern

* See pp. 350–1.

PREFACE

Ireland; Mr. Geoffrey Bonsall, Deputy Librarian of the University of Hong Kong; and Mr. A. N. L. Munby, Librarian of King's College, Cambridge, for the substantial help they have given me in my pursuit of Macartney documents. Mr. Kuo Ting-yee, Director of the Institute of Modern History, Academia Sinica, Taipei; Mr. V. T. Yang and Mr. Lo Hsiang-lin of the Department of Chinese, University of Hong Kong, for their generous help over problems relating to the Chinese side of the embassy. Dr. Joseph Needham, Sir William Dunn, Reader in Biochemistry in the University of Cambridge, for his valuable criticism of all references in the Journal to medicine, chemistry and scientific subjects in general; Professor Edmund Blunden, Professor of English in the University of Hong Kong, for first bringing to my attention the merits of Macartney's Journal, and for helping me to see it in relation to the literary background of that period; Mr. A. Shepherd, Lecturer in Geography, University of Hong Kong, for drawing the two sketch maps included in this book, and Mr. J. Macartney-Filgate, a collateral descendant of Lord Macartney, for information about the Macartney family.

In addition I wish to thank Sir Sydney Roberts, Master of Pembroke College, Cambridge; Mrs. Mildred Archer of the India Office Library; Mr. A. Grove, Curator of the Maidstone Museum; the Librarian and staff of the Wellcome Historical Medical Library; Dr. Laurence Picken; Dr. Nesca Robb and Dr. Barbara Rooke, who have all given me valuable help.

Finally, this list would not be complete without acknowledging the debt I owe my wife for her encouragement and help in copying, typing, correcting proofs and making the index, and to thank her for bearing cheerfully with my recurrent monologue on the Macartney embassy during the years in which this book was being prepared.

PASSAGES OMITTED FROM THE TEXT
THE JOURNAL

August 21. Macartney's calculations in a footnote to show how many men, wagons, etc., were employed to carry the presents, etc., from Tungchow to Peking.   p. 91

September 5. Dr. Gillan's opinion on whether the bricks of the Great Wall were fired in a kiln or not, and on the cause of their bluish colour.   p. 111

September 8. Abstract of the route from Peking to Jehol in the form of an itinerary giving names of villages and distances between them.   p. 116

OBSERVATIONS
(under POPULATION)

Footnote in which Macartney does a complicated sum to show that the populations of France and China were in a ratio of 24:37 at that time.   p. 246

INTRODUCTION

Introduction

Lord Macartney's embassy to China in 1793 was the first attempt by Britain to establish diplomatic contact with China. For almost a century English merchants had traded regularly at Canton, but although the East India Company, with all its prestige and wealth, controlled the English trade, its representatives at Canton were denied any direct access to the Chinese officials there. As merchants they were segregated and despised, and were forced to make their requests and complaints through an officially appointed body of Chinese merchants known as the Co-hong. In India, by the last decade of the eighteenth century, the East India Company administered as well as traded. Its members had power and prestige. But in Canton the Supercargoes* of the East India Company were regarded with suspicion as uncouth barbarian traders who must be kept firmly in their place by the scholar-officials of the Chinese empire.

Thus, when Macartney set out on his long voyage in the autumn of 1792 his chief object was to establish diplomatic relations with China. Having achieved this, his next task was to obtain a treaty of commerce and friendship between Britain and China in order to improve the conditions under which the English merchants traded at Canton, and if possible to open up new markets for British manufactures in northern China. Finally it was hoped that Macartney might be able to prepare the way for a representative of the King of England to reside permanently in Peking. But in seeking to establish diplomatic relations as if between two countries of equal status the government was instructing its ambassador to achieve the impossible. Other European nations had sent embassies to China in the past and their rulers had promptly been enrolled as 'tributary princes', and their ambassadors recorded as having performed the ceremonial kotow before the mighty Emperor of China. None had obtained any real concessions or established any conception of equal status. They had been treated on the same footing as other tribute-bearing countries such as Korea, the Liu-ch'iu islands, Burma and the various kingdoms of South-east Asia. No ambassador had succeeded in remaining more than a few months in Peking. The

* A person in a merchant ship appointed to take care of and sell the cargo.

INTRODUCTION

Russian embassies under Isbrand Ides in 1693 and Izmailov in 1720 had been more successful than those of the Portuguese and the Dutch. Russia, however, was a neighbouring country in contact with China on the river Amur, and ready to conduct the sort of caravan trade the Manchus understood. Yet even in the treaties which Peter the Great concluded with the Emperor K'ang-hsi the balance of advantage was decidedly in favour of China.*

To give a full account of Anglo-Chinese trade and relations at Canton in the century before Macartney's embassy in a short space would be impossible. In the summary which follows I have condensed heavily, and have been forced to leave out much detail since I do not wish to stand between reader and Journal any longer than is strictly necessary. The object of this book is to provide the complete text of Macartney's own Journal and to present it in such a way that anyone can take it up and read it for pleasure. Specialists who wish to make a fuller study of the pattern of Anglo-Chinese trade at Canton before the Macartney embassy can do so from the mass of extracts from the East India Company's papers published by H. B. Morse,† and from the excellent analysis of the whole subject by Earl H. Pritchard.‡ A more recent work by Michael Greenberg contains much information about the changing pattern of English trade at Canton from about 1784 onwards.§

SUMMARY OF ANGLO-CHINESE RELATIONS BEFORE THE MACARTNEY EMBASSY

At first sight it may seem strange that England sent no embassy to China until 1792. But the fact is that English trade with China was not firmly established until the beginning of the eighteenth century, and even then the Government left its management to the East India Company and showed little interest in the China trade until

---

* Among the papers attached to the manuscript of Macartney's Journal is a list of previous European embassies to China showing the length of their stay at the capital. Printed as Appendix E. For a modern list of embassies and a select bibliography on the subject see J. K. Fairbank and S. Y. Teng, *Ch'ing Administration: Three Studies* (Harvard University Press, 1960), pp. 160–1. (Page numbers quoted refer to foot of each page.)

† *The Chronicles of the East India Company Trading to China, 1635–1834*, 5 vols. (Oxford University Press, 1926–9).

‡ *The Crucial Years of Early Anglo-Chinese Relations, 1750–1800*, Research Studies of the State College of Washington, Vol. IV, Nos. 3–4 (Pullman, Washington, 1936).

§ *British Trade and the Opening of China, 1800–42* (Cambridge University Press, 1951).

after 1784, while the Company, noting the scant success of the previous foreign embassies, hesitated to press the Government to dispatch one. As far back as Charles II's reign a taste for tea-drinking had been developing in England, but at first the price was extremely high since it had to be re-imported from the Dutch. There was, therefore, every incentive to bring it direct from China in English ships.* As a result, between 1660 and 1700 various attempts were made to establish a factory† at Canton, and even on Formosa, and at Amoy in Fukien. But because of uncertain conditions in China itself, where the alien Manchus had recently overthrown the native Ming dynasty, the attitude of the Emperor and the local officials towards foreign trade was changeable. Nevertheless, by 1710 English merchants were trading regularly at Canton, although attempts to extend the trade to Chusan‡ and Amoy had been frustrated.

From the Chinese point of view it was never intended that foreign merchants should come to Chinese ports where and when they chose. Foreign trade was never recognized as a natural right which Chinese and foreign merchants might enjoy freely. It is worth trying to understand how this attitude grew up, because it contains the explanation to much that is puzzling in Sino-Western relations during the last two hundred and fifty years. Professor Fairbank, in a most illuminating article,§ has shown how foreign trade in China was tolerated but only under the guise of tribute. Any relations which existed between China and a foreign country must be of the suzerain-vassal kind, and permission to trade was granted as a gracious concession, not as a natural right. The origins of this theory go back into the distant past.

From earliest times China had been surrounded by barbarian peoples whose culture was clearly inferior. At no time did the Chinese come into direct contact with an equal civilization; countries on China's flanks such as Korea, Japan, Annam and Siam were strongly influenced by the culture of the 'Middle Kingdom'. From their previous contact with the barbarians around them the Chinese were conscious that their own superiority was not one merely of material power but of culture as well. So outstanding was the culture of the Middle Kingdom that the barbarians in contact with China

* See Morse, *Chronicles*, I, p. 9.
† A merchant company's foreign station where its 'factors' or agents lived.
‡ An island off Ningpo, on the coast of central China.
§ 'Tributary Trade and China's Relations with the West', *Far Eastern Quarterly*, I, No. 2 (1942).

turned towards her for their culture, thus supporting the Chinese conviction of superiority. 'After centuries of solitary grandeur as the centre of Eastern Asia, the Chinese developed what may be called, by analogy to nationalism, a spirit of "culturalism". Those who did not follow the Chinese way were *ipso facto* inferior....'.

According to Confucian teaching there was a certain power in right conduct which could influence others. The Emperor, because of his virtue, would irresistibly attract the barbarians outside the pale of Chinese civilization. The relationship between Emperor and barbarians symbolized the actual relationship between China and the countries round her. This relationship formed the theoretical basis for the tributary system, and it was taken for granted that the uncultured barbarian would recognize the superiority of Chinese civilization and would be so attracted to China that he would 'come and be transformed' and so partake in the benefits of the Empire. In return it was the function of the Emperor to be compassionate in his 'tender cherishing of men from afar'. These two phrases occur in all documents dealing with foreign relations, and were repeated more than once in the Chinese documents of the Macartney embassy,* and also in the documents of the Dutch embassy of 1794–5. In short, the Emperor showed compassion to 'men from afar', while the barbarian envoy showed his humble submission according to the prescribed Court ritual, part of which consisted of performing the full kotow. This involved three separate kneelings, each one followed by a full prostration with the forehead knocking the ground three times. The ceremony was performed to the shrill commands of an usher— 'Kneel, fall prostrate, rise to your knees', and so on. This rite was performed not once but many times during a short embassy, and left no doubt in the mind of the envoy as to who was the superior and who the inferior.† The tribute which barbarian countries sent was traditionally supposed to consist of native produce, the value of which in Chinese eyes was small and in no way commensurate to the valuable gifts bestowed on the vassal ruler and the members of his mission. 'The formalities of the tributary system constituted a mechanism by which formerly barbarous regions outside the Empire were given their place in the all-embracing Sinocentric

---

* See J. L. Cranmer-Byng, 'Lord Macartney's Embassy to Peking in 1793, from Official Chinese Documents', *Journal of Oriental Studies*, IV, 1 and 2, 1957–8 (Hong Kong, 1961).

† As an example of the many occasions on which it could be performed see J. J. L. Duyvendak, 'The Last Dutch Embassy to the Chinese Court (1794–5)', *T'oung Pao*, XXXIV (1938).

cosmos.' Thus, when the Europeans came to China this system was automatically applied to them.*

Throughout the reign of the Emperor Ch'ien-lung (1736–96), and indeed for forty years after, the geographical knowledge of even the greatest officials in China was extremely hazy and no clear differentiation was made between Britain and the other countries of Europe. They were all jumbled together somewhere in the 'Western Ocean'. In dealing with these Western Ocean barbarians everything must be carried out in accordance with the regulations dealing with tribute envoys, and these were recorded in the *Collected Statutes* of the Ch'ing dynasty (*Ta Ch'ing Hui-tien*). Thus in the 1764 edition of the *Collected Statutes* which were in effect when the Macartney embassy came to China, the regulations state: 'For a tribute envoy's entrance of the frontier and the tribute route which he follows, in each case there are fixed places. Not to follow the regular route, or to go over into other provinces, is forbidden.' In another section it stipulates: 'As to trade,—when the tribute envoys of the various countries enter the frontier, the goods brought along in their boats or carts may be exchanged in trade with merchants of the interior . . .'. A little later the regulations deal with 'barbarian merchants who themselves bring their goods into the country for trade', and state: 'For the countries beyond the seas, [the market] is at the provincial capital of Kwangtung. Every summer they take advantage of the tide and come to the provincial capital [Canton]. When winter comes they wait for a wind and return to their countries. All pay duties to the [local] officers in charge, the same as the merchants of the interior [China].'† Thus European merchants might come to Canton, but nowhere else, and here they would be regarded as subject to the laws of the Chinese empire, and be liable to customs duties (and 'squeeze') in the same way as the Chinese merchants. Also at Canton they were as far away from the capital as possible,‡ and were entirely under the control of the local officials who were expected to regulate foreign trade without reference to the Court except when peace was endangered.

---

* The two preceding paragraphs have been condensed from Professor Fairbank's article cited above, pp. 129–34. The footnotes are my own.

† Translated by Fairbank and Teng in *Ch'ing Administration*, op. cit., p. 144. In fact the Europeans came to Canton in the autumn and departed in the spring. The reason for this was that the sailing ships made use of the favourable monsoon winds which in autumn carried them steadily northwards and in the late winter carried them south again.

‡ Perhaps as far as 1,500 miles.

INTRODUCTION

At the head of the local administration was the Governor-General (Viceroy) who had charge of the two provinces of Kwangtung and Kwangsi, and was a very high official. Working in association with him was the Governor of Kwangtung with his headquarters at Canton. Under him were a number of Prefects and Magistrates, and under them various lesser officials. But independent of these two great Mandarins stood the Superintendent of Maritime Customs for Kwangtung who was the Emperor's financial representative at Canton. He was known to the English merchants as the Hoppo, this being a corruption of the Chinese name of the department of government at the capital under which he served, the *hu-pu* (Board of Revenue). The Hoppo caused the foreign merchants at Canton continual trouble by his rapacity and high-handed actions. He was usually appointed for a term of about three years, having first paid a large sum at Court for this privilege. During his term of office he would have to remit considerable sums of money to the Imperial Treasury, to say nothing of magnificent 'presents' to the highest officials at Court; yet during his short period of office as Hoppo he usually managed to amass a fortune for himself. This he did out of foreign trade.* From the outset a host of minor functionaries had also taken their share of the spoils. For instance there were the licensed pilots who guided the ships up the Pearl river to Canton, which lies about fifty miles inland from the sea. Then there were the linguists who were supposed to act as interpreters, but in fact were low-grade clerks who spoke a smattering of pidgin English, and the compradores who supplied the ships and factories with provisions. The services of these and other minions of the officials were compulsory. To all these, officials and minor functionaries alike, the foreign trade at Canton was a source of self-enrichment. The Supercargoes of the East India Company did what they could to protest at all new or increased dues and taxes. Coming from another part of the world where trade was usually by mutual consent for mutual profit they were constantly vexed by what seemed to them a capricious system which was controlled directly by the local officials. In India the Company's servants had grown accustomed to appeal direct to rulers over the heads of their deputies, or better still to play off one ruler against another. But in Canton the Emperor's great officials were all-powerful.

In the Confucian scheme of things, merchants, however wealthy, were a despised class, and trade a profession of low repute. The

---

* For an amusing confirmation of this see Macartney's *Journal* under October 7.

8

scholar-officials would not demean themselves by dealing in person with the barbarian merchants, but instead appointed Chinese merchants to trade with them and also to act as intermediaries. This was one of the main grievances of the foreign merchants at Canton, that they were not allowed to trade with whom they wished but only with a small number of licensed merchants. These were known as Hong merchants, the word *hong* meaning a firm. To be appointed a Hong merchant was not necessarily a valued privilege, and quite often Chinese merchants were forced to do so against their will. This was understandable because the Hong merchants were at the mercy of the Mandarins who exploited the lucrative foreign trade by squeezing them. The Supercargoes protested against a system which they disliked, but they were in a weak position. They could not appeal to the Emperor direct. The regulations stated: '. . . when a foreign country has something to state or request . . . in the provinces it may be memorialized on behalf (of the country) by the Governor-General and Governor concerned. Direct communication to the Court is forbidden'.* In any case, Peking was very far away, and the Supercargoes could neither write nor read Chinese. It was forbidden by law to teach foreigners the Chinese language; at the same time foreigners were forbidden 'to collect or buy works of Chinese history'. Thus Europeans at Canton were at the mercy of the local officials, whom they had to address through the Hong merchants, while the Hongists were naturally timid and easily coerced by authority. The Supercargoes could not even rely on the backing of the English Government if they wished to make a serious stand against the Canton system of trade. The copious extracts presented by Morse from the Company's Canton records give a vivid idea of their complaints against this system and the methods by which they tried to circumvent it.

Between 1700 and 1750 the Canton system was still evolving, and was still somewhat flexible, but the tendency was for the local officials continually to tighten their control over the foreign merchants and to impose heavier taxes and duties on them. For instance, by 1740 each foreign ship trading to Canton had to get a Hong merchant to stand security for the good behaviour of its crew and for the payment of Imperial dues on the ship's cargo. This gave the local officials even greater control over foreign trade and put the foreigner under a special obligation to one particular Hong

---

* Translated from the 1764 edition of the *Collected Statutes* by Fairbank and Teng, op. cit., p. 144.

INTRODUCTION

merchant. Meanwhile, by the middle of the eighteenth century the demand for Chinese goods in Europe had increased considerably; for silk, porcelain, lacquer-ware and other luxuries, and especially for tea. Furthermore, between about 1745 and 1775 there was a noticeable vogue in England for Chinese taste and culture. To give but one example, it was during this period that Sir William Chambers published his two books, *Designs of Chinese Buildings . . . etc.* (1757) and *A Dissertation on Oriental Gardening* (1772). But it was also during this period that conditions of trade at Canton became far more onerous, and the East India Company cast about for some means of easing them. In fact between 1750 and 1760 the whole system of trade was formally legalized by the Chinese authorities and became set in a rigid form. The immediate reason for this can be traced to disturbances in Canton at that time. The foreign seamen who came to that port were a rough lot, easily inflamed by the local drink which the Chinese shopkeepers were only too ready to sell them. As one Company report stated: 'The fact is that the Chinese shopkeepers in Hog Lane fill them with Samsu, a liquor more pernicious than Pariar Arrack, and when they are stupified they rob them of what money they have about them.'* As a result a Chinese shopkeeper might be injured by drunken sailors or the seamen of another European country be wounded in a brawl. Now the great object of the Manchu Government was to maintain peace throughout the Empire, while the particular duty of the Canton officials was to ensure the orderly behaviour of all foreigners in that city. Although Canton was far distant from Peking, nevertheless the officials there went in awe of the Emperor Ch'ien-lung and were constantly in fear of losing a rank or two in the official hierarchy. There may also have been deeper reasons for this hardening attitude towards foreigners which we can only guess at.

To begin with, the number of foreigners arriving at Canton to trade each season had increased considerably. Eventually foreign trade might become a dangerous weapon which the 'sea-barbarians' could use, first in order to gain access to the Empire, then to join with dissident Chinese within, and finally in order to overthrow the dynasty itself. Moreover, at this time, Ch'ien-lung was waging successful but long and costly campaigns against various Mongol tribes on China's Inner Asian frontiers. However, the Manchus had no

---

* Extract from a letter from the Secret and Superintending Committee of the East India Company dated Canton 25 November, 1792, now in the Wason Collection of Macartney documents, Cornell University. (Document No. 319.)

ANGLO-CHINESE RELATIONS

effective navy, so that the sea approaches were dangerously exposed, while from time to time there were risings against the Manchu régime within China itself. The problem which faced Ch'ien-lung and his ministers was to devise a system which would bring rich revenues into the Imperial treasury and at the same time keep the troublesome barbarians under firm control. It was not a question of increasing exports and imports, but of exploiting the barbarian demand for Chinese tea and luxuries. Again, European expansion in India and South-east Asia was not unknown to the Chinese at this time, though they may not have distinguished clearly between one foreign country and another. All Europeans were looked upon as quarrelsome and violent. Finally there was no satisfactory legal system for dealing with foreigners in China. The traditional Chinese principle of collective responsibility was extended to Europeans and 'the headman' of each nation was made responsible for ensuring that all men from his country conformed to Chinese law, while the Hong merchants were held responsible for the good conduct of foreigners generally. Furthermore, this principle held good in cases of homicide. Thus if a Chinese was killed in Canton, a ship or factory would be held responsible until someone, either the guilty person *or someone else*, was handed over for punishment. Consequently a few innocent Europeans had been strangled by order of the Canton magistrates. This caused further friction between the Western Ocean barbarians and the authorities. As a result of these various causes the Governor-General, in conjunction with the Hoppo, issued edicts in 1755 confirming the mass of restrictions which had grown up during the previous fifty years. These were solemnly and officially confirmed by an Imperial edict in 1760.

It was at this period that the idea of asking the Government in England to send an embassy to the Emperor of China was first put forward. One of the Supercargoes, Frederick Pigou, returned to England in 1754, and in a long letter to the Court of Directors made various suggestions for improving the conduct of the Company's business at Canton, and also proposed that an embassy should be sent in 1761 to congratulate the Emperor on the seventieth birthday of his mother, and that while so doing the ambassador should seek redress for the grievances of the Supercargoes. At the same time Pigou made a number of useful suggestions as to how the embassy should be conducted, some of which were later acted upon. However, at this time the Court of Directors decided not to send an embassy, and simply instructed the Supercargoes to renew their

INTRODUCTION

protests to the Governor-General, which they did, but without avail. Thus by 1760 the system was so firmly laid down that there was little chance of its being altered except by Imperial decree. The Supercargoes consoled themselves with the belief that if the Emperor knew of their grievances he would forthwith remedy them. In the same year that the Imperial edict was received confirming the whole system (1760), the Hong merchants formed themselves into an association—the Co-hong. Whether this was a spontaneous action or prompted by the local officials is not clear. The Co-hong was not really a monopolist body on the pattern of the East India Company, since each merchant still traded on his own account with his own capital, and the Co-hong rarely followed a policy of corporate bargaining. The main point is that the Co-hong members acted together under pressure from the local officials to ensure control over the foreign merchants. Their number was limited to twelve, although very often there were fewer, and this restricted the Supercargoes in their business. Moreover the Supercargoes were constantly afraid that the Co-hong would be used by the Canton officials as an even more efficient tool for 'squeezing' the foreign merchants. Its members were exposed to the greed and extortions of the local officials, especially the Hoppo and his crew, and bankruptcies were frequent.

Thus, after a half-century of trial and experiment, the Canton system had become stereotyped. From the point of view of the Emperor and his advisers it was almost perfect. China did not need the products of the Western Ocean barbarians; her economy based on agriculture, fishing and local handicrafts was self-sufficient.* The foreign trade at Canton was in luxuries. Furs and clockwork automata ('sing-songs') were pleasant to possess but not essential; nor were the woollens which the English were so anxious to sell in larger quantities. Yet the Emperor and his officials were not willing to stop the trade at Canton; it was too valuable to the Imperial treasury, and too many high Mandarins were able to use it for self-enrichment, or for obtaining cheaply splendid gifts to present to the Emperor and his favourite ministers and thus ensure future promotion. The Co-hong was a useful instrument for exacting the utmost from the foreigners. Canton was a large seaport as far away from the capital as possible. Here the local officials were firmly saddled with the duty of keeping the unpredictable foreigners under

---

* However, by the end of the eighteenth century there is some possibility that tin might be considered a necessity. See Gillan's remarks on page 296.

control. Some idea of recent European expansion in Asia, particularly in India, had reached the Emperor and his ministers. There must be no possibility of such a thing happening in China; hence the one-sided and exclusive methods of the Chinese. 'The Westerners who came in ships were "sea-barbarians"; their way of life was even more alien and disturbing to Chinese civilization than that of the northern barbarians. A Great Wall had to be erected against the invaders who came by sea.'* Thus foreign merchants might come to Canton each year to trade but only under strict regulations. They might stay in Canton only during the trading season, which was from about October until March; they might not possess property but only rent warehouses from the Hong merchants, and they had to obey various irksome restrictions designed to keep the foreign merchant under strict control.†

From the point of view of the Supercargoes the system as it now existed was well-nigh intolerable. They were at the mercy of the whims of the local officials, who could prevent them from complaining to the Emperor. They knew that the export of tea from China had expanded greatly, yet the sale of English manufactures in China had not increased in proportion. The potential market for English goods could not be exploited because of Chinese exclusiveness. They also knew that the people of Canton were of a 'trafficking nature' and willing enough to do business, but were not free agents. Sometimes conditions were so vexatious that they wondered if it would not be better to withdraw from China altogether. But there was always the spectre of trade rivals, the French and the Dutch, taking their place meanwhile and even expanding the trade. On the whole, since profits were still good it was better to stick it out,‡ to put up with uncertainty and humiliation, and to hope for better conditions in the future. But it was not trade as merchants in the rest of the world understood the term. It was too precarious and one-sided.

Furthermore, from about 1770 onwards the pattern of trade at Canton slowly became more complex because of the arrival of private merchants in the 'Country trade'. This term is usually applied to the trade which had grown up between India, South-east

---

* Greenberg, op. cit., p. 45.
† For a summary of the so-called 'eight regulations' which were restrictions of a personal kind, see Greenberg, op. cit., p. 58, and Pritchard, op. cit., pp. 133–4.
‡ Pritchard, op. cit., pp. 168–9, has worked out that during the period 1775–85 the East India Company made an average profit of 29 per cent per annum, while in the period 1785–95 they made an average profit of 21 per cent per annum on their Canton trade.

INTRODUCTION

Asia and China. The East India Company took part in this trade indirectly when it granted private merchants in India (both Indians and English residents) licences to trade at Canton. By the last quarter of the eighteenth century China was taking from India an increasing quantity of valuable goods such as cotton and opium, while in return she sent to India only goods of low value such as raw silk. On the other hand, ever since it had traded at Canton, the East India Company had been unable to sell sufficient goods to finance its large purchases of tea, and as a result had been forced to send great quantities of silver dollars to China to pay for its yearly purchases. The Company itself did not deal in opium, which was illegal in China, but gladly left this to the Country merchants trading under its licence.* They in turn found little trouble in smuggling opium into China from anchorages near Canton with the connivance of the local officials. Thus the growing value of the Country trade could be used to finance the traditional Company trade and so 'the resources of India were utilized to finance the purchase of China tea for England'.†

Meanwhile the Hong merchants themselves were trading under increasingly difficult conditions. On the one hand they had to bear the heavy exactions imposed on them by the local officials in the form of 'presents'. On the other hand they had to satisfy the English East India Company which now did considerably more trade at Canton than its other European rivals. The staple of the Company's trade was tea. In order to ensure good contracts for the valuable tea sales the Hong merchants had to agree to take certain quantities of English manufactures which they often sold at a loss. The volume of foreign trade had now increased considerably but the few Hong merchants who were allowed to take part in this trade were handicapped by their lack of liquid capital. Even the richest of them usually had a large part of their wealth tied up in land. As a result the Hong merchants began to borrow money at a high rate of interest from those Country traders who had been permitted by the Company to come to Canton. The Hong merchants from time to time ran up large debts as a result of an accumulation of loans at compound interest. This is an over-simplified explanation of a complex subject which is discussed fully in the study by Michael Greenberg already mentioned.‡ His conclusions are worth repeating. 'This

---

* For the opium trade see below, pp. 51–2.

† For details of how this worked see Greenberg, op. cit., pp. 11–13. This is an excellent study based primarily on an examination of the papers of the firm of Jardine, Matheson and Co.

‡ Op. cit., pp. 61–74. See also Pritchard, op. cit., pp. 199–212.

high rate of interest was, of course, an expression of the inchoate state of capital accumulation in China (as in medieval Europe), which was the fundamental reason why the Cohong could not cope with the expansion of British trade.' As a result a number of Hong merchants went bankrupt and were punished by the local officials under the harsh laws dealing with bankruptcy. The position in 1777 was so bad that only four of the Co-hong merchants could be depended on for business. The Country traders generally found it difficult to recover the interest on their loans, because the borrowing of money was prohibited by Chinese law and therefore they could expect little help from the Canton officials. As a result they appealed to the British Government to obtain redress for what they considered were their wrongs, and eventually their complaints fell on receptive ears. In 1784 William Pitt, acting in the spirit of Adam Smith's teaching,* introduced the Commutation Act by which duties on tea imported into England were reduced from over 100 per cent to $12\frac{1}{2}$ per cent. Before the passing of this act tea was being smuggled into England on a large scale. By reducing the cost of tea very considerably Pitt hoped to increase the Government revenue by greater legal sales. But if the price of tea in England was to remain reasonable it was necessary that conditions of trade at Canton should remain stable, and that no further increases should be made in the amount of duties, taxes and presents levied. Thus Pitt himself, as head of the Ministry, had good reason for considering an embassy. Furthermore it was about this time that the industrialists in England began to look round for wider markets for their growing volume of manufactures. Also there was still the fear that competition from France and Holland in the Canton trade might harm England. Finally, the East India Company, tired of the constant conflict between its Supercargoes and the Chinese officials at Canton, began to realize that perhaps the only way in which conditions might be improved was through an ambassador from Britain who could represent their case direct to the Emperor and his Court at Peking. In the year 1784 Pitt set up the Board of Control as an organ of government to deal with the affairs of the East India Company and of Britain in the East generally. Henry Dundas,† a boon companion

* *The Wealth of Nations* was first published in 1776.
† First Viscount Melville (1742–1811). Born into a legal and landed Scottish family. M.P. for Midlothian 1774. Chairman of Committee to report on state of British possessions in India 1781. Member of Board of Control from 1784, and President from 1793. Home Secretary 1791–4, Secretary for War 1794–1801. Macartney addressed his dispatches from China to Dundas who was then Home Secretary.

INTRODUCTION

of Pitt, especially over the port, was a member of this Board of Control. Dundas was regarded as the Government's authority on Eastern affairs, and since he himself was anxious to enlarge the trade both of England and India with China, all the conditions now existed for sending an embassy to the Emperor Ch'ien-lung.

In 1783 a Country trader put forward a plan to Dundas for improving English trade with China. He used the old but fallacious argument that if only the Emperor knew what was happening at Canton justice would be done to the foreign traders, and he proposed that an embassy should be sent to Peking at the expense of the East India Company. The possibility of expanding British exports to China, especially woollens, appealed to Dundas, and eventually in 1787 Lieutenant-Colonel Charles Cathcart* was appointed ambassador to China. Being a fellow Scot Dundas gave him preference over other candidates, but unfortunately at the time of his appointment he was in an advanced state of consumption. After elaborate preparations had been made, detailed instructions given, and valuable presents packed, the ambassador sailed from England aboard a frigate, only to die at sea on 10 June 1788 in the Straits of Banka, off Sumatra. Why Dundas failed to appoint a successor to take charge of the mission should the ambassador die on the outward voyage has never been explained. Why he appointed such a sick man in the first place also needs explaining. As a result the embassy returned to England and the idea was held in abeyance for a time. In 1791 Dundas was made Home Secretary, but retained his seat on the Board of Control. He now set about promoting another embassy to China, and considered the possibility not only of expanding British trade in China but of introducing it into Cochin China, Japan and Korea as well.† There was even an idea at this time of attempting to reach China through Tibet and so opening up a channel of communication between Calcutta and Peking and thus by-passing Canton.‡ Pitt supported this new project, and it so happened that there was available at the time a very able and experienced diplomat whom Dundas trusted—Lord Macartney. Preparations were therefore put in hand,

* Charles Allan Cathcart (1759–88). Born of an old and distinguished Scottish family. Second son of the ninth Baron Cathcart, who had been Ambassador to Russia 1768–71. He followed a military career, being promoted Quartermaster-General to the Bengal Army at an early age. M.P. for Co. Clackmannan from 1784.

† For these wider objects of the embassy see Alastair Lamb, 'Lord Macartney in Batavia, March 1793', *Journal of the South Seas Society* (Singapore), Vol. XIV (December 1958), pp. 57–68.

‡ See Alastair Lamb, *Britain and Chinese Central Asia* (Routledge and Kegan Paul, 1960), pp. 20–2.

and the experience gained in preparing the abortive Cathcart mission was of value in making the arrangements for the Macartney embassy. However, it was considered advisable to increase the size of the ambassador's suite, and the magnificence of the presents, and to send it out in a larger naval vessel.* Meanwhile it is time to introduce Lord Macartney without further preliminaries.

LORD MACARTNEY

George Macartney was born at Lissanoure Castle, overlooking Lough Guile in County Antrim, Northern Ireland, in 1737.† He attended a local school until he was thirteen, and was then admitted to Trinity College, Dublin, from which he graduated M.A. in 1759. Oliver Goldsmith and Edmund Burke had been students at Trinity College a few years previously, and when Macartney came to London after graduating he was soon on friendly terms with both Edmund and William Burke. He began by studying law, but soon gave it up and set out on the Grand Tour. While in Geneva he met Voltaire and spent several days as a guest at Ferney. Also while on his travels he made the acquaintance of Stephen Fox, son of Lord Holland and elder brother of Charles James Fox. On his return to England Macartney became a member of the Holland House set, and this may have decided him to seek a political career. Through Lord Holland he was introduced to Lord Sandwich who also became a friend and patron. It was also at this time that he met Sir Joshua Reynolds who painted the portrait of him, probably in 1764, which hangs today in Petworth House.

Macartney was just about to enter Parliament under Lord Holland's patronage when an opening occurred as envoy-extraordinary to the Court of Catherine the Great at St. Petersburg. At this time England was attempting to obtain a treaty of alliance with Russia in an effort to end English isolation in Europe and to strengthen herself against France, but the previous ambassador had failed to obtain such a treaty. Sandwich was now Secretary of State and it was due to his patronage that Macartney was appointed envoy to Russia, at the age of twenty-seven. He was knighted by the King before leaving England in 1764. After long and difficult negotiations Macartney succeeded in obtaining a treaty of commerce with Russia but failed to obtain the alliance which the Government desired. Russia

---

* For a detailed account of the preparations see Pritchard, op. cit., pp. 272–311.
† For details of his family history see Helen H. Robbins, *Our First Ambassador to China* (John Murray, 1908).

would only sign such an alliance if Britain would support her against the Ottoman Turks and give her subsidies. This the Government refused to do, and so the alliance fell through, though not because of any negligence on the part of Sir George Macartney. He returned to England in 1767 having proved himself a resourceful envoy with a flair for diplomacy. On his return from Russia he wrote an account of that country describing its character, history, government, commerce, and so forth.* In the introduction to this work he wrote: 'A knowledge of the history, manners, trade, power and policy of every nation with which Great Britain stands in any degree connected is of general use; but united as we now are with Russia by ties of friendship, commerce, and mutual advantage, even the minutest circumstances that relate to her, become particularly interesting and important.' Macartney had already started the habit of recording his observations while in posts abroad which was to culminate in his China Journal.

Soon after his return to England Macartney married Lady Jane Stuart, second daughter of Lord Bute, who, although now out of politics, still had some influence with the King. The marriage produced no children and does not seem to have been a warmly affectionate one, perhaps because Lady Jane was somewhat 'religious' and conventional in her views while Macartney was inclined to be somewhat sceptical. His main characteristic throughout his life was a powerful ambition to succeed in his career. Certainly they spent much of their time apart, Jane with her family whom she adored, and Macartney abroad. As a result of his three years at St. Petersburg Macartney was in debt and it was important that he should quickly secure some public appointment. At the beginning of 1769 he was made Chief Secretary for Ireland, a post which he held for the next three years, and on its termination was made a Knight Companion of the Bath. In 1775 he was appointed Captain-general and Governor of Grenada, the Grenadines and Tobago, and was raised to the Irish peerage with the title of Baron Macartney of Lissanoure. He reached Grenada in 1776, but in 1779 suffered the humiliation of having to surrender the island to Count d'Estaing who was in command of a French fleet which was attacking British possessions and ships in the West Indies in support of the American Colonists in their revolt

---

* *An Account of Russia, 1767*, printed for private circulation in 1768. See F. W. Reddaway, 'Macartney in Russia, 1765–1767', *Cambridge Historical Journal*, III (1931), pp. 260–94.

against England. Macartney was sent to Paris where he spent a short time as a prisoner-of-war before being exchanged.

It was about this time that Macartney first became a member of Dr. Johnson's circle. In a letter to Mrs. Thrale dated 11 November 1779 Johnson mentioned meeting him, as though for the first time.

> Yesterday I dined at Mr. Vesey's with Lord Lucan and Mr. Pepys. After dinner came in Lady Lucan and her three daughters, who seem all pretty people. In the evening there was Lord Macartney who had been taken by D'Estainge in America, and stripped by him almost naked. D'Estainge took from him [his] Lady's picture because I suppose it was set with stones. He is here now upon parole. He seems in some degree a literary man.*

Macartney was elected a member of The Club in May 1786 and it is known that he attended at least one meeting. Boswell, writing to Edmond Malone on 10 February 1791, mentioned that 'on Tuesday we had a Club of eleven. Lords Lucan (in the chair), Ossory, Macartney, Eliot, Bishop of Clonfert, young Burke, myself, Courtenay, Windham, Sir Joshua, and Charles Fox.'

A list of books in Macartney's library drawn up in 1786 shows that he possessed Johnson's *Political Tracts* (1776), *Lives of the Poets* (1779–81), and three volumes of his *Fugitive Pieces*. Furthermore, he possessed a copy of the first edition of Boswell's *Life of Samuel Johnson* which he annotated, and it was this annotated copy which Boswell used in preparing the second edition of his 'Life'. Boswell acknowledged this handsomely in his preface to this edition dated 1 July 1793.

> To enumerate those to whom I have been thus indebted, would be tediously ostentatious. I cannot however but name one whose praise is truly valuable, not only on account of his knowledge and abilities, but on account of the magnificent, yet dangerous embassy, in which he is now employed, which makes every thing that relates to him peculiarly interesting. Lord Macartney favoured me with his own copy of my book, with a number of notes, of which I have availed myself. On the first leaf I found in his Lordship's hand-writing, an inscription of such high commendation, that even I, vain as I am, cannot prevail on myself to publish it.

It would be interesting to read what Macartney wrote about Boswell on the flyleaf, but as far as I know the whereabouts of Macartney's annotated edition is not known. Macartney seems to have been an admirer of Johnson for he took the trouble to send Boswell a copy of a letter from Dr. Johnson to Lord Bute written in 1762 asking about his pension.†

* *The Letters of Samuel Johnson*, ed. R. W. Chapman (Oxford, 1952), Vol. II, p. 324. Both Johnson and Boswell spelt his name 'Macarteney'.
† R. W. Chapman, op. cit., Vol. I, p. 143.

INTRODUCTION

At the end of 1780 Macartney was appointed President of Fort St. George, the first Governor of Madras to be selected from outside the ranks of the East India Company's servants. He arrived in June 1781 at a time when England was still at war with France, and when Haidar Ali, the ruler of Mysore, had fought his way almost to the walls of Madras. Warren Hastings, Governor-General of Bengal, had sent Sir Eyre Coote, the most experienced British commander in India at that time, to take charge of the situation, which was made more critical because a French fleet was expected to arrive off the coast at any moment. However, the exertions of General Coote and Admiral Sir Edward Hughes eventually saved Madras. Although Macartney was Governor, Coote had been entrusted by the Government of Bengal with complete control over the conduct of the war, and this made for friction. Moreover, by the Regulating Act of 1773 the presidencies of Bombay and Madras had been made subordinate to Bengal, with the exception that in cases of emergency it was not necessary for them to obtain the consent of the Governor-General and Council of Bengal before starting hostilities or concluding treaties. Thus the authority of Bengal was not really supreme, and this helps to account for the hostility that existed between Macartney on the one side and Coote and Warren Hastings on the other.*

Haidar Ali died in 1782 and Coote in 1783. The new commander of the army, General Stuart, was soon at loggerheads with Macartney, and a good opportunity was lost of destroying the forces of Tipu, son of Haidar Ali. As a result of systematic disobedience to orders Macartney removed Stuart from his command and sent him to England under arrest. Macartney appears to have had a certain contempt for soldiers and their 'silly trade' as he termed it, and he preferred to try diplomacy instead. In 1784 he sent his secretary, George Staunton, to negotiate with Tipu, and the treaty of Mangalore was signed. Warren Hastings strongly disapproved of the terms as too conciliatory, and because the Nawab of the Carnatic had not been made a party to the treaty. Macartney, however, refused to alter them. Soon after arriving in Madras Macartney had persuaded the ruler of Arcot to make over to the Madras government the administration of the Carnatic revenues for the period of the war. A dispute over this which had developed with the government of Bengal was decided in June 1785 when the Government in England

---

* For details of Macartney's difficulties see *The Private Correspondence of Lord Macartney, Governor of Madras (1781–85)*, ed. C. Collin Davies, Camden Third Series, Vol. LXXVII (Royal Historical Society, 1950), Introduction.

annulled Macartney's action.* He therefore resigned. On leaving Madras he handed over a large sum to the treasury there, which in those days in British India was something of a marvel. Before quitting India finally he went to Calcutta in order to attempt to compose the differences between the Councils of Bengal and Madras. While in Calcutta he received an offer from the Board of Control of the Governor-Generalship of Bengal in the place of Warren Hastings, who had resigned and returned to England early in 1785. However, he declined the offer and sailed for England where he arrived early in 1786.† His conduct while at Madras was appreciated by the East India Company, which granted him an annuity for life of £1,500 especially to mark his great 'pecuniary moderation'. However, he had not been in England long before he was called out by General Stuart to fight a duel. This took place near the Tyburn turnpike, and Macartney was wounded in the arm by a ball from the General's pistol.‡ He was laid up for several months by the wound, and also by gout in both feet. However, a few years out of employment spent partly in London and partly at Lissanoure restored his health (except for recurrent gout), so that when, in the autumn of 1791, he was offered the appointment of ambassador to China he was ready to accept the post. In June 1792 he was created Viscount Macartney of Dervock in the county of Antrim.

Certainly in 1791 Macartney was the most outstanding diplomat and administrator available in England to fill the job. He already had experience of dealing with the autocratic ruler of a great empire—Catherine of Russia. He already had first-hand knowledge of the subtleties of oriental diplomacy from his negotiations with Tipu, ruler of Mysore. Moreover, he had the esteem of the Court of Directors of the East India Company and the support of influential friends in politics, including Dundas. He had trained himself from the outset to study and observe whatever country he happened to serve in, and to set down his impressions and opinions clearly on paper. Writing to the Secretary of War soon after his arrival in Madras he remarked: 'Your Empire hangs by a thread and one judicious effort may make it as strong as a cable.' Of General Stuart he wrote: 'He is old, over cautious, totally unenterprising and, I

---

* See C. C. Davies, op. cit., pp. xiv–xv, and C. H. Philips, *The East India Company, 1784–1834* (Manchester University Press, 1961), p. 36.

† For his reasons for declining the post see C. H. Philips, op. cit., p. 43.

‡ For an account of the duel by the seconds see Barrow, *Some Account of the Public Life and a Selection of the Unpublished Writings of the Earl of Macartney*, Vol. I, pp. 604–5.

think, a good deal impaired. He has made the last campaign in a go-cart, and I need not tell you the little respect which either that conveyance or his personal character will entitle him to from the troops.' Stuart, when writing to the Directors of the East India Company, related how he had lost a leg in battle 'while others at their ease are only dropping ink on their paper in black characters.' The cap fits Macartney rather well. In his public dispatches and private correspondence he tended to be prolix, even by the standards of his own times.

Macartney was a man of strong principles and firm character. He was never tempted to enrich himself by public office. He was a cool man in both judgment and feeling, hence he was able to keep his temper under control. If he had a high opinion of his own abilities he also had a high regard for the public service. He was ambitious, not for wealth and power but for the fame of having served his country successfully in his profession of diplomat and administrator. 'He was, moreover, a past master in the art of ingratiating himself with persons of importance whose assistance might at any time turn the scale in his favour.'* In short he was a natural diplomat. No other man in England at this time had such qualities or experience. If anyone could have succeeded in the infinitely difficult task of getting concessions from the Chinese Imperial Government, Macartney was the man to do it.

This was the first time that England had attempted to make diplomatic contact with China and to obtain a treaty of commerce. For over a hundred years ideas about China had been filtering into England. But knowledge of the Chinese empire had mostly been obtained at secondhand through the accounts of the Jesuits, which were apt to be over-enthusiastic, or from the superficial reports of previous European ambassadors. Here, then, was the opportunity of the century, a splendid chance to penetrate the subtleties of the Chinese character, to find out something of their method of government and the way their minds worked. In fact the Macartney embassy proved to be an early essay in penetrating the bamboo curtain of Chinese exclusiveness. It was something of a European reconnaissance, carried out by trained men, since in his suite Macartney took scientists ('natural philosophers'), draughtsmen, army officers and others, most of whom made copious observations and sketches of what they saw. Thus, when Macartney arrived back in England in September 1794, although he brought no treaty with him, he did

* C. C. Davies, op. cit., p. xvi.

bring back his Journal, a valuable contribution to the state of European knowledge of China at that time. In spite of the recent French Revolution the departure of the embassy in 1792 captured the imagination of many people in England at that time. A cartoon by Gillray, published on 14 September 1792, shows Macartney and his suite kneeling before the Emperor of China, proffering him presents, which are being spurned. But although the sceptics were ready to laugh, the general public was quick enough to buy the various accounts of the embassy written by those who took part in it, and published in the decade after their return.

Macartney's last public position was that of Governor of Cape Colony, which England had acquired from Holland as a result of the war against revolutionary France. He held this post from 1796 until he was forced by ill-health to resign in 1798. On returning to England he settled in a house at Chiswick, and here he lived quietly until his death, at the age of sixty-nine, on 31 March 1806. He was buried in Chiswick Churchyard and his grave lies near to that of Hogarth.

MEMBERS OF MACARTNEY'S SUITE

Macartney was willing to undertake the embassy provided that there was a reasonable chance of success. When Dundas consulted him on the best way to ensure this, Macartney stressed that the embassy should be conducted with a certain pomp and dignity. As a result he was promised H.M.S. *Lion*, sixty-four guns, Captain Erasmus Gower, to carry himself and part of his suite, and also the *Hindostan*, East Indiaman of 1,248 tons, Captain William Mackintosh, one of the largest and fastest of the East India Company's fleet, to carry the presents and the remainder of his suite. The total number of his entourage was ninety-five persons, of whom fifty-six sailed in the *Lion* and thirty-nine in the *Hindostan*. The complete list of names was given by Macartney on the first page of his Journal of the voyage from England to Cochin China.* Here follows a list of the more interesting members of the embassy:

Ambassador, George Viscount Macartney of Dervock, K.C.B.
Secretary (and Minister Plenipotentiary in the absence of the Ambassador), Sir George Leonard Staunton.
Two Under-Secretaries, Acheson Maxwell and Edward Winder (a relation of Lord Macartney's).

* For a note on this Journal, see p. 333.

INTRODUCTION

Two Interpreters, Jacobus Li and Pablo Cho (from the College for Chinese at Naples.*
Comptroller, John Barrow.
Surgeon, Dr. William Scott.
Physician (and 'natural philosopher'), Dr. Hugh Gillan, M.A. (Aberdeen), M.D. (Edin.).
Mechanic (experimental scientist), Dr. James Dinwiddie, M.A. (Edin.).
Painter, Thomas Hickey.
Draughtsman, William Alexander.
Metallurgist, Henry Eades.
Watchmaker, Charles-Henry Petitpierre.
Mathematical Instrument Maker, Victor Thibault.
Gardener and Botanist, David Stronach.
Page to Ambassador, Master George Thomas Staunton.
Valet to Ambassador, Aeneas Anderson.
Tutor to Master Staunton, Herr Hüttner.
Five German Musicians, John Zapfal (leader).

Military Escort: Lt.-Col. George Benson, Lt. Henry Parish, R.A., Lt. John Crewe, 10 Dragoons, 20 Artillerymen and 20 Infantry.

Conveying the embassy by sea: H.M.S. *Lion* (64 guns); Capt. Sir Erasmus Gower; 1st Lieut., Lieut. Campbell.
Hindostan, East Indiaman (30 guns), Capt. William Mackintosh.

Since the reader will be meeting several of these men regularly in the Journal, a short note on each of the following is given in Appendix A: G. L. Staunton, G. T. Staunton, Barrow, Gower, Dinwiddie, Gillan, Mackintosh, Alexander, Parish, Stronach, Jacobus Li.

CHINESE DEALINGS WITH THE EMBASSY

Although this book is concerned with Macartney's own Journal, it would be negligent not to consider from the Chinese point of view their dealings with the first English 'tribute envoy' and his embassy. Luckily these can be studied in the official Chinese documents preserved in various collections which have now been made available in print. The largest group of these is to be found in the *Chang-ku ts'ung-pien*, which contains, according to my reckoning, eighty-two documents concerning the embassy. These I have analysed and translated in part elsewhere.† However, at this stage it may be useful

* Maintained by the Congregation *De Propaganda Fide*.   † See footnote, p. 6.

for the reader to have some account, however simplified, of how the Emperor and his advisers dealt with the state business occasioned by the Macartney embassy.

At the centre of the web of Chinese government sat the Emperor, an autocrat grown old in the exercise of power, now, perhaps, relying too heavily on the judgment and character of his favourite minister, Ho-shen, but still shrewd, and able to strike terror into ministers who failed to please him. Ch'ien-lung ruled as well as reigned, yet he did so in a paternal way, often correcting or castigating his ministers much as a Chinese father would his sons. There are indications that in his last years he mellowed somewhat, and that he no longer inspired such terror as he had ten or fifteen years earlier at the height of the so-called Literary Inquisition. When Macartney saw him for the first time at the audience on 14 September 1793 he was favourably impressed. 'His manner is dignified, but affable and condescending, and his reception of us has been very gracious and satisfactory. He is a very fine old gentleman, still healthy and vigorous, not having the appearance of a man of more than sixty.' In fact at that time he was eighty-three. In spite of his age he still took an active part in affairs and was by far the most outstanding personality with whom Macartney had contact while in China.

The Emperor was born in 1711, the fourth son of the Emperor Yung-cheng. His personal name was Hung-li, and his reign title Ch'ien-lung. He is commonly referred to as the Emperor Ch'ien-lung except by pedants who call him correctly but clumsily 'the Ch'ien-lung Emperor'. He succeeded to the throne in 1736, and abdicated in favour of his son, the Emperor Chia-ch'ing, in 1796 in order to avoid reigning for more than sixty years, the length of the reign of his illustrious grandfather K'ang-hsi. His reign is famous in Chinese history for his extensive conquests among the tribes and kingdoms bordering on China's western and southern frontiers. Among his major victories was the subjection of the Sungars between 1755 and 1757, and the Mohamedans of Turkestan between 1758 and 1759, while he reduced the Burmese to suzerainty between 1766 and 1770, and the Annamese between 1788 and 1789. Finally the Gurkhas were driven out of Tibet and their own country invaded between 1790 and 1792. The conquest of Ili and Turkestan resulted in an increase of about 6,000 square miles to the empire and the elimination of a long-standing threat of invasion by the Mongols and Turks. Thus Ch'ien-lung enlarged the bounds of the Chinese empire till it reached its widest extent and its greatest prestige in

INTRODUCTION

history. But foreign conquests, however brilliant, were extremely costly. Towards the end of his reign a legacy of heavy taxation brought hardship and discontent to many provinces. The expense of the campaign against the Gurkhas was never officially disclosed. Apart from the cost of wars Ch'ien-lung was an extravagant ruler when he wished to indulge his fancy. Thus at his orders the simple pleasure gardens outside Peking, begun by his grandfather K'ang-hsi, were greatly extended and embellished during the early part of his reign. Buildings and fountains were added in the Italian style under the supervision of the versatile Jesuit priests Castiglione and Attiret, who acted as architects, Benoist who was in charge of fountains, and d'Incarville who was in charge of the European-style gardens. All this cost much to construct and keep up. Furthermore his six tours of the Yangtze valley between 1751 and 1784 were a heavy drain on the Imperial treasury. But his great officials were afraid to censure him for extravagance because they were intimidated by Ch'ien-lung's attitude towards criticism. Being a descendant of the Manchu conquerors of China in the previous century he was very sensitive to anything that might be construed as criticism, and was likely to interpret it as treason. The so-called Literary Inquisition which reached its climax between 1774 and 1788 helped still further to intimidate his officials. Even the most innocent expression of opinion could be twisted and made to seem treasonable. He was both a great emperor and a great autocrat. He did not allow his numerous sons to have any real share in government, but towards the end of his life leaned heavily on the advice of his favourite minister Ho-shen* to whom he gave increasing power. Eventually he handed over the government in 1796 to his fifteenth son, but even then he kept a hold over the more important functions of government. He died in 1799, at the age of eighty-eight. William Alexander,* the young draughtsman who accompanied the embassy, made a mass of colour-wash sketches on the spot and then worked a number of them up into finished water-colours on his return to England. One of his sketch books is preserved in the British Museum and it contains a vivid colour-wash drawing of the Emperor in 1793 which conveys exactly his outstanding qualities. It shows him as a tough, cunning, self-confident, autocratic ruler.

Macartney made some comments on the position of the Emperor as he saw it during his stay in China.† But he discovered little about

---

* For a note on him see Appendix A.
† See Journal 16 December, p. 201, and Observations, pp. 237–9.

the detailed working of the central government, and it may be worthwhile here to summarize how it worked so that the reader may be able more easily to imagine how the affairs of the embassy were dealt with. The chain of command went outward from the centre, but initiative in the first place usually came from the ministers themselves, especially the great officials in the provinces. The method was for an official to send a memorial to the throne, reporting an occurrence and suggesting a possible line of action, while reporting what had been done so far. Or he might memorialize about some irregularity in government, suggesting a remedy and punishments for the offenders. From the time that the Macartney embassy arrived off Macao until it was safely back there nearly seven months later there was a stream of memorials to the throne from the officials who were in contact with it. Specimens of these memorials in translation are given in my article cited above.

At the capital two bodies dealt with the business of state, acting as filters between the great officials and the Emperor.* The older body was the Grand Secretariat, but by the end of Ch'ien-lung's reign it dealt mainly with routine matters of administration. When a memorial was first received at the Grand Secretariat a minor official would draft a suggested answer to it. The memorial, together with the draft reply written in Manchu and Chinese, was passed to the Grand Secretaries for inspection. There were usually four Grand Secretaries (two Chinese and two Manchu) as well as two assistant Grand Secretaries. After the draft answer had been approved or altered it was presented to the Emperor at a dawn audience, together with the original memorial, by the Grand Secretary on duty. The Imperial decision was then given and if necessary an Imperial edict would be issued. In very special circumstances the Emperor wrote the endorsement of the document himself in red ink. Copies of the original memorial with its endorsement were then taken and finally the Imperial will was made known.

The second body, the Grand Council (sometimes called by Western scholars the Council of State) was of modern origin, being established in 1729. It was a less formal and more powerful body than the Grand Secretariat. Usually there were five or six Grand Councillors. They were selected from among the Grand Secretaries, the Presidents and Vice-Presidents of Boards, and even from the secretaries of the Grand Council itself. It was a compact body

* For an analysis of how they worked see J. K. Fairbank and S. Y. Teng, *Ch'ing Administration*, pp. 40–69. The following two paragraphs are based on this work.

working with secrecy, and dealt with an average of fifty memorials a day. The Grand Councillors followed the Emperor wherever he went, and special apartments were set aside for them both at Jehol and in the Summer Palace (Yuan-ming Yuan). They formed a kind of Imperial private secretariat. Having read a memorial the Emperor decided what should be done or indicated that he wished to discuss the matter with his Councillors. Finally the Imperial decision, either in the form of a separate edict or an endorsement to the memorial, was made known.

Also in the capital there were the six Boards or Ministries, in charge of administration. These were the Boards of Civil Office, Revenue, Ceremonies, War, Punishments and Works. Each Board had a Manchu and a Chinese President and two Manchu and two Chinese Vice-Presidents. There were also various other departments at the capital with all the paraphernalia of a highly developed civil service.

Provincial administration was under a hierarchy of officials: Governor-Generals, Governors, provincial Commanders-in-Chief of the Chinese army and Tartar Generals of the Manchu army, provincial Judicial Commissioners, Intendants of Circuits, Prefects, Magistrates, and District Magistrates. Also there were a number of specially appointed officials such as Salt Administrators, Grain Administrators, Commissioners for the Imperial Canal and others. These various posts dovetailed into one another in an elaborate way. The provincial officials held considerable responsibility but they also got into considerable trouble if they made a wrong decision.*

Luckily the day-to-day working of both the provincial and central administration can be studied in the Chinese documents dealing with the Macartney embassy printed in the *Chang-ku ts'ung-pien*. By the end of Ch'ien-lung's reign the Ch'ing bureaucracy had become stereotyped in organization, unimaginative in ideas and safety-first in operation. It also created for itself a great deal of paper work. This can be seen by the considerable exchange of memorials and rescripts between the provinces and the capital concerning the embassy. When confronted with an unfamiliar situation the officials were easily perplexed. Thus, when the English ships sailed up the coast to Tientsin instead of going to Canton as the regulations required, or when Macartney declined to take all the presents to Jehol because some were too bulky or fragile, the brushes of the

* For a fuller analysis see Macartney's tabulation of provincial officials in Observations, p. 252, and my footnote thereon.

bureaucrats flew up and down the paper in consternation, reiterating former precedents but never trying to evolve new methods to fit unusual circumstances. Rather they attempted to make the facts fit the old conceptions and so insure themselves against trouble. Many of the scholar-official class at this time were timid, precedent bound, and ready to pass on responsibility. At the same time the Emperor and his senior officials at the capital were always ready with advice for the officials on the spot, usually urging them to do the impossible as in a Court Letter of 24 July 1793 which stated: 'But when dealing with barbarians one ought to strike the mean between being too lavish and too frugal; only by so doing can you conform to the proper system. The practice of the provinces is either to err in doing too much or not enough.'* Ministers, even senior ones, could be rebuked in a paternal way by the Emperor, as witness part of a Court Letter aimed at Cheng-jui:

> What he memorialized was extremely silly. This really shows how unlucky the Salt Administrator is to be so muddle-headed. Because the people on board that country's ships [the *Lion* and *Hindostan*—Ed.] are unaccustomed to the climate the envoy wants to send them home in advance, and naturally we ought to let them please themselves. How could Cheng-jui advise them and suggest that it would be improper for the ships to return home in advance?†

Moreover, these documents give a valuable indication of the official Chinese attitude to the embassy. The main reaction was one of suspicion (because of the size of the embassy and the fact that it went direct to Tientsin and not Canton), mixed with dislike and disdain (when Macartney refused to practise the kotow and only bent one knee in front of the Emperor), finally changing to something like alarm when it was realized that Macartney was disappointed at the rejection of all his requests and it was felt that he might make trouble among the other Europeans on his return to Macao. However, on the surface, politeness was maintained and Macartney and Ho-shen appear to have behaved with elaborate courtesy towards each other. Thus 'face' was preserved. In fact all the great officials with whom Macartney and Staunton had dealings were outwardly gracious, except for Cheng-jui and Fu-k'ang-an who were openly hostile.‡ But there was no doubt that the officials in Peking sighed with relief when Macartney and his suite left the capital on 7 October, and were equally glad when they heard that

---

* J. L. Cranmer-Byng, op. cit., p. 132.
† Ibid., p. 153.
‡ For Fu-K'ang-an see footnote No. 18. For Cheng-jui see Appendix A.

INTRODUCTION

they had left Macao without incident.* It is a pity that we do not possess a diary written by one of the Chinese officials who had dealings with the embassy so that it could be contrasted with Macartney's Journal. However, we must be grateful for the mass of Chinese documents which have been preserved and which give us a good idea of how the Emperor and his ministers viewed the embassy. These documents do not often mince matters; after all it was not envisaged that the 'red haired barbarians of the western ocean' would ever peruse them.

RESULTS OF THE EMBASSY

The instructions which Henry Dundas, Home Secretary in Pitt's administration, handed Macartney before he sailed, can be summarized as follows. Macartney was to create as favourable an impression on the Chinese as possible, both by the good conduct of his suite and also by demonstrating England's scientific knowledge and technical achievements. He was also to obtain all the information possible about China, not only economic and political, but also military, intellectual, cultural and social as well as information about China's relations with Russia and other countries. The more important tasks of his embassy were the more specific ones. Briefly these were:

> To negotiate a treaty of commerce and friendship and to establish a resident Minister at the Court of Ch'ien-lung.
>
> To extend British trade in China by the opening of new ports, especially in northern China where British woollens might be sold.
>
> To obtain from China the cession of a piece of land or an island nearer to the tea and silk producing area than Canton, where British merchants might reside the whole year, and where British jurisdiction could be exercised.
>
> To abolish the existing abuses in the Canton system and to obtain assurances that they would not be revived.
>
> To create new markets in China, especially in Peking, for British products hitherto unknown, such as hardware and the like, samples of which were taken by the ambassador as presents.
>
> To open Japan and Cochin China to British trade by means of treaties.

The East India Company, in its instructions to the Ambassador, put rather a different point of view. It constantly urged him to be cautious. The gist of its instructions was not to upset the existing position of the Company in its trade at Canton but to create a

* For a revealing document which gives the point of view of the great officials at this juncture see J. L. Cranmer-Byng, op. cit., pp. 167-8.

RESULTS OF THE EMBASSY

favourable impression of the British character. To obtain permission to trade at one or more ports north of Canton. To obtain information about Chinese manufactures and trade, and to find out what new articles might profitably be exported from China to England.*

As it turned out, Macartney failed to achieve the specific tasks which the Government set him. Even the improvement of conditions at Canton, which Macartney hoped he had achieved through his good relations with Ch'ang-lin, the newly appointed Governor-General of Kwangtung and Kwangsi, did not last long. Macartney did not realize that in provincial administration the great officials rarely remained long in any post, while a newly appointed official would be more likely to discard the policy of his predecessor than to continue it. Ch'ang-lin, it is true, had issued two proclamations which, if enforced, might have improved the position of English merchants in Canton to some extent. The first, of 2 January 1794, laid down penalties for anyone who molested, plundered or defrauded the English. But it was aimed chiefly against the small fry who sold strong drink to the sailors. A second proclamation of 5 January was aimed at magistrates, military officers and others who might use their position to extort money from Europeans. But here again it was aimed only at the lesser officials. What the Supercargoes needed was an edict which would fix definitely the taxes, duties and regulations concerning trade, and be binding on the higher officials at Canton, especially the Hoppo. But this was an impossibility. Provincial officials, especially in Canton, had considerable powers delegated to them by the Emperor, and the Hoppo could easily lead the others in opposition to any unpopular measures which a new Governor-General might attempt, especially if their accustomed source of squeeze was threatened. In any case Ch'ang-lin was only Governor-General from September 1793 until August 1795 and spent even less than that period actually in Canton. Difficulties with the Hoppo continued, and in 1796 the Select Committee drew up a fresh list of requests which were presented to the Governor, but most of them were refused. Thus the position of English merchants in Canton was not perceptibly improved by Lord Macartney's embassy.

The question why Macartney failed to achieve his main objects remains to be answered. Was it because of any mistakes he may have made in the handling of his embassy or any conjunction of unfortunate circumstances? The Jesuit missionaries in Peking were

* For the detailed instructions see E. H. Pritchard, op. cit., pp. 307–9.

INTRODUCTION

inclined to attribute the failure of the embassy to trivial causes. Grammont, writing to the Spanish agent in Macao soon after the embassy had left Peking, accused Macartney of being ignorant of the proper etiquette of the Chinese Court, and blamed him for employing a Chinese interpreter who, he said, was not versed in Court ceremonial, instead of a European missionary who would have instructed him properly. This was merely sour grapes since Grammont had been angling for just such a post for himself. He even accused the ambassador of failing to give adequate presents, which is absurd. The reasons he gave were entirely superficial and had nothing to do with the failure of the embassy. A more sensible solution was put forward in a letter from Father Amiot to Macartney* in which he suggested that the embassy would have met with fewer difficulties if it had arrived before the great officials became alarmed by the news of the recent troubles in Europe. The French Revolution had broken out in 1789, but since even the most senior ministers did not clearly distinguish between the English and other Europeans this was only a general cause.

Macartney himself speculated on the reasons for the refusal to grant any of his requests when he wrote in his Journal on 4 October:

> Whether the difficulties we have met with arise chiefly from the particular humour and jealousy of the Court, or from the immutable laws of the Empire, which they talk so much of, must be left to time to determine. But from the observations which it has fallen in my way to make, I should rather imagine that the personal character of the Ministers, alarmed by the most trifling accident, the aversion they may naturally have to sudden innovation [i.e. Macartney's refusal to perform the kotow.—Ed.], especially at the Emperor's late period of life, and some recent events ill understood, joined, perhaps, to a paltry intrigue, have been among the chief obstacles to my business; for most of the principal people, whom I have had opportunities of knowing I have found sociable, conversable, good-humoured, and not at all indisposed to foreigners. As to the lower orders, they are all of a trafficking turn, and it seemed at the seaports where we stopped that nothing would be more agreeable to them than to see our ships often in their harbours.†

Macartney mentions the kotow ceremony. To what extent did his refusal to perform it prejudice the success of his mission? Here the Chinese documents shed some light. From the time that Macartney reached Tientsin instructions from Ho-shen to Cheng-jui show considerable concern that the envoy should practice the full kotow ceremony. Thus in a Court Letter on 14 August 1793 Ho-shen writes that Cheng-jui

> . . ought casually in the course of conversation to inform him tactfully that as

* See Journal, p. 151. † p. 153.

regards the various vassal states, when they come to the Celestial Empire to bring tribute and have an audience, not only do all their envoys perform the ceremony of the three kneelings and the nine knockings of the head, but even the princes who come in person to Court also perform this same ceremony. Now your King has sent you to bring birthday congratulations and naturally you should obey the regulations of the Celestial Empire.*

Again, instructions from the Grand Council to Cheng-jui dated 18 August state: 'But after he has arrived the tribute envoy must first practise the etiquette. If he still does not conform fully to the etiquette you must instruct him point by point. Only when he is versed in the salutation of the kotow may he be ushered into an Imperial audience.' A Court Letter of 9 September took up the same idea but more forcefully. '... However, the envoys who have come to Jehol are totally ignorant of the proper ceremonies and we are deeply dissatisfied. Recently, on their way to Peking, when they were well received by the various local officials and given supplies at various places along the route they were treated too generously which has caused them to become unwarrantably haughty.'† Later the same document states: 'These are ignorant barbarians, and it is not worth treating them with too much courtesy.'

Macartney had refused to practise the kotow and had sent Ho-shen a written statement on the subject. This statement was referred to in a Court Letter to the Princes and Ministers remaining at the capital.

> ... After the tribute envoy reached Jehol he procrastinated and feigned illness, and there were many instances in which he was ignorant of the etiquette. Yesterday we commanded the Grand Councillor [i.e. Ho-shen who is here writing as from the Emperor and using the royal 'we'.—Ed.] to summon the envoy to an interview. The chief envoy feigned illness and did not arrive but simply instructed the assistant envoy to come, and he presented a document, the wording of which showed ignorance. Thereupon Ho-shen and others personally refuted it with stern words and just reasons, and Ho-shen acted very much as befits his position as a great minister. At present instructions have been given for him to practise the ceremonial but he still pretends to be ill and procrastinates. We are extremely displeased at this unwarranted haughtiness, and have given instructions to cut down their supplies. ...‡

Nevertheless Macartney refused to practise it, and on 14 September he was received in audience by the Emperor without performing the kotow. Did his refusal prevent him from obtaining the concessions he sought? Very certainly it did not. Previous embassies

---

* Full text in J. L. Cranmer-Byng, op. cit., p. 145.
† Ibid., pp. 156–7.
‡ Ibid., p. 158.

INTRODUCTION

from Europe had performed the ceremony without obtaining any benefits. The members of the Dutch embassy under Isaac Titsingh and van Braam, who were in Peking at the beginning of 1795, kotowed readily on every occasion it was required of them, but to no advantage. In fact van Braam made himself a clown in the eyes of the Emperor, especially when his wig fell off while he kotowed at the frozen roadside as the Emperor was carried past. Naturally it was a blow to Manchu pride if an envoy did not kotow, but his refusal could always be put down to barbarian ignorance. If the Emperor and his advisers had wished to have closer ties with the English they would have done so whether the ambassador kotowed or not. Father Amiot, in his letter to Macartney,* was nearer the mark when he explained that the Chinese considered embassies as temporary ceremonies and that they had no favourable ideas towards treaties with distant powers.

The real reason for the failure of Macartney's mission was that from the very beginning it never stood the slightest chance of success.† There was never any common ground of understanding between England and China; the two countries possessed two different cultures with totally different outlooks. No treaty of commerce or alliance, no exchange of ministers could be effected while the attitude of those in power in China remained unchanged. To the Emperor and his ministers the Western Ocean barbarians seemed especially troublesome, warlike and even dangerous. With such people no relations, except that of suzerain and vassal, made sense. These foreigners must be kept under strict control and be allowed to trade only on Chinese terms. To Britain foreign trade was her life's blood. To Ch'ien-lung's ministers it brought luxuries and the opportunity of squeeze, which they would have been sorry to lose, but it was not a matter of national safety. Thus, as regards the main objects, the embassy might just as well have not been dispatched, because at no time could it possibly have succeeded. As Professor Pritchard has pointed out, the ambassador's task became impossible 'when he reached the barrier of Chinese custom, tradition and exclusiveness'.

As regards the general aims of the embassy, to what extent were they achieved? The answer is scattered throughout Macartney's Journal, in his dispatches to Dundas and the Directors of the East

---

* See Journal p. 151
† This can clearly be seen in the wording of the famous edict which Ch'ien-lung addressed to George III (translated in Appendix C).

RESULTS OF THE EMBASSY

India Company, and in the Observations appended to his Journal. Thus on 9 December 1793 Macartney recorded in his Journal that the Emperor had requested that if the King of England should send an envoy to China again he should come to Canton, which implied censure on Macartney for having sailed up the Gulf of Chihli. 'Nevertheless', wrote Macartney, 'I would not for any consideration that we had not, as by these means we are now masters of the geography of the north-east coasts of China, and have acquired a knowledge of the Yellow Sea, which was never before navigated by European ships.' This is borne out by the Journal of the voyage of H.M.S. *Lion* kept by Sir Erasmus Gower, where the navigational details of the passage through the Yellow Sea have been recorded in considerable detail. This was one result of the embassy—a knowledge of the northern coastline of China in case ports to the northwards should one day be opened to trade. Secondly Macartney and the members of his suite brought back to England with them a considerable amount of first-hand knowledge about China at that time, even if much of it was superficial. The Observations printed after the Journal show what they had succeeded in discovering, and how the Manchus and Chinese struck educated Englishmen. Furthermore, the embassy started young Staunton on his study of Chinese and impressed on those who took part the great importance of a knowledge of the Chinese language to any Englishman who might have dealings with the Chinese officials in the future. As a result of the embassy, ministers in England got a clearer idea of China and her rulers, and the problems which confronted the government in trying to establish better trading conditions and closer relations with the Court at Peking. But this information was gained at an enormous cost to the East India Company, probably in the region of £78,000.*
Finally, from the long-term point of view of the historian the most valuable by-product of the embassy was Macartney's own Journal, because it fixes a searchlight on one particular year at the end of Ch'ien-lung's reign.

Having said all this one might legitimately enquire how the embassy affected the rulers of China. What did the Emperor and his advisers—Manchu and Chinese—learn from it? The answer is *nothing*. Looking back from the present to these events it is possible

---

* The detailed figures have been worked out by E. H. Pritchard in 'The Instructions of the East India Company to Lord Macartney on his Embassy to China and his Reports to the Company, 1792–4', *Journal of the Royal Asiatic Society*, 1938, Pt. IV, pp. 508–9.

INTRODUCTION

to argue that Ch'ien-lung and his ministers missed a golden opportunity of beginning the task of modernizing their country, on equal terms with the West, in order to keep China's place in the changing world. They failed to face up to realities and to measure themselves against the Western barbarians. All the scientific appartaus which Macartney took with him, all the obvious superiority of H.M.S. *Lion*, a 64-gun ship, over the Manchu war junks, was wasted on these men. The efficiency of the six light brass cannon fired by trained artillery crews and the neat post-chaise which took Macartney from Peking to Jehol and back so comfortably, failed to make any impression on them. These outward proofs might have alerted the great officials to the danger which China would one day face from the West. But they had no effect whatsoever. Why was it that the rulers of Japan, in the mid-nineteenth century, woke up to their peril in time, and after a few years of passionate debate started a momentous programme of modernization, while the rulers of China would only admit the need to modernize at the end of the nineteenth century when the country was already under foreign spheres of influence? What were the factors in 1793 which inhibited officials of the Manchu–Chinese bureaucracy from feeling any sense of urgency or impending danger? These can be summarized as follows: First of all the date when the embassy took place. This was at the very end of Ch'ien-lung's reign, which had been a long and glorious one, a reign of continual military campaigns and almost unbroken military successes which had resulted in a very considerable expansion of the Chinese empire. To a man like General Fu-k'ang-an, who had only the previous year driven the Gurkhas out of Tibet in a successful winter campaign,* a few English soldiers and some howitzers did not seem impressive. Such men had faith in their own weapons, born of success against the peoples on their frontiers. Therefore they looked with complacency on the 'sea barbarians', their ships and their inventions. In any case, to have memorialized the throne about the possibility of defeat by the Western barbarians would have been most unpopular with Ch'ien-lung. Such a memorial might well have been treated as treason, or at least dismissed with contempt and loss of rank. The Manchu régime would not admit to any weakness, even when faced with a powerful warship on its coasts. The few great officials who came in contact with

---

* For the Nepalese side of the story see Mayura Jang Kunwar, 'China and War in the Himalayas, 1792–3', *English Historical Review*, vol. lxxvii (April, 1962), pp. 283–297.

the barbarian envoy and his suite appear to have treated them either with exaggerated politeness or with cold indifference.

The Chinese tradition, since the founding of the Empire in 221 B.C. was one of amazing continuity. There have been many *rebellions* in Chinese history aimed at overthrowing those in power, but until the present century no *revolution* aimed at overthrowing the methods of government and the organization of society. The reasons why China remained static and traditional for so long have been well analysed by R. H. Tawney* where, among other reasons, he points out that in China there was no relentless pressure of circumstances to compel her to undergo change. Furthermore the extreme stability of the Chinese gentry society, the ruling class in China until the present century, prevented change. It was this gentry society which prevented the development of modern science,† and it prevented, until too late, the modernization of the country, because it was wedded to the status quo. Through their positions in the bureaucracy as scholar-officials, through their possession of country estates as landlords, and their connection with city trade this class contrived to stay in power and to maintain the favourable conditions in which it flourished so robustly.‡ It was the scholar-official caste which reacted instinctively out of self-defence against any idea of adopting Western techniques, just as strongly as did the Manchus out of a feeling of cultural superiority.

Thus, if England failed to obtain a treaty of trade, or to improve her relations with China, the Chinese empire equally failed to take her first steps on the road to modernization which alone could have saved her from the humiliations of the Anglo-Chinese war of 1839–42, the Anglo-French campaign of 1858–60, her decisive defeat by Japan in 1894–5, and the general economic subservience to Japan and the West during the first forty years of the present century. At the end of the eighteenth century, helped by a treaty of trade and friendship with the foremost country of the West, China could have begun the painful but momentous changeover from a simple economy based primarily on land towards a complex modern economy, and the Manchu dynasty might have avoided the long and humiliating decline of the Chinese empire throughout the nineteenth century. But in 1793 China was stuck fast in a cycle of

* *Land and Labour in China* (Allen and Unwin, 1932), pp. 18–22.
† Joseph Needham in his magisterial work *Science and Civilization in China* proves that until about the fifteenth century science was flourishing in China.
‡ This theme is analysed in more detail by Derk Bodde in *China's Cultural Tradition* (Rinehart and Co., 1957), pp. 50–4.

INTRODUCTION

conservatism and exclusion which made certain the complete rejection without trial, of all ideas from outside. In its historical setting this failure to face up to the challenge of the West was inevitable, but it was nonetheless a tragic failure because from that time onward isolation was no longer a sound policy and China's relations with the West needed putting on a modern basis. From the English point of view Macartney's embassy failed to obtain better conditions for trade, but on the Chinese side the failure was more fundamental: it was a failure of perception, a failure to respond to challenge.

THE JOURNAL

Macartney kept two journals of his embassy. One gives a detailed account of the outward voyage from the day he set out from London to join the *Lion* at Portsmouth (11 September 1792) until the departure from Tourane Bay in Cochin China (15 June 1793). This account is concerned with almost everything except China. It is a journal of a voyage across the world, records visits to towns and people, and the natural history of lonely islands. It includes an account of a stay of over a month at Batavia, the capital of the Dutch East Indies, which is of considerable interest to historians, but contains little that directly concerns China. After reading an account of a voyage lasting nine months one is liable to feel a sense of anticlimax on actually reaching China. This was a criticism made against Staunton's account of the embassy when it was published; that he gave the reader more of the voyage than of the embassy. The second journal which Macartney kept, quite separately from the first, is concerned wholly with the embassy to China from the arrival of the ships off Macao in June 1793 until the safe return to Macao in January 1794. At the front of this second journal Macartney placed a very short summary of the outward journey which is just sufficient to put the reader in the picture before he starts the account of the embassy in China. It is this journal, together with the short summary of the outward voyage, which is printed in this book.*

The discipline of keeping a daily journal gave Macartney a form in which to set his thoughts, and on the whole his method is businesslike and straightforward, less diffuse than in his letters and dispatches. He describes in a direct way what he has seen, thought, and heard. Sometimes, given the right occasion, he lets his mind

* For a note on the MSS. of the two journals, their transmission and whereabouts, see p. 332.

soar and his pen paint. His set pieces of description are not too numerous, and we should be grateful for the detailed account of his audience with the Emperor Ch'ien-lung at Jehol on 14 September 1793 as well as for his description of the gardens there, which is all the more valuable because other European embassies were received at Peking and have left us accounts of the Capital but not of Jehol.* Macartney alone was able to see and describe the Manchu Emperors' hunting palace with its gardens and great temples near the Manchu homeland.

In describing diplomatic matters and tortuous negotiations Macartney is excellent, while the account of his conversations with the two conducting officials, Wang and Chou, especially the conversations of 15 and 16 August, are extremely lucid. Macartney was continually fencing with the Chinese, and trying to read between the lines in order to discover their motives. But he was truthful enough to admit that he did not understand everything. 'The Chinese character seems at present inexplicable.' (25 August). Only once in the Journal have I detected a piece of fine writing which may convey a misleading impression, and this is in Macartney's description of the temple of Pusa which he visited on 15 December during the return journey by waterways from Peking to Canton. The descriptions of the temple given by Staunton, Barrow and the Chinese local histories, to say nothing of a sketch of the place,† do not convey quite the same feeling of awe. Here, Macartney seems to have cast aside his usual accuracy and instead to have given rein to a Gothic imagination which can be compared to the writings of his contemporary, William Beckford. Macartney must have been aware of this exaggeration for he defends his own account in a spirited footnote:

> Upon lately reading this account of the temple of Pusa to one or two gentlemen who had visited it as well as myself, I find that though they perfectly agree in their recollection of all the principal features of the place, they think them rather heightened and surcharged. This I think is fair to take notice of, but at the same time I must add that I wrote the above description immediately on my returning to my yacht, merely for the purpose of aiding my recollection and certainly without any intention of imposing upon myself or upon others. Scarcely any two travellers, however, see the same objects in the same light, or remember them

---

* Jehol was used regularly by the early Manchu Emperors as a summer residence and as a hunting lodge. It lies about one hundred miles north of Peking and is outside the Great Wall. See note 28.

† Drawn by William Alexander and published as an engraving in the folio volume of illustrations to Sir G. L. Staunton's *An Authentic Account of an Embassy from the King of Great Britain to the Emperor of China*, 2 vols. (London, 1797), plate 43.

INTRODUCTION

with the same accuracy. What is involved in darkness to the optics of one man is often arrayed in the brightest colours to those of another. An impression vanishes or endures according to the material that receives it. . . .

One pleasing aspect of the Journal is Macartney's obvious interest in practical things and his exact observations on how they were made and how they worked. He describes the Great Wall in detail, giving exact measurements and explaining the method of construction; he describes how Chinese irrigation was carried out, and how the Grand Canal was constructed. This is quite in keeping with the England of his time when an educated man was also likely to be a 'natural philosopher' interested in the how and the why of things, and in obtaining exact information. Yet every now and then, in a passage of explanation or an account of some diplomatic matter, he gives us a tiny pen-picture of the scene, as when, in the entry for 4 September he writes: 'At one place where I alighted I saw a beautiful weeping willow hanging over a sweet pastoral stream on one side of the road. It measured fifteen feet in the girth and eight feet above the ground.' Or the entry for 24 November, which contains this film sequence: 'The mist grew every moment darker and heavier, and so magnified the objects around us that no wonder our senses and imaginations were equally deceived and disturbed, and that the temples, turrets and pagodas appeared to us through the fog, as we sailed along, like so many phantoms of giants and monsters flitting away from us, and vanishing in the gloom.' These brief pictures serve in the Journal much as do the coloured photographs and films of travellers today who use them to give immediacy to their lectures or writings. They are Macartney's personal attempt to capture and fix a scene which touched his imagination for a few moments during his travels.

If the reader finds that the first few pages of the Journal seem slow because of the author's preoccupation with wind and sea, let him start reading at the entry for 6 August when Macartney went ashore to meet the Governor of the province of Chihli, and the real business of the embassy began. From then onwards the narrative proceeds easily and the reader's interest is held except, perhaps, for the measurements of the Great Wall on the journey to Jehol which one may wish to omit. But in Macartney's day an opportunity of visiting the Great Wall was something to be dreamed of and envied. Dr. Johnson once became quite eloquent on the subject.

> He expressed a particular enthusiasm with respect to visiting the wall of China. I catched it for the moment, and said I really believed I should go and see

the wall of China had I not children, of whom it was my duty to take care. 'Sir,' (said he), 'by doing so, you would do what would be of importance in raising your children to eminence. There would be a lustre reflected upon them from your spirit and curiosity. They would be at all times regarded as the children of a man who had gone to view the wall of China. I am serious, Sir.'*

Macartney must have felt put on his mettle when he came to describe the Great Wall and was determined to note down all the details.

It is beyond my competence to discuss Macartney's style and to pronounce whether he wrote entirely in the Augustan manner of the eighteenth century, or whether in his descriptions there may not be a few glimpses of the romantic imagination. Although the Romantic movement is generally accepted as dating from the publication of the Preface to *Lyrical Ballads* by Wordsworth and Coleridge in 1798, presumably the ideas there expressed were in the air before that exact date. In Macartney's description of the temple of Pusa written in 1793 certain aspects seem to have an affinity with Wordsworth's famous description in *The Prelude* of how he stole a boat to enjoy an evening's row on a lake (Ullswater) and how the forbidding mass of 'a huge peak, black and huge', frightened him. Macartney himself set out 'in a small shallop', the water was 'motionless, silent, sullen, black', while 'the mountains frowned on us from on high'. Later he describes how 'a feeble taper glimmered from above ... we however looked forward to it as our pole star.'†
I hardly think that either Wordsworth or Coleridge could have read Macartney's description. Staunton's account was published in 1797, but his own description of the temple is more restrained, while Barrow did not quote from Macartney's description of it. In the main, however, Macartney's style is Augustan and classical. Certainly he read and admired Dr. Johnson, but there is less of the sonorous Johnsonian prose in his Journal, and perhaps more of Burke, while at other times he seems nearer to the style of Gray's letters and tours, or to Beckford's descriptions of his travels.‡ At least we know something of Macartney's taste in literature if a man's

---

* Boswell, *Life of Samuel Johnson*, 10 April 1778. Compare the remarks on the same subject by William Alexander quoted on p. 342 below.
† See *The Prelude*...., ed. Ernest de Selincourt, Book I (1850 text) lines 375 ff. Compare Book VIII, lines 74–99, where Wordsworth was writing under the influence of Macartney's description of the Imperial gardens at Jehol which Barrow quoted in his *Travels in China*, first published in 1804. De Selincourt's note on p. 550 refers.
‡ I am indebted to Professor Edmund Blunden, himself an admirer of Macartney's Journal, for these thoughts on Macartney's style.

INTRODUCTION

library is any criterion to go by. In the Wason Collection of Macartney papers at Cornell University there is a handwritten catalogue of his library dated 1786. Among other books it contained an account of Anson's Voyage round the World, Cook's Voyage to the Southern Hemisphere, as well as Du Halde's *History of China*, translated from the French in four volumes. Dr. Johnson was represented by his *Political Tracts, Fugitive Pieces* and *Lives of the Poets*, while Macartney had read and annotated Boswell's *Life of Samuel Johnson* in his own copy of the first edition. Milton was represented by *Paradise Lost*, and from a number of Miltonic echoes in the Journal, it seems that Macartney admired and remembered Milton. Also in his library were works by Locke, Voltaire, Chesterfield, Hume, Leibnitz and other seventeenth and eighteenth-century authors. He also possessed various books on medical subjects and natural history including Thomas Pennant's *Synopsis of Quadrupeds*.*

In reading Macartney's Journal a little historical knowledge and imagination is necessary in order to get the best out of it. One needs to remember how much of travel in those days was taken up with sailing ships; wind and weather and sailing terms played a large part in the journals of those who visited distant lands. Again, in travel overland horses and carriages predominated. Macartney showed legitimate pride in the craftsmanship exhibited in the carriage which he took to China, and in which he travelled to Jehol. 'In the course of these last two days both Wang and Chou took their turns to come into the post-chaise with me, and were inexpressibly pleased and astonished with its easiness, lightness, and rapidity, the ingenuity of the springs, and the various contrivances for raising and lowering the glasses, curtains, and jalousies' (*Journal*, 4 September 1793). Surely no other man in history has ridden post-chaise from Peking to Jehol and back? Again, it is worth remembering that those who took part in this embassy felt a tremendous sense of adventure. For them it was a great experience, a unique opportunity to visit a fabled land, about which the more they had read the more they began to wonder and doubt. Now they were to go there themselves and to live for a time among the inhabitants of China. They accepted the challenge and responded to it by reporting what they saw in their own notebooks.† But of the various first-hand accounts written Macartney's was the best, partly because he alone was fully in the know at each stage, partly because he alone was a practised observer,

---

* For Thomas Pennant, see footnote 61.

† For an annotated list of eye-witness accounts of the embassy, see Appendix D.

and because he alone had enjoyed a similar experience against which to measure it—his embassy to Russia. He never published his own account, perhaps because soon after his return to England he was sent on another diplomatic mission, this time to Verona to the Court of the exiled Louis XVIII,* while soon after his return from Italy he sailed for the Cape as Governor, and so never had the leisure necessary to edit it. Instead he allowed Staunton to draw heavily on his Journal when writing the official account of the embassy which was published in two large volumes in 1797. But Staunton's style, although weighty and worthy, lacks the personal touch which Macartney achieved. His account is less readable, is more of an official 'bluebook', less of a journal written for private pleasure. Macartney's manuscript was also used and quoted from by Barrow whose *Travels in China* was published in 1804, while Macartney was still alive. But as an account of the embassy it is episodic and rambling, and lacks the authority and direct eye-witness quality of Macartney's account.

One thing Macartney makes quite clear is that he noted down the material for his journal on the spot. Thus on 16 August he recorded: 'This day at half after six p.m. we arrived at the suburbs of Tungchow, where (our navigation being now ended) we quitted our yachts and went on shore, but before I proceed further I must set down a few particulars which have struck me, lest in the multiplicity of things before me they should slip from my memory. Indeed observations ought always to be written upon the spot; if made afterwards upon the ground of recollection they are apt to vary their hue considerably.'

On 15 December, after describing his visit to the rock temple of Pusa, he noted: 'In travelling through this country, whenever I meet with anything singular or extraordinary, I usually endeavour to recollect whether I have seen anything analogous to it elsewhere. By comparing such objects together and attentively marking their similitude and difference a common origin of principles, customs and manners may sometimes be traced and discovered in nations the most remote from each other.' Finally, the last paragraph of the Journal is addressed directly to the reader, and here Macartney explains his object and his method in keeping it.

> Should any accident throw this Journal under the eyes of a stranger unacquainted with me and the country I am now quitting, he might possibly imagine that I

---

* Louis-Stanislas-Xavier, Count of Provence and brother of Louis XVI, assumed the title of King in 1795 on the death of Louis XVII in prison.

> had too much indulged myself in local description and political conjecture. But nothing could be more fallacious than to judge of China by any European standard. My sole view has been to represent things precisely as they impressed me. I had long accustomed myself to take minutes of whatever appeared of a curious or interesting nature, and such scenes as I have lately visited were not likely to obliterate my habits or to relax my diligence. I regularly took notes and memorandums of the business I was engaged in and the objects I saw, partly to serve for my own use and recollection, and partly to amuse the hours of a tedious and painful employment. But I will not flatter myself that they can be of much advantage or entertainment to others.

This is certainly a clear statement of method. But does this mean that Macartney actually wrote the manuscript of his Journal while travelling in China? I think not. In order to answer this question it is necessary to examine the manuscript of the Journal which is preserved in Tokyo. This is not written in Macartney's own hand, though it has corrections and additions upon it, which I believe to be in Macartney's own handwriting. However, there are a number of documents preserved in the Wason Collection at Cornell which, from internal evidence, are in Macartney's writing and are initialled at the bottom by the single letter M. This hand is easy to identify once it has been seen a number of times. Thus, in the Commonplacebook which he kept, rather fitfully while in China, the entries are under subject headings and some of these are in his own hand. These he utilized in writing up the Observations on various subjects which he included after the Journal proper.* For instance, there is a note in his handwriting on government and another on women, both of which were drawn on when he came to write up his Journal.

Of greater significance are two small groups of notes preserved in the Wason Collection. They date from two separate periods. The first runs from 26 May until 3 August 1793 (Document no. 252), and the second from 1 January until 16 March 1794 (Document no. 290). These notes are on folded sheets of notepaper written in a very small but neat hand, and from internal evidence it appears that these were written by Macartney himself. These represent his rough, day-to-day notes about everything he thought worth recording at the time. However, not all these notes found a place in the Journal, and only served Macartney as a basis from which to write. Some have been crossed through and the gist of them transferred into the Journal, others were not used at all. At least one note is most revealing as it shows that Macartney and Captain Mackintosh of the *Hindostan* did not see eye to eye. It is dated Thursday, 1 August.

* See pp. 221–78.

> Captain Mackintosh not satisfied with my refusal of taking his furs, repeated the idea to Sir G. Staunton. Very hard on me. I don't understand him. At Chusan he wished us to go on by land and he to proceed no further. At Mietao and Ten-chou-fou he wanted me to send the things in the brigs to Tien-sing and discharge the ships. Now he wants to send trade to Pekin. He does not know his own mind and varies his plans and opinions as his interest seems to point, without any system.

But in his Journal there is no entry for that date. For 3 August the 'notes' read:

> The loading continues and it is hoped that it may be finished tomorrow. I went on board the *Clarence* and fixed to go in her. Captain Mackintosh came and talked a great deal, the bent of his discourse I understand but will not give way to. He may come to Pekin if he pleases but merely from curiosity and not from trade. Nothing can be produced lest it might be of prejudice to our own presents, if finer. Expressed my answer at his putting the chariot on board the junk and told him it must go back. I think he has behaved very ill in this matter.

In the Journal under date of 3 August the entry simply reads: 'The loading continues, and it is expected to be finished the day after tomorrow. The same Mandarin who attended yesterday returned today.'*

The other set of rough notes (1 January to 16 March, 1794) contains much information which was not put into the Journal, and in any case the Journal ends on 15 January. However, a few of these notes are reproduced in almost the same words in the Journal. For example the following is part of the rough note for Wednesday, 8 January which describes the parting from Wang and Chou.†

> Van-ta-gin and Chou-ta-gin came down to the *Lion* with us and dined on board with the Governor of Cae-chou-fou a red button, and two others. They then took leave of us and I should be guilty of great ingratitude to them if I did not bear testimony to their merits which towards us were very great. They all thro' behaved to us with great kindness and friendship and on every occasion when they could venture, served us effectually and did us justice in their reports. When they took leave of us they did it with strong marks of sensibility and shed many tears on the occasion. The next day they sent us a magnificent present of fruit, vegetables, etc., in twenty baskets at least.

If this is compared with the last paragraph of the entry for 8 January in the Journal it will be seen that while the sense remains the same the wording has been altered and shortened considerably in the version given in the Journal.

Along with these notes two loose pages of short observations

---

* For a note on Captain Mackintosh see Appendix A.
† For the probable identity of these two officials see Appendix A.

INTRODUCTION

have been preserved. One is interesting because it contains Macartney's thoughts on the difficulty of obtaining a true estimate of the population and resources of China.

> The Chinese are such puffs and exaggerators and so given to lying where even they have no motive, not even vanity, that everything I give as from them, must be received and credited with prodigious abatements. All the orientals are subject to this failing of exaggeration as is evident from the most ancient histories. In China they call the Emperor 'Ten thousand years'—that is his title, van-sary [*wan-sui*.—Ed.]—i.e. he ought and they wish him to live so long as if it were probable. They reckon their people by millions, their riches by ounces, and so on.

What then was Macartney's method of writing his Journal? From studying the documents I believe that he jotted down whatever he remembered of the day's events each evening on loose sheets of notepaper, without worrying much about the style. At some later date, perhaps on the voyage home, he used these notes as the basis for his Journal, which he then composed, improving the style and imposing order on his mass of material. The Tokyo manuscript of the Journal is not written in Macartney's own hand, but in a copy-book or clerkly hand. The writing has less character, and contains fewer flourishes than Macartney's own. Since he had with him on the embassy two under-secretaries, Acheson Maxwell and Edward Winder, and since presumably he was accustomed to dictating dispatches to secretaries, I think it reasonable to suppose that he dictated the Journal either to Maxwell or Winder. However, two copies of the 'Observations' on the Government of China, etc., exist, one in the same hand as the Journal and one in another hand. Whether Macartney wrote his Journal with the intention that it should eventually be read by the general public as well as by his family and friends it is hard to say.* But the final paragraph of the Journal beginning: 'Should any accident throw this Journal under the eyes of a stranger unacquainted with me and the country I am now quitting . . .' shows that he had thought of the possibility that one day those outside his circle of friends might read it. But even if

---

* Barrow, *Some Account of the Public Life and a Selection of the unpublished writings of the Earl of Macartney*, Preface, p. ix, mentions Macartney's Journal, 'a copy of which he transmitted to Mr. Dundas, then Secretary of State, as the public account of his proceedings on this new and extraordinary mission'. The East India Company requested Macartney to keep an account of the proceedings of the embassy 'with a Journal and Diary, to be delivered to us on your return to England'. See E. H. Pritchard, 'The Instructions of the East India Company to Lord Macartney on his Embassy to China and his Reports to the Company, 1792–4', *Journal of the Royal Asiatic Society*, 1938, Pt. II, p. 226.

to some extent he wrote up his Journal with an eye to posterity Macartney managed to retain a strong impression of immediacy, of day-to-day problems being faced and decisions made, and of his own vivid and personal reactions. Only when the Journal was adapted by Staunton for his official account of the embassy does the impact on the reader become second-hand and muffled.

Macartney's Journal contains many passages which have a special interest because they shed light on China at the end of Ch'ien-lung's reign, or because they have a certain familiar and topical ring about them. Here follow some samples:

Macartney's impression of the Chinese attitude towards truth (19 August, 3rd paragraph).

China's defenceless state in face of naval power, in the passage beginning: 'If the Court of Pekin is not really sincere can they possibly expect to feed us long with promises' (25 October).

A Manchu official's opinion of the Russians (13 November).

Why the rulers of China at that time were hostile to the reception of scientific ideas and inventions. This contains Macartney's declaration of faith in the inevitability of progress or 'amelioration' which is worth quoting because it is fairly typical of the outlook of the English gentleman of his time—an outlook of optimism tempered with Blackstonian complacency. 'It is, however, in vain to attempt arresting the progress of human knowledge. The human mind is of a soaring nature and having once gained the lower steps of the ascent, struggles incessantly against every difficulty to reach the highest.' To this is added a 'purple passage' footnote, in which Macartney elaborates on this theme beginning with the assertion 'Whatever ought to be will be' (4 December, paragraphs 3 and 4).

On 16 December (paragraph 6 onwards) he gives us an account of a typical day in the life of the Emperor which can also be found in the Helen Robbins edition of the Journal, but with the one significant alteration—she omits the last sentence which reads: 'A principal eunuch is always in waiting during the night in order to conduct to him any of the ladies whom he chooses to call for.' The Duty Eunuch—a pleasant picture.

INTRODUCTION

Some observations on the chief Hong merchants at Canton (26–8 December).

Finally, the entries for the period 2–7 January 1794 are lumped together under one long section which really comprises Macartney's summing up of the relations between China and England. Here Macartney is at his best, giving different aspects of the problem, and suggesting possible lines of action with their possible results in the best tradition of diplomatic dispatches. When he comes to define the status of China in the world of that time he does so in a passage of telling effect and in memorable words which can truly be described as prophetic.

> The Empire of China is an old, crazy First rate man-of-war, which a fortunate succession of able and vigilant officers has contrived to keep afloat for these one hundred and fifty years past, and to overawe their neighbours merely by her bulk and appearance, but whenever an insufficient man happens to have the command upon deck, adieu to the discipline and safety of the ship. She may perhaps not sink outright; she may drift some time as a wreck, and will then be dashed to pieces on the shore; but she can never be rebuilt on the old bottom.*

These words are so apt and so forcefully expressed that they deserve to be quoted in every history of modern China.

Not only did Macartney keep a day-to-day Journal, he also collected information under such headings as Manners and Character, Government, Justice, Property, etc. At the end of the Journal he explained why this information could not be incorporated in the Journal itself: '... I have added in the appendix a few papers relative to some particulars which I was desirous to be informed upon. They could not be inserted in their proper places, as it was frequently a long time after I had made my inquiries that I could obtain the answers, and when I did obtain them I was obliged to follow them up with further inquiries for explanation.' At the end of these observations on various subjects Macartney added a Conclusion† in which he explains how, before going to China, he 'perused all the books that had been written upon that country in all the languages I could understand', and obtained information from all he thought could help him. 'Having thus stored up in my mind all the materials within my reach I shut my books, and as soon as I arrived in the Yellow Sea I began a different course of study upon the same subject. Instead of reading any longer the accounts of others I turned to the

---

* See pp. 212–13.   † p. 278.

originals themselves, and lost no opportunity in my power of perusing and considering them.' These observations Macartney made for the benefit of the Government and the East India Company, so that those in authority in England might be more fully informed about the Chinese and their way of life. The Government would no longer have to rely on the observations of Supercargoes resident outside the walls of Canton, but could study the observations of a trained diplomat and his staff on a wide range of subjects.

However, we should not expect too much accurate and detailed information under these headings. Macartney was only in China for six months, and he had to rely on the services of a Chinese interpreter who understood Latin and Italian, but not French and English. Then, as now, the Chinese officials could tell the visiting foreigner what they wanted him to know, and he would have little chance of checking the information. Macartney realized this fully and never deceived himself over the value of the information he obtained.

> The intercourse of the Chinese with foreigners is, however, so regulated and restrained, and the difficulty of obtaining correct information so great that the foregoing papers must not be received without reserve nor regarded otherwise than as merely the result of my own researches and reflections, for I am sensible that, besides being defective in many points, they will be found to differ a good deal from the accounts of former travellers; but I am far from saying that the errors may not be in me, rather than in them.*

Would that some of our present-day pundits on China were as modest, and as undogmatic.

The general reader may find much of this information too specialized and detailed to be of interest. However, he may like to read the sections on Manners and Character, on Government, Justice and Property, and the observations made by Dr. Gillan on the state of Medicine in China. The remaining sections can well be left to historians of Ch'ing dynasty China, who will find embedded in them valuable scraps of information, but will need first the knowledge to disentangle what is misleading from what is true. The student of Chinese history may find it instructive to compare what Englishmen at the end of the eighteenth century knew about China at the end of Ch'ien-lung's reign, with what we today know of that period. He can measure how little or how much our historical knowledge has advanced since then.

Meanwhile, what is the value of the information which Macartney gives in these sections: is it perspicacious and detailed? The

* Conclusion, p. 278.

INTRODUCTION

answer is that these observations are very far from answering the questions one would like answered. Some of them are disappointingly thin, for instance the section on the Chinese language which is quite off the mark. Nor does Macartney show any knowledge of how the machinery of government worked at this time; he says nothing about the Grand Council, the Grand Secretariat and so on. He was forced to rely on what he saw or heard, and by placing all these separate details together to construct as full a picture as he could. Often his observations are acute and have the ring of exactness. About the common people he wrote:

> Superstitious and suspicious in their temper they at first appeared shy and apprehensive of us, being full of prejudices against strangers, of whose cunning and ferocity a thousand ridiculous tales had been propagated, and perhaps industriously encouraged by the government, whose political system seems to be to endeavour to persuade the people that they are themselves already perfect and can therefore learn nothing from others; but it is to little purpose. A nation that does not advance must retrograde and finally fall back to barbarism and misery.*

This is revealing not only of what is perhaps a continuing trait in the Chinese character, but also of a typical European attitude in the eighteenth and nineteenth centuries, a belief in the inevitability of 'progress', now generally discredited.

Another valid observation which Macartney continually makes is that there were two distinct nations in China at that time—the Chinese and the Manchus, and he adds: 'The government as it now stands is properly the tyranny of a handful of Tartars over more than three hundred millions of Chinese.' He concludes these remarks with: 'A series of two hundred years in the succession of eight or ten monarchs did not change the Mogul into a Hindu, nor has a century and a half made Ch'ien-lung a Chinese. He remains at this hour, in all his maxims of policy, as true a Tartar as any of his ancestors.'† The assimilation of the Manchus into the Chinese race did not take place until later.

Whenever he had the chance to observe for himself, and was not too handicapped by lack of the language, Macartney could be acute. For instance he was not overawed by the apparent stability and strength of the Manchu power. He diagnosed weakness and stress below the surface. 'In my researches I often perceived the ground to be hollow under a vast superstructure, and in trees of the most stately and flourishing appearance I discovered symptoms of speedy decay, whilst humbler plants were held by vigorous roots, and mean

* See p. 226. † See p. 237.

edifices rested on steady foundations.'* He then goes on to explain that the Chinese were recovering from the Manchu conquest and that a spark might 'spread flames of revolt from one extremity of China to the other'. Macartney's own explanation of the reason for this precarious situation is an interesting one, and not far from the truth.

> In fact the volume of the empire is now grown too ponderous and disproportionate to be easily grasped by a single hand, be it ever so capacious and strong. It is possible, notwithstanding, that the momentum impressed on the machine by the vigour and wisdom of the present Emperor may keep it steady and entire in its orbit for a considerable time longer, but I should not be surprised if its dislocation or dismemberment were to take place before my own dissolution.†

Since Macartney died in 1806 and the Manchu dynasty finally abdicated in 1912, this was very wide of the mark, nevertheless the emperors who succeeded Ch'ien-lung were in a weak position, threatened by growing internal unrest, and later by attacks from outside by the Western Ocean barbarians. The dynasty nearly perished in the mid-nineteenth century at the hands of the Taiping rebels.

On trade between Europe and China Macartney naturally had much to say. In the course of his observations he mentioned that in 1792 'the illegal and contraband trade of opium consists of two thousand five hundred chests . . .'. At this point it is necessary to say something about the opium trade as it then existed. Except for one occasion, in the season of 1782, when the East India Company itself sold opium at Canton because it was short of bullion with which to purchase tea, its policy was to confine its activities to the production of opium in India and to leave its distribution in China to private merchants. The British power in India had assumed a monopoly of the sale of opium inside its dominions in 1773 and later in 1797 assumed a monopoly of its manufacture. This monopoly came to yield a substantial part of the total revenue of British India. There were three sources of the supply of opium at this time: Bengal, where the Company controlled the sale, in the Native Provinces of Central India, where it was controlled by means of transit passes, and in Turkey where it was bought in small quantities by American traders. The best quality opium known as Patna and Benares came from Bengal, while an inferior kind called Malwa was produced in the Native States of India. The opium trade to China was thus in private hands. Because the Emperor had forbidden its import it had

* See p. 239. † See p. 239.

INTRODUCTION

to be smuggled into Kwangtung by the country merchants, who, as already explained (p. 14), were useful to the East India Company because they could supply the funds upon which the Company depended for its large purchases of tea. Thus, tea purchases were financed by two staple products—raw cotton and opium—both of which came from India.

As it happened, Macartney was in China at an interesting stage in the development of England's trade with that country. As yet the balance of this trade was in favour of China because of the huge purchases of China tea. But Macartney had already foreseen a problem which was to alarm the Chinese government into taking action against the opium trade about forty years later. Macartney wrote in the section entitled Trade and Commerce:

> Before I conclude the head 'Commerce' I cannot avoid adding a word or two, as not entirely foreign to the subject. If the China trade of the Dutch, French, Danes, Swedes, Americans, etc., by which the Chinese have hitherto received a considerable balance, should fall to the ground, and our trade continue to improve as it now seems to promise, that is to say, that the value of exports and imports between England and China should become nearly equal, and the balance between China and India remain still in favour of the latter, may not the Chinese take alarm at so much silver being sent out of their country in discharge of the balance?

The answer is they did, and this was one of the reasons why the Chinese government eventually made a stand against the smuggling of opium into the country. From the Chinese angle opium had been known as a useful drug for centuries. However, when it began to be in demand to satisfy a vicious habit rather than as a useful drug it was prohibited by Imperial decree. The first edict was issued in 1729, and a very definite ban was placed on its importation and use in 1797. This second edict shows that by the end of the eighteenth century indulgence in this vice had spread beyond the coastal provinces of Kwangtung and Fukien. But two obstacles prevented the Chinese government from actively stamping out the smuggling of opium. The chief difficulty was the corruptness of the Mandarins who got a fat squeeze out of leaving the smugglers alone, and also the naval weakness of the Manchus. The ships of the foreign smugglers were faster and better armed than the Imperial war junks.

Macartney discussed other facets of foreign trade with China, and in mentioning Russian trade wrote:

> The returns to China are made chiefly in furs, leather and woollen cloth, the latter mostly German with a small quantity of English superfine. In my road to Jehol I met several strings of camels laden with these woollens, and so ignorant in matters of trade were many of the Chinese that they believed them to be the

manufacture of Tartary, just as several English articles which I saw at Pekin were supposed to be the production of Canton.

The section on Arts and Sciences is interesting not so much for what Macartney tells us, as for his attitude towards Chinese technical achievements. He reveals the slight extent of his information on this subject when he states: 'In respect to science the Chinese are certainly far behind the European world. They have a very limited knowledge of mathematics and astronomy, although from some of the printed accounts of China one might be led to imagine that they were well versed in them.'* Though it is true that throughout Ch'ien-lung's reign there was little interest in scientific and technical matters, this had not been so previously. For proof of this one only has to glance at any volume in Dr. Needham's important work, *Science and Civilization in China*. Therefore in the section on the Arts and Sciences included in the Observations, and in the section on Medicine, Surgery and Chemistry I have been at pains to take up Macartney and Gillan in my notes wherever they have made sweeping statements which are not true, and I have given references so that the reader can satisfy himself on the true position in each instance.† However, this does not alter the fact that Macartney and the members of his entourage were eager to learn all they could about Chinese science and technology, and had they been given better information they would not have been so inaccurate. But the low esteem in which scientific and technical matters were held at the end of Ch'ien-lung's reign, together with the almost impassable language barrier, prevented them from satisfying their curiosity. Dinwiddie's *cri de coeur* sums up the position neatly: 'What information could we derive respecting the arts and sciences in a country where we could not converse with the inhabitants?'‡ It was not entirely the fault of the English that no one in the factory at Canton could speak Chinese. Foreigners were expressly forbidden to learn it and Chinese caught teaching them were punished. No wonder that Dr. Gillan's survey was mostly a tangle of misstatements. Had the Chinese from whom he tried to obtain the information been reasonably informed on the subject of medicine and surgery themselves, or willing to find out, and had he not been forced to rely on an interpreter, his account would not have been so wide of the mark. As it was he

* See p. 264.
† I wish to acknowledge here the considerable debt I owe to Dr. J. Needham and his research associate Dr. Lu Gwei-Djen. They not only discussed the content of these notes with me but kindly supplied me with the references as well.
‡ See Appendix D, p. 347.

INTRODUCTION

had to rely on the help of Jacobus Li who gave in Italian the gist of what he understood from another Chinese who may, himself, have been but slightly acquainted with the subject.* As proof of the indifference with which the great officials viewed scientific and technical matters at that time, Macartney relates that although Dr. Dinwiddie took with him all kinds of apparatus for making experiments, the officials at the capital appeared quite uninterested in these matters.

> But the Mandarins in Pekin manifested very little disposition of this kind; none of them discovered the slightest notion of the pressure of fluids, the principles of optics, perspective, electricity, etc., although several of them had seen air-pumps, electrical machines, spy glasses, prisms, magic lanterns, and show-boxes. Nevertheless, it was observed that most of the great men who came to see the globes, the planetarium, the barometers, and pendulums put up at the Yuanming Yuan affected to view them with careless indifference, as if such things were quite common and familiar to them, and the use of them well understood.†

It was a pity that the great officials at Peking were so contemptuous of technical inventions, otherwise the Chinese in the capital might have witnessed the diverting spectacle of Dr. Dinwiddie making an ascent in an air balloon over the roofs of the Imperial Palaces, or descending under the waters of the Northern Lake in Smeaton's diving bell. But in such matters they were probably ready enough to take their cue from the aged Emperor who was contemptuous of such inventions and was reported by Dr. Dinwiddie as being heard to say when inspecting an air pump, 'These things are good enough to amuse children.'‡ While people in Europe were flocking to see balloon ascents by Montgolfier and Lunardi and demonstrations of all the latest inventions, in China at that time they ignored such things.

These observations by Macartney on various aspects of China at the time of his embassy are uneven, but contain a fair number of interesting ideas and comparisons. The modesty of his conclusion to them is disarming.

---

* In a Commonplace Book in which Macartney put down information obtained during his China embassy there are notes on venereal disease and smallpox written in Italian, the information being supplied by 'Andrea Plumb', i.e. Jacobus Li. (Wason Collection, Cornell University.) For Jacobus Li see Appendix A.
† p. 266.
‡ Quoted in W. J. Proudfoot, *Biographical Memoir of James Dinwiddie*, p. 53. This statement is corroborated by William Alexander in his own MS. Journal, p. 26a. 'We hear from Deodati the Italian missionary that the Emperor had seen the presents of which he had spoken lightly, intimating that some were fit only for the amusement of children.'

Whatever I did see, or could learn from good authority, I have made it a point most faithfully to represent and report. The picture may seem harsh, cold or ill-coloured, but the fancy of the painter has intruded nothing into the picture that did not appear to him in the original from which he drew. He meant neither to embellish nor disfigure, but solely to give as just a resemblance as he could.

Macartney was aware that his descriptions of China were far less flattering than those translated into English from the writings of the Jesuits, which had such a vogue in the mid-eighteenth century. In fact one of the valuable results of Macartney's embassy was that it supplied Europe with a sober and matter-of-fact account of China which gradually replaced the optimistic and often imaginary accounts which the Physiocrats found so useful to quote when attacking the French monarchy before the revolution. By the end of the eighteenth century in Europe the picture of China contained in *Le Despotisme de la Chine** had given place to the information contained in Macartney's Journal.

Finally, it is worth remembering that the Journal, together with the Observations, is of interest not only for what Macartney says about China, but also for what he lets fall about Europe and England in his own times. These scattered references I have taken up in my own notes in the hope that they will interest the general reader and also be of some use to the student of that period. In reading the Journal one should try to keep in mind the background and the assumptions against which Macartney wrote it. If we take the thirty years from 1760 until 1790 as the period during which Macartney formed his impressions and gained his knowledge of England and Europe, we shall be able to imagine the background against which he lived. In England, during these years, educated men were influenced by the massive common sense of Dr. Johnson, who died in 1784, by the taste of the Adam brothers in architecture, by Josiah Wedgwood in design, and by Sir Joshua Reynolds on the principles of art.† In matters of law and the English Constitution, most men were lulled by the complacency of Blackstone and the praise of the French *philosophes*. It was a period of strong contrasts, the new ideas and the old jostling together. Some men were influenced by Adam Smith's new economic ideas while others were quite content

---

* By François Quesnay. Published in 1767 as a series of articles in which he pointed to China as an example of a country ruled in accordance with the principles of Natural Law.

† Reynolds delivered fifteen Discourses to the students of the Royal Academy, the first in 1769, very soon after the Academy's foundation, and the last in 1790.

INTRODUCTION

with monopoly and the mercantile attitude. In religious matters a number of serious-minded citizens were Methodists, but many others were freethinkers, or were satisfied with the complacency of the Anglican Church. Edward Gibbon, perhaps the most outstanding of the rationalists, was writing the *Decline and Fall of the Roman Empire*, which was published between 1776 and 1788.

But the second half of the eighteenth century in England was notable in more ways than in politics and the arts. This was a great age of exploration and expansion overseas. While Britain was losing her American colonies she was exploring the Pacific and preparing the way for her colonization of Australia. Cook's three great voyages of 1769–71, 1772–5 and 1776–9 set a precedent and a pattern, so that Macartney's embassy to China was partly a diplomatic mission and partly a voyage of discovery. It was not by accident that he took with him two botanists, two artists and an officer who could draw plans and maps.* Meanwhile the British were beginning to expand their foothold both in Canada and in India, and the first settlement was established in Australia in 1788. Equally typical of this period was a widespread interest in natural philosophy among educated men who might be amateur astronomers, geologists, botanists, zoologists or experimental chemists and physicists. Geographical exploration was paralleled by exploration of the forces of nature. Banks accompanied Cook on his first voyage as a gentleman botanist, and his activities on the coast of Australia are commemorated to this day in the name Botany Bay.† Sir Joseph Banks, just as much as Dr. Johnson, was typical of his age. As President of the Royal Society from 1778 until his death in 1820 he had considerable influence on practical affairs in his time, advising the King on how to improve his breed of sheep, advising the Government on the best methods for settling New South Wales, and advising Macartney on the best methods for bringing tea plants from China to Bengal. Moreover, the new Linnean system of classification had by now made possible a more scientific study of natural history. In astronomy Cook and Charles Green, an assistant astronomer at the Royal Observatory at Greenwich, had successfully observed the Transit of Venus on 3 June 1769 from the island of Tahiti, while in England Sir William Herschel was immersed in the construction of huge

---

* Lieutenant Parish. See p. 313. For botanists see p. 317.

† Cook recorded in his Journal of the voyage of the *Endeavour*: 'The great quantity of plants Mr. Banks and Dr. Solander found in this place occasioned my giving it the name of Botany Bay.' Quoted in H. C. Cameron, *Sir Joseph Banks* (Batchworth Press, 1952), p. 31.

telescopes which were considerably more powerful than previous ones. Joseph Priestley, another man typical of his age, was conducting experiments and adding his discoveries to the advance in knowledge of chemistry and electricity which was taking place in Europe in the late eighteenth century. Even Dr. Johnson was fond of 'chemical experiments'. This was also the age of the Scottish surgeons William and John Hunter who did much to advance medical knowledge by their study of human anatomy. In the same spirit George Stubbs, when he painted his horses, gave a more natural representation of them because he was a close student of animal anatomy. It was during this period that the Universities of Glasgow and Edinburgh turned out many eminent men in the world of medicine and 'natural philosophy'. In fact it was the beginning of a great age for Edinburgh, which now became a leading city of culture and learning. It was no accident that among Macartney's entourage were included two professional men of medicine and science, Dr. Gillan and Dr. Dinwiddie, and that they both held degrees from Edinburgh University. Meanwhile advances in scientific knowledge were quickly being turned to practical use by technical inventions. It was during the last forty years of the eighteenth century that the Industrial Revolution in England began to thrust forward mainly because of this inter-relation between scientific discovery and technology.

It is against this background that Macartney's Journal should be placed. Again and again Macartney shows his interest not only in diplomacy and commerce but also in technical and scientific matters. At this time an educated man could still read the Greek and Latin classics, the best authors of his native country, and at the same time feel a strong curiosity about the workings of the natural world and a practical interest in technical advances. It is this questing, thrusting spirit of England in the later eighteenth century that Macartney catches admirably in his Journal.

Finally, the story which Macartney relates is of topical interest. After one hundred and seventy years Britain is still trying to establish satisfactory relations with China. Some progress has been made since Macartney voyaged to Peking, but far less than might be expected. The present *impasse* may be temporary, and is perhaps the product of the world situation. But the thoughtful reader, comparing the difficulties which Macartney experienced in 1793 with those encountered by British diplomats and businessmen at the present time may discover certain similarities. Some of the reasons for

INTRODUCTION

Britain's failure to establish normal trade and diplomatic relations with China at the end of the eighteenth century still exist even now. If this is true, then a study of Macartney's embassy would seem of value to those who wish to understand China's relations with the Western world today.

THE JOURNAL

Journal from England to Cochin China*

I embarked at Spithead on board the *Lion* man-of-war of sixty-four guns, commanded by Sir Erasmus Gower, on Friday 21 September 1792 and sailed from thence on Wednesday 26th, the wind not permitting us to proceed sooner. The *Hindostan* Indiaman (on board of which were some of the gentlemen of my train, some of the guard, and the greater part of the presents) and the *Jackall* brig, tender, got under way at the same time, but a gale of wind coming on, the *Jackall* was obliged to put back, and we saw no more of her till the March following when she overtook us in the Straits of Sunda. The *Hindostan* kept company with us during the whole voyage from the Channel to the Peiho river in the Gulf of Pei-chihli.

We touched at Madeira for a few days from whence we proceeded to Teneriffe where we passed a week, the *Lion* having occasion to take in a quantity of wine for the ship's company during the voyage. We then proceeded to St. Jago, the capital of the Cape de Verde Islands (in order to renew our water and stock) and found it very much distressed, no rain having fallen there for three years past.

From St. Jago we sailed to Rio Janeiro where we remained about a fortnight. In our way from thence to the Straits of Sunda we visited the desert island of Tristan da Cunha as also the islands of Amsterdam and St. Paul. From the Straits of Sunda we hastened to Batavia at which place we were most hospitably entertained and most magnificently feasted by the Dutch Government. After leaving Batavia we anchored at several of the Malay islands, particularly Pulo Condore, which little spot has undergone almost as many revolutions within these few years as the greatest empires in a series of ages. Our next stage was Tourane Bay in Cochin China which afforded us a fine harbour, excellent water, plenty of provisions and accommodation for our sick. And after some days (when our good intentions and pacific deportment became unequivocally evident to the natives) we received distinguished civility and substantial kindness from the King of the country, whose place of residence was at the distance of

---

* [This is Macartney's brief summary of the outward voyage. For a note on the complete Journal of the voyage see p. 333. The China Journal begins on p. 63 below.—Ed.]

two days' journey from our berth. He sent us presents of rice and vegetables, spices and cattle, in short everything that we had occasion for, and in such abundance that there remained a surplus above our wants which I delivered to the English factory in China to be disposed of for the account of the East India Company.

In return for his Cochin Chinese Majesty's hospitality I made him a present of my fine steel-hilted sword, also one of Ellicott's[1] gold watches and a pair of bayonet-pistols and some camlet and other lesser articles, which pistols and camlet, etc., I was obliged to purchase from an officer on board the *Hindostan* and from another ship then at anchor in the bay, not being able to get at our own packages. This place affords a most excellent harbour and there is a spot where a fort might be built and garrisoned at a small expense sufficient to withstand any attempt, against any force likely to be brought against it from any power of this part of the world. The riches or commodities of the country are summed up in one distich by Father Loureiro, a Portuguese missionary, who resided long in the country.

> Xylaloin, myrrham, piper ardens, sacchara profert
> Pluraque, si repetas, officiosa dabit.[2]

But besides the above articles it produces excellent cinnamon, common rice and mountain rice in vast abundance and has many rich mines both of gold and silver, one of the latter at no great distance from Tourane Bay.

I have desired a sketch to be taken of this place* and of the site for a fort, together with many other useful particulars, nor have I neglected the island of Cambello in the offing, which I have also had visited and described so that the East India Company may have before them all the information in my power to procure for them, in case they should ever think proper to make a settlement at this place.†

* Vide plans, etc., in the appendix. [Omitted here—Ed.]
† [This description of the island of Callao is preserved in the Wason Collection of Macartney documents at Cornell University. (Document no. 362.).—Ed.]

Saturday, June 15. This day we sailed on board the *Lion* from Tourane Bay, in Cochin China, accompanied by the *Hindostan* and the two little brigs, *Jackall* and *Clarence*.

Wednesday, June 19. At two o'clock p.m. we saw the mainland of China, bearing N.N.E. distant . . .* leagues.

Thursday, June 20. At six o'clock a.m. we came to an anchor off the Grand Ladrone in eleven fathom water, within view of several small islands. The city of Macao bearing seven leagues N.W. of our berth.

I sent Sir George Staunton, Mr. Maxwell and Captain Mackintosh on shore for intelligence. None of the trading-ships of the season being yet arrived, all the gentlemen of the different European factories were still at Macao.

Saturday, June 22. This afternoon Sir George Staunton returned on board the *Lion*. The information from Macao was that the news of an Embassy from England had been received at Court with great satisfaction, that the Emperor considered it as no small addition to the glory of his reign that its close should be distinguished by such an event, and that orders had been dispatched to all the seaports of China to give the most hospitable and honourable reception to His Majesty's ships whenever they should appear on the coasts. At the same time it was perceived that the Embassy had excited great jealousy and apprehension in the minds of some of the Europeans at Macao, particularly of the Dutch and Portuguese. With respect to the former, they were soon quieted by our assurances, and by the letters we brought from Batavia; but with respect to the latter, it was easy to discover that, whatever face they might wear towards us, we had to expect from them every ill office and counteraction in their power. It is singular enough that, of the Europeans at Macao, none seemed better disposed to us than the Spanish agents Messieurs Agoti and Fuentes, who not only testified their goodwill by several

* [Word omitted.—Ed.]

little services, but gave us an essential proof of their confidence by sending me a manuscript plan and chart of the city of Macao* and the river of Canton, taken upon the spot by M. Agoti himself, the result of several years' observation and labour.

Sir George Staunton left the missionaries Nyan and Vang on shore, as also one of our intrepreters, Padre Cho, who suddenly took fright, and was so impressed with an apprehension of the Government at Pekin that he could not be persuaded to proceed with us. We indeed regret the loss of him the less as his companion, who remains with us, though not so complete a scholar is a man of much better temper, has a very good understanding, an excellent disposition, and is sincerely attached to us.† In the place of Padres Nyan and Vang we, at the earnest request of the Italian missionaries of the Propaganda at Macao, to whom we owe some obligations, have consented to give a passage to two others, who had been waiting for an opportunity of proceeding to Pekin and of entering into the Emperor's service there as mathematicians and astronomers.

Sunday, June 23. Sailed this morning from the Grand Ladrone at six o'clock a.m. with the *Hindostan, Jackall* and *Clarence* in company. Our course N.E. Passed Pedro Blanco, a large white rock above the water at four o'clock p.m. The Chinese coast still in sight nine leagues distant.

Friday, June 28. Lost sight of the *Hindostan* and the two brigs in the dark weather, and sailed for the Quesan‡ or Patchcock Islands, where we expect to fall in with the *Endeavour* brig, Captain Proctor, whom the Company's Commissioners had dispatched some time before, with orders to cruise there for us till the 30th inst.

Saturday, June 29. Passed the Heusan§ islands and arrived off the Quesans. Anchored in eleven fathoms soft mud, Patchcock island two leagues west from us.

Sunday, June 30. We saw nothing of the *Endeavour*, neither could we learn any news of her from the Chinese fishing-vessels, several thousands of which covered the sea all round us.

A Chinese pilot came on board with some of his people, who seemed never to have seen such a ship as the *Lion* before. They

* Vide plan and chart in the appendix, no. 1 AA. [Omitted here—Ed.]
† [See p. 319.—Ed.] ‡ [? Kiu-shan.—Ed.]. § [? Hu-shan.—Ed.]

examined everything with great curiosity, and observing the Emperor of China's picture in the cabin, immediately fell flat on their faces before it, and kissed the ground several times with great devotion.

Monday, July 1. At three o'clock p.m. we were joined by the *Hindostan, Jackall* and *Clarence.* Ever since we made the coast of China on the 19th of last month the weather has been (excepting one day) always dark, heavy, rainy, moist, or stormy.

Wednesday, July 3. This day we came to an anchor in Chusan Roads in six and a half fathom water, between Plowman's island and Buffalo's nose, a most excellent safe harbour, sheltered from all winds. The city of Chusan is about fifty miles west of us. Sir George Staunton went in the *Clarence* to Chusan in order to procure pilots from the Governor to conduct us to Tientsin.

Sunday, July 7. Sir George Staunton returned and brought with him the pilots, who, on being informed of the *Lion's* draft of water, said that a ship of her size could not proceed further than Miao Tao, near the city of Tengchowfu, at the entrance of the Gulf of Pei-chihli, but that all sorts of convenient vessels could be procured at that place to convey us from thence in safety to Tientsin, and the passage could be made in four days. The Gulf of Pei-chihli is represented by them to be without any good anchoring ground, very shallow, and in many places full of shifting sands.

Sir George Staunton had a good deal of difficulty in procuring the pilots. The Governor of Chusan, to whom he had applied, told him that his authority extended no further than to furnish us with pilots to conduct us to the adjoining province, where others would in the like manner be supplied to proceed with us to the next, and so on along the coast till we reached our last port. But as this mode of management did not at all suit us Sir George requested him, if possible, to find some persons who would take care of our navigation the whole way from Chusan to Tientsin, without stopping at any intermediate place, adding that if such pilots could not be had at Chusan, they might perhaps be had from Ningpo. Upon this the Governor, fully sensible of the Emperor's orders with regard to the Embassy, and apprehensive that we might address ourselves to his superior Mandarin at Ningpo, exerted himself so effectually that at last two men were discovered, who, having formerly been owners and masters of vessels in the trade, had frequently been at Tientsin; but it was with the greatest reluctance, and indeed, under a sort of compulsion, that they undertook the charge. And, after all, considering the little nautical skill they seem to possess, we don't expect any great assistance from them, but must trust a good deal to our own.

Monday, July 8. This day we sailed for Miao Tao from Chusan roads.

Thursday, July 16. I sent my proclamation* to Captain Mackintosh relative to the conduct of his people on board the *Hindostan*, also a duplicate to Lieutenant-Colonel Benson and to Mr. Barrow to be communicated to the soldiers and servants on board that ship.

Friday, July 19. We came to anchor this morning in Tchi-tao Bay, which our pilots had mistaken for Miao Tao. They seem grossly ignorant and timid, were frightened out of their wits when they observed that on our passage along the coast on shoaling our water we always stood out to sea, and were puzzled beyond measure by our manoeuvres, seeing us work to windward without minding weather, tide, or monsoon. I delivered my proclamation to Sir Erasmus Gower who ordered it to be read to the crew of the *Lion*.

Saturday, July 20. We got a new pilot from the shore, and in a few hours came abreast of the city of Tengchowfu. We now discovered that the Miao Tao is an island to the northward of us instead of being an harbour on the main as we had been led to imagine. It lies about three and a half miles eastward of Tengchowfu. We came to an anchor half way between them in eight fathom water, but veering off to fifteen. The road is bad and dangerous.

For several days past the weather has been very unsettled, sometimes extremely boisterous, and at others almost calm with frequent fogs, the latter always the concomitants of an easterly wind. Whenever it cleared up we eagerly turned our eyes towards the shore which afforded us great variety of prospect. The background of the province of Shantung as we sailed along it appeared generally barren, mountainous and rocky, but wherever we could perceive the smallest interval of cultivable ground it smiled under the hand of industry.

* Vide no. 2 among the enclosures of my dispatch to Mr. Secretary Dundas, dated 9 November 1793. [Omitted here—Ed.]

We could not well distinguish the kinds of grain that were growing, but they seemed to be Indian corn, millet, beans and peas. From Mandarin's bonnet to Tengchowfu there are pleasant villages to be seen on the shore at every half mile's distance, in which many of the houses are built of stone, the elevation of their roofs at an angle of forty-five degrees, covered with tiles very neatly arranged. The coast is often indented with small sandy bays and there are many safe harbours for vessels of a moderate size, formed by islands at a short distance from the main. The sea is of very unequal depth, often varying within an hour from five to forty-two fathoms, which last it never exceeded.

In the evening, about three hours after we had let go our anchor, the Governor of Tengchowfu, a Mandarin of high rank, came on board to visit me. He told me he had received orders from his Court to entertain us, to render us all services in his power, and to provide for us proper means of conveyance if we chose to proceed by land from Tengchowfu to Pekin. His visit lasted upwards of two hours, during which he talked a great deal, and with as much ease and frankness as if we had been old acquaintance. He is about thirty-five years of age, courteous, intelligent, and inquisitive.

Sunday, July 21. Dispatched the *Jackall* under the command of Mr. Campbell, First Lieutenant of the *Lion*, across the Gulf of Pei-chihli towards Tientsin to explore the navigation. At noon the Governor of Tengchowfu who was here last night, sent on board us a present of four bullocks, eight sheep, eight goats, five measures of white rice, five measures of red rice, two hundred pounds of flour, and several baskets of fruits and vegetables, which was acknowledged by a proper return.

An old man of seventy years of age has been put on board as pilot, who says that the Gulf of Pei-chihli is always perfectly safe in the months of July, August, and September, so that the *Lion* has nothing to apprehend from the weather for some time to come; that the boats for carrying our baggage and the presents are now ready at the mouth of the river leading up to Tientsin, and waiting for our arrival; and that they are large and convenient, and so constructed that there is no danger of our packages being wetted or damaged.

Tengchowfu is a city of the first rank in the province of Shantung about a mile and a half in length, but much less in breadth. At the southern extremity it includes a large space of ground that is not built upon and at the northern end is a rocky elevation with an extensive pagoda upon it which overlooks and commands the whole city. The walls and bastions are crenelled* and kept in perfect repair, but there is no appearance of any guns upon them.

This evening we were joined by the *Endeavour* brig, Captain Proctor of the Bombay Marine, which the Company's Commissioners had dispatched from Macao with letters for us. Not knowing of our intentions of calling there they had, a little before our arrival on the coast, ordered this vessel to the northward in hopes of her meeting us before we got the length of Tientsin.

Monday, July 22. Sailed from Tengchowfu leaving Miao Tao on our right hand and some small islands on our left. The passage is safe.

Tuesday, July 23. Our observations at noon today gave us 38.42 north latitude. We are now got into that part of the Yellow Sea called the Gulf of Pei-chihli which is remarkably smooth and clear. We have had a light breeze that carries us four or five miles per hour and at four o'clock this evening were out of sight of land.

Wednesday, July 24. At daybreak saw the land about twelve miles distant from us. It is low, flat and sandy, with a heavy surf beating upon it with great violence. We sounded, and had ground at six and a half fathoms. We suppose ourselves to be ten leagues to the south-east of Tientsin river. It is thought that the coast is laid down in the chart too far to the westward, or that too much breadth is given to the gulf which, by our reckoning, can not be three degrees from east to west.

Thursday, July 25. This morning at sunrise we discovered at about two or three miles distance a prodigious number of Chinese vessels all around us. Our pilots did not precisely know where we were; we supposed ourselves to be eight or nine miles from the river that goes up to Tientsin, as houses and trees were just discernible from the masthead to the north and south, and we found, when Lieutenant Campbell and Mr. Hüttner returned in the *Jackall* this evening, that we had not been much mistaken. They told us that when they arrived in the mouth of the river some inferior Mandarins had come on board, and finding they belonged to the Embassy, had conducted them on shore, and presented them to two great men, who had been stationed at that place for some time past in expectation of my

* [Crenellated.—Ed.]

coming. They were received with many marks of respect and treated with great hospitality. A thousand questions were asked relative to every particular of the Embassy; the number of persons, their ages and qualities, the presents brought for the Emperor, and what they consisted of, the size and force of the *Lion* and the other ships attending us, etc. The answers to all which were written down by the secretary in waiting. At their departure they were desired to inform me that everything was ready for my reception, and that as soon as the *Lion* approached the bar two great Mandarins would be sent on board to compliment me. We are now above five leagues distant from the bar.

It appears that the expectations of the Chinese have been raised very high, by the manner in which the Embassy was announced, of the presents which it is to be accompanied with. When Sir George Staunton was at Macao he found, on conversing with the gentlemen there, that they were conceived to be of immense value, and when he mentioned what they were, it was thought that the Chinese would be much disappointed. From these considerations Mr. Browne was induced to add his fine telescope to what we had already brought, and I have this day completed our apparatus with Parker's great lens,[3] which Captain Mackintosh brought out with him on a speculation, and which he has been prevailed upon to part with on very reasonable terms, forgoing all the profit which he had the prospect of deriving from the sale of so valuable and so uncommon an article. As this lens is an object of singular curiosity, I was apprehensive that if it fell into the hands of the Chinese merchants and were presented through their channel to the Emperor it might tend towards the disparagement of our fine things, and perhaps be imagined to eclipse them. I therefore thought it advisable, for the public service and the honour of the Embassy, to join it to the other presents; and now being possessed of Mr. Browne's fine telescope and this extraordinary lens, I flatter myself we have no rivalship to apprehend at Pekin from the appearance of any instruments of a similar kind. This evening I sent back Mr. Hüttner in the *Endeavour*, Captain Proctor, in order to explain to the Mandarins whom he had seen a number of particulars relative to our going on shore, and to make inquiry about several things which it is necessary for us to be previously acquainted with.

Friday, July 26. It rained most violently at the forenoon, and in the evening we had for several hours together such a series of lightning and thunder as I never remember before. The lightning seemed to overspread the whole sky with immeasurable sheets of livid flame, accompanied by continued volleys of thunder that resembled the rolling fire of well-disciplined troops at a review. The sea, however, remained perfectly smooth and unruffled by these concussions of the atmosphere, and we rode at single anchor all the time.

Saturday, July 27. A clear fine day. The sun seems to rise with new brightness and serenity after the turbulence of the night. I delivered to Sir Erasmus Gower my letter to him of this date.*

Sunday, July 28. Several inferior Mandarins came on board, and informed us that everything was preparing for our landing, that a number of boats were already in waiting, and that the remainder would be down to-morrow. We shifted our berth and moved a little nearer to the bar in six fathom water. Our station was ascertained this day by an exact observation; $38.51\frac{1}{2}$ north latitude and 117.50 east longitude from Greenwich. The variations of the compass by an amplitude; 27 July 1° 29" west, and 28 July 1° 25" west. The rise of the tides here is eight or nine feet, the ebb and flow all round the compass, but the strength of the flood is from south-east and of ebb from north-west.

Monday, July 29. Nothing material occurred.

Tuesday, July 30. The *Endeavour* returned and brought us all the information we had desired. Some of the Mandarins having said that they intended to purchase watches and swords when they came on board, seemed a little disappointed when Mr. Hüttner told them that as we were not merchants we had nothing to sell.

It would seem however, from this, that they expect presents of the kind, and unluckily, our baggage where those articles are cannot easily be come at. I must, therefore, I believe, purchase from some of the officers of the *Hindostan* a few small things for the purpose.

Wednesday, July 31. The wind blowing all day very strong from the eastward prevented any boats coming from the shore. At noon two Mandarins of high rank attended by seven large junks laden

---

* Vide no. 3 among the enclosures of my dispatch to Mr. Secretary Dundas, dated 9 November 1793. [Omitted here—Ed.]

with a variety of provisions for our ships, came alongside. The profusion of these was so great and so much above our wants that we were obliged to decline accepting the larger part of them. I here insert the list.

20 bullocks, 120 sheep, 120 hogs, 100 fowls, 100 ducks, 160 bags of flour, 160 bags of rice, 14 boxes of Tartar bread, 10 chests of tea, 10 chests of small rice, 10 chests of red rice, 10 chests of white rice, 10 chests of tallow candles, 1,000 water melons, 3,000 musk melons, 22 boxes of dried peaches, 22 boxes of fruit preserved with sugar, 22 boxes of other fruit, 22 boxes of ochras, 22 boxes of other vegetables, 40 baskets of large cucumbers, 1,000 squash cucumbers, 40 bundles of vegetables, 20 measures of peas in the pods, 3 baskets of earthenware or coarse porcelain.

In truth, the hospitality, attention, and respect which we have experienced at Tourane, Chusan, Tengchowfu, and here are such as strangers meet with only in the Eastern parts of the world.

The two chief Mandarins are called Wang *ta-jen* and Chou *ta-jen*.* Wang and Chou are their family names; *ta-jen* is the title annexed to their rank, and signifies Great Man. Wang is a war Mandarin, has a peacock's feather and a red coral flourished button on his cap, which is the second order. Chou, who wears a blue button, which is a degree inferior to the red, is a civilian and a man of letters. After a number of compliments and civilities in the Chinese manner, we proceeded to business, and Chou wrote down from time to time such particulars as he thought necessary.

We have settled with them everything relative to our going ashore, the mode of conveying our baggage and the presents, and the kind and number of vessels for the purpose. I find it will be a work of four or five days at least before we can leave the ship.

These two Mandarins seemed to be intelligent men, frank and easy in their address, and communicative in their discourse.

They sat down to dinner with us, and though at first a little embarrassed by our knives and forks, soon got over the difficulty, and handled them with notable dexterity and execution upon some of the good things which they had brought us. They tasted of our wines of different kinds, and also of our spirits, from gin, rum, and arrack, to shrub, raspberry, and cherry brandy, the latter of which seemed to hit their palates in preference to the rest, and they shook hands with us like Englishmen at their going away. They were much struck with the appearance of the guard and Marines (which were drawn up

* [See Appendix A, pp. 325–31.—Ed.]

on the quarter deck to salute them as they passed), listened with attention to our music, and departed, I believe, very much pleased with our manner of entertaining them. They were very inquisitive about the presents, and when I explained to them their nature they seemed to think them very proper, and requested a list* of them to be transmitted to Court, which I have promised.

Friday, August 2. This day the junks came from the shore alongside of the *Hindostan*, and began to take in the articles which are to be carried from on board her. A Mandarin of the third order with a blue button on his cap came with them to superintend the business, and stayed till the vessels were loaded.

Saturday, August 3. The loading continues,† and it is expected to be finished the day after to-morrow. The same Mandarin who attended yesterday returned to-day.

Sunday, August 4. This day the people worked with great alacrity, the loading was completed, and all the baggage and presents put on board the large junks, to be transhipped into smaller ones, at Taku, in order to be conveyed up the river to Tungchow (within twelve miles of Pekin), where the navigation discontinues. The Chinese sailors are very strong and work well, singing and roaring all the while, but very orderly and well regulated, intelligent and ingenious in contrivance and resource, each of them seeming to understand and exercise his proper share of the business and labour going forward. In each vessel were inferior Mandarins who received the articles and gave accountable notes for them, so that no loss or mistake is likely to happen.

All the Chinese whom we have yet seen, from the highest to the lowest, have their heads close shaved, except on the crown where the hair is left untouched by the razor for about a couple of inches in diameter and is suffered to grow to a great length, being considered as a very becoming ornament. It is always black and as strong and coarse as horse hair, which it much resembles. It is plaited in a tress and falls down the back like a Ramillies queue.‡ I have seen some of

---

* Vide no 5 among the enclosures in my dispatch to Mr. Secretary Dundas, 9 November 1793. [Omitted here—Ed.]

† Vide drawing of the *Lion* and a junk loading alongside, in the appendix no. 2B. [Omitted here—Ed.]

‡ [A wig with a long plaited tail fashionable in eighteenth-century England. Named after Marlborough's victory over the French at Ramillies in 1706.—Ed.]

them a yard long. Those who can afford it wear bonnets of bamboo with a red silk fringe round them. The lower sort have straw hats but many of them go quite bareheaded.

Tomorrow we shall proceed ashore. From the very distinguished reception which we have met with, and from every appearance being so much in our favour, I think it will be best to send the *Hindostan* to Chusan with the *Lion* (which is now so sickly that she must get into the first possible safe port for recruiting her people), in hopes that we may be able to obtain permission for her (the *Hindostan*) to take in a cargo there, by way of a beginning to the expected extension of our commerce in China.

Captain Mackintosh himself comes with us to Pekin, and I propose to dispatch him from thence with the permission, if procured, to join his ship at Chusan, and to carry our dispatches from thence to England, which we flatter ourselves will then be very interesting.

Monday, August 5. This day at nine a.m. we left the *Lion* man-of-war, and embarking in smaller vessels (myself and the gentlemen of the Embassy in the *Clarence*, *Jackall*, and *Endeavour*, the servants, guards and other attendants with the baggage, presents, etc., in Chinese junks), proceeded to the mouth of the Peiho river, the distance being about eighteen to twenty miles. Having a good breeze and a spring tide in our favour we, in a few hours, got over the bar on which we found from seven to nine feet water. At the bar and within it the water is very thick and turbid, although between the bar and the *Lion*'s berth the sea was remarkably green and clear. The coast is so low that it can scarcely be seen till you approach within a couple of miles of it and is only then to be distinguished by the buildings which rise above it. On entering the river we were perfectly astonished and confounded by the inconceivable number of vessels of all sorts with which it was covered.

The troops were drawn up on the southern bank and made a tolerably good appearance. The Mandarins, Wang and Chou, who had dined with us on board the *Lion*, now came to visit us, and pressed us much to accept their invitation to a banquet on shore which had been prepared for us, but being a good deal fatigued I declined it, and proceeded up the river about a mile further to the yacht provided to convey me to the city of Tungchow, within twelve miles of Pekin. This yacht was large, clean, comfortable, and convenient, and here I found the Mandarins Wang and Chou to welcome me, and to inquire whether anything was further necessary for my accommodation. Similar care and attention seemed to have been paid to all the other gentlemen.

The river here appeared to be as broad as the Thames at Gravesend. Great numbers of houses on each side, built of mud and thatched, a good deal resembling the cottages near Christchurch in Hampshire, and inhabited by such swarms of people as far exceeded my most extravagant ideas even of Chinese population. Among those who crowded the banks we saw several women, who tripped along with such agility as induced us to imagine their feet had not been crippled in the usual manner of the Chinese. It is said, indeed, that this practice, especially among the lower sort, is now less frequent in the northern provinces than in the others. These women are much weather-beaten, but not ill-featured, and wear their hair, which is universally black and coarse, neatly braided, and fastened on the top of their heads with a bodkin.

The children are very numerous and almost stark naked. The men in general well-looking, well-limbed, robust and muscular. I was so much struck with their appearance that I could scarce refrain from crying out with Shakespeare's Miranda in the 'Tempest':

> Oh, wonder!
> How many goodly creatures are there here!
> How beauteous mankind is! Oh, brave new world
> That has such people in it!

Tuesday, August 6. This morning early, provisions for the day were distributed with great order and regularity and in vast abundance among all the different departments of the Embassy, and soon after, several Mandarins of high rank came to visit me, and to inform me that the *Tsung-tu* or Viceroy of the province of Peichihli,* whose usual residence is at Paotingfu, one hundred miles distant, was arrived here, having been sent by the Emperor to compliment me on my entrance into his dominions, and to give proper orders upon the occasion. At eight a.m. I went on shore accompanied by Sir George Staunton, his son, and our interpreter, passing from my yacht over a temporary wooden bridge erected for this purpose, covered with mats, and having rails on each side decorated with scarlet silk.

Here we found palanquins prepared for us, which are neat light chairs made of bamboo, and covered with satin, and carried by four stout fellows, two of them before and two of them behind. In these

* [For a note on the functions of provincial officials see note 102.—Ed.]

we set out escorted by a troop of horse for Hai-chin-miao, or the temple of the Sea God, where the Viceroy had taken up his quarters; and though the distance was near a mile, yet the same men carried us at a pretty smart pace the whole way without resting.

Before the gates of the temple were several tents pitched of various colours, white, red, and blue (but the latter seemed to predominate), having each a distinguishing pennant, and before them were drawn up several companies of soldiers with sabres in their hands (no fire-arms), and dressed in a uniform blue stuff or cotton, laced with a broad red galloon. Besides the troop of horse which escorted us, there was another body of cavalry attending at the temple, each cavalier having a bow and a quiver of arrows, but no sword or pistols.

The Viceroy received us at the gate with distinguished politeness and an air of cordiality, and led us into a great saloon, which was soon filled with his officers and attendants, from whence, after drinking tea, he removed to another apartment, to which we passed through a spacious square court, each side of which was formed by magnificent buildings, much resembling those in my book of Chinese drawings. The ornaments were so brilliant and so diversified that I at first imagined them to be of wood, painted and highly varnished, but on a nearer inspection I found them to be of porcelain and tiles of various moulds and colours. Though the Chinese architecture is totally unlike any other, and most of its combinations and proportions contradictory to ours, yet its general effect is good and by no means displeasing to the eye.

We now entered upon the business. The Viceroy began by many compliments and inquiries about our health, and talked much of the Emperor's satisfaction at our arrival, and of his wish to see us at Jehol in Tartary* (where the Court always resides at this season), as soon as possible. To these we made the proper return of compliment, and then informed the Viceroy that the train of the Embassy consisted of so many persons, and that the presents for the Emperor and our own baggage were so numerous, and took up so much room that we should require very spacious quarters at Pekin. That as we found it was the Emperor's wish for us to proceed to Jehol we should prepare ourselves accordingly, but that we should find it necessary to leave a great part of the presents at Pekin, as many of them could not be transported by land to such a distance without being greatly damaged, if not totally destroyed. We explained to him the high

* [See note 28.—Ed.]

compliment intended by the first sovereign of the Western world to the sovereign of the East by sending the present Embassy, and hoped it would be attended with all the good effects expected from it. That as it was equally my duty and inclination to promote these views to the utmost of my power, I requested the Viceroy would be so kind as to give me such information and advice as might enable me to render myself and my business as acceptable to the Emperor as possible. I also mentioned to him that, as the *Lion* and the other ships that came with me were very sickly, and stood in need of an hospital and of refreshments on shore for the accommodation and recovery of their people, it would be necessary for Sir Erasmus Gower to be furnished with a diploma by virtue of which he might be entitled to those advantages at such ports as he might find it most convenient to repair to on the coast of China, either Miao Taó, or Chusan, for the advancing season required his speedy departure out of the Gulf of Pei-chihli.

It is impossible to describe the ease, politeness and dignity of the Viceroy during the whole conference, the attention with which he listened to our requests, and the unaffected manner in which he expressed his compliance with them. With regard to the ships, imagining their stores must have been exhausted in so long a voyage, he offered to supply them with twelve months' provisions immediately. I hope this does not forbode his wishes for our speedy departure. He is a very fine old man of seventy-eight years of age, of low stature, with small sparkling eyes, a benign aspect, and a long silver beard, the whole of his appearance calm, venerable and dignified.[4] During the course of this visit I was particularly struck with the apparent kindness and condescension with which the people of rank here speak to, and treat, their inferiors and lowest domestics.

When we returned to our yachts, we found a most magnificent and plentiful dinner prepared for us, which had been sent as a present by the Viceroy.

Wednesday, August 7. Early this morning Wang came to visit me and said it was the intention of the Viceroy to wait upon me at ten o'clock a.m. He then turned the discourse upon the Viceroy's great age and debility of body, which, however, he said, would not prevent him from paying his compliments to me in person, although it would be attended with great inconvenience to him to walk from the shore over the wooden bridge to my yacht; the descent from the bank being very steep, and not quite safe for a feeble old man. I

PREPARATIONS FOR DEPARTURE

immediately saw what he was driving at, and therefore told him that I should be very sorry to be the occasion of the Viceroy's risking either his person or his health for the sake of a visit of ceremony; as for other points of ceremony I was unacquainted with the Chinese customs myself, but as the Viceroy knew them perfectly, I was sure he would do, in regard to them, whatever was right, and which the Emperor would most approve of his doing. Upon this, Wang said that the Viceroy would come in his palanquin to the end of the bridge, and send in his visiting-ticket to me, and hoped I would consider it the same as if he had come across the bridge in person into my yacht. I repeated what I had said before, and told him I left the matter entirely to the Viceroy himself. He seemed to go away very well pleased, and at ten o'clock the Viceroy came in great state with the parade of guards, and a very numerous attendance of Mandarins and officers, who, as soon as his palanquin was set down, all dismounted from their horses and kneeled down to pay him their obeisance. He sent an officer with his visiting-paper, which is a large sheet several times doubled, and painted red, and inscribed with the owner's titles in large characters, and which my interpreter received from him. This business being performed, the Viceroy returned to his quarters in the same form, ceremony, and order with which he came.

This day and the next were chiefly employed in preparing for our departure, and arranging the order of our progress. In this we were assisted by the different Mandarins appointed to attend us, with regularity, alertness, and dispatch that appeared perfectly wonderful. Indeed, the machinery and authority of the Chinese Government are so organized, and so powerful, as almost immediately to surmount every difficulty, and to produce every effect that human strength can accomplish.

The gentlemen of the Embassy, the servants, artists, musicians, and guards, together with the presents and baggage, were embarked on thirty-seven yachts, or junks, each yacht having a flag flying at her mast-head to distinguish her rank and ascertain her station in the procession. There was, besides, a great number of other boats and vessels of various sorts for the Mandarins and officers who were allotted to our service, and who amounted to near one hundred of different degrees, wearing the red, blue, white and yellow buttons, by which their respective qualities are denoted.

Friday, August 9. This morning I dispatched Mr. Proctor in the *Endeavour* from the river. He was obliged to take back with him the two Macao missionaries, Hanna and Lamiot,[5] without their ever coming ashore. We found, indeed, that if they accompanied us to Pekin they would be considered as belonging to the Embassy and obliged to depart with it, whereas their intention is to enter into the Emperor's service and to remain the rest of their lives in China, like the other missionaries.

At noon the gongs or copper drums began to beat with a most deafening noise, and gave the signal for all being ready for departure. In less than an hour our whole fleet was under sail, and we proceeded up the river with a good breeze and flowing tide at the rate of about four miles per hour.

Sunday, August 11. This morning we arrived at the city of Tientsin. It is about eighty miles distant by water from the mouth of the river, but only forty-five by land. Here the Viceroy had arrived the night before in order to receive us, and here we were met by Chengjui,* a Tartar Mandarin in high office at this place, who was styled the Emperor's Legate, having been deputed, together with Wang and Chou, to accompany us from thence to Jehol, the Viceroy's age and infirmities disabling him from any fatiguing service. Our yachts stopped almost in the middle of the town before the Viceroy's pavilion. On the opposite quay, close to the water, was erected for this occasion a very spacious and magnificent theatre, adorned and embellished with the usual brilliancy of Chinese decorations and scenery, where a company of actors exhibited a variety of dramas and pantomimes during several hours almost without intermission.

Both sides of the river were lined for near a mile in length with the troops of the garrison, all in uniform, accompanied by innumerable flags, standards, and pennants, and by the clangour of various instruments of war-like music. At noon I disembarked with all the gentlemen of the Embassy and my whole train of servants, musicians, and guards. I was received at my landing by the Viceroy and the Legate, and conducted to their pavilion, where as soon as we were seated the conversation began, and continued for some time in the same general strain of mutual compliments and profession as our former one at Hai-chin miao. We then descended to particulars, and after a very long discussion, during which I easily discovered a perverse and unfriendly disposition in the Legate toward all our concerns, and which struck me the more forcibly when contrasted with the urbanity and graciousness of his superior the

* [See Appendix A, pp. 322-5.—Ed.]

Viceroy, it at last was settled that we should proceed upon the river up to Tungchow, a city within twelve miles of Pekin, which would take us up seven days, and consequently carry us to the 18th of August.

From Tungchow we were to travel the rest of our journey by land, but we should probably be detained at that place for several days, on account of the trouble of removing the presents and baggage out of the boats, of procuring porters and carriages for their conveyance, and a variety of other arrangements necessary to be made for the accommodation of the Embassy previous to our settlement in the capital. I calculated that thus we should scarcely be able to reach Pekin sooner than the 26th, and that we should then require at least ten days to repose ourselves, to settle my family, to separate the presents, and prepare for our further journey into Tartary, which I supposed we might be able to begin about 5 September. The planetarium, the globes, the great lens, the lustres, the clocks, and some other articles, I declared my intention of leaving behind at Pekin, and expressed my wishes of taking with me such of the other presents only as were not likely to suffer by a long land carriage. The journey from Pekin to Jehol would not exceed six or eight days at most, so that we might expect to reach the Emperor's Court some time before his birthday, which we understood was to fall on 17 September.

According to these ideas, which seemed to be approved of, I took my measures, but to my great surprise soon after the Legate, who now began to come forward with an air of greater importance, took up the subject of our conversation anew, started objections to some parts of the arrangements, and pressed me very urgently to let all the presents go to Jehol at once. I told him that nothing could be more agreeable to me than to accommodate myself to his ideas, but that from the nature and mechanism of several of the presents (which I explained to him), it would be impossible to transport them in the manner he wished without irreparable damage. Of my reasons he seemed to have no comprehension, but adhered to his own opinion, and added that he believed the Emperor would insist on having all the presents carried to Jehol and delivered at the same time. I answered him that the Emperor was certainly omnipotent in China, and might dispose of everything in it as he pleased, but that as the articles which I meant to leave at Pekin would certainly be totally spoiled if managed according to his notions, I requested he would take them entirely into his own hands, for that I must be excused from presenting anything in an imperfect or damaged state, as being unworthy of His Britannic Majesty to give and of His Chinese Majesty to receive.

This consideration startled him and, together with the Viceroy's opinion, who perfectly comprehended and felt my reasoning, induced him to recede and to acquiesce in the first arrangement; but I could not avoid feeling great disquiet and apprehension from this untoward disposition so early manifested by the Legate.

Having now adjusted this matter we took our leave and returned to our yachts, where a magnificent dinner was sent us by the Viceroy with wine, fruits, sweetmeats, etc., together with presents of tea, silk, and muslins, not only for myself and gentlemen of my train, but even for all the servants, mechanics, musicians and soldiers. Although of no great value, they were accompanied with so many obliging expressions and compliments that we received them in the manner we thought most likely to please the person who made them, especially as his whole deportment to us had been so handsome and satisfactory; and as he was to proceed directly to Jehol, where, no doubt, he would give an account of us to the Emperor, and we flattered ourselves from our conduct that it would not be to our disadvantage. During the evening we received many visits from the principal Mandarins of Tientsin and the neighbourhood. They seemed to examine everything belonging to us—our dress, our books, our furniture—with great curiosity and attention; were very inquisitive, lively, and talkative, and totally void of that composure, gravity, and seriousness which we had been taught to believe constituted a part of the Chinese character.

This evening I received two letters from Mr. Grammont, a missionary at Pekin,[6] offering me his services, and cautioning me against a Portuguese missionary, who, he says, has been appointed interpreter to the Embassy. We received no information of this kind from the Viceroy, the Legate, or Wang or Chou. However, without taking notice of it, or showing that I knew it, I seized the first occasion to request that we might be allowed, when we arrived at Pekin, to select one of the European missionaries in the Emperor's service to attend us, and assist us in our affairs, whose language we are acquainted with. They promised to write to the Court on the subject, and said they had no doubt of success.

The city of Tientsin is one of the largest in the empire. I think its extent along the river cannot be less than from Milbank to Limehouse. Along the quays on each side are many conspicuous buildings, chiefly temples, warehouses, magazines and public edifices.

TIENTSIN

The private houses make no great figure and present only a dead wall to the street, for all the windows look into the courts within. The population is said to exceed 700,000 souls. The crowds of people (males only) whom we observed both on shore and in the boats on the river were quite astonishing. The numbers of vessels of different kinds were no less so; they certainly must amount to many thousands. Several of them are of great size: from 100 to 160 feet long though seldom more than 25 feet broad. They are built very strong, of the shape of a long flat-bottomed trough curved upwards at each end, but the poop considerably higher than the prow and projecting a vast way behind the sternpost which thus appears almost in the middle of the vessel. The sails are of mats or of cotton, made like a fan to fold up with bamboo sticks, and when wanted to be set are drawn up from the deck with great labour (for they are ignorant of the use of the double pulley) by rings or hoops of rattan round the mast which is of one stick and of enormous thickness, and which having no shrouds is supported by a stout . . .* in the kelson below and by strong wedges driven in at the partners above. The depth of the hold from the deck is only eleven feet, and the draft of water about five or six. These vessels frequently make considerable voyages along shore, trading to Lai-chou-fu,† Tengchowfu, Ningpo, Amoy and even to Canton but are frequently wrecked and lost upon the coasts from the extraordinary ignorance of the Chinese in the art of navigation, for although above two hundred and fifty years are elapsed since they have been acquainted with Europeans, and although they see and admire our ships and our seamanship yet have they never in the slightest point imitated our build or manoeuvres but obstinately and invariably adhere to the ancient customs and clumsy practice of their ignorant ancestors; and this negligence is the more extraordinary as there is no country where naval skill is more requisite, for the interior provinces are all connected by innumerable canals, rivers and lakes and the maritime ones are chiefly subsisted by the fishery.‡ They have no forestaff, sextant, octant or quadrant or other instrument for taking the latitude, neither do they make use of any log-line to ascertain their run. The only directions they have are their soundings and compass, and their guess of the distance from headland to headland. About the middle

---

* [Word illegible.—Ed.]
† [Now Yeh-chou. Near Tengchow.—Ed.]
‡ [But by the end of the embassy Macartney had revised his opinion. See p. 274.—Ed.]

of the town the river divides; the branch which we have ascended flows almost due east, the other takes a southern direction. Our course is on the main stream N.W. which we are to pursue without stopping, except for a short time to make visits and to receive the provisions for our tables, which are regularly distributed every day early in the morning.

Monday, August 12.   This morning we arrived at Yong-siun.* The tide comes no higher up than to this place which is thirty-three miles from Tungchow, and from hence our yachts are drawn up against the stream by trackers on shore. There are usually fourteen or fifteen men to each yacht, so that the number now employed by us amounts to upward of five hundred. The people engaged in this service are comely and strong made, but remarkably round-shouldered, owing, I suppose, to their mode of labour. They appear to be coppercoloured from their constant exposure to the sun; but they are naturally fair, as we observed when they stripped to plunge into the water. As in summer they go naked from the waist upward, their complexion is, of course, very dark, but in the parts below where they are usually clothed is not so.

We are much troubled with mosquitoes, or gnats, and other insects, among which is a *phatana* or moth of a most gigantic size, not less than a humming-bird, and we are stunned day and night by the noise of a sort of cicada which lodges in the sedgy banks and is very obstreperous. Its music is not of the vocal kind as I at first imagined, but seems to be occasioned by a strong oscillation of the wings where they articulate with the dorsal vertebrae.†

The country on each side of the Peiho is quite flat and subject to inundations, the inconveniences of which are guarded against by different precautions. In some places great bastions of cut stone (granite) are built at particular reaches of the river to resist the floods, at others the banks are bordered by causeways of the same material for a considerable length, with sluices at proper distances to let off the water which is then distributed with great care and impartiality

---

* [? Yang-tsun.—Ed.]

† Upon further enquiry I find myself mistaken and that this chirping is produced by the motion of two flaps, or *lamilla*, which cover the abdomen. It is the signal or invitation of the male insect to allure the female, which latter is quite mute and unprovided with these organs of courtship. These insects nestle in the long sedge and often sit upon trees. It would seem that in this country everything that has life is multiplied to the highest degree, for so numerous is this noisy race that we are almost deafened by their incessant . . . [word illegible.—Ed.]

for the improvement of the neighbouring grounds. What we principally observed growing here were Indian corn, the *holcies* sorghum or Barbados millet, the *panicium italicum* or small yellow millet, the *panicium milliacum*, a new kind of *phaseolus* or kidney bean, several varieties of rice, cucumbers, water melons, apples, pears, plums and peaches but very few timber trees, and those only willows, but of very large size. Famines often happen in this part of the province arising sometimes from want of rain and sometimes from the depredations of locusts. On these occasions robberies are frequent, and not to be repressed by all the power of government, but as they are only committed through absolute hunger and necessity, so they usually cease at the return of plenty.

Tuesday, August 13. Some of the provisions which were brought for us this morning being found tainted (which was not to be wondered at, considering the extreme heat of the weather, Fahrenheit's thermometer being at 88), the superintending Mandarins were instantly deprived of their buttons, and all their servants bambooed, before we knew anything of the matter. So sudden and summary is the administration of justice here. As soon as we saw Wang and Chou we interceded in favour of the degraded delinquents, but though we were heard with great attention, and received very flattering answers, we easily perceived that no indulgence or relaxation of discipline was to be expected on such occasions.

Wednesday, August 14. This morning we passed by a very beautiful building on the north bank of the river. It is a pleasure house erected for the Emperor's accommodation in his progresses through this country. The roof is covered with a sort of yellow tiles, which, when the sun plays upon them, shine like burnished gold.

Today we had pleasant, cool weather, flying clouds frequently obscuring the sky but never descending in rain. Travelling here would be agreeable enough were it not for the confounded noise of the copper drums, which the people in the forecastle are perpetually rattling upon. This, we are told, is meant as a compliment and to do us honour, but I observe that it serves also as a signal of direction to regulate the motions of the accompanying yachts.

Thursday, August 15. We now observe with pleasure some picturesque blue mountains at thirty or forty miles distance. They contribute a good deal to enliven our prospects, which have hitherto been confined to the level uniformity of the circumjacent country. We found the river here considerably swelled by the late rains in Tartary, where it takes its rise, and the floods extended so far over the banks that the trackers of our yachts were usually up to their middles in the water.

During the greater part of the passage our conductors, Cheng-jui the Legate, together with Wang and Chou, visited me almost every day, but this morning they came with an appearance of more formality than usual. Their business was to acquaint me that the Emperor was much pleased with the accounts which he had heard of us, and that he was disposed to let our arrangements take place as we had proposed; that he had ordered two houses to be prepared for us, one in the city of Pekin, and the other in the country about six miles from it, near the Emperor's palace of Yuan-ming Yuan.* That we might choose which we liked best, but that they believed we should prefer the one in the country, because of its gardens and its neighbourhood to Yuan-ming Yuan. That after we had been presented, and had assisted at the ceremony of the Emperor's birthday at Jehol, it was intended we should immediately return to the capital, and that the Emperor himself would soon follow us. They added that as our stay in Tartary would be very short, they wished us not to carry the field-pieces and howitzers with us, which we had told them made a part of our presents, as there would not be time nor opportunity there to exercise or exhibit them.

They then introduced the subject of the Court ceremonies with a degree of art, address, and insinuation that I could not avoid admiring. They began by turning the conversation upon the different modes of dress that prevailed among different nations, and, after pretending to examine ours particularly, seemed to prefer their own, on account of its being loose and free from ligatures, and of its not impeding or obstructing the genuflexions and prostrations which were, they said, customary to be made by all persons whenever the Emperor appeared in public. They therefore apprehended much inconvenience to us from our knee-buckles and garters, and hinted to us that it would be better to disencumber ourselves of them before we should go to Court. I told them they need not be uneasy about that circumstance, as I supposed, whatever ceremonies were usual for the Chinese to perform, the Emperor would prefer my paying him the same obeisance which I did to my own Sovereign. They said they supposed the ceremonies in both countries must be nearly alike,

* [See p. 95.—Ed.]

that in China the form was to kneel down upon both knees, and make nine prostrations or inclinations of the head to the ground, and that it never had been, and never could be, dispensed with. I told them ours was somewhat different, and that though I had the most earnest desire to do everything that might be agreeable to the Emperor, my first duty must be to do what might be agreeable to my own King; but if they were really in earnest in objecting to my following the etiquette of the English Court, I should deliver to them my reply in writing as soon as I arrived at Pekin. They then talked of the length and dangers of our voyage, and said that as we had come to such a distance from home our King would naturally be anxious for our return, and that the Emperor did not mean to hunt this autumn as usual, but to remove with his Court very early to Pekin on purpose that we might not be delayed. I told them His Imperial Majesty would judge from the King's letter and from my representations what was expected from me at my return to England, and what time would be sufficient to enable me to transact the business I was charged with, and to describe to my Sovereign the glory and virtues of the Emperor, the power and splendour of his empire, the wisdom of its laws and moral institutes, the fame of all which had already reached to the most distant regions.

I was then asked if I had brought any presents to the Emperor from myself, besides those from the King. This question disconcerted me not a little; however, I replied without hesitation that I had brought a chariot, which was indeed (as it ought to be) much inferior in value to those sent by the King, yet, being of a different form, and remarkably elegant of its kind, I hoped the Emperor would condescend to accept it from me. I added that I flattered myself I should have some other present to offer him at New Year's Day, meaning to impress them with an idea that I expected to be allowed to stay beyond that period; for all along, ever since our departure from Tientsin, I have entertained a suspicion, from a variety of hints and circumstances, that the customs and policy of the Chinese would not allow us a very long residence among them. In all the different visits and conferences that have passed between us and our conductors, I observe, with great concern, a settled prejudice against the Embassy in Cheng-jui the Legate, though often attempted to be concealed by him under extravagant compliments and professions. I have taken great pains to conciliate him, but I suspect he is not of a conciliable nature. With regard to Wang and Chou, I think we have interested them much in our favour. When we have had opportunities of conversing with them in the absence of the Legate they have scarcely disguised their sense of the Emperor's partiality to the Tartars in preference to his Chinese subjects; nor do they seem much to like their colleague the Legate, who is a Tartar, but being the first in the commission has the exclusive privilege of corresponding with the Court upon our affairs, and whom they consider as a sort of crazy morose man. They said that we seemed very early to have discovered his character, and that they admired us much for the complaisance and patient attention of our deportment to him.

Tuesday, August 16. This day at half after six p.m. we arrived at the suburbs of Tungchow, where (our navigation being now ended) we quitted our yachts and went on shore, but before I proceed further I must set down a few particulars which have struck me, lest in the multiplicity of things before me they should slip from my memory. Indeed observations ought always to be written upon the spot; if made afterwards upon the ground of recollection they are apt to vary their hue considerably.

In the whole course of the river from Tungchow to the sea there is not at present a single permanent bridge, nor is there a bridge of any other kind whatsoever except one of boats at Tientsin which is occasionally opened or removed for the passage of vessels. I observed, however, this morning about a dozen miles before we arrived here the remains of a noble arch of solid masonry and near it were several ruins of walls and buildings as if some considerable city formerly stood there. The whole country which we passed through was, as far as we could see, cultivated with uncommon neatness and industry. We are told, however, that the agriculture here is very inferior to what is practised in many other provinces. The number of villages is wonderful and the population almost incredible. Not a day passed that we did not meet or overtake many hundreds of vessels laden with merchandise and the produce of the neighbourhood, and crowded with such multitudes of owners and passengers as left it almost doubtful whether the inhabitants on the water did not equal those upon the land.

During one of the visits that passed between us and our conductors they turned the discourse upon our dominions in Bengal, and affirmed that some British troops from thence had lately given assistance to the insurgents in Tibet. I was very much startled with this intelligence, but instantly told them that the thing was impossible, and that I could take upon me to contradict it in the most decisive manner. It came out on farther conversation that the Emperor's troops had met with a check on the western borders, which was so unexpected that they could account for it no otherwise than by supposing their enemies to be supported or assisted by Europeans, and they pretended that several persons with hats had been particularly remarked in one of the engagements. I hope that by the manner in which I treated this intelligence any ill impression which such a report might occasion to our prejudice will have been done away. Perhaps it was merely a feint or artifice to sift me and try to discover our force or our vicinity to their frontiers, and I am the more disposed to think so because a day or two after, on resuming the subject, they asked me whether the English at Bengal would assist the Emperor against the rebels in those parts. As I had told them before that one of the reasons why the story could not be true was the distance of our possessions from the scene of action, their question seemed calculated to catch me; for if, from eagerness or complaisance, I had answered in the affirmative, they would have concluded against my sincerity, because if our troops could come thither to the assistance of the Emperor's troops, they could equally have come to the assistance of his enemies.

Our yachts have been all along the passage most plentifully supplied with provisions, China wine, fruits, and vegetables of various kinds, and served with great sedulity and attention. At all the military stations we passed (which were very numerous) the soldiers were drawn out, with their colours and music, and if at night, with the addition of illuminations and fireworks. Whatever little articles we seemed to want we were immediately supplied with, and no entreaties could prevail for our being allowed to purchase them.

The most refined politeness and sly good breeding appeared in the behaviour of all those Mandarins with whom we had any connection; but although we found an immediate acquiescence in words with everything we seemed to propose, yet, in fact, some ingenious pretence or plausible objection was usually invented to disappoint us. Thus when we desired to make little excursions from our boats into the towns, or into the country, to visit any object that struck us as we went along, our wishes were seldom gratified. The refusal, or evasion was, however, attended with so much profession, artifice, and compliment that we grew soon reconciled and even amused with it.

We have indeed been very narrowly watched, and all our customs, habits and proceedings, even of the most trivial nature, observed with an inquisitiveness and jealousy which surpassed all that we had read of in the history of China. But we endeavoured always to put the best face upon everything, and to preserve a perfect serenity of countenance upon all occasions.

I therefore shut my eyes upon the flags of our yachts, which were inscribed 'The English Ambassador bringing tribute to the Emperor of China', and have made no complaint of it, reserving myself to notice it if a proper opportunity occurs.

Saturday, August 17. We shall be obliged to remain some days at Tungchow in order to land the presents and our baggage from the yachts, and to put them in proper order for carriage to Yuan-ming Yuan, whither it is meant that we should go directly without stopping at Pekin. From Tungchow to Pekin the distance is twelve miles, and from Pekin to Yuan-ming Yuan about seven.

The presents and baggage were lodged in two great pandals* built for the purpose in the suburbs near the river. Each of them was two hundred and seven feet long and thirteen feet broad, thirteen feet from the ground to the rafter or wall plate, and thirteen feet from the ground to the middle angle of the roof. The materials were strong bamboos and close matting impervious to the rain. Between the pandals was a passage or street of forty-two feet wide. The whole was shut up with gates at each end, guards posted there, and placards stuck up forbidding any persons from approaching the place with fire. These pandals were erected in a very few hours. Everything belonging to us was landed from thirty-seven vessels in less than one day. Such expedition, strength, and activity for the removal of so great a number of packages, many of which were of enormous weight, awkward shape, and cumbersome carriage, in a few hours cannot, I believe, be paralleled or procured in any other country than China, where everything is at the instant command of the state, and where even the most laborious tasks are undertaken and executed with a readiness and even a cheerfulness which one would scarcely expect to meet with in so despotic a government. The Chinese seem able to lift and remove almost any weight by multiplying the power; thus they fasten to the sides of the load two strong bamboos; if two are not sufficient they cross them with two others, and so proceed quadrating and decussating the machine, and applying more bearers, till they can master and carry it with ease.

Our quarters were in the suburbs of the city at a *miao* or temple,

* [A shed for temporary use; from the Tamil word *pendal* (Shorter O.E.D.).—Ed.]

consisting of several courts and spacious apartments. Here we were all very commodiously lodged during the time we stayed, and as usual supplied abundantly with whatever we had occasion for. This temple or *miao* was founded by a munificent bigot some centuries ago for twelve bonzes, and endowed with considerable revenues. The *sanctum sanctorum* forms but a small part of the building, and is solely appropriated to the worship and the images of Fo-hi and his subaltern deities.[7] The rest is a kind of choltry or caravanserai, where travellers of rank are lodged in their journeys through this place upon public service.

My train was so numerous that we took up almost the whole of the temple; only one bonze remained in it to watch over the lamps of the shrine: all the rest removed to another temple in the neighbourhood. The Chinese Government (I speak in a general sense of those who administer the Government) though all under one omnipotent head have, in fact, no rational, established state religion. They leave the people to follow the accidental superstition of their education and places of nativity, but wisely obviate the mischiefs that might arise from it as much as possible by turning into public utility by quartering useful subjects upon useless devotees, by frustrating the intention without forbidding the practice of mortmain, and by converting the follies of the dead to the benefit of the living.

Sunday, August 18. Wang called upon me this morning at breakfast and told me that the porters and wagons would be all ready on Tuesday, that our things might begin moving early that day, and be all carried away before the following night. He added that we should set out ourselves on Wednesday morning, pass through Pekin, and proceed to Yuan-ming Yuan, where a Colao[8] of high rank was appointed by the Emperor to meet us, together with a European missionary. He could not inform me of the name or nation of the missionary, but I suspect him to be Joseph-Bernard d'Almeida,* the Portuguese whom we had been so often cautioned against.

Wang and Chou both came together to visit me in the evening, and brought me the Tartar's excuse for his not accompanying them, saying that he was somewhat indisposed, but it would seem that his staying away proceeded rather from pride and ill-humour than from real illness. I, however, sent a very civil compliment to him on the occasion expressive of my concern at his illness and my intention to visit him next day.

* [See p. 93.—Ed.]

JOURNAL—AUGUST

Monday, August 19. I went down to the pandals this morning, where I met the Tartar Legate, Wang and Chou, and several other Mandarins, who were assembled there to give orders for the operations of the next day. On this occasion I proposed to amuse them with the exercise of our small brass field-pieces, which were now mounted and prepared for moving with the rest of our presents and baggage. Though they were remarkably well cast and of a most elegant form, fixed on light carriages, and in every respect completely well appointed and well served, and fired from twenty to thirty times in a minute, yet our conductor pretended to think lightly of them, and spoke to us as if such things were no novelties in China. I have good reason, however, to suppose that there is nothing like them in the whole Empire, and that these gentlemen are at bottom not a little mortified by this small specimen of our art and superiority.

On our return from the pandals Wang and Chou walked up with us to our quarters, and told us that the Emperor's answer was come to our request of having a European missionary to attend us, and that we might choose any of the Europeans in the Emperor's service then at Pekin. That the Emperor was disposed to favour us as much as possible, having already conceived the highest esteem for us from the accounts he had heard of our appearance, deportment, and conversation ever since our arrival in his dominions.

They then renewed the subject of the ceremonial relative to which they had been perfectly silent for several days. It seems to be a very serious matter with them, and a point which they have set their hearts upon. They pressed me most earnestly to comply with it, said it was a mere trifle; kneeled down on the floor and practised it of their own accord to show me the manner of it, and begged me to try whether I could not perform it. On my declining it, they applied to my interpreter to do it, who though a Chinese, said he could only act as I directed him; they seem a little disappointed in finding me not so pliant in this point as they wished. As to themselves, they are wonderfully supple, and though generally considered as most respectable characters, are not very scrupulous in regard to veracity, saying and unsaying without hesitation what seems to answer the purpose of the moment. Their ideas of the obligations of truth are certainly very lax, for when we hinted to them any contradictions that occurred, or deviations from their promises in our affairs, they made very light of them, and seemed to think them of trifling consequence. We entertained them with a concert of music, which they appeared to be much pleased with, and when they left us repeated the same flattering expressions and compliments which they had set out with in the beginning of their visit.

This night died of dysentery after a long illness Henry Eades, a cunning artist in brass and iron, who, hearing of my intention to take with me to China a person in his branch, had strongly importuned both me and Sir George Staunton in London to give him a preference to other candidates. Finding him well qualified, I consented, and had reason to be well satisfied with him, as he was not only skilful and ingenious, but a quiet, well-behaved man. As the sea did not seem to agree with him at the beginning of our voyage, I proposed to him to return from Madeira, but he unfortunately determined to persevere.

Tuesday, August 20. Eades was buried this morning, all the servants, musicians, and guard attending his interment; the funeral service was read upon the occasion, and a volley of small arms was fired over his grave. Vast numbers of Chinese were spectators of the ceremony, and seemed to be a good deal affected by its order and solemnity. After it was over our baggage began to move, and a great part of it was dispatched before night.

Wednesday, August 21. We rose very early this morning and found the palanquins, horses, carriages and everything ready for our departure. The Tartar Legate, Wang, Chou and several other Mandarins of rank waited for us at the great gate, and set off at the same moment that we did. We passed through the city of Tungchow which is of great extent, encompassed with very high walls, washed by the river on one side and defended by a broad wet ditch on the others.* There are no guns mounted on the ramparts, nor did I observe anything of that sort except a few small swivels near the gates. It took us about two hours to get through the town. Several of the streets are broad and straight and the shops on each side often present a gay picturesque appearance, but we observed no magnificent houses or distinguished buildings. A few triumphal arches are erected in the principal street which have an agreeable effect but they are merely of wood, painted, gilded and varnished. In many

* Note of the number of men, waggons and horses, etc., employed in carrying the presents, baggage, stores, etc., of the Ambassador and suite from Tungchow to Yuan-ming Yuan. [Macartney here makes elaborate calculations which give a grand total of 85 waggons, 39 handcarts, 209 horses, 2,495 men.—Ed.] These were all for the use of the Embassy exclusive of the vast number belonging to the Mandarins and other attendants.

places awnings of mats are extended across from house to house, as a shelter from the sun and rain, which are easily drawn backward and forward by small cords, as the state of the weather may require. We stopped at a village half-way between Tungchow and Pekin to breakfast and to repose ourselves, the day being very hot and the roads very dusty. From thence we reached Pekin in about two hours (six miles), and after taking some refreshments of tea and fruit at the Palace gate, we proceeded to Yuan-ming Yuan, where we arrived about three o'clock p.m. and found the greater part of our baggage already come; the remainder soon followed.

The road from Tungchow to Pekin and from Pekin to Yuan-ming Yuan passes through a fine level country, is very broad and bordered with trees on each side, chiefly willows of great size, much beyond any I have ever seen in Europe. The middle part of the road is a causeway or flat pavement about seven or eight yards wide composed of large stones cut smooth, many of them twenty feet in length and three or four feet broad. On the way from Tungchow to Pekin we crossed the river over a most beautiful bridge of white marble forty feet wide, there are five arches, the centre one I suppose not less than . . .* feet. On this journey we were preceded by a great number of soldiers, brandishing long whips in their hands, which they were continually exercising in order to keep off the enormous crowds which incessantly thronged about us and obstructed the passage. The suburbs of Pekin are very extensive. We were fifteen minutes from our entering the east suburb to the east gate. We were above two hours in our progress through the city, fifteen minutes from the west gate to the end of the west suburb and two hours from thence to Yuan-ming Yuan. The house at this last place allotted for our habitation consists of several small courts and separate pavilions, and is situated in a little park or garden, laid out in the Chinese manner with serpentine walks, a narrow winding river forming an island with a summer-house in the middle of it, a grove of various trees interspersed with a few patches of grass ground diversified with inequalities and roughened with rocks, the whole surrounded with a high wall and guarded by a detachment of troops at the gate. Some of the apartments are large, handsome, and not ill-contrived, but the whole building is so much out of repair that I already see it will be impossible to reside in it comfortably during the winter. It appears, indeed, to be only calculated for a summer dwelling, though I understand it is the best of the hotels at this place

* [Word illegible. —Ed.]

destined (as several more are) for the reception of foreign ambassadors.

We had been promised that the European missionaries should come to us as soon as we arrived here, but none of them have as yet made their appearance.

Thursday, August 22. The Tartar Legate came this morning to compliment me on my arrival at Yuan-ming Yuan. He said that there was a Grand Secretary on the road from Jehol particularly appointed to attend to our affairs, and that he would send one or two of the European missionaries to me to-morrow. As the Legate seemed to be in better humour than usual I took the opportunity of mentioning the subject of my quarters, which I told him were very handsome, but somewhat out of repair, and rather inconvenient to us Europeans, whose modes of living were different from the Chinese, and that I hoped he would give directions for our removal to Pekin, where I thought we should be more at our ease. He seemed to agree with me on this point, and said he thought there could be no objection.

Friday, August 23. This day the Tartar Legate sent to announce his intention of visiting me, and of bringing several of the European missionaries with him. He accordingly arrived at ten a.m. with Joseph-Bernard d'Almeida, André Rodrigues and another Portuguese; Louis de Poirot, Joseph Panzi and Peter Adeodato, Italians; Joseph Paris, a Frenchman, and one or two others.[9]

The Emperor had, on occasion of the Embassy, distinguished some of these missionaries by his favour, and had conferred white buttons on Poirot and Adeodato, and a blue one (which is of a higher rank) on d'Almeida. This latter is the person against whom I had been particularly cautioned from Macao, and from other quarters, as a man of a malignant disposition, jealous of all Europeans, except those of his own nation, and particularly unfriendly to the English, and, indeed, I have seen enough this day to convince me of the truth of the representation. This man, who was bred a Jesuit and is upwards of seventy years old, has been a great many years in China, and now belongs to the College of Mathematics, though of a very limited knowledge in that science. He has some skill in surgery, and having attended the Minister Ho-shen, who is afflicted with a rupture, availed himself of that circumstance to obtain the Emperor's appointment of him to be interpreter to my

Embassy. Whether from vanity of being selected for such an office, or from the hope of being able by that means to frustrate its success, I know not, but, unfortunately for him, when he was introduced to me for that purpose, it appeared to the Legate and the other attending Mandarins that he was unqualified for the office, being entirely ignorant of the languages most familiar to us. His mortification upon this occasion he had not sufficient temper to conceal, and almost instantly expressed very unfavourable sentiments of the Embassy to an Italian missionary who stood near him. As they conversed in Latin, he probably imagined I should not understand or overhear him, but his looks and gestures would have been alone sufficient to discover the state of his mind if his tongue had been silent.

At this visit I reminded the Legate of my wishes to remove to Pekin, on which occasion d'Almeida very impertinently interfered, and advised him against the measure, pretending that it would retard our journey to Jehol and be otherwise unadvisable; but his objections were over-ruled by a superior authority, although the Legate seemed much disposed to admit them.

All the other missionaries seemed shocked at and ashamed of his behaviour, and interposed their endeavours to bring him to a proper composure. During the whole time I remained perfectly calm, and seemed not to perceive or notice his behaviour, but on the contrary was pointed in my civilities to him, and at his going away told him, through the channel of a French missionary, how much I regretted my not understanding the Portuguese language, as it deprived me of the advantage of so able an assistant and interpreter. He came back soon after, and seemed indeed to be a good deal softened, and even gave me assurances of his services and good disposition; but after what I have seen it is necessary to be uncommonly circumspect. It will be right to cultivate and make use of him, if possible, but it would be egregious folly and dupery to confide in or depend on him.

About an hour after, Wang and Chou returned in order to acquaint us that the Grand Secretary Chun,[10] a cousin of the Emperor, who had been announced to us, was come, and that it was now settled for him and Wang and Chou to manage all our affairs, without the interference of the Tartar Legate.

In consequence of this arrangement, Wang, accompanied by our interpreter and Mr. Maxwell, one of my secretaries, went this evening to Pekin to view the palace intended for my residence, and to give directions for putting it into proper order for our reception.

Whilst they were employed on this business, Chou came to take us to the Emperor's palace of Yuan-ming Yuan, or the Garden of Gardens, as the name imports, and to ask our opinion of the fittest apartments to place the globes, the clocks, the lustres, and the planetarium in. This place is truly an Imperial residence; the park is said to be eighteen miles round, and laid out in all the taste, variety, and magnificence which distinguish the rural scenery of Chinese gardening. There is no one very extensive contiguous building but several hundreds of pavilions scattered through the grounds and all connected together by close arbors, by passages apparently cut through stupendous rocks, or by fairyland galleries, emerging or receding in the perspective, and so contrived as to conceal the real design of communication and yet contribute to the general purpose and effect intended to arise from the whole. The various beauties of the spot, its lakes and rivers, together with its superb edifices, which I saw (and yet I saw but a very small part), so strongly impressed my mind at this moment that I feel incapable of describing them.[11]

I shall therefore chiefly confine myself to the great hall or presence chamber of the Emperor.* It is one hundred and fifty feet long and sixty feet wide; there are windows on one side only, and opposite to them is the Imperial Throne, of carved mahogany brought from England, and elevated by a few steps from the floor.

Over the Chair of State is an inscription in Chinese:

CHENG-TA-KUANG-MING-FU

the translation of which signifies:

VERUS, MAGNUS, GLORIOSUS, SPLENDIDUS, FELIX.'†

And on each side of the Chair of State is a beautiful Argus pheasant's tail spread out into a magnificent fan of great extent. The floor is of chequered marble, grey and white, with neat mats laid upon it in different places to walk upon. At one end I observed a musical clock that played twelve old English tunes, the 'Black Joke', 'Lillibullero', and other airs of the 'Beggars' Opera'. It was decorated in a wretched old taste, with ornaments of crystal and coloured stones but had been, I dare say, very much admired in its time. On the dial appeared in large characters, 'George Clarke, Clock and Watch Maker, in Leadenhall Street, London.'‡

This saloon we determined on for the reception of some of our

---

* Vide the drawing in the appendix, No. 3G. [Omitted here—Ed.]

† [A free translation of the Chinese might be: Upright, great, illustrious, famous, fortunate.—Ed.]

‡ [See note 1.—Ed.]

most magnificent presents, which were to be distributed as follows: on one side of the throne was to be placed the terrestrial globe, on the other the celestial; the lustres were to be hung from the ceiling, at equal distances from the middle of the room; at the north end the planetarium was to stand; at the south end Vulliamy's clocks, with the barometer and Derbyshire porcelain vases and figures, and Fraser's orrery; an assemblage of such ingenuity, utility and beauty as is not to be seen collected together in any other apartment, I believe, of the whole world besides.[12]

Before I quit the palaces of Yuan-ming Yuan I must observe a singularity in the Chinese taste which has not yet reached us, and which in truth is by no means worthy of our copying. Although you ascend to the principal buildings by regular flights of smooth or chiselled stone stairs, yet there are several others, even pavilions of elegant architecture, to which the approach is by rugged steps of rock, seemingly rendered rough and difficult by art, in order to imitate the rude simplicity of nature. In such situations the impropriety is glaring and argues a sickly and declining taste, meant solely to display vanity and expense. The cost of sending for such enormous masses from the mountains of Tartary must be very great, for in my whole route through the province of Pei-chihli from the mouth of the Peiho to the city of Pekin I did not see a single pebble big enough to make a seal of.

At Yuan-ming Yuan we were met by the Grand Secretary Kunsan,* who went round the palaces with us, and entertained us with a collation of fruits and sweetmeats, at which the Tartar Legate assisted; for, to my great surprise after what I had been told, I found him at my elbow almost every step I took during the evening. I have reason to believe that he does not mean to resign his charge of us; I suspect he has contrived means of settling the matter with the Grand Secretary. This will be an unpleasant circumstance, because, as he is a Tartar and has powerful connections at Court, our friends Wang and Chou are obliged to pay him great deference, and dare not exert themselves in our favour as much as they are inclined to do. We have, however, found them already very useful to us in many instances.

At eight o'clock Mr. Maxwell returned from Pekin, and reported that he had seen and been all through the palace at Pekin intended for us. It is an immense building containing eleven courts, and ample room for every purpose we can require.

* [See note 10.—Ed.]

Saturday, August 24. Sir George Staunton went to Yuan-ming Yuan, and took with him Mr. Barrow, Dr. Dinwiddie, Thibault, and Petitpierre, and other artists and workmen,[13] to give them directions about arranging the machinery and disposing in their proper places the planetarium, orrery, globes, clocks, lustres, etc. These gentlemen are to remain for this purpose at the Yuan-ming Yuan during our journey into Tartary, but it is thought they will not be able to dispatch it in less than six or seven weeks at soonest.

Some of the Chinese workmen, not accustomed to handle articles of such delicate machinery, were interrupted in their attempts to unpack them by our interpreter, who told them that, till put up and delivered, they must still be considered as under our care; upon which the Legate interposed and said, no, they are *cong-so*,* tributes (*oblata*) to the Emperor, and consequently we had nothing more to do with them. Our interpreter replied that they were not tributes (*cong-so*), but presents (*sung-lo*).* The Grand Secretary put an end to the conversation by saying that the expression of *sung-lo*, or presents, was proper enough.

On his return to quarters our interpreter came to me (as he said) from Wang and Chou, and told me that, although the Emperor's allowance for defraying the Embassy was very considerable, yet that it did not equal the expense, and that it was expected that I should make them a very handsome present to supply the difference. I answered that I was very willing to do so, and asked what he thought they would be satisfied with. Upon recollecting himself a little, he said he believed that five hundred dollars apiece would be a proper sum, which I made no scruple immediately to agree to, as they so strongly professed themselves our friends, as they certainly have weight with the Grand Secretary sufficient, we trust, to counteract the Legate's practices with him to our prejudice, and as, if they misbehave, we shall have them at our mercy. Besides, being engaged in our business and having once tasted of our bounty they are likely to endeavour to deserve further favour by further services; as it is observed of certain beasts of prey that having once smacked human blood, they never afterwards have a relish for any other.

Sunday, August 25. Notwithstanding what I have written in the preceding paragraph, our interpreter told me this morning that he was then just come from Wang and Chou, who desired him to say that, though they had the highest respect and regard for me, they

* [? *kung-shou* and *sung-li*.—Ed.]

could not possibly think of accepting any presents of money; that it was true the expense they incurred by their attendance on the Embassy was considerable, but that it chiefly fell upon Chou, who was very rich and well able to bear it; that Wang was not rich, and did not therefore contribute to it; but then, he had the principal share of the fatigue of the business, in reviewing and stationing the boats, hiring the porters, horses, and carriages, superintending the provision department, punishing delinquents, etc., whilst Chou did little else than receive the reports, write out the register, and pay the disbursements. All this seems very extraordinary and I know not how to account for it, first to signify a disposition to take our money, and then to refuse it, at the same time preserving their friendship for us, and actually rendering us every service in their power.

The Chinese character seems at present inexplicable. The Tartar Legate, having delivered to me yesterday a letter, written by Sir Erasmus Gower from Tengchowfu, which had come by the Emperor's couriers, I directed an answer to be prepared, and requested to have it forwarded. He asked me what was in Sir Erasmus's letter, and in the answer. I had them both interpreted off-hand, and added with great good-humour that we had no secrets but what he was welcome to know.

Before he went away he mentioned the subject of the ceremonial, and was desirous of practising it before me; but I put an end to the subject by telling him I had a paper relative to it, which would be ready to deliver to him at Pekin in a day or two.

Monday, August 26. This morning we removed to Pekin, and are not only comfortably, but most magnificently lodged in the Tartar town in a vast palace consisting of eleven courts, some of them very spacious and airy.* It took us an hour and a half to come from Yuanming Yuan to the suburbs and from thence to our habitation an hour and a half more. It is situated, as all the private houses here are, in a narrow lane, the great streets being entirely occupied by shops or public buildings.

Tuesday, August 27. Father Raux, a French missionary of the Congregation of St. Lazarus at Paris, a native of Hainault, came and informed me that he had permission to attend us, and that he would

* Vide drawing no. 4D. in the appendix. [Omitted here—Ed.]

wait upon me every day to receive our commands and execute our commissions. He is a tall, corpulent man, of easy manners and conversation, with a great volubility of speech. He understands both the Chinese and Manchu languages, and seems to be perfectly contented with his lot here. He is well informed, and extremely communicative and fond of talking, so that I imagine it will not be difficult to learn from him everything he knows.[14]

Wednesday, August 28.   Mr. Barrow returned from the Palace of Yuan-ming Yuan, and said they had put up in the saloon of the throne Parker's two lustres, had set the globes in their proper places, as also the orrery and Vulliamy's clocks, figures, and vases, and had laid the floor for the planetarium, and that the whole would have a very fine effect. Three of the Emperor's grandsons had been to look at them, and were much delighted with the sight. They particularly admired the clocks and the vases of Derbyshire porcelain. They, however, asked which we thought, our porcelain or theirs, to be preferable. The answer returned to them was that ours was considered as very precious of its kind, otherwise it would not have been offered to the Emperor; but that the value we set upon theirs was easily to be seen by the great quantities which were every year purchased by our merchants at Canton and sent in our shipping to England; and they seemed to be very well satisfied with this indirect explanation. The great Mandarin attended, and seemed to be much struck with the attention manifested by our bringing several spare glasses for the dome of the planetarium, one of the panes of which happened to be cracked, and which, without such a precaution, could not be repaired in China.

Thursday, August 29.   This day I put up the state canopy and their Majesties' pictures in the presence chamber, and delivered my paper* relative to the ceremonial to be transmitted to Jehol. I had a good deal of difficulty in persuading Father Raux to get it translated into Chinese and to put it into the proper diplomatic form, so much is every person here afraid of intermeddling in any state matter without the special authority of Government; and he only consented on condition that neither his writing nor that of his secretary should appear, but that I should get it copied by some other hand. Little

---

* Vide no. 8 enclosed in my dispatch to Mr. Secretary Dundas of 9 November 1793. [Omitted here—Ed.]

Staunton was able to supply my wants on this occasion, for having very early in the voyage begun to study the Chinese [language] under my two interpreters, he had not only made considerable progress in it, but he had learned to write the characters with great neatness and celerity, so that he was of material use to me on this occasion, as he had been already before in transcribing the catalogue of the presents.

In the paper I expressed the strongest desire to do whatever I thought would be most agreeable to the Emperor, but that, being the representative of the first monarch of the Western world, his dignity must be the measure of my conduct; and that, in order to reconcile it to the customs of the Court of China, I was willing to conform to their etiquette, provided a person of equal rank with mine were appointed to perform the same ceremony before my Sovereign's picture that I should perform before the Emperor himself. The Legate shook his head, but Wang and Chou said it was a good expedient, and offered immediately to go through the ceremony themselves on the spot; but as they had no authority for the purpose, I civilly declined their proposal. I received a very kind letter and message,* together with his portrait, from old Father Amiot, who has been near sixty years in China, lamenting that his age and infirmities prevented him from coming to wait upon me, but expressing the strong interest he takes in the success of my Embassy, and promising me every information, advice, and assistance in his power.[15]

Friday, August 30. Having now nearly completed the selection of such presents as I judged most eligible to carry with me to Jehol, I gave notice to the Legate and our other conductors that we should be ready to set out on Monday next 2 September (which, according to their method of computation, answers to the 27th of the seventh month, their year beginning on the 1st of February), and that I proposed to employ one of the intervening days in viewing the buildings, triumphal arches, and other things most worthy of observation in the city of Pekin. But I found I had miscalculated in this instance, as much as I had done on some former ones of a similar nature, for I was requested to repress my curiosity till after my return from Tartary, as it was improper that an ambassador should appear in public at Pekin till after he had been presented to the Emperor. On this occasion the question was repeated to me what present I

* Vide letter in the appendix. [Omitted here—Ed.]

meant to offer the Emperor from myself, for that, instead of the chariot, which I had mentioned to them before, it would be proper to provide something portable to be delivered into the Emperor's hands by my own at the time of my introduction, no ambassador approaching him for the first time without one. I told them I was prepared with one, and when my baggage was all unpacked I would show it to them. I was a good deal at a loss what to fix upon, all the principal articles that we had brought having been already inserted in the catalogue and announced to them as presents from the King. Luckily, it happened that Captain Mackintosh had with him some watches of very fine workmanship, which he was persuaded to cede to me at the usual estimate of profit upon things of this kind brought for sale from Europe to Canton. This was the more fortunate, as I had been informed, besides, that not only valuable presents were to be made to the Emperor, but also that his sons and the principal great men in the Ministry expected to be gratified in the same manner. The persons pointed out to me were Pa-ye, Che-y-ye, Che-ou-ye and Chet-si the Emperor's sons, Mien-cul-ye his eldest grandson,[16] the great general A-kuei, and Ho-shen* and Fu-ch'ang-an, the two favourite Ministers, Li-pu Shang-shu the President of the Court of Rites,† and a few others. I was, however, told at the same time that nothing of this kind was to be offered till my return from Jehol, after the Emperor had seen and accepted the presents destined for him.

When Father Raux came today, as usual, to attend me, he brought me a present from his convent of several acceptable articles, some excellent French bread, sweetmeats and confections, very fine large figs, and a quantity of grapes, both red and white, the latter of a most delicious flavour, and without stones. He told me they were originally brought to the Jesuits' garden from Chamo, on the borders of the great desert of Gobi, on the north-western frontier of the Empire, and had much improved by the transplantation. From him I learned more particularly what I had been already told by Wang and Chou relative to the state of the Court, and I understand that the Emperor has had twenty sons, four only of which now remain alive.‡ He is of so jealous a nature that no person as yet knows with certainty which of them he intends for his successor. He does not allow any of them to interfere in his government, but manages it in a great measure alone, reading all the dispatches himself, and often entering

---

* [See Appendix A, pp. 320–2—Ed.]   † [See note 32.—Ed.]
‡ Viz., the fourth, eleventh, sixteenth and seventeenth.

into the minutest detail of affairs. His principal Minister is Ho-shen, a Tartar of obscure origin but considerable talents, whom he has raised by degrees from an inferior post in his guards to his present elevation, having been struck with the comeliness of his person at a review twenty years ago and confirmed in the prepossession by finding his character correspond to his figure. He is in such high favour that the Emperor not long since gave one of his daughters in marriage to this Minister's eldest son, and conferred on him many other marks of distinction. The second favourite Minister is Fu-ch'ang-an,[17] a young Tartar, whose elder brother has by his means also obtained in marriage a daughter or niece of the Emperor and several of the most important employments in the State, having been Commander-in-Chief in the war of Formosa, Viceroy of Canton, and latterly General of the forces on the Tibet frontier.[18]

The A-kuei,[19] whose exploits are so particularly celebrated in the *Mémoires sur la Chine,* has a still higher rank of precedence than the Minister whom I have mentioned, but, being much advanced in years, and notwithstanding his great merits, far from being a personal favourite of the Emperor, he now lives a good deal retired, and seldom meddles in public affairs.

The three other Grand Secretaries of the first tribunal of state are men of great abilities and of long experience, but, being of Chinese families, possess little influence, though their opinions are highly respected.[20]

Father Raux says that there are above five thousand Chinese Christians in the city of Pekin alone, and he computes the number throughout the whole Empire at a hundred and fifty thousand. He confirmed to me what we read of in most of the histories of China—that it is a common practice among the poor to expose their children. The police send a cart round the city at an early hour every morning, which takes them up and conveys them to a fosse or cemetery appointed for their burial. The missionaries often attend and preserve a few of these children which appear to them to be healthy and likely to recover.* The rest are thrown indiscriminately, dead or alive, into the pit. But Father Raux assured me very seriously that his brethren always first christened those that appeared to have any life remaining in them, '*pour leur sauver l'âme*'.

The Chinese, he says, seem to be less jealous of religious con-

---

* Father Noël in 1763 says that 20,000–430,000 children are exposed every year in Pekin and that 3,000 of them are baptized by the missionaries or catechists. The whole might be baptized, he says, if they had twenty or thirty catechists.

versions than formerly, owing to the discretion of the present missionaries, whose zeal, I presume, is not now quite so ardent as that of their predecessors. Nevertheless, they engage not a little of the attention of Government, and within this twelve months past all their letters, which usually went free by the common post between Pekin and Canton, are constantly opened and examined. The Chinese, have indeed, an indistinct idea of there being at this time great disturbances and rebellions in Europe, and the Legate has often repeated the questions to me on our road whether England was really at peace with all the world, as I asserted.

The Bishop of Pekin had permission to visit me this day in form. He is a Portuguese of about forty years old, of a dignified appearance and conciliating manners, but said to be of false and crafty nature, and to possess no great measure of learning.[21] He, however, speaks Latin with great fluency, and made me a speech in that language of a quarter of an hour long. He was attended by two Portuguese missionaries, and by several others of different nations, and in their presence made me the strongest professions of friendship and attachment; several of them, however, took an early opportunity of advising me not to trust him. I think, indeed, there is some reason, from what I have seen, to believe that the Portuguese have formed a sort of system to disgust and keep out of China all other nations. Between them and the rest of the missionaries there appears to be great jealousy and enmity—*odium plusquam theologicum*. In a conversation with an Italian a few days ago, he told me that all the missionaries except the Portuguese were our warm friends, but that the Portuguese were friends of nobody but themselves. Bernard d'Almeida has never come near me since our first meeting at Yuan-ming Yuan, but I understand that he has been sent for to Jehol.

Saturday, August 31. Father Grammont, the French missionary from whom I received the two letters at Tientsin, and also some intelligence since my arrival at Pekin, visited me in the afternoon, apologized for not having done it sooner, owing, as he said, to a jealousy entertained of him by the Legate on account of his having talked so much on the subject of the Embassy, of the power and grandeur of the English nation, of the magnitude of its commerce with, and its importance to the Chinese Empire. Father Grammont was bred a Jesuit, is now advanced in years, and has been a long time in China. He is certainly a very clever fellow and seems to know this country well, but as he is said to be of a restless, intriguing turn it is necessary to be a good deal on one's guard with him.

Sunday, September 1. Busily employed this day in making preparations for our journey to Jehol, as we are to set out tomorrow. To the occurrences at Pekin, which I have already noted, I must now add that, besides our conductors and the missionaries, we were every day visited by numbers of Mandarins of the higher ranks, some engaged to it by the duty of their stations and employments, others allured by curiosity, and not a few by my band of music, which performed a very good concert in one of my apartments every evening.[22] Among these visitors was the chief Mandarin of the Emperor's orchestra, who attended constantly and listened to the performance with all the airs of a virtuoso. He was so much pleased with some of our instruments that he desired leave to take drawings of them. I was willing to give them to him as a present, but he civilly declined my offer, and I found, indeed, they would have been of no use to him. He, however, sent for a couple of painters, who spread the floor with a few sheets of large paper, placed the clarinets, flutes, bassoons and French horns upon them, and then traced with their pencils the figures of the instruments, measuring all the apertures and noting the minutest particulars, and when this operation was completed they wrote down their remarks, and delivered them to their master. I was told that his intention is to have similar instruments made here by Chinese workmen, and to fit them to a scale of his own. The Chinese have long since adopted our violin although it is not yet very common and have lately learned to note their music on ruled paper, which seems to show that there are some things at least which, notwithstanding their vanity and conceit, they are not above being taught. They were totally ignorant of punctuation till they observed it in their Chinese books printed by the Jesuits for the instruction of youth, since which it is now frequently used by many of the first scholars in the Empire.[23]

But what seemed to attract more general notice than anything in the house were the King and Queen's pictures in their royal robes, by Sir Joshua Reynolds,[24] which were hung up opposite the state canopy, in the grand saloon through which we usually passed to the concert room. Indeed, so very great was the crowd of people to see them, as soon as they came to be talked of, that I was obliged to apply to Wang to regulate the number and quality of the visitors and the hour of admittance.

Their admiration has been also much excited by the presents and specimens of different manufactures which we have to distribute, and by the various little articles of use and convenience which Europeans are accustomed to, our dressing-tables, shaving-glasses, and pocket instruments; but we have been sometimes sufferers a little on these occasions from the eagerness of their curiosity, and from their awkwardness in handling them. The flexible sword-blades of Mr. Gill's manufactory at Birmingham,[25] they were particularly struck with, and Wang, to whom as a military man distinguished by wounds and long service I gave a couple, seemed more pleased with them than if I had offered him any other present of a hundred times the value. I am persuaded that if we can once introduce them into China as an article of trade there will be a very great demand for them.

I know it is the policy of the East India Company to increase principally the export of the coarser woollens, and I have little doubt that in a very few years China will call for more of them than we can easily supply; but I would recommend also the sending out our very finest cloths (for what we call superfine in the invoices are really not the very finest), together with assortments of kerseymeres and vigonias.[26] Those we wore ourselves I observed everybody greatly admired. The Emperor has lately permitted cloth to be worn in his presence in the spring and autumn—that is to say, from the 1st of October to 20th November, and from the 1st of February to the 1st of April. Light silk is the dress of summer, and satins or damasks, lined with fine furs, of the winter.

It being all settled that we should set out early tomorrow to Jehol, the Grand Secretary Keen-san,* attended by two Mandarins of high quality with red buttons on their caps, came late this evening to wish me a good journey, and to repeat that the Emperor was impatient to see us, having particularly remarked and being much pleased with our prudence and circumspection in having desired a separate hospital at Chusan for the sick people of the *Lion*, and a boundary-line to be drawn in order to prevent the sailors from straggling. The Emperor, he said, highly approved of it, and had given orders that Sir Erasmus Gower should do as he wished, that he might stay there as long as he pleased and go away when he pleased. From all this it is evident that every circumstance concerning us and every word that falls from our lips is minutely reported and remembered.

* [See note 10.—Ed.]

Monday, September 2. At six o'clock a.m. we began our journey. Young Staunton and myself travelled in a neat English post-chaise which I had provided, and which was drawn by four little Tartar horses not eleven hands high, being, I believe, the first piece of Long-acre manufactory[27] that ever rattled upon the road to Jehol. Sir George Staunton, having a touch of the gout, went in a palanquin; the other gentlemen of my train, as also the servants, musicians, artists, guards, etc. were accommodated with horses or carriages in such manner as they preferred. Our whole cavalcade now amounted to seventy persons, of which forty composed the guard; the rest of our people, amounting to twenty-one, remained behind, some being employed in putting together and arranging the presents at Yuan-ming Yuan, and the others either invalids or attendants necessary to be left to take care of the house during our absence.

To carry the presents and our beds and baggage, I dare say, exclusive of horses and carriages, there were at least two hundred porters employed who regularly made the same daily journeys that we did. From my hotel, through the city of Pekin to the gate are four and a half miles, and from thence our first stage was of five miles to Ching-ho,* a small fort enclosed with a wall, where we breakfasted.[28] Here are several cross-roads leading into the country in all directions. From Ching-ho are eleven miles to Lin-coo,† a little village where the Emperor has built a lodge for stopping at when he travels this way. Six miles and a half further stands the palace of Nan-chut-see, which terminates our first day's journey. The road hitherto is pretty straight, over a sandy level, which seems to have been anciently covered with the sea though now fifty or sixty miles from it; on each side every cultivable inch is cultivated. We observed the *holcus* sorghum, *panicum crus galli*, *panicum milliacium* and *italicum*, horse beans, horse peas and sesamum, all sown in drills between which another successive crop was often rising in the same ground. Scarcely any trees to be seen but the crack willow with a very rough bark (*salix fragilis*) which even in this sandy soil grows to a vast size. Two or three ashes and a few mulberries of a particular species. To the northwest of Lin-coo we crossed the river which though narrow is yet deep enough in summer to admit the passage of the Chinese boats of which several are employed on it. Its course, like all the other rivers in this tract runs to the southward and eastward. Nan-chut-see is situated at the foot of the mountains, which here approach very near one another and form a pass of nearly

* [? Chen-ho.—Ed.]   † [? Liu-k'o Chung.—Ed.]

a mile across. They are not varied like the mountains of Shantung by bold elevations and depressions but present a long rough-set outline of shallow indentures. In the spring when the snows melt I should suppose most of this plain to be under water. During all this day, the neat husbandry of the country, the industry of the people,

Macartney's route from Tientsin to Jehol

and the air of business that appears in their faces, the goodness of the road, and the circumstance of travelling in a post-chaise, almost made me imagine myself in England, and recalled a thousand pleasing ideas to my remembrance.

JOURNAL—SEPTEMBER

Tuesday, September 3. From Nan-chut-see, which we left this morning at five a.m., we reached the suburbs of Hoai-ziou-chien,* a city of the third order (eight and a half miles), in less than two hours, and after breakfasting there, we, in two hours and a half more (twelve miles), came to a palace of the Emperor near Min-yu-chien,† a city of the third order also, where we proposed to sleep. The road was much the same as yesterday. The mountains were tumbled about very agreeably, and must have a cheerful appearance when clothed with verdure; at present they are very brown and dusky. They have not the slightest volcanic character, but much resemble the mountains about Vellore in the Carnatic, being of various shapes and magnitudes, each standing on its own basis and rising singly from a circumferent level and often crowned with trees and pagodas. Some of them appeared to have been originally conical and rounded off or shortened by the lapse of time. At about two-thirds of the way between Hoai-ziou-chien, and Min-yu-chien we passed a river (whose course is southward) over a bridge built on caissons of wattles filled with stones. I understand that such bridges are very common in this part of the country. The caissons are of different dimensions according to the spread of the flood; they are from four to eight feet broad and their lengths are equal to the width of the bridge. The distances between them also vary. They are usually about one and a half the breadth of the caissons. The caissons are fixed by perpendicular spars more or less frequent according to the depth of the river and rapidity of the current. In broad or navigable streams this caisson-work is discontinued in the middle, and large flat-bottomed boats are substituted. Over the whole are laid planks, hurdles and clay. When the Emperor is expected to pass additional bridges are constructed. Near this place a part of the Great Wall, stretching over a high, steep hill, was visible on our left distant about nine or ten miles from the road.

This evening a Tartar officer of high rank, and commander of the troops in this district, paid us a visit, and brought a small present of fruit and sweetmeats. A sensible, gentlemanlike man, and sufficiently informed, as appeared in his conversation, of the pre-eminence of Great Britain in Europe as a civilized, ingenious, and powerful nation. Wang, though decorated with the same button and of the same military rank, yet would scarcely venture to sit down in his presence, so great is the respect affected by the Chinese towards the Tartars of the Court.

* [? Huai-jou hsien.—Ed.]   † [? Mi-yün hsien.—Ed.]

RIDING POST-CHAISE

Wednesday, September 4. Our first stage this morning from Min-yu-chien was about six and a half miles to a bonze's temple called Kiow-song-chang and our next was of fifteen miles to You-chin-sa where we have dined and shall sleep. Near this palace is a small walled town called Che-siou, resembling in the mode of its fortification and defence, to most of the other cities which we have passed through in China. And here I must say a word or two on the subject of them. They have usually four or five rectangular projections from each front according to their size, answering to the purpose of bastions and are about one hundred yards from each other. They contain generally three or four embrasures in front and two in each flank and are distant from centre to centre three yards. The walls are from twenty-five to thirty-five feet high, the gates are defended by projections of different figures and dimensions, but usually forty or fifty yards square. Sometimes the angles are taken off by a curve, and sometimes the whole projection is semicircular. This space is entered from without, in some instances in the front, but oftener in one of the flanks. A second gate then opens into the town, in the middle of that side of the enclosure that is formed by the city wall. These are, I understand, the general principles of defence that prevail in China. The walls are seldom surrounded by a regular ditch or strengthened by outworks. Where these cities happen to stand upon a canal a small branch of it is sometimes led round them. Artificial mounts are often to be found within short commanding distances, probably raised in very ancient times. I never saw artillery mounted on the walls of any of these fortified towns, and I suspect they have none in their arsenals. Chou says it is not necessary, as no enemies with artillery are to be apprehended. The chief use, therefore, of walled towns at present is for securing the treasure, tributes and taxes of the Emperor, as they are received; for the protection of the public granaries and for the safety of the prisons. The road this day, though very rough, has been pleasant and romantic; it is uphill the whole way and so I find it will continue to Jehol. Cultivation now is seldom practicable except on the edges of ravines. Great numbers of goats and horses appear from time to time on the mountains and run along the most dangerous precipices without apprehension or accident. In the course of these last two days both Wang and Chou took their turns to come into the post-chaise with me, and were inexpressibly pleased and astonished with its easiness, lightness, and rapidity, the ingenuity of the springs, and the various contrivances for raising and lowering the glasses, curtains, and jalousies. At one place where

I alighted I saw a beautiful weeping willow hanging over a sweet pastoral stream on one side of the road. It measured fifteen feet in the girth and eight feet above the ground. It comes out in conversation that the Legate has never dispatched my letter to Sir Erasmus Gower,* and this day he has returned it to me with a trifling excuse for his not sending it. He said it did not appear from what I had told him to be of any importance, and in truth it was of very little. What can be the meaning of this?[29] To-morrow he is to leave us in order that he may get to Jehol a day or two sooner, and have things ready there for our reception.

Thursday, September 5. From You-chin-sa to Ku-pei-k'ou, where we stopped to breakfast, are thirteen miles. About the half way the road ascends a steep hill and passes through Min-nan-tien, which stands on the summit and signifies the gate of the southern heaven.† Between Min-nan-tien and the Great Wall which now begins to show itself is a valley of considerable extent and of uncommon picturesque beauty, watered by a clear winding stream. The sides of the valley are formed by rocky mountains, not sloping but rising almost perpendicularly at right angles from the plain. These mountains, gradually approaching, almost close the passage, leaving only a narrow defile or ravine through which there is barely room for the road, and a small rivulet that runs in the bottom. Across the road is built a tower of eighteen feet wide (with the gate in the centre) and forty-five feet long. This pass had been formerly quite closed by the side walls of the tower continuing up the hills both on the east and west, but on the latter it was now open, for both the arch through which room had been left for the stream to flow and the wall raised upon the arch have been destroyed and there now appears a complete disruption of the whole from top to bottom. Through the lower gate we proceeded on for a considerable way, I suppose near 1,000 yards, through a large extent of ground with several houses built upon it enclosed by high walls connected with the great one, till we came to another gate and from thence to the town of Ku-pei-k'ou which is very populous and strongly enclosed by two or three rows of walls, which at a few miles distance converge together and unite with the main one. After breakfast we set out from Ku-pei-k'ou in order

---

* Vide letter from Sir George Staunton to Sir Erasmus Gower dated 29 August 1793. [Omitted here—Ed.]
† [? T'ien-nan men.—Ed.]

to visit this celebrated wall which we had heard such wonders of, and after passing through the outermost gate on the Tartar side, we began our peregrination on foot, there being no other method of approach. In less than half an hour, after travelling over very rough ground, we at last arrived at a breach in the wall, by which we ascended to the top of it. I shall here minute down all the particulars relative to it which I can either recollect myself or have been reminded of by my companions.

The wall is built of blueish coloured brick, not burnt but dried in the sun,* and raised upon a stone foundation, and as measured from the ground on the side next Tartary, it is about twenty-six feet high in the perpendicular. The stone foundation is formed of two courses of granite equal to twenty-four inches or two feet. From thence to the parapet including the cordon which is six inches are nineteen feet four inches, the parapet is four feet eight inches. From the stone foundation to the cordon are fifty-eight rows of bricks and above the cordon are fourteen rows; and each row, allowing for the interstices of the mortar and the insertion of the cordon may be calculated at the rate of four inches per brick. Thus then fifty-eight and fourteen bricks equal to seventy-two give two hundred and eighty-eight inches, or twenty-four feet, which together with the stone foundation make twenty-six feet. The wall on the inside, I presume, measures nearly the same. At the bottom the walls are five feet thick, and diminish gradually as they rise, being only four feet two inches at the cordon, and one foot and a half at the top of the parapet. The space or terrepleine between the walls, which is filled with earth and rubbish up to the level of the bottom of the cordon and paved with square bricks is eleven feet in the clear, so that there is room for two coaches or five horsemen abreast. This great wall is strengthened and defended by square towers at one hundred and fifty to two hundred feet distance. They are of different dimensions. I entered one which projected eighteen feet from the ramp on the Tartar side; there is no projection on the Chinese. It is forty feet long at the bottom and gradually diminishes so as to form a square of only thirty feet at the terrepleine. The perpendicular height is about

* From the colour of the bricks we were led to imagine that they had not felt the fire, but I have been since assured from good authority that they were certainly burnt in a kiln.

[Macartney then adds, in a footnote, the opinion of Dr. Gillan on the subject after he had carried out two experiments. His conclusion was that the colour was caused by iron existing in the original clay and also because of iron in the ashes and the coal used.—Ed.]

JOURNAL—SEPTEMBER

thirty-six feet eight inches. This tower stands of four courses of stone, each course equal to fourteen inches, which gives fifty-six inches, or four feet eight inches, and above the stone work to the top of the parapet are ninety-six rows of bricks, which at four inches to each brick and making allowances, as before, for the cordon, produce three hundred and eighty-four inches or thirty-two feet. Total thirty-six feet eight inches. The parapet of the wall is cut with embrasures at nine feet distance from centre to centre and there are loop holes between the embrasures of twelve inches long and ten wide, and scarped away below, which appear much better calculated for musketry than for arrows. This circumstance, together with that of the holes of the embrasures of the tower being pierced, as we observed with small holes, similar to those used in Europe for receiving the swivels of wall pieces, would seem to countenance a conjecture that the Chinese had the use of some sort of firearms in very ancient times; for all their writing agree that this wall was built above two hundred years before the Christian era.* It is carried on in a curvilinear direction often over the steepest highest and craggiest mountains as I observed in several places, and measures upwards of one thousand five hundred miles in length from its commencement in the Gulf of Pei-chihli in the province of Shantung east of Pekin, to its termination in the province of Shensi, west of Pekin.[30]

If the other parts of it be similar to those which I have seen, it is certainly the most stupendous work of human hands, for I imagine that if the outline of all the masonry of all the forts and fortified places in the whole world besides were to be calculated, it would fall considerably short of that of the Great Wall of China. At the remote period of its building China must have been not only a very powerful empire, but a very wise and virtuous nation, or at least to have had such foresight and such regard for posterity as to establish at once what was then thought a perpetual security for them against future invasion, choosing to load herself with an enormous expense of immediate labour and treasure rather than leave succeeding generations to a precarious dependence on contingent resources. She

---

* Since the above hasty account was written I have been favoured with a plan, section and measurements and observations on this celebrated wall by Lieutenant Parish of the Royal Artillery, which from his approved skill and accuracy as an engineer and draftsman are to be considered as highly valuable and supersede everything that has been hitherto written on this subject. They are annexed to this journal in the appendix No. 5EEEE. [See Sir G. L. Staunton, *An Authentic Account . . .*, folio volume of plans etc., plate 23—Ed.]

must also have had uncommon vigilance and discernment so as to profit by every current event and to seize the proper moment of tranquility for executing so extensive and difficult an enterprise. But besides a defence against her enemies she possibly had other objects in view. She might intend it to shut out from the fertile provinces of China the numerous and ferocious beasts of the wilds of Tartary, to ascertain and fix her boundary, and to prevent emigration. Till the establishment of the present dynasty on the throne she seems to have entertained no project of foreign conquests, and it is still a favourite point of her policy to confine her subjects with the limits of the empire. Those who depart from China without licence are inevitably punished with the utmost vigour if ever brought back. The wall is still in some places which I saw quite perfect and entire, and looks as if recently built or repaired, but in general it is in a ruinous condition, and falling fast to decay, very little care being taken to preserve it. Indeed at present its utility in point of defence seems to be almost at an end. For the Emperor now reigning has extended his territory so far beyond it that I doubt whether his dominions without the wall are inferior to those within it.

It was not without a little management that we contrived to examine this wall so much at our leisure, for some of our conductors appeared rather uneasy and impatient at the length of our stay upon it. They were astonished at our curiosity, and almost began to suspect us, I believe, of dangerous designs. Wang and Chou, though they had passed it twenty times before, had never visited it but once, and few of the other attending Mandarins had ever visited it at all. From Ku-pei-k'ou are eleven miles to Liou-king-fong,* which ends this day's journey. A little incident has happened at this place which strongly marks the jealousy that subsists between the Chinese and the Tartars. A Tartar servant of the lowest class attending at the Palace had, it seems, stolen some of the utensils furnished for our accommodation, and when taxed with the theft by Wang and Chou, answered with so much impertinence that they ordered him to be smartly bambooed on the spot, The moment he was released he broke out into the most insolent expressions, and insisted that a Chinese Mandarin had no right to bamboo a Tartar without side of the Great Wall. The punishment was, however, repeated in such a manner as to make him not only restore the stolen goods, but repent I believe, of his topographical objection to it. I suspect, however, that there was some sort of ground for his distinction, but that the

* [? Liang-chien-fang.—Ed.]

commission of our conductors was sufficiently extensive to overrule it, and supersede any local immunities.* Chou tells me he has every reason to believe that my proposal relative to the ceremonial will be approved of.

Friday, September 6. Our journey to-day was very short, it being only thirteen miles from Liou-king-fong to Ching-chang-you, where we mean to sleep. The further we advance among the mountains we find the weather grow colder. It was remarkably sharp this morning, although yesterday the thermometer (Fahrenheit's) stood at 82, and at 78 the day before.

We now observe many people with very large goitres or wens growing on the outside of their throats as in the Valais and the Tyrol. The snow lies here several months in the year and to the use of snow water the Chinese attribute this deformity. How justly I do not know, but it is certain that there are no goitres to be seen in the southern provinces where probably the waters are not less impregnated with the tufa stone than in the northern ones.[31] The country here indeed has a very Alpine appearance much resembling Savoy and Switzerland.

This evening our interpreter amused us with an extract from one of the Tientsin gazettes, which seem to be much on a par with our own newspapers for wit and authenticity. In an account given there of the presents said to be brought for the Emperor from England the following articles are mentioned: several dwarfs or little men not twelve inches high, but in form and intellect as perfect as grenadiers; an elephant not larger than a cat, and a horse the size of a mouse; a singing-bird as big as a hen, that feeds upon charcoal, and devours usually fifty pounds per day; and, lastly, an enchanted pillow, on which whoever lays his head immediately falls asleep, and if he dreams of any distant place, such as Canton, Formosa, or Europe, is instantly transported thither without the fatigue of travelling. This little anecdote, however ridiculous, I thought would not be fair to leave out of my journal.

Saturday, September 7. From Ching-chang-you are eleven miles to Wan-ha-you, where we stopped to breakfast and from Wan-ha-you to Co-la-cho-you are seven miles more; here we have dined and

* On this occasion Wang could not help saying to our interpreter: 'A Tartar will always be a Tartar.'

propose to sleep. The road to-day has been very rough and stony. The country opens and grows less romantic but still pleasant.

Sunday, September 8.   This morning we set out from Co-la-cho-you, which is twelve miles from Jehol, and observed as we passed a very remarkable appearance on the right hand of the road called Schwong ta-shang.* It is a double rock on the top of a high hill rising up quite bare from its base, somewhat resembling what the Needles were a few years since. It is perforated in two places,† the one near the bottom and the other equidistant from the top. The height of the highest part of the rock from the base is about two hundred and thirty feet—a drawing of it is annexed. We stopped at K'uang-wu-lan, two miles short of Jehol, in order to dress and marshal the procession for my public entry. It was arranged in the following manner, and made a very splendid show:

> An hundred Mandarins on horseback.
> Lieutenant-Colonel Benson.
> Four Light Dragoons.
> Four Light Dragoons.
> Four Light Dragoons.
> Lieutenant Parish.
> Drum.   Fife.
> Four Artillerymen.
> Four Artillerymen.
> A Corporal of Artillery.
> Lieutenant Crewe.
> Four Infantry.
> Four Infantry.
> Four Infantry.
> Four Infantry.
> A Sergeant of Infantry.
> Two Servants ⎫
> Two Servants ⎪ in a rich green and gold
> Two Servants ⎬   livery
> Two Servants ⎪
> Two Servants ⎭
> Two Couriers   Ditto

* Vide, the drawing no. 6F in the appendix. [? Shuang-ta-shan. Omitted here—Ed.]

† It had this appearance from the road at the place from whence I saw it, but Lieut. Parish who went close up to it found that it was not quite joined above at the top.

Two musicians	} in a rich green and gold livery	
Two musicians		
Two gentlemen of the Embassy	} in a uniform of scarlet embroidered with gold	
Two gentlemen of the Embassy		
Two gentlemen of the Embassy		
Lord Macartney	} in a chariot	
Sir George Staunton and son		
A servant in livery behind	ditto	

We were near two hours from K'uang-wu-lan to the palace prepared for us at Jehol, which is spacious and convenient. All the baggage, presents, etc., etc., were already arrived before us.

Being now at the end of our journey I shall here insert a few notes and observations before I proceed to a detail of our transactions at this place.

[Here follows an 'abstract of the route from Pekin to Jehol', in the form of a detailed itinerary giving the names of the villages passed through and mileage covered from place to place, the total being shown as 489 Chinese *li* or 136 miles. Also included in this abstract was a note of the 'northing' and 'easting' made and the observed latitude of Pekin and Jehol—Ed.]

Our journey upon the whole has been very pleasant and, being divided into seven days, not at all fatiguing. At the end of every stage we have been lodged and entertained in the wings or houses adjoining to the Emperor's palaces. These palaces, which occur at short distances from each other on the road, have been built for his reception on his annual visit to Tartary. They are all constructed upon nearly the same plan and in the same taste. They front the south and are usually situated on irregular ground near the bases of gentle hills which together with their adjoining valleys are enclosed by high walls and laid out in parks and pleasure grounds with every possible attention to picturesque beauty. Whenever water can be brought into the view it is not neglected; the distant hills are planted, cultivated or left naked according to their accompaniments in the prospect. The wall is often concealed in a sunk fence, in order to give an idea of greater extent. A Chinese gardener is the painter of nature, and though totally ignorant of perspective as a science, produces the happiest effects by the management of or rather pencilling of distances, if I may use the expression, by relieving or keeping down the features of the scene, by contrasting trees of a bright, with those of a dusky foliage, by bringing them forward, or throwing them back according to their bulk and their figure, and by introducing buildings of different dimensions, either heightened by strong colouring, or softened by simplicity and omissions of ornament.* Having arrived one day pretty early in the afternoon at Min-yu-chien, one of the stages of our journey, I had a drawing made of the palace there, from whence a general idea may be formed of the accommodation such buildings afford. The wings, in one of which we were all conveniently lodged (being above seventy persons) are sufficiently accurate, but the centre part, which is set apart for the Emperor, was not allowed to be examined. However, the gentleman who made the drawing had an opportunity after sunset of pacing the extent of its front, and of hastily collecting the form and distribution within.

The common road from Pekin to Jehol is, in general, pretty good for the two first days, but I must observe that there is another road parallel to it, which is laid off for the sole use of the Sovereign, no other person being permitted to travel upon it, a circumstance of Imperial appropriation which I don't recollect even in Muscovy or Austria. As the Emperor is expected to return to Pekin in the latter end of this month the repair of this road is already begun, and we calculated that in the hundred and thirty-six miles from Pekin to Jehol above twenty-three thousand troops were employed upon it. They are usually divided into working parties of ten men to every hundred yards. Almost close to the road at various distances are towers or military posts (about one to every five miles) each post having from six to fifteen soldiers attached to it, who all turned out as we passed along, and fired a salute for us from three small chambers of iron fixed vertically in the ground, while a brass gong rattled upon the parade and a yellow flag fluttered upon the battlements.

The garrison of Jehol during the Emperor's residence is about a hundred thousand men.

Jehol, Sunday, September 8 (continued). Soon after we arrived at this place the Legate came and gave me back my paper about the ceremonial, and said that if I delivered it myself to the Minister I should receive the answer. Our interpreter also came and told me from Wang and Chou that the Emperor had seen my entry and procession from one of the heights of this park, and was much pleased

---

* Vide drawing no. 79 in the appendix. [Omitted here—Ed.]

with them, and that he had immediately ordered the first Minister and another Grand Secretary to wait upon me. In the meantime Wang and Chou themselves arrived, and told me that as there would not be sufficient room in my apartment for all the first Minister's suite, he, the first Minister, hoped I would excuse him from coming to me in person, and that it would be the same thing if I would be so good as to come to him. He added that the first Minister had received a hurt in his knee, which rendered it inconvenient and painful to him to move much about. It being very hot weather, and the servants greatly hurried and fatigued with the operations of the day, and our baggage, etc. not being yet unpacked or put into order, I excused myself with a civil compliment, but told them that if there was any business necessary to mention immediately, Sir George Staunton should attend the first Minister in the evening. They then informed me that the Tartar Legate had been censured by the Emperor for some misrepresentations with regard to the Embassy, and had been already punished by a degradation of three ranks.*

Soon after, several Mandarins of high rank came to visit me, some of them wearing yellow vests, which are marks of particular favour from the Emperor.

The Minister having signified a desire this afternoon of seeing Sir George Staunton, he immediately went with his son and our interpreter to the Minister's house, which is above a mile from my hotel, having passed through a great part of the town of Jehol in his way to it. There he found the Legate at the door, who conducted him to an apartment, where the Minister was sitting, attended by four other Grand Secretaries, all having red buttons on their caps, and two of them dressed in yellow vests. On Sir George's return I found that the Minister's objects were to know the contents of the King's letter to the Emperor (of which a copy was accordingly promised to be given to him), and to contrive means of avoiding, if possible, the compliment to His Majesty, in return for my compliance with the Chinese ceremony, as proposed in my paper,† which it was apparent the Minister had seen before the Legate had given it back to me. Sir George now delivered it to the Minister officially from me.

---

* The Emperor having heard that I had his picture in my cabin on board the *Lion*, asked the Legate whether it was like him, upon which it came out that the Legate had never been near the *Lion*, which he had been ordered to visit. It was said that he was afraid of the water, and therefore would not venture, not suspecting that his omission would be discovered.

† Vide paper no. 8 among the enclosures in my letter to Mr. Secretary Dundas dated 9 November 1793. [Omitted here—Ed.]

Monday, September 9. The Legate, Wang and Chou came this morning to urge me to give up the reciprocal compliment I demanded, but I dwelt upon the propriety of something to distinguish between the homage of tributary Princes and the ceremony used on the part of a great and independent sovereign. I understand privately that the Emperor is not acquainted with the difficulties that have arisen on this subject, but that when he is the matter will probably be adjusted as I wish.

Tuesday, September 10. This day the Legate, Wang and Chou renewed the conversation of yesterday relative to the ceremony, in the course of which I told them it was not natural to expect that an ambassador should pay greater homage to a foreign prince than to his own liege Sovereign, unless a return were made to him that might warrant him to do more. Upon which they asked me what was the ceremony of presentation to the King of England. I told them it was performed by kneeling upon one knee and kissing His Majesty's hand. 'Why then,' cried they, 'can't you do so to the Emperor?' 'Most readily,' said I; 'the same ceremony I perform to my own King I am willing to go through for your Emperor, and I think it a greater compliment than any other I can pay him.' I showed them the manner of it, and they retired seemingly well satisfied. In the afternoon Chou came to me alone, and said that he had just seen the Minister, and had a long conference with him upon this business, the result of which was that either the English mode of presentation (which I had shown them in the morning) or the picture ceremony should be adopted, but he had not yet decided which. I said nothing.

Soon after the Legate arrived, and declared that it was finally determined to adopt the English ceremony, only that, as it was not the custom in China to kiss the Emperor's hand, he proposed I should kneel upon both knees instead of it. I told him I had already given my answer, which was to kneel upon one knee only on those occasions when it was usual for the Chinese to prostrate themselves. 'Well then', said they, 'the ceremony of kissing the Emperor's hand must be omitted.' To this I assented, saying, 'As you please, but remember it is your doing, and according to your proposal, is but half the ceremony, and you see I am willing to perform the whole one.' And thus ended this curious negotiation, which has given me a tolerable insight into the character of this Court, and that political address upon which they so much value themselves.

JOURNAL—SEPTEMBER

Wednesday, September 11. At half-past nine a.m. the Legate, Wang and Chou came to my house to attend me to the Minister or chief Grand Secretary. His palace is very spacious, and consists of several courts, through which we passed before we arrived at his apartment, which is small and has nothing magnificent in furniture or appearance. He received us with great affability, and seemed, as Sir George Staunton told me, quite a different sort of person from what he appeared a few days before. He is a handsome, fair man about forty to forty-five years old, quick and fluent. On his right hand was the Fou-liou,* a handsome, fair man also, of about thirty years old, and on his left two old Chinese Grand Secretaries, one the President of the Court of Rites and the other the President of the Tribunal of Finance,³² and at the end of all was another great man in a yellow vest, but who did not seem to be of equal authority with the others.

I began by saying that, being now recovered from the fatigue of my journey, I was happy to have an early opportunity of waiting upon him and expressing my wishes to present the King's letter to the Emperor as soon as possible, every difficulty being now obviated. I said that in the meantime I had made many inquiries about the Emperor's health, and was rejoiced to hear that it was so good as to promise long life to him for many years, and consequently much happiness to his subjects, and that it would give sincere pleasure to the greatest Sovereign in the West to hear such good news from me of the greatest Sovereign of the East. The Minister made some compliments in return, and said that, on account of the very great distance from which the Embassy had been sent, and of the value of the presents, some of the Chinese customs (which had hitherto been invariably observed) would now be relaxed, and that I might perform the ceremony after the manner of my own country, and deliver the King's letter into the Emperor's own hand. So now these preliminary difficulties are over, and Saturday next, being a great festival at Court, is fixed for the day of my introduction. In the course of this conversation, which lasted a considerable time, he asked me several questions relative to our voyage—where we had stopped on our way, and for what purposes. Having mentioned our putting in at Tourane Bay, in Cochin China, for water, he observed to me that that country was a tributary and dependance of China. He inquired how far England was from Russia, and whether they were good friends together, and whether Italy and Portugal were not near

---

* [i.e. Fu-ch'ang-an, a personal name and not a rank. Macartney used it correctly as a name in his first references. See note 17.—Ed.]

England and tributary to it. I explained to him the distance between England and Russia in Chinese measure, and repeated that we were at present at peace with all the world, and with the Empress of Russia as well as with others, but that there did not seem to be the same cordiality at present as formerly, on account of the King of England (who is a lover of peace and justice, and a friend of the distressed) having once interfered to repress a spirit of encroachment shown in some of her measures with regard to Turkey. As to Italy and Portugal, they were not tributaries of England, but, from the same motives of general justice and equity before mentioned, the King of England had often afforded them protection and shown them marks of his friendship. When I arose to go away the Minister took me by the hand, and said he should be happy to cultivate my acquaintance, and hoped to have frequent opportunities of seeing me familiarly at Yuan-ming Yuan, as the bustle and hurry of business and the festivals of the Emperor's anniversary must necessarily engage the greater part of his time whilst the Court remained at Jehol.

In the afternoon our friends Wang and Chou visited us, and repeated a great many flattering things which they assured us the Minister had said of us, and that he had made so favourable a report to the Emperor that he was quite impatient for Saturday.

Then the Tartar [Cheng-jui—Ed.] arrived, and brought us a present of fruit and sweetmeats from the Minister, with a compliment similar to that brought by Wang and Chou. We employed the rest of the day in getting the presents put in order.

Thursday, September 12. And this day they were sent to the Palace to be viewed. Soon after the Legate came to visit me, and brought another present of fruit and sweetmeats, but seemed much out of sorts.

Friday, September 13. Wang and Chou called on us to say that the presents were much approved, but it was wished that somebody might be sent to show how the telescopes were to be put up and used; upon which Dr. Gillan and our interpreter went and taught the eunuchs how to join them together, to adjust the day and night glasses, and to manage the rack-work. Notwithstanding their complete ignorance, these gentry pretended to understand, at half a word, all the machinery of these instruments, but Dr. Gillan did not leave them till he thought he had really made them masters of

JOURNAL—SEPTEMBER

it. To-morrow being the grand festival at Court, and the day appointed for our first presentation, we are busily employed in getting ready for the occasion.

Saturday, September 14. This morning at four o'clock a.m. we set out for the Court under the convoy of Wang and Chou, and reached it in little more than an hour, the distance being about three miles from our hotel. I proceeded in great state with all my train of music, guards, etc. Sir George Staunton and I went in palanquins and the officers and gentlemen of the Embassy on horseback. Over a rich embroidered velvet I wore the mantle of the Order of the Bath, with the collar, a diamond badge and a diamond star.

Sir George Staunton was dressed in a rich embroidered velvet also, and, being a Doctor of Laws in the University of Oxford, wore the habit of his degree, which is of scarlet silk, full and flowing. I mention these little particulars to show the attention I always paid, where a proper opportunity offered, to oriental customs and ideas. We alighted at the park gate, from whence we walked to the Imperial encampment, and were conducted to a large, handsome tent prepared for us on one side of the Emperor's. After waiting there about an hour his approach was announced by drums and music, on which we quitted our tent and came forward upon the green carpet.

He was seated in an open palanquin, carried by sixteen bearers, attended by numbers of officers bearing flags, standards, and umbrellas, and as he passed we paid him our compliments by kneeling on one knee, whilst all the Chinese made their usual prostrations. As soon as he had ascended his throne I came to the entrance of the tent,* and, holding in both my hands a large gold box enriched with diamonds in which was enclosed the King's letter, I walked deliberately up, and ascending the side-steps of the throne, delivered it into the Emperor's own hands, who, having received it, passed it to the Minister, by whom it was placed on the cushion. He then gave me as the first present from him to His Majesty the *ju-eu-jou* or *giou-giou*,[33] as the symbol of peace and prosperity, and expressed his hopes that my Sovereign and he should always live in good correspondence and amity. It is a whitish, agate-looking stone about a foot and a half long, curiously carved, and highly prized by the Chinese, but to me it does not appear in itself to be of any great value.

The Emperor then presented me with a *ju-eu-jou* of a greenish-

---

* Vide two drawings of the tent in the appendix no. 8H.H. [See Frontispiece—Ed.]

coloured stone of the same emblematic character; at the same time he very graciously received from me a pair of beautiful enamelled watches set with diamonds, which I had prepared in consequence of the information given me, and which, having looked at, he passed to the Minister. Sir George Staunton, whom, as he had been appointed Minister Plenipotentiary to act in case of my death or departure, I introduced to him as such, now came forward, and after kneeling upon one knee in the same manner which I had done, presented to him two elegant air-guns, and received from him a *ju-eu-jou* of greenish stone nearly similar to mine. Other presents were sent at the same time to all the gentlemen of my train. We then descended from the steps of the throne, and sat down upon cushions at one of the tables on the Emperor's left hand; and at other tables, according to their different ranks, the chief Tartar Princes and the Mandarins of the Court at the same time took their places, all dressed in the proper robes of their respective ranks. These tables were then uncovered and exhibited a sumptuous banquet. The Emperor sent us several dishes from his own table, together with some liquors, which the Chinese call wine, not, however, expressed from the grape, but distilled or extracted from rice, herbs, and honey. In about half an hour he sent for Sir George Staunton and me to come to him, and gave to each of us, with his own hands, a cup of warm wine, which we immediately drank in his presence, and found it very pleasant and comfortable, the morning being cold and raw.

Amongst other things, he asked me the age of my King, and being informed of it, said he hoped he might live as many years as himself, which are eighty-three. His manner is dignified, but affable, and condescending, and his reception of us has been very gracious and satisfactory. He is a very fine old gentleman, still healthy and vigorous, not having the appearance of a man of more than sixty.

The order and regularity in serving and removing the dinner was wonderfully exact, and every function of the ceremony performed with such silence and solemnity as in some measure to resemble the celebration of a religious mystery. The Emperor's tent or pavilion,* which is circular, I should calculate to be about twenty-four or twenty-five yards in diameter, and is supported by a number of pillars, either gilded, painted, or varnished, according to their distance and position. In the front was an opening of six yards, and from this opening a yellow fly-tent projected so as to lengthen considerably the space between the entrance and the throne.

* Vide the drawing of the tent in the appendix no. 8H.H. [See Frontispiece—Ed.]

JOURNAL—SEPTEMBER

The materials and distribution of the furniture within at once displayed grandeur and elegance. The tapestry, the curtains, the carpets, the lanterns, the fringes, the tassels were disposed with such harmony, the colours so artfully varied, and the light and shades so judiciously managed, that the whole assemblage filled the eye with delight, and diffused over the mind a pleasing serenity and repose undisturbed by glitter or affected embellishments. The commanding feature of the ceremony was that calm dignity, that sober pomp of Asiatic greatness, which European refinements have not yet attained.

I forgot to mention that there were present on this occasion three ambassadors from Tatze or Pegu and six Mohammedan ambassadors from the Kalmucks of the south-west, but their appearance was not very splendid.[34] Neither must I omit that, during the ceremony, which lasted five hours, various entertainments of wrestling, tumbling, wire-dancing, together with dramatic representations, were exhibited opposite to the tent, but at a considerable distance from it.

Thus, then, have I seen 'King Solomon in all his glory'. I use this expression, as the scene recalled perfectly to my memory a puppet show of that name which I recollect to have seen in my childhood, and which made so strong an impression on my mind that I then thought it a true representation of the highest pitch of human greatness and felicity.

Sunday, September 15. The Emperor, having been informed that in the course of our travels in China we had shown a strong desire of seeing everything curious and interesting, was pleased to give directions to the first Minister to show us his park or garden at Jehol. It is called in Chinese Wan-shu Yuan, which signifies the paradise of innumerable trees.

In order to have this gratification (which is considered as an instance of uncommon favour) we rose this morning at three o'clock, and went to the Palace, where we waited, mixed with all the great officers of state, for three hours (such is the etiquette of the place) till the Emperor's appearance. At last he came forth, borne in the usual manner by sixteen persons, on a high open palanquin, attended by guards, music, standards and umbrellas without number, and observing us as we stood in the front line graciously beckoned us to approach, having ordered his people to stop. He entered into conversation with us, and, with great affability of manner, told us that he was on his way to the pagoda, where he usually paid his morning

THE GARDENS AT JEHOL

devotions; that, as we professed a different religion from his, he would not ask us to accompany him, but that he had ordered his first Minister and chief Grand Secretaries to conduct us through his garden, and to show us whatever we were desirous of seeing there.

Having expressed my sense of this mark of his condescension in the proper manner, and my increasing admiration of everything I had yet observed at Jehol, I retired; and whilst he proceeded to his adorations at the pagoda, I accompanied the Ministers and other Grand Secretaries of the Court to a pavilion prepared for us, from whence, after a short collation, we set out on horseback to view this wonderful garden. We rode about three miles through a very beautiful park, kept in the highest order, and much resembling the approach to Luton in Bedfordshire;[35] the grounds gently undulated and chequered with various groups of well-contrasted trees in the offskip. As we moved onward an extensive lake appeared before us, the extremities of which seemed to lose themselves in distance and obscurity. Here was a large, magnificent yacht ready to receive us, and a number of smaller ones for the attendants, elegantly fitted up and adorned with numberless vanes, pennants, and streamers. The shores of the lake have all the varieties of shape which the fancy of a painter can delineate, and are so indented with bays or broken with projections, that almost every stroke of the oar brought a new and unexpected object to our view; nor are islands wanting, but they are situated only where they should be, each in its proper place and having its proper character. One marked by a pagoda, or other building, one quite destitute of ornament, some smooth and level, some steep and uneven, and others frowning with wood, or smiling with culture. Where any things particularly interesting were to be seen we disembarked, from time to time, to visit them, and I dare say that in the course of our voyage we stopped at forty or fifty different palaces or pavilions. These are all furnished in the richest manner, with pictures of the Emperor's huntings and progresses; with stupendous vases of jasper and agate; with the finest porcelain and japan, and with every kind of European toys and sing-songs;*
with spheres, orreries, clocks, and musical automatons of such exquisite workmanship, and in such profusion, that our presents must shrink from the comparison and 'hide their diminished heads'.†
And yet I am told that the fine things we have seen are far exceeded by others of the same kind in the apartments of the ladies and in the

* [See Note 1, p. 355—Ed.]
† [Milton, *Paradise Lost*, Bk. IV, 35—Ed.]

European repository at Yuan-ming Yuan. In every one of these pavilions was a throne, or Imperial state, and a *ju-eu-jou*, or symbol of peace and prosperity placed at one side of it, resembling that which the Emperor delivered to me yesterday for the King.

It would be an endless task were I to attempt a detail of all the wonders of this charming place. There is no beauty of distribution and contrast, no feature of amenity, no reach of fancy which embellishes our pleasure grounds in England, that is not to be found here. Had China been accessible to Mr. Brown or to Mr. Hamilton[36] I should have sworn they had drawn their happiest ideas from the rich sources which I have tasted this day; for in the course of a few hours I have enjoyed such vicissitudes of rural delight, as I did not conceive could be felt out of England, being at different moments enchanted by scenes perfectly similar to those I had known there, to the magnificence of Stowe, the soft beauties of Woburn or the fairy-land of Painshill.[37]

One thing I was particularly struck with, I mean the happy choice of situation for ornamental buildings. From attention to this circumstance they have not the air of being crowded or disproportioned; they never intrude upon the eye but wherever they appear always show themselves to advantage, and aid, improve and enliven the prospect.

In many places the lake is overspread with the nenuphar, or lotus (nymphea) resembling our broad-leaved water-lily. This is an accompaniment which, though the Chinese are passionately fond of, cultivating it in all their pieces of water, I confess I don't much admire. Artificial rocks and ponds, with gold and silver fish are perhaps too often introduced, and the monstrous porcelain figures of lions and tigers usually placed before the pavilions, are displeasing to an European eye. But these are trifles of no great moment, and I am astonished that now, after a six hours critical survey of these gardens I can scarcely recollect anything besides to find fault with.

At our taking leave of the Minister he told us that we had only seen the eastern side of the gardens, but that the western side, which was the larger part, still remained for him to show us, and that he should have that pleasure another day. Of the great men who accompanied us on this tour the principal were, 1st, the Minister, or great Grand Secretary Ho-shen; 2nd, the Fou-liou,* or Second Minister; 3rd his brother Fu-k'ang-an, formerly Viceroy of Canton, but lately named Viceroy of Szechwan; and 4th, Sung-yun,[38] a young man of

* [i.e. Fu-ch'ang-an.—Ed.]

high quality—all Tartars, and, if I may use the expression, Knights of the Yellow Vest.

Sung-yun had, not long since, been employed upon the frontiers of Russia, to accommodate the disputes with that nation; and knowing that I had been formerly the King's Minister at Petersburg, he talked to me a good deal about his own mission. He said that he had negotiated at Kiahkta with a great Russian general, who wore a red ribbon and a star like mine, and they very soon understood each other and concluded their business. He was particularly pointed in his civilities to us, seemed very intelligent, and asked many proper questions relative to the riches and power of Russia. It would seem as if he had been selected on purpose to try the extent of my knowledge, or of my sincerity, by comparing my answers with his own notions upon the subject.

During the whole day the first Minister, or Grand Secretary, paid us very great attention, and displayed all the good breeding and politeness of an experienced courtier, though I am afraid I can already perceive that his heart is not with us, for, on my mentioning to him this morning, as we rode along, that the creation of such a paradise as Jehol in so wild a spot was a work worthy of the genius of the great K'ang-hsi, he seemed to be quite astonished how I came to know that it was undertaken by K'ang-hsi, and asked me who told me so. I said that, as the English were a wise and learned nation, and acquainted with the history of all countries, it was not to be wondered at that they should be particularly well informed of the history of the Chinese, whose fame extended to the most distant parts of the world. Notwithstanding this compliment was a natural and a flattering one, he did not seem to me to feel it so; and I suspect that at bottom he rather wonders at our curiosity than esteems us for our knowledge. Possibly he may consider it as impertinent towards them and useless to ourselves.

The Fou-liou* or second Minister's deportment towards us was very gracious. Not so that of his brother, which was formal and repulsive. I mentioned above that he had been Viceroy of Canton, and it would appear that he has not been an inattentive observer of European manner and character. I could not avoid remarking it this morning, for, happening to be next to me at the moment I approached the Emperor, and perhaps not thinking me quick enough in my motions, he pulled me by the sleeve, and at the same time, though with an air of complaisance and respect, touched my hat

* [i.e. Fu-cha'ng-an.—Ed.]

with his hand to indicate his wishes that I should take it off on the occasion, a thing that could scarcely have occurred to any of his brother courtiers, as the salutation of the hat is entirely a European custom, and only used by Europeans, the Asiatics never uncovering their heads, even in the presence of their most elevated superiors.

Well aware of his connections and consequence, I was desirous of conciliating him to our interests, and endeavoured to soothe his vanity on the points where he was thought most accessible. I told him that I had often heard of his reputation as a warrior, and therefore I hoped that the exercise of my guard and their military evolutions, with the latest European improvements, might afford him some pleasure and entertainment. But he declined the proposal with great coldness and a mixture of unreasonable vanity, saying that nothing of that kind could be a novelty to him, though I have my doubts whether he ever saw a firelock in his life; at least, I am sure I have never yet seen anything above a matchlock among all the troops in China. But another incident in the course of our tour more strongly marked his indisposition towards us. The Minister having informed me that an account was just received of the arrival of the *Lion* and the *Hindostan* at Chusan, I seized the opportunity of requesting that Captain Mackintosh (in whose ship the greater part of the presents for the Emperor had been brought), having paid his obeisance to the Emperor, might be permitted to proceed, and join his ship at the port where she now lay, but Fu-k'ang-an interposed, and said that it was improper, and against the laws of China for strangers to be permitted to travel about in such a manner through the provinces of the Empire. Nor could any reasoning of mine, though conveyed to him in the gentlest and most flattering terms, induce him to relax from his opinion, or draw even a smile from him the rest of the day. Whether whilst at Canton he may have met with some unintentional slight, or whether, which is more probable, he may have remarked (for he is certainly a man of capacity) and felt, with regret and indignation, that superiority which, wherever Englishmen go, they cannot conceal from the most indifferent observer. Finding this moment so unfavourable, I declined pressing the matter further, but requested the Minister to allow me a short conference with him, either the next day or the day following. I found, however, that, though infinitely gracious and civil in his manner and expression, I could gain no ground upon him. He excused himself on account of the approaching ceremony of the birthday, and the load of business on his hands requiring dispatch before the departure of the Court from Jehol, and repeated to me, as he had done in his first conference, that he hoped to have frequent opportunities of seeing me at Yuan-ming Yuan and cultivating my friendship there. I therefore take it for granted it has been a settled point from the beginning to do no business with me at Jehol. I, however, before we parted, persuaded him to consent to receive a short note, which I said I should take the liberty of sending him in a day or two. This is now my only resource, and I must therefore set about it without delay.

Monday, September 16.   Having now twice paid our obeisance to the Emperor, we conceived, from what had been told us before we left Pekin, that we might go freely about and walk abroad without constraint and impediment. To avoid anything, however, that might commit my character, I continued within doors but Sir George Staunton and some of the other gentlemen made a little excursion into the country to-day, but they were followed the whole way by a number of Mandarins and soldiers who, though they never attempted to direct their motions, still attended them at no great distance.

Thus I see that the same strange jealousy prevails towards us which the Chinese Government has always shown to other foreigners, although we have taken such pains to disarm it, and to conciliate their friendship and confidence. Perhaps our conductors are apprehensive that, from the novelty of our appearance and the singularity of our dress, we may be subjected to rude curiosity, and that some disturbance might arise for which they must be responsible, it being, as I am informed, a maxim of the Chinese Government never to excuse an officer for any accident that may happen in his department.

This morning Ho-shen, the first Minister, sent for Dr. Gillan, and without hesitation explained to him all his ailments—his rupture, his rheumatism, etc., etc.—and desired the doctor's opinion of his case. The doctor is now preparing it, and has promised me a copy.*

I received a visit this afternoon from a genteel young Tartar, decorated with a smooth red button and a peacock's feather of two eyes. His Manchu name is Poo-ta-vang, his Chinese one Mou-liou. He affects to be well informed of the geography and history of his

---

* Vide Dr. Gillan's paper in the appendix. [Not included in the Tokyo version of the Journal and appendices.—Ed.]

country. He told me that the present Emperor is descended from Co-be-li, or, as we call him, Kublai Khan, a son of Genghis Khan, who, in the thirteenth century, conquered China, and whose family (called the dynasty of Yen-tchao*) held it under the Mongol yoke for near one hundred years, till dethroned by the dynasty of Ming. The Mongols, who then fled into the country of the Manchu, inter-married and mixed with them, and from one of these alliances sprung the Bogdoi Khans,[39] who invaded China in 1640, and have reigned over it ever since.† Poo-ta-vang says that all the Tartar Princes who dined with us in the Emperor's tent are persons of great consequence, have numerous clans dependent upon them, and can bring large bodies of troops into the field. They are often called upon in time of war, and have their respective stations, rank, and duty assigned to them under the grand banners of Tartary. Their lands, or fiefs, were formerly hereditary by primogeniture, and are properly so still; but it is now necessary for the eldest son, on the death of his father, to receive a sort of investiture from the Emperor, who, if no objection arises, never refuses it. They seem like the honours of the *Casas Titulares* in Portugal. These Tartar Princes usually marry the daughters and nieces of the Imperial family, and hold a certain rank at Court in consequence of the alliance. They are obliged to come every year to attend the Emperor's birthday, and they then return home, being seldom detained, or employed in China in offices that require much literature, as their education is usually directed to military pursuits.

Their weapons are chiefly the scimitar and the bow and arrow, in the exercise of which they are remarkably expert. They seemed a good deal surprised when I once told them, in answer to their inquiries, that we had left off the use of the bow in Europe, and fought chiefly with firearms in its place. The bow is the Emperor's favourite instrument of war, and I observe that he is always represented in the pictures as shooting at stags, wolves and tigers with arrows, and never with a musket.

Poo-ta-vang says that Mukden, or Chin-yan-tsin,‡ as the Chinese call it, the Emperor's Tartar capital, which is about two hundred miles off, is larger than Pekin and that the Emperor has immense treasures there. Scarcely any Chinese have ever been at Mukden, or, indeed, many miles beyond Jehol.

* [Yuan-ch'ao—Ed.]
† I don't find upon inquiry from others that this genealogy is quite unequivocal.
‡ [? Shen-yang.—Ed.]

THE EMPEROR'S BIRTHDAY

Tuesday, September 17. This day being the Emperor's birthday, we set out for the Court at three o'clock a.m., conducted by Wang, Chou and our usual attendants. We reposed ourselves for above two hours in a large saloon at the entrance of the palace enclosure, where fruit, tea, warm milk, and other refreshments were brought to us. At last notice was given that the festival was going to begin, and we immediately descended into the garden, where we found all the great men and Mandarins in their robes of state, drawn up before the Imperial pavilion. The Emperor did not show himself, but remained concealed behind a screen, from whence, I presume, he could see and enjoy the ceremonies without inconvenience or interruption. All eyes were turned towards the place where His Majesty was imagined to be enthroned, and seemed to express an impatience to begin the devotions of the day. Slow, solemn music, muffled drums, and deep-toned bells were heard at a distance. On a sudden the sound ceased and all was still; again it was renewed, and then intermitted with short pauses, during which several persons passed backwards and forwards, in the proscenium or foreground of the tent, as if engaged in preparing some *grand coup de théâtre*.

At length the great band both vocal and instrumental struck up with all their powers of harmony, and instantly the whole Court fell flat upon their faces before this invisible Nebuchadnezzar. 'He in his cloudy tabernacle shrined sojourned the while.'* The music was a sort of birthday ode or state anthem, the burden of which was 'Bow down your heads, all ye dwellers upon earth, bow down your heads before the great Ch'ien-lung, the great Ch'ien-lung.' And then all the dwellers upon China earth there present, except ourselves,[40] bowed down their heads, and prostrated themselves upon the ground at every renewal of the chorus. Indeed, in no religion either ancient or modern, has the Divinity ever been addressed, I believe, with stronger exterior marks of worship and adoration than were this morning paid to the phantom of his Chinese Majesty. Such is the mode of celebrating the Emperor's anniversary festival according to the Court ritual.

We saw nothing of him the whole day, nor did any of his Ministers, I imagine, approach him, for they all seemed to retire at the same moment as we did. Of them the first, or great Grand Secretary Ho-shen, the Fou-liou,† the Fou-liou's brother Fu-k'ang-an, and

---

* [Milton, *Paradise Lost*, Bk. VII, 247–9:—'for yet the sun/was not; she in a cloudy tabernacle/sojourned the while'. The word 'shrined' occurs in Bk. VI. 671–2—Ed.] † [i.e. Fu-ch'ang-an.—Ed.

TOUR OF THE WESTERN PARK

s and colours.* All seemed to be nearly at
ld convey me within reach of them.

out to us by the Minister a vast enclo-
, was not more accessible to him than to
t by the Emperor, his women, and his
n its bounds though on a smaller scale
ch distinguish the eastern and western
lready seen, but from everything I can
f the fanciful descriptions which Father
hambers have intruded upon us as reali-
rivate retreats various entertainments of
ve nature are prepared and exhibited by
numerous (perhaps some thousands) to
s ladies, I have no doubt; but that they
ths of extravagance and improbability
htioned I very much question as from
(and I have not been sparing to make
ufficient reason to warrant me in accord-
counts which they have given us. When
n Russia several years ago, I remember
Empress's palaces the image of a town,
ps, and warehouses, pretended trades-
siness of common life represented in a
amusement of the Court which much
m Chambers' picture, than anything I
China. If any place in England can be
similar features to the western park
it is Lowther Hall in Westmorland,[42]
years ago) from the extent of prospect,
cts, the noble situation, the diversity of
ds, and command of water I thought
an of sense, spirit, and taste the finest
ns.

s tour, as in the former, we were enter-
s with a collation of *petits pâtés*, salt
dishes, with fruits and sweetmeats, milk
s we rose from table a number of yellow

of what we call in England sheet cows, also sheet
ottled and spotted, the latter chiefly strawberry.
d sheet cow and a literary example of its use in
a broad white band round the body'. The com-
the O.E.D.—Ed.]

boxes or drawers were carried in procession before us, containing several pieces of silk and porcelain, which we were told were presents to us from the Emperor, and we consequently made our bows as they passed. We were also amused with a Chinese puppet-show, which differs but little from an English one. There are a distressed princess confined in a castle, and a knight-errant who, after fighting lions and dragons, sets her at liberty and marries her, wedding-feasts, jousts, and tournaments. Besides these there is also a comic drama, in which Punch and his wife, Bandimeer and Scaramouch, perform capital parts. This puppet-show, we were told, properly belongs to the ladies' apartments, but was sent out, as a particular compliment to entertain us. One of the performances exhibited drew great applause from our conductors, and I understand it is a favourite piece at Court.

I could not help admiring the address with which the Minister parried all my attempts to speak to him on business this day, and how artfully he evaded every opportunity that offered for any particular conversation with me, endeavouring to engage our attention solely by the objects around us, directing our eyes to the prospects, and explaining the various beauties of the park and buildings. I, nevertheless, found an occasion to remind him of his promise to peruse the note which I meant to send him, and told him that it would be ready to-morrow. It was now near three o'clock, when, he said, he must take his leave of us, at the same time expressing his concern that affairs of consequence required his attendance; but he added that he left us under the care of the Grand Secretary Sung-yun, who would accompany us to the grand pagoda at Potala, and the others in its neighbourhood.[43] The Fou-liou and his brother* went away with the first Minister.

These pagodas, which all adjoin the park, are surrounded by a great wall and each pagoda is in a separate enclosure of its own. I dare say we visited at least a dozen of them all differently situated, some on gentle elevations, some on the plain, and some on the tops of high hills, approachable only by rocky stairs of difficult ascent, or by long passages leading through gloomy caverns, or under the shadow of enormous rocks which seem to threaten the passenger at every step with instant annihilation. They are all buildings of great extent and magnificence, but Potala, which may be considered as the grand cathedral, is infinitely superior to the rest in point of magnitude, splendour and celebrity. It is an immense edifice, and

* [i.e. Fu-ch'ang-an and Fu-k'ang-an.—Ed.]

THE POTALA AT JEHOL

with the offices belonging to it covers a vast deal of ground (not less than twenty to twenty-five acres) and contains, I should conceive, a greater quantity of materials than St. Paul's. The principal temple, or monastery in it, in which eight hundred lamas, or priests of Fo-hi are lodged, is a square of four fronts, each front of upwards of two hundred feet long, enclosing a quadrangle of above one hundred and thirty feet each side, in the centre of which is the Golden Chapel, which including the projection of the roof is near eighty feet square and seventy feet high. A spacious corridor below and open galleries above connect the apartments of the quadrangle, the depth of which apartments with corridor is forty-seven feet in the clear.* The height of the building from the ground on the outside, including the terraces, is two hundred and fifty feet and consists of eleven stories, three in the terrace and eight above it.†

In the chapel we found all the monks or lamas busily engaged in their devotions, dressed in yellow vestments, with books in their hands and chanting their liturgy in a kind of recitative, not unlike our cathedral service, and not disagreeable to the ear. The paraphernalia of religion displayed here—the altars, images, tabernacles, censers, lamps, candles, and candlesticks—with the sanctimonious deportment of the priests and the solemnity used in the celebration of their mysteries, have no small resemblance to the holy mummeries of the Romish Church as practised in those countries where it is rich and powerful. In the middle of the chapel is a small space railed off and elevated by three steps above the floor, which presents three altars richly adorned, and three colossal statues, one of Fo-hi, one of Fo-hi's wife, and the other of some great Tartar divinity, whose name I forget, all of solid gold.‡ Behind these altars is the *sanctum sanctorum*, which is dimly lighted by an expiring lamp, seemingly placed there for the purpose of inspiring religious horror or exciting pious curiosity. As we approached it, the curtain, which had just before been drawn a little aside, was suddenly closed, as if on a sudden alarm, and shut out the shrine from our profane eyes. This pagoda is dedicated to Potala, one of the transmigrations

---

* Apartments, 37 feet
    Corridor, 10 feet
        total, 47 feet

† Vide an elegant drawing together with a plan and section of Potala by Lieut. Parish of the Royal Artillery annexed to this Journal, no. 10K.K.K. [See Sir G. L. Staunton, *An Authentic Account* . . . , folio volume of plans etc., plate 26—Ed.]

‡ [See note 7.—Ed.]

of Fo-hi; for Fo-hi, like Brahma, the supreme divinity of the Hindus, has condescended from time to time to leave the heavenly mansions, and to become incarnate among men and beasts in this earthly world below. Hence he is represented in his temple as riding upon dragons, rhinoceroses, elephants, mules, and asses, dogs, rats, cats, crocodiles, and other amiable creatures, whose figures he fancied and assumed, according to the lama mythology, for the edification and instruction of Tartars. There are, in some of these pagodas, a thousand of these monstrous statues, all most horribly ugly, and so ill-represented, and so unlike anything in heaven or earth, or in the waters under the earth, that one would think they might be safely worshipped even by the Jews without incurring the guilt of idolatry. There are also niches filled with the images of saints and bonzes without number, fully sufficient to match the longest catalogue of the Romish calendar. The Emperor, it is affirmed, thinks that he is not only descended in a right line from Fo-hi himself, but, considering the great length and unparalleled prosperity of his reign, entertains of late a strong notion that the soul of Fo-hi is actually transmigrated into his Imperial body, *Nihil est quod credere de se non possit*, etc., etc., so that the unbounded munificence he has displayed in the erection of these pagodas may be looked on as not quite so disinterested for, according to this hypothesis, there has been nothing spent out of the family.

We went up to the top of Potala in order to examine the roof of the chapel which, as our conductors assured us in the most solemn manner, is covered with plates of solid gold. It may be so, but without such an extravagance, so enormous is the profusion of all other expense, so vast the undertaking and so perfect the execution, that such a monument as Potala, of grandeur and stability, required not only all the fervour and enthusiasm of the most munificent bigot, but all the exertion and authority of the most powerful and most opulent monarch of the East. Our expedition of this day, from the time of our leaving home in the morning till our return in the afternoon lasted upwards of fourteen hours.

Wednesday, September 18. We went this morning to Court, in consequence of an invitation from the Emperor, to see the Chinese comedy and other diversions given on the occasion of his birthday. The comedy began at eight o'clock a.m. and lasted till noon. He was seated on a throne opposite the stage, which projects a good deal into the pit; the boxes are on each side without seats or divisions.

THEATRICAL ENTERTAINMENTS

The women are placed above, behind the lattices, so that they can enjoy the amusements of the theatre without being observed. Soon after we came in the Emperor sent for me and Sir George Staunton to attend him, and told us, with great condescension of manner, that we should not be surprised to see a man of his age at the theatre, for that he seldom came thither, except upon a very particular occasion like the present; for that, considering the extent of his dominions and the number of his subjects, he could spare but little time for such amusements. I endeavoured in the turn of my answer to lead him towards the subject of my Embassy, but he seemed not disposed to enter into it farther than by delivering me a little box of old japan, in the bottom of which were some pieces of agate and other stones much valued by the Chinese and Tartars, and at the top a small book, written and painted by his own hand, which he desired me to present to the King, my master, as a token of his friendship, saying that the old box had been eight hundred years in his family. He at the same time gave me a book for myself, also written and painted by him, together with several purses for areca nut. He likewise gave a purse of the same sort to Sir George Staunton, and sent some small presents to the other gentlemen of the Embassy. After this several pieces of silk and porcelain, but seemingly of no great value, were distributed among the Tartar Princes and chief courtiers, who appeared to receive them with every possible demonstration of humility and gratitude.

The theatrical entertainments consisted of great variety, both tragical and comical; several distinct pieces were acted in succession, though without any apparent connection with one another. Some of them were historical, and others of pure fancy, partly in recitative, partly in singing, and partly in plain speaking, without any accompaniment of instrumental music, but abounding in love-scenes, battles, murders, and all the usual incidents of the drama.

Last of all was the grand pantomime, which, from the approbation it met with, is, I presume, considered as a first-rate effort of invention and ingenuity. It seemed to me, as far as I could comprehend it, to represent the marriage of the Ocean and the Earth. The latter exhibited her various riches and productions, dragons and elephants and tigers and eagles and ostriches; oaks and pines, and other trees of different kinds. The Ocean was not behindhand, but poured forth on the stage the wealth of his dominions under the figures of whales and dolphins, porpoises and leviathans, and other sea-monsters, besides ships, rocks, shells, sponges and corals, all performed by concealed actors who were quite perfect in their parts, and performed their characters to admiration.

These two marine and land regiments, after separately parading in a circular procession for a considerable time, at last joined together, and forming one body, came to the front of the stage, when, after a few evolutions, they opened to the right and left to give room for the whale, who seemed to be the commanding officer, to waddle forward, and who, taking his station exactly opposite to the Emperor's box, spouted out of his mouth into the pit several tons of water, which quickly disappeared through the perforations of the floor. This ejaculation was received with the highest applause, and two or three of the great men at my elbow desired me to take particular notice of it, repeating at the same time '*Hoha, hung hoha*' ('Charming, delightful!')*

As the entertainment lasted some hours, and there was an uninterrupted communication between the Court boxes where we were and the others, several of the principal Mandarins took the opportunity of entering into frequent conversation with us, and from what passed I have certainly derived much matter of observation and reflection. It did not escape me that most of these Mandarins were Tartars, scarcely any real Chinese coming near us, but among those that addressed us the most familiarly I particularly remarked two, who appeared to have a more confident and disengaged manner than the rest, and who asked us whether we could speak Persian or Arabic. It seems they are Mussulmen and chiefs of those hordes of Kalmucks who, not long since, on occasion of some discontent or misunderstanding with Russia, migrated in great numbers from the coasts of the Caspian Sea to the frontiers of China, and put themselves under the Emperor's protection.[44] He gave them a very favourable reception, and has decorated these two leaders, or *mirzas*, with transparent blue buttons and peacocks' feathers to their caps as an earnest of his accepting their submission and allegiance.

A little before one o'clock p.m. we retired, and at four we returned to Court, to see the evening's entertainments, which were exhibited on the lawn in front of the great tent or pavilion where we had been first presented to the Emperor. He arrived very soon after us, mounted his throne, and gave the signal to begin. There were wrestling and dancing, and tumbling, and posture-making, which appeared to us particularly awkward and clumsy from the performers being mostly dressed according to the Chinese custom, one

* [i.e. *hao, hen hao*, which literally means, 'good, very good.'—Ed.]

ACROBATICS AND FIREWORKS

inseparable part of which is a pair of heavy quilted boots, with the soles of an inch thick. The wrestlers, however, seemed to be pretty expert, and afforded much diversion to such as are admirers of the *palaestra*.

A boy climbed up a pole or bamboo thirty or forty feet high, played several gambols and balanced himself on the top of it in various attitudes, but his performance fell far short of what I have often met with in India. A fellow lay down on his back and then raised his feet, legs and thighs from his middle perpendicularly so as to form a right angle with his body. On the soles of his feet was placed a large round empty jar, about four feet long, and from two and a half feet to three feet diameter. This he balanced for some time, turning it round and round horizontally, till one of the spectators put a little boy into it, who after throwing himself into various postures at the mouth of it, came out and sat on the top. He then stood up, then fell flat upon his back, then shifted to his belly, and after showing a hundred tricks of that sort, jumped down upon the ground and relieved his coadjutor.

A man then came forward and after fastening three slender sticks to each of his boots, took six porcelain dishes of about eighteen inches diameter, and balancing them separately at the end of a little ivory rod which he held in his hand and twirling them about for some time, put them one after the other upon the points of the six boot-sticks above mentioned, they continuing to turn round all the while. He then took two small sticks in his left hand and put dishes upon them in the same manner as upon the others and also one more upon the little finger of his right hand so that he had nine dishes annexed to him at once, all twirling and spinning together, which in a few minutes he took off one by one, and placed them regularly on the ground without the slightest interruption or miscarriage. There were many other things of the same kind, but I saw none at all comparable to the tumbling, rope-dancing, wire-walking, and straw-balancing of Sadler's wells; neither did I observe any feats of equitation in the style of Hughes's and Astley's amphitheatres,[45] although I had been always told that the Tartars were remarkably skilful in the instruction and discipline of their horses. Last of all were the fireworks, which in some particulars exceeded anything of the kind I had ever seen. In grandeur, magnificence, and variety they were, I own, inferior to those of Batavia,* but infinitely superior in point of

---

* [Where Macartney had stayed on the outward voyage. See Robbins, op. cit., p. 215—Ed.]

novelty, neatness, and ingenuity of contrivance. One piece of machinery I greatly admired, a green chest of five feet square was hoisted up by a pulley to the height of fifty or sixty feet from the ground, the bottom was so constructed as then suddenly to fall out, and make way for twenty or thirty strings of lanterns enclosed in the box to descend from it unfolding themselves from one another by degrees, so as at last to form a collection of at least 500, each having a light of a beautifully coloured flame burning brightly within it. This devolution and development of lanterns (which appeared to me to be composed of gauze or paper) were several times repeated and every time exhibited a difference of colour and figure. On each side was a correspondence of smaller boxes which opened in like manner as the others and let down an immense network of fire, with division and co-partments of various forms and dimensions, round and square, hexagons, octagons, and lozenges, which shone like the brightest burnished copper, and flashed like prismatic lightning with every impulse of the wind. The diversity of colours indeed, which the Chinese have the secret of clothing fire with, seems one of the chief merits of their pyrotechny. The whole concluded, as at Batavia, with a volcano or general explosion and discharge of suns and stars, squibs, bouncers, crackers, rockets, and grenadoes, which involved the gardens for above an hour after in a cloud of intolerable smoke. Whilst these entertainments were going forward the Emperor sent to us a variety of refreshments, all of which, as coming from him, the etiquette of the Court required us to partake of, although we had dined but a short time before.

However meanly we must think of the taste and delicacy of the Court of China, whose most refined amusements seem to be chiefly such as I have now described, together with the wretched dramas of the morning, yet it must be confessed there was something grand and imposing in the general effect that resulted from the whole spectacle, the Emperor himself being seated in front upon his throne, and all his great men and officers attending in their robes of ceremony, and stationed on each side of him, some standing, some sitting, some kneeling, and the guards and standard-bearers behind them in incalculable numbers. A dead silence was rigidly observed, not a syllable articulated nor even a laugh exploded during the whole performance. Before we left the Court, Wang told me that all the ceremonies and diversions of Jehol were now finished, and that, as the Emperor had fixed the time for his departure for Yuan-ming Yuan to be on the 24th instant, it would be proper for us to set out some days before him. He therefore proposed to me the 21st, and hoped it would not be inconvenient. So we must get ready accordingly.

I have now just received the translation of my note to the first Minister, in which I request that Captain Mackintosh, having safely delivered all the presents brought in the *Hindostan*, and paid his obeisance to the Emperor, may be allowed to repair without delay to Chusan, to resume the care of his ship there; that his Purser may be permitted to purchase a cargo of tea, or such other produce as that port and its neighbourhood can furnish; and that the officers may have leave to dispose of their private trade, in case they should have any. I have also recommended to send a European missionary with Captain Mackintosh, who may (if thought proper) conduct the two mathematicians who had come to Taku in order to enter into the Emperor's service,* but were still on board the *Hindostan*; and I have repeated my desire to have a free communication with Canton for the purpose of epistolary correspondence. But after all I am now under some difficulty about the transmission of my note. I can't trust the Legate, and none of the missionaries have as yet had leave to come near us since we have been at Jehol. Neither would it be proper to send it by a common messenger, if such could be procured and depended on. Wang and Chou say they can't venture to interfere in the matter, as it is solely in the Tartar's department. *Il faut y penser.*

Thursday, September 19. This morning very early my interpreter contrived to elude the vigilance of all our attendants, and to make his way with my note to the first Minister's house. His undertaking was, however, not a little difficult, for being dressed in the European habit, it was not without some obstruction and even insult from the populace that he was able to pass. The Minister not being visible, my paper† was delivered to Ma lao-yeh,‡ one of his secretaries, who promised to deliver it and obtain a speedy answer. The interpreter offered him a handsome present in money for this service; but he declined accepting it, saying, however, that when he returned to Pekin he should not be averse to receive from me some little European article as a mark of my favour. Late this evening the Legate, Wang and Chou came here together. The Tartar took out of his

---

* See note 5.

† Vide no. 9 among the enclosures in my letter to Mr. Secretary Dundas of 9 November 1793. [Omitted here—Ed.]

‡ [*Lao-yeh* is a title, the English equivalent being something like 'master'.—Ed.]

pocket a paper, which he said was an answer to my note of this morning to the Minister, and read to me the contents, which were as follows. That Captain Mackintosh, having come with me, could not be allowed to separate, but must go away at the same time with me; that his ship might sell at Chusan what goods she had brought, and take in a loading there in return, for which she should be exempt from any duties. That the two European mathematicians should be allowed to come to Pekin, and enter into the Emperor's service, and that the Minister would give proper directions for the purpose without our interference.

I requested a copy of the paper from the Legate, but he refused it, and in the whole of this conference showed himself as much indisposed to us as ever. But what gives me much more serious concern is that I apprehend a decided disinclination towards the Embassy in a more important quarter. A council, I find, was lately held on our subject, to which the first Minister had called the attendance, not only of the late Viceroy of Canton, Fu-k'ang-an, but had brought the former Hoppo of Canton out of prison (where he had long lain under sentence of various crimes)[46] and consulted him at the Board. The particulars of what passed there I have not been able to learn, but I can't avoid auguring the worst from the convention of such a divan.

Friday, September 20. The Emperor's presents for the King, consisting of lanterns, pieces of silk and porcelain, balls of tea, some drawings, etc., were finally packed up this morning in the presence of the Mandarins. I ordered 'George III. Rex.' to be marked on each box to prevent any mistake or confusion. They don't appear to me to be very fine, although our conductors affect to consider them as of great value.

We have been busied all this day in making preparations for our journey of to-morrow. I understand from Wang and Chou that, as we are now less encumbered than we were before, we shall be only six days upon the road instead of seven. The Tartar Legate came and made us a visit to-day, but had nothing more to mention to us relative to the business of yesterday. He said he should accompany us to Pekin, and hoped to visit us at the different stages where we meant to stop at.

Saturday, September 21. This morning at seven a.m. we set out for Pekin from Jehol, much in the same manner and order as we had travelled before to Jehol from Pekin. The road was so very heavy (it having rained in the night for six hours without intermission) that we did not reach this place (Cola-chou-you), where we are to sleep, till four o'clock p.m., although the distance is little more than a dozen English miles. I went this evening to the top of a high hill near our stage from whence I had a very delightful prospect. It was an amphitheatre of considerable extent formed by a spacious green level surrounding the eminence I stood upon, watered by a fine river that almost rendered it an island, and apparently terminated by a circular screen of mountains overlapping each other, but which all rising separately and singly from the plain left open in reality innumerable passages between them. The weather has been cold and windy, though not unpleasant in the sun. This day died Jeremy Reid, one of my guard, belonging to the Royal Regiment of Artillery. His disorder was occasioned by a surfeit of fruits, the man having eaten no less than forty apples at a breakfast.

Sunday, September 22. This morning we buried Reid, the gunner who died yesterday, and we proceeded to our present stage (Ching-chang-you), being eighteen miles, where we have dined and shall stay to-night. The Legate made us a short visit this evening.

Monday, September 23. Our journey to Ku-pei-k'ou this day has been twenty-four miles. For upwards of an hour before we reached it we had a very fine view of the Great Wall in front of us and on each side of us. Some of the gentlemen of the Embassy were desirous of paying another visit to it, in order to examine it with greater accuracy than formerly, but the passage or breach where they had mounted before having been stopped up during our absence with stones and rubbish, and consequently now rendered impracticable, they were obliged to look out for another place of access, which having discovered, they were enabled to gratify their curiosity a second time.

Tuesday, September 24. Having a long journey of thirty-five miles to perform to-day, we set out very early in the morning and in about nine hours reached this place (Min-yu-chien), where we propose remaining to-night. The Legate made us another visit this afternoon.

Wednesday, September 25. Our stage to-day was twenty-seven miles from Min-yu-chien to Nan-chut-see. We saw nothing of the Legate to-day.

JOURNAL—SEPTEMBER

Thursday, September 26. We set out this morning at four o'clock a.m., and arrived about noon at my hotel at Pekin (twenty-seven miles), having performed the journey from Jehol in five days and a half. We were lodged and entertained at the Emperor's houses on our return, in the same manner and with the same attentions as in our former journey. Wang and Chou continue their friendly disposition towards us, and on every occasion do us all the good offices in their power; but the Legate still preserves the same vinegar aspect without relaxation.

Pekin, Friday, September 27. We were all this morning employed in arranging the remainder of the presents to be sent to Yuan-ming Yuan. Our conductors seem pressing for us to finish this business, which, added to our own observations and intelligence from others, induces us to imagine that it is not intended we should pass the winter here.

Saturday, September 28. The greatest part of the presents are delivered, and my interpreter is gone to Yuan-ming Yuan, in order to assist the gentlemen and artists (whom I left there) to translate and explain everything relative to the machinery and management of the planetarium, orrery, globes, clocks, etc., so that the missionaries and others, who are to have the charge of them, may be able to keep them in order after our departure.

The Legate visited me to inform me that the Emperor was to arrive on Monday next, and that it was the custom for ambassadors, as well as for the great Mandarins of the Court to go and meet him on the road at a place about twelve miles off. He therefore proposed to me seeing that I was much indisposed with the rheumatism, that, in order to lessen the fatigue, I should sleep at my former quarters at Yuan-ming Yuan, which were half-way, and proceed the next day to attend the Emperor. Though in very great pain at the moment, I told him I should exert myself to the utmost on such an occasion, and hoped I should be able to travel to-morrow.

Sunday, September 29. I kept myself quiet till the afternoon, and then set out for this place (Yuan-ming Yuan) where I now am, very much fatigued, and going to bed to recruit for to-morrow's expedition.

Monday, September 30. This morning at four o'clock we were all in motion, and arrived at our ground in less than two hours. We were conducted into a large saloon, where refreshments were prepared for us, and then proceeded to the spot where the Emperor was to pass and to take notice of our attendance. Our station was on a high bank on the left of the road; on each side of us, and opposite to us, were several thousands of Mandarins, household troops, standard-bearers, and other Court officers, lining the way for several miles, as far as our eyes could reach. The Emperor himself soon made his appearance, carried in a kind of sedan chair, and followed by a clumsy state chariot upon two wheels without springs, which must be so rough and disagreeable a machine that I think he will be delighted with a transition to the elegant easy carriages we have brought for him.*

We paid our compliment to him as he passed, and he sent me a message importing that as he understood I was not well, and as the cold weather was approaching, it would be better for me to return immediately to Pekin than to make any stay at Yuan-ming Yuan. The Minister Ho-shen soon followed the Emperor, and gave me a very gracious salute as he passed by, but he did not stop a moment, as I imagined he would do from what the Legate had said yesterday.

As soon as the cavalcade was at some distance, and the crowd a little dispersed, I returned to Yuan-ming Yuan, and, after resting myself there a short time, came on to Pekin, where I arrived this afternoon, extremely tired and very much out of order.

Tuesday, October 1. This day the gentlemen and artists who had been employed in the arrangement of the planetarium, lustres, globes, etc., at the palace of Yuan-ming Yuan returned there to finish that business, and to put up Parker's great lens, which I had procured from Captain Mackintosh, and which seemed to strike the Chinese in a most particular manner; and yet, so ignorant are they in matters of the kind, that they asked Mr. Barrow whether he could not make such another for them; and when he told them that it was made by the artist who had executed the lustres, and whose sole profession was to compose works of glass and crystal, and that there was not such another lens in the world beside, they shook their heads as if they doubted his veracity, but having asked Dr. Gillan the same question apart, and receiving a similar answer, they appeared to be somewhat satisfied. They, however, requested that it might be fixed in its place immediately; and when they were informed that it would require some time, they expressed the utmost

* [See note 27.—Ed.]

astonishment, and were scarcely made to comprehend how it could admit of any delay, as they said it was the Emperor's order to have it done instantly, for he was impatient to see it, and our gentlemen might have an hundred, two hundred, or any number of hands that they chose to call for, to assist them.

The Legate, indeed, testified no less surprise upon a former occasion, on being told that it would take several weeks to combine all the different movements of the planetarium, imagining that labour, not skill, was the only thing necessary, and that putting together so complicated a machine as a system of the universe was an operation almost as easy and simple as the winding up a jack. By this intercourse with the palace a new channel of communication and intelligence has been opened and which we have already derived some advantage from. This is the more fortunate, because none of the missionaries, except Father Kosielski, have been allowed to frequent us since we returned from Jehol.

It seems that before our arrival and the presentation of the King's letter, some of the Emperor's Ministers had given it as their solemn opinion that we should be desired to depart at the end of our forty days, which period is pretended by the Chinese to be the term fixed by the laws of the empire for the stay of a foreign embassy.

To obviate this notion in time and to rectify some other mistakes, I sent a note* to the Minister (Ho-shen) expressing my thanks to the Emperor for his gracious permission that Captain Mackintosh's ship should load at Chusan, but repeating that, as nothing could be done but under the inspection of Captain Mackintosh himself, for whose discretion and good conduct I would be responsible, I hoped he might be allowed to rejoin his ship at Chusan without delay. That with regard to myself, I proposed to return to Europe by way of Canton, for which place I should ask the Emperor's permission to set out as soon after the new year as the season would allow, as I expect the King's ships would be then arrived at Macao, in order to convey me home. The Minister's answer to this note is a desire to see me at Yuan-ming Yuan to-morrow morning.

Wednesday, October 2. This morning, though much indisposed, I went to Yuan-ming Yuan, and found the Minister sitting with Fou-liou† and the Fou-liou's brother Fu-k'ang-an, but no other Grand

---

* Vide no. 10 in the enclosures to Mr. Secretary Dundas in my letter of the 9 November 1793. [Omitted here—Ed.]

† [i.e. Fu-ch'ang-an.—Ed.]

AN INTERVIEW WITH HO-SHEN

Secretaries attending. He began by delivering to me some letters which he said were just arrived by the post from Chusan. One of them was for Captain Mackintosh from his First Mate, and there were two from Sir Erasmus Gower to myself. On asking me what news they brought, I immediately told him the contents, which were that the *Lion* was preparing to leave Chusan with all expedition, but that the *Hindostan* could not depart till her commander should join her. I then freely put into his hands the letters themselves, in order to remove from his mind any doubt he might entertain of the authenticity of my information to him. He said he hoped the *Lion* was not gone, for he imagined that, after so long an absence from home, I must be very desirous of soon returning to it; and that the Emperor, upon first hearing that I was ill and that I had lost some of my people by death since my arrival in China, remarked how much foreigners were liable to suffer from the cold winters of Pekin, and had expressed his apprehensions that we should run great risk of injuring our health if we did not set out from it before the frost set in. The Minister added that, as to the feasts and ceremonies of the New Year, which, he observed, I had mentioned in my note, they were nothing more than a repetition of the amusements I had already seen at Jehol. To this I answered that I had been accustomed to cold climates, and was therefore not much afraid of feeling inconveniency from that of Pekin, especially as I had taken precautions to guard against its ill-effects. After a few more words upon this subject, I begged to recall to his recollection the flattering hopes he had given me when at Jehol that I should have frequent opportunities of seeing him at Yuan-ming Yuan, the earliest of which I wished to take, in order to explain to him fully my Sovereign's instructions to me, and to enter into negotiation upon the points contained in them; that as yet I had barely opened my commission, but it was the King's wish that I might be allowed to reside at his (the King's) expense constantly at the Emperor's Court, according to the custom in Europe, for the purpose of cultivating and cementing a firm friendship between two such powerful monarchs. I said that, with this view, I had been directed to propose that the Emperor would please to send a reciprocal Embassy to England, the care of which I would undertake to have managed in such a manner as I was sure would be highly satisfactory, as I should have proper ships with every accommodation prepared for the purpose of conveying it to England and bringing it back to China in safety, with every possible mark of honour and respect. I

JOURNAL—OCTOBER

then explained to him in general terms the favours I had chiefly to ask, endeavouring to state them in such a manner, and in such terms as to take away any appearance of demand and merely to convey a sense of their propriety in themselves, unattended with the slightest inconvenience of any kind whatsoever to China; and an assurance to him that they would be received as strong marks of benevolence and friendship towards the Prince who had sent me to request them, and whose subjects would always endeavour to render themselves deserving of the Emperor's favour and protection.

The Minister, with his usual address, avoided entering into any discussion of these points, which I had taken so much pains to lay before him, and turned the discourse upon the state of my health, assuring me that the Emperor's proposal for my departure arose chiefly from his anxiety about it, for that otherwise my stay could not but be agreeable to him.

Although from the course of the conversation and from the deportment of the Minister and his two assessors I was led to draw rather an unfavourable inference relative to my business, yet, when I rose to take my leave, nothing could be more gracious or more flattering than the expressions which he made use of to me upon the occasion, insomuch that my interpreter congratulated me on the fair prospect of my negotiation, and said that he expected the happiest issue from it. Nevertheless, since my return home I have received two different communications, by which I am informed that the Emperor's answer to the King's letter is already prepared and sent to be translated into Latin from the Chinese. This, I find, is an infallible indication of the Court's intentions and as a signal for us to take our leave. I am afraid there is good ground for my apprehensions, as Wang and Chou, who have just been here, tell me that I shall have a message from the Minister to meet him to-morrow at the palace. They say that the Emperor's letter for the King will probably be then delivered to me, (for they pretend not to know certainly that it will), in which case they advise me to ask permission to depart without delay. I suppose they have been directed to hold this discourse to me; but they appear much dejected, for besides the loss of such advantages from us they might expect should we obtain the objects of the Embassy, they have now little hopes of the advancement and preferment at Court which they had conceived hopes of from being selected to attend us.

Padre Cho, the interpreter who left me at Macao, having resumed his Chinese dress, is now come to join his family here and brings me a letter from Mr. Irwin, one of our Commissioners at Canton, dated the 2nd July, communicating to me the principal occurrences in Europe down to the 10th January last by which it appears that a war with the French Convention is almost inevitable.

Thursday, October 3. The Legate came early this morning to acquaint me that the first Minister and several other Grand Secretaries were to assemble at the palace of the city, and hoped that I would meet them there in ceremony as soon as I could be ready. Being ill in bed when he came, and scarcely able to rise, I don't remember ever having received an unpleasanter message in my life. However, I got up immediately and gave directions, in consequence of this summons, to prepare everything for the occasion. It was not long before I set out, but I need not have been so punctual, for we were kept waiting near three hours before the Minister and his co-adjutors were in proper order for our reception. At last we were conducted through several spacious courts, and over several magnificent bridges, to the foot of the great stairs of the Imperial Hall,[47] where I found a fine yellow silk arm-chair, representing the majesty of China and containing the Emperor's letter to the King. After making our usual reverences, we proceeded to the hall, the chair and letter being carried up in great state before us.

The Minister explained to me the meaning of all this formality, and told me that the letter, which was now uncovered, would be sent to my house in the same pomp, but he did not tell me what was in it. He then pointed to some tables upon which were arranged in great regularity a number of bundles with yellow wrappers over them, and said they were the remainder of the Emperor's presents to the King, and also some presents for myself and for all the persons who had come with me from England.

All that had now passed was not only without the Minister's usual graciousness of manner, but with a degree of constraint and stiffness that appeared to me not natural, but assumed for the occasion. I soon, however, discovered his real indisposition towards us by his decisive refusal of some magnificent presents which I had made him, and which I had every reason from himself to imagine he had accepted, as he had informed me into whose charge they should be delivered. The other Grand Secretaries were equally steady in their refusal, and had declined what I sent.

I was now almost fainting with fatigue and therefore requested the Minister's leave to retire, but first reminded him of the points

I had mentioned to him yesterday, which I had had my Sovereign's commands to solicit (although not particularly specified in his letter), and requested that he would allow Sir George Staunton to continue the subject with him, as I was unable to speak longer. He said I might send him a note of my requests, but he said it in such a tone as gives me no great hopes of success from it, especially as he chose to be quite silent on the subject of my former note, which from the manner of our parting yesterday, I had reason to think he would have mentioned to me to-day.

Soon after my return home this afternoon the Emperor's letter* to the King was brought to my house in great ceremony, accompanied by sixteen Mandarins of rank and their attendants. The presents followed it, and those for the King were immediately packed up in boxes and marked as before.

It is now beyond a doubt, although nothing was said upon the subject, that the Court wishes us to be gone, and if we don't take the hints already given, they may possibly be imparted to us in a broader and coarser manner, which would be equally unpleasant to the dignity of the Embassy and the success of its objects.

That no time might be lost, or advantage taken, I have dispatched to the Minister the note† which he desired me this morning to send to him. It consists of six principal articles extracted from my instructions, and compressed into as narrow a compass as possible.

The first is a request to allow the English merchants to trade to Chusan, Ningpo, and Tientsin.

2nd. To allow them to have a warehouse at Pekin for the sale of their goods, as the Russians had formerly.

3rd. To allow them some small, detached, unfortified island in the neighbourhood of Chusan as a magazine for their unsold goods, and as a residence for their people to take care of them.

4th. To allow them a similar privilege near Canton, and some other trifling indulgences.

5th. To abolish the transit duties between Macao and Canton, or at least to reduce them to the standard of 1782.

6th. To prohibit the exaction of any duties from the English merchants, over and above those settled by the Emperor's diploma, a copy of which is required to be given to them (as they have never yet been able to see it) for their unequivocal direction.

* Vide no. 11 enclosed in my dispatch to Mr. Dundas dated 9 November 1793. [Omitted here—Ed.]

† Vide no. 12 among the enclosures in my dispatch to Mr. Dundas of 9 November 1793. [Omitted here—Ed.]

Friday, October 4. Yesterday evening Father Amiot, who had sent me the earliest notice of the Emperor's letter to the King being prepared, and several other pieces of important intelligence, and who seemed watchful over our interests and anxious for our success, found means of letting Sir George Staunton know (for I was very ill and obliged to go to bed) his sentiments on the state of our affairs here at this juncture for my speedy information. He is of opinion that the Chinese consider embassies as mere temporary ceremonies, sent on particular occasion only, none of those from Europe having been of any considerable duration, and the last from Portugal, though very well received, of less than six weeks; that they have as yet no favourable ideas of treaties with distant powers, but that they might be rendered sensible of them if applied to and solicited without precipitation, and managed with caution and adroitness, for nothing was to be expected as attainable on the sudden.

He thinks that the Embassy would have met with fewer difficulties at its outset if it had arrived before the Government had been alarmed by the news of great troubles in Europe, the inhabitants of which are indiscriminately considered by them as of a turbulent character; but, nevertheless, that my Embassy has been so brilliant, and has made such an impression in the country, as must in the end be productive of very happy consequences, notwithstanding any different appearance at present. He advises that the ground gained by sending an Embassy from the King to the Emperor should by no means be lost, but be followed up by an intercourse of letters between them, which the annual ships might convey, and which might be still improved, and perhaps carried to the most desirable effect by a person resident at Canton, with the King's commission, in order to ensure him access to the Viceroy, and to enable him to appear at Court, and negotiate with authority, in case he should be invited to attend there on occasion of the accession of a new Emperor, or any other solemnity. He desired me to be told that he was afraid my illness had been occasioned by disappointment here, but that I ought not to give way to feelings of that sort, as both those who had planned the Embassy and had undertaken it might well forego the satisfaction of momentary promises in favour of the more solid and permanent advantages which must gradually follow from it. In conclusion, his judgment was that it would be most for our interests at present to signify my wishes to return home as soon as I could conveniently set out.

This is nearly the sum of the good Father's opinion and advice, though mixed with many other observations and ideas relative to the late subversion in France, which are needless to insert here, but which strongly mark the horror it has inspired, and which may probably prove advantageous to us. But I don't require many arguments at present to induce me to follow my own sentiments which, since the receipt of Mr. Irwin's letter, strongly lead me to depart, both on account of the propriety of the measure in itself and the beneficial service which, if the *Lion* be not gone, I may possibly be able to render to the Company in case, when I arrive at Canton, I should find Mr. Irwin's apprehensions realized of a war with the French Convention.

Nevertheless, having been selected for this commission to China, the first of its kind from Great Britain, of which considerable expectations of success had been formed by many, and by none more than by myself, I cannot help feeling the disappointment most severely. I cannot lose sight of my first prospects without infinite regret. The consciousness of doing all in a man's power to do in the exercise of public employments is an ultimate consolation against most evils that can happen, but it requires no ordinary strain of philosophy to reconcile him at once to the immediate failure of success in a favourite undertaking, be the remote consequences ever so flattering. In Father Amiot's letter* to me before I set out for Jehol he desired me not to be disturbed or discouraged by any untoward accidents, and to be assured that, in the end, the objects of the Embassy might be attained by patient perseverance and unruffled attention; and his opinion seems not to be changed by what has happened since. From living half a century in this country, possibly from well-grounded knowledge and experience, he is become a very warm admirer of the Chinese nation, and has taken much pains, and in some instances, not without success, to remove several false ideas entertained in Europe of their character, customs, and policy. I have been but so short a time in the country, and he has been so long in it; I have seen so little of it, and he has seen so much; he is, besides, a man of such probity and universal charity that his opinion is entitled to considerable respect from me. Nevertheless, from the great deference and veneration which the Chinese have long paid to his acknowledged virtue and abilities, he may have insensibly contracted too great partiality for them, and may view their Government through a flattering medium. His apostolic zeal,

* Vide the letter in the appendix. [Omitted here—Ed.]

too, which is a predominant feature in his character, may tend to render him sanguine. He knows that without a better intercourse between Europe and China, or a miraculous interposition from above, the Gospel is likely to make but a slow progress in this part of the world; and he knows that if the trade of China were once properly opened to us, it would wonderfully facilitate the business of conversion, and those of his own faith would still have the vineyard to themselves, for he has no jealousy of the English interfering with them in the proselyte branch.

At this time it is a prevailing opinion among the missionaries, and such whose minds are solely employed upon religious objects, that the crisis of Catholicism is at hand, and that the Church of Rome is to rise triumphant and universal from all the troubles and convulsions that now assault and distract it. These considerations naturally lead the good father to contribute his endeavours, and to wish us not to relinquish an object which certainly no other power is more likely to attain. He, possibly, is afraid that I may imbibe hasty prejudices, and that my vanity may be wounded by finding that our appearance and address, which we had reckoned so much upon, had availed us so little here, and he is therefore solicitous to set me right, and prevent my going wrong.

Whether the difficulties we have met with arise chiefly from the particular humour and jealousy of the Court, or from the immutable laws of the Empire, which they talk so much of, must be left to time to determine. But from the observations which it has fallen in my way to make, I should rather imagine that the personal character of the Ministers, alarmed by the most trifling accident, the aversion they may naturally have to sudden innovation, especially at the Emperor's late period of life, and some recent events ill understood, joined, perhaps, to a paltry intrigue, have been among the chief obstacles to my business; for most of the principal people, whom I have had opportunities of knowing, I have found sociable, conversable, good-humoured, and not at all indisposed to foreigners. As to the lower orders, they are all of a trafficking turn, and it seemed at the seaports where we stopped that nothing would be more agreeable to them than to see our ships often in their harbours. With regard to their immutable laws, what laws are really so I know not; but I suppose the phrase has no very precise meaning, and is only made use of as a general shield against reason and argument, for we know that they have broken through some of their laws that were declared to be unalterable. The recent instance of the ceremony in my own case is one, not to mention others, which the accession of the present dynasty to the throne must have often rendered necessary.* I have written down these reflections as they arise in my mind; how far they are just it is not at this moment in my power to ascertain, but at all events it appears to me the wisest measure for the public service and my own character is to retire with as good a grace as I can, and to signify my intentions to do so without delay. The more distant objects of my mission must be for future consideration, and depend on circumstances, on my finding the *Lion* still at Chusan, and on such further news as I may learn at Canton.

Dispatched a note† to the first Minister, in which, after a few compliments, I acquainted him that, as soon as I should receive a written answer to the requests of my former note, I wished to have the Emperor's leave to depart, and to proceed to Chusan, from whence it was possible that Sir Erasmus Gower was not yet sailed, and for whom, in that hope, I enclosed a letter‡ desiring him to wait for my arrival; but that, in case Sir Erasmus should have sailed, it would be necessary for me to proceed to Canton, as the *Hindostan*, which must remain till Captain Mackintosh joined her, could not accommodate half my train and baggage; and I concluded, as I began, with the customary compliments and professions.

Late this evening the Legate came to inform me that the Minister had dispatched my letter for Sir Erasmus Gower, and that my desire of taking leave and of proceeding to Chusan was agreed to; and that to prevent any likelihood of our being surprised by bad weather, the Emperor had fixed the 7th instant for the beginning of our journey, and given orders that every honour and distinction should be paid us on the road. He added that I should receive the answer to my requests when I took leave of the Minister, who would come into the city on the morning of my departure for the purpose of delivering it to me, and of wishing me a prosperous return home.

Saturday, October 5. So this matter is now settled. Wang and Chou tell me that the Emperor has appointed two very great men, Sung-yun and I-shon,§ to conduct us. The latter I remember to have seen

---

* [See note 40.—Ed.]

† Vide no. 13 enclosed in my dispatch to Mr. Secretary Dundas dated 9 November 1793. [Omitted here—Ed.]

‡ Vide no. 14 enclosed in my dispatch to Mr. Secretary Dundas dated 9 November 1793. [Omitted here—Ed.]

§ [Not identified. Only Sung-yun appears to have accompanied Macartney.—Ed.]

at Jehol; the former is my acquaintance who had been on the frontiers of Russia, and who accompanied us on our visit to the garden of Jehol and to the pagodas of Potala and its environs.

The Legate is to go no further with us than to Tientsin, but Wang and Chou say they are not yet informed how far they are to attend us, but they suppose not beyond the limits of their province.

Sunday, October 6. The Legate, Wang and Chou came early this morning in order to assist us in our preparations for departure tomorrow, and to give directions for providing us with whatever accommodations we may require. They say all will be ready to a minute, so that we may set out as soon as I receive notice of the Minister's being prepared for the ceremony of my taking leave. I understand that there is a considerable number of great people at Court who have expressed their being much pleased with us, and who wished that we had continued here longer.

Tungchow, Monday, October 7. This day at noon we set out from my hotel at Pekin on our road to Chusan. In my way through the city I stopped at the Minister's pavilion, where I found him ready to receive me, attended by the Fou-liou, the Fou-liou's brother Fu-k'ang-an, and several Grand Secretaries of distinction, all dressed in their robes of ceremony. He pointed to a table covered with yellow silk on which were placed two large rolls; one of them he told me, contained the Emperor's answer* to my paper of requests, the other a list† of all the Emperor's presents. I said I hoped the answer was favourable to my wishes, as it might contribute in some degree to soften the regret which it was natural to feel on leaving the place of His Imperial Majesty's residence. He seemed as if surprised with the courtliness of such an address considering the circumstances of the moment, and feeling himself embarrassed to make a suitable return, changed the subject, and among other things said he hoped our tables had been properly served during our stay. He then mentioned to me the Emperor's nomination of Sung-yun to conduct me to Chusan, as a matter which, I suppose, he imagined would be agreeable to me. The Minister had a smile of affected affability on his countenance during the greater part of the time, but I thought the

---

* Vide no. 15 among the enclosures in my letter to Mr. Dundas of 9 November 1793. [Omitted here—Ed.]

† Vide no. 16 among the enclosures in my letter to Mr. Dundas of 9 November 1793. [Omitted here—Ed.]

JOURNAL—OCTOBER

Fou-liou and his brother looked confoundedly sour at us. I have reason to suspect that there is some mystery in this appearance, and that a Court intrigue, which may be still on foot, relative to the affairs of the Embassy, has occasioned a disunion or difference of opinion among these great personages.

Before we took our leave a Mandarin of the fifth order, decorated with a white transparent button on his cap was called forward, who immediately kneeled down, and continued in that posture till the Emperor's letter and the list of presents were fastened on his back by broad, yellow ribbons tied round both his shoulders. As soon as this operation was performed, he rose and immediately mounted his horse* and thus accoutred, rode before us the whole way to this place (Tungchow), where he delivered his charge into my hands in the same humble posture that he had received it. From the time we quitted the Minister it took us near two hours before we arrived at the last gate of the eastern suburb of Pekin.

Notwithstanding what I have observed of the wonderful populousness of this country in general yet that of Pekin seems less in proportion than that of Tientsin and some other places. Though a sight so novel as that of my Embassy drew immense crowds of the inhabitants into the streets, yet I doubt whether London would be much behind hand on any great day of ceremony. I should think that when the King went to St. Paul's after his illness[48] there were more people to be seen out of doors and at the windows where he passed along than appeared in the streets of Pekin either this afternoon when I came away, or the morning when I arrived. I must not, however, forget that Pekin one scarcely meets with any but men, as the women seldom stir abroad. The houses in China are of one story only, and in general are very closely inhabited, it being no uncommon thing for a dozen people to be crowded into one small chamber that in England would be considered as a scanty accommodation for a single person. I should think that Pekin stands on at least a third less ground than London, including Westminster and Southwark, but still it is one of the largest cities in the world, and justly to be admired for its walls and gates, the distribution of its quarters, the width and allineation of its streets, the grandeur of its triumphal arches and the number and magnificence of its palaces.

There are two streets, each of which are scarcely less than a league in length, they are near one hundred feet wide and are chiefly inhabited by merchants and traders, whose shops and warehouses are

* Vide the drawing no. 11 L in the appendix. [Omitted here—Ed.]

JOURNEY TO CANTON

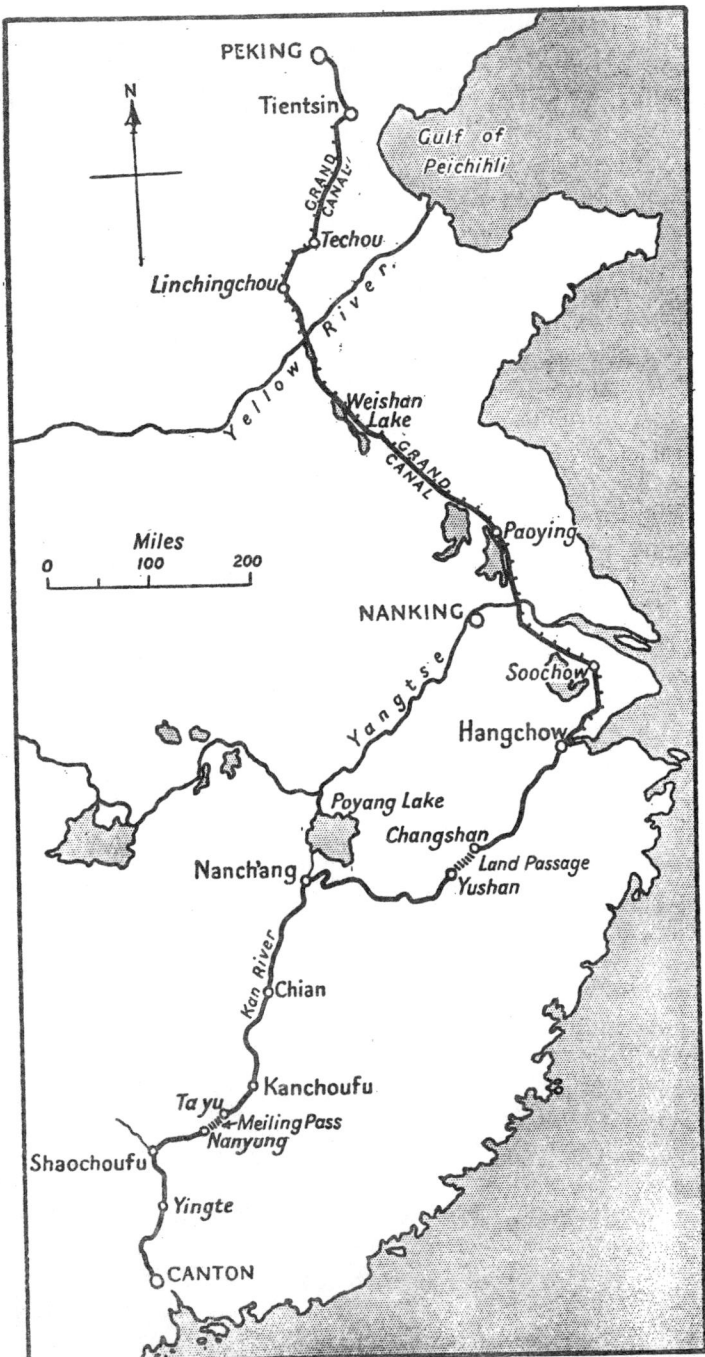

Macartney's route from Peking to Canton

most profusely decorated with every ornament that colours, gilding and varnish can bestow. The hotels of the great are mostly situated in retired, narrow streets. The one I inhabited was near the city wall, and had not been long built. It is supposed to have cost near £100,000, and was erected by a former Hoppo of Canton, who has been degraded for his crimes, and has long lain under sentence in prison.* As all his fortune was forfeited to the Crown my hotel made part of the confiscation, and we were told by one of the missionaries that the wits of Pekin had been much diverted with its being allotted for our residence, and said it was but a fair retribution as the house had been built by the Hoppo out of his extortions from our countrymen at Canton.

None of the streets are paved so that in wet weather they are covered with mud and in dry weather the dust is excessively disagreeable pervading every place and everything, but what renders it intolerably offensive is the stench with which it is attended, for though proper care is taken to have all the streets cleaned very early every morning from the filth and ordures of the preceding night, yet the odour generally continues floating in the air for the greatest part of the day.

The police is singularly strict. It is indeed stretched to an extent unknown I believe in any other city, and strongly marks the jealousy of the Government, and their unceasing apprehension of danger. At night all the streets are shut up by barricadoes at each end and a guard is constantly patrolling between them so that no person can pass after a certain hour without assigning satisfactory reasons or being liable to punishment if disapproved of. A number of watchmen are also stationed at short distances who carry a rattle and every two or three minutes proclaim their vigilance by the exercise of their instrument. One or two of these guardians of the peace had their stands so near to my house that I could not sleep a wink for the first three or four nights, but by degrees I became used to the noise and grew to mind it as little as the ringing of a church bell.

From Pekin we were near three hours in our journey to this place (Tungchow) and we are now lodged at our old quarters in the great *miao* or bonze temple which has been again prepared for us. The civil officer or Mandarin of this place, a Manchu Tartar (Wang, the military commander, is a Chinese),† has been just here to pay me a visit and offer his services. Mentioning to me in conversation that the waters were now very low and daily decreasing, he took occasion

* [See note 46.—Ed.]   † [See p. 325.—Ed.]

to observe how attentive and considerate it was in the Emperor to fix an early day in the season for our departure. A few days later the river would have become too shallow to float our yachts, and it would be excessively inconvenient and uncomfortable to go in small boats or to travel by land. This is certainly true, and shows how quickly the Court lesson reached this gentleman, and how aptly he had already learned it.

Our conductors inform us that the yachts and everything else will be ready for our embarkation to-morrow morning.

Tuesday, October 8. This morning I walked down to the waterside and found it would be some hours before the final arrangements could be made for our setting out. I went on board my own yacht, and some of the others, and observed with pleasure the same care and attention for our accommodation down the river that we had experienced before in ascending it. It was six o'clock this evening before we sailed from Tungchow.

Wednesday, October 9. We made but little progress last night, as the waters were low, and the yachts frequently got aground. This has happened two or three times again to-day. The weather is cold during the night and early in the morning, but grows very warm towards the middle of the day.

Thursday, October 10. This afternoon Wang came to tell me that Sung-yun had just received a letter from the Emperor, the contents of which he wished to communicate to me, and soon after I saw his yacht approaching mine very fast. I therefore desired Wang to tell him that as soon as he came alongside I would pay him a visit. I accordingly went on board him, and immediately began by reminding him of his former civilities to me at Potala and the gardens of Jehol, and renewing my acknowledgments of them, and I then expressed how happy I felt from his being appointed the superintendent of our present voyage. He received me with every possible mark of consideration, expressed the highest satisfaction at having been chosen upon the occasion to accompany us, and then read to me the Emperor's letter, the purport of which was that he (Sung-yun) should take us under his particular care, and render everything agreeable to us in the course of our voyage. That he should conduct us to Chusan, and see us embarked on board our ships, if they should be still there; if not, that he should proceed with us to Canton. I discovered from him, however, that my letter for Sir Erasmus Gower, desiring him to wait for me at Chusan, had not been sent. They suspected I know not what, and had therefore suppressed it. I told him that Sir Erasmus, having performed the King's order to land the Embassy in China, would certainly proceed upon other service, unless he heard reasons from me to detain him. I therefore requested him not to lose a moment in having my letter dispatched. He said he would immediately write to Pekin upon the subject, and did not doubt that it would be done. I then took my leave, and in about half an hour after he came on my yacht to return my visit. Here the conversation became less formal. He talked to me a good deal about the Russians, who, he said, though fierce and barbarous, were by no means a bad people. Understanding from me that I had resided three years in Russia as the King's Minister, he expressed much surprise, and asked me what I could be doing there so long. I explained to him the laws and customs of European nations with regard to their mutual intercourse, and told him that the Sovereigns of Europe usually kept ambassadors constantly resident at each other's Courts for the purpose of cultivating reciprocal friendship, and preventing misunderstandings. He answered me that it was otherwise in China, which never sends ambassadors to foreign countries; that ambassadors from foreign countries were only occasionally received, and, according to the laws of the Empire, allowed but forty days' residence, although on particular occasions it might have happened that the term was extended to eighty days. He mentioned some other niceties relative to the etiquette of the Court, and entered a good deal into the manners and customs of China, which, he said, he knew were different from ours; but they could not be broken through without inconvenience and perhaps mischief to the State, and that therefore foreigners should not be surprised or dissatisfied at them. I expressed my concern on account of the ignorance I had been kept in with regard to many things which he now told me, adding that I had endeavoured to do, as were equally my wishes and my duty to do, everything which I imagined could render me agreeable to the Emperor and his Ministers, and that if anything were omitted, it was not my fault, as I had been so much restrained in my intercourse with the European missionaries who had lived long in China, and could consequently have assisted me with information and instruction. His answer was that of a complete courtier, assuring me that our behaviour had been such as showed we required nothing of that kind, but entitled us to every favour and regard that the laws of the Empire could authorize, that he did perfect justice to my sentiments and declaration, and would not fail to transmit them faithfully to Court.

After he went away Wang and Chou remained with me a great part of this evening. In the course of conversation, they said that including all the yachts, baggage-boats, and those of the attending Mandarins, there were forty vessels employed in our present expedition, and upwards of a thousand persons attached to this service.* That the Emperor allows five thousand taels per day (each tael equal to 6s. 8d.) for defraying the expense of it, and that if that sum should fall short it must be levied on the provinces we pass through. That fifteen hundred taels per day were allotted for the expense of our residence at Pekin, and that they were scarcely sufficient. Although the maintenance of the Embassy must have undoubtedly been very considerable, I can by no means conceive it in any degree adequate to so large an amount. That it has been fully charged to the Emperor is highly probable, but between the money charged and the money actually expended I understand there is usually a very material difference; for though the Emperor's warrant may be signed for a great sum, yet the cheques of office, as they are called, are so numerous and so burdensome, that before it arrives at its last stage it is almost sweated to nothing. I remember Chou telling me one day, as an instance of this, that an inundation in the course of last year had swept away a village in the province of Shantung so suddenly that the inhabitants could save nothing but their lives. The Emperor (who, from having formerly hunted there, was well acquainted with the place) immediately ordered one hundred thousand taels for their relief, out of which the first *li-pu*[49] took twenty thousand, the second ten thousand, the third five thousand, and so on till at last there remained no more than twenty thousand for the poor sufferers. So we find that the boasted moral institutes of China are not much better observed than those of some other countries, and that the disciples of Confucius are composed of the same fragile materials as the children of Mammon in the western world.

Friday, October 11. This day we made very little way. The river was in some places so shallow that our yachts were often dragged along the bottom by mere bodily force. One of them being somewhat larger than the others, and more heavily laden, was not able to

* Vide the estimate in the appendix by Mr. Barrow. [Omitted here—Ed.]

proceed, and Mr. Maxwell, Captain Mackintosh, and Dr. Gillan, etc., were obliged to remove into smaller boats and divide the baggage.

Sunday, October 12. This day I paid another visit to Sung-yun, who told me that by the latest accounts from Chusan our ships were still there. He said that as, on account of the shallowness of the water our progress was very slow, we might have time to amuse ourselves if we chose it by going on shore and viewing the country on the banks, only taking care not to lose sight of our vessels. His attention and civility continuing so pointed, and his good opinion and esteem so unaffectedly expressed, I had the less difficulty in engaging him to converse freely upon the subjects which are now most interesting to me. I renewed the topic of my former conference with him, and endeavoured to impress him with high ideas of the compliment meant to be paid to the Emperor by the King's sending an Embassy from so great a distance, with such distinguished marks of consideration and regard. I said I had hoped to find frequent opportunities of fulfilling the purposes of it, which were to testify the sincere interest my Sovereign took in the Emperor's welfare, to improve the connexion between them, and to recommend the King my master's subjects in China to protection and favour. To this he replied with quickness that the Emperor had lately given fresh orders to treat the English and other Europeans at Canton with indulgence and liberality. I told him I had no doubt of the Emperor's good disposition towards us, and that he should always find the gratitude of our merchants in the respect and obedience which they would pay to his orders; but that they wished to be precisely informed what those orders, that related to them, really were, which hitherto had not been the case, as for these twelve years past several new duties had been levied on them without their being able to learn the reason; that these duties were every year increasing, and that if not soon regulated the English commerce, which is now carried on in sixty large ships annually, must be relinquished and given up, as unable to bear so heavy burdens. It was therefore become an object of such consequence that I could not but hope proper steps would be taken thereupon. He answered me that certainly there would, but that the duties and taxes could not be fixed absolutely, because they must necessarily vary from time to time, according to the exigencies of the state, or of the particular provinces where they were levied. I observed to him that they should be reduced to their former level as soon as the extraordinary occasion was past, but that ever since the year 1782 they had been regularly augmenting at Canton, and were now become an insupportable grievance. He confessed that the duties at Canton had been increased of late years on account of the wars of Tongking and Tibet, but that as there was peace at present they would certainly be diminished.* I expressed to him the pleasure I felt in receiving this information, together with what he had mentioned before of the Emperor's orders in favour of the English, from so high an authority and in so agreeable a manner, and I begged leave to request the continuance of his good offices in our affairs. It is much to be regretted that as the first Minister was determined not to give me such opportunities as I sought for conversing upon business with him, he had not appointed Sung-yun to attend to us from the beginning instead of the Legate, as possibly we might have been able by his means or through his channel to enter into negotiation, whereas the Legate did everything in his power to obstruct and disappoint us. I just hinted this to Sung-yun, who said that possibly it might have been so, but that I should find him as ready now to convey our sentiments and explain them to the Minister as he could have been then. Through all his discourse there is such an air of candour, frankness and amity that if I am deceived in him, he must be the most consummate cheat in the world.

Sunday, October 13. This day we arrived at Tientsin, where we were served with a most sumptuous provision for our tables, excellent mutton, pork, venison, and poultry of all kinds, fruits in great variety—peaches, plums, apples, pears, grapes, chestnuts, walnuts, and several others quite new to me. I should not mention this entertainment particularly had it not been intended as a personal compliment from Sung-yun himself for in general we have been always supplied in great abundance. And here I cannot avoid remarking a singular proof of attention shown to us in this journey. The Chinese seldom use milk as any part of their food (it being appropriated entirely to the nourishment of the calves), but, observing that we had been much accustomed to it, and that we always mixed it with our tea when we could get it, they have taken care that we shall not want that article on the road, for they have brought with us a couple of cows in a boat fitted up on purpose, by which means we shall have a constant supply of milk all the way, an accommodation of no inconsiderable value to English travellers.

* [See note 79 for Tongking. For Tibet see note 18.—Ed.]

JOURNAL—OCTOBER

How are we to reconcile the contradictions that appear in the conduct of the Chinese Government towards us? They receive us with the highest distinction, show us every external mark of favour and regard, send the first Minister himself to attend us as cicerone for two days together through their palaces and gardens; entertain us with their choicest amusements, and express themselves greatly pleased with so splendid an embassy, commend our conduct and cajole us with compliments. Yet, in less than a couple of months, they plainly discover that they wish us to be gone, refuse our requests without reserve or complaisance, precipitate our departure, and dismiss us dissatisfied; yet, no sooner have we taken leave of them than we find ourselves treated with more studied attentions, more marked distinction, and less constraint than before. I must endeavour to unravel this mystery if I can. Perhaps they had given way to impressions which they could not resist, but are ashamed to confess; perhaps they begin to find their mistake, and wish to make some amends for it.

Monday, October 14. We now ascended the river Yu-ho* which falls into the Peiho at this place (Tientsin). It is about eighty feet wide and the stream is so strong as to require eighteen or twenty towers to each yacht and we are not supposed to go at the rate of more than a mile and a half per hour, but the beauty of the scene makes some amends for the slowness of our motions. The banks slope gently down and are planted on the top with fine large shady trees, the fields neatly divided and admirably well cultivated, the farm houses picturesque, and every three or four miles are canals of different breadths either falling into the river or branching from it into the country.

Tuesday, October 15. The weather was remarkably cold this morning, but grew excessively hot towards noon. At six o'clock a.m. the mercury in Fahrenheit's thermometer stood at forty-seven and at two o'clock p.m. had risen to seventy-four, a variation of twenty-seven degrees in eight hours which is much greater than I remember to have observed anywhere before. These sudden vicissitudes begin already to affect the health of our people, and several of the guard are growing sickly. Their living in the midst of such

* [Literally 'the Imperial river'; i.e. the Grand Canal. Also called the Yun (liang)-ho, i.e. grain transportation river, because tribute rice from southern China to Peking was carried along it. See note 114.—Ed.]

plenty without much restraint or exercise may, however, contribute also to their complaints.

Wednesday, October 16.   The course of the river to-day is very serpentine. In wet seasons it rises very high and overflows its banks, although they are elevated in some places near twenty feet above the present level of the water. It is said the great Yellow River anciently ran here and took this route to discharge itself into the Gulf of Peichihli, although its present mouth is near two hundred miles to the southward of it. The country is sandy and dry in appearance but you can't dig a foot deep anywhere without finding water in abundance. The willow plantations continue with some fruit trees, chiefly plums intermixed with them.

Thursday, October 17.   Passed by several large burying-grounds, from which I conclude we are not far from some large town or city. The population seems prodigious, and we are told it increases the farther we go southward. To-day we observed a great many women mixed with the men, but few of them handsome. They labour in the fields at harvest and other country business just like their husbands.

Friday, October 18.   We observed several towns and walled cities at some distance which, added to the general appearance of the country, give it some resemblance to Flanders and Holland. I find that the weather here is always warm and pleasant when a southerly wind blows, but cold and pinching whenever it shifts to the northward. Owing to this circumstance the thermometer was yesterday at fifty-three at sunrise and to-day at forty-six. Wang and Chou own that in the winter a great many poor people die in these provinces for want of sufficient clothing. It is chiefly their clothing that the Chinese trust to for a defence against the cold weather. They have no fireplaces nor fixed stoves in their houses; they employ pans of charcoal for their culinary purposes and sometimes have braziers brought into their chambers, but these give only a short temporary heat and require too much trouble and attention to be regularly kept up. We arrived this evening at Chun-siou,* which is a very large city on the left bank of the river. The troops were all drawn out with flags, standards, music, torches, lamps and lanterns in honour of our approach.

* [? Present-day Te-chou.—Ed.]

Saturday, October 19. The appearance of the country to-day is rather dreary, no trees or shrubs to be seen except the *ricinus*, which produces what we vulgarly call in England the 'Palma Christi', or castor oil. In Europe and the West Indies I believe it is only used in medicine, but I am informed that the Chinese have the secret of depriving it by some process of its purgative quality and of rendering it esculent and palatable. The thermometer was at fifty this morning at six o'clock and at sixty-eight about noon.

Sunday, October 20. The country much the same as yesterday; the weather cold, the sky gloomy, the sun seldom shining out. A few drops of rain in the afternoon but scarcely to be called a shower.

Monday, October 21. This morning I paid a visit to Sung-yun, and had a very long conference with him. The Emperor's letter to the King made a principal subject of it.

The secretary who had penned the last letter, and who was now in the train of Sung-yun, was present, and endeavoured to excuse that part of it which I complained of, in which it is said that the requests made in the Ambassador's note of 3 October were supposed to have come rather from him than from the King. According to the explanation given me it is a sort of political conundrum, a Court artifice to elude an ungrantable demand, for Chinese urbanity does not admit a supposition that one sovereign can desire of another what is possible to be refused. It is, therefore, concluded that the request has never been made, or if made that the Ambassador has been guilty of an error in the delivery of his message, and to have asked from his own head what had never entered into that of his master.

This mode of interpretation, however respectful it may be pretended to the King, is certainly not very flattering to his representative; but I was willing to understand the matter in their own way and let it pass so. All private and personal considerations must merge in the pursuit of public objects, and in diplomatic transactions there is a wide difference between negotiating with an European and an oriental prince, between a king of Spain or king of Prussia, and an emperor of China or Japan. Even Louis XIV on occasion of one of his ships being fired at in the archipelago said there was no point of honour with such people as the Turks. When I mentioned to Sung-yun my surprise at finding myself supposed, in the letter, to be desirous of introducing the English religion into

China, he said they had taken it for granted we were like the other Europeans, who it was well known, had always been industrious and active in propagating their faith. To this I replied that whatever might be the practice of some Europeans, the English never attempted to dispute or disturb the worship or tenets of others, being persuaded that the Supreme Governor of the Universe was equally pleased with the homage of all His creatures when proceeding from sincere devotion, whether according to one mode or another of the various religions which He permitted to be published. That the English came to China with no such views, as was evident from their merchants at Canton and Macao having no priests or chaplains belonging to them, as the other Europeans had; and that, so far from an idea of that kind entering into my mind or my commission, I had not in my whole train any person of the clerical character, and that it was such persons only who were employed as the instruments of conversion; that it was true, as stated in the letter, the English had been anciently of the same religion as the Portuguese and the other missionaries, and had adopted another, but that one of the principal differences between us and them was our not having the same zeal for making proselytes which they had. I added, however, that I could not but be surprised at its being known in China that we had formerly been of the same faith as the missionaries, and that I supposed it must have come from the missionaries themselves. He answered that no such thing was inserted in the letter, at least in the Chinese and Tartar copies, and that if it was to be found in the Latin it must arise from the blunder or malice of the translator.[50]

I continued my observations on the letters, and said that in the first the Emperor had chiefly dwelt upon the request of an English Minister being allowed to reside constantly at Pekin (which was not complied with), but that he had avoided touching particularly on the other points of my mission, confining himself to a general assurance that the English merchant should be treated with kindness and favour, and that in the second letter, besides imputing to me the strange religious project which I had already mentioned, he seemed to accuse us of an unfair design to obtain exclusive privileges, which I totally disavowed. It was true, I admitted, that we had only asked for ourselves, but that, however grateful we should be for any favours granted to us, we by no means presumed to desire that his bounty should not be extended to others. I renewed the subject of the grievances complained of at Canton which, I observed, were so disguised in the Emperor's letter that it was not surprising that they should be disregarded; but that they were of the most serious consideration to us, and if not speedily remedied the trade of Canton would fall to decay, than which nothing could be more prejudicial to China. Sung-yun begged me to lay aside the uneasiness I seemed to feel from the perusal of the letters which, he declared, were not meant to convey anything unfavourable or unpleasant to the Embassy or myself, but he wished to remind me that the laws and usages of China were invariable, and that the Emperor was so strictly observant of them that no consideration could ever induce him to infringe them. That he was therefore upon his guard against the slightest appearance of innovation, and had declined any immediate compliance with the particular requests we had made; but that we were not to infer from thence a disinclination in him towards us or our concerns, for that notwithstanding any surmises of others, he entertained very kind intentions with regard to us, and that the English at Canton would soon find the good effects of them. He said that from the mechanism of their Government a great deal must be left to the discretion and recommendation of the Viceroys, whose conduct might possibly be sometimes not unexceptionable, but that, as a particular mark of attention to us, Ch'ang-lin,[51] a Mandarin of high rank and allied to the Emperor, was just appointed *Tsung-tu*, or Viceroy, of Canton, a man of remarkable benignity to strangers, and whose justice and integrity displayed in his late government of Chekiang had pointed him out as the fittest person for this new employment. That orders had been sent to him to make the most minute inquiries at Canton into such vexation and grievances as may exist there, and, as soon as he has maturely considered them, to rectify everything amiss by the most effectual exertion of his authority. That this would probably take some time, and the good consequences could scarcely be felt till the ensuing season when, upon proper notice being given to him of the arrival of our ships, every reasonable indulgence will be allowed them. To these agreeable declarations I was not backward in expressing how satisfactory they were to me, but I insinuated to him that to render them completely so to my Sovereign a third letter from the Emperor, confirming the flattering hopes now given me, would be very desirable, as it would remove every doubt that might arise upon the others, and that it was the more necessary as, from the singular variation in the translation from the original in one particular instance, it was not unreasonable to imagine some other mistake or insertion might be found there. Sung-yun seemed sensible enough of the value I put upon obtaining a third letter, but said it could make no difference whatsoever as to the public advantages in consideration, and that he was afraid, as I had taken leave, a new dispatch would be incompatible with the etiquette of the Court. He told me that it appeared to him that the Emperor was every day more and more pleased with the compliment of the Embassy, and he added that the assurances which he had given me of the Emperor's favourable intentions were by no means to be taken as effusions of his own friendship, or the compliments of his office, but as the literal words (which they really were) of the Emperor's dispatches to him, and that when I came to converse with Ch'ang-lin, whom I should find at Hangchowfu, he would confirm all he had mentioned in the fullest manner. I find that scarcely a day passes without Sung-yun's receiving and dispatching letters, so that it would seem we form no small object of Court solicitude. The Chinese couriers are so expeditious that, I am told, it is no uncommon thing to convey a letter fifteen hundred miles in ten or twelve days.[52]

Tuesday, October 22. At sunrise the thermometer was fallen so low as forty-eight. We observe large plantations of cotton on each side of the river which here meanders so much that we have had the sun ahead and astern of us twenty times in a few hours. At four o'clock p.m. we passed by Lin-chin-chou,* a large walled city that poured out such myriads of its inhabitants to see us sail along as quite astonished me although I have been so much accustomed to the sight of Chinese population.

The largest and tallest poplars I ever saw, particularly the quaking asp, are in vast numbers here. Before dark this evening we quitted the river and entered through a sluice into a narrow canal.†

Wednesday, October 23. The canal now enlarges to the breadth of fifty or sixty feet and is very muddy. It winds like a river and is in fact I suppose a river aided and improved by art. The banks are unequal, in some places very high, in others scarcely elevated above the plain.

Thursday, October 24. This day we passed through three sluices. Received a message from Sung-yun that he had received a letter

* [Now called Lin-ching-shih.—Ed.]
† Vide drawing and sections of a sluice and mode of passing through it in the appendix no. 12 M.M.M.M. [See p. 269 footnote—Ed.]

from the Emperor, and would communicate the contents when convenient to me. I was taken very ill this morning, and have not stirred out of bed all day, but I hope to be well enough to-morrow to see Sung-yun.

Friday, October 25. Sung-yun told me that the Emperor was very much pleased with the accounts he had been enabled to give him of our prosperous journey, and had sent me a testimony of his benevolence (a cheese and some sweetmeats) with a gracious repetition of kindness and regard.

We had a good deal of desultory conversation upon the general subjects of our last meeting, during which he took occasion to say that we should find it an easy matter to set everything to rights with the new Viceroy of Canton, who was so reasonable and so just that I might depend upon it he never would countenance the most trifling oppression. He again declared that greater indulgence and favour were intended to be shown to the English than they had ever experienced before, and seemed anxious to impress this opinion upon me. If the Court of Pekin is not really sincere can they possibly expect to feed us long with promises? Can they be ignorant that a couple of English frigates would be an overmatch for the whole naval force of their empire, that in half a summer they could totally destroy all the navigation of their coasts and reduce the inhabitants of the maritime provinces, who subsist chiefly on fish, to absolute famine?

Saturday, October 26. Continued our course on the canal, which is now supplied from a very extensive lake on our left hand. The idea of the great canal in Russia which at certain distances runs about parallel to the shores of the Ladoga and is filled from it seems to have been borrowed from hence. The bank here between the canal and the lake occasionally varies in breadth being in some places not less than half a mile thick, and in others scarcely more than two hundred yards. Though the lake is very extensive yet I could see its extreme boundaries from the deck of my yacht. The prospect of it this morning at sunrise was most delightful, the borders fringed with wood, houses and pagodas on the sloping grounds behind, and the lake itself covered with numberless vessels crossing it in different directions, according to all the various modes of navigation that poles, paddles, oars and sails can supply. On our right are many villages on the bank, which is here and there pierced with

A MOST NOBLE CANAL

sluices, in order to turn the water for the purposes of agriculture. In the background at four or five miles distance are several pretty round hills rising singly from the plain and crowned with trees and pagodas. The weather has been uncommonly fine, neither too cold nor too warm, much like our mild October in England.

Sunday, October 27. The canal is now conducted over a great morass, which appears without limits on each side, and above which it is raised and embanked by immense mounds of earth very high and very thick. It is a most stupendous work as Chou has explained it to me. Imagine a vast surface of inundation narrowed and forced up by human skill and industry into an artificial channel several yards above its former bed, and flowing along in that airy state, till it finds a corresponding level where it unites with many other streams. It then becomes a most noble canal improved and adorned with sluices and bridges of singular workmanship and beauty, and after a long course through one of the finest provinces in China gently falls into the Yellow River or Hwang Ho.

Monday, October 28. I have observed for some days past that there are eighteen trackers and one driver uniformly attached to each yacht. The regulation had been sometimes departed from before, so I suppose the police here is more strict. The districts through which the canal passes are obliged to furnish the people for this service, as the post-masters in France and Germany are bound to supply a certain number of horses for travellers. The wealthiest farmer in China would be obliged to perform the work himself if he did not provide a substitute.

Tuesday, October 29. A lively breeze sprang up from the southwest this morning which makes the feel of the air uncommonly pleasant. A fine grey marbled sky, which from time to time discloses such a proportion of the sunbeams as to render the hue of the weather more cheerful. Sung-yun came to say that he had received a letter acquainting him that the *Lion* and the smaller vessels had sailed away from Chusan on the 16th instant, so there only remained the *Hindostan* to convey us to Macao. I told him she was totally incapable of accommodating us, being built for trade, and not calculated for passengers, that from our manners and habits of life we required a good deal of room; and that a general sickness was the inevitable concomitant of a crowded ship. He said he would immediately write these particulars to Court, and did not doubt that he should receive such orders thereupon as would be perfectly agreeable to us. He proposed that, if we proceeded to Canton through the inland provinces, we should send away our heavy baggage by the *Hindostan*. To this I made no objection, as I wished to travel with as little encumbrance as possible, but I could not avoid reminding him of my letter to Sir Erasmus Gower, and observing that if it had been forwarded as I requested, the inconvenience we now felt from his departure would have been prevented. He seemed perfectly conscious of this, and rather confused at my mentioning it, as he knew very well the unfavourable inference that might be drawn from the omission. Thus, from the suspicious character of the Court which is so disposed to imagine some deep design in almost every proceeding of an European, we are now very seriously disappointed. Sir Erasmus Gower, hearing nothing from me, and knowing nothing of the state of things in Europe, is gone to the eastward and will not return before May. Our valuable China ships must therefore sail home without a convoy which, should we have a French war, would be attended with very great danger. Sung-yun says he proposes when we come to Yangchow to stop there for two or three days.

Wednesday, October 30. The wind rose so high in the course of last night and continues so violent and so contrary that I find we are not to think of lifting our anchor before to-morrow.

Thursday, October 31. Sung-yun made me a visit this morning and repeated to me what he had mentioned some days before, that the Emperor had strongly expressed in his last dispatch his satisfaction at the accounts which had been transmitted to him of our deportment and conversation, and that the more he reflected on the circumstances of the Embassy the better he was pleased with it, being now convinced that it had not been sent from any improper views or mischievous curiosity, but solely to do him honour and solicit commercial privileges and protection. He added that the new Viceroy of Canton was fully impressed with the Emperor's sentiments, and that he was to allow our merchants to have free access to him, in order to lay before him their complaints in person instead of sending them to him through the channel of the Co-hong.* I said I was infinitely sensible of the Emperor's goodness, and nothing could

* [See Introduction, p. 12.—Ed.]

render it more valuable but some paper or writing to the purpose of what he had said which I might have to show my Sovereign, who, whatever credit he might be disposed to give to his Ambassador, would pay much more attention to anything of that sort from the Emperor himself. But to this he answered that the Emperor had his own method of doing business, and nobody presumed to prescribe to him a different one; that it was his style to give general assurances, not specific promises, and that it was not at all unlikely we might find the former turn out more to our advantage than the latter could do. He told me that he had already mentioned in one of his dispatches my wishes to have a third letter, and that he should be glad that they were gratified, but he feared it was contrary to usage, adding however that he had as yet received no answer upon that subject.

Friday, November 1. Since passing the last sluices yesterday the canal has widened very much, and is now as broad as the Thames at Putney.

Saturday, November 2. This morning we fell down the canal into the Hwang Ho, or great Yellow River, which, where we crossed it, was about three miles wide and very muddy. We then struck into another canal, and are now proceeding to the southward in our way to Yangchow, where it is intended to stop for some days.

Sunday, November 3. This day just before we came to Chin-chan* we passed through the largest sluice I have as yet seen in China. The fall was between three and four feet. These sluices which in some districts occur at the distance of a few miles from one another properly form locks of that distance. The boats collect in great numbers at the sluice, the valves open, and in a few minutes the whole fleet passes through, the flood gates are then let down and the canal soon recovers its former level. Chin-chan is an immense town; from its extent on both sides of the water and the prodigious number of vessels and people, I should suppose it to be nearly equal to Tientsin.

Monday, November 4. This day we pass by Poan-gin,† a large walled city on our left, and observe on our right a large lake at about a mile's distance.

* [? Ching-chiang.—Ed.]
† Here the surface of the canal was on a level with the top of the walls of the town. [? Pao-ying.—Ed.]

Tuesday, November 5. We arrived at Yangchow, which is a considerable trading town, and expected to stop here, but Sungyun has altered his intentions and means to go on to Hangchowfu.

Wednesday, November 6. At daybreak we fell into the Yangtze River, commonly called the Kiang-ho, which was about a mile and a half wide at the place where we crossed it. On the southern shore stands the town of Tchin-chien,* which is large, well situated, well built, and well inhabited, but the walls seem to be much out of repair and going fast to decay.† A garrison of at least two thousand men all turned out to show themselves, with colours and music, and appointed as if going to be reviewed. They consisted of different corps, differently dressed and armed, according to their respective services, some with matchlocks, some with bows and arrows, and some with halberds, lances, swords and targets. Many of them wore steel helmets, as they are supposed to be, though I suspect they are only of burnished leather or glittering pasteboard. The uniforms which are very showy and of different colours, red, white, blue, buff and yellow, must be very expensive, but after all these troops have a slovenly, unmilitary air, and their quilted boots and long petticoats make them look heavy, inactive and effeminate.

Wang tells me that all these fine regimentals and steel caps belong to the Emperor, are carefully kept in a public wardrobe, and never worn but upon great holidays and occasions like this. As to the steel helmets he says they are merely for show and are too heavy to be used on active service. I wished to procure one, but was disappointed. About half a mile from the town and nearly in the middle of the river is an insulated conical rock‡ of considerable height and extent, built from the water's edge to the top with temples, turrets and belvederes on regular terraces or stories one above the other, intermixed with evergreen trees of various volumes and shades of verdure, contrasted in so happy a taste and distributed in such a manner as to give to the whole the air of a fairy edifice suddenly raised upon the river by the magic of an enchanter. It has a very striking effect and almost realizes the extravagant paintings of China fans and screens, which I am now inclined to think have been done from real views and not from the fancy of the artist. The people's complexions here are the fairest we have observed since we left Pekin.

---
* [? Chen-chiang.—Ed.]
† Vide drawing no. 13N. [Omitted here—Ed.]
‡ Vide drawing no. 14O in the appendix. Usually called by the people 'the Golden Mountain'. [Omitted here—Ed.]

Possibly they may be of a less mixed race than the others. Several men-of-war junks were lying before the town, manned with soldiers in uniforms like the troops, who showed themselves on the decks and affected a warlike appearance, but though there were a few port holes cut in the sides of the vessels I did not see a single cannon peeping through any of them.

Thursday, November 7. Proceed this morning to Tchan-chou-fou,* and pass through a very noble bridge† of three arches, the centre one so high that my yacht had no occasion to lower her masts in going under it. Tchan-chou-fou is a city of the first order and was formerly very considerable, but is much declined. Most of the houses next to the water are of wood, the walls are falling down in many places and the people, I thought, looked dispirited. The removal of the Court to Pekin from Nankin, which is the capital of this province of Kiangnan,‡ is still felt and regretted by the inhabitants. Nothing indeed but very strong political considerations could have induced the Sovereign to prefer the northern regions of Pei-chihli on the confines of Tartary to this part of his empire which is the most beautiful that can be imagined and abounds with everything to render life convenient and delicious. All the advantages of climate, soil and production have been lavished here by nature with an unsparing hand. This evening we passed through the fine city of Soochow, which is called by travellers, the Paradise of China.

Friday, November 8. The country seems to be one continued village on both sides as far as we can see,§ wonderfully beautiful and rich. Many mulberry trees are planted round the houses, but most of them have been stripped of their leaves. We are now in the silk country but we have as yet had no opportunities of making the observations and enquiries we wish to do. We passed through three small lakes and at one place under a very long bridge of one hundred arches.[53]

Sung-yun has shown me a letter just received from Court, by which he is directed to put the Embassy, as soon as we arrive at Hangchowfu, under the care of the new Viceroy of Canton, who is

* [? Ch'ang-chou.—Ed.]
† Vide drawing no. 15P. in the appendix. [Omitted here—Ed.]
‡ [Corresponding approximately to the modern provinces of Kiangsu and Anhwei.—Ed.]
§ Here, from Tan-too to Tan-yun-chien the depth of the canal is above one hundred feet.

soon to set out for that place, and to conduct us thither. Captain Mackintosh is to join his ship at Chusan, and I told Sung-yun that I should send on board him the presents and all the baggage which we should not have occasion for in the remainder of our journey, also a part of my guard and of my other attendants. He seemed to receive this information with pleasure, and said he should himself go as far as Ningpo, on the way from Chusan to Hangchowfu, to give orders that the *Hindostan* might have every indulgence and assistance necessary for her dispatch, and that he should then return to Pekin to render an account of his commission to the Emperor, and he was happy to say that we had enabled him to give a very agreeable and satisfactory one. He desired me to tell Captain Mackintosh that if, from the shortness of time or from any other difficulties, he was disappointed of a cargo at Chusan, he should nevertheless have the same privileges when he came to Canton that were promised for Chusan and that, as a particular compliment to the Embassy and on account of the ship's connexion with it, she should be exempted from the payment of any measurage or other duties.

Saturday, November 9. We stopped this morning at a village without the walls of Hangchowfu, and found that the new Viceroy of Canton* had come up in his yacht to confer with Sung-yun, and that he would soon be alongside of mine to welcome us on our arrival here. Whether I was prejudiced in his favour or not by the accounts I had heard of him, I thought his appearance much to his advantage. He is perfectly well bred, and the whole of his manner candid and gentleman-like. He confirmed to me everything Sung-yun had said upon business, and particularly mentioned the Emperor's instructions to him to pay the greatest regard to the English at Canton, who, on every occasion, he said, should have free access to him in person or by letter. He then asked me some questions about my passage from England and the length of the voyage back, and said that it was very flattering to the Emperor to have an embassy sent to him from so great a distance; that the Emperor had charged him to repeat his satisfaction from it, and to deliver to me an additional present for the King, consisting of some pieces of gold silk, some purses taken from his own person and—what was of very high value—the 'paper of happiness' inscribed by the Emperor's own hand, which is known to be the strongest mark a Sovereign of China can give to another Prince of his friendship and affection.[54]

* [Ch'ang-lin. See note 51.—Ed.]

A paper was also sent to me of a similar import, as a testimony of his approbation of the Embassy and an earnest of his proposed attention to its objects. The Viceroy then said that he hoped, in four or five days, everything would be ready for us to proceed, and that he expected much pleasure from seeing us and conversing with us frequently in the course of the voyage. As for Captain Mackintosh, etc., Sung-yun would take care of them, but he was afraid the Captain would not find it easy to get a loading either at Ningpo or Chusan. Upon this I begged leave to send for Captain Mackintosh, to whom he then explained the difficulties he was likely to meet with. The Viceroy told him that the merchants there were not accustomed, like those of Canton, to trade with Europeans and to purchase English goods; that they were probably not at present provided with such articles as Captain Mackintosh might want, and that whatever they sold to him they would expect to be paid for in ready money. He mentioned some other objections, which I endeavoured to obviate, but observing so many impediments and thinking it better not to urge further a business which we plainly saw they wished us to decline, and which it was in their power to defeat, we gave it up with a good grace upon the Viceroy's repeating the assurances given before of the *Hindostan*'s being exempted from the payment of measurage and duties at Canton. This night finished my dispatch to Mr. Dundas.

Sunday, November 10. The *Tsung-tu*, or Viceroy, paid me a visit, and repeated in still stronger terms than yesterday the assurances and declarations of the Emperor's favour and of his own particular good wishes and disposition towards us. Hangchowfu is a very populous, extensive and flourishing city. A vast quantity of silk is produced in its neighbourhood. Having asked the people of my yacht what kind of mulberries chiefly grow here I was informed by some that it was the red and by others the white, from whence I conclude they are both equally common. I hope from the measures I have taken to be able to learn something relative to the culture of silk here, but the shyness and jealousy of the Chinese in all matters where they observe us to be curious and inquisitive are inconceivably great.

Monday, November 11. This afternoon I received a letter from Sir Erasmus Gower, dated at Chusan 15 October which, through the singular jealousy and suspicion of the Chinese Government, had been kept from me until now. From this letter I have received news of the *Lion*'s people being very sickly, and of the surgeon and his first mate not being likely to recover. That the ship was in such want of medicines, particularly of bark and opium, that it became necessary to have a speedy supply of both, and therefore he (Sir Erasmus Gower) was returning for that purpose to the mouth of the river at Canton, but should proceed again from thence to the northward without delay. Having mentioned to the Viceroy that Sir Erasmus Gower was probably now in Macao Roads, and that it was possible a letter from me might reach him if dispatched immediately, he has promised to send it away this night by a special messenger to Mr. Browne at Canton, who will know how to forward it. Wrote my letter to Sir Erasmus telling him that I was upon my road to Canton, and requesting him to remain off Macao till he either saw me or heard from me again.

Tuesday, November 12. The Viceroy made us another visit and improves upon us every time we see him.

Wednesday, November 13. Received a farewell visit from Sung-yun, who seemed to be quite melted at parting from us. Among other things, he said to me in a strain of liberality scarcely to be expected in a Tartar or a Chinese, that as all distant countries must necessarily have different laws and customs, we should not be surprised that theirs varied from ours, that we owed each other mutual indulgences, and he therefore hoped I should not carry with me to Europe any impressions to the disadvantage or disparagement of China.

He possesses an elevated mind, and during the whole time of our connexion with him has on all occasions conducted himself towards us in the most friendly and gentleman-like manner. This kind of behaviour is not only agreeable to his natural character, but I believe he thinks it will be agreeable to his Court, as no part of it can be concealed or misrepresented; for notwithstanding his high rank and situation, such is the caution and circumspection of this Government, that two considerable Mandarins (one of whom was the secretary who penned the Emperor's letters to the King) were always present at our conferences. Sung-yun declined accepting the presents I offered him, but excused himself in a very becoming and unaffected manner.

Before I quit this subject I must not omit that our discourse together sometimes turned upon Russia, of which he endeavoured to speak as of a country they had no apprehensions from. He said that when disturbances happened on the frontiers they were usually occasioned by disorderly people whom, when complained of, the Court of Russia always disavowed, and delivered to be punished as soon as they could be taken hold of, and that at bottom the Russians were not a bad sort of people, though very ignorant and unpolished. It appears not only from Sung-yun, but from several others whom I have conversed with, that the Chinese are no strangers to the Czarina's character, nor to the manner of her mounting the throne.⁵⁵

Thursday, November 14. This morning we proceeded from Hang-chowfu on our journey to the southward. I travelled in a palanquin and was upwards of two hours in passing through the city, which I found still larger and more populous than I at first imagined. It is very closely built and the streets very narrow; they are paved with broad flat stones and put one much in mind of the courts in London that run parallel with the Strand. Almost every house is a shop. I observed in some of them, as I went along, great quantities of furs, broad cloth and long ells, mostly imported, I believe, in English bottoms to Canton. The environs of the town are very beautiful, embellished by an extensive lake,* a noble canal with several inferior ones, and gentle hills cultivated to the summit, interspersed with plantations of mulberries and dwarf fruit-trees, sheltered by oaks, planes, sycamores, and camphors.

After travelling about six miles from the east gate through this charming scene, we came to a broad tide-river, where we found the yachts ready for our embarkation. These vessels† have cotton or canvas sails and something of a European air, being sharp both fore and aft. Although their bottoms are quite flat they sail well and draw very little water, not more than ten inches even when laden with two tons and a half weight. In this short stage we passed three military posts at which we saw a few guns that seemed to have been brought forward on purpose for us to take notice of them. They are from two to four pounders, very heavy and very clumsy, the thickness of the

---

* On one side of the lake is a pagoda in ruins, which forms a remarkably fine object. It is octagonal, built of fine hewn stone, red and yellow, of four entire stories besides the top, which was mouldering away from age. Very large trees were growing out of the cornices. It was about two hundred feet high. It is called the Tower of the Thundering Winds, to whom it would seem to have been dedicated, and is supposed to be two thousand five hundred years old. Vide drawing no. 16 Q.Q.Q.Q. [Omitted here—Ed.]

† Vide the drawing in the appendix No. 16 Q. [Omitted here—Ed.]

metal at the mouth being equal to the bore of the gun. Though scarcely fit for service they are preserved with great care, each of them having a wooden roof over it. There are not above a dozen of them in the whole. At the different stations on the road the troops always turned out to salute us, which they frequently did by falling down on their knees, but there was a large body of five hundred to a thousand drawn up to receive us at the waterside, dressed and armed in their best manner who made a very handsome appearance. They seemed, indeed, to look more like soldiers than any I had seen in China before, and to show a marked admiration of my guards as they marched along to embark noticing every particular, their dress, their arms, the cadence of their movements, their quick and slow step, their erect figures, their manly air and military mechanism.

Friday, November 15. This morning at daylight I found we had advanced up the river above the reach of the tide; it is still very broad, not less than half a mile across. Yesterday we sailed, but now we are towed. The country on each side is full of mountains with fertile valleys between them. Near the banks grows a great variety of trees, among which were particularly pointed out to me the tallow tree and the camphor tree which I had not remarked before.

Saturday, November 16. The country is beautiful and romantic somewhat resembling the scenes on the river Conway between Lanroost and the sea. I made a visit to the Viceroy at which Wang and Chou were present. It was intended these two latter gentlemen should leave us at Hangchowfu, but as they were well known to the Viceroy, and as he observed that they were agreeable and accustomed to us, he desired them to come on and accompany the Embassy to Canton. Very little was said in this conversation relative to our affairs. I thought it better to avoid entering upon that subject abruptly, and to wait for more favourable opportunities of introducing it, many of which must occur in the long journey now before us. I left it to him to lead the discourse as he liked, which though chiefly upon general topics, he artfully contrived to intermingle with many expressions of compliments to me and professions from himself.

Sunday, November 17. The Viceroy returned my visit and began of his own accord to talk to me of the trade carried on between

Great Britain and China of which he owned he was but imperfectly informed. He therefore desired me to explain to him the principal points in which I wished his assistance when we came to Canton. When I had done this he requested me to give it to him in writing, which I told him should be done as soon as possible. He said his reason for asking it was that he might read it at his leisure, in order to be master of the subject, for he was determined to do what was equitable and proper, to grant what was reasonable and to deny what was not so. He was sensible that some change of conduct towards us would be right, both for the sake of justice and the reputation of his country. But he confessed that, though his affinity to the Emperor and his rank in the state afforded him strong ground to stand on, yet he had measures to keep and delicacies to observe, for he was well aware of the counter-action he must expect at Canton from those who may perhaps be interested in the continuance of those very grievances we suffered and that he had heard of the prejudices entertained against us by some of the great people at Court, particularly Fu-k'ang-an, his predecessor, who would not be much pleased to see him adopt a new system the reverse of his own. But there was another thing which he would candidly mention. He said he knew the refusal that had been given by Ho-shen to the requests of the Embassy, and the disappointment resulting from it. It was therefore to be apprehended that the English might be led from thence to infer an unfavourable disposition in the Court towards them which it really had not, and to conduct themselves in such manner as to defeat any indulgences meant to be granted to them, and consequently render him culpable for any representations he might make in our favour.[56] For this reason he requested me to satisfy him fairly how I considered matters to stand relative to this point. I told him I should answer him with the utmost frankness and own that, from the reception my requests had met with, I naturally concluded the Court of Pekin to be indifferent, if not unfriendly to Great Britain; and that I should have represented it so in my dispatches home if Sung-yun had not taken such pains to impress me, as he declared he had the highest authority to do, with the Emperor's favourable sentiments towards us and our concerns, and if he, the Viceroy himself, had not confirmed them at the first conference I had with him in the presence of Sung-yun. That the solemn assurances then given to me by him and Sung-yun had not only prevented me from writing in the manner that I had intended, but induced me to inform my Court, that notwithstanding what had passed at Pekin, I had since that time received so many kind messages and promises from thence that I could not doubt of a very serious attention being paid to my representations. That thus the matter now stood, and that it rested with him to determine whether I had deceived my own Court or not. It was from what he should do, not what I should write, that they would form a judgment. Soon after the Viceroy left me he sent presents of tea, fans, and perfumes to me, and to all the gentlemen of the Embassy.

We have now quitted the mountains and are got into a charming fruitful country. Here the tea tree grows in great abundance on the dry rising grounds. The mulberry flourishes most on the loamy flats. I have given directions to have some young tea plants taken up, if possible, as also the varnish tree and tallow tree, with an intention of sending them to Bengal, in hopes of Colonel Kyd's being able to nurse them and bring them to maturity, so that one day or other they may be reckoned among the commercial resources of our own territories.[57] I shall add the eggs of the silk worms which I at last, and with great difficulty have been so fortunate to procure. The Chinese, whether from jealousy or superstition or both could scarcely be persuaded to part with them.

Monday, November 18.   The river spreads here a good deal, and is very shallow. The banks rich, pleasant and generally level, but we see the mountains at a distance before us, and approach them very fast. I suppose we shall be amongst them to-morrow.

This evening Wang brought two genteel young men with him on board my yacht, and presented them to me as the ambassadors from the King of the Liuchiu islands, now on their way to Pekin. Regularly once in two years this prince sends such ambassadors to Amoy, in the province of Fukien (no other port being open to these strangers), from whence they proceed by this route to carry their master's homage and tribute to the Emperor. They speak Chinese well, but have a proper language of their own, whether approaching to the Japanese or Korean I could not well comprehend. They told me that no European vessel had ever touched their islands, but if they should come they would be well received. There is no prohibition against foreign intercourse; they have a fine harbour capable of admitting the largest vessels not far from their capital, which is considerable in extent and population. They raise a coarse kind of tea, but far inferior to the Chinese, and have many mines of copper and iron. No gold or silver mines have as yet been discovered among them, which may in some measure account for these islands being so little known.

The dress which these ambassadors wore I particularly remarked. It is a very fine sort of shawl made in their own country, dyed of a beautiful brown colour and lined with a squirrel skin, or *petit-gros*. They wore turbans very neatly folded round their heads; one was of yellow silk and the other of purple. They had neither linen nor cotton in any part of their dress that I could perceive. The fashion of their habit was nearly Chinese. They were well-looking, tolerably fair complexioned, well-bred, conversable, and communicative. From the geographical position of these islands they should naturally belong either to the Chinese or the Japanese. They have chosen the protection of the former, and when their Sovereign dies his successor receives a sort of investiture or confirmation from Pekin. It would seem that the Japanese give themselves no sort of concern about their neighbours. Concentrated and contented in their own Empire, they seldom make excursions beyond their own coasts, and are equally averse that their coasts should be visited by others. If circumstances permit, I think it may be worth while to explore these Liuchiu islands. The climate is temperate, rather cold in winter, but not very hot in summer.[58]

Tuesday, November 19. The river is nearly of the same breadth to-day as yesterday, but very unequal in its depth; in some places not less than ten or twelve feet, and in others so shallow that we were often suddenly stopped in our progress. It is quite wonderful to see the strength and expertness of the Chinese boatmen, who by main bodily might often dragged or lifted, over sands and gravel almost dry, the yachts we travelled in, some of which were heavy-laden and seventy feet in length by twelve feet in the beam. The banks of the river and the views are wild, but not unpleasant, the grounds varied by cultivation in the valleys and by plantations in the hills, which are neither high nor steep. The people have a boorish, rustic aspect, and are less polished than any we have yet met with. This is a cross passage; the great route from Pekin to Canton is by way of Nankin and through the Poyang lake but as we left Nankin on our right hand in order to come to Hangchowfu we deviated from the common track by which means we have had an opportunity of seeing a part of China which probably no European ever visited before. I am just informed by Chou that the Viceroy has received a dispatch from Court with an account of Sir Erasmus Gower's arrival in Macao Roads on the 31st of last month, so that a letter from Canton to Pekin and from thence to this place, including every delay, has been transmitted in less than twenty days,* so good a look-out do the Chinese keep on their coasts, and so watchful have they been of the motions of our ship of war.

Wednesday, November 20. This evening we arrived at the end of our first navigation from Hangchowfu, and to-morrow we are to cross overland to Yu-san-chien, where we are to embark again.

Soon after we came to an anchor the Viceroy visited me and made me an apology for our accommodation, saying that it was not so good as he wished it to be on account of the road being very little frequented. Our accommodation has, nevertheless, been very good, and I told him I thought so, and that it had been less good, yet as it was exactly the same as he had himself, I could not be discontented.

He seemed still somewhat apprehensive, whether from his own reflections, or from those of his superiors, that I must feel much dissatisfaction at bottom, as I certainly do, in not having succeeded in the points I had solicited, and that consequently my representations home might be the occasion of future trouble or mischief. He was, however, much pleased when, on his renewing the subject of our former conversation, I repeated to him exactly what I had said to him upon it a few days before. But still doubtful of my sincerity, I found he was desirous of putting it to a test, by his asking me whether I would authorize him to tell the Emperor that the King my master would always continue in friendship with him, and in testimony of it would write to him, and send an ambassador again if the Emperor were willing to receive him. I said that though what I solicited was refused, yet in every other respect I had no reason to complain, as the Embassy had been very honourably received and entertained, and that the Emperor had sent presents to the King as marks of his friendship in return for those sent by the King to the Emperor. That therefore I had no doubt that the King might go so far as to write to the Emperor to acknowledge the receipt of the presents, and the marks of distinction conferred on the Embassy. As to matters of business, they stood on a different ground. That the King's original idea was to have an ambassador usually resident in China, and if I had found my staying at Pekin had been agreeable I should have remained there a considerable time, but that frequent or temporary embassies from so great a distance were attended with

* [See note 52.—Ed.]

much trouble and expense to both Courts. Nevertheless, I thought that possibly another Minister might be sent to China if there was good ground to expect that such a measure would be requited by adequate advantages, but that my state of health and many other circumstances rendered it impossible for me to think of undertaking a second embassy. He then asked me if the King were to send here another Minister, how soon it could be; but that he did not mean to propose to me a repetition of so great and splendid an embassy as mine, which he was sensible could not be equipped without great charge and inconvenience. I told him it was not in my power to say how soon or to calculate any time, the space between England and China being so vast, and sea voyages so precarious. Before he went away he assured me he had received the greatest satisfaction from the different conversations he had had with us, and should immediately write to the Emperor, who would be highly pleased in every respect with his accounts of us. I gave him the paper* which he had desired a few days ago, containing a short sketch of the points I wished to obtain at Canton,† also a letter to be forwarded to Sir Erasmus Gower, and he then returned to his yacht. But in a few minutes afterwards he came back and said that, as he was going to send a dispatch to Court, he thought it would be the more agreeable to the Emperor if accompanied with a few words from me to him (the Viceroy) in the Chinese style, of general compliment and acknowledgment of the Emperor's attention to us and anxiety for our welfare. I thanked him for the suggestion and told him I should not fail to follow it. Every time we see this gentleman he gains upon our good opinion, and I do not despair of the Company's receiving many advantages by his means. It is true that he has art and address, and an air of candour to disguise them with, but he has prudence, sagacity, and a sense of character.

Thursday, November 21. At ten o'clock a.m. set out on our journey by land, and dined at the half-way house, which marks the boundary of the provinces of Chekiang and Kiangsi. We then came on to this place, Yu-san-chien, having performed the whole journey of twenty-four English miles in less than nine hours. The mode of travelling is either on horseback, in a covered palanquin, or an open chair. Our gentlemen had the choice of their conveyance, but as the

---

* Vide no. 1 enclosed in my dispatch to Mr. Secretary Dundas of 23 December 1793. [Omitted here—Ed.]
† Vide letter of 19 November 1793. [Omitted here—Ed.]

weather was uncommonly pleasant most of them preferred riding. We found this short transition from the water to the land very agreeable, and were highly delighted with the face of the country we passed through. It is much diversified by hills of a moderate size which, like all I have seen in China, either rise singly from the plain or in small groups of three or four and never run into a chain as is generally the case in other mountainous regions. I did not see a spot in the whole way that was not cultivated with infinite industry and compelled to produce every grain and vegetable of which it was capable. The soil is naturally indifferent, which renders the farmer wonderfully active in his endeavours to fertilize it; the care with which everything convertible into manure is preserved would appear ridiculous elsewhere, but is here fully justified by the effect.[59] Wherever the sides of the hills admit of it they are wrought into terraces, graduated with different crops and watered by the chain pump.* The ponds and reservoirs are a public concern and great justice is observed in the distribution of their contents. The plough is the simplest in the world, has but one handle, is drawn by a single buffalo and managed by a single person, without any assistance.

The husbandry is singularly neat, not a weed to be seen, everything is sown in drills, and there are never less than two crops in the year and often there are three.† For horse and foot the road is excellent but admits of no wheel carriage and at every mile there is a village which is generally extensive and populous.

I must not omit that the Viceroy, observing our curiosity about everything relative to natural history, allowed us to collect seeds and fossils as we came along, and to take up several tea plants in a growing state with large balls of earth adhering to them, which tea plants I flatter myself I shall be able to transmit to Bengal, where I have no doubt that by the spirit and patriotism of its Government an effective cultivation of this valuable shrub will be undertaken and pursued with success.‡

The place where we procured our tea plants is nearly in twenty-eight north latitude. The summers here are very hot and the winters extremely cold, but not attended with frost or snow. The Viceroy has also with great liberality of mind sent a Mandarin to the distance of forty miles with orders to get for us some pieces of petuntse

---

* The husbandman carries the chain pump with him from place to place.
† The mountains are all newly planted with trees, chiefly firs, a great many thousands of acres. This is the case almost the whole way from hence to Canton.
‡ [See note 57.—Ed.]

and kaolin[60] and other materials used by the Chinese in the manufacture of their porcelain. In talking with a Chinese one day who came on board my yacht with some plates and dishes, I thought, if I understood him rightly that he said the asbestos or incombustible fossil-stone entered into the composition of China ware.

Friday, November 22. We have been detained all day at this place (Yu-san-chien) by the violent rain which has now fallen for four and twenty hours without intermission.

Saturday, November 23. Leave Yu-san-chien and proceed down the river which is about eighty yards wide, shallow and rapid, with steep and well wooded banks on either side.

I delivered to the Viceroy the note of compliment,* which he had suggested to me the idea of, to be transmitted with his letter to Pekin. Observing the character of the writing to be remarkably neat, he inquired who had transcribed it, and when I informed him that it was little George Staunton, he would scarcely believe that a boy of twelve years old could have already made such a progress. Nor was he perfectly satisfied till he had actually seen him add, at the bottom of the paper in Chinese characters, that it had been written by him.

Sunday, November 24. Last night we continued our voyage, but so dense a vapour had risen in consequence of the late rains and overspread the atmosphere that, though the river widened and deepened considerably, our navigation seemed often attended with danger. Our vessels frequently struck upon the shelves, and sometimes ran foul of each other with a sudden crash, thus contributing not a little to the dismal character of the night, which was still, moist, cold, and comfortless. The mist grew every moment darker and heavier, and so magnified the objects around us that no wonder our senses and imaginations were equally deceived and disturbed, and that the temples, turrets, and pagodas appeared to us through the fog, as we sailed along, like so many phantoms of giants and monsters flitting away from us, and vanishing in the gloom. At noon we stopped at Ho-cou, a large handsome village built close upon the water's edge opposite to a singular range of hills shaped like reversed punchbowls, and composed chiefly of black rock, in the rifts of which several very large trees were growing. We have now changed our

* Vide no. 2 enclosed in my letter to Mr. Secretary Dundas, dated 23 December 1793. [Omitted here—Ed.]

JOURNAL—NOVEMBER

yachts for vessels of a large size, and are proceeding in them. The small ones were very pleasant and convenient, but had not sufficient room for the proper stowage of our baggage.

Monday, November 25.   Came this morning to Qui-te-chou, a large village, and stopped some hours.

Tuesday, November 26.   The river expands to the breadth of half a mile; a fine level country, not naturally very fertile but wonderfully well cultivated. The Chinese are certainly the best husbandmen in the world. Most of the province of Kiangsi that I have yet seen is a poor soil. We arrived this evening at Poyang-hou near the great Poyang lake. I can hear nothing about the fish here that Mr. Pennant desired me to enquire for.[61]

Wednesday, November 27.   Proceeded at a little after midnight as soon as the moon was up. The famous town of Ching-te-chen (the capital of the porcelain manufactory of the Empire) lies at no great distance from our route and it would have been very desirable to have seen it, but we were so circumstanced that it was not to be done without many difficulties, which I thought it better to avoid.[62]

Thursday, November 28.   The weather this morning was very sharp. Fahrenheit's thermometer at fifty-six at noon. Passed by Nan-chou-fou,* a very large city on a low sandy point where the river divides into two broad branches. The shores flat, and barren high mountains to the north-west at fifteen or twenty miles distance.

Friday, November 29.   We stopped all last night at a village about four miles from Nan-chou-fou, where the Fuyuen, or Governor of the province,† paid us a visit and brought us presents of tea and teacups, some beads, pieces of silk and red Nankin.‡ I returned his compliment with a pair of pearl watches, an assortment of hardware, knives, scissors, wine, and brandy.

Saturday, November 30.   The river still continues wide, but in general very shallow. The shores are flat and sandy, and in the wet season the whole country must be under water to a vast extent. No trees or houses to be seen but on a few elevated spots. The weather cold, no sun.

* [? Nan-ch'ang-fu.—Ed.]   † [See note 102—Ed.]   ‡ [i.e. nankeen.—Ed.]

Sunday, December 1. This morning we approached the mountains and our course now lies among them, and generally close to the foot of them, although there is sometimes on the other side of us a plain of two or three miles across. We observe several buildings on the tops of them, which have the appearance of watchtowers, somewhat resembling those I have seen on the coast of Spain between Carthagena and Malaga. There are also some very pretty white pagodas of nine stories high, newly built on lesser eminences near the banks. Stopped for a few hours at the town of Ki-gan-fou.* The weather cold, no sun.

Monday, December 2. Our voyage to-day was through a country that afforded very beautiful scenery. The river is still shallow but very broad, spreading over a vast bed of small round pebbles. A forest of many miles in extent covered all the eastern bank. I observed several very large firs of different kinds and among them the *pinaster*, but the predominant trees were of broad leaf, though I could not well distinguish their species. We caught here some fish, but not like any I am acquainted with. We passed a great many floats or *balzas* of timber,† some of several hundred feet long.‡ They are navigated with a mast and sail and have houses raised upon them for the habitation of the skippers and their families. Such numbers of children as poured out from them to see us can only be compared to bees rushing from their hives at the time of swarming. The weather cold, no sun.

Tuesday, December 3. The river now becomes much narrower and deeper, being pent up between the mountains which shut it in so closely and approach so near to each other that till the moment we came to the opening we can scarcely imagine the possibility of a passage.

To the left is the walled town of Ouan-gan-keen,§ which we pass[ed] without stopping and came to this village where we are to remain for the night. The weather still cold and no sun.

---

* [? Chi-an-fu.—Ed.]

† [The Spanish word for a raft is *balsa*. The Balsa tree, which grows in South America, is so named because its timber is very light, and is used by the natives to make rafts and canoes.—Ed.]

‡ The tops of hills and every other space where nothing but timber will grow are planted with trees of different sorts. From Hangchowfu to Canton many millions of acres are covered with young fir trees besides the great old woods.

§ [? Wan-an-hsien.—Ed.]

Wednesday, December 4. Continued our voyage this morning, the country less mountainous and more diversified. Several pretty white pagodas lately erected and generally in happy situations appear within view and show that whatever may be the case elsewhere, the devotion of the inhabitants here is by no means in the wane.

The Viceroy, accompanied by Wang and Chou, paid me a long visit this evening. They came at eight o'clock and stayed till this moment. It is now midnight. The Viceroy was uncommonly civil and sociable and talked freely on a great variety of things. He asked several questions relative to Canton, to the value and amount of our trade there and that of other nations; and what surprised me, he seemed to know already the difference between the Country ships from India and the ships of the Company.* He suspects great peculation among the public officers at Canton and that the Emperor is much defrauded in his revenue there. I answered him with a proper reserve saying that, as I had never been at Canton, I could not speak with precision, but that when I arrived there I would endeavour to procure for him any information in my power that he wished to have. He requested that I would, and at the same time desired Chou, who is the man of letters and business, to take notes of what I should mention to him.

Having occasion to light his pipe, and his attendants being absent, I took out of my pocket a small phosphoric bottle, and instantly kindled a match at it. The singularity of a man's carrying fire in his fob without damage startled him a good deal. I therefore explained to him the phenomenon and made him a present of it. This little incident led to a conversation upon other curious subjects, from which it appeared to us how far the Chinese (although they excel in some branches of mechanics) are yet behind other nations in medical or surgical skill and philosophical knowledge. Having often observed numbers of blind persons, but never having met a wooden leg or a deformed limb here, I concluded that good oculists were very rare and that death was the usual consequence of a fracture. The Viceroy told me I was right in my conjecture. But when I told him of many things in England, and which I had brought people to instruct the Chinese in, if it had been allowed, such as the reanimating drowned persons by a mechanical operation, restoring sight to the blind by the extraction or depression of the glaucoma, and repairing or amputating limbs by manual dexterity, both he and his companions seemed as if awakened out of a dream, and could not

* [See Introduction, p. 13—Ed.]

conceal their regret for the Court's coldness and indifference to our discoveries.[63]

From the manner of these gentlemen's inquiries, the remarks which they made, and the impressions which they seemed to feel, I have conceived a much higher opinion of their liberality and understanding. Whether in these two respects the Minister be really inferior to them, or whether he acts upon a certain public system, which often supersedes private conviction, I know not. But certain it is that in a conversation with him at Jehol, when I mentioned to him some recent inventions of European ingenuity, particularly that of the air balloon,[64] and that I had taken care to provide one at Pekin with a person to go up in it, he not only discouraged that experiment, but most of the others, which from a perusal of all the printed accounts of this country we had calculated and prepared for the meridian of China. Whatever taste the Emperor K'ang-hsi might have shown for the sciences, as related by the Jesuits in his day, his successors have not inherited it with his other great qualities and possessions. For it would now seem that the policy and vanity of the Court equally concurred in endeavouring to keep out of sight whatever can manifest our pre-eminence, which they undoubtedly feel, but have not yet learned to make the proper use of. It is, however, in vain to attempt arresting the progress of human knowledge. The human mind is of a soaring nature and having once gained the lower steps of the ascent, struggles incessantly against every difficulty to reach the highest.* I am indeed very much mistaken if all the authority and all the address of the Tartar Government will be able much longer to stifle the energies of their Chinese subjects. Scarcely a year now passes without an insurrection in some of the provinces. It is true they are usually soon suppressed, but their frequency is a strong symptom of the fever within. The paroxysm is repelled, but the disease is not cured.[65]

Thursday, December 5. The sun shines out this morning, which after so long an absence is a very welcome and cheerful appearance.

---

* Whatever ought to be will be. The resistance of adamant is insufficient to defeat the insinuation of a fibre. Time is the great wonder worker of our world, the exterminator of prejudice and the touchstone of truth. It is endless to oppose it. Power becomes enervate and efforts ridiculous. The tyranny or spectre of a state may stalk abroad in all its terrors and for a while may force a base currency on the timorous multitude, but in spite of those terrors there is always a certain counteraction fearlessly working in the mind of common sense, industriously refining the ore and imperceptibly issuing or emitting a standard metal whose intrinsic value soon degrades and baffles every artifice of impure coinage.

JOURNAL—DECEMBER

High hills rise on each side of the river, planted and cultivated with trees and grain on terraces and embellished with small, neat villages perched on ledges of rock wherever the projection could sustain a superstructure.

Stopped this evening at Kian-chou-fou, a large walled city of the first order. On our arrival before the town we had a profusion of military honours. I may here remark once for all that at every place on the way where troops were stationed they always turned out for us, unfurled their colours, sounded their music, and saluted with three guns, which number is never exceeded on such occasions. They also frequently sent us little presents of fruit and other refreshments.

Friday, December 6. A fine sun-shiny day again. We now observe vast plantations of sugar canes (ripe and fit for cutting) on the flats at each side above the river, which here sinks twenty feet below the surface of the country. The water is, however, easily raised to the level required by a wheel which the current gives motion to. The nave is made of strong timber, but the other parts, the fellies, the spokes, the scoops, etc., are chiefly of light bamboo. As this machine appeared to me equally simple and efficient I desired a model and a drawing* to be made from it. Our latitude at noon twenty-six north.

Saturday, December 7. So shallow was the river to-day in many places that our yachts were actually forced along the bottom by mere corporal exertion. They draw from ten to twelve inches and the depth of the water where I measured it was not eleven. We are now obliged to change them and to-morrow shall proceed in smaller ones.

Sunday, December 8. This distant prospect is mountainous but all the level ground is covered with sugar canes. The thermometer at sixty-eight. The weather very pleasant.

Monday, December 9. The weather is still delightful, but the country more barren than any we have observed in our progress. In this province the women of the lower sort whom we saw have their feet generally of the natural size, and go without shoes or other covering of the sort. They are mostly ill-favoured and, except by

* Vide the drawing and description in the appendix, no. 17 R. [Reproduced on p. 273—Ed.]

wearing their hair and having rings in their ears, are scarcely distinguishable from their husbands.*

At nine p.m. we arrived at this place (Nan-gan-fou).† Here the Viceroy showed me a paper or edict from the Emperor addressed to him, of which I am to have a copy.‡ As it was explained to me it seems conceived in very friendly terms, saying that if the King should send a Minister again to China he would be well received. But in such case it is desired that he should come to Canton, which implies a sort of disapprobation of our having come up the Gulf of Pei-chihli. Nevertheless, I would not for any consideration that we had not, as by these means we are now masters of the geography of the north-east coasts of China, and have acquired a knowledge of the Yellow Sea, which was never before navigated by European ships.

The Viceroy told me that he had sent my letters to Canton at the time I delivered them to him. He had not yet received any news from thence about the *Lion*, which makes me very apprehensive that Sir Erasmus Gower may be gone away.

Tuesday, December 10. This morning we set out by land from Nan-gan-fou, which is a large walled city situated on the side of a steep hill rising abruptly from the left shore of the river. We travelled in the same manner as in our former expedition, some in palanquins and some on horseback, according to the conveyance they liked best.

From Nan-gan-fou to You-chan where we stopped to dine are fifteen miles, through a romantic Alpine country and over a mountain that divides the provinces of Kiangsi and Kwangtung. This mountain is, I believe, one of the highest in China, being the source of some rivers which run into the sea in opposite directions, one discharging itself to the north-east and another to the south-west. By making a considerable detour we might have avoided it, but the industry of the Chinese has rendered any deviation unnecessary by cutting a safe and commodious horse road over it in a gentle zig-zag from the bottom to the top.⁶⁶ There is then a regular inclined plane of eighteen miles to this place (Nan-chou-fou) forming one of the richest countries in the world, entirely covered with rice on terraces, which though not approved of by some, I believe to be very strong

---

* They are so strong and accustomed to labour that it is said many Chinese come into Kiangsi from the other provinces to improve their fortunes by marrying what they call a working wife.

† [? Nan-an-fu.—Ed.]

‡ Vide no. 3 in my enclosures to Mr. Secretary Dundas of 23 December 1793. [Omitted here—Ed.]

and wholesome food. The common people who live chiefly upon it and who have but a spare allowance are extremely vigorous, hardy and cheerful, four of them carrying my palanquin without effort and stepping under it with agility. In our navigation from Hangchowfu the boatmen were usually wet up to their knees twenty times in a day, and sometimes almost the whole day, dragging our yachts along and often actually lifting them by mere bodily force over the shallows that occurred so often in the course of the rivers which we travelled upon. I have seen two Chinese raise nearly a ton weight between them, and pass it from one vessel to another. I doubt whether the labour of a negro in our West Indies be near so constant, harassing, toilsome, or consuming as that of the Chinese boatmen. They seem to work night and day with very little intermission and every exertion they make is accompanied by such vocal efforts, such a screaming symphony as would alone exhaust an European more than any manual employment.

The whole distance from Nan-gan-fou to Nan-chou-fou* is about thirty-three miles, and we performed the journey in nine hours, the time of baiting included. The horses on this road are remarkably small, but hardy and nimble. They have not handsome foreheads, but are otherwise well shaped, with limbs as clean and slender as those of a stag.†

Wednesday, December 11. The city of Nan-chou-fou is very extensive and wonderfully populous. We were upwards of an hour in passing from our entrance at the first gate to our quarters, which were in a spacious public edifice with a large hall in the centre of it, where the provincial candidates for literary degrees (which alone qualify for civil offices in China) are examined and received. Here most of the gentlemen of the Embassy slept, but as my yacht was ready prepared I preferred settling myself in it at once. The towns we have seen since leaving Tungchow generally resemble one another. The streets long, straight and narrow. The houses dark and dismal, most of them shops, populous and busy.

This day we left Nan-chou-fou and proceeded on our voyage. A little below the place of our embarking we passed under a bridge of three hundred yards long built with stone piers, over which are laid great balks and beams of rough timber and then a floor of planks.

* [Nan-hsiung-fu.—Ed.]
† To the southward of this place the people seem less civilized than on the other side of the mountain.

The river below the bridge is very shallow, and the navigation becomes every day more difficult, for the banks are of a loose sand which the least swelling of the waters washes into the channel and forms into spits and ridges that scarcely any industry can remove. Our present boats are therefore small, but we are to change into larger at Chao-chou-fou,* where the river begins to deepen. From Nan-chou-fou the passage to Canton is usually made in seven or eight days, but we shall probably be longer in order to give time to the Viceroy to get there a little before us to prepare for our reception. He has been constantly with us till now ever since we left Hang-chowfu. When he took leave of us to-day he told us that he had written to the Emperor in such terms upon our subject that he was persuaded we should leave China, not only without dissatisfaction but with essential proofs of the Emperor's favour. I said that his indulgence to the King my master's subjects at Canton would be the most essential and acceptable favours he could possibly confer upon me. I have now good reason to know that Wang and Chou have sincerely endeavoured to promote our interests. The Viceroy appears to have much confidence in them and to treat them with great respect and regard.

Thursday, December 12. The weather to-day is very fine and cool, the river still shallow, the country sandy, barren and wild. We expect to reach Chao-chou-fou to-morrow at noon.

Wang, who is an old soldier and of high reputation in his profession, told me that he calculated the military force of China to be equal to 1,800,000 men, and on my close questioning him said he would give me a statement of it in writing.† In like manner Chou, who is a civil officer and has been Governor of several extensive districts, estimates the population of the Empire at above three hundred and thirty millions and the annual revenue at fifty to sixty millions sterling, of which after paying the civil and military expenses near ten millions came net into the Emperor's coffers. He affirmed that there could be no question of the accuracy of this account as he had received it from the heads of office in Pekin, who were his particular friends, and he added that if I had any doubts he would give me a copy of it.‡ How far the information of these gentlemen may be exact, or approaching to truth (for it is natural to

---

* [? Shao-chou-fu. ? Present-day Shao-kuan.—Ed.]
† Vide in the appendix, the head, Military. [See pp. 253—Ed.]
‡ Vide in the appendix, the head, Population and Revenue. [See pp. 245–51—Ed.]

amplify upon such subjects) may be conjectured with more probability when I peruse the details which they have promised me, and compare them with other documents, but great allowances must be made for the particular light in which they see things and the manner in which they consider them, both perhaps very different from our ideas relative to similar objects. I suspect indeed from what dropped in the conversation that Wang in his computation of the army reckons the Tartar Banners,[67] and that Chou in his statement of the population of the Empire comprehends the old Manchu dominions of the reigning family, and the new conquests in west Tartary, and that under the head of revenue he includes without discrimination whatever is levied upon the subject. Now, if I were asked the amount of the revenue of Great Britain I should naturally answer off hand sixteen or seventeen millions without thinking of Ireland, of India, of tithes, poor rates, roads, turnpikes, canals or parish asses,* which amount to a prodigious sum, but, though levied on the people and felt as severely as any other taxes, do not enter into the King's treasury. Neither would I have reckoned in the military establishment the troops in Ireland, nor the Company's army in India, because not paid by, nor accounted for to the British Parliament, although certainly on a great view of our Empire all these things, which I should have omitted, ought properly to be included. But when it is considered that China, exclusive of the Emperor's Tartar dominions, is about eight times as big as France, infinitely more populous in comparison to its extent, far better cultivated and receiving annually for ages a great commercial balance in its favour, it is possible that my friends may not be guilty of so much exaggeration as one at first sight would imagine.

Friday, December 13. Arrived before Chao-chou-fou at one o'clock a.m. Our course this morning was through a pleasant, romantic, but barren country. The river grows gradually wider and deeper, the mountains on each side are composed of a dark coloured stone, in regular strata of eight to ten feet thick. Here and there are a few stunted fir trees, but I saw nothing like timber. The lesser hills are either burial grounds or military stations with signal houses erected on them. From Chao-chou-fou which is a large city we fell down the river about four or five hundred yards to a sort of suburb or village on the opposite bank where we quitted our smaller yachts and went into the larger ones that were prepared for us. It is observable that

* [Assessments.—Ed.]

TEMPLE OF PUSA

the rendezvous for boats and travellers is usually without the walls of the cities so that the interior, where the prisons, granaries and public offices are kept is preserved free from the noise, bustle and turbulence which must necessarily prevail where there is a perpetual concourse of watermen who are commonly more disorderly than the other classes of the people.

Saturday, December 14. Proceeded to-day from Chao-chou-fou and came to this place (Quan-yung-gan).* Here we mean to pass the night, that in the morning we may have an opportunity of visiting the neighbouring *miao*, or temple of Pusa,[68] who is said to have been a near relation of Fo-hi, and is much in vogue among the devotees of this province.

Sunday, December 15. My curiosity being much excited by the accounts which I had heard of the Temple of Pusa, I rose at an early hour and embarked in a small shallop in order to avoid interruption or encumbrance. The morning was remarkably fine, the sun rose with uncommon brilliancy, and the whole face of nature was lighted up with cheerfulness and beauty. Before we had proceeded many hundred yards we were attracted to the left by an arm of the river, which after stretching itself considerably from the main stream had bent and elbowed itself into a deep cove or basin, above which enormous masses of rocks rose abruptly on every side, agglomerating to a stupendous height and menacing collision. The included flood was motionless, silent, sullen, black. The ledge where we landed was so narrow that we could not stand upon it without difficulty. We were hemmed round with danger. The mountains frowned on us from on high, the precipice startled us from beneath. Our only safety seemed even in the jaws of a cavern that yawned in our front. We plunged into it without hesitating, and for a moment felt the joys of a sudden escape. But our terrors returned when we surveyed our asylum. We found ourselves at the bottom of a staircase hewn in the rock, long, narrow, steep and rugged. At a distance a feeble taper glimmered from above and faintly discovered to us the secrets of the vault. We, however, looked forward to it as our pole star. We scrambled up the steps, and with much trouble and fatigue arrived at the landing-place. Here an ancient bald-headed bonze issued from his den, and offered himself as our conductor through this subterraneous labyrinth. The first place he led us to

* [Barrow, *Travels in China*, writes Quan-gin-shan. ? Kuan-yin-shan.—Ed.]

was the grand hall or refectory of the convent. It is an excavation forming nearly a cube of twenty-five feet, through one face of which is a considerable opening that looks over the water and is barricaded with a rail. This apartment is well furnished in the taste of the country with tables and chairs highly varnished, and with many gauze and paper lanterns of various colours, in the middle of which was suspended a glass lantern of prodigious size made in London, the offering of an opulent Chinese bigot at Canton. From hence we mounted by an ascent of many difficult steps to the temple itself, which is directly over the hall, but of much greater extent. Here the god Pusa is displayed in all his glory—a gigantic image with a Saracen face, grinning horribly from a double row of gilded fangs, a crown upon his head, a naked scimitar in one hand and a firebrand in the other. But how little, alas, is celestial or sublunary fame: I could learn very few particulars of this colossal divinity. Even the bonzes who live by his worship scarcely knew anything of his history. From the attributes he is armed with, I suppose he was some great Tartar prince or commander of antiquity; and if he bore any resemblance of his representative he must have been a most formidable warrior, and probably little inferior in his day to the King of Prussia or Prince Ferdinand in our own. A magnificent altar was dressed out at his feet with lamps, lanterns, candles and candlesticks, censers and perfumes, strongly resembling the decorations of a Romish chapel, and on the walls were hung numerous tablets inscribed in large characters with moral sentences and exhortations to pious alms and religion.

Opposite to the image is a wide breach in the wall, down from which the perpendicular view requires the finest nerves and the steadiest head to resist its impression. The convoluted rocks above shooting their tottering shadows into the distant light, the slumbering abyss below, the superstitious gloom brooding upon the whole, all conspired to strike the mind with accumulated horror and the most terrifying images. From the chapel we were led through several long, narrow galleries to the rest of the apartments, which had been all wrought in the rock by invincible labour and perseverance into kitchens, cells, cellars, and other recesses of various kinds. The bonzes, having now learned the quality of their visitors, had lighted an additional number of torches and flambeaux, by which means we were enabled to see all the interior of the *souterrain*, and to examine into the nature of its inhabitants and their manner of living in it. Here we beheld a number of our fellow-creatures, endowed

THE CORK CONVENT

with faculties like our own ('some breasts once pregnant with celestial fire'), buried under a mountain and chained to a rock, to be incessantly gnawed by the vultures of superstition and fanaticism. Their condition appeared to us to be the last stage of monastic misery, the lowest degradation of humanity. The aspiring thoughts and elegant desires, the Promethean heat, the nobler energies of the soul, the native dignity of man, all sunk, rotting or extinguished in a hopeless dungeon of religious insanity. From such scenes the offended eye turns away with pity and disdain, and looks with impatience for a ray of relief from the light of reason and philosophy.

At my departure I left among this wretched community a small donation, which was, however, so far above their expectations that I think it not unlikely they will insert a new clause in their litany, and heartily pray that the Chinese Government may adopt a more liberal policy, and open the country to the free inspection and curiosity of English travellers.*

I remember to have seen in Portugal near Cape Roxent, a Franciscan monastery that this temple of Pusa put me a good deal in mind of. I mean what is usually called the Cork Convent,[69] which is an excavation of considerable extent under a hill, divided into a great number of cells, and filled up with a church, sacristy, refectory and every requisite apartment for the accommodation of the miserable Cordeliers† who burrow in it. The inside is entirely lined with cork; the walls, the roofs, the floors are covered with cork, the tables, seats, chairs, beds, couches, the furniture of the chapel, the crucifixes and every other implement all made of cork. The place was certainly dismal and comfortless to a great degree, but it wanted

---

* Upon lately reading this account of the temple of Pusa to one or two gentlemen who had visited it as well as myself, I find that though they perfectly agree in their recollection of all the principal features of the place, they think them rather heightened and surcharged. This I think is fair to take notice of, but at the same time I must add that I wrote the above description immediately on my returning to my yacht, merely for the purpose of aiding my recollection and certainly without any intention of imposing upon myself or upon others. Scarcely any two travellers, however, see the same objects in the same light, or remember them with the same accuracy. What is involved in darkness to the optics of one man is often arrayed in the brightest colours to those of another. An impression vanishes or endures according to the material that receives it. I have therefore often thought what amusement and instruction might be derived from a perusal of the journals kept (if such have been kept) by the different persons belonging to my Embassy. Even the memorandums of a *valet de chambre* might be of some value. [See Aeneas Anderson, appendix D below.—Ed.]

† [Franciscan monks.—Ed.]

the gigantic form, the grim features, the terrific aspect which distinguish the temple of Pusa.

In travelling through this country, whenever I meet with anything singular or extraordinary, I usually endeavour to recollect whether I have seen anything analogous to it elsewhere. By comparing such objects together and attentively marking their similitude and difference a common origin of principles, customs and manners may sometimes be traced and discovered in nations the most remote from each other.

Monday, December 16. The river now flows between two rows of high, steep, green hills, broad, smooth and deep. On the side of one of these hills I observed a black patch of very considerable extent enclosed within a pale, and found upon a nearer approach that it was a great mass of coal emerging above the surface; and I understand that all this part of the country abounds with that substance, although very little use is made of it by the Chinese.

The weather for these two days past has been very sharp, with a clear, frosty air. The thermometer at fifty this morning and at sixty-three in the middle of the day.

We stopped at Tchin-yuen,* and Wang and Chou passed the whole evening with me.

Having observed many barren spots and wild mountains at different distances in the course of our journey from Pekin and particularly in this neighbourhood, I took occasion to ask them some questions on the subject, and I learned from them that all uncultivated or desert lands are supposed to belong to the Sovereign. But any person, on giving notice of his intention to the nearest magistrate, may cultivate them if he chooses it, and thereby acquire the property of them, for there is no such thing in China as a waste or common depending upon a manor or lordship for the purpose of feeding the game or the vanity of an idle paramount. But in truth, I believe there is scarcely an acre of cultivable land in China that is not cultivated. Although a general resemblance runs through the whole nation as viewed in the gross, yet almost every province has its own particular mode of husbandry, and varies also from the rest in many other points. The boats of the different rivers are all of different builds, adapted to the nature of the stream. We have sailed in five or six of perfectly distinct construction between Tungchow and this place.

* [? Ch'ing-yüan (hsien).—Ed.]

Wang and Chou gave me the following particulars of the Emperor's usual course of life, when not engaged in hunting or in other excursions.

He rises at three o'clock a.m., and then goes to his private pagoda to worship Fo-hi. He then reads the dispatches of the different officers who, from their stations, are permitted to write to him directly. At seven o'clock a.m. he breakfasts, after which he amuses himself about his palaces and gardens with his women and eunuchs. He then sends for the first Grand Secretary, or chief Minister, with whom he transacts the current business, and then has a kind of levee, which is attended by all the Grand Secretaries and great Mandarins who have the entrée. He dines usually at three o'clock p.m., and then goes to the theatre or other diversion of the day, after which he retires and amuses himself with reading till bed-time, the hour of which is never later than seven o'clock in the evening. A principal eunuch is always in waiting during the night in order to conduct to him any of the ladies whom he chooses to call for.

The female establishment is one Empress, now dead, two Queens of the first rank, six Queens of the second rank, and one hundred concubines. He has four sons by the late Empress, and has others by his Queens and concubines, also several daughters, who are married to Tartar Princes and other Tartars of distinction, but none of them to Chinese. He is a man of great parts, learning and application, religious and charitable, affable and affectionate to his subjects, vindictive and relentless to his enemies; much elated with his greatness and prosperity, and impatient of the slightest reverse or mischance; jealous of his power, suspicious of his ministers, and when angry not easily appeased. He has never admitted any of his sons to the smallest share of his confidence or authority, although some of them are upwards of forty years old. Nor is it known or presumed whom he intends for his successor. Mien-cul-ye, his eldest grandson, is a man of capacity, has been employed in affairs, and is supposed to be much in his favour.*

Some years since the Emperor had pretended that he was weary of the throne, and fixed a time for his retiring from it, but as the period approached he began to think it better to defer his resignation to a more distant day. At present it stands for 1796, but it is by no means certain that it will then take place.† He is naturally of a

* [See note 16.—Ed.]
† [In fact Ch'ien-lung did hand over the government to his fifteenth son, Chia-ch'ing, in 1796.—Ed.]

healthy constitution and of great bodily strength, and though upwards of eighty-three years old, is as yet but little afflicted with the infirmities of age. These particulars relative to this great personage I have set down as I received them from my two friends, who have given them to me, I am persuaded, according to the best of their knowledge and opinion. From their rank and situation they have certainly had good opportunities of obtaining intelligence and of forming their judgments.

Tuesday, December 17. The river grows very broad and meets the tide here, being thirty miles above Canton. The mountains on each side are at seven or eight miles distant. We stopped at San-chou-hien,* where the state yachts were in waiting to convey us to Canton. But as the Viceroy's preparations for our reception are not yet quite completed, I understand that we shall not arrive there till Thursday.

Wednesday, December 18. Early this morning we passed by the town of Fou-sang,† which is a very considerable one and arrived before noon at a garden-house belonging to the Chinese Hong merchants of Canton, where we found Messieurs Browne, Irwin, and Jackson, the Company's Commissioners, together with Mr. Hall, the secretary. They had come up from Canton to meet us, and brought with them our letters and packets from Europe, which after a fifteen months' absence were singularly acceptable. By these we have learned the state of affairs between Great Britain and France. It now remains to consider how far the motions of the Embassy are to be regulated by it. The Commissioners inform me that my letters had been forwarded to Sir Erasmus Gower, and that the *Lion* is now lying below the second bar. They presented to me the Hong merchants, who had come from Canton on purpose to pay their respects to the Embassy. To-morrow we make our entry into Canton.

I can't omit remarking that in the course of our navigation from Nan-chou-fou,‡ we have had an uncommon profusion of military honours lavished upon us everywhere as we passed along, which I attribute to the Viceroy's having given particular directions for the purpose as he preceded us. As the Chinese consider the province of Canton to be the most obnoxious to invasion from the sea, the

* [? San-shui-hsien.—Ed.]
† [? Fo-shan (Fatshan.)—Ed.]   ‡ [? Nan-Ch'ang-fu.—Ed.]

military posts in it are very numerous. There seemed to be an affected reiteration of salutes wherever we appeared, in order, I presume, to impress us with an idea of the vigilance and alertness of the troops, and to show that they were not unprepared against an enemy.* Nevertheless, as they are totally ignorant of our discipline, cumbersomely clothed, armed only with matchlocks, bows and arrows, and heavy swords, awkward in the management of them, of an unwarlike character and disposition, I imagine they would make but a feeble resistance to a well-conducted attack. The circumstance of greatest embarrassment to an invader would be their immense numbers, not on account of the mischief they could do to him, but that he would find no end of doing mischief to them. The slaughter of millions would scarcely be perceived, and unless the people themselves soon voluntarily submitted, the victor might indeed reap the vanity of destruction, but not the glory or use of dominion.

Thursday, December 19. At eleven o'clock a.m. we set out in the state barges for Canton, and at half an hour after one were landed at the great stairs of the island house, which had been prepared for our reception. From the stairs we walked upon a stage of fifty or sixty yards long, covered with carpets, till we reached the place where it united with terra firma. Here we were received by the Viceroy, the Fuyuen or Governor, the Hoppo or Treasurer, and the principal Mandarins of rank in this neighbourhood, all dressed in their robes of ceremony. We were then conducted into a very large apartment, with double semi-circular rows of arm-chairs on each side. The Viceroy and his assessors took their stations opposite to us, and a conversation began, which lasted about an hour. It chiefly turned upon the incidents of our journey from Pekin and the arrival of the *Lion*, which the Viceroy requested might come up to Whampoa. We then adjourned to the theatre, on which a company of comedians (who are reckoned capital performers, and had been ordered down from Nankin on purpose) were prepared to entertain us. And here we found a most magnificent Chinese dinner spread out upon the tables, and a display of the presents upon this occasion. The Viceroy conducted the whole ceremony with the greatest dignity and propriety, distinguishing us by the most pointed marks of respect and regard (things quite new and astonishing to the Chinese here, who are totally unused to see foreigners treated with any

* [See note 56.—Ed.]

attention), and evincing in every instance the high consideration which the Embassy was held in by the Government.

Our quarters are in an island, opposite to the English Factory, which is situated on the mainland in the suburbs of the city of Canton.[70] The river that divides us is about half a mile broad. These quarters consist of several pavilions or separate buildings, very spacious and convenient, and some of them fitted up in the English manner with glass windows and fire-grates, which latter at this season, although we are on the edge of the tropic, are very comfortable pieces of furniture. Our habitations are in the midst of a large garden, adorned with ponds and parterres, and with flowers, trees, and shrubs, curious either from rarity or beauty. On one side of us is a magnificent *miao*, or bonze temple, and on the other a large edifice from the top of which is a very fine view of the river and shipping, the city and the country to a great extent.

Friday, December 20. The theatre, which is a very elegant building with the stage open to the garden, being just opposite my pavilion, I was surprised when I rose this morning to see the comedy already begun and the actors performing in full dress, for it seems this was not a rehearsal, but one of their regular formal pieces. I understand that whenever the Chinese mean to entertain their friends with particular distinction, an indispensable article is a comedy, or rather a string of comedies which are acted one after the other without intermission for several hours together. The actors now here have, I find, received directions to amuse us constantly in this way during our time of our residence. But as soon as I see our conductors I shall endeavour to have them relieved, if I can do it without giving offence to the taste of the nation or having my own called in question.

In case His Imperial Majesty Ch'ien-lung should send Ambassadors to the Court of Great Britain, there would be something comical, according to our manners, if my Lord Chamberlain Salisbury were to issue an order to Messrs. Harris and Sheridan, the King's patentees, to exhibit Messrs. Lewis and Kemble, Mrs. Siddons, and Miss Farren[71] during several days, or rather nights together, for the entertainment of their Chinese Excellencies. I am afraid they would at first feel the powers of the great buttresses of Drury Lane and Covent Garden[72] as little affecting to them as the exertions of these capital actors from Nankin have been to us.

We have found here five Indiamen almost ready to sail for England, viz.: the *Bombay Castle*, the *Brunswick*, the *Minerva*, the

VISITS FROM OFFICIALS

Chesterfield and the *Bellona* (a Botany Bay ship),*⁷³ and this day news is come of the arrival of the *Thurlow*, the *Abergavenny*, the *Osterley*, the *Glatton* and the *Ceres* from Manila, at which place they called in their way hither.† Several more are expected from England; cargoes are provided and ready not only for all these but for two more. The two more, however, will not be wanted this season, as the *Princess Royal* has been taken by the French in the Straits of Sunda and the destination of another expected ship has been altered at home.

Saturday, December 21; Sunday, December 22; Monday, December 23. These three days have been chiefly taken up in receiving visits from the Viceroy, the Fuyuen or Governor, the Hoppo or Treasurer, the *Tsung-ping*, or Governor of Chao-chou-fou,⁷⁴ and several other great Mandarins, some of whom I find are come from a considerable distance to see us. The great public honours and respect paid here to the Embassy cannot fail, I think, to have a very good effect upon the people in favour of our factory. In these visits I explained at length the different grievances of our trade. The Hoppo was averse to any alterations and wished everything to remain as he found it. The Viceroy thought every reasonable alteration should be made, and they debated together with great earnestness for a considerable time. The subject was renewed again and again, and I should hope from the Viceroy's profession and assurances that we have got the better of the Hoppo.

We have also been employed in consulting and settling with the Commissioners the destination and departure of the ships, and in preparing our letters for England.

After maturely considering all the circumstances before me, reflecting upon the state of the ships now ready to sail and upon the value of the cargoes provided for loading the ships lately arrived and those still expected this season (which cargoes, when sold, I can scarcely estimate at less than three millions sterling), ascertained of the capture of the *Princess Royal* in the Straits of Sunda and of a French force there; carefully perusing the letters lately received from Batavia,‡ having no notice or intelligence of any convoy intended to

---

* Besides these were the *Triton*, *Warley* and *Royal Charlotte* from the Coromandel Coast and the *Exeter* from Bombay, which had arrived a few days before but were not yet loaded.

† The *Walsingham*, *Hawke* and *Henry Dundas*, who left England in the beginning of July, arrived eight or ten days after them.

‡ Vide Titsingh's letter to me in appendix. [Not printed in this book.—Ed.]

be sent from home, aware of the present situation in Cochin China,* both in respect to its internal commotions, and its pretended dependence of this Empire, combining all these things together, I have now, however painful to me, been obliged to dismiss from my mind many of the flattering ideas which I had entertained at the commencement of my Embassy, of distinguishing it by some happy discovery, some signal and brilliant success, in the prosecution of our political and commercial interests in these distant parts of the world. I have given up my projected visit to Japan, which (though now less alluring in prospect) had been always with me a favourite adventure as the possible opening of a new mine for the exercise of our industry and the purchase of our manufactures.[75] All these ideas I have resigned at present, and adopted the measures which appear to afford the most probable substantial advantages to the public. It is therefore determined that the *Bombay Castle*, the *Brunswick*, the *Minerva*, the *Chesterfield*, and the *Bellona* shall proceed immediately for England, the two first are strong, well armed and well-manned ships, and Captain Montgomery of the *Bombay Castle*, a man of known spirit, skill and experience, being the senior officer, is to command this little fleet and to conduct it in the manner which he judges most essential to its security. The other ships (probably thirteen) will proceed when ready, under the convoy of His Majesty's ship the *Lion*. Thus, by the speedy departure of the five ships, not only their demurrage will be saved, but if they arrive safe, the Court of Directors will be the earlier enabled to judge of their China resources. By the *Lion*'s convoying the remainder, an immense property will be secured from danger in these seas and, I trust, reach England in safety.

Tuesday, December 24. Our interpreter came and mentioned to me the different persons who expected to receive presents from the Embassy. I have desired Mr. Barrow to select and deliver them, and to put whatever remains unexpended into the hands of Mr. Browne, according to the Company's instructions, and to take a receipt for the same.†

Wednesday, December 25. This day being Christmas Day, we all went over and dined with the British Factory. The captains of the *Bombay Castle*, the *Brunswick*, the *Minerva*, the *Chesterfield* and

* [See note 79.—Ed.]
† Vide Mr. Barrow's papers and accounts. [Omitted here—Ed.]

the *Bellona* took leave of me. My dispatches for England are sent on board the *Bombay Castle*, the duplicates on the *Brunswick*.

Thursday, December 26; Friday, December 27; Saturday, December 28. I have had some conversation with the principal Hong merchants of this place. Pan-ke-qua is one of the principal, a shrewd, sensible, sly fellow. Chi-chin-qua is the next in point of consequence, but not inferior in point of opulence. The latter is the younger man and of a franker character.[76] To me he affected much regard for the English nation, and declared without reserve his willingness to try experiments in trade with any new articles our Factory desired him. Mr. Irwin and Mr. Jackson were present when he said this to me. Pan-ke-qua wears a white opaque button on his cap, and Chi-chin-qua wears a crystal one, which is a degree superior to Pan-ke-qua's, but I soon learned the reason. Pan-ke-qua is more prudent and less ostentatious. Chi-chin-qua owned to me that he had also a blue button, but that, though he always wears it at home in his own family, he never appears with it abroad, lest the Mandarins in office should visit him on that account and make use of it as a pretence to squeeze presents from him, naturally supposing that a man could well afford them who had given ten thousand taels (each tael is equal to 6s. 8d.) for such a distinction. These different ranks of buttons are sold here to the wealthy merchants, but confer no official authority. When I say sold, I do not mean that the Government sells them, but the suitor certainly buys them by the large presents which he makes to the great men at this extremity of the Empire who have interest enough at Court to procure them.

I mentioned to these Hong merchants several things,* which from what I had observed were well adapted in my opinion to the northern parts of the Empire and would, I believed, be acceptable articles at Pekin, but they seemed to know as little of Pekin as of Westminster; not one of those whom I conversed with had ever been in the capital. They scarcely ever stir from the place of their nativity, unless compelled by authority or incited by the strongest motives of interest, but grovel on at Canton from generation to generation very unlike the Chinese whom I have had occasion to see in other places. These merchants have no trade beyond Nankin; Nankin is the great commercial metropolis; to Nankin they send most of their Europe goods, from Nankin they receive a considerable part of the goods intended for Europe, so that the Nankin

---
* Vide my list in the appendix; head, Trade and Commerce. [See pp. 257–8—Ed.]

merchants are in fact the real masters of the Chinese market; a circumstance which renders our admission to trade directly to Chusan and Ningpo doubly desirable, and it is not to be despaired of. We once had it.[77]

Sunday, December 29.   Sir Erasmus Gower had brought the *Lion* up to Whampoa and from thence came here himself last night. He returned again this day and I went down with him in his barge, and took Wang along with us. It is about eleven miles from Canton and we were three hours in the passage, but it is often made in less than two. I observed lying there nine Company's ships, three Country ships, one English–Ostend ship called the *City of Genoa,* under Genoese colours and commanded by a Captain Snyders, an Englishman, and three or four Americans, the largest of which latter did not exceed six hundred tons. They are called by the Chinese 'second chop' Englishmen, the teas which are the principal articles they take are of a very inferior kind and are chiefly paid for in dollars.

The river of Canton is quite covered with boats and vessels of various sorts and sizes, all, even the very smallest, constantly and thickly inhabited. The country is pleasant, flat near the water, but rising into mountains at ten or twelve miles distance. On the left is the village of Whampoa, where the bankshalls[78] (temporary huts built for the accommodation of our people and the reception of their stores) are situated. On the right, a little further down, are two islands, commonly called French island, and Danish island, which I particularly showed to Wang (whom I had brought with me for this purpose) and explained to him our wishes to have leave to build accommodation for our people upon them. He said he would report to the Viceroy that there could not be any objection. We returned here (to Canton) in the evening.

Monday, December 30; *Tuesday, December* 31.   The accounts which we had heard of the commotions in Cochin China have been now confirmed to us by good authority. We are informed that the King of Donai (the southern region) had attacked the King of Tongking, or Nangan, as the Chinese call the reigning Prince, in the neighbourhood of Tourane Bay, which we had visited; that the town of Taifo had been taken and plundered, that the King of Nangan himself had fled to the northward, and that the whole country was in the utmost of confusion.[79] As it is probable that these troubles will not be speedily composed, perhaps if a settlement in Cochin China be thought advisable a more favourable season may not offer. It is a measure that with proper precautions may, I believe, be accomplished. There is a most happy spot, a perfect Gibraltar, on the east point of Tourane Bay marked out by nature for the purpose.* A battalion of Sepoys and a company of European artillery would be fully sufficient to defend it against any force that is ever likely to be mustered for attacking it.

Wednesday, January 1, 1794. This morning the Viceroy visited me in great ceremony and said he had received a letter from the Emperor, the contents of which he was ordered to communicate to me. It contained, as usual, a repetition of the Emperor's satisfaction from the Embassy, his good disposition towards the English, and promises to them of his future favour and protection. These seem to be expressed in stronger terms than the former, and the Viceroy himself was particularly courteous and caressing. He told us he had already issued two proclamations, denouncing the severest punishments against any persons who should attempt to injure Europeans, or practise extortion in dealing with them. These proclamations† are published and it is hoped it will have a good effect.‡ [80]

This being New Year's Day we all went over and dined with our Factory.

Thursday, January 2; Friday, January 3; Saturday, January 4; Sunday, January 5; Monday, January 6; Tuesday, January 7. As none of the gentlemen of our Factory had ever been within the city of Canton, except the Commissioners, when they went to deliver the Chairman's letter announcing my intended Embassy, I had a strong curiosity to see it. I entered it at the great water-gate and traversed it from one end to the other. It covers a great extent of ground and is said to contain a million of inhabitants. This account may possibly exaggerate, but the population everywhere in China is so vastly disproportionate to what we have been accustomed to observe in Europe that it is difficult for us to determine upon any rule or standard of our own to go by. I can, therefore, only repeat upon this point what I have learned from the best informed of the

* Vide the plan in the appendix. [Omitted here—Ed.]
† Vide the enclosures, no. 3 and no. 4, in my letter to Mr. Secretary Dundas, 7 January 1794. [Omitted here—Ed.]
‡ I here delivered to the Viceroy a more particular account of the grievances at Canton. Vide no. 1 enclosed in my dispatch to Mr. Dundas of 7 January 1794, also his answer, no. 2. [Omitted here—Ed.]

natives. The streets are narrow and flat paved, much resembling those of Hangchowfu. No wheel carriages are admitted, nor did I see any horses in the town except those which my servants rode upon. It is full of shops and trades, and has in general a gloomy appearance, except in two or three large open squares, where the Viceroy and other great men reside.

All the people seemed very busily employed, chiefly in making either silk boots or straw bonnets, in the working of metals, and the labours of the forge, and most of them wore spectacles on their noses. The walls are kept in good repair, but no guns are mounted on them. The ordinary troops here, instead of a blue uniform and red lace as elsewhere, are clothed in red with a blue lace. I am informed that several persons have been punished for petty extortions practised against some strangers here, notwithstanding the late proclamations. But there are many other things that depend a good deal on ourselves which, I believe, would be more likely to secure us than proclamations and punishments. We no doubt labour under many disadvantages here at present, but some of them we have it in our own power to remove. Instead of acting towards the Chinese at Canton in the same manner as we do towards the natives at our factories elsewhere we seem to have adopted a totally opposite system. We keep aloof from them as much as possible. We wear a dress as different from theirs as can be fashioned. We are quite ignorant of their language (which, I suppose, cannot be a very difficult one, for little George Staunton has long since learned to speak it and write it with great readiness, and from that circumstance has been of infinite use to us on many occasions). We therefore almost entirely depend on the good faith and good-nature of the few Chinese whom we employ, and by whom we can be but imperfectly understood in the broken gibberish we talk to them.[81] I fancy that Pan-ke-qua or Mahomet Soulem would attempt doing business on the Royal Exchange to very little purpose if they appeared there in long petticoat clothes, with bonnets and turbans, and could speak nothing but Chinese or Arabic. Now I am very much mistaken if, by a proper management, we might not gradually and in some years be able to mould the China trade (as we seem to have done the trade everywhere else) to the shape that will best suit us. But it would certainly require in us great skill, caution, temper and perseverance, much greater perhaps than it is reasonable to expect. I dare say there are many hasty spirits disposed to go a shorter way to work, but no shorter way will do it. If, indeed, the Chinese were provoked to interdict us their commerce, or do us any material injury, we certainly have the means easy enough of revenging ourselves, for a few frigates could in a few weeks destroy all their coast navigation and intercourse from the island of Hainan to the Gulf of Pei-chihli and if I were to indulge the speculations of an ambitious or vindictive politician, I doubt not but we might vulnerate them as sensibly in many other quarters. We might probably be able from Bengal to excite the most serious disturbances on their Tibet frontier by means of their neighbours there, who appear to require only a little encouragement and assistance to begin. The Koreans, if they once saw ships in the Yellow Sea acting as enemies to China might be induced to attempt the recovery of their independence. The thread of connexion between this Empire and Formosa is so slender that it must soon break of itself, but a breath of foreign interference would instantly snap it asunder.

The Portuguese, who, as a nation, have been long really exanimated and dead in this part of the world, although their ghost still appears at Macao, hold that place upon such terms as render it equally useless and disgraceful to them. It is now chiefly supported by the English, and on the present footing of things there the Chinese can starve both it, and those who support it, whenever they please. If the Portuguese made a difficulty of parting with it to us on fair terms, it might easily be taken from them by a small force from Madras, and the compensation and irregularity be settled afterwards. Or with as little trouble and with more advantage we might make a settlement in Lantao* or Cow-hee, and then Macao would of itself crumble to nothing in a short time.[82] The forts of the Bocca Tigris† might be demolished by half a dozen broadsides, the river would be impassable without our permission, and the whole trade of Canton and its correspondencies annihilated in a season. The millions of people who subsist by it would be almost instantly reduced to hunger and insurrection. They must overrun the country as beggars or as robbers, and wherever they went would carry with them misery and rebellion. In such distractions would Russia remain inactive? Would she neglect the opportunity of recovering Albazin and re-establishing her power upon the Amur? Would the ambition of the great Catherine, that has stretched beyond Onalaska to the eastward, overlook the provinces and partitions within grasp at her door?[83]

* Vide drawing in the appendix. [Omitted here—Ed.]
† Vide the plans and description in the appendix, no. 19 I. [Omitted here. Note 58 refers—Ed.]

JOURNAL—JANUARY

Such might be the consequence to this Empire if we had a serious quarrel with it. On the other hand let us see what might be the consequence to ourselves. It is possible that other nations, now trading or expecting to trade with China, would not behold our success with indifference, and thus we might be involved with much more formidable enemies than Chinese. But I leave that consideration aside and proceed to others.

Our settlements in India would suffer most severely by any interruption of their China traffic which is infinitely valuable to them, whether considered singly as a market for cotton and opium, or as connected with their adventures to the Philippines and Malaya.

To Great Britain the blow would be immediate and heavy. Our great woollen manufacture, the ancient staple of England, would feel such a sudden convulsion as scarcely any vigilance or vigour in Government could for a long time remedy or alleviate. The demand from Canton for our woollens alone can't now be less than £500,000 to £600,000 per annum, and there is good reason to believe that with proper care it may in some years be stretched to a million. We should lose the other growing branches of export to China of tin, lead, copper, hardware, and of clocks and watches, and similar articles of ingenious mechanism. We should lose the import from China not only of its raw silk, an indispensable ingredient in our silk fabrics, but of another indispensable luxury, or rather an absolute necessary of life: tea. We should also in some measure lose an excellent school of nautical knowledge, a strong limb of marine power, and a prolific source of public revenue.

These evils, it would seem, must infallibly follow from a breach with China. Whether in time other markets might not be found or created to make us amends, I am not yet sufficiently acquainted with this part of the world (and still less with the disposition of the Court of Spain) to hazard a decision; but it is not impossible that, though prodigious inconveniences and mischiefs would certainly be felt at the moment from a rupture, means might be discovered to reverse or repair them. But all these inconveniences and mischiefs which I have stated as objects of apprehension may happen in the common course of things without any quarrel or interference on our part. The Empire of China is an old, crazy, First rate man-of-war, which a fortunate succession of able and vigilant officers has contrived to keep afloat for these one hundred and fifty years past, and to overawe their neighbours merely by her bulk and appearance, but whenever an insufficient man happens to have the command upon

SPECULATIONS

deck, adieu to the discipline and safety of the ship. She may perhaps not sink outright; she may drift some time as a wreck, and will then be dashed to pieces on the shore; but she can never be rebuilt on the old bottom.

The breaking-up of the power of China (no very improbable event) would occasion a complete subversion of the commerce, not only of Asia, but a very sensible change in the other quarters of the world. The industry and ingenuity of the Chinese would be checked and enfeebled, but they would not be annihilated. Her ports could no longer be barricadoed; they would be attempted by all the adventurers of all trading nations, who would search every channel, creek, and cranny of China for a market, and for some time be the cause of much rivalry and disorder. Nevertheless as Great Britain, from the weight of her riches and the genius and spirit of her people, is become the first political, marine and commercial power on the globe, it is reasonable to think that she would prove the greatest gainer by such a revolution as I have alluded to, and rise superior over every competitor.

But to take things solely as they now are, and to bound our views by the visible horizon of our situation, without speculating upon probable events (which seldom take place according to our speculations), our present interests, our reason, and our humanity equally forbid the thoughts of any offensive measures with regard to the Chinese, whilst a ray of hope remains for succeeding by gentle ones. Nothing could be urged in favour of an hostile conduct, but an irresistible conviction of failure by forbearance.

The project of a territory on the continent of China (which I have heard imputed to the late Lord Clive) is too wild to be seriously mentioned, and especially if all can be quietly got without it, that was expected to be got with it. By my Embassy the Chinese have had, what they never had before, an opportunity of knowing us, and this must lead them to a proper way of thinking of us and of acting towards us in future. If, when the dispute happened in the year 1759, a royal ambassador had been sent to the Court of Pekin, I am inclined to think the affair would have taken a very different turn. They would certainly have received the Embassy with respect, possibly indeed with less honours and distinctions than mine, on account of the difference between compliment and complaint; and though they might then have granted no favours, yet the caution of the Government would at least have guarded them from doing injustice.

On the footing that Mr. Flint was sent, what could have been expected? A private individual commissioned by a few other individuals trading at Canton, whom the Chinese had not yet learned to respect as they ought, was dispatched without a passport in a small vessel to Tientsin (an irregular proceeding in itself and in the teeth of a particular law), to accuse the regency of Canton, then consisting of persons appointed and supported by those who were to judge them.[84]

At present, after reflecting upon all the incidents of the Embassy, the complexion of the Court of Pekin, and the footing of our Factory at Canton, I cannot but be of opinion that nothing is more likely to contribute essentially to the promotion of our interests than having a King's Minister, or a Company's Minister with a King's Commission always resident at Canton, totally unconcerned with trade of any kind and clearly known to be so. The first object is to preserve the ground we have lately gained. It is no small advantage arising from the Embassy that so many Englishmen have been seen at Pekin, from whose brilliant appearance and prudent demeanour a most favourable idea has been formed of the country which had sent them. Nor is it any strain of vanity to say that the principal persons of rank who, from their intercourse with us, had opportunities of observing our manners, tempers and discipline very soon dismissed the prejudices they had conceived against us, and by a generous transition grew to admire and respect us as a nation and to love us as individuals. Gained by our attentions, we found them capable of attachment; though in public ceremonious, in private they were frank and familiar. Tired of official formalities they seemed often to fly to our society as a relief, and to leave it with regret. Dispositions like these, an able Minister would not fail to improve. By his intercourse with the Viceroy, the Fuyuen, and the Hoppo, he would be able to excuse irregularities and clear up mistakes. He would discover the proper seasons for advancing or receding, when to be silent with dignity and when to speak with confidence and effect. But above all the King's Commission would authorize him to write to, and entitle him to be heard by, the Court of Pekin itself, a circumstance probably alone sufficient to awe the regency of Canton and keep them within the bounds of justice and moderation. These opinions I have formed, and these conclusions I have drawn, from what experience I have had of this country, from what observations I made upon the characters of the people that were within my reach to converse with, and the Emperor's letter to the Viceroy, no.

3 enclosed in my dispatch from Canton to Mr. Secretary Dundas of the 23rd of last month.*

I am aware that a measure of this kind may seem to interfere with the Company's servants of Canton, but it ought to have no such operation. It should neither lessen their emoluments nor their consequence, but have a contrary effect. I believe that nothing has contributed more to render our merchants at Lisbon and St. Petersburg respectable and important than the residence of His Majesty's Ministers at those ports to maintain our commercial rights and protect them from wrong. The Chinese, it is true, are a singular people, but they are men formed of the same materials and governed by the same passions as ourselves. They are jealous of foreigners; but are they jealous of us without reason? Is there any country on the globe that Englishmen visit where they do not display that pride of themselves and that contempt of others which conscious superiority is apt to inspire? Can the Chinese, one of the vainest nations in the world, and not the least acute, have been blind and insensible to this foible of ours? And is it not natural for them to be discomposed and disgusted by it? But a better knowledge of the better parts of our character will calm their disquiets, weaken their prejudices and wear away their ill-impressions. Every day we shall have fewer enemies and rivals to injure us in their opinion. The French, who had long flourished here, have given up the trade and disappeared, and other nations also must either soon abandon it or be content to carry it on, as the Dutch and Americans do, with little credit and little advantage.

Having now no particular business to detain the Embassy longer at Canton, and unwilling to trespass further on the hospitality of the Court of China, at whose expense we have been entertained ever since we landed in the Empire (they not permitting us to maintain ourselves, though often pressed by me and entreated to let us do so), I told the Viceroy of my intention of going to Macao, and of waiting there till our ships should be ready to sail for England under the *Lion*'s convoy. And to prevent his taking umbrage, or imagining I was not perfectly pleased with my reception and residence here at Canton (which have certainly been as honourable and agreeable to me as possible), I put my removal chiefly upon the ground of my state of health, which has been much impaired, and which it is thought the sea air would be favourable to. I fixed with him the time of my departure for to-morrow, and as I proposed to embark from

* [A copy has been preserved in the India Office Library.—Ed.]

the wharf of the Factory, I invited him to breakfast with me there, in order that I might have the opportunity (which he had before promised me) of introducing and recommending the Company's Commissioners to him, to the Fuyuen, and the Hoppo in the most public and the most distinguished manner. He was particularly inquisitive about the nature of these gentlemen's office and their rank. I endeavoured to explain the matter to him as well as I could, but there is no making the Chinese understand the wide difference there is between an English merchant and a merchant of any other nation.

Wednesday, January 8. This day at ten o'clock a.m. we set out from our quarters and crossed over the river to the English Factory, where I was met by the Viceroy, the Fuyuen, the Hoppo, and the other principal Mandarins. I presented the Commissioners, to whom they gave a very gracious reception, with liberal promises of access and attention. This ceremony being finished, we all sat down together to the collation prepared for us, which our Chinese friends did ample justice to, some of them seeming to relish much the good things set before them and nothing more than our sweet wine and cherry brandy.

At one o'clock p.m. Sir George Staunton, Sir Erasmus Gower, Lieutenant-Colonel Benson and I took our leave of them and embarked on the *Lion*'s barge. The other gentlemen went in the pinnaces and boats of the Indiamen, which their Captains had obligingly brought up from Whampoa for this occasion, with pennants flying, and the crews all dressed in uniform, so that our procession down the river was very numerous and splendid. Wang and Chou, together with the *Tsung-ping* of Chao-chou-fou, a man of high quality, with a red button and peacock's feather on his cap, and of a sociable, pleasant humour accompanied us in a state yacht and dined with us on board the *Lion*. And here our friends Wang and Chou took leave of us. They shed tears at parting, and showed such marks of sensibility and concern as could proceed from none but sincere and uncorrupted hearts. If I ever could forget the friendship and attachment of these two worthy men, or the services they rendered us, I should be guilty of the deepest ingratitude.

Thursday, January 9. Received this morning a most liberal present of fruit and vegetables of all kinds in twenty large baskets, sent us by Wang and Chou as a farewell token of their remembrance. Their respective duties and employments now call them away to very distant provinces, and they are not likely to see any of us again. Of this little attention I therefore confess myself the more sensible. But I consider it in two ways, as equally intended to be a mark of their public consideration for us, attaching to their characters as men of high station in this country, and of particular regard to us as their private friends of another.

Chou *ta-jen* is a man of letters and capacity. He stands high in the opinion of the Viceroy, whose universal reputation, joined to his connexion with the Imperial family, will probably elevate him one day to the first situation at Court. I have more than once talked with Chou on the subject of office and preferment, and from his prospects of advantage being enlarged by what he has seen here, his pretensions heightened by his connexion with us, and his ambition dilated by the patronage of the Viceroy, I think it not at all improbable that he may soon be sent here in a high employment. The place of Hoppo, which is usually of three years' duration, seems to be the object of his present views. *Honores mutant mores,* and it is possible that promotion might have the same effect upon him as upon his predecessors, but as he is of an age before which a man's principles have usually been settled and his character decided, I have reason to believe that if he ever obtains the appointment we shall receive the most essential advantages by it. But from the very circumstance of his connexion with us, our address to him and management of him would require the more care and dexterity.

The Commissioners, Messieurs Browne and Jackson, and Mr. Hall the Secretary, came and dined with us on board the *Lion*. We expected Mr. Irwin, but his illness deprived us of the pleasure of his company.

Friday, January 10.   We fell down the river below the first bar, and anchored for the night.

Saturday, January 11.   We set sail this morning with hopes of being able to get below the second bar, but the wind heading us, we were under the necessity of coming to an anchor.

Sunday, January 12.   This day we passed the second bar and then came to an anchor for the night.

Monday, January 13.   At eight o'clock a.m. we made sail and in about a couple of hours passed the two forts which have been erected by the Chinese to guard the mouth of the Pe-kiang-ho, as they call it, or the Bocca Tigris as it is usually styled by the Europeans from the Portuguese denomination. The lesser fort is built on a small island to the west, the principle one is on the mainland with a steep hill rising close behind it. Both of them very despicable in our eyes when viewed in the light of defence.* There are a great many embrasures, but several are unfurnished with guns and of the few guns which they have the largest does not exceed a six pounder. The passage between the two forts is less than a mile across and any ship might go through it almost harmless with the wind and tide in her favour. As we sailed by the Chinese made a prodigious military parade, manned the walls with a numerous garrison, and extended an encampment of five hundred or six hundred men all along the eastern beach, with their standards, colours, streamers, music and other appurtenances of war. There were several armed junks lying in the road, crowded with soldiers who took great pains to show themselves on the deck, but did not salute us as the forts did, having nothing but swivels mounted on their quarters, though they had several sham ports below. The largest of them did not appear to exceed two hundred and fifty tons. It is said that there is another passage behind the eastern fort of Anunchoi, leading into the country to the north-east above Canton, by which the largest ships may run up within a short distance of that city, but the Chinese keep it a secret from Europeans as much as possible, and endeavour to prevent anything larger than a boat from navigating it.[85]

In the afternoon at four o'clock p.m. we came to an anchor in five fathom water in Macao roads, the town bearing west about six miles distant. Lieutenant-Colonel Benson and Lieutenant Campbell went ashore in the pinnace. From the deck we see the *Jackall*, the *Clarence* and a large Portuguese ship all at anchor in the mouth of the Typa.†

Tuesday, January 14. It blew very hard all this day till four o'clock p.m. when (the weather moderating a little) the Governor's boat ventured out with his aide-de-camp on board, who came with the Governor's compliments and an offer of his best services.

Wednesday, January 15. This day at ten o'clock a.m. I went on shore at Macao with all the gentlemen of the Embassy and was

---

* Vide the plan and description in the appendix, no. 19 T. [Omitted here—Ed.]
† [Also Tipa or Taipa. An island off Macao, but here used as the name of an anchorage.—Ed.]

received at landing by the Governor, Don Manuel Pinto, and the *Desembargador*, Don Lazaro de Silva Ferreira, who is the principal civil officer of the place. A company of foot, mostly negroes and mulattoes, but commanded by European officers, were drawn up in military order on the quay, and endeavoured to make as good an appearance as they could. Their undersize, motley complexion, and shabby regimentals impressed us, however, with no very high ideas in their favour.

We were very handsomely entertained at dinner by the Governor, who is a well-bred reasonable man of about forty years old, and has the rank of Lieutenant-Colonel in the Portuguese service. His wife, a native of Goa, is of an agreeable figure, and did the honours of her house extremely well. The *Desembargador** has parts, observation and address, and speaks very good French.

Most of the gentlemen of the Embassy are lodged at the English Factory. My quarters are at a house in the upper part of the town, rented by Mr. Drummond, who has been so good as to lend it me during his absence. It is most delightfully situated, and has a very pleasant romantic garden adjoining to it of considerable extent. The tradition of Macao says it was formerly the habitation of the celebrated Camoens, and that here he composed his *Lusiad*.[86]

At this place we propose to stay till our homeward-bound ships, now thirteen in all, are ready to sail (which it is calculated will be in less than six weeks), and then proceed on the *Lion* as their convoy to England.

I now close my China Journal, in which I have written down the transactions and occurrences of my Embassy and my travels through this Empire, exactly as they passed and as they struck me at the time. To these I have added in the appendix a few papers relative to some particulars which I was desirous to be informed upon. They could not be inserted in their proper places, as it was frequently a long time after I had made my inquiries that I could obtain the answers, and when I did obtain them I was obliged to follow them up with further inquiries for explanation.

Should any accident throw this Journal under the eyes of a stranger unacquainted with me and the country I am now quitting, he might possibly imagine that I had too much indulged myself in local description and political conjecture. But nothing could be more fallacious than to judge of China by any European standard. My sole view has been to represent things precisely as they impressed me. I

---

* [Chief Judge.—Ed.]

had long accustomed myself to take minutes of whatever appeared of a curious or interesting nature, and such scenes as I have lately visited were not likely to obliterate my habits or to relax my diligence. I regularly took notes and memorandums of the business I was engaged in and the objects I saw, partly to serve for my own use and recollection, and partly to amuse the hours of a tedious and painful employment. But I will not flatter myself that they can be of much advantage or entertainment to others.

LORD MACARTNEY'S OBSERVATIONS ON CHINA

viz.:

> Manners and Character
> Religion
> Government
> Justice
> Property
> Population
> Revenue
> Civil and Military Ranks and Establishments
> Trade and Commerce
> Arts and Sciences
> Hydraulics
> Navigation
> Chinese Language
> Conclusion

Manners and Character

If I venture to say anything upon the manners and character of the Chinese, I must begin by confessing that I am very far from being a competent judge of them. Though assisted by an honest and able interpreter, though possessed of many advantages from the intercourse which my station afforded me with persons of the first rank and abilities, and from the extent of my travels through the country of China; yet I am sensible that it was impossible to avoid falling into mistakes. From my not knowing the language, from sometimes misconceiving those who did, from misinterpreting looks and gestures, where our hands and our eyes were to perform the offices of our tongues and our ears, I may have formed wrong judgments and have deceived myself; but as I do not mean that others should be deceived, I fairly own my disadvantages, and give previous notice of the nature of the information that may be expected from me. It will be chiefly the result of what I saw and heard upon the spot, however imperfectly, not of what I had read in books or been told in Europe.

It should never be absent from our recollection that there are now two distinct nations in China (though generally confounded together by Europeans), the Chinese and the Tartars, whose characters essentially differ (notwithstanding their external appearance be nearly the same) and whose minds must naturally be differently bent by the circumstances which respectively govern them. They are both subject to the most absolute authority that can be vested in a prince, but with this distinction, that to the Chinese it is a foreign tyranny; to the Tartars a domestic despotism. The latter consider themselves as in some degree partakers of their sovereign's dominion over the former, and that imagination may perhaps somewhat console them under the pressure of his power upon themselves; like the house servants and house negroes belonging to a great landlord in Livonia, or planter in Jamaica, who, though serfs themselves, look down upon the peasantry and field negroes of the estate as much their inferiors.[87]

If opinions were solely to be formed of China and its inhabitants from the accounts of the first travellers and even of later missionaries, they would often be inadequate and unjust; for those writers, although they probably did not mean to deal in fiction, yet when they do tell the truth, they do not always tell the whole truth, which is a mode of narration that leads to error almost as much as falsehood itself.

When Marco Polo, the Venetian, visited China in the thirteenth century, it was about the time of the conquest of China by the western or Mongol Tartars, with Kublai Khan, a grandson of Genghis Khan, at their head. A little before that period the Chinese had reached their highest pitch of civilization, and no doubt they were then a very civilized people in comparison of their Tartar conquerors, and their European contemporaries, but not having improved and advanced forward, or having rather gone back, at least for these one hundred and fifty years past, since the last conquest by the northern or Manchu Tartars; whilst we have been every day rising in arts and sciences, they are actually become a semi-barbarous people in comparison with the present nations of Europe. Hence it is that they retain the vanity, conceit, and pretensions that are usually the concomitants of half-knowledge, and that, though during their intercourse with the embassy they perceived many of the advantages we had over them, they seemed rather surprised than mortified, and sometimes affected not to see what they could not avoid feeling. In their address to strangers they are not restrained by any bashfulness or *mauvaise honte*, but present themselves with an easy confident air, as if they considered themselves the superiors, and that nothing in their manners or appearance could be found defective or inaccurate.

Their ceremonies of demeanour, which consist of various evolutions of the body, in elevating and inclining the head, in bending or stiffening the knee, in joining their hands together and then disengaging them, with a hundred other manoeuvres they consider as the highest perfection of good breeding and deportment, and look upon most other nations, who are not expert in this polite discipline, as little better than barbarians. Nevertheless having once shown off and exhausted all these tricks of behaviour, they are glad to relapse into ease and familiarity, and seem never so happy as when indulging in free conversation with those whom they do not distrust, for they are naturally lively, loquacious and good-humoured. They were certainly much surprised to find us so mild, sociable, and cheerful.

The court character is a singular mixture of ostentatious hospitality and inbred suspicion, ceremonious civility and real rudeness, shadowy complaisance and substantial perverseness; and this prevails through all the departments connected with the Court, although somewhat modified by the personal disposition of those at their head; but as to that genuine politeness which distinguishes our manners, it cannot be expected in Orientals, considering the light in which they regard the female world.

Among the Chinese themselves, society chiefly consists of certain stated forms and expressions, a calm, equal apathetical deportment, studied, hypocritical attentions and hyperbolical professions.

Where women are excluded from appearing, all delicacy of taste and sentiment, the softness of address, the graces of elegant converse, the play of passions, the refinements of love and friendship must of course be banished. In their place gross familiarity, coarse pleasantry, and broad allusions are indulged in, but without that honesty and expansion of heart which we have sometimes observed to arise on such occasions among ourselves. Morality is a mere pretence in their practice, though a common topic of their discourse. Science is an intruder and gaming the resource. An attachment to this vice accompanies even the lowest Chinese wherever he goes. No change of country divests him of it. I have been assured that the Chinese settled in our new colony at the Prince of Wales's island, pay not less than ten thousand dollars per annum to the government for a licence to keep gaming-houses and sell opium.[88]

Every Chinese who aspires to preferment attaches himself to some Tartar of consequence, and professes the utmost devotion to his service; but such is the strong and radical dislike in the client to the patron, that scarcely any benefits can remove it and plant gratitude in its place. As the nature of dependence is to grow false, it cannot be wondered at if these Chinese are not strict observers of truth. They have indeed so little idea of its moral obligation, that they promise you everything you desire, without the slightest intention of performance, and then violate their promises without scruple, having had no motive for making them that I could perceive, unless it were that they imagined what they said might be agreeable to you just at the moment. When detected or reproached they make light of the matter themselves, and appear neither surprised nor ashamed; but nevertheless it was evident that they particularly remarked our punctuality and our strict attention to truth in all our transactions with them, and respected us accordingly.

Although the difference of ranks be perhaps more distinctly marked in China than in any other country, yet I often observed that the Mandarins treat their domestic servants with great condescension and talk to them with good nature and familiarity; but in return an unremitted attention and obedience are expected and never withheld.

A Chinese family is regulated with the same regard to subordination and economy that is observed in the government of a state; the paternal authority, though unlimited, is usually exercised with kindness and indulgence. In China children are indeed sometimes sold, and infants exposed by the parents, but only in cases of the most hopeless indigence and misery, when they must inevitably perish if kept at home; but where the thread of attachment is not thus snapped asunder by the anguish of the parent, it every day grows stronger and becomes indissoluble for life.

There is nothing more striking in the Chinese character through all ranks than this most respectable union. Affection and duty walk hand in hand and never desire a separation. The fondness of the father is constantly felt and always increasing; the dependence of the son is perfectly understood by him; he never wishes it to be lessened. It is not necessary to coax or to cheat the child into the cutting off an entail, or the charging his inheritance with a mortgage; it is not necessary to importune the father for an irrevocable settlement. According to Chinese ideas, there is but one interest in a family; any other supposition would be unnatural and wicked. An undutiful child is a monster that China does not produce; the son, even after marriage, continues for the most part to live in the father's house; the labour of the family is thrown into one common stock under the sole management of the parent, after whose death the eldest son often retains the same authority, and continues in the same union with his younger brothers.

The houses of the better sort exhibit a certain show of grandeur and magnificence, and even of taste and elegance in their decorations, but at the same time discover, at least to our eyes, evident marks of discomfort and inconvenience. There is a want of useful furniture. They have indeed lanterns of gauze and paper and horn and diaphanous gum, most beautifully coloured and disposed, and they have tables, couches, and chairs, loosely covered with rich carpeting, with gold and silver damasks, and other silks; but they have no bureaux, commodes, lustres, or looking-glasses; they have no sheets to their beds, neither does their bedding itself seem well adapted or agreeable. They don't undress themselves entirely as we do, when they go to rest, but lay themselves down upon alcoved benches, which are spread with a single mat or thin mattress, and adjusted with small pillows and cushions. Their apartments are not well contrived or distributed, according to our ideas of utility and propriety, having seldom any doors that shut with locks or proper fastenings, but in lieu of them screens and curtains, which are removed or drawn back as occasion requires. In the cold weather they are warmed by flues under the floor, for there are neither stoves, fire-places, nor fire-grates in the rooms; but sometimes braziers filled with charcoal are brought in and occasionally renewed.

The people, even of the first rank, though so fond of dress as to change it usually several times in a day, are yet in their persons and customs frowzy and uncleanly. Their outward garment of ceremony is richly embroidered with silks of different colours (those of the highest class of all with golden dragons), and their common habit it of plain silk, or fine broadcloth; but their drawers and their waistcoats (of which they usually wear several according to the season) are not very frequently shifted. They wear neither knit nor woven stockings, but wrap their legs round with a coarse cotton stuff, over which they have constantly drawn a pair of black satin boots without heels, but with soles nearly an inch in thickness. In summer everybody carries a fan in his hand, and is flirting it incessantly.

They wear but little linen or calico, and what they do wear is extremely coarse and ill washed, soap being never employed by them. They seldom have recourse to pocket handkerchiefs, but spit about the rooms without mercy, blow their noses in their fingers, and wipe them with their sleeves, or upon anything near them. This practice is universal, and what is still more abominable, I one day observed a Tartar of distinction call his servant to hunt in his neck for a louse that was troublesome to him.

At their meals they use no towels, napkins, table-cloths, flat plates, glasses, knives nor forks, but help themselves with their fingers, or with their chopsticks, which are made of wood or ivory, about six inches long, round and smooth, and not very cleanly. Their meat is served up ready cut in small bowls, each guest having a separate bowl to himself. Seldom above two sit together at the same table, and never above four. They are all foul feeders and eaters of garlic and strong-scented vegetables, and drink mutually out of the same cup which, though sometimes rinsed, is never washed or wiped clean. They use little vinegar, no olive oil, cyder, ale, beer, or grape wine; their chief drink is tea, or liquors distilled or prepared from rice and other vegetables, of different degrees of strength according to their taste, some of which are tolerably agreeable and resemble strong Madeira.

They almost all smoke tobacco and consider it as a compliment to offer each other a whiff of their pipes. They also take snuff, mostly Brazil, but in small quantities, not in that beastly profusion which is often practised in England, even by some of our fine ladies.

They have no water-closets nor proper places of retirement; the necessaries are quite public and open, and the ordure is continually removing from them, which occasions a stench in almost every place one approaches.

They have no wheel-carriages for travelling on a better construction than that of a higler's cart; the best are set upon four clumsy wheels, and drawn by five horses or mules, two abreast in the shafts and three leaders abreast before them. They are without springs, consequently very uneasy. The saddles, bridles and accoutrements of their horses are inelegant and ill-contrived, much heavier than is requisite, and equally inconvenient to the beast and his rider. Although so much prejudiced in favour of their own customs and fashions they could not, after some time, withstand the superiority of ours in a variety of instances. The lightness, neatness, and commodiousness of my post-chaise, in which I travelled to Jehol, they were quite delighted with; but the fearlessness and celerity and safety with which my postilions drove it along almost petrified them with astonishment. The elegance and finishing of our saddles and other parts of horse-furniture particularly struck the Tartars, some of whom I think are likely to adopt them by degrees.

Our knives and forks, spoons, and a thousand little trifles of personal conveniency were singularly acceptable to everybody, and will probably become soon of considerable demand, although the government is certainly averse to all novelties, and wishes to discountenance a taste for any foreign article that is not absolutely necessary; but luxury is stronger than law, and it is the prerogative of wealth to draw from abroad what it can't find at home. One great advantage indeed of the embassy is the opportunity it afforded of showing the Chinese to what a high degree of perfection the English nation had carried all the arts and accomplishments of civilized life; that their manners were calculated for the improvement of social intercourse and liberal commerce; that though great and powerful they were generous and humane, not fierce and impetuous like the Russians, but entitled to the respect and preference of the Chinese above the other European nations, whom they have any knowledge of. This favourable impression of us may be confirmed and improved in them by a continuance of our own attention and cautious conduct. The restriction and discipline of our seamen at Canton are among the proper regulations for this purpose, not to mention some other arrangements that will naturally be made there, in consequence of the ground we now stand upon.

The common people of China are a strong hardy race, patient, industrious, and much given to traffic and all the arts of gain; cheerful and loquacious under the severest labour, and by no means that sedate, tranquil people they have been represented. In their joint efforts and exertions they work with incessant vociferation, often angrily scold one another, and seem ready to proceed to blows, but scarcely ever come to that extremity. The inevitable severity of the law restrains them, for the loss of a life is always punished by the death of the offender, even though he acted merely in self-defence, and without any malice prepense.

Superstitious and suspicious in their temper they at first appeared shy and apprehensive of us, being full of prejudices against strangers, of whose cunning and ferocity a thousand ridiculous tales had been propagated, and perhaps industriously encouraged by the government, whose political system seems to be to endeavour to persuade the people that they are themselves already perfect and can therefore learn nothing from others; but it is to little purpose. A nation that does not advance must retrograde, and finally fall back to barbarism and misery.

A Chinese boy who was appointed to wait upon young George Staunton would not for a long time trust himself to sleep in the house with our European servants, being afraid, he said, that they would eat him. The Chinese, however, at all the seaports where we touched were quite free from these foolish notions; and I flatter myself that the Embassy will have effectually removed them in all the provinces which it passed through.

The lower sort most heartily detest the Mandarins and persons in authority, whose arbitrary power of punishing, oppressing and insulting them they fear, whose injustice they feel, and whose rapacity they must feed. The Mandarins themselves are equally at the mercy of their superiors, the Ministers and Grand Secretaries of the Court, and are punishable by confiscation, and even by death, not only for their own offences, but for what others may do amiss within their department. They are responsible for whatever happens in the place where their authority extends; accident is construed into intention, and unavoidable error into wilful neglect. But this is not all, for the penalty is often inflicted on the offender's whole family, as well as on the offender himself. The Ministers and Grand Secretaries too are liable to any indignity which the caprice of the Emperor may chance to dictate. The bamboo is one of the grand instruments of discipline from which no rank or elevation is exempt or secure. The Emperor's nearest relations, even his own sons, are subject to it, and there are two of them now living upon whom it is well known to have been inflicted. But this is an argument of obedience which will probably one day refute itself.

Although the Emperor, as the father of his people, affects and professes impartiality, and wishes to have it understood that he makes no distinction between Tartars and Chinese, neither Tartars nor Chinese are imposed upon by the pretence. The care taken to preserve the Manchu language among all the Tartars settled in China forms one unequivocal line of demarcation, exclusive of the others which I have occasionally taken notice of in these sheets. After a short residence in the country, I found no difficulty in distinguishing a Tartar from a Chinese, although their mode of dress and forms of behaviour are precisely the same, but there was always something (I know not well how to describe it, *quod sentio tantum*) that indicated the difference in a moment.

In any attempt at a general sketch of the manners and character of a nation, candour and experience will naturally suggest a number of exceptions, and Christian charity will make large allowances. The composition of mankind, in all countries, is a mixture of the same materials, though blended in different proportions; but there is usually one particular essential ingredient that pervades and leavens the whole mass, as from a predominating feature results the general cast of the countenance. If therefore the majority of the people, whom I have been describing, should be less perfect than might be wished, it is not very difficult to conjecture the cause. The Tartars perhaps imagine that their own selfish government derives a good deal of its vigour even from the unwholesome state of the juices in the body of the nation; and as a healthy constitution might be the consequence of a proper fermentation of them, the interested physician, who wishes to keep the patient as long as possible under his hands, will be in no haste to cure a disease whose duration he thinks may be long protracted without becoming fatal. The fault therefore is less in the people than in those who have the care of them.

If among others with whom we were conversant we met with a few superior characters the merit is entirely their own and to themselves, not to education or example, they chiefly owe those virtues and good qualities by which we distinguished them. For notwithstanding the high-flown eulogiums to be found in books of Chinese morality, it is in general of a very flimsy texture and little understood. The tincture is more relished than the essence; the frame is more looked at than the picture; the parade of duty almost stifles duty itself.

It so happened that of our four principal connections, the Grand Secretary

Sung-yun, the Viceroy Ch'ang-lin, and our constant companions Wang and Chou, two were Tartars and two were Chinese; and although their respective nationalities could not escape us, yet they seemed perfectly united in their friendly and honourable conduct towards us, and made us therefore the more regret our ill fortune in having known so few others that resembled them.

As my knowledge of the female world in China was very limited, I have little to say upon the subject, but it may not be improper to say that little. The women of the lower sort are much weather-beaten, and by no means handsome. Beauty is soon withered by early and frequent parturition, by hard labour and hard fare. They have however a smart air, which arises from their manner of tying up their hair on the crown of their heads, and interspersing it with flowers and other ornaments. In the neighbourhood of Pekin I met some ladies of the higher ranks in their carriages, who appeared to have fair complexions and delicate features. They were all painted, as indeed are many of the inferior classes.

There is no law to prohibit intermarriages between the Tartars and the Chinese, but they very seldom intermarry. The Manchu and Mongol Tartars chiefly marry together, and scarcely ever with any of the other Tartar tribes. The Manchus often give a large portion with their daughters; the reverse is the case among the Chinese, where the parent usually receives a consideration or handsome present from his son-in-law.

The Tartar ladies have hitherto kept their legs at liberty, and would never submit to the Chinese operation of crippling the feet, though it is said that many of their husbands were desirous of introducing it into their families. I made many inquiries relative to this strange practice, but with little satisfaction. Chou admitted that no very good reason could be given for it. Its being an ancient custom was the best he could assign, and he confessed that a religious adherence to ancient customs, without much investigation of their origin, was a principal feature in the Chinese character. He added, however, that it possibly might have taken its rise from oriental jealousy, which had always been ingenious in its contrivances for securing the ladies to their owners; and that certainly a good way of keeping them at home was to make it very troublesome and painful to them to gad abroad. The rendering useless and deformed one part of the human body that is connate with the rest is little less strange than the practice of totally cutting off another; and yet we express no disgust nor surprise at the operation of circumcision, which prevails among a large proportion of mankind, and the Italian opera has long reconciled us to the indecency of castration.

It is inconceivable from whence arises the dissatisfaction at our natural form that seems to be felt by the whole human species, from the politest nations of Europe to the most barbarous islanders of the South Seas. Boring the ears, painting the face, and dusting and plastering the hair with powder and grease are equally fashionable in London and Otaheite;[89] but this perverseness and disfiguration are not confined to ourselves, but extended by us to the inferior creation. A noble lord of my acquaintance in Ireland contrived to put out all the eyes of Argus and extinguish the brilliant plumage of his peacocks, and to propagate in their stead a breed of whites, greys and cream colours. The good

BOUND FEET

wives of Dorking have added a supernumerary claw to all the chickens of their hatching; and our jockeys, by their docks and crops, their fan-tails, short tails, and no tails at all, make their horses as little like what God made them as can possibly be imagined. We find beauty in defects and we create defects where we don't find them.

I by no means want to apologise for the Chinese custom of squeezing their womens' pettitoes into the shoes of an infant, which I think an infernal distortion. Yet so much are people subject to be warped and blinded by fashion, that every Chinese above the vulgar considers it as a female accomplishment not to be dispensed with. Nay, a reverend apostolic missionary at Pekin assured me that in love affairs the glimpse of a little fairy foot was to a Chinese a most powerful provocative. Perhaps we are not quite free from a little folly of the same kind ourselves. We have not yet indeed pushed it to the extreme the Chinese have done, yet are we such admirers of it, that what with tight shoes, high heels and ponderous buckles, if our ladies' feet are not crippled they are certainly very much contracted, and it is impossible to say where the abridgement will stop. It is not a great many years ago that in England thread-paper waists, steel stays, and tight lacing were in high fashion, and the ladies' shapes were so tapered down from the bosom to the hips that there was some danger of breaking off in the middle upon any exertion. No woman was thought worth having who measured above eighteen inches round at the girdle. At present a contrary mode prevails. Prior's comeliness of side is exploded, and protuberance is procured wherever it can be fitted.[90] The Chinese ladies, like other Asiatics, never alter the costume of their dress, and I suppose the gowns they now wear are much of the same cut as those of their great grandmothers on board of Noah's Ark; but though the habit is the same, they are a little more changeable and coquettish in the choice and disposition of their ornaments.

The shift is of silk netting, the waistcoat and drawers are usually of silk and trimmed or lined with furs in cold weather. Over all they wear a long satin robe made full and loose which is gracefully gathered round the waist and confined with a sash. These different members of their apparel are usually each of a different colour, and in the selecting and contrasting of them, their taste and fancy are chiefly displayed. They adorn and set off their hair with ribbons and flowers, with bodkins, and pearls, but wear neither powder nor pomatum, diamonds nor feathers. Many of the mysteries of an European toilet they have never heard of, though perfectly versed in all those of their own, to which they devote no small portion of their time. They have not yet been initiated in the secrets of captivation by false pretences and love-swindling, or of eking out a skeleton figure by a cork rump, a muslin bosom and a buckram stomacher; for though they reckon corpulence a beauty in a man, they think it a most palpable blemish in their own sex. They therefore pay particular attention to the slimness of their shape, and have the art of preserving it in all its ease and delicacy without effort or compression.

Though a Chinese has properly but one wife at the head of his family, the number of his concubines depends on his own opulence and discretion. So far

OBSERVATIONS

in this point Chinese and European manners seem pretty much alike, but they differ widely in another. The mistresses of a Chinese live in tolerable harmony together in the same house, and even under the authority of the wife, who adopts and educates their children, and these children inherit from the father equally with hers.

I have been the less reserved in what I have said upon this subject, because I was willing to convey an impartial idea of some things in China, which to our local vanity and prejudice appear monstrous or incredible. Nor was I sorry to have this opportunity of remarking how little right we have to despise and ridicule other nations on the mere account of their differing from us in little points of manners and dress, as we can very nearly match them with similar follies and absurdities of our own.

Religion

The project of an alliance between church and state does not seem to have entered into the contemplation of the politicians of China. Perhaps the pride of despotism disdained the support of religion, or the wisdom of government rendered the aid of superstition unnecessary. The Europeans who first visited the country were astonished to find a general toleration of religious worship and opinions prevail, and to observe lamas and bonzes, Parsees, Jews and Mahometans living together in peace, and believing as they pleased, without molestation; a state of society, as yet uncommon in Europe, and at that time little expected to be found in Asia. It is therefore not improbable that Christians would have enjoyed the same indulgence, had it not been for the rashness of their missionaries. The pious zeal of these good fathers outran their discretion, and they seemed desirous of anticipating the promised call of the Gentiles without patiently waiting for the day of the Lord. The jealousy of the state was naturally alarmed and measures were adopted to repress an innovation which, if not regulated, might soon become dangerous, but if it were found innocent, might be afterwards allowed. And now, notwithstanding the disturbances at different times occasioned by their apostolic labours, and the persecutions, as they are fond of terming them, which have raged against the Christians in China, they are neither forbidden nor restrained in the exercise of their religion at Pekin, where the steeples of Christian churches and the pinnacles of pagan pagodas are to be seen rising in the same city. They enjoy a perfect personal toleration, and are capable of holding offices in the state. Nothing more is required of them than not to interrupt the public tranquility by working at conversions, and fishing for proselytes. In these regulations they now apparently acquiesce, and conduct themselves, I believe, with much more prudence and circumspection than their predecessors, but they never lose sight of their vocation. They are silently but unceasingly raising recruits for the church, and adding to the number of the elect. Some few of their neophytes may perhaps be adult persons, but the greater part are foundlings saved by them from perishing, or children purchased from indigent parents. To aid them in their pious labours, they send some of the most promising of these youths to be educated in the Chinese community at Naples,[91] who at their return are usually commissioned into the distant provinces. Those of them whom I had occasion to know the best appeared to be persons of acute understandings, of gentle manners and sincere piety, zealous for the propagation of their faith, but possessing little energy or powers of persuasion.

Although it is affirmed that there are at present about one hundred and fifty thousand Christians in China, the number at the same time is confessed to be much smaller than it was a century or two ago; but I much question whether many of those, who were then called Christians, could fairly come under that description. The first evangelical adventurers there highly magnified their own merits, and the success of their labours. They indiscriminately honoured with the name of Christian every person whom they baptized, and the outward and visible sign was rated as equivalent to an inward conviction. And this, I believe, has been pretty much the real history of most of the other oriental missions, which we read such exaggerated accounts of in the *Lettres édifiantes* and other Jesuitical publications.[92] There appear to be indeed several unfavourable circumstances to the rapid growth of Christianity in China. It is attended with no worldly advantage to the professor, and a Chinese is more likely to be allured by an immediate though transitory benefit, than by a distant reversion, however valuable and lasting. The prohibition or restriction of sensual gratifications, in a despotic country where there are so few others, is difficult to be relished. Confession is repugnant to the close and suspicious character of the nation, and penance would but aggravate the misery of him whose inheritance is his labour and poverty his punishment. Against it also is the state of society in China, which excludes women from their proper share of influence and importance.* A religion like that of Mahomet can only be extended by violence and terror, for the natural stubbornness of men does not readily give way to novel impressions; but the mild spirit of the Gospel is only to be infused through the means of gentleness, persuasion, and imperceptible perseverance. These are the proper instruments of conversion and peculiarly belong to the fair sex whose eloquence, on such occasions, gives charms to devotion and ornaments to truth. The earliest stages of Christianity received no small support from female agency and example; and for what show of religion still appears in our churches, we are surely not a little indebted to the piety and attendance of the women.

The missionaries at Pekin, with the exception of one or two of the youngest, appear perfectly reconciled to their situation, and to live as contentedly and

* A religion which requires that women should at stated times communicate to priests in private their thoughts and actions, must be particularly disgusting to a Chinese husband, who had not himself been suffered to see his wife till the day of his marriage, and who but seldom suffers her afterwards to see even her near relations of another sex.

OBSERVATIONS

happily as they probably would do in any other place. Among them the Italians and French are best informed, the most learned, and the most liberal in their sentiments; but their coadjutors the Portuguese still retain a considerable share of ancient bigotry and rancour. They all wear the Chinese dress, acquire the language of the country, and in outward appearance are scarcely to be distinguished from the other inhabitants.

I come now to speak of the profane religions that are current in China. As far as I could observe none of them have much influence on the conduct of those who profess them; whatever difference may be in the dogma, the morality is pretty nearly the same, and the practice of the same social duties approved and recommended. But men's virtues do not always depend on their theological notions, and the sinners of one sect are, I believe, seldom less numerous than those of another.

There is properly no established religion in China, none to which any monopoly of particular privileges is attached, none that excludes the professors of another from office and command. The employments of the state are open to all subjects, whether they pray in a *miao* or a pagoda. Of those deputed by the Emperor to attend my Embassy, the legate followed the doctrine of the lamas, Wang was a disciple of the bonzes, and Chou a Confucianist, and all three were joined together in the same commission.

The Tartars for the most part profess the court religion which is the worship of Fo-hi, according to the doctrine and discipline of the grand Dalai Lama, the pope or patriarch of Lhasa in Tibet, of whom so many fables have been related and credited in Europe. By the most correct accounts he is a kind of ecclesiastical sovereign, under the direction of a regency, whose dominions are in themselves very considerable, but whose spiritual jurisdiction stretches from the shores of the Caspian to the sea of Kamchatka, and from the mountains of Bhutan to the frozen Ocean, an extent of belief not inferior to that of Islamism or Christianity, and hitherto as prosperous as either. The Emperor Ch'ien-lung, as I have observed in my journal, is not only firmly persuaded of the truth of this religion, but from the unexampled success of all his undertakings during a fifty years' reign, seriously entertains an idea that his progenitor, the great Fo-hi himself, has condescended to become incarnate in his person, and actually at this moment to animate his imperial body.*

However wild and extravagant such a conceit may be regarded, we know from history how much even the best understandings may be perverted by prosperity, and that human nature, not satisfied with the good things of this world, sometimes wishes to anticipate the condition and felicity of the next. If Alexander scorned to have less than Jupiter Ammon for his father, if many Roman emperors extorted altars and sacrifices in their life-time, if even in the reign of Queen Elizabeth an English nobleman encouraged the belief of his descent from a swan, and was complimented in a dedication† upon his feathered pedigree, a similar infatuation may be the less inexcusable in Ch'ien-lung, a monarch,

* [See note 7.—Ed.]
† See note relative to Stafford, Duke of Buckingham, in Shakespeare's *Henry VIII*.

the length and happiness of whose reign, the unlimited obedience of whose incalculable subjects, and the health and vigour of whose body have hitherto kept out of his view most of those circumstances that are apt to remind other men of their misery and mortality. At all events, he is a most scrupulous practitioner of every form of the Lama religion, and the numerous and superb convents and temples, which he has erected at Jehol, the first in the world for costliness and grandeur, are incontestible evidences of the sincerity of his faith and the fervour of his piety. The mass of the people in China are gross idolators, and also worship a deity by the name of Fo or Fo-hi;* but he is understood to be a different deity from the Fo-hi of the Court, although he is reported to have come from the westward, as well as his namesake, and to have preached his revelation at a very remote period of time, long before the Christian era. The *miaos* or temples dedicated to this mode of religion, and the confraternities of bonzes and bonzesses who administer it, are prodigiously numerous in all parts of China. The vulgar, as elsewhere, are in general excessively superstitious. They are strict observers of lucky and unlucky days, and many of them, like their betters, are dabblers in chiromancy,† divination and astrology. In the course of my journal I have had occasion to notice the striking resemblance between the trumpery of Chinese worship and the apparatus of the Church of Rome. In several of the *miaos* and pagodas there is a recess or alcove carefully concealed by a close curtain, the removal of which discovers the image of a beautiful woman with a crown upon her head, surrounded by a glory, and two little boys sitting at her feet; the whole seeming like a parody upon popery, or a typification of the Virgin Mary, our infant Saviour, and the young Evangelist St. John. The female figure is called the mother or parent of the gods,‡ and is therefore sometimes represented with a number of arms branching from her shoulders, each furnished with some characteristical emblem, a sword, a spear, a sickle, a sheaf of corn, etc. A thousand legends are related and implicitly believed of this lady and her children, which are said to originate in very high antiquity, probably coeval with the Cybele of the Greeks and the Isis of Egypt. Nevertheless among all these absurdities and contradictions the Chinese, like the Indians, have a confused idea of a unity in the Godhead, and both equally pretend that though Fo-hi and Brahma are supposed to split themselves into a number of divinities, who are called the god of the Sea, the god of the Mountain, the goddess of Pleasure, the goddess of Plenty, etc., yet that these are merely parts or emanations of one only supreme God over all, whose providence divides itself into separate functions for the better government and instruction of this sublunary world.

The higher ranks of the Chinese and those of good education are many of them what in England we courteously call free thinkers and philosophers, the rest are mostly disciples of Confucius, of whom there are two sects. The one consider their founder to have been a man of great wisdom and charity, endowed with talents and virtues much superior to the age he lived in. They venerate his name, sing his praises at their feasts and drink bumpers to his memory, in

* [See note 7.—Ed.]   † [Palmistry.—Ed.]   ‡ [? Kuan-yin.—Ed.]

the same manner as the Whigs of Ireland do in honour of the glorious King William. But among the other Confucianists this grateful recollection has degenerated into a corrupt superstition; the toast has changed into a libation, and what originally expressed a tribute to deceased merit is become a mixture of sanctified ceremony and convivial abuse. Even here the perversion did not stop. Sacrifices were added, and sheep and oxen are now immolated to the manes of Confucius. These rites are celebrated at stated times and every person who presents the offering acts as hierophant himself, for this sect of enthusiasts, like the Quakers among ourselves, has always kept clear of an exclusive priesthood.

Although I have only mentioned the religions most prevalent, I must not omit that several Jews and Mahometans are to be found in China; but their number is not considerable, and they are melting fast into the common mass. I have been told that the Arabs or Mussulmans came into the country at a period so early as the ninth century. The Jews can boast of a much higher origin, and are pretended to be a remnant of the captivity. I have particularly noticed the case of these nations, in order to show that the Chinese are not intolerant of any religion, from which no danger is apprehended, and to disprove a common opinion prevalent in Europe that, by the ancient laws of the empire, foreigners were not allowed to settle there. This notion was originally insinuated by the Jesuits, with an exception as to themselves, and more particularly disseminated by the Portuguese, but it is in a great measure erroneous. The fundamental caution and circumspection of the government, which is awake to the slightest alarm, and perhaps not groundlessly jealous of European enterprise, naturally keep them on their guard, and prevent them from being quite so prone to encourage strangers as many other nations are. The immense population of the country renders such recruits unnecessary, but I do not find that their policy in this respect goes beyond its mark.

Lay Europeans, as well as missionaries, assuming the dress and manners of the Chinese, and desirous of entering into the Emperor's service at Pekin, would I believe be received and naturalized without much difficulty. They might establish and propagate themselves there like Jews and Mahometans, and be christened or circumcised as they liked, without any notice of such practices by the magistrates or any malediction of their neighbours. I saw nothing at Canton to hinder any Englishman, who would wear the Chinese habit and speak the Chinese language, from becoming a Chinese if he chose it, and of becoming even a Hong merchant if possessed of money and address. It is true, he could not easily quit the country and return home without a particular permission. Several missionaries however have found means of procuring it, and are now actually resident in Europe. But whilst we are startled with such difficulties in China, how can we forget that at this hour no person whatever can depart from Russia without a formal passport from the Chancery? An attempt to escape from such a restriction would be highly criminal and incur a most rigorous punishment. Every foreigner whatsoever, even the most respectable English merchant at St. Petersburg, is subject to this regulation, as much as the meanest peasant in the empire.

The missionaries remaining at Pekin are considered upon the same footing as, or perhaps in some respects a better than the other subjects of their rank in the immediate service of the Court. Some of them have been honoured by the Sovereign with particular marks of distinction and favour; and if the indispensable celibacy of their order had not prevented them from contracting matrimonial engagements in China, we might possibly have now found several of their posterity possessing high offices, and yet retaining their religion. It was formerly a part of their institution to keep at a distance as much as they could, all Europeans who were not closely connected with, or entirely dependent upon the missions; and the Portuguese Jesuits who remain alive still adhere to this maxim. But since the abolition of their Society* a great change has taken place in the sentiments and policy of the other missionaries, and, I believe, most of them are now of opinion that an unqualified admission of Europeans into China would be rather favourable to their interests than prejudicial to their views.

I should not have omitted that the different missions possess, beside their churches and communities, several shops and houses in the city of Pekin, which they let out to the Chinese, and receive a handsome rent from them. They have also villas and vineyards in the country to retire to for health and devotion. The French Jesuits formerly had a very large estate there, but it was dissipated on the dissolution of their Society, and only a very small part of it now remains in the hands of the order of St. Lazarus.† The revenue of the two Portuguese seminaries at Pekin amounts to 12,000 taels, or £4,000 a year. That of the Congregation de Propaganda Fide is very trifling, and the deficiencies are chiefly supplied from Rome. The French Missions Etrangères, which are a distinct body from the Lazarists, and have their particular establishment in China, were maintained by their superiors at Paris before the late subversion,‡ but since that event they are in a most deplorable situation.

In treating of the religions of the Chinese I should have mentioned the Taoists who are the most ancient of all the superstitions, being as is pretended, some thousand years antecedent to the revelation of Fo. But as they are not at present very numerous it was the less necessary to be particular on their subject. For the same reason I have not noticed the various subdivisions of the other religions, which are from time to time branching into new sects and fraternities, like the Methodists, Seceders, Swedenburghers, Moravians, and Muggletonians in England.[93]

* [The Society of Jesus was disbanded by order of Pope Clement XIV in 1773.—Ed.]
† [i.e. the Lazarists.—Ed.]
‡ [The French Revolution, which broke out in 1789.—Ed.]

OBSERVATIONS

Government

The ancient constitution of China differed essentially from the present. Although the Emperor was styled despotic, and decorated with all the titles and epithets of oriental hyperbole, the power and administration of the state resided in the great councils or tribunals, whose functions were not to be violated or disturbed by court intrigue or ministerial caprice. It was a government by law, and when attempts were made by their princes to render it otherwise, as often happened, rebellion was the consequence and expulsion the penalty. Hence according to history the regular succession of the crown was broken through, new sovereigns elected, and the former constitution restored. The present family on the throne is the twenty-second distinct dynasty whose hands have swayed the sceptre of China. The government as it now stands is properly the tyranny of a handful of Tartars over more than three hundred millions of Chinese.

An uninterrupted succession of four Emperors, all endowed with excellent understandings, uncommon vigour of mind and decision of character, has hitherto obviated the danger of such an enormous disproportion, and not only maintained itself on the throne, but enlarged its dominions to a prodigious extent.[94]

Various causes have contributed to this wonderful phenomenon in the political world. When the Tartars entered China a century and a half ago, the country had long languished under a weak administration, had been desolated by civil wars and rebellions, and was then disputed by several unworthy competitors. The Tartars availing themselves of these circumstances, at first took part as auxiliaries in favour of one of the candidates but they soon became principals, and at last by valour and perseverance surmounted every obstacle to their own establishment. The spirit of the Chinese was now effectually subdued by the weight of calamity; they were wearied with contending for the mere choice of tyrants among themselves, and the less reluctantly submitted to a foreign usurpation. The conquerors, however terrible in arms and ferocious in their manners, were conducted by a leader of a calm judgment as well as of a resolute mind, who tempered the despotism he introduced with so much prudence and policy that it seemed preferable to the other evils which they had so recently groaned under. A state of tranquil subjection succeeded for some time to the turbulence and horrors of a doubtful hostility; the government, though absolute, was at least methodical and regular. It menaced but did not injure; the blow might be dreaded, but it seldom was felt.

Chinese preceptors of the highest reputation for learning and virtue were appointed to conduct the education and instruction of the young Tartar princes, from whom were to spring the future sovereigns of the empire. The Chinese language was preserved as the language of the state, the highest veneration was affected for the ancient institutes and laws; the established forms of office and pageantry of administration were retained, and the external manners and deportment of the vanquished were assumed by the victors. All these contributed at first to impose upon the people, and to reconcile many of them to the new government. From hence has arisen a vulgar mistake that the Tartars had indiscriminately and sincerely adopted all the maxims, principles and customs of the Chinese, and that the two nations were now perfectly amalgamated and incorporated together. So far as respects the habits and head-dress they are certainly assimilated; but it is not the Tartar who has conformed to the Chinese costume, but the Chinese who has been obliged to imitate the Tartar. The nature and character of each continues unchanged, and their different situations and intrinsic sentiments cannot be concealed under any disguise. Superiority animates the one, depression is felt by the other. Most of our books confound them together, and talk of them as if they made only one nation under the general name of China; but whatever might be concluded from any outward appearances, the real distinction is never forgotten by the sovereign who, though he pretends to be perfectly impartial, conducts himself at bottom by a systematic nationality, and never for a moment loses sight of the cradle of his power. The science of government in the Eastern world is understood by those who govern very differently from what it is in the Western. When the succession of a contested kingdom in Europe is once ascertained, whether by violence or compromise, the nation returns to its pristine regularity and composure. It matters little whether a Bourbon or an Austrian fills the throne of Naples or of Spain, because the sovereign, whoever he be, then becomes to all intents and purposes a Spaniard or Neapolitan, and his descendants continue so with accelerated velocity. George the First and George the Second ceased to be foreigners from the moment our sceptre was fixed in their hands. His present Majesty is as much an Englishman as King Alfred or King Edgar, and governs his people not by Teutonic but by English laws. The policy of Asia is totally opposite. There the prince regards the place of his nativity as an accident of mere indifference. If the parent-root be good, he thinks it will flourish in every soil and perhaps acquire fresh vigour from transplantation. It is not locality, but his own cast and family; it is not the country where he drew his breath, but the blood from which he sprung; it is not the scenery of the theatre, but the spirit of the drama that engages his attention and occupies his thoughts. A series of two hundred years in the succession of eight or ten monarchs did not change the Mogul into a Hindu, nor has a century and a half made Ch'ien-lung a Chinese. He remains at this hour, in all his maxims of policy, as true a Tartar as any of his ancestors.

The Viceroys of the provinces, the commanders of the armies, the great officers of state are almost all Tartars. The detail of business indeed, and the laborious departments are chiefly carried on by the Chinese, as being more regularly educated, more learned and more patient than the Tartars, who in general have a different turn, and prefer active military duty to tranquil or sedentary occupations. In all the tribunals of justice and finance, in all the courts of civil or military administration, an equal number of Tartar assessors is indispensably necessary to be present, in order to watch over and control the others. A Chinese

OBSERVATIONS

may preside at the Board,* and pronounce the opinion, but the prompter and manager is a Tartar who directs and governs the performers. These regulations and precautions sufficiently disclose the sovereign's real opinion of his tenure of the empire, and how little he depends upon the affections and loyalty of his Chinese subjects. The government of China, as now instituted, may not inaptly be compared to Astley's amphitheatre,† where a single jockey rides a number of horses at once, who are so nicely bitted and dressed that he can impel them with a whisper, or stop them with a hair. But at the same time he knows the consequence of mismanagement or neglect, and that if they are not properly matched, curried and fed, patted and stroked, some of them will be liable to run out of the circle, to kick at their keepers and refuse to be mounted any longer. Considering then all circumstances, the original defect of title to the inheritance, the incessant anxiety of forcible possession, the odium of a foreign yoke, the inevitable combats of passion in a sovereign's breast, when deceived by artifice, betrayed by perfidy, or provoked by rebellion, the doubtful and intricate boundaries of reward and punishment, where vigour and indulgence may be equally misapplied, the almost incalculable population, the immense extent of dominion, the personal exertions requisite in war, and the no less difficult talents of administration in peace—considering, I say, all these circumstances, the government of such an empire must be a task of inconceivable vigilance and toil; and yet it is a task that has hitherto been performed with wonderful ability and unparalleled success. That such singular skill in the art of reigning should have been uninterruptedly transmitted through a succession of four princes for upwards of a century and a half would be very difficult to account for, if we did not constantly bear in mind a fundamental principle of the state. All power and authority in China derive solely from the sovereign, and they are not only distributed by him in his life time, but attest their origin after his decease. The appointment of his successor is exclusively vested in him. Without regard to primogeniture, without the fondness of a parent, without the partiality of a friend, he acts on this occasion as the father of the state, and selects the person of his family, whom he judges the most worthy to replace him. Every choice of this kind as yet made has been unexceptionably fortunate. K'ang-hsi proved as great a prince as his father; Yung-cheng was inferior to neither, and Ch'ien-lung surpasses the glory of all his predecessors. Who is the Atlas destined by him to bear this load of empire when he dies is yet unknown, but on whatever shoulders it may fall, another transmigration of Fo-hi into the next emperor will be necessary to enable him to sustain it on its present balance; for though within the serene atmosphere of the Court everything wears the face of happiness and applause, yet it cannot be concealed that the nation in general is far from being easy or contented. The frequent insurrections in the distant provinces are unambiguous oracles of the real sentiments and temper of the people. The predominance of the Tartars and the Emperor's partiality to them are the common subject of conversation among the Chinese whenever

* [See note 32.—Ed.]   † [See note 45.—Ed.]

they meet together in private, and the constant theme of their discourse. There are certain mysterious societies in every province who are known to be disaffected, and although narrowly watched by the government, they find means to elude its vigilance and often to hold secret assemblies, where they revive the memory of ancient glory and independence, brood over recent injuries, and meditate revenge.*

Though much circumscribed in the course of our travels we had opportunities of observation seldom afforded to others, and not neglected by us. The genuine character of the inhabitants, and the effects resulting from the refined polity and principles of the government, which are meant to restrain and direct them, naturally claimed my particular attention and inquiry. In my researches I often perceived the ground to be hollow under a vast superstructure, and in trees of the most stately and flourishing appearance I discovered symptoms of speedy decay, whilst humbler plants were held by vigorous roots, and mean edifices rested on steady foundations. The Chinese are now recovering from the blows that had stunned them; they are awaking from the political stupor they had been thrown into by the Tartar impression, and begin to feel their native energies revive. A slight collision might elicit fire from the flint, and spread flames of revolt from one extremity of China to the other. In fact the volume of the empire is now grown too ponderous and disproportionate to be easily grasped by a single hand, be it ever so capacious and strong. It is possible, notwithstanding, that the momentum impressed on the machine by the vigour and wisdom of the present Emperor may keep it steady and entire in its orbit for a considerable time longer; but I should not be surprised if its dislocation or dismemberment were to take place before my own dissolution.† Whenever such an event happens, it will probably be attended with all the horrors and atrocities from which they were delivered by the Tartar domination; but men are apt to lose the memory of former evils under the pressure of immediate suffering; and what can be expected from those who are corrupted by servitude, exasperated by despotism and maddened by despair? Their condition, however, might then become still worse than it can be at present. Like the slave who fled into the desert from his chains and was devoured by the lion, they may draw down upon themselves oppression and destruction by their very effort to avoid them, may be poisoned by their own remedies and be buried themselves in the graves which they dug for others. A sudden transition from slavery to freedom, from dependence to authority, can seldom be borne with moderation or discretion. Every change in the state of man ought to be gentle and gradual, otherwise it is commonly dangerous to himself and intolerable to others. A due preparation may be as necessary for liberty as for inoculation of the smallpox which, like liberty, is future health but without due preparation is almost certain destruction.‡ Thus then the Chinese, if not led to emancipation by degrees, but let

* [See note 65.—Ed.]
† [Macartney died in 1806. The last Manchu Emperor abdicated on 12 February 1912.—Ed.]
‡ [A topical reference. See note 143—Ed.]

loose on a burst of enthusiasm would probably fall into all the excesses of folly, suffer all the paroxysms of madness, and be found as unfit for the enjoyment of freedom as the French and the negroes.

Justice

In the ancient accounts of China, the administration of its justice, the strict impartiality observed in rewarding desert and in inflicting punishments, the equal security afforded to all men by the laws, are mentioned in such high strains of eulogy, that we are tempted to suppose this was the spot where the last footsteps of Astraea* were imprinted. So long a period has elapsed since that time that the marks are a good deal effaced, and seem to be wearing out every day. This is the natural consequence of a convulsion in the ancient government, and particularly of the last grand revolution, when it could scarcely be expected that the balance of justice should be held with an equal hand between the conquerors and the conquered. It is, however, pretended by many that little or no alteration has been made; the common modes of procedure are continued, the usual formality in the pleadings is observed, and the same solemnity of decision is practised as before; but the consumption of the body cannot be concealed by the fullness of the robe.

My friend Chou (who as civil governor of a city of the first rank on which several others are dependent, has a very extensive judicial range and jurisdiction)† endeavoured to impress me with an idea of the equity and regularity of the courts where he presided, and as I entertain a very favourable opinion of him, I dare say that few of the others are better ordered or more pure; but it escaped from him in conversation that considerable presents were often made by the suitor to the judge. I took this occasion of explaining to him as well as I could the nature and principles of our jurisprudence and establishments, which placed the dispensers of justice above temptation by the magnitude of their salaries, and therefore rendered the acceptance of presents as unnecessary as improper. To this he answered that the circumstance of presents in China ought not to be misinterpreted, and that the offering and receiving them formed a part of their ceremonies, and were an established usage from which no mischief was to be feared. He seemed so much prejudiced in favour of the manners of his country in this instance, and so little aware of what they must lead to, that he further informed me that the presents on these occasions were always proportioned to the opulence of the donors, and to the rank of the persons to whom they were made; and when I expressed my suspicion that a poor man who had little to give, must run a bad chance in a law-suit with a rich man who had much, he assured me that perquisites of office (as these things are considered)

* [Astraea was the goddess of justice in Roman mythology.—Ed.]
† [See p. 328.—Ed.]

had seldom any influence of the determination of a cause. Perhaps he did not wish to deceive me, for there are some favourite points on which men are often apt to deceive themselves. But allowing his own particular conduct to be as unexceptionable as he meant me to believe it, yet I have strong ground to suspect the general course of justice to be very much otherwise, and that this practice of presents, sanctioned as it is by usage and authority, is perverted to the worst purpose and grown into an intolerable abuse. A missionary indeed, in talking to me once upon this subject, seemed to apologize for the Chinese by saying that they give and receive these presents rather from custom and fashion than from bad motives, and that if they are corrupt, they are so without being aware of it. The true meaning of all which is that, through an appearance of decency and gravity of proceeding, justice wears a double face, and that integrity is professed though bribery be allowed. Another person, who had still better opportunities of knowing these matters, made no scruple of dashing out to me that money was well known to be the great instrument of decision in their courts which generally found reason in the bottom of the longest purse. But the influence of preliminary presents is supposed to prevail also in the other departments. No introduction can be obtained, no business effected without it. A refusal would be considered by the suitor as an unequivocal mark of hostility. This infamous system is universal among the Orientals, and is, I conceive, a principal cause of their decay and subversion. All the other great monarchies of the east, which we are acquainted with, have been overturned by it, one after another, and it will probably some day have its share in the catastrophe of China. In the criminal department capital punishment is not so comprehensive as with us.[95] Fine and imprisonment, flagellation and exile are the usual inflictions, except in cases of blood, which admit of no pardon or commutation.

There are six modes of capital punishment.

1st Cutting into ten thousand pieces.
2nd Cutting into eight pieces, or what is called double quartering, both of which operations are performed upon the living subject.
3rd Beheading.
4th Strangling, which is the least infamous of all, but excessively barbarous, the patient being nine times drawn up and let down, the cord nine times restricted and relaxed, before the final suffocation.
5th Burning with green faggots.
6th Beating to death with cudgels.

The Sheriff's calendar is said to be usually very large; but there is a general gaol delivery once in every year at which the prisoners are either punished or released, unless where particular circumstances require a longer detention.

I had been informed that a delinquent was sometimes allowed, when sentenced to be bambooed, to hire another person to undergo the punishment in his place, but the fact was strongly denied. Neither did I find it now to be true, though possibly it may have been so in former times, that a son might substitute himself for his father's punishment.

OBSERVATIONS

The order and administration of the gaols are said to be remarkably good; the debtor and the felon are confined in separate places and not permitted to approach each other. This is an excellent regulation; it seems equally impolitic and immoral to associate guilt with imprudence, and confound wickedness and misfortune by promiscuous imprisonment. By the laws of China the case of a debtor is, in other respects, extremely cruel. Although he should resign every farthing of his property, yet if it be insufficient to discharge the whole of his debt, and his relations cannot or will not make up the deficiency, he is condemned to wear a neck yoke in public for a certain period. If his insolvency be incurred by gaming, he is liable besides to a corporal punishment.

A man may sell himself in some cases, as for instance to discharge a debt to the crown, or to procure money for enabling him to bury his father, but if he behaves himself well during his servitude, he is entitled to his liberty at the end of twenty years, if otherwise, he continues a slave for life, and his children also if he had included them in the original agreement. The Emperor's debtors, if fraudulently such, are strangled; if such only by common misfortunes, their wives and children and property of every kind are sold, and themselves banished into the wilds of Tartary. Oaths are not required in civil or criminal causes; if voluntarily offered they are always suspected; and yet, what is singular, the torture is sometimes used in both to procure evidence and confession.

It is not invariably, though generally, true that all sentences of death are signed by the Emperor. There have of late been several occasions where the first magistrate has taken upon himself to execute criminals upon the spot for treason, rebellion, atrocious murder, etc. He takes his chance for approbation and usually obtains it.

Property

As in China the interests of the Emperor are always the first consideration, no property can be secured against his claims. In cases of delinquency, confiscation is inevitable.

Entails are unknown and a man may dispose of his fortune, real and personal, in the manner most agreeable to himself. By law he may even devise it to the bonzes or other religious fraternities, but of late such bequests are very rare, for the policy of the state, although unwilling positively to prohibit any ancient right, however imprudently exercised, yet renders its abuse as little hurtful as possible, by quartering officers, travellers, couriers, and others upon most of the *miaos* and temples that are endowed in mortmain, so that posthumous folly is defeated, and idleness made to contribute to the maintenance of industry.

A testator often leaves his estates to his wife, especially in the case of the

MONEY MATTERS

minority of his children; but if a man dies without a will, his lands and personalty are equally divided among his sons, reserving a proper dower for the widow, which varies according to the province where she chooses to reside. The daughters have nothing but are maintained, till married, by their brothers and if there be no brothers, by their next inheriting relations.

There are many great landed estates in China, some even to the amount of £100,000 per annum, accumulated by various means, by legacies, by clandestine trade, that is to say, by trade carried on by inferior agents with the capitals of great men to whom trade is directly forbidden, by usury, by employments, by presents, etc. A widow at Tientsin, whose husband had been enriched in this manner, and who left her his fortune (his four sons being minors) not long since sent a million of taels of silver (£333,333 sterling) as a present to the Emperor towards the expense of the Tibet war.

The legal interest of money is twelve per cent, but it is commonly extended to eighteen and sometimes even to thirty-six. Usury is punishable by the laws but, as in most other countries, is rarely punished. Usury, like gaming, is a dishonourable mode of getting money, but by a sort of compact between necessity and avarice, between affluence and distress, the prosecution of a Jew or a sharper is considered as not very honourable even in those who suffer from them.

In farms (which are usually let for three, five or seven years, resumable by the landlord or relinquishable by the tenant at the end of any of those terms according to the contract) the owner divides the crop with the cultivator. The latter has one half entirely to himself, the former takes the other half and pays out of it the Emperor's tax, which is considered to be always the same, whether the season be plentiful or scanty. If, however, it prove to be very unusually bad, an abatement may be made upon due representation. Five per cent is said to be the Emperor's proper share of the valued crop, but the valuation (which is an arbitrary one of the crown officer) is generally fixed so much higher than the current price of produce, that the landlord's commutation with the Crown is sometimes not less than eight or ten per cent instead of five. Though twelve per cent be the legal interest, yet land sells for twenty years' purchase in the neighbourhood of Pekin.

The only current money in China is a thin brass or copper coin, about the breadth of a shilling, with a hole drilled through it for the purpose of being strung. A thousand of these pieces, which are called by us *sapecas*, are esteemed at a tael* or Chinese ounce of silver, and ten drachms or *chens* make a tael, or 6s. 8d. sterling.[96]

A measure of rice or other grain is taken as a pound or *chin* and ten measures or *chins* go to a *tou* or Chinese peck and so on. The Chinese mode of reckoning is all by decimals.

I here annex the prices current of several articles at Pekin, as I collected them from the best information I received on the spot.

* *Sapeca* and tael are the names introduced by the Portuguese, but the proper Chinese words are *li* and *liang*.

OBSERVATIONS

	Taels	Sapecas
A common horse	20 to 25	
An ox	15 to 20	
A cow	10 to 15	
A pound of beef		40
A pound of mutton		50
A pound of veal		45
A pound of pork		50
A pound of ham		80
A fowl		100
A duck		150
A goose		500
An egg		3
A pound of rice		24
A pound of flour		20
The complete dress of a peasant	2 or perhaps	2500
Ditto of a Mandarin of rank	20	
Ditto of an inferior Mandarin	8	
The complete robe of ceremony of a high Mandarin	100	
Ditto if enriched	1000	
A saddle and bridle	16 to 25	
A pair of black satin boots	2½	
Ditto of leather	2	
A cap or bonnet	2 to 4	
Tea		—
Salt per pound		35

A Chinese peasant can maintain himself for fifty *sapecas* a day. Our boatmen, who drew the yachts in the provinces which we passed through, generally were paid eighty *sapecas* a day, or one *sapeca* for each *li*, each *li* being equal to three hundred and sixty geometrical paces.

A common weaver, joiner or other tradesman earns little more than a bare subsistence, unless he should prove remarkably expert and ingenious, in which case he would be paid according to his abilities. It does not appear that there is always sufficient employment for the people, whose multitude is so great as to exceed the means of subsistence by labour, so that many who are able and willing to work are obliged to depend upon the alms of private charity, or seek for support in the public hospitals; and notwithstanding these resources it is affirmed that in every year vast numbers perish of hunger and cold. The summers are so warm that the common sort go almost naked, and the winter is so rigorous that the mortality is very great from the want of clothing and shelter. In the different provinces of the empire there are often partial famines, and whenever they are attended with very serious or fatal consequences the Mandarin of the district is punished, according to Chinese policy, for not having foreseen the calamity and replenished the magazine sufficiently to remedy the accident. From the misery to which a large proportion of the people are thus exposed (the majority is indeed very wretched in all respects) it is not to be wondered that they should lose every sense but that of self-preservation; that they should forget the other ties of nature, and sell their children without scruple if they find a chapman, and desert them without pity if they don't. This is the common reproach of strangers to the Chinese, but it should not be made with too much precipitation and severity, for I believe, where the parent has any possible means of supporting his offspring, there is no country where paternal affection is stronger than in China; and it is natural that it should be so, because there is no country where filial respect and gratitude are so strong.

Population

The population of China has been always considered by Europeans as much greater in proportion to its extent than the population of any other country. The printed accounts of it vary much. My friend Father Amiot's calculations, as given in Grosier's description of China,[97] seem not to have been well understood by the person who copied or digested them; for in one place he is made to say that the population in 1743 amounted to near 200 millions, exclusive of the province of Fukien; and in another place that in the same year it exceeded 280 millions. I wished to have had this difficulty reconciled, but the good father being in a dying condition when I was at Pekin, and consequently not well able to review his notes, I was disappointed of the correct information which I expected from that quarter. There is another table of the population in 1761 given by Grosier, where it is stated at upwards of 198 millions, and he tells us that it is founded on the best authority. Monsieur Pauw,[98] and some other writers of his turn have amused the public with their speculations upon China, and are disposed to undervalue everything that belongs to it, and particularly to dispute its populousness. On the other hand I have received an enumeration strongly asserted to be genuine, which assigns no less than 333 millions.

A foreigner, from an imperfect knowledge of the language, from misapprehension or misinterpretation, from want of access to public offices, or from the scantiness or inaccuracy of private information, is often liable to argue ignorantly and falsely, sometimes to take things for granted that should be denied, and sometimes to reject what ought to be received. Whatever, therefore, I may say upon this subject, is not meant to be delivered in a tone either of conviction or disbelief in myself, but solely for the disquisition and judgment of others.

China proper, exclusive of the Tartar dominions, contains about 831,000,000 acres, or about 1,298,000 square miles. France contains about 103,000,000 acres, or about 162,000 square miles. If China then be eight times as large as France, 333 millions are not so high a calculation as at first sight it would appear to be. Messieurs Moheau and Necker estimate the population of France at 26 millions and Dr. Price carries it beyond 28 millions. Supposing then the two countries to be equally populous in proportion to their extent, China should contain 216 millions, taking 27 millions as the medium between Dr. Price and the other two gentlemen. But having formerly travelled over the greatest part of France,

OBSERVATIONS

and resided a considerable time in that kingdom, when in its most flourishing state long before the late subversion, and having very lately travelled through China from its northern to its southern extremity, I should be inclined to say without hesitation, that China was twice as populous as France. Now the above account of 333 millions to 216 millions admits the population of China to be in proportion to that of France as to one and thirteen twenty-fourths to one, or only a third and a thirty-seventh greater than that of France.* In truth, the immense numbers which occurred in every part of China where I passed in the towns, the country, on the rivers, and the seas that wash its coasts, very far exceeded any idea that I had formed on the subject, especially as all the people who appeared (very few excepted, perhaps not 500 in all) were males. The state of the population, as marked in the table, was given to me by Chou, a Mandarin of high rank, and supreme governor of Tientsin, who was one of those appointed by the Emperor to attend my embassy from the moment of my arrival on the coast of Pei-chihli. He was a man of letters and information, and from habit and frequent converse contracted a strong friendship and affection for me. He nevertheless had all the vanity of a Chinese, and the more he was impressed with the manifest superiority of the Europeans, which he could not avoid being very sensible of in his long intercourse with us, the more was he disposed to exaggerate the grandeur of his country, its population and other circumstances of national fondness.

Table of the Population and Extent of China Proper, within the Great Wall

PROVINCES	POPULATION	SQUARE MILES	ACRES
Pei-chihli	38,000,000	58,949	37,727,360
Kiangnan (2 Provinces)†	32,000,000	92,961	59,495,040
Kiangsi	19,000,000	72,176	46,192,640
Chekiang	21,000,000	39,150	25,056,000
Fukien	15,000,000	53,480	34,227,200
Hupeh ⎫ Hukuang	14,000,000 ⎫	144,770	92,652,800
Hunan ⎭	13,000,000 ⎭		
Honan	25,000,000	65,104	41,666,560
Shantung	24,000,000	65,104	41,666,560
Shansi	27,000,000	55,268	35,371,520
Shensi	18,000,000 ⎫	154,008	98,565,120
Kansu	12,000,000 ⎭		
Szechwan	27,000,000	166,800	106,752,000
Kwangtung	21,000,000	79,456	50,851,840
Kwangsi	10,000,000	78,250	50,080,000
Yunnan	8,000,000	107,969	69,100,160
Kweichow	9,000,000	64,554	41,314,560
Total	333,000,000	1,297,999	830,719,360

* [In a footnote here Macartney does a complicated sum to show that for every twenty-four persons in France, China will have thirty-seven.—Ed.]
† [Kiangsu and Anhwei.—Ed.]

Thus have I given the table of population as I received it from Chou. How far it may be exact I have no means of ascertaining, but he assured me that I might depend upon it. When I expressed my doubts upon the subject he laughed, as if he thought it ridiculous to question a matter of such notoriety,[99] and added that it appears by an ancient authentic register of two hundred years old, that then above 57 millions of males from twenty to fifty years of age were assessed to the capitation, such being at that time the mode of levying the taxes, which was afterwards altered, and the whole burden laid upon the land. Since the accession of the present Emperor's family to the throne the influx of people from Tartary must have greatly increased the number of inhabitants.

The contents in square miles and acres, as given in the table above, are extracted from the Jesuits' map of China, undertaken and completed in the reign of K'ang-hsi by his special command.[100]

If one-fourth of the surface of China were to be deducted for roads, canals, marshes, mountains, and other uncultivable grounds, there would still remain 623,039,520 profitable acres, or one and nine-tenths acres to each individual, supposing the population to amount to 333 millions, or 337 persons to a square mile.

As to the population of Chinese Tartary, it was impossible to obtain any intelligence, the Chinese being almost as ignorant of that country as we are, scarcely any of them having ever seen it, except a few officers sent on military duty, and persons banished to it for crimes. The Chinese talk of Tartary as of a country half as big as the rest of the world besides, but their conceptions of its limits are very dark and confused. There is a wide difference between pretension and possession.

When I was the King's minister at St. Petersburg* the common idea prevalent at court there was that the Russian dominions comprehended one-twelfth part of the land upon the globe, and since that time they have been very considerably enlarged. Upon the whole I should think that the extent of the two empires of China and Russia is pretty nearly equal; and that the two together make one-sixth part of the land on the earth's surface, and about one twenty-third of the whole terraqueous globe.

Revenue

The revenues of this great empire are said to be little less than 200 millions of taels,† equal to £66,666,666 sterling, or about four times those of Great Britain, and three times those of France before the late subversion. They consist of

    1st The impost upon land.

---

* [1764–67. See Introduction, p. 17.—Ed.]

† I have given the revenue in round numbers, but the Chinese, who have a fanciful predilection for odd numbers call, it 199,999,999.

OBSERVATIONS

    2nd The gabelle upon salt.
    3rd The customs and other smaller taxes.

From the produce of these all the civil and military expenses and incidental and extraordinary charges are first paid on the spot out of the treasuries of the provinces where such expenses, etc., are incurred, and the remainder is remitted to the imperial treasury at Pekin. This surplus amounted in the year 1792 to the sum of 36,614,328 taels, or £12,204,776 sterling, according to the following account which I received from Chou.

Account of Revenue received into the Imperial Treasury at Pekin from the different Provinces of China Proper

PROVINCES		TAELS	TOTAL IN IN TAELS	MEASURES OF RICE AND OTHER GRAIN	POPULATION
Pei-chihli		2,520,000 land 437,000 salt 79,000 taxes	3,036,000	none	38,000,000
Kiangnan		5,200,000 land 2,100,000 salt 910,000 taxes	8,210,000	1,440,000	32,000,000
Kiangsi		1,900,000 land 220,000 taxes	2,120,000	795,000	19,000,000
Chekiang		3,100,000 land 520,000 salt 190,000 taxes	3,810,000	780,000	21,000,000
Fukien		1,110,000 land 87,000 salt 80,000 taxes	1,277,000	none	15,000,000
Hukuang	Hupeh	1,300,000 land 10,000 taxes	1,310,000	100,000	14,000,000
	Hunan	1,310,000 land 35,000 taxes	1,345,000	100,000	13,000,000
Honan		3,200,000 land 13,000 taxes	3,213,000	230,000	25,000,000
Shantung		3,440,000 land 130,000 salt 30,000 taxes	3,600,000	360,000	24,000,000
Shansi		3,100,000 land 510,000 salt 112,000 taxes	3,722,000	none	27,000,000
Shensi		1,660,000 land 40,000 taxes	1,700,000	none	18,000,000
Kiangsu		300,000 land 40,000 taxes	340,000	220,000	12,000,000
Szechwan		640,000 land 30,000 taxes	670,000	none	27,000,000

THE IMPERIAL TREASURY

Kwangtung	1,280,000 land } 50,000 salt } 10,000 taxes }	1,340,000	none	21,000,000
Kwangsi	420,000 land } 50,000 salt } 30,000 taxes }	500,000	none	10,000,000
Yunnan	210,000 land	210,000	220,000	8,000,000
Kweichow	120,000 land } 10,000 salt } 15,000 taxes }	145,000	none	9,000,000
	Total Taels	36,548,000	4,245,000	333,000,000

From the preceding table, the surplus revenue of 1792 received into the Emperor's treasury at Pekin, after all the public expenses are defrayed, will stand as follows:

Land, salt, and taxes   36,548,000 Taels or £12,182,666 sterling
4,245,000 measures of rice at 1¼d.
 per measure   66,328 ,, 22,109
         36,614,328 = £12,204,775 sterling

The ordinary military establishment I have calculated at 74,974,450 taels or £24,991,483,* and the civil establishment at 2,960,000 taels = £986,666,† which two sums being doubled for extraordinaries, and allowing 7,500,000 taels = £2,500,000 for unforeseen expense, and adding the Emperor's residue of 36,614,328 taels = £12,204,775 will give the sum of 199,983,228 taels = £66,661,076, or very nearly the total estimated revenue of China.

At Pekin are two treasuries, one called the State Treasury, into which the surplus above mentioned of 36,614,328 taels = £12,204,776 is paid, and out of which are issued all monies for the Emperor's expenses, his palaces, pagodas and other buildings, his stables, his gardens, wives, concubines, sons, grandsons and more distant princes of the blood, and the general charges of the Court. The other, called the Secret Treasury, receives the confiscations, the presents, the Tartar tributes, and some other articles, all which, together with the residue from the State Treasury, form what may properly be considered as the Emperor's privy purse. This is the regular course of business; but as the present government is entirely despotic, the Emperor may act according to his pleasure in revenue matters, as in all others; but it is said he has not been known to interrupt the usual administration. His treasures are supposed to be immense, arising solely from the regular unavoidable savings of the State Treasury and Secret Treasury, his revenue from thence very far exceeding his disbursements. The greater part is kept in Mukden, the capital of Manchu Tartary, for I doubt whether the Tartars yet think themselves secure at Pekin, considering the prodigious disproportion between them and the Chinese, and their mutual jealousy and antipathy. Scarcely a year passes without an insurrection in some of the

* Vide, head, Military.   † Vide, head, Civil.

OBSERVATIONS

distant provinces, and there are actually at present some very serious disturbances in Szechwan, to quell which Fu-k'ang-an (so often mentioned in my journal), who was formerly Viceroy of Canton, and afterwards commanded in Tibet on the frontier of Nepal, has been lately appointed.*

Having said above that the 36,614,328 taels = £12,204,775 remitted to the State Treasury of Pekin were the Emperor's share of the general revenue, after all expenses first paid, it would seem from thence as if it were liable to variation, and that in some years it might be more and in others less; but I have reason to imagine that it seldom, if ever, falls below that sum, because Sung-yun, who accompanied me from Pekin to Hangchowfu, informed me that whenever any extraordinary aids or supplies became necessary on occasion of wars and other occurrences, they were levied by additional taxes on the provinces adjacent to the scene of action; and upon this ground it was that he accounted for the increased duties on the commerce of Canton, which our merchants complained of. Those duties, he said, had been laid on towards the support of the war in Tongking, which province adjoins Canton, but that the war being finished, they would hereafter be reduced.

In the administration of so vast a revenue, especially in the distant provinces, those to whom it is entrusted have, no doubt, frequent opportunities of committing great abuses; and that they do not always neglect them is pretty evident from the immense confiscations accruing to the Emperor. It is indeed affirmed that much corruption and oppression prevail in most of the departments of the state. To what degree this may be true I know not, but admitting it in a very great extent, the subject in China may be considered as more favoured in point of taxation than the subjects of any other country, for if the whole revenue were to be reduced to a capitation, it would not amount to more than five shillings per head on the population of the empire. By an analogous computation the people of Ireland would pay to government eight shillings per head, the people of France (before the subversion) sixteen shillings per head, and the people of Great Britain thirty-four shillings per head.

With regard to the revenue which the Emperor of China draws from his Tartar dominions, I could not procure any information to be depended upon of its amount. Besides what he may receive from his demesnes there, the chiefs of the Tartar Banners and their vassals pay a certain tribute which is every day increasing, either because they are now more able, or because they are more willing to pay it than formerly.

Tartar goods, or goods imported into China by the way of Tartary, such as furs, leather, woollen cloth, etc., are liable only to a very moderate custom at the Great Wall on entry into China, but all China goods exported to Tartary pass duty free.

I observed in the beginning of this head of 'Revenue' that it consisted of three branches, first the land, second the salt, and third the smaller taxes. The first is levied according to a certain fixed rule upon the produce of the land (*vide* head, 'Property'); the second, or salt, is a monopoly, or exclusive privilege of

* [See note 65.—Ed.]

making that article, granted by the Emperor to particular persons, for which they pay to the crown a fixed proportion according to the local circumstances of the province where it is manufactured, one third being the rate settled in one district, one fourth in another, and so on. The third branch consists of certain taxes or customs upon goods passing over bridges, canals and roads, and entering into cities and walled towns; also on the sale of cattle, and some other minuter objects. In the collection of these revenues I understand that the subordinate officers have considerable fees and perquisites, for in China, as in some other countries, no business can be expedited through the lower departments without them.

Export and import duties ought regularly to be levied *ad valorem* of the articles, but the collector often takes upon himself arbitrarily to estimate the value according to his own fancy. Thus, for instance, I have heard he has been sometimes known at Canton to tax a bale of coarse cloth as highly as a bale of superfine; and that in weighing off raw silk at the custom-house beam he has called 120 lb. a picul, levied the duty accordingly, and discharged the scale, although a picul be really $133\frac{1}{3}$ lb. and not 120 lb. Thus these taxes, though possibly not in themselves exorbitant, are yet so liable to abuse in the administration, as often to become serious grievances, and foreigners must remain exposed to them till they have taken the trouble of learning the language of the country, and can make themselves heard and understood; for however rapacious a Chinese officer may be, he is apt to shrink from a bold and clamorous complainant, as he is sure that though the latter may possibly not be redressed, yet notorious delinquency in himself is not likely to pass unpunished.

Civil and Military Ranks and Establishments

In China there is properly no hereditary nobility. The children and collaterals of the sovereign enjoy a certain degree of consideration dependent on the favour with which they are regarded at Court; but as that advantage is liable to grow weaker by their lengthening distance from the throne, or fountain of honour, they may in process of time sink into the mass of the people, and be scarcely distinguished from them otherwise than by their yellow and red girdles, which none but such as are of the imperial blood are privileged to wear. Those who descend from the reigning (which pretends to be the elder) branch are adorned with a yellow sash, those who descend from the younger with a red one.

It is affirmed that the posterity of Confucius, who are still extant, enjoy certain hereditary honours transmitted to them from their great ancestor, but I am not precisely informed of the nature of them, nor of the advantages which they confer.

Rank in China is generally supposed to be the reward of merit and service, and it frequently is so; but there appears to be one glaring partiality in the

OBSERVATIONS

distribution of it. A Chinese seldom attains the highest degree till very advanced in life, but I have seen Tartars already possessed of it at the age of five or six and twenty.

Formerly persons in office were chiefly known by their robe of ceremony, but as it was not constantly worn in common, the present Emperor Ch'ienlung invented or founded the distinction of the bead or button, which being fixed on the top of the cap, evidently and immediately denotes the title of the wearer. Of these buttons he established eight classes attainable by the civil and military without distinction, which are as follows[101]

1st The button of red coral, smooth.
2nd The button of red coral, carved or flourished.
3rd The button of light transparent blue.
4th The button of light opaque blue.
5th The button of clear white crystal.
6th The button of opaque milk white.
7th The button of brass gilt, smooth.
8th The button of brass gilt, engraved and flourished.

And besides these there is another distinction superior to all, being a ruby-coloured or rather amethyst-coloured button, and of a larger size than the others, which is only conferred on Tartar princes and persons allied to the Emperor.

In all the public acts and papers a Mandarin is invariably styled according to the order of his button, and if he should be degraded to an inferior one on account of delinquency, as very frequently happens, he is obliged to be the herald or publisher of his own shame, and to write himself ——Mandarin, formerly of the —— class, but now degraded to the —— class. This mode of punishment is considered rather as a kind of fatherly correction from the Emperor to a faulty child, than as a mark of much severity, and the culprit, after a certain term of contrition and probation, is usually restored to his former dignity.

In so extensive an empire the number of Mandarins, or persons employed in the different civil and military situations, must be prodigiously great; but I shall content myself in this sketch with giving only a list of the chief officers of business, observing at the same time that under them there are some thousands of Mandarins who wear the gilt button, appointed by Viceroys, commanders of armies and presidents of tribunals, who are allowed that privilege when the necessity of the service requires it, but are punished if found to abuse it.

A List of the Chief Civil Officers,[102] distinguishing their Number, Station and Salaries

NO.		SALARY OF EACH TAELS PER ANNUM.	TOTAL
11	The *Tson-tou*, or Viceroy over one or more provinces	20,000	220,000
15	The *Fo-yen*, or Governor under him of each province	16,000	240,000

CHINESE SOLDIERS

19	The *Hoo-poo*, or Fiscal, the Chief Officer of revenue	9,000	171,000
18	The *An-ʒa-tʒe*, or President of the criminal tribunals	6,000	108,000
86	The *Tao-quen*, or Governor presiding over more than one city of the first order and their dependencies . . .	3,000	258,000
184	The *Foo-quen*, or Governor only of one city of the first order, and its dependencies	2,000	368,000
149	The *Kiou-quen*, or Governor of a city of the second order	1,000	149,000
1305	The *Sieu-quen*, or Governor of a city of the third order	800	1,044,000
17	The *Siou-jou*, or President of science and examinations		
117	The *Cho-tao*, or Inspectors-General .	3,000	402,000
	Total taels		2,960,000

The salaries of these officers are sometimes lessened or increased according to the varying state of the provinces and cities, some decaying, and others improving, which is regularly reported to the *Cho-taos* or inspectors every year. Extraordinary allowances are also paid to these officers on occasion of any extraordinary trouble or expense incurred in their departments, such as by the passage of great persons, ambassadors, etc., through the places where they are to do the honours to them of their respective stations.

My information relative to the military of China is principally derived from Wang, an officer of high rank in the army who, together with Chou (the Mandarin particularly mentioned under the heads of 'Population' and 'Revenue'), was deputed by the Emperor to attend to my embassy, and who remained with me from the moment of my landing in China to my departure from Canton. Wang is a man of good understanding and of great bodily strength. Being an excellent soldier he has raised himself from an inferior station to the rank of *Fu-chiang*, or the third military degree, and to the flourished red coral button, which is the second class or order of precedence in the state. In consequence of having received three wounds in the service, he has besides been honoured with a peacock's feather, which is worn pendant from the back of his cap, and is a distinction solely appropriated to the army.

There are, in time of peace, 1,800,000 troops within the Great Wall; that is to say 1,000,000 of infantry, and 800,000 cavalry; but in time of war, considerable detachments from them are sent abroad.

The Tartar troops, properly so called, are mostly stationed in Tartary beyond the Great Wall, attached to the banners under the command of their respective chiefs, and upon quite a different footing from the 1,800,000 regular Chinese troops above mentioned; but a vast number of these latter are Tartars who have a higher pay than their Chinese fellow-soldiers; and the principal officers of confidence in the army are Tartars also.

The soldiers are all volunteers, and none are received into the service but such as are expert, healthy, strong, and sightly. Beside their ordinary pay, the Emperor makes them certain presents upon particular occasions, such as when they marry, when they have male children born, and when their parents die. When they themselves die, their families are entitled to a gift of consolation. Thus, then, the condition of a soldier in China is by no means an undesirable one, and when a man is once enrolled in the military he is generally looked upon as well provided for.

The allowances are as follows:

A Chinese horseman has three ounces and three drachms of silver* and fifteen measures of rice per month.

A Tartar horseman in the Chinese army has seven ounces and twenty measures of rice per month.

A Chinese foot soldier (in whose rank are included the artillery, pioneers and all who do not serve on horseback) has one ounce and six drachms of silver, and ten measures of rice per month.

A Tartar foot soldier in the Chinese army has two ounces and six drachms and ten measures of rice per month.

The Emperor furnishes the arms and accoutrements, and the upper garment which for the infantry is commonly of a dark blue cotton stuff bound with a red galloon, coarse, clumsy and inconvenient for active service. The horsemen† and the sword and target men are differently clothed, some in yellow, some in white; the particular reason of which distinctions I know not, but I conclude it to be of no moment.

To every division is a certain proportion of match-lockers, archers, sword and target men, and cavalry. To every two hundred men is an imperial ensign or standard; but at a parade every tenth man carries a showy triangular pennon of red, blue, green, or yellow taffeta, I presume according to the fancy of the commanding officer.

It is pretended that in the arsenal of every province there are five hundred firelocks in store.‡ All the other arms are matchlocks, bows and arrows, and swords and bucklers.

Of eighty thousand Chinese troops employed in the last expedition to Tibet, only thirty thousand had fire-arms and those all matchlocks.

A matchlock in China costs $1\frac{1}{2}$ ounce or tael of silver.

A sword costs half an ounce.

A bow costs 3 ounces, 6 drachms.

* A Chinese ounce of silver is equal to eighty pence sterling. Ten drachms are equal to an ounce.

† The cavalry in China carry no pistols and are only armed with swords and bows and arrows.

‡ Query. Why don't the Chinese use firelocks instead of matchlocks? Wang said the flints were apt to miss fire, but that the matchlocks though slow were always sure. The truth is, I believe, that there are no good flints in China, and the Chinese maxim is to do as well as they possibly can without foreign supplies. I doubt whether the flints brought from Europe to China be of the best kind; a change of climate could not extinguish their natural vivacity.

MILITARY OFFICERS

A sheaf of arrows costs 3 ounces, 6 drachms.
A uniform costs 4 ounces.

In every walled town there is a garrison proportionate to its size, for the security of the revenue, the magazines of provisions and the prisoners, whether debtors or criminals, lodged in the gaols there. It is said that in these there are great guns belonging to every town of this description, but I never saw any mounted on the walls or bastions not even at Pekin. The gates are generally very high and consist of several stories, one above the other, with portholes which are shut with doors, on the outside of which are painted the representations of cannons which at a distance look somewhat like the sham ports of our men-of-war; but if real cannon were mounted there they would be of little use, as on account of the lowness of the stories the smoke would not suffer the peoples remaining to serve them.

A List of the Chinese Chief Military Officers,[103] their Number, Ranks and Salaries

NO.	RANK	SALARY OF EACH IN TAELS PER ANNUM.	TOTAL TAELS
18	The *Tou-ton*	4,000	72,000
62	The *Zun-ping*	2,400	148,800
121	The *Foo-zien*	1,300	157,300
165	The *Tchoo-zien*	800	132,000
373	The *Giou-zi*	600	223,800
425	The *Tou-tze*	400	170,000
825	The *Sciou-foo*	320	264,000
1680	The *Zien-zun*	160	268,000
3622	The *Pa-zun*	130	470,870
44	Commissaries of corn and provisions of the first rank (*Sciou-zun*)	320	14,080
330	Commissaries of corn and provisions of the second rank (*Zien-zun*)	160	52,800
		Total Taels	1,974,450

A rough Calculation of the Military Establishments of China

	TAELS	
1,000,000 infantry at two ounces or taels of silver each per month, provisions included	24,000,000	
800,000 cavalry at 4 ounces each ditto	38,400,000	
If 800,000 horses cost at 20 ounces each, 16,000,000 ounces, the annual wear and tear at 10 per cent will be	1,600,000	
Uniforms for 1,800,000 men once a year at 4 ounces each	7,200,000	
Yearly wear and tear of arms, accoutrements, contingencies, etc., at 1 ounce per man for 1,800,000 men	1,800,000	
		73,000,000
	Total Taels	74,974,450

OBSERVATIONS

N.B.—No allowance being made in the above estimate for the expense of artillery, tents, war equipage, nor for boats, vessels of force, etc. I include them in the extraordinaries of the army, which are probably equal to the ordinaries.

Trade and Commerce

For near forty years past our knowledge of the commerce of China has been confined to Canton. The Europeans frequenting that port, being chiefly engaged in the mere business of buying and selling on the spot, wanted leisure or curiosity to make inquiries beyond the sphere of their immediate and most interesting concerns, and the Chinese merchants, whether from ignorance or policy, were little qualified or disposed to give them very accurate information. It is however certain that a considerable intercourse, though perhaps less than formerly, is still maintained between China and Japan, the Philippine islands, the isles of Sunda, and the countries of Cochin China and Korea. From Canton to Tengchowfu, at the entrance of the gulf of Pei-chihli (to say nothing of the country within the gulf itself) is an extent of coast of near two thousand miles, indented with innumerable harbours, many of them capable of admitting the largest European ships, and all of them safe and sufficiently deep for the vessels of the country. Every creek or haven has a town or city upon it; the inhabitants, who abound beyond credibility, are mostly of a mercantile trafficking cast, and a great part of them, from their necessary employment in the fishery, which supplies them with a principal part of their subsistence, are accustomed to the sea and to the management of shipping. But according to the present regulations of the empire, all trade with any of these places is absolutely interdicted to Europeans, and Canton is the only port which they are allowed to frequent. I shall therefore at present turn my chief attention to the commerce carried on at Canton, and particularly to those branches of it which are most interesting to Great Britain and her dependencies in India.

A few years ago the exports to China on the Company's account in English goods and on English bottoms scarcely exceeded one hundred thousand pounds per annum, and the private trade might perhaps be as much more. The balance was paid in silver; but, since the Commutation Act, the exports have been gradually rising, and have not yet, I am persuaded, reached their highest point.*
There were imported into Canton from England during the last season (*anno* 1793), in sixteen Company's ships, to the amount of above 2,911,000 taels, or about £970,333 sterling,† in lead, tin, woollens, together with furs and other

* [See Introduction, p. 15.—Ed.]

† | Taels | | £ | |
|---|---|---|---|
| 2,335,000 | = | 778,333 | Company's trade. |
| 576,000 | = | 192,000 | Private trade at £12,000 per ship on 16 ships. |
| 2,911,000 Taels | | £970,333 | |

articles of private trade. The order for woollens* only in the present year is above £250,000 higher than that of the former, so that this single article of woollens has grown to be between £700,000 and £800,000 and will probably increase. Thus then our exports from England to China alone will be £1,200,000 at least, or six times as much as they were a dozen years ago.

The value of exports from China to England in eighteen Company's ships† this season is above 4,583,326 taels, or £1,527,775 prime cost,‡ which when sold will certainly produce above £3,000,000 sterling.

As I have endeavoured to be very moderate in the above estimate, I have confined myself solely to the trade carried on in the Company's ships, making no allowance for any imports into China by the Ostend interlopers under Genoese, Tuscan, Prussian and other foreign colours, which are well known to be the actual property of English traders, and probably laden with a considerable proportion of English goods. But without making any allowance on such account I have little doubt that in a few years our exports to China from England alone will balance the first cost of our imports to England from China.

To the items of our exports from England which are now chiefly confined to woollens, tin, lead (exclusive of the private trade, the particulars of which I am not well informed about) I shall here give a list of such articles as, from my own observation, I should think by the proper management of the Hong merchants at Canton, might grow into general demand at Pekin.

Bronze figures.
Agate and blood stone, much valued in large pieces—amber ditto.
Green serpentine stone, also in high request.
Derbyshire spar for girdle clasps, also cut into various shapes, particularly into small round beads or globes of half an inch to one inch in diameter, to intersperse in the Mandarins' collars of ceremony.
Gill's swords, plain and also handsomely mounted.§

---

* The wearing of broadcloth at Court in the Emperor's presence has been lately permitted, is now universal during the months of March, April, May, September, October and November, by all who can afford it in the northern provinces, and is pretty common during the cold months in the southern ones.

† Only sixteen ships came in regular course from England to China this season, but the *Hindostan* which attended the embassy and the *Bellona*, Botany Bay ship, added to them make these eighteen loaded ships from Canton. Cargoes were ready for two more that were expected, but one, the *Princess Royal*, was taken by the French in the Straits of Sunda, and the other (the *Woodcot*, I believe) was differently disposed of.

‡
Taels		£	
3,969,436	=	1,323,145	Company's trade.
613,890	=	204,630	Private trade on 18 ships (Tea, 1,814,400 lb.)
Taels 4,583,326	=	£1,527,775	

§ Arms are not permitted to be brought to China for sale without particular permission, but from the admiration expressed of ours I should imagine the Hong merchants could obtain leave for a few to be imported, and as they came to be better known, the prohibition would probably be entirely taken off.

OBSERVATIONS

> Fowling pieces with good agate flints.
> Coarse linen.
> Writing paper.
> Saddles of the Chinese fashion.
> Waistcoats and stockings of fleecy hosiery.
> Spring garters.
> Vigonia cloth.
> Whips with lashes fixed to wooden handles.
> Knives, forks and spoons, one of each in one small case.
> Penknives with several blades.
> Brushes and combs, scissors, files, and various lesser articles of hardware.
> Plated goods; pocket-books with instruments.
> Necklaces and earrings for women.
> Telescopes, spring glasses and spectacles, prints and pictures.
> Nails of all sorts and sizes.
> Plate glass, and small looking glasses, convex and concave.

Some of these articles, I dare say, already make a part of the private trade, but not being possessed of any very correct information upon that subject, I have thought it best to give as extensive a list as I could of the articles likely to find sale in the northern part of China, which is as yet in a great degree a *terra incognita* to most of the merchants of Canton.*

I imagine that at Birmingham we can manufacture everything in iron cheaper than the Chinese can do. I should therefore recommend the making a few experiments according to the Chinese patterns. A pair of tailor's shears made at Canton costs ten pence English, which I suppose may be afforded in England for half the price. In truth, if we keep our ground (I think we may improve it) our trade by prudent management may be gradually enlarged to an immense extent. The demand for our tin† (now that the Chinese understand its quality, and that their prejudices in favour of the Banca tin, which they had been in the habit of preferring, are worn off) is likely to increase. At present it is equal to £100,000 sterling per annum, and a certain quantity of our lead, not less than twenty to thirty thousand pounds sterling value is pretty sure of finding a market at Canton. But there is another article of export to China which, though I observe it is of late almost discontinued, may perhaps be revived, and, if I

---

* [Cp. a similar list in the Wason Collection of Macartney documents at Cornell, no. 322.—Ed.]

† They say our tin does very well in utensils, but they pretend it is not so easily hammered and beat into leaf as the Banca tin. They can't, however, distinguish the difference between our leaf tin, and the Banca leaf tin when shown to them. Would it not be advisable to send them a part of our tin in leaf? Our tin having the Company's mark upon it, passes all through China without difficulty or examination, which is not the case of the Banca tin, the Chinese having often discovered the latter to be adulterated. Indeed the Company's good faith seems perfectly well established, and our woollens, with the Company's mark also freely pass unopened from hand to hand in the way of trade.

am not mistaken in my conjectures may be rendered of considerable importance—I mean copper. Upon this subject I have endeavoured to procure the best information in my power, and I shall here insert the result of my inquiries.

White copper or tutenag seems to be composed of red copper, zinc, and a small portion of iron. To prove this the following experiments were made.

Experiment 1st. A quantity of copper ore was divided into two parts. One of these parts being completely roasted was revivified *per se*. The produce was common red copper, which proved that the ore originally contained nothing but red copper.

Experiment 2nd. The remaining portion of the ore was next completely roasted and revivified. It was then fused with . . .* parts of zinc and a small portion of *ferrum vitriolatum* previously calcined. The result was a mass of white copper, or something so like it as scarcely to be distinguished from it.

These experiments prove that white copper may be made from copper ore, with a proper addition of zinc and *ferrum vitriolatum* calcined. Tutenag in China is supposed to be sheer zinc, and of the finest sort; but this can't be true, for zinc is a semi-metal, which although it be not readily broken with the hammer, yet cannot be much extended under it, whereas the tutenag of China has very different properties and extends easily under the hammer. The consumption of white copper in China is immense. The price at Canton is seldom lower than one hundred dollars per picul of $133\frac{1}{3}$ lb. or about four shillings per pound. Red copper in ingots was sold in London in July 1792 (vide prices current) at one shilling per pound. Would it not then be much better for us (supposing white copper could be made in England for 2s. or 2s. 6d. per lb.) to export it to China instead of attempting to push the red copper, which is considered as a losing article, and is not likely to be rendered a lucrative one; for the Hong merchants are obliged by government to sell it at a fixed price, and they pretend that they lose fifty per cent upon every picul of it which they take from us in the way of trade.† The principal use that English red copper is applied to in China is the coinage of small money or cashes, of which one thousand are equal to a tael, or 6s. 8d. sterling. The houses are covered with tiles, which are so very cheap and answer the purpose so well, that our red copper is not likely to be substituted for roofing. Neither do I think that its use can be introduced for many other purposes. The small boilers of the Chinese are commonly of earthenware, and their large ones of cast-iron. Great quantities of tutenag are exported from China to India; our Country ships sometimes take near £100,000 worth in the season, so that if we can make it in England, a new and profitable article is added to our exports.

I have said nothing of the fur trade to Canton, although I am inclined to imagine that, if it were solely in the Company's hands (and it in a great measure depends upon them that it should be so) it might be rendered of very great value. In the present state of it, the Chinese at Canton purchase furs from us,

---

* [Blank space in text.—Ed.]

† It is probable that they really do lose by it, for if there were any profit, however small, they would not think it below their attention.

and from other nations frequenting that port, to the amount of more than £200,000 per annum.

With regard to toys, jewellery, etc., commonly called sing-songs,* paints, dyeing-stuffs, etc., it is better to leave them at large as objects of speculations for private traders, whose habits of industry and individual activity are better calculated than the magnificent system of a great commercial body for a traffic in such articles.

Having now given a sketch of the direct trade between Great Britian and China, it remains to speak of the commerce of our dependencies in India with China, which commerce is of high concern to us, and merits particular attention and regulation. The amount of the legal trade of 1792, imported to Canton in twenty of our Country ships, was 1,608,544 taels,† to which is to be added the value of 473,000 taels in cotton brought in the Company's ships from Bombay, making together 2,081,544 taels, or about £693,848. The illegal and contraband trade of opium consists of two thousand five hundred chests,‡ which at four hundred dollars per chest will give £250,000, so that the whole imports from Bengal and Bombay to Canton are not much short of a million sterling, or £943,848. The exports from China in the above mentioned twenty Country ships cost at Canton 968,632 taels,§ or £322,877. There appears then a balance of £620,971 in favour of India in her China trade, and it seems likely to increase, for the cotton of Bombay and the opium of Bengal are now become in a

---

* [See note 1.—Ed.]
† The principal articles were as follows:

	Piculs		Taels
Cotton	112,854 at 11 taels per piculs		1,241,394
Tin	5,261 at 15	ditto	78,915
Pepper	5,567 at 15	ditto	83,505
Sandalwood	8,780 at 20	ditto	175,600
Elephant's teeth	330 at 37	ditto	12,210
Bees' wax	564 at 30	ditto	16,920
		Taels	1,608,544
Add Cotton	43,000 at 11 by Company's ships		473,000
		Taels	2,081,544

‡ [See Introduction, p. 51.—Ed.]
§ The articles were as follows:

	Taels
Raw silk	352,600
Tutenag	256,046
Sugar	130,490
Sugar-candy	107,490
Allum	37,516
Wrought silk	31,600
China ware	30,000
Camphor	18,750
Nankin cotton cloth	2,750
Quicksilver	1,150
Turmeric	240
Total value Taels	968,632

THE HOPPO'S EXTORTIONS

great measure necessaries in China, the latter having grown into general demand through all the southern provinces, and the former being preferable to silk for common use, as a cheaper and pleasanter wear.*

The profits of the Hong merchants upon their foreign trade must be very great to enable them to bear the expense of the numerous and magnificent presents which they make to the superior Mandarins at Canton who, in their turn, send a part of these presents to the Emperor and his ministers and favourites at Pekin. By what I saw at Jehol and Yuan-ming Yuan, and by the reports concerning the things I did not see (particularly in the ladies' apartments, and the European palace, which latter is entirely furnished and enriched with articles from Europe) I am led to believe what I have been assured of, that the Emperor possesses to the value of two millions sterling at the least in various toys, jewellery, glass, musical automatons, and other figures; instruments of different kinds, microcosms, clocks, watches, etc., etc., all made in London.

It is generally supposed that the system of administration at Canton has been corrupt and oppressive to a great degree, and it is certain that several of the Hoppos or treasurers at their return to Pekin have been called to a strict account. Some have suffered large confiscations and others a severer punishment; but the distance from the metropolis is so great, the temptations so strong, and the chances of impunity so many, that the faithful discharge of such a duty requires more integrity than is usually to be found here united with power and opportunity.† Hence arise the peculations and extortions so much complained of, and many of them I believe very justly complained of at Canton. There is one which I am qualified particularly to speak upon. In consideration of Captain Mackintosh having accompanied my embassy, and brought the presents to the Emperor on board of his ship, he was assured she should be exempted from all the Emperor's duties payable at the port where she loaded. Being disappointed of the goods expected at Chusan, he proceeded on the *Hindostan* to Canton, and took in there a usual cargo for England; but the privilege that had been promised was not understood by the Hoppo in the same manner that it had been understood by us, for after the accustomed duties for all the ships had been paid by the Hong merchants, of which 30,000 taels were the *Hindostan*'s proportion, the Hoppo repaid into Mr. Browne's hands only 14,000 dollars instead of the whole 30,000 taels as was expected, saying that so much was the exact amount of the Emperor's duties, but not saying nor explaining what became of the remainder. It is, however, of some advantage to us to have learned from such an authority what the Emperor's real duties are, and may be a step to relieve us from the others, which it is probable are for a great part absolute extortions.

The trade of the Dutch, French, Americans, Danes and Swedes with China is so much declined, and so likely in a few years to be almost annihilated, that it

---

* Another reason may be given for the great rising demand in China for India cotton. As the inhabitants every day seem to increase beyond the usual means of subsistence I suspect they are obliged to convert many of their cotton plantations into provision grounds. † [Cf. note 46.—Ed.]

is the less necessary for me to dwell upon the subject. The Danes and Swedes have in a great measure given it up and will, I believe, send but few more ships to Canton. Many years must elapse before it can be revived in France. The Americans, with all their contrivances and industry are not likely, as I am well informed, to pursue it with much advantage;[104] and as for the Dutch, the affairs of their Company in these parts of the world are in so deplorable a condition that it is scarcely possible to contemplate them without compassion, or to approach them without shrinking. They afford an awful lesson for our instruction.[105]

The total imports of all these different nations to Canton in 1792, when summed up together, amount to £200,000 and their exports from thence to between £600,000 and £700,000 which gives a balance of near half a million against them, and what renders it more unfavourable is that very little of what they bring to China is of their home production.

The trade between China and Russia, which had been long interrupted, is now open again. Mr. Coxe, in his account of it some years since, states it to be much more considerable than I could have imagined.[106] I have not his book with me to refer to, but as well as I recollect he computes the value of silks, Nankin cloth, tea, porcelain, etc. brought over land from China into Russia at several hundred thousand pounds per annum. In 1767, when I left St. Petersburg, it was supposed to be very, very far short of his estimate, and indeed I do not conceive that either the necessities or faculties of Russia could warrant it even at this day. The returns to China are made chiefly in furs, leather and woollen cloth, the latter mostly German with a small quantity of English superfine. In my road to Jehol, I met several strings of camels laden with these woollens, and so ignorant in matters of trade were many of the Chinese that they believed them to be the manufacture of Tartary, just as several English articles which I saw at Pekin were supposed to be the production of Canton.

Among the various novelties and projects which the Empress of Russia's fertile fancy has imagined, I am somewhat surprised that the sending a ship or two to Canton never occurred to her. The magnificent idea of holding, from such a distance, an intercourse with the two extremities of China, and of showing to that empire that it was accessible to her by sea as well as by land, would seem perfectly congenial with her character, and naturally to arise in so ambitious and adventurous a mind.[107]

Having mentioned under the head 'Arts and Sciences' that the Chinese excelled in the art of dyeing, it may be proper to observe that nevertheless the China Nankin, which from its cheapness, pleasantness, and colour is of such general wear in England, is not dyed as is commonly imagined but is fabricated from a native brown cotton wool, which is chiefly cultivated in the provinces of Kiangnan and Chekiang. I am informed from good authority that this kind of cotton grows also in the neighbourhood of Manila in the island of Luzon.*

---

* Since writing the above I have been told that the brown cotton of Kiangnan, when transplanted to Canton loses its original colour in two or three generations of the plant.

BALANCE OF PAYMENTS

As fifty thousand to sixty thousand bales of cotton of four hundred pounds each, worth ten to twelve taels per picul, are annually imported from India to Canton, which is from three to five taels less than the price of the native cotton of China, I should think it might be worth while for our gentlemen at Bombay and Surat to procure the brown cotton plant from Manila, if not from China, and cultivate it in India. The Bombay cotton is chiefly used by the Chinese for making what is called the white Nankeen, but which is rather of a cream colour than of a clear white.

Perhaps it may not be improper to consider here the effects that might possibly follow from cultivating the brown cotton in India and sending it to England. East India white cotton now sells for ten pence per pound in London (vide prices current of June 1794), but suppose it to sell for one shilling a pound, which is about one-third cheaper than the average price of West India cotton, this circumstance then, with the reduction in the cost of labour by the use of our machinery (never likely to be produced in China) and the dye saved besides, might enable the people of Manchester to afford their Nankins at so low a rate as in a short time entirely to exclude that article of our present import from Canton.

The Chinese have a method of dyeing their cotton wool in scarlet much superior to any with which we are acquainted. It is said they employ some strong astringent vegetable juice for fixing that colour, but from what plants it is extracted we are entirely in the dark. The chief excellence of their colours in general, which we so much admire, arises from their indefatigable care and pains in washing, purifying and grinding them, for many of them are not the produce of China, but imported from Europe.

Before I conclude the head 'Commerce' I cannot avoid adding a word or two, as not entirely foreign to the subject. If the China trade of the Dutch, French, Danes, Swedes, Americans, etc., by which the Chinese have hitherto received a considerable balance, should fall to the ground, and our trade continue to improve as it now seems to promise, that is to say, that the value of exports and imports between England and China should become nearly equal, and the balance between China and India remain still in favour of the latter, may not the Chinese take alarm at so much silver being sent out of their country in discharge of the balance? Also what is likely to become of that silver when the Country ships shall no longer have the resource of remitting the amount of it as formerly by bills upon Europe through the treasuries at Canton? I have been told that some silver has of late been carried away by the Country ships from Canton to India, and that the Hong merchants, considering silver as mere merchandize, did not appear sensible of any disadvantage from such a trade; but any conjectures or questions that might occur to me upon these points have been, I dare say, already anticipated and resolved by the honourable East India Company and their servants at Canton.

OBSERVATIONS

Arts and Sciences

The Chinese possess great skill in many branches of the arts, particularly in the manufacture of silk stuffs, and of certain kinds of cotton cloth. They excel in the secrets of dyeing and fixing their colours, in the process also of grinding and preparing their pigments for limning, in composing and laying on varnishes, and in neatness of joinery and cabinet-work. But what they are supposed to understand in a very superior degree is the pottery, or art of moulding clay or earth to every purpose of which it is capable, and of shaping, glazing, colouring, and hardening it as they please. Hence the beauty and variety of their porcelain, the smoothness and brilliancy of their tiles, and the neatness and solidity of their bricks. With regard to the latter, to say nothing of the Great Wall, I must observe that we saw some buildings at Yuan-ming Yuan which, as pieces of brickwork, are superior both in point of materials and workmanship to Tyrconnel House in the south-west corner of Hanover Square, which is boasted of as the most perfect thing of the sort in England.[108] Whatever they undertake they appear to perform with ease and dexterity. After Parker's two great lustres had been put together by our people from England, and hung up in the great hall of Yuan-ming Yuan, an operation that required considerable time, pains and intelligence, it being found necessary to remove them to another place, two common Chinese took them down piece by piece in less than half an hour without the smallest assistance or instruction. A Chinese with his rude instrument quickly cut off a slip from the edge of a curved plate of glass belonging to the dome of the planetarium, which our artists could not effect after repeated attempts with a diamond. This appeared the more extraordinary as the use of glass is not yet familiar to the people, their table utensils being mostly of porcelain, their mirrors of metal, and their windows of oyster-shell or of paper. They execute all kinds of embroidery and needlework with admirable elegance, and the commonest articles of their dress, though clumsy and cumbersome in its fashion, are yet sewed and made up with singular precision and contrivance.*

In respect to science the Chinese are certainly far behind the European world. They have but a very limited knowledge of mathematics and astronomy, although from some of the printed accounts of China one might be led to imagine that they were well versed in them.[109] A great part of their astronomy is mere astrological trifling, whose chief end is to point out the proper times for certain ceremonies, upon the strict observance of which the happiness of the empire and individuals is supposed to depend. Their affectation of the science of astronomy or astrology (for they have but one word in their language to express both) induced them at a very remote period to establish a mathematical

---

* They can copy an European picture with great exactness, but they appear to be strangers to the principles of perspective in painting, their own original pieces being without any distribution of light and shade. This is the more extraordinary, as, from the laying out of their gardens and pleasure-grounds, one would be tempted to imagine that they understood it perfectly.

college or tribunal, the duty of which is to prepare and furnish to the nation an annual calendar, somewhat like our *Poor Robin's Almanack*, with lists of all the lucky and unlucky days of the year, predictions of the weather, directions for sowing and reaping, etc., etc. This branch is entirely confided to and conducted by the Chinese doctors, who are chosen for the purpose from among the most celebrated philomaths of the nation, but the real astronomical parts (the calculation of eclipses, the phases of the moon, the conjunction of the planets, etc.) are at present committed to the charge of three European missionaries, viz. Gouvea, the Bishop of Pekin, his secretary, and Padre Antonio, all of them Portuguese, but none of them eminently qualified for the business. The Chinese could not venture to depend on the calculations of their own people, as they are known to be never quite accurate, and to be often, indeed generally, very erroneous. They have, however, a tolerable idea of the circles of the sphere, of the annual and diurnal motions and the common phenomena, but are entirely strangers to physical astronomy.* The first introduction of Europeans into the mathematical tribunal is said to have arisen from a circumstance which in itself is alone sufficient proof of the gross ignorance of the Chinese in astronomical matters.

Their computation of time being solely lunar soon became necessarily erroneous from their defect of knowledge in the irregularities and the periodical revolutions of the moon. The consequence then would naturally be that these errors must increase from time to time till a palpable change of seasons should become perceptible, and till their calendar were corrected in a certain degree by the addition or subtraction of a month, where it was found to be necessary. A growing error of this kind was detected by one of the European missionaries in 1670 and pointed out by him to the Chinese before it was too gross to be observed by the senses. He showed them the proper method of rectifying it, which was done by striking off the intercalary month that they had inserted at a wrong time, where the year ought only to have been considered as a common one of twelve lunar months. As the Chinese are not very nice in their calculations, the Europeans have not had much difficulty since that time in keeping their calendar pretty near the truth. The cycle of nineteen years, called by the Greeks and Romans the cycle of the moon, answers this purpose sufficiently well, the intercalated months being in the second, fifth, eighth, tenth, thirteenth, sixteenth and eighteenth years. From this accident the missionaries derived many advantages, and began to acquire some consideration at Court. To what height their attainments in science may have reached I know not; but we have good reason to think, that their successors of the present day have not soared many degrees above the Chinese; for, according to their own confession to Mr. Barrow, they never give themselves the trouble of calculating the eclipses themselves, and even in those of the sun when applied to the meridian of Pekin, they are entirely inattentive to parallax. They expressed much uneasiness and apprehension that the subversion in France would prevent the Paris *Connoissances des Temps* from being regularly transmitted to them as formerly, and were there-

* Vide Long's astronomy and Pauw's researches.

OBSERVATIONS

fore highly gratified by our furnishing them with the latest of our printed nautical almanacks, and a manuscript supplement calculated for a few years to come. With regard to geometry, the Chinese know a few of the most useful propositions; but whether they had learned them previous to the arrival of the missionaries I cannot ascertain. They have also some tincture of plain trigonometry, but are totally ignorant of spherical. A table of logarithms has been published in Chinese but I believe it was introduced by the Jesuits. Algebra is quite unknown among the Chinese.[110] Gouvea, the present Portuguese Bishop of Pekin, who belongs to the tribunal of mathematics, said that it had hitherto been found impossible to render the principles and operations of algebra intelligible to them, because they have no alphabet; but his reverence did not seem perfectly to understand the subject himself, for algebraical quantities may certainly be represented by any mark or character, as well as by the letters of an European alphabet. The truth indeed is, that the present missionaries are very little conversant in algebra, or fluxions, and but poor proficients in any other branches of science. Some of those who were patronized by the Emperor K'ang-hsi, about fourscore years ago, were men of considerable knowledge, and of indefatigable industry. They attempted to introduce experimental philosophy into China, and from the accounts given by them of the taste of the Court, and of the avidity with which their lessons and exhibitions were received, we were induced to provide and carry with us expensive apparatuses of different kinds and of the latest inventions; but we had very little occasion to make use of them, for almost everything of this nature, that had been taught by the Jesuits, seemed to be either entirely forgotten or considered of no value. Neither Ch'ien-lung himself nor those about him appeared to have any curiosity in these matters. It is, besides, the policy of the present government to discourage all novelties, and to prevent their subjects as much as possible from entertaining a higher opinion of foreigners than of themselves. Dr. Dinwiddie gave a few lectures and exhibited some experiments at Canton to the English factory, which were constantly attended by the principal Chinese merchants, who seemed highly delighted with them, and showed the strongest desire of further instruction. Had Dinwiddie remained at Canton and continued his courses, I dare say he might have soon realized a very considerable sum of money from his Chinese pupils alone.* But the Mandarins in Pekin manifested very little disposition of this kind; none of them discovered the slightest notion of the pressure of fluids, the principles of optics, perspective, electricity, etc., although several of them had seen air-pumps, electrical machines, spy glasses, prisms, magic lanterns, and show-boxes. Nevertheless, it was observed that most of the great men who came to see the globes, the planetarium, the barometers, and pendulums put up at Yuan-ming Yuan affected to view them with careless indifference, as if such things were quite common and familiar to them, and the use of them well understood. They could not, however, conceal their sense of the beauty and elegance of our Derby porcelain, when they saw the ornamental vases belonging to Vulliamy's clocks.† Three young princes, sons of the Emperor's eleventh son,

* [See p. 310.—Ed.] † [See note 12.—Ed.]

frequently visited our artists whilst engaged at Yuan-ming Yuan, and expressed great admiration of the workmanship and appearance of the globes, clocks and orrery, but candidly owned that they did not comprehend the purposes of them. Though the father of these princes is the patron or inspector of the college of mathematics, it is probable he does not hold the elements taught there in very high estimation, as his children were not instructed in them, their education being solely confined to the acquirement of the Chinese and Manchu languages, the study of their ceremony, or ethics, and of the history of their own empire.

The Chinese bridges are generally of an elegant appearance, but I presume of a slight construction, for there are very few of them over which wheel-carriages are allowed to pass. The elliptical arch is unknown to them, as it was to the ancient Greeks and Romans.[111] Instead of a keystone, in the form of a truncated wedge as with us, the crown of their semi-circular arch is usually a curved stone segment of a considerable span, from whence it may be presumed that their geometrical skill is not very great in the construction of bridges.

It sometimes happens that men by mere dint of natural parts, without the advantage of education (such as Arkwright and Brindley,[112] etc.) will hit upon methods of accomplishing great undertakings, where the most plausible theories have been found insufficient or inapplicable to the purpose; but this can rarely happen except in a country like Europe, where the general effect of the mechanical powers is familiar to the vulgar, from the daily observance of their universal use. Thus every common person will have recourse to a pulley, a lever, a tooth and pinion wheel, because he has seen them perform their functions a thousand times, and although he has no just idea of their exact powers, yet by repeated trials he is certain of succeeding. But in a country like China, where the sciences, which first pointed out those artificial powers, are little known and little cultivated, difficulties when they occur can only be surmounted by the increase and exertions of numbers. Perhaps it would not be refining too much to suppose that the Chinese neglect of science as applicable to practice is the result of reflexion, and that it is true wisdom in the government to discountenance the use of the mechanic powers, or at least never to employ such artificial aid but where it is absolutely unavoidable, because the existence of so many millions of their people depends chiefly upon their manual labour.[113] Most of the things which the Chinese know they seem to have invented themselves, to have applied them solely to the purpose wanted, and to have never thought of improving or extending them further. They know so far as that natural bodily force may be assisted by means of the single pulley and the lever. The first we observed at Taku in the transhipping our packages from the sea junks into the river ones, for which operation they employed three or four single pulleys each with an equal number of falls* in order to lift the heavy articles out of the holds of the vessels. The pulleys were fixed to an horizontal rope running between the masts, and four or five men were applied to each fall. So far they have proceeded in the use of this contrivance but no further, because, as from the

* [Usually 'block and fall'; rope of hoisting-tackle.—Ed.]

immense population of the country, any number of hands can be easily procured. Their principle is rather to gain in time than in power, otherwise having already employed the single pulley, the double one would have naturally occurred to them. For raising the anchors of the large sea junks that make distant voyages, they have a machine or kind of windlass, to which several levers are fixed and which, instead of being stopped by pawls, is stopped by a wedge inserted between the rollers and the deck. A machine of the same kind, placed vertically, is said to be used for drawing their vessels up a glacis from the lower level of a canal to an upper one; but of this singular method of overcoming inequalities of surface on inland navigation, without the use of locks and sluices, I am not qualified to give a proper account, as nothing of the sort occurred in the course of our passage, but it is often practised in several other parts of China. There are indeed no undertakings of utility and invention for which the Chinese are more celebrated than the numberless communications by water through the interior of their country. None have excited greater admiration among foreigners. As a considerable part of our journey from Pekin to Hangchowfu was upon what is usually called the Grand or Imperial Canal, I am enabled to give some account of it. This great work was executed for the purpose of laying open to each other the northern and southern provinces of the empire. It is more properly an improved river than an entirely artificial canal, according to our general acceptation of the term, for it has a descent in almost every part, and generally runs with considerable velocity. Although it is evident that the projectors were very little, if at all, acquainted with the principles of levelling, they possessed sufficient sagacity to avail themselves of all the natural advantages resulting from the ground over which the water was to be conveyed. If we turn our attention to that particular part of the canal which lies between the Yu-ho and the Hwang Ho, and which effects the communication of these two rivers, a tolerable idea may be formed of the extent of Chinese knowledge and contrivance in enterprises of this nature. The direct distance of the Yu-ho to the Hwang Ho, where the canal unites them, may be about two hundred miles. The beds of these two rivers are pretty nearly on the same level, but the interjacent country rises from each with an imperceptible ascent and is highest about midway. The Chinese had no instrument or other means of art to ascertain this point of elevation, but nature indicated it to them by the course of a river which, rising in Shantung to the eastward, and running westward in the intermediate space between the Yu-ho and Hwang Ho is obstructed in its passage, and then divides into two branches, one of which takes a northern course and falls into the Yu-ho, the other pursues a southern route and descends into the Hwang Ho. The northern stream seems to have been generally traced according to all its windings, the bed of it enlarged and formed with an uniform descent, and its navigation improved by flood-gates thrown across at certain distances, sometimes of two, three or more miles asunder, in order to prevent too great or too sudden a loss of water. These flood-gates are no more than a few loose planks, sliding between two grooves, cut in the stone piers or abutments, which project on each side from the banks of the canal, and approach so near as to leave in the middle only a sufficient space for the largest junks to pass through. A few miles before the northern branch joins the Yu-ho, instead of following, as formerly, the natural meanders of the stream, it is carried straight forward in one direction, by a deep cut of forty feet through a partial elevation of the surface of the ground. The task was not difficult, as the soil is a mixture of light sand and clay, entirely free from rocks or any sort of stone. But the southern branch required more management and address, as its progress was to be directed over a great extent of swampy grounds and lakes, and from thence through an ascending country to the Hwang Ho. On approaching this morass they were obliged to cut very deep below the surface of the ground, for the purpose of giving the water a velocity sufficient to force itself between two high banks raised above the inundated country with incredible labour and expense. In one place it traverses a vast lake, whose surface is far below its own, and there its branches are rivetted with enormous blocks of marble, clamped together at the top with irons; and lest the body of water in the canal should prove too strong for the resistance of the banks, they are intersected with sluices at certain distances, through which the superfluous water passes into deep ditches or hollows formed on each side in the middle of the banks themselves. The surface of the water let into these ditches or hollows, being kept at a mean height between the surfaces of the canal and the lake or inundation, the pressure of the body of water is diminished by one half, and all danger of disruption removed. The canal then proceeds through a rising country, being often thirty and forty feet below the surface of the ground, and falls into the Hwang Ho with a current of two to three miles per hour.[114]

From the above account it may be inferred that the Chinese in flat or nearly flat countries are chiefly directed by the apparent course of the natural streams, follow it as nearly as possible, without regarding the labour or expense attending such a system, and when they come to a difficulty not easily surmounted by their other means, they have recourse to a glacis, up and down which the vessels are passed between two canals of different levels.*

* Since writing the above I have received the following note from Dr. Dinwiddie who, having separated from me at Hangchowfu in order to proceed to Chusan for the purpose of embarking on the *Hindostan* for Canton, had an opportunity of examining more at leisure not only the common canals, but also the others whose communication is preserved by means of a glacis.

'The flood-gates in the canals of China are preferable to English locks in every situation where the canal is nearly level, and are constructed at a quarter of the expense. The inclined plane down which the boats are launched and up which they are drawn is a mode superior to our practice, for besides their being cheaper they are much more expeditious. The power employed consists of two windlasses, placed opposite to each other on the banks or abutments of the canals, the axis perpendicular, the gudgeons of the lower end supported on a stone and the upper end turning between two stones, sustained in an horizontal position on four upright stones. Each windlass has four bars which are manned with twelve to sixteen persons. The time employed in one instance observed was two minutes and a half, and in another about three.'

(Vide Mr. Alexander's drawing.) [Reproduced in Staunton, *An Authentic Account*, Folio Vol., p. 34—Ed.]

OBSERVATIONS

The Chinese have an excellent method of carrying heavy packages, by dividing the burden equally among the bearers. This is effected by applying two long poles parallel-wise to the object of conveyance, and by crossing these at their extremities with two others. Eight men are thus admitted to an equal participation of the weight. By lengthening the first poles with four others, and by applying to their extremities two transverse ones as before, sixteen men may be engaged together in this machinery, and so on to a greater number; but I don't recollect to have seen more than thirty-two men employed at once in the carrying of a single burden. I had already slightly mentioned this method of carrying packages in my journal of the 17th August 1793.

As it is generally supposed that the art of printing is of great antiquity among the Chinese, I must not pass it by without some notice. Their printing, such as I saw, is merely a wooden cut, or rather an embossing or carving in alto-relievo upon a flat board or tablet, which when wetted with ink and impressed by the paper, delivers a reversed copy of itself. From the size of the page, which is incapable of decomposition, from the necessary accuracy of the process, and the tediousness of the execution, it would seem that new publications are not very frequent, and that knowledge is not so rapidly disseminated in China as in England by reviews, magazines and such other periodical oracles of taste and literature.

Du Halde and Grosier tell us that the Chinese have moveable types made of wood, not of cast metal as with us, but that they use them only for the corrections and changes in the Pekin Court Register, or list of public officers, which is renewed every three months. In this case, however, I suspect that they have no letter fount, but that they cut away the old characters or names that are to be altered, and fill up the space by glueing or otherwise fastening the new ones upon it. The weekly gazettes published in most of the great cities of the empire are, I believe, struck off in their common method of block-printing.

Whether printing as practised by us be an original European invention, or whether the first hint of it was derived from China, I will not presume to determine, but it is certain that the art was not known in Europe till one hundred and fifty years after Marco Polo's return from China. As he did not impart the discovery I conclude he was ignorant of it, and that such books as he may have seen there he mistook for manuscripts, and indeed to the eye of a stranger they have much of that appearance.[115]

The structure of the Chinese language, which, it is said, consists of eighty thousand words or characters, each word however originally formed being a distinct, indivisible hieroglyphic or representation of an idea, is such as to render the use of moveable types totally inapplicable to Chinese printing; for as the Chinese have no alphabet of letters, or elements of composition as we have, it would be necessary for them (instead of a fount of twenty-four divisions which are sufficient for languages like ours) to have a fount of eighty thousand divisions for theirs, or a division for every separate character, a project impossible to be reduced to practice.

The skill of the Chinese in medicine, surgery and chemistry is certainly very limited, notwithstanding what we have read in many authors of their proficiency in those arts. Doctor Gillan, at my request, was so good as to investigate the matter and to examine into their pretentions. I therefore refer to his very ingenious papers upon the subject.*

The excellent quality of the China silk, and the beauty of the stuffs which are manufactured with it, have claimed the admiration of the world from the earliest ages. The raw material itself is, I understand, superior to any of the same kind of any other country; but I have been assured that the fabrics of Lyons and Spitalfields are sometimes even superior to those of Nankin. Of this I cannot pretend to judge, but admitting that the Chinese can weave the best silks in the world, it is no less true that they also make the worst, for they suffer nothing to be lost; the flosses, combings, refuse, etc., are all carefully saved and worked into some useful texture or other, such as nettings, curtains, gauzes, girdles, etc. All that I could learn relative to the silk, silk-worms, and mulberry-trees of China is contained in my answers to the Honourable East India Company's queries to which I refer.† I am concerned to say that they are not very satisfactory, for I found it impossible to obtain all the information I wanted.

With regard to the agriculture of the Chinese, who are certainly most admirable husbandmen, such observations and remarks as I had occasion to make upon the subject during the course of my travels, being interspersed through my journal, it is unnecessary to repeat them here.

Having given an extensive description of the Emperor's gardens at Jehol, in my account of that place, I have the less to add upon Chinese scenography, or art of laying out pleasure-grounds, upon which they value themselves so highly, as they do indeed upon everything else that affords them the slightest pretension. Whether our style of gardening was really copied from the Chinese, or originated with ourselves, I leave for vanity to assert, and idleness to discuss. A discovery which is the result of good sense and reflection may equally occur to the most distant nations without either borrowing from the other. There is certainly a great analogy between our gardening and the Chinese; but our excellence seems to be rather in improving nature, theirs to conquer her and yet produce the same effect. It is indifferent to a Chinese where he makes his garden, whether on a spot favoured or abandoned by the rural deities. If the latter, he invited them or compels them to return. His point is to change everything from what he found it, to explode the old fashion of the creation and introduce novelty in every corner. If there be a waste, he adorns it with trees; if a dry desert, he waters it with a river or floats it with a lake. If there be a smooth flat, he varies it with all possible conversions. He undulates the surface, he raises it in hills, scoops it into valleys and roughens it with rocks. He softens asperities, brings amenity into the wilderness, or animates the tameness of an expanse by accompanying it with the majesty of a forest. Deceptions and eye-traps the Chinese are not unacquainted with, but they use them very sparingly.

* [See below, pp. 279–303.—Ed.]
† [Not in Tokyo MS. Preserved at Cornell, Wason Collection, document no. 379.—Ed.]

OBSERVATIONS

I observed no artificial ruins, caves or hermitages.* Though the sublime predominates in its proper station, you are insensibly led to contemplate it, not startled by its sudden intrusion; for in the plan, cheerfulness is the principal feature and lights up the face of the scene. To enliven it still more the aid of architecture is invited. All the buildings are perfect of their kind, either elegantly simple or highly decorated according to the effect that is intended to arise, erected at suitable distances and judiciously contrasted, never crowded together in confusion, nor affectedly confronted and staring at each other without meaning. Proper edifices in proper places is the style which they admire. The summer-house, the pavilion, the pagoda, have all their respective situations, which they distinguish and improve, but which any other structures would injure or deform. The only things disagreeable to my eye are the large porcelain figures of lions, tigers, dragons, etc., and the rough-hewn steps and huge masses of rock-work which they seem studious of introducing near many of their houses and palaces. Considering their general good taste in the other points I was much surprised at this, and could only account for it by the expense and the difficulty of bringing together such incongruities; for it is a common effect of enormous riches to push everything they can procure to bombast and extravagance, which are the death of taste. In other countries, however, as well as in China, I have seen some of the most boasted seats, either outgrowing their beauty from a plethora of their owner's wealth, or becoming capricious or hypochondriacal by a quackish application of it. A few fine places, even in England, might be pointed out that are labouring under these disorders; not to mention some celebrated houses where twisted stair-cases, window-glass cupolas, and embroidered chimney-pieces convey nothing to us but the whims and dreams of sickly fancy, without an atom of grandeur, taste, or propriety.

The architecture of the Chinese is of a peculiar style, totally unlike any other, irreducible to our rules, but perfectly consistent with its own. It has certain principles from which it never deviates; and although, when examined according to ours, it sins against the ideas we have imbibed of distribution, composition and proportion, yet upon the whole it often produces a most pleasing effect; as we sometimes see a person without a single good feature in his face, have nevertheless a very agreeable countenance.

Hydraulics

The Chinese have a method of raising water from rivers to the high banks, not exceeding forty feet, for the purposes of irrigation which is at once simple, ingenious and effective. A machine constructed at a very trifling expense and

* [They were hardly necessary in China. By the end of Ch'ien-lung's reign there were ample natural ruins, centuries old. For example, see p. 179 n.—Ed.]

worked without labour or attendance furnishes a reservoir on the highest parts of the ground with a constant supply of water from whence it is conveyed through a variety of small channels to any part where it may be wanted.[116]

A perspective view of this machine is annexed in which AAA, BBB is an undershot water wheel with a double periphery made of bamboo. AA being about one foot in diameter greater than BB. The diameter of the wheel is about forty feet.

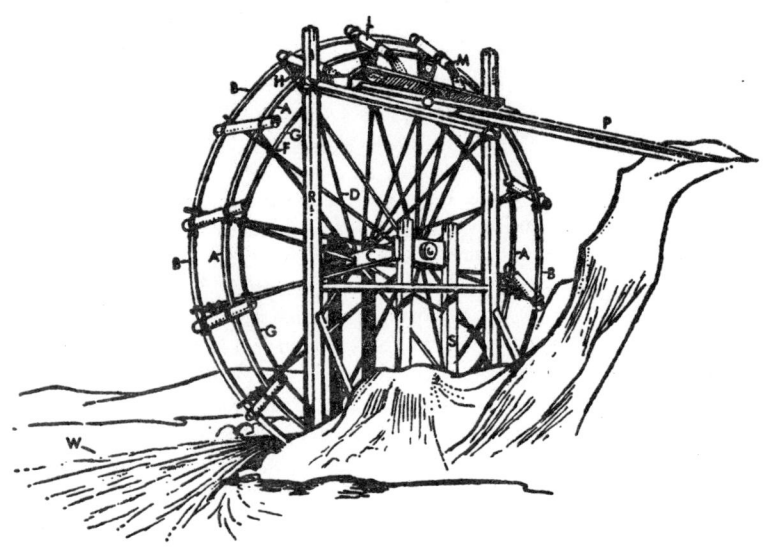

Elevation of a wheel used by the Chinese for raising water

(Based on an engraving reproduced in Sir G. L. Staunton's *An Authentic Account of an Embassy from the King of Great Britain to the Emperor of China,* 1796.)

C. The nave about nine feet long and six inches in diameter; near each extremity of the nave are inserted sixteen or eighteen spokes of bamboo DD; these spokes cross each other at F where they are bound together and strengthened by the concentric ring of split bamboo GG; from hence they are continued to the five peripheries of the wheel to which they are bound with cordage made of twisted bamboo.

HH. The floats or ladle-boards by which the wheel is turned. These are a kind of basket work, made of split bamboo and fixed between the spokes, extending in breadth from one periphery to the other, and in depth towards the centre of the wheel about three feet.

LL. Scoops of bamboo attached to the two peripheries at an angle of twenty-five to thirty degrees with the horizon; the elevated end (M) is open and directed towards the part where the water is to be conveyed. These bamboos are about four feet long, and two inches diameter in the clear.

OO. A long trough supported by the posts RR; into this trough are inserted two wooden pipes PP to convey the water from thence into the reservoir. SS. Posts to support the transoms on which the wheel turns. By the diminution of the inner periphery of the wheel and the angle at which the scoops are placed to them it is obvious that the water taken up at (W) will be retained in them till they become horizontal near the vertex; the end of the scoop that was before elevated will then begin to be inclined, and the water will fall into the trough OO, which may be placed a few inches or a foot at the utmost below the inner periphery of the wheel.

The only material employed in the construction of this wheel, except the nave and the posts on which it is supported, is bamboo.

The quantity of water raised by this wheel may be roughly estimated as follows.

Suppose the length of the scoops four feet and the diameter in the clear two inches (the general dimensions as nearly as I could judge) each scoop will contain six-tenths of a gallon; a slender wheel of this sort seems capable of supporting about sixteen scoops; these will contain $9\frac{6}{10}$ gallons. Suppose the wheel to make three revolutions in one minute, for which a very small stream of water will serve, there will be twenty-eight gallons deposited in the trough, allowing a gallon for waste, or one thousand six hundred and eighty gallons in an hour; therefore in twenty-four hours this very simple and slight machine will raise forty thousand three hundred and twenty gallons or one hundred and sixty tons of water.

Navigation

In my journal of the 11 August 1793 I gave some account of the junks and shipping employed by the Chinese, and expressed my astonishment at their obstinacy in not imitating the ingenuity and dexterity of Europeans in the build and manoeuvre of their vessels, after having had such striking examples before their eyes for these two hundred and fifty years past; but I must now, in a good measure, retract my censures upon this point, as from what I have since observed in the course of my several voyages on the rivers and canals of China, I confess that I believe the yachts and other craft usually employed upon them for the conveyance of passengers and merchandize, and the Chinese boatmen's manner of conducting and managing them, are perfectly well calculated for the purposes intended, and probably superior to any other that we in our vanity might advise them to adopt.[117]

With regard to vessels of a different kind for more distant voyages to Batavia, Manila, Japan, or Cochin China, I am informed that the Chinese of Canton, who have had frequent opportunities of seeing our ships there, are by no means insensible of the advantage they possess over their own; and that a principal merchant there some time since had ordered a large vessel to be constructed according to an English model, but the Hoppo being apprized of it, not only forced him to relinquish his project but made him pay a considerable fine for his delinquency in presuming to depart from the ancient established modes of the Empire which, according to his notions, must be wiser and better than those of the barbarous nations which come from Europe to trade there. It is indeed, as I have before remarked, the prevailing system of the Tartar government to impress the people with an idea of their own sufficiency, and to undervalue in their eyes as much as possible the superior invention of foreign nations; but their vigilance in this respect, and the pains they take for the purpose, evidently betray the conscious fears and jealousy they entertain of their subjects' taste for novelty, and their sagacity in discovering and wishing to adopt the various articles of European ingenuity for use, convenience and luxury, in preference to their own clumsy old-fashioned contrivances.* The government also probably apprehend danger from our teaching their subjects things of which they are now ignorant, but which they would be willing enough to learn. No precaution can stand before necessity; whatever they want from us they must have, and every day they will want more, and elude all means of prevention in order to procure them. Cotton, opium, watches, and broadcloth and tin they can't do without, and I have little doubt that in a short time we shall have almost a monopoly of those supplies to them.

But to return from this digression to the subject of Chinese navigation. It is a very singular circumstance that, though the Chinese appear to be so ignorant of that art, and have neither charts of their coasts or seas to direct them,[118] nor forestaff, quadrant or other instrument for taking the sun's altitude,[119] yet they have for many years past been acquainted with the use of the mariner's compass;† they even pretend that it was known to them before the time of Confucius. Be that as it may, the best writers agree that it was not known to us in Europe till the latter end of the thirteenth dentury, after the conquest of China by the Mongol Tartars; but whether communicated by Marco Polo on his return from China, or by some other adventurer remains undecided.[120] The plan of it, according to its division into thirty-two points, seems to indicate it to be rather an intended European improvement upon something already discovered than to be an original invention. The Chinese compass being divided only into twenty-four points it was easy to add eight more, and yet even with their improvement the European compass in one respect labours under one disadvantage when compared with the Chinese one, for in the latter the calculations are much easier, each point answering to fifteen degrees without odd minutes.

* I am assured that several smart young Chinese at Canton are in the habit of wearing breeches and stockings *a l'Angloise* in their houses, and when they come abroad cover them over with their usual Chinese accoutrements.

† *Ting-nan-chen*, or the 'South deciding needle'.

OBSERVATIONS

Whoever it was that originally introduced the mariner's compass as now used of thirty-two points could not have been extensively versed in science, for long before the discovery of the magnetic needle philosophers of all nations had agreed to divide the circle into three hundred and sixty equal parts or degrees, a degree into sixty minutes, a minute into sixty seconds, etc., etc.[121] The reason, I presume, of the general adoption and continuance of these numbers is the convenience of their being divisible into integral parts by so many different numbers. The points of our mariner's compass, however, happen not to be among these numbers, for three hundred and sixty divided by thirty-two gives $11\frac{1}{4}$ degrees so that, except the four cardinal points and their four bisecting points, all the others, converted into degrees, are involved with fractions; a circumstance of great inconvenience, although thought immaterial by seamen who have tables for every minute of a degree ready calculated to their hands. Now it is submitted whether the Chinese, without any pretensions to science, have not fallen upon a more convenient division of the card of their compass than the Europeans have adopted with all their pretentions to science. It is quartered by the four cardinal points in the same manner as ours, and each of these is subdivided into six points, making twenty-four points in the whole card, so that every point contains fifteen degrees, or the twenty-fourth part of three hundred and sixty.

After all perhaps a division of the card into thirty-six points would be found more advantageous than any other, for then every point would be equal to ten degrees, half a point to five degrees, etc., etc.

Chinese Language

Without presuming to decide upon the merits or demerits of a language which I have so little acquaintance with, I shall however set down that little which I have. It appears to me to be a universal character for this part of the world, as the Japanese, the Cochin Chinese, the people of Pulo Condore, etc., though they could not understand the language of our Chinese interpreters when spoken to them, yet perfectly comprehended whatever our interpreters wrote, in the same manner as all the musicians in Europe of every different country understand equally well the musical scale and read written music, whether Italian, German, English, or of any other school; and as all nations in Europe equally understand the Arabic numerals, and the various signs used by astronomers, mathematicians, chemists, etc. If it be true, to the extent it is said to be, that the Chinese language consists of as great a diversity of characters as scarcely any one man is capable of learning them all, it is no doubt a very great defect. Let us, however, consider for a moment how few there are who really understand the meaning of every word that occurs in the lexicon of our own language (the English). To him who does not, the word not understood is exactly the same as an unknown or unlearned character in the Chinese language to a Chinese.

From the progression of science within these two hundred years, I suppose there may be nearly a fourth more words in the English language at present than had been received in Queen Elizabeth's time; and if the range of our knowledge enlarges, the number of words to express our knowledge must be enlarged also. In the actual state of our language I believe there are very few men not capable of acquiring a thorough acquaintance with every word of it, and each word is certainly a character, being only a different combination of letters from any other word, and expressing an idea, just as each Chinese character is a different combination of marks or strokes, but each expressing an idea. Now I imagine it very possible to find several individuals in Europe (particularly in Germany) who are perfect masters of Greek, Latin, English, French, Italian, Spanish, Portuguese and German. Perhaps the various vocables of these eight languages put together may turn out to be not fewer than all the Chinese characters, which have been so much censured on account of their number and variety. I dare say that Sir William Jones, now one of the judges in Bengal, knows several languages more than I have enumerated, consequently if he had been born a Chinese, and applied himself solely as the Chinese do to the study of the Chinese language, he would have very easily mastered every character and combination which it consists of.[122] The Chinese, by studying their own language, are likely to know it well, and every Chinese studies it more or less; and as to the great difficulty of learning it, for which we blame it, I am persuaded that it is much exaggerated, for I never heard it complained of by the Chinese themselves, and, among them I observe that everybody, even the meanest people, can write it sufficiently for their business and the common purposes of life.

Sir George Staunton's son, a boy of twelve years old, during our passage from England learned, in a few broken lessons from a very cross master and by his own attention, not only such a *copia verborum* and phraseology as enabled him to make himself understood, and to understand others when he arrived in China, but acquired such a facility in writing the Chinese character, that he copied all our diplomatic papers for the Chinese government (the Chinese writers being afraid of their hands being known) in so neat and so expeditious a manner as to occasion great astonishment among them.* And here, in confirmation of what I have said above, let me observe that this young gentleman possesses already five languages, English, Latin, Greek, French, and Chinese, a thing scarcely to be paralleled at so early an age.

The Chinese language seems, however, to have one material defect. It is liable to be equivocal, and appears to depend in a great measure upon the tone or pronunciation of the words used by the speakers, for I took notice that in their conversation together they were often subject to mistake one another, and to require frequent explanations. The same word as written having different significations according as it is spoken with a grave or with an acute accent.

* [See p. 352.—Ed.]

OBSERVATIONS

Conclusion

Before I set out upon my embassy to China I perused all the books that had been written upon that country in all the languages I could understand. With everybody from whom I had hopes of information I endeavoured to converse, and where that could not be done, I corresponded with them by letter. Having thus stored up in my mind all the materials within my reach I shut my books, and as soon as I arrived in the Yellow Sea I began a different course of study upon the same subject. Instead of reading any longer the accounts of others I turned to the originals themselves, and lost no opportunity in my power of perusing and considering them.[123]

The intercourse of the Chinese with foreigners is, however, so regulated and restrained, and the difficulty of obtaining correct information so great that the foregoing papers must not be received without reserve nor regarded otherwise than as merely the result of my own researches and reflections, for I am sensible that, besides being defective in many points, they will be found to differ a good deal from the accounts of former travellers; but I am far from saying that the errors may not be in me, rather than in them. I may have seen neither so well, nor so much as they did, but whatever I did see, or could learn from good authority, I have made it a point most faithfully to represent and report. The picture may seem harsh, cold or ill-coloured, but the fancy of the painter has intruded nothing into the picture that did not appear to him in the original from which he drew. He meant neither to embellish nor disfigure, but solely to give as just a resemblance as he could.

DR. GILLAN'S OBSERVATIONS ON THE STATE OF MEDICINE, SURGERY AND CHEMISTRY IN CHINA

Medicine and Surgery

The state of physic, both as a science and a profession, is extremely low in China; as a science indeed it can hardly be said to exist among them.[124] There are no public schools or teachers of medicine, no professors of the sciences connected with it, no regular united body or college of physicians throughout the whole Empire.[125] They are totally ignorant of the anatomy and physiology of the human body, which is never dissected in China;[126] nor do they seem to have any idea that such knowledge could be of any use to them in the treatment and cure of diseases. Their pathology and therapeutics must of course be extremely deficient and are for the most part erroneous.[127] Natural history, natural philosophy and chemistry, as sciences, are equally unknown to them. Their *materia medica* in consequence of this is extremely limited; their medicines are few in number and are almost altogether taken from the vegetable kingdom. There is no general catalogue of the *materia medica*, no public authorized pharmacopoeia for the *formulae medicamentorum*, composed or used in China.[128] It does not appear that they use directly or indirectly as a medicine any animal substance whatever, except their celebrated asses skin glue, nor any preparation from the mineral kingdom but mercury, sulphur, saltpetre and common salt.[129] Several of the branches of these sciences, however, exist as arts among the Chinese, which use and experience have taught their mechanics the practice of, and in their Encyclopaedia there is a treatise expressly composed upon herbs; but it appears written much more with a view to agricultural and culinary purposes than to medicine.[130] Accordingly they have no fixed rule or standard for the choice and preparation of their medicines. Every practitioner is left to his own judgment and experience to select and exhibit them as he thinks proper. The composition, the doses, and the method of administering them of course are arbitrary and capricious, and vary not only in different provinces and towns but in the hands of every physician and dabbler in physic. Hence physic in China must be vague and uncertain in its principles and practice, and the profession itself necessarily becomes low and obscure. Medicine is not divided in China into three branches as it is in Europe.[131] The same person acts as physician, surgeon and apothecary, and as it frequently happens in other countries, many of them take advantage of the obscurity in which their own art is involved and of the ignorance and credulity of the people to gain money by the sale of nostrums and secrets of their own, which they pretend to be of wonderful efficacy in the cure of the greatest number of diseases incident to the human body. They have hand-bills printed for this purpose, setting forth their medicines, and attested cures annexed to them, which they take all possible means to circulate among the people.

As there are no public schools or professors of medicine in China, a young man who wishes to become a physician has no other way of acquiring a knowledge of the practice of physic but to engage himself to some practitioner as an apprentice for a certain period of time and upon such terms as the master chooses to prescribe. During the time of his apprenticeship the young man has an opportunity of seeing his master's practice, of visiting his patients along with him, and of acquiring such parts of his knowledge and secrets as he chooses to communicate to him. Physicians seldom make fortunes in China, nor can their patients afford in general to pay them high fees. I understand that about forty cash (about 3d. sterling) is the usual fee among the people, and two hundred cash (about fifteen pence sterling) among the Mandarins. But almost all the great Mandarins and princes of the blood have physicians of their own, who live always with them and follow them wherever they go. The Emperor has several who always remain in Court. His physicians, like almost all the rest of his attendants to whose charge he commits his principal affairs and especially his domestic concerns, are eunuchs. The Emperor's physicians and those of the princes and Mandarins are not much better instructed, or much more skilful than the generality of the physicians of the Empire, but they are held in much higher estimation, and when they become favourites they are frequently promoted to honours and fortune.

In the distinction, discernment and cure of diseases the Chinese physicians draw their indications chiefly from the state of the pulse, in the knowledge of which they boast the highest skill. Père du Halde has given a translation of one of their celebrated treatises on this subject, which seem to contain a pretty just account of the ideas they entertain and of the strange system they have formed on this head.[132] But it is evident from the nature and structure of the human frame, as well as from the circulation of the blood, that the general doctrines of the Chinese physicians upon this point must be false. Nothing indeed but the grossest ignorance of anatomy and physiology could make them believe such absurdities. There is certainly a very close connection established by Nature between the state of the pulse and the general affection of the system, with regard to frequency, force, fullness, hardness, softness, etc., by which we are enabled to form our judgments respecting the nature and cure of many diseases. But the Chinese physicians carry their pretensions far beyond this. According to their ideas, every viscus and every part of the body has a particular pulse belonging to itself, which indicates with certainty what part of the system suffers, and how it is affected in disease. They pretend that the pulse, like a general interpreter of animal life, explains every state and condition of the body and that by means of it alone they can immediately discover the seat, nature and cause of disease without asking any question of the patient, or those around him, and without being informed of any other circumstance respecting him. I had an opportunity of seeing and ascertaining this point at Jehol.[133] The Grand Secretary,* for several years past had been frequently indisposed at various times, and always complained of violent pains during the periods of his illness which generally attacked him about the beginning of spring and at the end of autumn. These pains affected chiefly the larger joints of his arms and legs, his back and his loins. Sometimes all these parts were affected at once, but for the most part the pain shifted from one place to another, often alternating its situation, and accompanied with a considerable degree of inflammation and swelling. It often happened too that he felt excruciating pain about the lower part of the abdomen, and a large swelling appeared beginning at the ring of the external oblique muscle on the right side, and extending all along the spermatic chord down to the scrotum. This pain and swelling sometimes occurred at the same time with the articular lumbar and dorsal affections, but more frequently they happened at different times.

They were much more frequent in their recurrence; they did not at all seem to affect spring and autumn as the first did; they were shorter in their duration and frequently appeared and disappeared all at once, and particularly upon his making any sudden exertion, and after a free and natural stool. All these circumstances I learned from himself, and he seemed a good deal surprised at my asking him so many particular questions, which it is not customary for physicians in China to do in any case. In the treatment of this disease his physicians had exhausted all their skill, but to no purpose. The original complaints still continued to recur as usual and had latterly been much more violent than at any former period. After a full examination of his pulses his physicians had early decided that the whole of his complaints and all their change of place and symptoms were owing to a malignant vapour or spirit which had infused itself into, or was generated in his flesh, which shifted itself from place to place, and always excited pain, inflammation and swelling in the part where it fixed itself. In consequence of this opinion respecting the nature and cause of the disease, the method of cure was to expel the vapour or spirit immediately, and this was to be effected by opening passages for its escape directly through the part affected. This operation had been frequently performed and many deep punctures made with gold and silver needles (which two metals only are admissible for this purpose) with exquisite pain and suffering to the patient. Still, however, the disease continued its usual course, nor did the Grand Secretary ever find any permanent benefit from the operation; but this, from the authority and information of his pulses, was entirely owing to the obstinacy of the vapour, which either remained in part in the body in spite of every effort to dislodge it, or was generated in fresh quantities in other parts, after being expelled from the seat it had first occupied.

They had proposed the same method of treatment for the pain and swelling of the lower part of the abdomen, which they considered in the same light as

* [Ho-shen.—Ed.]

the former, and as a part of the same disease. But this the Grand Secretary, apprehensive of injury to some part of the genitalia, could never be persuaded to submit to, and very fortunate it was for him that he continued obstinate on this point. It was under these circumstances, and about ten years after the first attack of his complaint, that I visited him at his own palace at Jehol, in consequence of his own request to His Excellency the Ambassador for his physician to go and see him. After the first ceremonies were over, and the tea, fruits and sweetmeats were taken away, he made me sit down on the couch (or platform covered with cloth, which in Chinese they call . . .* signifying a throne) beside him and presented me first his right arm, and next his left, rested upon a small pillow covered with yellow silk and embroidered with gold, that I might feel and examine his pulses, believing that from their indications alone I could tell him everything respecting the nature, cause and actual state of his complaints. In compliance with the customs and prejudices of his country, and that I might not at first shock himself or his physicians, who stood around us, by neglecting such an important function, I felt with seeming attention and gravity all his pulses on both arms and continued to do so for a long time. Having gone through this preliminary part, I then told him that we were not accustomed to examine the pulses in various parts of the body in Europe, that we usually felt it in one place only, because we know that all the pulses corresponded together and communicated with the heart and each other by means of the circulation of the blood, so that from knowing the state of one artery, or pulse, we knew the state of all the rest. He seemed to listen to me with astonishment and immediately expressed his surprise to his physicians, who stood around us and appeared equally amazed at the novelty of such a doctrine. The interpreter observed to me that they were much embarrassed and disconcerted in their answers to the Grand Secretary. At my request, and to satisfy himself on this subject, he applied the forefinger of his right hand to the left temporal artery, and the same finger of his left hand to the right ankle, and to his great surprise he found the beats of his pulses simultaneous. He appeared much pleased and expressed his satisfaction to those around him. I next told him that, besides feeling and examining carefully the pulse, we were accustomed to take many other circumstances into consideration in ascertaining the nature of diseases, and particularly that we asked a variety of questions respecting internal sensations and external circumstances, the answers to which enabled us to form a better and more accurate judgment. It was in consequence of this that I obtained the information above stated, and upon full investigation it appeared that he laboured under two distinct complaints. The first was rheumatism, which first attacked him in the mountains of Tartary where he had been long exposed to cold and rainy weather, previous to the accession of his complaint, at the period above mentioned. At that same time he was confined to his tent a whole month, with a . . .† fever and a severe pain and swelling in both his knees; the fever abated, and the inflammation and swelling of the knees gradually subsided, so as to leave him very [un]well for some time afterwards. The pain, swelling and

* [Space left blank in the original.—Ed.] † [Word illegible.—Ed.]

other symptoms recurred however the succeeding spring, in cold moist weather, and had continued to recur, at different periods, ever since.

When I asked him more particularly respecting the pain and swelling of the lower part of the abdomen, he confessed he had from his infancy had some little swelling near the ring of the external oblique muscle and sometimes a little way along the spermatic chord. It had, however, never given him any pain or uneasiness till about eight years ago when it suddenly increased to a very large size when he was making an exertion to mount a very tall horse. It gave him exquisite pain at the time and for two days afterwards. I examined the part and found a complete formed hernia. Had he been punctured here, as his physicians had proposed, in all probability the worst consequences would soon have followed. When the interpreter translated to him my explanation of the nature of his complaints, and the method of cure, he seemed quite lost in astonishment. He conversed again with his physicians and at last desired the interpreter to tell me that my ideas and all that I had said were so extraordinary that it appeared to them as if it had come from an inhabitant of another planet.

Surgery does not exist in China as distinct, either in profession or practice, from that of physic; the same person, as has been already stated, unites in himself all the three branches of Physic, Surgery and Pharmacy. Surgery is indeed in a state still lower than the practice of physic among them, and the surgical operations (if such they can be called) are very simple and few in number in China. It has always been found in every age and in every country that the progress of surgery depended upon that of anatomy, without an accurate knowledge of which it is impossible for anyone ever to excel as a surgeon. But in China, where anatomy is altogether unpractised and unknown, it is particularly remarkable how ignorant they seem to be of every kind of surgical operation. I neither saw nor heard of any they perform except the following.

1st. Puncturing with gold and silver needles any inflamed and swelled part, to give issue to the malignant vapour or spirit which, according to their theory, is the cause of such pain, swelling and inflammation.[134] This is the operation in greatest vogue among them and most frequently performed. As it is performed in the same manner and with the same views in Japan, it has been alleged the Chinese had borrowed it from thence, but the well-known attachment of the Chinese to their own practices, opinions and inventions, and the difficulty with which they receive and modify anything foreign, make it much more probable that the Japanese learned it from China.

2nd. Cutting of corns and nails. In this they excel and are very expert, although their instruments are extremely rude and clumsy. They are made of hard tempered steel, ground to a fine edge, and all the rest left rough and unpolished as joiners' and carpenters' tools are in England.[135] I had often heard of their being dexterous chiropodists, and had an opportunity of seeing them perform this operation, so as to be satisfied that they merited the reputation bestowed upon them in this respect.

3rd. Cleansing the ears. In this too they are very expert.

4th. Applying adhesive plasters to sores, and various parts of the body in case of deep-seated pain, and to occasion a revulsion when they apply the plaster at a distance from the part affected, and to draw it to the surface of the body when they apply it directly over that part. Plasters of this kind too are frequently applied to various parts, from motives of religion and superstition. The composition of these is in the hands of the bonzes, who alone pretend to understand and direct the use and situation of them. They sell and apply them for money to the people, whom they teach to expect great advantage from them. Many of them are pretended to be aphrodisiac, and these fetch the greatest price and are most in demand.

5th. Castration. This operation they not only perform upon young children, in order to make them eunuchs for the Emperor, and in hopes that the family and their relations shall one day become rich and happy, when the eunuch grows up and gets in favour at Court, but also upon adults and these past the middle age of life. It seems there is some ancient law or custom by which every man who makes himself an eunuch must be provided for by the Emperor. We heard of several examples of this voluntary castration at Pekin among poor indigent persons, and in times of great scarcity and want. In performing the operation they amputate penis, testes and scrotum, or *rasibus* as the missionaries call it. No fatal accident or haemorrhage is ever known to happen from this operation in China. The missionaries pretend that the Chinese have a particular art in performing it, and that they manage it with such dexterity that the eunuch is able to walk about in a few days. All their skill, however, has not entirely extinguished the jealousy of the Emperor respecting the possibility of a regeneration of some of the parts. As they alone have the care of the Emperor's wives and concubines he causes them to be visited once or twice a year, that no offensive part may have time to become to him an object of jealousy.

The use of general remedies or such as act upon the whole system is equally unknown to them both in physic and surgery. In both cases they think only of topical applications and medicine, and seem not at all to conceive the necessity or advantages of general ones. They never bleed in any case.[136] I never heard of blisters, cupping or scarifying. Amputation they never perform. When accidents requiring it occur it seems they leave the patient to nature and chance, and sometimes he recovers but more frequently dies, especially when an artery is wounded, when the inflammation runs high, or when mortification succeeds. We did not see one person in all China who wanted either leg, arm or any part of a limb.

In the composition of their medicines they are very simple and seem to possess little pharmaceutical skill. They consist chiefly of vegetable powders, decoctions and a few extracts. These they seldom mix or combine, but for the most part exhibit them in a simple form.[137] Their chief remedies consist of rhubarb, ginseng, ginger, pepper, camphor, tea, opium and oil. They make no use of chemical medicines excepting one preparation of mercury for the cure of the venereal disease, which shall be mentioned afterwards. This preparation and the use of it they learned undoubtedly from some of the missionaries. It is single in its kind and is even from that very circumstance a proof of its having come to them from a foreign quarter, and of their ignorance in general of chemical compositions.

The prevalent diseases in China, as far as I could learn or observe, are such as arise from alternate ...* of heat and cold, and among the lower classes of people those which originate in debility and inanition. In the hot seasons inflammatory fevers, *coups de soleil*, phrenitis, hepatitis and cholera morbus prevail. In the cold seasons catarrhs and peripneumonies,† and among the poor people fluxes, dropsies, and typhus fever are the reigning diseases. I heard of no disease peculiar to China. It has indeed been remarked that the natives are much subject to opthalmia and blindness, and there appears some foundation for it. In the provinces we passed through I observed many who had sore eyes and I saw several who were blind. It has been supposed and alleged by many writers that the rice, which is the principal food of the Chinese, is the cause of these disorders of the eyes, but this by no means appears to be the case. If the rice occasioned them, these diseases ought to be much more general than they are, since all the inhabitants of China depend upon this article for their chief subsistance, and the same cause would naturally produce the same effect in a greater or less degree among all those who were subject to its influence. It appears to me more rational to ascribe it to the excessive heat and light of the sun, from which the small round caps they wear do not defend the eyes. I am persuaded, also, that this is really the chief cause of the complaint from having observed that almost all those I saw affected with it, were labouring people whose occupations obliged them to be much abroad and constantly exposed to the action of the solar rays.

The air and climate of China must undoubtedly be various in such an extensive empire. But it does not appear that they have any peculiar effects upon foreigners different from those which depend upon the evident properties of the atmosphere, with regard to the different degrees of heat, cold and moisture; properties which in all countries produce similar effects, and always proportionate to their degrees of intensity, although modified by external circumstances. In the northern provinces, where the soil is chiefly composed of mud and clay and the land extremely level and low, the water is in general very impure, and even when allowed to remain in vessels at rest, it hardly ever deposits the whole of the impurities it contains.[138] The quantity of earthy sediment that falls to the bottom from the water of the province of Pei-chihli exceeds everything known in Europe. The deposition is made more quickly and more completely by boiling the water, and it is not improbable that these circumstances may have contributed to the universality of the practice of drinking everything warm in China. Their common beverage is made by pouring boiling water upon a small quantity of tea leaves in a cup. They allow it to remain a little, and then drink the infusion quite hot, without any addition of sugar or milk, as we are accustomed to use it in Europe. This process has a double effect. The boiling of the water frees it in a great measure from the earthy impurities it contains, and the tea leaves, besides giving a grateful taste to the infusion, serve as a filter for

* [Word illegible.—Ed.]   † [Pneumonia.—Ed.]

rendering it still more pure. When drunk cold and by itself this water is found to produce pains in the stomach and bowels, and frequently too it brings on fluxes. This happened to several of the soldiers and servants, and I had no doubt but it was owing to the great quantities of impurities the water contained. The Chinese opinion was that it was owing to the coldness of the water. They contend that nature, having given us hot blood and fluids, meant that everything we took into the system should be of the same temperature with our fluids, and they always make their own practice conform to their theory; but besides drinking everything hot I do not remember ever to have seen anyone in China drink water pure and unmixed. Tea was their constant drink from morning till night. They keep it constantly prepared in all their houses and always present a cup of it to all visitors when they enter the hall, and another when they go out. In many places there are people who take their stand upon the high road and prepare and sell it at the rate of from one to three cash to the travellers who pass by; and at different distances there are temples or pagodas for poor travellers to stop at and repose themselves and pass the night if they . . .* it. In these pagodas there are public servants appointed whose business it is to have tea always ready and give it to these travellers gratis; but no other refreshment is given them besides tea and shelter. To these places, too, persons meeting with any accident or suddenly taken ill by the way may be carried, but there is no medical assistance appointed for them. These are the only places like public hospitals in China as far as I could learn. It seems they have no infirmaries or dispensaries with medical assistants appointed to them in any part of the Empire.[139] That part of Tartary immediately adjoining to the province of Pei-chihli and separated from it only by the Great Wall is extremely wild and mountainous. The face of the country changes all at once, and the air and climate appear totally different. Those who have travelled in the Alps are immediately struck with the general resemblance between this country and many parts of the Valais. The mountains are not so much covered with wood, and the hills and valleys are more arid and dry than those of the Valais, but in most other respects the coincidence is very complete; the air is keen and penetrating, the cold in winter is very intense, the snow lies upon the mountains and in the hollows for . . .† months and all the water the inhabitants use is chiefly from melted snow and ice. As we advanced into the narrow valley between the mountains we remarked a very considerable difference in the looks and appearance of the inhabitants and saw a great number of them with goitres or wens upon their necks.‡ These goitres were of a much larger size than any I had ever seen in the Valais or in the Tyrol. They begin immediately below the parotid gland and generally reach round under the jaws from ear to ear affecting all the submaxillary glands on their whole course; some of them were of an enormous size, and by their breadth and weight had distended the skin so as to hang very . . .§ the breast. It appeared upon a general estimation that nearly one-sixth of all the inhabitants we saw were affected with this deformity. Among

* [Word illegible.—Ed.]   † [Word illegible.—Ed.]
‡ [See note 31.—Ed.]   § [Two words illegible.—Ed.]

themselves they do not esteem it such, and what is very remarkable, they all ascribe it to the snow water they use. The same cause has been assigned for it in Europe, but it by no means accounts for the phenomena of the disease. But what seems very remarkable here, too, is that the goitres seemed to be confined to a certain district or extent of country. They began to disappear as we approached Jehol, whose situation however is still higher above the level of the sea, and after we came to the Palace . . , close by the town . . . situated on the banks of the river . . .* we saw no more of them at all. I do not remember to have seen one single goitre all the time we were at Jehol, although there was a prodigious number of inhabitants in the place and curiosity had brought great crowds from all the adjacent country to see the Embassy.

The venereal disease in all its forms is common in China. I could not learn anything positive respecting its antiquity from any authentic documents, and had it not been that our Mandarins assured us the general belief in China was that the disease was always known among them even in the remotest periods of their empire, I should have been inclined, from a variety of concurring circumstances, to have believed it of a more recent date. It is certain that, although the disease be one of the most disagreeable in its symptoms, and dangerous in its consequences, of all those that afflict the human race, they continue extremely ignorant of its nature and cure in China.[140] Their ignorance of anatomy and surgery sufficiently accounts for their deficiency in the cure of many of the local affections of the genitalia and urinary passages. But one would naturally think that anxiety on the part of the patient and inquiry and multiplied experience for ages on the part of the physicians, would at least have found out the means of cure for the systemic disease, had it really been of such great antiquity among them. They do not appear to have any distinct name for it in Chinese. About Canton, where it is most frequent, and where they understand best its nature and cure in consequence of their communication with the Europeans, they call it *ts'ao-pi-t'eng*, i.e. the parts of the man diseased, and *ts'ao-chi-pa-t'eng*, i.e. the parts of the woman diseased. In the northern provinces they call it *pau-mei* or *t'ien-p'ao-ch'uang*, which signify various symptoms of the disease according to their external appearances, as warts, etc.[141] But besides these names they frequently speak of it under the appellation of the Canton ulcer, a term which would imply its having been first spread through the country from that town, where it had first appeared, and where probably it had been originally introduced by the Europeans trading to that port. Many of the missionaries are decidedly of this opinion, in support of which they further add that the only mercurial preparation the Chinese use for the cure of it was communicated to them by one of the missionaries, and they continue it unchanged to this day. The Chinese, however, who ought to know best, maintain that the disease has always existed and been known in China.

I had an opportunity of learning these circumstances, and at the same time of seeing the disease in its various stages, in the persons of the four chief Mandarins who accompanied us to Canton. Chou and Wang had caught the

* [Blanks left in the original.—Ed.]

infection from some of the ladies of Hangchowfu and about a fortnight after it appeared in both in the form of chancre and gonorrhoea. Wang, the military Mandarin, applied to me first and was soon cured of his complaints. He seemed exceedingly surprised when I first suggested an injection into the urethra. He had never heard of such a thing before. However he submitted to it readily enough, and afterwards took the syringe and injection and applied it himself according to my directions. His friend Chou, seeing the good effects of the remedies he had taken, wished very much to try the same course, but as a civil Mandarin he was more ashamed to acknowledge his situation. He therefore requested Wang to demand a fresh supply as it were for himself, and to give them privately to him. Wang, whose free, frank, open manners lead to no concealment, could not disguise the matter when he demanded the medicines with directions for using them. I told him he was perfectly cured already and that he did not want any unless he meant to prepare himself for his return to Hangchowfu. He burst out into a fit of laughter, and immediately told me the medicines were for his friend Chou, whose modesty would not permit him to appear in person. He soon got the better of his modesty, however, and was perfectly cured in a short time. As both of them had experienced the good effects of our medicines, and so quick a cure, they anxiously requested a stock of them for future contingencies with written directions how to use them, and instructions how to prepare and compose them, both of which requests were readily granted to them.

To *ta-jen*, the Military Commander at Mam-cham-fou,* who came with us from that city to Canton, had been ill of the complaint for several years. He had many scabs and eruptions on various parts of his body, and as his father had died of a similar disease he was extremely apprehensive of his own fate, All the symptoms, however, readily yielded to frictions with mercurial ointment. and he too got a supply for future use.

The *Tsung-tu*† was affected much in the same way and treated in a similar manner, with the same success; he was so much pleased with the effects of the medicines he took that the very day we left Canton where he came to take leave of the Ambassador at the English factory, he applied for the receipts of the different compositions he had used, and made Chou translate them into Chinese characters through the interpreter's explanations.

From the concurring testimony of these four gentlemen it is certain that the venereal disease is now at least very frequent in China, but that the treatment and cure of it are very ill understood. After the running from the urethra has ceased and the external sores have disappeared they generally consider themselves cured. They seldom continue the use of mercury long enough to cure the constitutional infection, and in consequence of this neglect venereal sores, blotches and scabs often break out on the surface of the body; some time afterwards exostoses of the bones succeed, and many unhappy patients, after leading in this manner a miserable life of a few years, die in the utmost distress.

It is a common opinion in China that the infected parent communicates a

* [? Nan-chou-fou.—Ed.] † [i.e. the Viceroy, Ch'ang-lin.—Ed.]

diseased constitution to his offspring, insomuch that some families are supposed to have the venereal taint hereditary. The Viceroy and To ta-jen both believed this respecting themselves. During the mercurial course they sometimes assist the operation of the mercury with infusions of ginseng and tea, and solutions and mixtures of camphor. Occasionally, too, they make use of the warm bath, but in general they only employ warm bathing in the second state of the disease when the secondary eruptions appear which they do not at all rightly understand the nature of, but call them leprosy, and in general they consider this state of the complaint is incurable.

In Canton and the neighbourhood of it they use mercurial ointment for the cure of the *lues venerea*, the use and preparation of which they have learned from the Europeans residing there. But in Pekin and all the northern provinces they employ mercurial pills, prepared according to the following formula which was communicated by Chou. It appears, from the ingredients and proportions of the formula to have been introduced by some of the missionaries, as they themselves declare, and from the ignorance of chemical skill it manifests, and the uncommon acrimony of the pills resulting from the operation, we may easily believe their assertion that it was communicated by them a long while ago. Chou could not tell exactly what was the number of pills formed from the sublimed mass, how much each pill weighed, nor how many were taken for a dose; but he knew very well that their operation was violent and that they frequently produced violent vomiting and purging and severe pains in the bowels. These inconveniences and the pain resulting from them were the principal reasons that prevented patients in China from continuing the use of the medicine long enough to complete the cure. The formula is as follows:

> ℞   Nitre ℥vii
> Sulphuris ℥viii
> Hydrargyri ℥ix

Having first reduced the saltpetre and sulphur to a fine powder, mix all the ingredients together in an earthen pot or jar, cover this jar with a porcelain vessel, and place this apparatus on the fire. Collect the smoke or vapour arising from this mixture and condensed in the upper porcelain vessel and form it into pills. Give these pills to those who labour under the venereal complaint and in a few days they will be rid of the complaint. It appears, however, that they distinguish between the treatment of gonorrhoea and *lues venerea*. In the first they recommend the mildest and most simple food, abstinence from . . .* wine, oil, vinegar and all aromatic condiments, to drink tea and along with it to take every day and at several times a decoction of the root of peony (called in the Chinese language *pung-fu-lin*)[142] and by observing this regimen the patient will recover his health, they say, in a hundred days.

The mercurial pills, prepared according to the formula, are only to be employed in confirmed *lues venerea* after chancres and other symptoms of general infection have appeared.

* [Word illegible.—Ed.]

The smallpox is a very common and fatal disease in China. From the beginning of the disease and during the whole of the eruptive fever they keep the patient as warm as possible, and according to the usual practice, which prevails at all times in all situations and among all ranks in China, they give everything to eat and drink as hot as it can swallowed. It is not surprising that under these circumstances the confluent smallpox, or as they are often called, the malignant species, should often occur and sweep off many thousands at a time. This frequently happens in China and the contagion spreads widely through the country. The natural heat of the climate and the warm regimen the patients are kept upon certainly contribute much to the aggravation of the disease and in many instances determine the confluent instead of the distinct species. They understand the practice of inoculation which has very long been known among them, and they often perform it,[143] but I could not learn they thought it necessary to prepare the body by previous medicines; or that they chose one season of the year as more favourable for the disease than another. Their method of performing inoculation is quite different from ours and is undoubtedly much inferior in every point of view. It seems to be only a more certain method of communicating the smallpox in the natural way, either by conveying the contagion along with the respired air into the lungs, or with the saliva into the stomach. Their method is this. They take a small quantity of cotton, which they impregnate with recent variolous matter and then stuff it into one of the nostrils of the patient. After this the external opening of the nostril is plugged up with wax, rosin or plaster, and in this state the patient remains for three days, after which they withdraw the whole apparatus from the nostrils and wait the issue of the operation. Should it not succeed it is repeated again exactly as before, and thus continued until the smallpox at last appears. In consequence of this method it generally happens that the whole inside of the nostril, of the mouth, the tongue and *fauces** are covered with pustules, which circumstance occasions that difficulty of respiration and deglutition which is remarked to be more particularly connected with the inoculated than with the natural smallpox in China. They are very anxious to guard against the pits or marks this disease so frequently leaves behind it, and they use oil for anointing the scabs that form on the bases of the pustules, in order to detach them more easily in the same way as is done in Europe. They do not however understand the advantages of cool air and a cooling regimen, from which we derive so much benefit in Europe.

Respecting the measles I could get very little information. I was however told that they are frequent and as troublesome in China as in Europe, and that they understand less their nature and cure than of any of the other epidermical diseases that prevail through the empire.[144]

* [Latin word meaning 'throat.'—Ed.]

Chemistry

Chemistry cannot be said to exist as a science in China, although several branches of it are practised in various parts of the Empire as chemical arts.[145] None of these arts, however, appear to have been brought to any great degree of perfection by the Chinese, excepting the manufacture of porcelain or china, in which they have long been acknowledged to excel. It seems to be a just remark that in all mechanical arts and manufactures the Chinese content themselves with the processes and methods of operation already known, which they imitate without the smallest change or deviation, and without ever enquiring whether they might be improved by any addition or alteration in the mode of conducting them.[146] As soon as the product of any art or manufacture has appeared to them to answer the general purpose for which it was intended they seem never to have sought to make any further progress in it, either in elegance, ornament or increased utility. I had an opportunity of seeing the processes they follow, and the products resulting from several of these arts; but I could not learn that they had any general name or term, under which to denominate several kindred arts, or to mark them out as connected together by the same general principles, or conducted with similar views and operations.[147] They have all the perfect metals except platina, and of the semi-metals I saw cobalt, zinc and mercury. I shall briefly state the few observations I had an opportunity of making on each of these metals, and on a few other articles of Chinese manufacture, and the processes they follow in making them.

GOLD

There are said to be several mines of this precious metal in China, but they do not work them. Almost all the gold they have is collected in the provinces of Yunnan and Szechwan. It is found in small grains among the sand in the beds of the rivers and torrents which carry it down along with them as they descend from the mountains, and perfectly pure and free from any alloy. Gold is not coined into money, nor is it much used in China except for making a few trinkets and ornaments, and especially at Canton where the Chinese artists manufacture it into fans, buckles, snuff boxes, tooth pick cases, seals, watch chains, etc., for the Europeans who trade there. The natives themselves do not use or purchase any of these articles, but the Mandarins and women of rank wear large bracelets or rings of it round their wrists, both by way of ornament and superstitition. It is a general belief among them that these bracelets or rings possess a certain secret charm of preserving the wearer from a variety of diseases.[148] This custom and belief are so prevalent that those who cannot afford the gold wear silver ones, and the lower classes of the people have them of brass and tin. The carvers and gilders use gold leaf for gilding and ornamenting their works as in Europe. All the tiles of the roof of the great temple of

Potala were beautifully gilt, and all the numerous statues of their deities and heroes were ornamented in the same manner. Their silk and velvet weavers use it in their gold tissues and in their embroideries, in the same manner as it is used by the manufacturers of Lyons, and a small portion of it is employed in making gilt paper for burning at the altars of their gods, and in the funeral ceremonies of the great. Gold is sold in China as an article of commerce. The proportion it bears to an equal weight of silver varies a little at different times, but is always much lower than in Europe. The gold dust when collected is melted in crucibles, and cast into ingots of various size and shape. It is extremely soft and ductile and of a very pale colour on account of its perfect purity.

SILVER

Silver is found in greater abundance in China than gold. It is not coined into money, but, after being smelted in crucibles and rendered as pure as possible by cupellation, it is cast into little masses of different shapes and weight; in this form it is current, like money, for the purchase of merchandise and various commodities, its value being determined by its weight, and the current price of the market. The Emperor's treasury consists of silver in this form, and out of it he pays his troops and public officers of state. Silver too is drawn into threads and used by the silk weavers in their silver tissues in the same manner as the the gold is. Not only the native silver of the country is melted down into these forms, but also a very great number of the dollars carried to China by the Europeans, for the purchase of the various articles they import from thence into Europe.*

COPPER

Copper is found in great plenty. All the coin or cash† of the Empire is made of it, but for this purpose they employ copper of a very inferior quality. It is very ill smelted, quite brittle, and contains a great deal of the impurities of the ore, from which it is extracted. For the composition of bell metal, they use a mixture of copper and tin in somewhat different proportions, and evidently containing more tin than ours does in Europe. The bells of the bonzes' temples made of this composition appear to be more sonorous than ours, but also more brittle and of course much more liable to be broken. The gongs, which are in such general use, are made of a composition of the same metals, but with a much greater proportion of copper, and in several of them there is a small quantity of tutenag mixed with the copper and tin.

The Chinese white copper, called by them *pe-tung*, has long been celebrated and imported into Europe as an article of commerce, to a considerable amount annually.[149] It has a beautiful silver-like appearance; it has a very close grain, takes a fine polish, and many articles of neat workmanship in imitation of silver are made from it; the nature of this metal was for a long time entirely unknown

* [See note 96—Ed.]   † [A small Eastern coin. Singhalese *kasi*, a coin.—Ed.]

in Europe. The different companies were satisfied with importing and selling it as other merchandise, and the artists with the manufacture and sale of the various articles they made of it, without enquiring further into the natural history or extraction of it. The missionaries, who seem in general to magnify things in their accounts of China and its productions (especially when they write about things they do not properly understand) have presented this metal as a native production of the earth,* but tarnishing a little after a long exposure to the air. They pretend that the *pe-tung* owes its whiteness and lustre only to its own native qualities and texture, and not to any adventitious metal or composition mixed with it, and that on the contrary its original splendour is rendered more dim and obscure by the addition of a small proportion of silver and tutenag which the workmen find it necessary to mix with it, on account of its brittleness which prevents them from being able to work it by itself. This, however, is certainly a mistaken account of the matter; for the addition of tutenag would increase instead of diminishing the native brittleness of the *pe-tung*, which, instead of being a simple metal, is always found to be a compound substance. An accurate analysis has determined it to consist of copper, zinc, a little silver, and in some specimens, a little vitriolated iron and nickel has been found. The iron has accidentally adhered to the zinc, when separated from the calamine, as all the ores of zinc are found to contain some iron mineralized by sulphur. In consequence of this circumstance, which seems only accidental, some artists have been inclined to believe that vitriolated iron, in a small proportion, entered as a necessary ingredient into the composition of white copper. In this, however, they are mistaken, for zinc and iron, or copper and iron, do not unite well together, much less when the iron is in a saline form. Iron too would render the colour darker in proportion to the quantity contained in the composition of the mixed metal.

Tutenag is the name the Chinese give to zinc, which they extract from a very rich ore of calamine, by pounding the calamine into a fine powder and then mixing it with charcoal dust, and distilling the mixture from earthen jars, in a common distilling apparatus placed on a slow fire. The zinc rises in the form of flowers or sublimate, passes through the worm or pipe of the head of the still, which is luted to the earthen jar, containing the calamine and charcoal powders, and is received under water in a vessel placed for the purpose, into which the extremity of the pipe plunges. The water condenses the flowers of the zinc, which fall in consequence to the bottom, and, when a sufficient quantity has been thus obtained, they are collected out of the vessel, and then put into melting pots, and fused into the masses, which are commonly sold under the name of tutenag. The ore from which the Chinese extract their tutenag is extremely rich and very pure. It generally contains from six-tenths to nine-tenths of its weight of pure zinc, and it has the peculiar advantage of containing hardly any iron, and not a particle of lead or arsenic; all of which extraneous impurities are generally found in the calamine and blende ores, from which zinc

* And not a composition of art. They describe it as of a shining white colour, brightest when newly dug out of the earth.

is extracted in Europe. On these accounts the manufacturer gives a decided preference to the Chinese zinc or tutenag because the European zinc is not purified by subsequent processes, as it might be, from these adventitious ingredients, which will so far tarnish the colour of the metal, and prevent its compositions from receiving so fine a polish as they otherwise would do. I was informed at Canton that, besides the advantages resulting from the purity of their tutenag, there was another circumstance which contributes much to the beauty of their *pe-tung*. Instead of simply melting together in the furnace the proper proportions of *pe-tung* and tutenag, they first reduce the copper into as thin sheets or lamina as possible, these thin plates they make red hot, and increase the fire almost to a melting heat, so that the copper is rendered quite soft and almost ready to flow. In this state they are suspended over the vapour of their purest tutenag, placed in a subliming vessel over a brisk fire; the vapour of the sublimate in this state penetrates the hot sheets of copper, and unites very intimately with it, so as to remain fixed with it, and not easily dissipated or calcined by the succeeding fusion it has to undergo. When the copper plates have thus imbibed as much of the sublimed tutenag as they can absorb, they are immediately withdrawn and put into melting pots, and the surface of the whole covered with charcoal powder; if the artist thinks the sheet of copper has not absorbed a sufficient proportion of the tutenag he adds in the melting pots what he thinks sufficient for making up the deficiency; the melting pots are now placed in a furnace, when a brisk fire is kindled, and the whole fused together very completely; the fire is then withdrawn and the pots allowed to cool very gradually; when it is quite cool the *pe-tung* is withdrawn, and is found to be of a brighter and much closer and finer grain when prepared by this process than it is in the common way; and the nature of the operation evidently leads to this conclusion, and appears very well calculated for the desired effect. With respect to the *pe-tung* itself, which the missionaries pretend to be found only in China and nowhere there but in the mountains of Yunnan, it is possible that there may there exist a natural ore of copper and tutenag blended together, from the smelting of which there would result brass or white copper, according to the proportion of tutenag contained in the ore, just in the same manner as these substances result from the artificial mixture of these ores in the usual processes for producing them. But whether this be the case or not, the result of the operation in either case would be the same and possess similar properties.

Tutenag or zinc is not the only substance employed in whitening copper. Both tin and arsenic produce the same effect; zinc and arsenic can both be easily separated from this composition by exposing it for a long time to a violent heat, and the copper is then found in its simple and natural state. Tin cannot be separated in this way, but it may by other easy processes, in so far as tin is contained in *pe-tung* the colour is rendered less brilliant and is of a bluish watery colour and arsenic diminishes its malleability. Tutenag used always to be imported from China, but of late years its ores, calamine and blende (or black Jack as the English miners call it) have been found in great abundance in various parts of England, and the art of extracting the zinc is now so well understood

CHINESE IRON

that very probably it may soon cease to be an article of commerce from China. In consequence of the improved state of chemistry, white copper is now made in England, and so like the Chinese *pe-tung* as not to be distinguished from it; any little difference that may be found by experiment may be supposed to proceed from original qualities of the ores, whence the ingredients of the composition are extracted, and from the processes employed in smelting and combining and working them; for in this respect not only the mines of different countries vary in their properties, but also those of the same country and province differ very much in hardness, softness, malleability, ductility, colour, specific gravity, etc. This fact has been long known to mineralogists and metallurgists. Perhaps too some difference may arise from the use of coked pit-coal in England for smelting the ores, as it is impossible entirely to free it from iron and sulphur or vitriolated iron, whereas the Chinese only use charcoal of wood in all their processes.

IRON

There are several mines of iron ore, and the metal itself is in great abundance all over the Empire.[150] They apply it in general to the same uses as we do in Europe, but in the manufacturing of it they appear much inferior; it is not so soft, nor so malleable and ductile as ours, which probably arises from its not being so well managed in roasting and smelting the ore. Their nails, hinges, and in general all their smith work, are exceedingly brittle and very apt to snap across when any attempt is made to bend them. Their tools of it are very clumsily made and not at all polished. They understand, however, the art of casting it very well, and they make pots and other vessels of it extremely thin. They understand too the conversion of it into steel by cementation, and give it a pretty good temper, but in both respects they are much below the English artists, whom on this point they in vain attempt to imitate. Many of the Europeans, however, and of the missionaries particularly, had boasted much of the skill of the Chinese in this respect. According to their accounts the artists of Canton are said to possess peculiar secrets for tempering their steel instruments so highly as to cut all sorts of stones and the thickest glass with them, as we do in Europe with diamonds. This account was confirmed to me by several of the gentlemen at Canton, and it was therefore thought worth while to ascertain the fact. We went through the workshops where the artists were employed in their respective branches, and saw them all indeed seemingly cut glass with great ease by means of a steel rod they held in their hands; but upon examining these steel rods, we found every one of them armed at the extremity with a small diamond. Our gentlemen all returned convinced of their mistake, which arose from their never having before taken the trouble of examining the instruments closely, and trusting entirely to what they saw at a distance. They have indeed an instrument shaped like a small chisel at both ends, with which they can cut their own thin glass, and a good penknife might do the same. But the Chinese themselves did not pretend that they possessed any such tools, as had been reported of them, nor did they know any secret whatever for giving such a temper to steel. I bought one of their instruments with which they sometimes cut their own glass, but it appears of a very ordinary temper.

LEAD

This metal is little in use among the Chinese. I only remember to have seen a few sheets of it, nailed as ornaments on the sideboards and cable posts of some of the junks of the Pei-ho, and a few knobs or balls of it on the tops of the poles erected before the gates of the Mandarins' houses and the temples of the bonzes. It is chiefly used at Canton in very thin sheets for lining the tea chests.

TIN

Tin is in great use. Large quantities of it are consumed daily and it is an article of great request through the whole of the provinces of the Empire. At Canton they employ a mixture of it in a small proportion with lead for forming the very thin plates which the tea packing cases are lined with, and everywhere kitchen stoves lined with clay, and ornaments for sedan chairs and their poles are made of it. But the chief consumption of tin is in the offerings and sacrifices they make at the altars of their idols, and in the funeral ceremonies of their dead. After having reduced the tin to as thin a foil as possible they cut it into slips of various size and form and gum it upon square bits of paper, numbers of which are burnt in vessels before the altars and images of their temples by almost every individual daily throughout the whole year. When one considers the immense popularity of this it will give an idea of the great quantity of tin that must be consumed in this way. The greatest part of their imported tin comes from England, but it is not equal to the Malacca and Banca tin imported to them by the Dutch, and the Chinese accordingly give them the preference. The Banca and Malacca tin is quite pure, and on this account more easily rolled into thinner foil, and of a brighter lustre. The English tin naturally contains in its ores a small proportion of iron, copper and arsenic, the fire necessary for smelting the tin fuses also along with it the iron and copper, and the arsenic continues adhering to, or combined with it, and hence the block tin formed from such ore must contain a small quantity of these three substances, all of which contribute to debase its quality. The iron and copper tarnish the colour and give it a yellowish hue, and the arsenic renders it more brittle and difficult to form into foil. Lead too is sometimes purposely mixed with the block tin, it being much cheaper than tin and difficult to detect, and hence the manufacturers have great temptations to adulterate it. The use of coked pit coal too is liable to the same inconveniences as in the smelting of zinc from calamine or blende. It would not be difficult to purify the tin from all these foreign substances and so to make the English rival the Banca tin, if the manufacturers found it their interest and were inclined to do it.

MERCURY

This semi-metal is very common at Canton, but I saw it nowhere else. At Canton they employ it chiefly in tinning small mirrors or looking glasses which they make there of a very diminutive size, but in great numbers, and at a very low price, not much exceeding a penny sterling. The toys, too, commonly known under the name of Chinese balancers and tumblers, are partly filled and the changes of their equilibrium effected by mercury. All the chemical uses and preparations of it are unknown to them. A general idea prevails among the low people that the use of mercury in the venereal disease would render the men impotent and the women barren, and although they know it produces no such effects on Europeans, this they contend (and they firmly believe it) is owing to their being formed of a different structure of body; their own expression is that a Chinese inside is quite different from an European's.

PIT-COAL

There are different mines of pit-coal in different provinces, but there are few of them wrought.[151] I saw and entered into one of them in the province of Canton. The entry or drift was low down on the side of a very high mountain and only a few feet above the level of the river down which we came in our junks. It was pierced through the mountain in a horizontal direction, and the roofs and sides of it were supported with upright and cross bamboos. The excavations were made, and the coal dug out, on every side horizontally. They had neither risen high up nor sunk below the level of the entrance of the drift. There was very little water in it, and what there was ran in a small canal dug for it by the side of the foot-walk of the drift, and fell into the river flowing by the foot of the mountain. The passage was lighted by lamps placed at different distances, and the coal which resembled very much that of Whitehaven[152] was carried out on men's shoulders in baskets; each man carried out two baskets suspended at the ends of a bamboo, laid across his neck and shoulders, in the usual way in which burdens of all kinds are carried in China.

There were but few miners employed, and the quantity of coal dug out of the pit appeared to be very inconsiderable. The chief consumption of it seemed to be for burning lime, great quantities of which are made from the marble and limestone of the mountain itself in which the coal is found, and of all the adjoining ones, through which in all probability the stratum of coal passes. The Chinese prefer charcoal of wood for fuel, but in some of the northern provinces where wood is scarce and very dear they use coked pit-coal, prepared in the same way as we do in England. But although they must have long observed the prodigious quantity and disagreeable smell and suffocating nature of the smoke issuing from the crude pit-coal during the process of coking, it does not appear that they have ever examined the properties of it, or thought of considering it either from motives of curiosity, investigation or utility. This coked coal, as far as I could learn, is only used for culinary purposes, for baking of bricks and burning of lime. It was frequently served to us for fuel in the junks, in the provinces of Pei-chihli and Shantung, and as far as I could judge appeared in every respect inferior to our English coke. We brought with us specimens of the coked and crude coal, of the coked from Pei-chihli and Shantung, and of the crude from the mine of the province of Canton.

PORCELAIN

I had no opportunity of seeing the manufacture of the china porcelain, formerly so much in repute in Europe, and in the making of which they still excel. The superior excellency of this article is certainly owing to the greater purity of the petuntse and kaolin, and the superior quality of the blue colours which their china is painted with, and I was informed that they formerly prepared the ingredients for making it from their own cobalt, but now great quantities of smalt (which is the powder of a glass, made from one part of calx of cobalt, usually called zaffre in commerce, and two parts of powdered flint mixed and melted together) are carried out to them from Europe; and of late Prussian blue has been imported for them, which still gives a finer and deeper colour. But since the English East India Company has ceased to import china into England the manufactory of it has diminished much in quantity and in quality.[153]

CAMPHOR

This article is in great repute and bears a high price. The best kind is the native camphor, which they get from Japan, which is sold at an extravagant rate; but the quantity of it is very small. By far the greatest part of their camphor is made in China and extracted from the leaves, twigs, branches and wood of the *laurus camphora* which grows plentifully in the country and which they call *chang shu*. They take the branches, leaves and twigs of this tree, chop them into small pieces and infuse them in a large cauldron of boiling water. They make the water continue to boil till the whole of the camphor is extracted from the fibres of the leaves and branches, and when they observed it adhere in a glutinous form to the sides of a wooden rod with which they constantly stir the mixture, they then withdraw the fire, pick out the branches and leaves and decant the water or pass the whole through a fine sieve.

The camphor remains behind and congeals by degrees into a glutinous mass which they now take and mix with clay and lime; this mixture is now put into an earthen vessel, which they cover with another of the same kind, and lute the juncture of the vessels carefully with a paste of rice or of clay and paper. The apparatus is then placed over a slow fire and the camphor gradually sublimes through the clay and lime into the upper vessel to the sides of which it adheres, forming a cake whose shape corresponds to the interior sides of the upper vessel into which it rises, while the clay and lime retain the impurities it formerly may have contained. When they want to have the camphor very pure they repeat this process and sublime it three or four times. This is the method of extracting and preparing the camphor at Hangchowfu.

GLASS

There was formerly a glass manufactory established at Pekin under the direction of some of the missionaries, but it is now neglected and no glass is made in China.[154] The Canton artists, it is true, collect all the broken fragments of European glass they can find, which they pound and melt again in their furnaces; when melted they blow it into large globes or balloons which they afterwards cut into pieces of various shapes and magnitude as they want it. The chief use they make of it is for small looking glasses and a few toys. This is the only kind of glass they now make in China, and as they blow it extremely thin they find it easy to cut it with the steel chisels formerly mentioned; they do not seem to understand the manufacture of glass from the crude materials, nor to know exactly what they are. The glass beads, and buttons of various shapes and colours, are imported to them from Europe and chiefly from Venice.

The Chinese make great use of spectacles, which they hang upon their ears by loopholes from each end of them. The eye glasses are all made of rock crystal. Large crystals are found in various parts, but the finest are got in the mountains of Canton. The Canton artists cut these crystals into thin lamina with a kind of steel wire saw, formed by twisting two or more wires together and laying them like a bow string to the end of a small flexible bamboo. When they proceed to work with this saw they undo one end of the wire string, pass it round the crystal in the place they mean to cut, and then fix the crystal between two pivots and saw it in the same manner as our watchmakers do when they saw or cut any piece of brass or other metal. Below the crystal there is a small trough full of water into which the siliceous powder of the crystal falls as it is cut by the revolutions of the steel wire. With this mixture they frequently moisten the wire and the groove formed in the crystal by it during the whole of the operation. The powder of the crystal, like that of the diamond, helps to cut and polish itself. I examined a great number of the polished eye glasses after they were ready for setting, but I could not observe any diversity of form among them; they all appeared to me quite flat with parallel sides. The workmen did not seem to understand any optical principles for forming them in different manners so as to accommodate them to the various kinds of imperfect vision.

COMMON SALT

The quantity of sea salt made in China is almost incredible and the Emperor derives a great revenue from it. There are mines of rock salt in some of the provinces but these I did not see, nor any specimens of the salt produced from them either in China or in Tartary. These resemble exactly what used to be called *Sel de Gabelle* in France. It is made from the spontaneous evaporations of salt water by the heat of the sun on the sea coasts of the maritime provinces, especially those of Canton and Fukien.[155] When the tide rises the sea water is let into shallow pits or beds prepared for it; the bottom of these pits is made of clay; there is a mound or bank raised between them and the sea, which is let into them at high water by means of sluices. The whole process is conducted exactly in the same manner and upon the same principles as it is done in the south of France, adjoining to the Mediterranean, in Spain, Italy and Portugal. The salt found in this manner contains the same kinds of impurities as the Gabelle salt, but the Chinese use it without boiling down and refining it a second time. From the sea coasts it is distributed through every part of the Empire. There is an immense magazine or store of it laid up at Tientsin, which seems to be the general repository for Pekin and all the northern provinces. The salt is deposited on the ground, with mats and straw only below it, in long ranges like rows of houses, and the top and sides of the heaps are only covered with bamboo mats of the same kind to defend it from the wet and the rain. In this position it remains till it be carried away for use. A considerable portion of it is dissolved and lost by every shower, and some part of it too is spoiled by the dirt and mud that mix with the bottom parts of it, but the quantity naturally and annually produced is so great that these trifling losses are overlooked as of no consequence. As nearly as I could be informed the price of the salt at Tientsin, including the duty or impost paid to the Emperor, is about 1⅜ penny sterling per lb. At Pekin it is dearer, and at Canton cheaper. This is owing to the impost being different at different places, and to the price of carriage which increases in proportion to the distance from the place where the salt is made.

SALTPETRE

All the other combinations of salt, or as they are called by the chemists neutral salts, are unknown in China, excepting common salt and saltpetre.[156] They do not know the constituent parts, the acids and the alkalis of which these salts are composed, nor do they think they are compound substances. They believe them on the contrary to be simple and elementary. They have, however, the two alkalis, fossil and vegetable. The vegetable alkali they obtain by lixiviating the ashes of their wood fire, but I do not know where they get the fossil. I made particular inquiry, but the only answer I obtained was that it came from Tartary; how that could be I do not understand. They confound those alkalis together by the name of *ken*,* and they use them for washing and cleansing their clothes. They do not understand the manufacture of soap, although they have plenty of oil with which, and their *ken*, they might make it exceedingly good.[157] We tried to make some at Pekin, and in the junks, and found it answer very well.

Saltpetre is found native in the soil of a great many places particularly in the province of Pei-chihli. This soil is collected in heaps and the nitre is extracted from it by lixiviation with boiling water, and by filtering and evaporating the solution afterwards, in the same manner as in India and Europe. The specimens I saw of it were not pure, and it seems they are not very anxious about the

---

* [Cantonese *kan*; Mandarin *chien*.—Ed.]

perfect purification of it. They conceive easily enough that the earthy impurities mixed with it may debase it somewhat, but they have no notion of the existence of the calcareous muriates and nitrous selenites and common salt, etc., contained in it. The whole of the saline substances they believe to be nitre only. The chief purposes for which they employ it are for making gunpowder and artificial fireworks. The first they pretend to have long known and that it is of very great antiquity among them, and in the last they are still thought to surpass most other nations.[158]

GUNPOWDER

There is no particular manufactory for making gunpowder in any part of the Empire.[159] They have but few fire-arms and trust much more to their sabres and bows and arrows than to their muskets, of which they seem not to understand well the advantages or management. They have, however, among their troops a few companies of soldiers armed with matchlocks; of these every soldier makes his own powder. There seems to be no general rule for the proportions of the ingredients, which are saltpetre, sulphur and charcoal, as in Europe. Their charcoal is very ill prepared and they have no choice in the kind of wood from which they prepare it. The most general proportions are two parts of nitre to one part of roll sulphur and one part of charcoal, so that 100 lb. weight of Chinese powder would consist of the following ingredients and proportions:

Nitre	50 lb.
Roll Sulphur	25 lb.
Charcoal	25 lb.
Total	100 lb.

It is easy to be conceived, however, that in a country where there is no particular manufactory or established proportions, but where every individual makes his own, the rates of ingredients will vary a good deal in different places. The nitre, sulphur and charcoal, when reduced separately to fine powder, are thrown into wooden vessels, then moistened with a little water and afterwards mixed as intimately as possible by continued trituration with wooden rods or pestles. After the mixture is completed it is taken out of the troughs and dried in the sun. They never granulate it as we do in Europe, but use it in the form of fine powder or black dust, such as it comes out of the trough, and is dried by the sunbeams, although the specimens I saw of it were sensibly moist and in general very ill prepared. When they use it they first put the charge into the piece, and then ram it down with moist earth or sand; they then rest the piece on the ground by means of a fork attached to it and prime it; they have a long projecting match from, and sometimes a train of powder communicating with, the touch-hole. They set fire to this match or train and then run off to a little distance, till the discharge takes place. The report is not near so loud as an equal quantity of European gunpowder would give, and the smoke is extremely thick and black, as might be expected from so large a proportion of charcoal and sulphur.

ARTIFICIAL FIREWORKS

The composition of those I had not an opportunity of ascertaining. They are not the same everywhere. Every artist endeavours to keep his own composition secret. Among other ingredients, however, which they mix in general with gunpowder, they make much use of filings of zinc and camphor. For producing the vivid red flame and sparkling stars they mix together filings of zinc, nitre and camphor, and a mixture of the same filings with camphor and gunpowder produces the brilliant white stars and lucid globes of fire.

TANNING OF LEATHER

The Chinese do not use tanned leather for making boots and shoes as we do. I saw some leather, however, at Pekin which appeared very well dressed and tanned. The missionaries informed me that they understood the art of tanning very well, although they seldom use it, and from the specimen I saw I could easily believe it. They excel in the preparation of fur skins.

VEGETABLE EXTRACTS, SPIRITUOUS LIQUORS, ETC.

They make a great many extracts, infusions, decoctions and preparations from vegetables and particularly an excellent extract from tea which I never saw nor heard of before. But all these preparations are used for the kitchen and condiments, and they form the principal part of their cookery, which is more varied and consists of a greater number of dishes even than the French cookery.

Their oils are all expressed from the seeds and kernels of fruits; they have no essential oils by distillation. The greatest part of their oil is expressed from the kernel of the seeds of the *tcha-wha*.[160]

The only distilled spirituous liquors they have is their *son-tchou*; it is made from a fermented infusion of rice, and distilled in the same manner as British spirits are prepared from malt.[161] They always distil it with a high heat which gives it an empyreumatic taste that renders it disagreeable to strangers. It is distilled a second time with a slow fire when they want to have it strong, and in this state it is considerably above proof. They have plenty of grapes but they eat them either fresh or as raisins and do not employ them for making wine. The missionaries have a vineyard at Pekin and find that the soil answers very well for the vine; they make wine enough for their consumption but the Chinese, attached in everything to their customs, do not choose to imitate them, nor do they relish the taste or flavour of European wine unless it be very strong Madeira. The Chinese wine is all made from the juices of a particular fruit which they call . . .* mixed with *son-tchou*. It is generally of a yellow colour, has a burnt smell and a dry empyreumatic taste.

* [Space left blank in text.—Ed.]

PAPER

Their paper, which is well known, is all made of the thin filmy membranes that line the interior cavities of the bamboo. They reduce it to the consistence of a fine pulp with water, and afterwards form it into large sheets which are exceedingly thin and of various degrees of whiteness and fineness, according to the purposes for which they are wanted. Their paper is so thin that it will not bear the ink on both sides; hence all their books are doubled in the leaves and printed only on one side.

They have a particular kind of gum which they melt and blow into large lanterns. These lanterns are quite pellucid, and so like thin transparent horn that at first we mistook them for such, and thought the Chinese must have possessed some art of softening and incorporating the substances of various horns together in order to form lanterns of such enormous size. It was in consequence of this idea that we learned they were not horn but of a particular kind of gum, or gum resin, which I could not ascertain the nature of nor get further information respecting it.

APPENDICES

APPENDIX A

Biographical Notes on Some Personalities, English and Chinese

ENGLISH EMBASSY

Sir George Leonard Staunton (1737–1801). Born in Galway, Ireland, where his family had been settled for over a hundred years. Studied medicine at Montpellier and took his M.A. there in 1758. Settled in London in 1759 and wrote on medical subjects. Went to the West Indies in 1762 where he practised as a doctor and made enough money to enable him to give up medicine after a few years and to become a landed proprietor in Grenada. Thus, when Macartney reached Grenada as Governor in 1776, Staunton was one of its leading inhabitants. His influence was of considerable help to Macartney and the two men became friends. At the time of the capture of Grenada by the French, Staunton was aide-de-camp to the Governor, and as a result lost all his possessions in the looting which followed the surrender, and was sent to Paris as a hostage for a short period. In 1781 when Macartney went to Madras he took Staunton with him as his Secretary. In this capacity Staunton negotiated a treaty of peace in 1784 between Macartney, as Governor of Madras, and Tipu, ruler of Mysore. On his return to England he was awarded a life pension of £500 a year by the East India Company and made an Irish Baronet by the King. Staunton had a literary turn of mind and corresponded with Dr. Johnson, Edmund Burke and other distinguished men of his day. He was made a Fellow of the Royal Society in 1787 and was granted an honorary Doctorate of Civil Law by Oxford University three years later.

In 1792 he was appointed Secretary to the embassy and Minister Plenipotentiary in the absence of the ambassador, with authority to carry on the embassy in case of Macartney's death or incapacity. There was a faint hope that if matters went very favourably Macartney might eventually leave Staunton in China as Britain's first permanent Minister to the Court of Peking. After his return to England he was entrusted by Macartney with the task of compiling the official account of the embassy, which was published in two volumes in 1797.* He suffered a stroke shortly afterwards and died in 1801, and was buried in Westminster Abbey.

---

* Its merits and defects are discussed on p. 350.

Staunton had an active, enquiring mind, and was particularly interested in botany, being a Fellow of the Linnean Society. He was a hard worker who had the happy knack of getting on well with Macartney.

He took with him to China his only son, GEORGE THOMAS STAUNTON (1781–1859), who, during the outward voyage picked up the elements of the Chinese language from the two Chinese priests, Cho and Li, who were accompanying the ambassador as interpreters.* He was received in audience by the Emperor at Jehol, and kept a diary while in China, part of which has survived in manuscript.†

In 1798 G. T. Staunton became a writer in the East India Company's Factory at Canton, and in 1804 a Supercargo. He inherited his father's title in 1801. In 1808 he was appointed interpreter and in 1816 became President of the Select Committee. In the same year he accompanied Lord Amherst on his abortive embassy to Peking. In 1817 he retired from the Company's service in Canton and settled in England. He became a member of Parliament and was often consulted by the Government on Chinese affairs. While in Canton he translated the *Ta-ch'ing lü-li*, the Statutes and Rescripts of the Ch'ing dynasty.‡ This work was a codification of the customs, precedents and laws of China in existence when the code was promulgated. Various editions were published throughout the Manchu dynasty. In 1823 he co-operated with H. T. Colebrooke in founding the Royal Asiatic Society, and gave the Society a collection of Chinese books, consisting of 186 separate works.§

SIR JOHN BARROW (1764–1848). Born in humble circumstances in north Lancashire, he became interested in mathematics, scientific experiments, and nautical science. Hardworking and ambitious, he got the job of teaching mathematics at a school in Greenwich, and by a piece of luck was engaged by Sir G. L. Staunton to give young Staunton private tuition. Through Staunton's patronage he obtained the post of Comptroller to the embassy. On returning to England from China he lived with Sir George Staunton in London, helping him with his library, and no doubt helping him with the official account of the embassy. In 1804 he published his own book about

---

* See p. 319.
† Discussed on p. 351.
‡ *Ta Tsing Leu Lee, being the Fundamental Laws, and a Selection from the Supplementary Statutes of the Penal Code of China* (T. Cadell, London, 1810).
§ For a note on this subject see J. L. Cranmer-Byng, *Journal of the Hong Kong Branch of the Royal Asiatic Society*, Vol. I (1960–1), pp. 124–6.

the embassy entitled *Travels in China*, and in 1807 published a Life of Lord Macartney.*

The main part of his career falls after the China embassy, but can be summarized briefly. When Macartney went out to the Cape as Governor he took Barrow with him as his Private Secretary. Barrow stayed there until 1802, and then returned to England. Henry Dundas, while First Lord of the Admiralty, appointed Barrow Second Secretary to the Navy, a post which he occupied for the next forty years. At the time Dundas is alleged to have said that he and Pitt had been so taunted with giving away all the good things to Scotsmen that he was glad to have chosen an Englishman for once. Barrow's advice was asked by Government on various occasions in dealing with the Chinese empire. He published numerous articles in the *Quarterly Review*, and repeated his observations on China in his autobiography, published in 1847. His account of *The Mutiny and Piratical Seizure of H.M.S. Bounty* (1831) is a minor classic.†

Barrow was an ambitious man, ready to turn his hand to anything and to master fresh knowledge. He had a high opinion of his own abilities, especially in the literary field. His career demonstrates how, in eighteenth-century England, a bright boy could rise in the world from humble circumstances to an enviable position, provided that he was industrious and had the good luck to secure patronage early in his career.

SIR ERASMUS GOWER (1742–1814). He entered the Navy in 1755, serving in various stations abroad, and distinguishing himself in the Indian Ocean between 1781 and 1783. If he had not been on the important Newfoundland Station in 1787 he would have commanded the frigate detailed to take Colonel Cathcart to China. However, he was later appointed to take Lord Macartney on the same embassy. His biography in the *Dictionary of National Biography* states that from 1792 until 1794 he commanded the *Lion*, 'taking out to China Lord Macartney and his embassy, for which service he was rewarded with the honour of Knighthood'. This sounds as if he were knighted after returning from China, but in fact the Macartney papers in the Wason Collection at Cornell prove that he was knighted on 1 August 1792. Macartney, in a letter to Dundas dated 31 July, added a P.S.: 'Sir George Staunton and I propose

---

* *Some Account of the Public Life and a Selection from the Unpublished Writings of the Earl of Macartney*, 2 vols. Both books are discussed in Appendix D.

† Printed in *The World's Classics* (O.U.P.), 1914 and subsequently.

being at St. James' tomorrow to take leave, and Captain Gower will attend for the same purpose and for receiving the Honour, which you were so good as to say you would recommend to His Majesty. They will both have the honour of waiting upon you at dinner according to your invitation which I communicated to them.'* Francis Baring, in a letter to Macartney, dated 4 August puts 'Sir Erasmus Gower', and Macartney writing to Evan Nepean, Under-Secretary of State, on 6 August, also puts 'Sir Erasmus Gower'. He was promoted Rear Admiral in 1799, Vice-Admiral in 1804 and Admiral in 1809.

DR. JAMES DINWIDDIE (1746–1815). Born into a Scottish family of small farmers. His father spelt his name Dinwoody, but the son preferred the spelling Dinwiddie. He was educated at Dumfries Academy and Edinburgh University where he took his M.A. in 1778. From an early age he showed ability in mathematics and 'a curiosity for mechanical contrivances'. After graduating he collected together various pieces of scientific equipment suitable for demonstrating experiments and then started on a series of public lecture tours, his stay in Dublin being particularly successful. He incorporated into his equipment items which caught the public imagination of his day, including some 'philosophical fireworks' of varied and beautiful colours, and an air balloon, which he constructed himself. In August 1792 he was made a Doctor of Laws of Edinburgh University, and about the same time was engaged as 'mechanic' to Macartney's embassy. The term mechanic caused some confusion and Dinwiddie asked to be called 'machinist', defining his duties, in a letter to Macartney, as: 'The erecting and regulating the planetarium; the constructing, filling and ascending in the balloon; descending in the diving bell; together with experiments on air, electricity, mechanics, and other branches of experimental philosophy; astronomical and other calculations.'† Needless to say, the Chinese would have none of these things, and Dinwiddie's scientific experiments had to wait until he reached India.

When the embassy left China in March 1794, Dinwiddie sailed for India in the *Jackall*, taking with him his scientific apparatus. He was also entrusted by Macartney with several cases of tea, tallow and varnish plants as well as some silkworms' eggs, all of which he

---

* Wason Collection, document No. 161.
† Quoted in William Jardine Proudfoot, *Biographical Memoir of James Dinwiddie* (Liverpool, 1868), p. 27.

delivered to Dr. Roxburgh, the superintendent of the Company's Botanical Garden in Calcutta. He arrived there in September 1794, and soon began to lecture to eighty of 'the first ladies and gentlemen in the settlement' on natural philosophy and chemistry, as well as giving a course of lectures on China and private instruction in various branches of science and art. He repeated his lectures in Madras, and then in 1800 was appointed Professor of the newly opened Fort William College (Calcutta). He finally left India in 1805. When he set out with the Macartney embassy in 1792 he was £500 in debt, but when he returned to England from India he was worth about £10,000. While in China he had kept a journal and fragments of this record were printed by his grandson, W. J. Proudfoot.*

DR. HUGH GILLAN (?–1798). A native of Moray, he studied at Aberdeen University graduating M.A. in 1779. He studied medicine at Edinburgh University, and received his M.D. in 1786. His thesis, *De igne*, was published in the same year and copies have survived. He accompanied the embassy as physician, and at the request of Lord Macartney put together some notes on Chinese medicine, surgery and chemistry which exist in a manuscript attached to Macartney's own Journal.† On his return to England he became a Fellow of the Royal Society on 19 February 1795 and a Licentiate of the Royal College of Physicians of London on 30 March 1795. In the same year he became a physician in the army under Major-General Alured Clarke, but I have been unable to find out any more about his career. He died on 19 May 1798.‡

The surgeon who accompanied the embassy, William Scott, does not appear to have written anything about Chinese surgery. According to Barrow, 'Doctor Scott had been a surgeon in the Navy, had read a great deal and talked much more.... Dr. Scott contributed nothing that I am aware of towards elucidating the manners, customs, character or general knowledge of the Chinese.'§

CAPTAIN WILLIAM MACKINTOSH. An employee of the East India Company. In accordance with the custom of the Company the officers of their ships trading to Canton were allowed to trade on

---

* See Appendix D. † Printed on pp. 279–303.
‡ I am indebted to Mr. L. M. Payne, Librarian of the Royal College of Physicians, London, and to Mr. D. E. Griffiths of the Department of Manuscripts, University of Edinburgh Library, for supplying me with this information about Dr. Gillan.
§ *An Autobiographical Memoir of Sir John Barrow, Bart.* (London, 1847), p. 48.

their own account and to have free space for their goods on board ship. A captain was usually allowed to carry fifty-six tons free of charge. In the Company documents of this period Captain Mackintosh is shown as trading at Canton from 1784 onwards. He commanded the *Hindostan* on her first voyage from England to Madras, Canton and back (1789–91), on her second voyage when she accompanied the embassy (1792–4), and on her third voyage to Bombay, Canton and back (1796–9). During the course of the embassy he was expressly forbidden by the East India Company to transact private trade except at Canton. Pritchard has worked out that on this particular voyage Mackintosh was allowed £9,632 worth of private trade.*

He appears to have been well thought of by William Richardson, Secretary at East India House, who had suggested him as a possible member of the Select Committee at Canton.† Certainly in the early stages of the preparations for the embassy Macartney had relied on the opinions and information of Richardson and Mackintosh. Macartney, therefore, had asked Dundas for Mackintosh to be attached to the embassy to convey the presents. But having once been a merchant and enjoyed the Company's 'privilege trade' he naturally had an eye to the main chance and wanted to trade in Peking itself. This Macartney forbade, but after considerable trouble obtained permission for him to trade at Chusan. While at Canton young Staunton, in his Journal for 28 December 1793, recorded: 'This evening we went to see some curious machines in clockwork (Singsongs) at Captain Mackintosh's factory. One among the others was particularly curious being a beautiful pyramid with golden serpents continually twirling up it and four dragons at its base spitting pearls and round it continually walking an elephant who at the same time both moves his trunk and tail.'‡ The Dutch Embassy took two automata to Peking as presents which they bought at Canton. They represented a fortune-teller with birds and a butterfly. Captain Mackintosh had bought them in London and carried them to Canton as part of his private trade.§ William Alexander, who

* E. H. Pritchard, 'The Instructions of the East India Company to Lord Macartney on his Embassy to China ...', *Journal of the Royal Asiatic Society*, 1938, Pt. II, p. 228, n.1.

† E. H. Pritchard, *The Crucial Years* ..., pp. 273–4, 280.

‡ The MS. of this Journal is in the Library of Duke University, North Carolina. See Appendix D, p. 351.

§ See van Braam Houckgeest, *Voyage de l'ambassade de la Compagnie des Indes orientales hollandaises, vers l'empereur de la Chine, dans les années 1794 et 1795...*, 2 vols. (Philadelphia, 1797–8), II, p. 377.

returned to England on the *Hindostan*, states that Mackintosh dined with Pitt and Dundas at Walmer Castle when the embassy arrived off Folkestone.*

LIEUTENANT HENRY WILLIAM PARISH. Macartney took with him not only a military escort, but also six brass cannon together with twenty artillerymen under the command of Lieutenant Parish. However, Parish was not merely an artillery officer but had been trained to make plans and sketches and to take measurements. Although Macartney left Hickey and Alexander behind in Peking, he did have Parish with him on the trip to Jehol. Thus when the ambassador and his party reached the Great Wall on 5 September he wrote an account of it in his Journal, but added in a footnote:

> Since the above hasty account was written I have been favoured with a plan, section and measurements and observations on this celebrated wall by Lieutenant Parish of the Royal Artillery, which from his approved skill and accuracy as an engineer and draughtsman are to be considered as highly valuable and supersede everything that has been hitherto written on this subject.

While at Jehol Parish made a number of sketches including a view of the eastern side of the Imperial park, one of the Potala, and another of the Imperial tent at the time of Macartney's audience with the Emperor, together with a plan and key to the scene depicted in it. These three sketches were used by William Alexander as the basis for his larger colour-wash drawings. After the embassy returned to Macao, Parish was ordered to go on board the *Jackall* to survey a number of islands between Macao and Hong Kong island. As a result of this expedition he wrote a report for Lord Macartney dated 28 February containing his observations on Lantao.† He also made a sketch map of Lantao and the neighbouring islands which is preserved in the British Museum.‡ Other reports written for Lord Macartney by Parish concern Tourane Bay, the Bocca Tigris, military posts on the route from Peking to Jehol, the defences of Macao, and the order of parade of Chinese troops at Tientsin. Barrow, in his autobiography, gives information of his untimely death:

* See Appendix D, p. 343.
† Wason Collection of Macartney documents, Cornell University (no. 371). See also note 82.
‡ In 'Maps, plans and sketches of places and scenes in China by Henry W. Parish.' (Add. MS. 19822 folio 13.) A sketch plan of the audience ceremony and tent is also preserved in this collection, folio 8. For other sketches by Parish see Add. MSS. 35300 and 33931.

Lieut. Parish, of the artillery, was a good officer and an excellent draughtsman in the engineer department, as his drawings of a section and view of the Great Wall of China and other subjects will testify, though generally they were taken by stealth. On his return to England, he was appointed aide-de-camp to the Marquis Cornwallis, as Governor-General of India, fell overboard on the passage out, and was drowned.*

WILLIAM ALEXANDER, R.A. (1767–1816). Born at Maidstone. As a young man he studied under Julius Caesar Ibbetson who had accompanied the abortive Cathcart embassy as far as Java in the capacity of 'painter'. Ibbetson was offered a similar post with the Macartney embassy but declined.† However, he recommended his young pupil for employment. In the event Thomas Hickey was appointed 'painter' and William Alexander was included in the embassy as 'draughtsman'. Throughout the course of the embassy Alexander kept a journal‡ from which we know that he and Hickey sailed in the *Hindostan* and returned to England together in the same ship. He also tells us that Hickey went to Peking but not to Jehol. For some reason Macartney decided not to take his artists to Jehol and Alexander, much to his annoyance, was also left behind at Peking. However, this did not deter him from making a vast number of sketches during his stay in China, some of which, on his return to England, he worked up into finished colour-wash drawings. A number of these were engraved and reproduced in Staunton's account of the embassy.

In contrast Hickey seems to have produced almost nothing, although his salary of £200 per annum was twice that of Alexander. As the frontispiece to Barrow's *Travels in China* there is a coloured engraving of Wang, one of the two officials conducting the embassy, which was made from a drawing by Thomas Hickey. It seems a crude portrait and compares unfavourably with the colour-wash sketch of Wang by Alexander which is in the British Museum. But this may be the fault of the engraving. There is also one pen-and-ink sketch (slightly tinted in water colours) of some Chinese trackers hauling on a tow rope while others watch them, which is

* *An Autobiographical Memoir of Sir John Barrow, Bart.* (London, 1847), p. 47. However, Cornwallis was Governor-General from 1786–93, while Parish did not return to England from China until 1794. It is true that Cornwallis was appointed Governor-General for a second time in 1805, but this was more than ten years after Parish returned from the China embassy. Perhaps Barrow meant to write Wellesley, who went out to Bengal as Governor-General in 1798.

† See Rotha Mary Clay, *Julius Caesar Ibbetson, 1759–1816* (Country Life, Ltd., 1948), p. 24.

‡ See Appendix D.

signed with the initials T.H., and is preserved in the British Museum. It seems inferior in skill to Alexander's known work. Apart from these two works, and a thumb-nail sketch also signed T.H. which is preserved in the India Office Library, I have been unable to discover any paintings or drawings made by Hickey during the embassy; that is from September 1792 until September 1794. It seems possible that this does in fact represent the sum of his efforts during those two years, because Barrow, in his Memoirs, tends to corroborate this. 'Mr. Hickey, an indifferent portrait-painter, was a countryman of Lord Macartney, whose portrait he had painted; and being now out of employment, his Lordship, it was said, took him out of compassion; I believe he executed nothing whatever while on the embassy, but in conversation he was a shrewd, clever man.'*

On the other hand the results of William Alexander's industry while in China can be seen in profusion. In the India Office Library are preserved two folio volumes which contain between them a total of 870 small colour-wash drawings. These appear to be first sketches and give a vivid picture of how China and the Chinese must have appeared to the members of the Macartney mission. The British Museum has an album of 'Drawings taken in China' which contains eighty-two colour-wash drawings. These are rather more substantial and more finished than those in the India Office Library. However, they are still in the nature of sketches. In addition, the British Museum has a number of finished water-colour drawings which Alexander worked up from his preliminary sketches after his return to England. These include a picture of the Emperor Ch'ienlung being carried in a palanquin to his large Mongolian-type marquee in the grounds of Jehol to receive Lord Macartney in audience on 14 September 1793. To some extent this work is an exercise of the imagination, for Alexander did not himself see this event but had to rely on a sketch made by Lieutenant Henry W. Parish. However, Parish was no mean draughtsman himself as his plans and sketches preserved in the British Museum show. While in Peking Alexander had the chance of seeing the Emperor carried in his palanquin in procession and thus he could imagine the scene at Jehol with some accuracy.

The largest collection of finished drawings of China by William Alexander is housed, appropriately enough, in the Museum of his native Maidstone. Here, there are over twenty large colour-wash drawings which represent his polished work and give a good idea of

* *An Autobiographical Memoir of Sir John Barrow, Bart.*, p. 49.

the scenery and costume of the Chinese. Finally there are seven large colour-wash drawings in the Victoria and Albert Museum, one of which is an attractive view of the Potala at Jehol, also based on a sketch by Henry Parish.

Thus nearly fifty large colour-wash drawings by Alexander are known to have been preserved as well as nearly a thousand sketches. Furthermore, two books published during his lifetime were illustrated by coloured engravings made from his work, which show his skilful use of gay colours in portraying Chinese costume.* In his sketch of the Emperor Ch'ien-lung preserved in the British Museum the Imperial robes are painted in vivid yet pleasing colours.

In 1808 Alexander became Assistant Keeper of Antiquities at the British Museum, in which capacity he had charge of the collection of prints and drawings. Between 1794, when he returned to England from China, and his death in 1816 he made various sets of drawings most of which were engraved and published.†

He was buried in Boxley churchyard near Maidstone, and there is a memorial tablet inside the church which reads in part:

> Near this place lies the remains
> of
> William Alexander Esqre. F.S.A. and L.S.
> One of the Librarians of the British Museum.
> He accompanied the Embassy to China
> in 1792
> and by the power of his pencil introduced
> into Europe a better knowledge of the
> habits and manners of China
> than had been before attained. . . .

Barrow, who was not lavish in his praise of other members of the embassy said of him: 'Mr. Alexander drew beautifully and faithfully in water-colours, and omitted nothing that was Chinese, from the human face and figure, down to the humblest plant, and so true were his delineations, that nothing before or since could be compared with them.'‡

---

* *The Costume of China* (with 48 coloured engravings), London: William Miller, 1805. *Picturesque representations of the Dress and Manners of the Chinese* (with 50 coloured engravings), London: John Murray, 1814.

† See *The Gentleman's Magazine*, Vol. LXXXVI, pt. ii (1816), pp. 279–80, 369–71.

‡ *An Autobiographical Memoir of Sir John Barrow*, p. 49.

It is high time that a biography of William Alexander was written and a catalogue of his drawings published.

BOTANISTS

One botanist, DAVID STRONACH, was officially appointed to accompany the embassy. His name appears at the beginning of Macartney's Journal of the voyage from England to Cochin China where he is listed among the ambassador's suite as 'gardener and botanist'. During the outward voyage, in the passage from Rio de Janeiro to Batavia the embassy anchored off Tristan da Cunha and Macartney records in his Journal for 18 December 1792 that Staunton, Barrow, Gillan and Parish were to go ashore the following morning attended by Haxton and Stronach as botanists. In fact during the night a fresh wind blew up and they had to sail away without landing. Thus two botanists actually accompanied the embassy. Staunton, himself an amateur naturalist, in mentioning the composition of the ambassador's suite, wrote:

> It is to be regretted that to this list cannot be added any professed naturalist, who might have made the most of the opportunities for observation which such a voyage afforded.... The zeal of naturalists was not, however, wanting; and two botanic gardeners were provided, one at the public charge, and one at the expense of an individual of the Embassy, for the purpose of collecting specimens of whatever productions worthy of observation that nature might furnish in the course of the expedition.*

From various sources we can glean a little information about the activities of the two botanists during the embassy. Thus William Alexander, in his manuscript Journal, describes how on 20 August 1793 the members of Macartney's suite set out on the overland journey from Tungchow to Peking, most of them riding in carts, but that the gardener 'went on horseback for the more easily procuring plants'. Staunton mentions that certain members of the suite were left behind at Peking and the Yuan-ming Yuan early in September, among them being 'one of the botanical gardeners'. While there he collected specimens of the many plants of the Province of Chihli, and Staunton prints a list of these containing about one hundred and twenty names. Staunton reproduces three further lists of plants, viz.: plants collected on a journey between Peking and

* Staunton, *An Authentic Account* . . ., Vol. I, p. 37. Staunton himself engaged Haxton. See the 'List of the gentlemen who composed the retinue of Earl Macartney', printed at the front of Aeneas Anderson's *A Narrative of the British Embassy to China*, where under Staunton's name two servants and a gardener are shown as being in his employment.

BRIEF BIOGRAPHIES

Jehol, plants collected in the provinces of Shantung and Kiangnan, and plants collected in Kiangsi and Kwangtung.* Bretschneider,† who is the authority on this subject, devotes considerable space to the Macartney embassy, mentioning Haxton but not Stronach. He suggests that Staunton presented his collection of plants from China to Sir Joseph Banks. Certainly Staunton's name is commemorated in the names of several species of Chinese plants cultivated in the West.

On reaching Macao early in 1794 Stronach compiled a list of plants in the Camoens garden, which is preserved in Cornell University,‡ while Haxton appears to have collected for Sir Joseph Banks specimens of *Enkianthus quinqueflorus* under the Chinese name of *tiao-chung* ('hanging bells').§ Lieutenant Parish in his report on a survey of Lantao and neighbouring islands mentions that at Cowhee [Ma Wan.—Ed.] they went ashore and the gardener found ginger, guava and wild figs.

Apart from collecting specimens of Chinese plants the embassy had a more specific aim. Macartney had been requested to obtain specimens of young tea plants and to send them to Bengal where they might come to maturity 'so that one day or another they may be reckoned among the commercial resources of our own territories'.‖ On 10 August 1792 Francis Baring, Chairman of the Court of Directors of the East India Company, wrote to Macartney: 'Sir Joseph Banks has collected some memorandums about the tea trade with a view to its culture in Bengal which he will communicate to your Lordship.'¶ Presumably these 'memorandums' correspond to the instructions preserved at Cornell University entitled 'Note relative to the method of bringing to England seeds from China and Japan in a state of vegetation.' This note contains detailed instructions about the boxes and earth to be used, about watering the plants, as well as 'a list of curious plants, natives of China and Japan, wished to be obtained from thence'.**

We get a last glimpse of the results of Staunton's enthusiasm and the work of the botanists in a letter from Dr. Gillan dated 16

* See Staunton, op. cit., Vol. II, pp. 165, 274, 435, 524.
† E. Bretschneider, *History of European Botanical Discoveries in China* (London, 1898), Vol. I, pp. 156–83. He reproduces Staunton's lists of plants and gives additional information.
‡ Wason Collection of Macartney documents (no. 407).
§ Bretschneider, op. cit., Vol. I, p. 217.
‖ See Journal, 17 November, and note 57 which deals specifically with the attempt to introduce the tea plant from China into India.
¶ Wason Collection of Macartney documents (no. 177).
** Wason Collection of Macartney documents (no. 429).

September 1794, in which he informed Macartney that he was going to Deptford to inspect the plants on board the *Bombay Castle*, East Indiaman, and that if Lady Mendip's tea tree was dead he would endeavour to replace it. Finally on 20 September he wrote to Macartney that he was now 'ready to deliver the specimens of dried plants and seeds' to Macartney's house in Curzon Street.*

INTERPRETER

JACOBUS LI (alias Jacob Ly, alias Mr. Plumb). When Macartney wished to obtain an interpreter to accompany the embassy to China he had some difficulty in finding anyone. Eventually Staunton went to Naples where he found two Chinese, Paolo Cho and Jacobus Li, who had completed their training for the priesthood. They were members of the Chinese College at Naples which had been founded in 1732 by Father Ripa and was directed by the Congregation *De Propaganda Fide*.† In exchange for a passage to China the two priests were to act as interpreters to the embassy, being qualified to interpret between Chinese and Italian or Latin. As related in the Journal, Padre Cho went ashore at Macao in June 1793 but declined to continue with the embassy. He arrived in Peking at the end of September, having travelled overland. Jacobus Li, however, served Macartney faithfully throughout, and coped with the difficult job of sole interpreter. He tried to serve Macartney's interests and to represent his point of view as strongly as possible, but he must have felt somewhat constrained in the presence of the great officials with whom Macartney conversed. Once or twice Macartney says that his interpreter refused to be intimidated. According to young Staunton, Li had a brother, a Mandarin with a blue button, who arrived at Peking on 30 September 1793.‡

Barrow gave Li a warm word of praise in his *Travels in China* when he wrote:§

> On the conduct of Lee, our Chinese interpreter, any praise that I could bestow would be far inadequate to his merit. Fully sensible of his perilous situation, he never at any one time shrunk from his duty. At Macao he took an affectionate leave of his English friends, with whom, though placed in one of the remotest provinces of the Empire he still contrives to correspond. The Ambassador, Lord Macartney, has had several letters from him, the last of which is of so late a date as March 1802....

* Macartney documents preserved in the Public Record Office of Northern Ireland at Belfast, Vol. 19, nos. 173 and 175.
† See note 91.
‡ MS. Journal kept by G. T. Staunton. See Appendix D. § p. 604.

BRIEF BIOGRAPHIES

Aeneas Anderson also mentions that Li left the service of the ambassador at Macao. 'At this place Mr. Plumb quitted the service of the embassy. He was very amiable and obliging in his conduct to everyone engaged in the same service with himself. He was offered a suitable provision, if he would return to England; but though he appeared to part from his European friends with a sensible regret, he very naturally preferred to return to the bosom of family and friends, from whom he had been so long separated. . . .'*

Two letters from Li to Macartney, written in Latin, are preserved in the Public Record Office of Northern Ireland at Belfast. One is dated 21 February 1801 and the second dated 3 July 1802, both written from the province of Shansi.† Unfortunately they contain no news except the fact that 'the way here from Macao is almost blocked because of the fury of the rebellion which is daily growing in the provinces of Hu-kuan, Shensi and Szechwan.' He signed his name Jacobus Ly in one letter and Jacobus Plumb in the other. Since he was referred to as Mr. Plumb by some of Macartney's suite it is likely that he bore the common Chinese surname of Li ('plum tree'), though I have been unable to discover his personal names.

CHINESE OFFICIALS

HO-SHEN (1750–99). A Manchu of the Plain Red Banner who rose swiftly by means of the Emperor's favour from being a guard at the palace gate to becoming the most powerful minister in the empire. He held Ch'ien-lung's complete confidence from 1775 until the Emperor's death in 1799. His promotion was rapid. In 1776 he was appointed a Grand Councillor, at the age of twenty-six, and in 1780 president of the Board of Revenue. In the same year his son was betrothed to the Emperor's favourite daughter; they were married ten years later. In 1784 he was made president of the Board of Civil Office and became an assistant Grand Secretary. He retained control over the lucrative Board of Revenue until Ch'ien-lung's death. Throughout his career he held many administrative and military posts as well as positions in the Imperial Household, often holding several concurrently. He was granted a succession of titles of nobility until in 1798 he attained the coveted rank of duke.

Although without military talent he was an adroit courtier. Macartney, from his contact with Ho-shen during the embassy, drew quite a sympathetic picture of him, stressing his finesse as a

* *A Narrative of the British Embassy to China* (Debrett, 1795), p. 264.
† Macartney MSS, nos. 77 and 174.

diplomat. Their first meeting was on 11 September 1793 when Macartney went to his palace at Jehol. 'He is a handsome, fair man about forty to forty-five years old, quick and fluent.' On 15 September Ho-shen and other great officials accompanied Macartney and his immediate suite on a visit to the Imperial Park at Jehol (the Wan-shu Yuan). After this sightseeing tour Macartney noted: 'During the whole day the first Minister, or Grand Secretary, paid us very great attention, and displayed all the good breeding and politeness of an experienced courtier. . . .' But when he wanted to discuss business Macartney the diplomat failed to get his way with Ho-shen the courtier. 'I found, however, that, though infinitely gracious and civil in his manner and expression, I could gain no ground upon him.' On the following day Dr. Gillan was sent to examine Ho-shen for various ailments. The doctor gave an account of this incident in his report on the state of medicine in China. He found that Ho-shen had a completely formed hernia of some years' standing, and that in addition he suffered periodically from sharp attacks of rheumatism.* On 17 September Ho-shen again showed Macartney round the Imperial Park, this time the western part, and again Macartney tried to introduce into the conversation the objects of his mission but without success. 'I could not help admiring the address with which the Minister parried all my attempts to speak to him on business this day, and how artfully he evaded every opportunity that offered for any particular conversation with me, endeavouring to engage our attention solely by the objects around us. . . .' Finally on 2 October, after his return to Peking, Macartney made one final effort to discuss with Ho-shen the main purpose of his embassy, but without avail. 'The Minister, with his usual address, avoided entering into any discussion of these points, which I had taken so much pains to lay before him, and turned the discourse upon the state of my health, assuring me that the Emperor's proposal for my departure arose chiefly from his anxiety about it, for that otherwise my stay could not but be agreeable to him.'

Macartney met Ho-shen at the height of the latter's power when he was firmly entrenched in the Emperor's favour, and no Censor dare accuse him, and attempts to implicate him obliquely had failed. To what extent he was controlled by the Emperor and to what extent he consulted with other great ministers, if at all, has not been precisely determined. But it is certain that Ho-shen placed a number of his supporters in important posts and that most ambitious

* See pp. 281–3.

officials gave him lavish 'presents' so that eventually he amassed a fortune which rivalled the Emperor's own. In eighteenth-century England patronage was usually extended in return for political support, but Ho-shen's patronage was given in return for more material gains. His relations with Cheng-jui, mentioned immediately below, are just one example of his corrupting influence on the official class at this time. Most Chinese historians have portrayed him as cunning, avaricious and self-seeking. He was, however, completely loyal to his master, Ch'ien-lung.

When the Emperor resigned the throne in 1796 in favour of his fifteenth son, Chia-ch'ing, the position was not materially changed, because the aged Emperor still protected his favourite. Chia-ch'ing had to stifle his hatred of Ho-shen and wait for his father's death. Immediately this happened Ho-shen was arrested, his huge horde of gold, silver and jewels was confiscated, and after a number of serious charges had been made against him he was given Imperial permission to commit suicide.

Ho-shen was a symptom of the disease which Macartney perceived underlying the Chinese empire in the last years of Ch'ien-lung's reign. His position was made possible because of Ch'ien-lung's autocratic rule, because the Emperor was extremely sensitive to any criticism of his management of affairs, and by extension of this to any criticism of the conduct of his favourite minister. As a result no effective protest could be made against Ho-shen's corruption and against his irregular position, which was not the result of success in the Imperial examination system combined with long and competent service in the bureaucratic system, but of direct Imperial favour.*

CHENG-JUI (? 1734–1815). In his Journal Macartney continually referred to an official whose name he spelt as Chin, and whom he described as the Emperor's Legate. This was Cheng-jui, a Manchu of the Plain White Banner who, at the time of the embassy, was salt administrator at Tientsin.

Cheng-jui started his career as 'keeper of the stores' at the Yuanming Yuan. By the thirty-eighth year of Ch'ien-lung's reign (1773–4) he had risen to be a second-rank secretary in the Imperial

---

* For his biography see the article by Knight Biggerstaff in Hummel, *Eminent Chinese of the Ch'ing Period*, Vol. I, p. 288. For a stimulating analysis of his relationship with the Emperor and the case against him see D. S. Nivison, 'Ho-shen and his accusers' in *Confucianism in Action*, ed. D. S. Nivison and A. F. Wright (Stanford, 1959), pp. 209–243.

Household. His subsequent career was one of slow promotion, but broken by occasional setbacks whenever he was sent an Imperial rebuke. Thus he was made superintendent of the Imperial silk factory at Hangchow in the year 1778–9, and salt administrator of Liang-Huai in 1786–7. In the following year he sent the Emperor a gift of two pairs of engraved lacquered screens inlaid with flower patterns in real pearls. An Imperial edict refusing the screens stated:

> Wall screens are merely for occasional display at festivals. Why should one be too extravagant over them? Now Cheng-jui has had real pearls inlaid in these useless objects which simply shows that he is good at 'playing the courtier'. It looks as if he has been enjoying luxury so much that his mind has become muddled. Apart from returning these screens an edict should also be sent severely rebuking him.

However, this did not prevent his being made Superintendent of the Imperial silk factory at Soochow shortly afterwards. In the first month of the fifty-eighth year of Ch'ien-lung's reign (1793) he was appointed salt administrator of Changlu (Tientsin). His biography states: 'At that time England sent an embassy bringing tribute. The Emperor commanded Cheng-jui to look after the tribute envoy and bestowed upon him the honour of wearing the peacock feather.' Later, however, because of his memorial about the English ships at Chusan, and because he did not memorialize jointly with Chin Chia and I-ling-a, but in his own name alone, an edict was issued reprimanding him.*

For a while after the embassy, Cheng-jui's affairs seem to have prospered, and two separate memorials from him were received favourably by the throne. He was invited to attend the feast held during the first year of Chia-ch'ing's reign for the thousand 'grand old men'. However, in the fifth year of Chia-ch'ing's reign (1800–1), one of Cheng-jui's personal servants got into trouble for illegally soliciting contributions (in Cheng-jui's name) in order to rebuild a dilapidated temple. During the investigations into this case it came to light that Cheng-jui had once presented two hundred thousand taels of silver to Ho-shen. An Imperial edict was then issued which is revealing because it shows the way in which officials at that time sought Ho-shen's favour by giving him 'presents'. The relevant part of the edict reads:

> Although Cheng-jui owed the Government many sums of money [from public funds.—Ed.] which he had delayed repaying for a long time with the intention of

---

* For details see J. L. Cranmer-Byng, op. cit., pp. 152–5.

defaulting, yet he tried to present two hundred thousand taels of silver to Ho-shen. When Ho-shen declined it Cheng-jui did not pay back his debts to the Government with this silver. Instead he used this money to purchase official rank for his son, and also to set up shops. Thus he regarded government money, which he ought to have refunded, as a matter that could be delayed, while he thought it an urgent matter to bribe a powerful family. Now that he is at our temporary palace and has been interrogated by us personally he has stated that the two hundred thousand taels of silver were offered to Ho-shen as a present because Ho-shen's wife had died. However, at that time Ho-shen thought it was not enough, and wanted him to increase it to four hundred thousand taels, and that is why he refused to accept it. Nevertheless, in the past he did once offer Ho-shen two hundred thousand taels which were accepted immediately. Apart from this the satins and curios which Ho-shen commanded him to buy were innumerable.

It is then suggested, in his biography,* that his motive was to ingratiate himself with Ho-shen who would then become his protector. In this way Cheng-jui might hope to remain at his post as Salt Administrator of Liang-Huai (a lucrative one) without being transferred elsewhere. Luckily for Cheng-jui the case against Ho-shen was wound up with the latter's death, and thus he escaped punishment on this count. However, he was punished for his part in the rebuilding of the temple. According to the edict already quoted:

> . . .—not only the wealthy shopkeepers were burdened but also the small men who could not afford it were also compelled to contribute, thus placing heavy burdens on them. . . . Now, when he comes for an audience, if we still show him our favour without punishing him ignorant people would suspect that Cheng-jui had made a gift to hush up the matter and had, therefore, received a full pardon. At the present time when discipline is being tightened up how can he be let off, with the result that a bad man would be allowed to remain in the ranks of the highest ministers? Let Cheng-jui be dismissed and be sent under escort to the Imperial Tombs to work, and let him ponder over his misdeeds and his punishment, and also pay money to redeem himself.

Such a punishment under the paternal government of Ch'ien-lung and his immediate successors was not normally permanent, and by the tenth year of Chia-ch'ing's reign he had been regranted the right to wear the peacock feather, and in the fourteenth year (1809–1810) he was appointed Grand Minister of the Imperial Household. However, he still showed a propensity to have a say in state affairs by submitting memorials. As a result of one particularly foolish memorial an Imperial edict was issued depriving him of the peacock feather. He was lucky not be punished more severely, as the edict

---

* Cheng-jui is not mentioned in Hummel, *Eminent Chinese of the Ch'ing period*. I have taken the information given here from his biography in the *Kuo-ch'ao ch'i-hsien lei-cheng*, chüan 96, pp. 37a–41b, and the edicts quoted therein.

says: 'But considering his old age and dotage only a slight punishment has been given him, so that he may be warned and know what to fear.' In the nineteenth year of Chia-ch'ing's reign (1814–15) he reached the highest post in his career, that of Left (i.e. Senior) Vice-Minister in the Department of Works. However, one last memorial on a matter that was none of his business angered the Emperor and he again lost his peacock feather, being also deprived of his post as a Vice-Minister, his position in the Imperial Household and the honour of riding a horse inside the Imperial Palace. He died in the first month of the twentieth year of Chia-ch'ing's reign (1815). He was over eighty years old at the time of his death.

This brief account of his career gives some idea of the official with whom Macartney came into contact continually during the course of his embassy. Cheng-jui appears to have been touchy, vain, stubborn and not a little muddleheaded. He was a Manchu who perhaps had been given more power than his capabilities and character warranted.

WANG. When Macartney transferred from the *Lion* on to the junk provided to take him up the Peiho to Tungchow, two Chinese officials were assigned to conduct him throughout his stay in China. He refers to them in his Journal as Van-ta-gin and Chou-ta-gin, explaining that *ta-gin** means 'great man'. However, to leave these two names in Macartney's romanization without attempting to identify them would be most unsatisfactory, and would condemn these two officials, whom the reader will get to know quite well, to remain mere names without identities.

Since 'Van' is not a Chinese syllable the true pronunciation of his name must have been slightly different. Luckily Macartney offers some clues in his Journal which help to identify 'Van' with certainty. These are:

31 *July* 1793.   'Van is a war Mandarin, has a peacock's feather and a red coral flourished button on his cap, which is the second order' (p. 71).

On 25 August Macartney recorded that he was prepared to give 'Van' and 'Chou' a present because of the expense they would incur over the embassy. However, they refused to accept any money: 'It was true that the expense they incurred by their attendance on the embassy was considerable, but that it chiefly fell upon

* Wade-Giles romanization *ta-jen*.

BRIEF BIOGRAPHIES

Chou, who was very rich and well able to bear it; that Van was not rich, and did not therefore contribute to it. . . .' (p. 98).

Under the entry for 1 September he recorded: 'Van, to whom as a military man distinguished by wounds and long service I gave a couple [of swords] . . . .' (p. 105).

On 7 October when Macartney and his party had reached Tungchow on the journey from Peking to Canton he wrote: 'The civil officer or Mandarin of this place, a Manchu Tartar (Van, the military commander, is a Chinese), has been just here to pay me a visit . . .' (p. 158).

Barrow, in his *Travels in China*, first published in 1804, gave a valuable clue when he wrote: 'Chou is at present in a high situation at Court, but Van, the cheerful good-humoured Van, has paid the debt of nature, having fallen honourably in the service of his country' (p. 604). This information Barrow probably obtained from one or other of the missionaries remaining at Peking who still occasionally wrote to Macartney or Staunton.

Finally, young Staunton, in his manuscript Journal of the embassy,* spells his name Vang with a 'g', which is an approximate romanization for Wang. Since young Staunton made a definite study of the Chinese language under the Chinese interpreters on the outward voyage his attempt to romanize the sound of 'Van's' name is likely to have been more accurate than those of Macartney and Barrow.

In the list of office-holders printed in the Tungchow local history covering this period of Ch'ien-lung's reign the military commander (*Fu-chiang*) at Tungchow at the time of the Macartney embassy was named Wang Wen-hsiung.† His biography is given in *Ch'ing-shih kao* (355, 1a), and in *Kuo-ch'ao ch'i-hsien lei-cheng* (366, 1a–12b). According to these biographies the details of Wang Wen-hsiung's career correspond so closely to what we know of the official 'Van' that I am satisfied that Macartney was in fact conducted throughout his embassy by Wang Wen-hsiung. Briefly stated the main facts of Wang's career are as follows:

Born of a Chinese family in Kweichow province he entered the army and rose from the ranks. He saw action in the campaigns in Burma and on the borders of Yunnan, and received various promotions until he commanded a battalion. In the fortieth year of Ch'ien-lung's reign (1775–6) he led his troops in an attack on a mountain

* Discussed in Appendix D.   † *T'ung-chou chih, chüan 6, Kuan-shih chih.*

fortress, climbing up first. Although wounded in the leg he refused to withdraw. For this action he was awarded the blue feather, and after further promotions, the peacock feather. In the fifty-seventh year (1792–3) he was promoted commander (*Fu-chiang*) of the Tungchow brigade, a post which he held until 1796. There is no mention in the biographies of him that he accompanied Lord Macartney to Jehol and throughout the embassy. But presumably this was not considered an important assignment since Wang and 'Chou' were acting in a subordinate capacity under Cheng-jui, who received the praise (and blame) for conducting the ambassador. In any case escorting a barbarian envoy was hardly an important episode in the career of a military official.

In the first year of Chia-ch'ing (1796–7) he was sent with a force into Hupeh to suppress bandit sects there. He was promoted to the rank of *T'i-tu* (provincial Commander-in-Chief) in 1798. He took part in various other campaigns against the rebels in Shansi and Szechwan and during one of these campaigns he was taken ill and vomited blood. As a result he was granted sick leave. After recovering he was again in command of troops. On the twenty-fourth day of the seventh month of the fifth year of Chia-ch'ing (12 September 1800) he was fighting against rebels in Shensi province. His force was outnumbered and surrounded. He received several wounds but continued to fight. Finally his left arm was severed, and he fell from his horse and died.

We can now compare the evidence from Macartney and Barrow with the facts set down in Wang's biographies. Both the English and Chinese accounts agree that he was a professional soldier, that he was not wealthy (he served in the ranks), that he had been wounded on active service and had been awarded a peacock feather. That in 1793 he was military commander at Tungchow. That he was killed in battle, 'having fallen honourably in the service of his country'. The Chinese sources give a picture of a thorough-going soldier, continually on active service, fearless and tough. Macartney and various members of his embassy give the impression that 'Van' was cheerful, good-humoured and bluff; a proper soldier. From this evidence I feel that it is reasonable to identify Macartney's 'Van' with Wang Wen-hsiung, an historical figure of flesh and blood.

There is a coloured print of him as the frontispiece to Barrow's *Travels in China*, about which Barrow wrote: 'The portrait of this gentleman, drawn by Mr. Hickey, is so strong a likeness, and he was deservedly so great a favourite of every Englishman in the train of the British ambassador, that I am happy in having an opportunity of placing it at the head of this work' (p. 184).

Note. I wish here to acknowledge the great help I have received from Mr. Kuo Ting-yee, Director of the Institute of Modern History, Academia Sinica, Taiwan, in preparing this note on 'Van' and the following note on 'Chou'. He very kindly searched through the *T'ung-chou chih* (which was not available to me in Hong Kong) and sent me the Chinese characters of Wang's name. From this I have been able to trace his biography in the usual works of reference.

CHOU. The official whom Macartney calls 'Chou' was most probably Ch'iao Jen-chieh, a Taotai at Tientsin at the time of the embassy. In his Journal Macartney gives the following information about 'Chou'.

> 10 *October* 1793. I remember Chou telling me one day ... that an inundation in the course of last year had swept away a village in the province of Shantung so suddenly that the inhabitants could save nothing but their lives. The Emperor ... immediately ordered one hundred thousand taels for their relief, out of which the first *li-pu* took twenty thousand, the second ten thousand, the third five thousand, and so on till at last there remained no more than twenty thousand for the poor sufferers. (p. 161)

> 9 *January* 1794. Chou *ta-jen* is a man of letters and capacity. He stands high in the opinion of the Viceroy, whose universal reputation, joined to his connexion with the Imperial family, will probably elevate him one day to the first situation at Court. I have more than once talked with Chou on the subject of office and preferment, and from his prospects of advantage being enlarged by what he has seen here. ... I think it not at all improbable that he may soon be sent here [i.e. Canton.—Ed.] in a high employment. The place of Hoppo, which is usually of three years' duration, seems to be the object of his present views (p. 217).

In the Observations Macartney also mentions him. 'My friend Chou (who, as civil governor of a city of the first rank on which several others are dependent, has a very extensive judicial range and jurisdiction) endeavoured to impress me with an idea of the equity and regularity of the courts where he presided, and as I entertained a very favourable opinion of him, I dare say that few of the others are better ordered or more pure. ...' (Observations, 'Justice', p. 240).

Again, in another place Macartney noted: 'The state of the population, as marked in the table, was given to me by Chou, a Mandarin of high rank, and supreme governor of Tientsin, who was one of those appointed by the Emperor to attend my embassy from the moment of my arrival on the coast of Pei-chihli. He was a man of letters and information, and from habit and frequent converse contracted a strong friendship and affection for me' (Observations, 'Population', p. 246).

Barrow, writing some time before 1804, stated that Wang had been killed, but that 'Chou is at present in a high situation at Court.'*

Finally, young Staunton, in his Journal, provides us with the most important clue when he romanizes Chou's name as Chiow, which produces approximately the same sound as the Wade-Giles romanization of Ch'iao. Again, I feel inclined to accept the evidence of someone who, although a schoolboy, had made a real attempt to learn something of the language from Chinese teachers.

Mr. Kuo Ting-yee very kindly searched through the local histories of Tientsin for any official holding office at the time of the Macartney embassy who might be described as 'Governor of Tientsin',† and also having a family name which might be changed into Chou by mispronunciation. The only name which could possibly be corrupted into the romanization 'Chou' is that of an official called Ch'iao Jen-chieh. Unfortunately this man has not been given a biography in any of the standard biographical works devoted to the Ch'ing period. Mr. Kuo therefore abstracted from the various local histories of the Provinces in which Ch'iao Jen-chieh served the main points of his career, and I have drawn on Mr. Kuo's extracts in compiling the following biographical note.

Ch'iao Jen-chieh was born in the province of Shansi. He became a provincial graduate (*chu-jen*) in the year 1765. He later served as a District Magistrate and proved himself to be a good administrator. He was promoted Military Administrative Taotai (*Ping-pei-tao*) of Tientsin, holding this post from 1790–3. This was a civil appointment in spite of its title. The holder was an Intendant of a Circuit, and as such would be in charge of two or more Prefectures. But because he also had control over the military forces within his area he was officially designated Military Administrative Taotai. There had been bad floods near Tientsin in 1792 and as a result the famine-stricken people swarmed through the district of Tientsin on their way to the north. Ch'iao started a relief campaign among the officials and gentry and set up points for serving congee (rice gruel) outside the four main gates of the city to feed the hungry refugees.

---

* *Travels in China*, p. 604.
† See *Tientsin fu-chih*, chüan 12, Chih-kuan chih; chüan 40, Huan-chi chuan. Hsü Tientsin hsien-chih, chüan 9, Chih-kuan chih; chüan 11, Ming-huan chuan.

BRIEF BIOGRAPHIES

This may have been the flood which 'Chou' described to Macartney on 10 October 1793. If he was the chief instigator of relief measures he would naturally be indignant about the small amount of relief money which eventually found its way to Tientsin. There is no mention that he conducted Macartney on his embassy, but this fact was of no local importance, and in any case may not have been considered of significance to Chinese historians.

In Chia-ch'ing's fifth year (1800–1) he was promoted to be Provincial Judicial Commissioner (*An-ch'a-shih*) of Chihli. Since Chihli was the metropolitan province in which Peking was situated this post was an important one and would bring Ch'iao into contact with high officials at the capital. In the following year (1801–2) he was transferred to a similar post in Fukien, and in 1802–3 to Hupei, also as *An-ch'a-shih*.

When Barrow says that 'Chou is at present in a high situation at Court' it is possible that he is referring to the post of Provincial Judicial Commissioner for Chihli which Ch'iao held some time in 1800–1. Now, if one of the missionaries at Peking who had got to know Macartney and Staunton during the embassy wrote to either of them towards the end of 1800 or in the early part of 1801, he would naturally report 'Van's' death, which occurred in September 1800, and the promotion of 'Chou' to a post which might be loosely described as 'a high situation at Court'. Unfortunately I have not discovered any mention of this news in the letters from missionaries written at this time which I have examined. However, it is possible that further letters may come to light which will yield more definite information.

Ch'iao Jen-chieh is recorded as having left his post in Chia-ch'ing's ninth year (1804–5), but no reasons are given. Presumably he retired from public service. Thus he had held the highest judicial post in three different provinces over a period of five years. One biographical note states that 'he was skilled in civil administration and particularly capable in unravelling complex legal cases and therefore he was well known for his good official conduct'. Ch'iao obviously seems to have specialized in judicial work, and this seems to bear out what Macartney wrote about him. 'My friend Chou (who ... has a very extensive judicial range and jurisdiction) endeavoured to impress me with an idea of the equity and regularity of the courts where he presided....'

Thus there is strong evidence for identifying Macartney's friend Chou with Ch'iao Jen-chieh who was Military Administrative Taotai at Tientsin in the period 1790–3. However, since this identification leaves certain problems still unsolved I do not wish to claim categorically that Macartney's Chou was in fact Ch'iao Jen-chieh. Therefore I have not adopted the spelling Ch'iao through the Journal although it corresponds closely to young Staunton's romanization of the name which, I feel, is more likely to be correct than Macartney's Chou.

APPENDIX B

Note on the Transmission of the Manuscript of the Journal

WITH ORIGINAL TABLE OF CONTENTS

The manuscript of Macartney's Journal, from which the text here printed has been taken, is now preserved in the Tōyō Bunko (The Oriental Library) in Tokyo. It consists of three folio volumes. The history of the manuscript is as follows:

It remained in the possession of Lord Macartney's heirs until 1854, when his books and documents were sold by Puttick and Simpson, the number given to the Journal in their catalogue being 1040.* As a result of this sale the manuscript of the Journal, together with many of Macartney's other documents, passed into the collection of the great nineteenth-century bibliophile, Sir Thomas Phillipps. In the catalogue of the Phillipps collection the three volumes of the Journal were given the numbers 13414, 13415 and 19001 and these numbers can still be seen, written in pencil, in the inside front covers of the three volumes preserved in Tokyo.

Part of the Phillipps collection, including the Journal, was sold by Sotheby's on 23 May 1913. It was item no. 913 in their sale catalogue, and was described as 'A Journal of the Embassy to China in 1792, 1793, 1794 by George Lord Macartney, to which are added several explanatory Notes and References with an Appendix of Documents, the original manuscripts. 3 vols. folio.' It was bought by a dealer in rare books and manuscripts and eventually came into the library of G. E. Morrison (1862–1920), *The Times* Correspondent in Peking in the early years of this century, who at that time owned one of the best libraries of books and manuscripts dealing with the Far East. In 1917 the bulk of his library was bought by Baron Iwasaki, and it was this collection which formed the nucleus of the Tōyō Bunko. The three volumes of the Journal are described in the *Catalogue of the Asiatic Library of Dr. G. E. Morrison; Now a Part of the Oriental Library, Tokyo, Japan; Part I, English Books,* on page 396.† The description given in the catalogue is attributed to Morrison himself.

The Observations attached to the Journal exist in two manuscript

---

* Puttick and Simpson sale catalogue no. 352 of February 1854.
† Published in 2 vols. by the Oriental Library (Tokyo, 1924).

versions. The first eight sections appear in both versions, but the section by Dr. Gillan in only one. These two versions are clearly meant to be the same and contain only a few very minor differences in wording. One version is in the same handwriting as the Journal, the other version is in a different hand. I have followed this second version since the one in the same hand as the Journal appears to have been altered in a number of places to make it conform to the second version. Why there should have been two versions of the Observations and only one of the Journal itself I do not claim to know.

Apart from the Journal of the actual embassy to the Emperor of China, printed in this book, Macartney kept a separate Journal of the outward voyage from the time he went on board H.M.S. *Lion* on 11 September 1792 until he left Tourane Bay in Cochin China on 15 June 1793. This manuscript also passed into the Phillipps Collection and was sold at Sotheby's on 23 May 1913. The Phillipps catalogue number of this Journal was 14197, and the item number in Sotheby's sale catalogue was 911. The first page is headed simply 'Memoranda from London to China'. Opposite the first page, in a different hand, is the following note: 'This journal was written by Lord Macartney on board the *Lion* merely for his own amusement and to pass away a few heavy hours on a very long sea voyage. J.B.' The initials were presumably those of John Barrow who had the opportunity of studying the two Journals while writing his *Life* of Macartney. This Journal was bought by a dealer for £11 and later passed into the hands of Maggs Bros., the antiquarian booksellers, and was described in their *Bibliotheca Asiatica* (No. 452) of 1924, item number 694. From Maggs it passed to Stevens, the book auctioneers from whom it was finally bought by the Wellcome Historical Medical Library in September 1930 for £15.* Ten pages (pp. 118–127 inclusive) have been torn out of this manuscript at a point where Macartney was describing the entertainment given by the Dutch to the members of the embassy during their stay at Batavia. This corresponds with the gap noted by Helen Robbins when she printed her version of this Journal in *Our First Ambassador to China*.

* I am most grateful to Mr. A. N. L. Munby, Librarian of King's College, Cambridge, for bringing to my attention the existence of this Journal in the Wellcome Historical Medical Library, and also for putting his great knowledge of the Phillipps Collection at my disposal. Five volumes of his detailed study of Sir Thomas Phillipps and the Phillipps Collection have been published by the Cambridge University Press, 1951–60. A final volume is to follow.

TRANSMISSION OF THE JOURNAL

I have deliberately referred to Macartney's Journal of the voyage from England to Cochin China and his Journal of the actual embassy in China as quite separate journals, which they clearly are. As Barrow states, the Journal to Cochin China was kept for his own amusement to pass the tedious hours of a long voyage. But on reaching China Macartney started a new Journal, not to pass away the time but to record what he saw and experienced. The two Journals are clearly separated by the short résumé of the voyage which Macartney wrote as an introduction to his China Journal. Both Barrow and Helen Robbins in their biographies of Macartney have ignored this fact.

Barrow prints Macartney's summary of the outward voyage, but makes no reference to his Journal of it, while Helen Robbins prints the Journal of the voyage but omits, without comment, the short résumé.

It is a thousand pities that the large collection of Macartney documents should have been scattered piecemeal over the world by sales which have continued from 1854 until as recently as 1945; a calamity only surpassed in extent by the dispersal of the vast collection of Sir Joseph Banks' manuscripts by auction at Sotheby's in 1886. Anyone who succeeds in making a detailed list of the whereabouts of these scattered Macartney documents will be doing a great service to scholars of eighteenth-century European history; but the task is likely to be a long and arduous one.

Note. Here follows the original Table of Contents included in the MS. of Macartney's Journal.

A JOURNAL OF THE EMBASSY TO CHINA
IN 1792, 1793, 1794

To which are now added several explanatory notes and references, with an appendix containing:

1. A register of the thermometer and barometer in China from the 23rd June 1793 to the 17th March 1794.
2. A list of the different embassies to China in the last century and the present.*
3. A letter from Father Amiot to Lord Macartney dated Pekin 27th August 1793.

    * [Included in this edition of the Journal as Appendix E—Ed.]

ORIGINAL TABLE OF CONTENTS

4. A letter from Mr. Irwin to Lord Macartney dated Macao July 2nd 1793.
5. A letter from Mr. Titsingh, one of the Supreme Council of Batavia to Lord Macartney, dated Batavia 4th November 1793.
6. Several papers containing Lord Macartney's observations upon China under different heads.* Viz.:

> Manners and Character
> Religion
> Government, Justice and Property
> Population
> Revenue
> Civil and Military Ranks and Establishments
> Trade and Commerce
> Arts and sciences
> Navigation
> Hydraulics
> Language.

7. Portfolio of charts, plans, drawings, etc.
8. Queries and answers relative to silk.
9. Dr. Gillan's papers upon the state of medicine, surgery, chemistry, etc., in China.*
10. Dr. Gillan's opinion of the case of the Grand Secretary Ho-shen.

* [Included in this edition of the Journal.—Ed.]

APPENDIX C

An Edict from the Emperor Ch'ien-Lung to King George the Third of England

The majority of the Chinese documents dealing with the Macartney embassy printed in the *Chang-ku ts'ung pien* are concerned with routine administrative matters. There are instructions from the Grand Council about the transport of the presents, the reception and entertainment of the envoy and his suite, the efficient manning of their posts by the military, and so forth. Suddenly, among all these tedious and prosaic matters one long Imperial edict stands out like a monolith on a desert plain. It is written in powerful and elegant Chinese and puts to shame the memorials and Court Letters concerning the embassy which often lack just such style and precision. This is one of the very few Chinese documents dealing with the Macartney embassy which has been translated into English and is the only one known to historians generally. The translation from which quotations are usually given was published by E. Backhouse and J. O. P. Bland in their *Annals and Memoirs of the Court of Peking.** However, they do not state from which collection of Chinese documents they made their version. It is more in the nature of a paraphrase than a close translation, so that Chinese ideas are sometimes made to fit into English conceptions and phrases. Their translation has the convincing ring of English legal and diplomatic jargon, but when compared closely with the Chinese is apt to seem too anglicized. This version has held the field for fifty years but perhaps the time has come when this edict should be studied in a literal translation which attempts to bring out the full flavour of the Chinese. For instance, many of the characters used have a haughty and condescending tone, so that the edict echoes classical Chinese phrases and is full of nuances of superiority which must have been extremely satisfying to the Emperor and his officials but were lost on the western barbarians in their English translation. In fact the worthy Jesuit fathers who were charged with translating this edict from Chinese into Latin deliberately modified expressions here and there which they thought would offend the English.†

In the *Chang-ku ts'ung-pien* this edict is prefaced by a memorandum

* London, 1914. † See note 50.

336

EDICT FROM CH'IEN-LUNG

from the Grand Council dated the twenty-seventh day of the sixth month (3 August 1793) which states:

> We have respectfully drafted an edict to the country of England which we now submit. As soon as it has been sent down* it should be translated into Manchu and Western Ocean characters [i.e. Latin.—Ed.], and again submitted. It should then be reverently copied out, and as soon as the tribute envoy sets out to return to his country it should be given to him in accordance with precedent. Respectfully memorialized.

This is interesting because it shows that even before Macartney stepped ashore in China an edict ordering his dismissal existed in draft. According to the editors of the *Chang-ku ts'ung-pien* this edict was promulgated on the nineteenth day of the eighth month (23 September 1793). This means that the final version was approved by the Emperor nine days after he had received Macartney in audience. The Latin translation was actually delivered to the ambassador on 3 October 1793. It is perhaps as well for subsequent Anglo-Chinese relations that neither Macartney nor the English Government realized quite how condescending was the original Chinese version of the edict.†

AN EDICT

'We, by the Grace of Heaven, Emperor, instruct the King of England to take note of our charge.

'Although your country, O King, lies in the far oceans, yet inclining your heart towards civilization you have specially sent an envoy respectfully to present a state message, and sailing the seas he has come to our Court to kotow and to present congratulations for the Imperial birthday, and also to present local products, thereby showing your sincerity.

'We have perused the text of your state message and the wording expresses your earnestness. From it your sincere humility and obedience can clearly be seen. It is admirable and we fully approve. As regards the chief and assistant envoys who have brought the state message and tribute articles, we are mindful that they have been sent from afar across the sea, and we have extended our favour and courtesy to them, and have ordered our ministers to bring them

---

* I.e. approved by the Emperor and sent to the Grand Council for action.

† See J. L. Cranmer-Byng, op. cit., p. 134, n. 45. I am indebted to the Editorial Board of the *Journal of Oriental Studies*, University of Hong Kong, for permission to reproduce this translation, which originally appeared in my article published in Volume IV, nos. 1–2 of that Journal.

to an Imperial audience. We have given them a banquet and have repeatedly bestowed gifts on them in order to show our kindness. Although the officers, servants and others, in charge of the ships more than six hundred in number, returned to Chou-shan [Chusan. —Ed.] and did not come to the capital, yet we have also bestowed gifts on them generally so that all should receive favours equally.

'As to what you have requested in your message, O King, namely to be allowed to send one of your subjects to reside in the Celestial Empire to look after your country's trade, this does not conform to the Celestial Empire's ceremonial system, and definitely cannot be done. Hitherto, whenever men from the various Western Ocean countries have desired to come to the Celestial Empire and to enter the Imperial service we have allowed them to come to the capital. But once having come, they were obliged to adopt the costume of the Celestial Empire, they were confined within the Halls,* and were never allowed to return home. These are the fixed regulations of the Celestial Empire, and presumably you also know them, O King. Now, however, you want to send one of your subjects to reside at the capital. But he could neither behave like a Western Ocean man who comes to the capital to enter our service, remaining at the capital and not returning to his native country, nor could he be allowed to go in and out, and to have regular correspondence.† So it would really serve no purpose.

'Moreover, the territories ruled by the Celestial Empire are vast, and for all the envoys of vassal states coming to the capital there are definite regulations regarding the provision of quarters and supplies to them and regarding their movements. There never has been any precedent for allowing them to suit their own convenience. Now, if your country retains someone at the capital his speech will not be understood and his dress will be different in style, and we have

---

* This refers to the four halls or Churches in Peking where the various foreign missionaries and laymen in the Emperor's service lived at this time. Sir G. T. Staunton in *Miscellaneous Notices Relating to China* has a note on the missionaries in Peking at the time of the Macartney Embassy, and lists the churches as follows:

The Greater Portuguese Church	Nan-t'ang (Southern Hall)
The Lesser Portuguese Church	Tung-t'ang (Eastern Hall)
The French Church	Pei-t'ang (Northern Hall)
Church of the Sacred Congregation of the Propaganda	Hsi-t'ang (Western Hall)

† I think the idea implied is that such a person would not be allowed to send information home as a regular matter. At this time the Celestial Empire was, as always, very suspicious lest foreign countries should gain knowledge of her internal affairs, and the Jesuits at Peking had recently had their letters opened and examined.

EDICT TO GEORGE III

nowhere to house him. If he is to resemble those Western Ocean men who come to the capital to enter the Imperial service we must order him, without exception, to change his dress to that of the Celestial Empire. However, we have never wished to force on others what is difficult to do. Besides, if the Celestial Empire desired to send someone permanently to reside in your country surely you would not be able to agree to it? Furthermore, there are a great many Western Ocean countries altogether, and not merely your one country. If, like you, O King, they all beg to send someone to reside at the capital how could we grant their request in every case? It would be absolutely impossible for us to do so. How can we go as far as to change the regulations of the Celestial Empire, which are over a hundred years old, because of the request of one man—of you, O King?

'If it is said that your object, O King, is to take care of trade, men from your country have been trading at Macao* for some time, and have always been treated favourably. For instance, in the past Portugal and Italy and other countries have several times sent envoys to the Celestial Empire with requests to look after their trade,† and the Celestial Empire, bearing in mind their loyalty, treated them with great kindness. Whenever any matter concerning trade has arisen which affected those countries it has always been fully taken care of. When the Canton merchant Wu Chao-p'ing‡ [Wayqua.—Ed.] owed money to foreign ships we ordered the Governor-General to advance the money out of the Treasury and to pay his debts for him at the public expense, and to have the debtor-merchant severely punished. Presumably your country has also heard about this. Why, then, do foreign countries need to send someone to remain at the capital? This is a request for which there is no precedent and it definitely cannot be granted. Moreover, the distance between Macao, the place where the trade is conducted, and

---

* It would have been more accurate if the edict had said 'Canton', since it was here that the actual English trade was carried on. The merchants were forced by Imperial edict to live in Macao during the off season, but they did not trade with the Chinese there. They were only allowed at Canton during the trading season, which was approximately from October to March.

† Presumably with requests that they might be allowed to appoint someone to look after the interests of their trade at the capital. However, the text may not mean more than that they petitioned the Emperor for redress of abuses by Chinese officials in Macao and Canton. In any case Italy did not send a mission. If Italy is meant, then a Papal envoy is referred to, but this mission would be for diplomatic and not trade reasons.

‡ See Morse, *Chronicles*, II, p. 25, and Pritchard, *Crucial Years*, p. 201.

the capital is nearly ten thousand *li*,* and if he were to remain at the capital how could he look after it?

'If it is said that because you look up with admiration to the Celestial Empire you desire him to study our culture, yet the Celestial Empire has its own codes of ritual which are different from your country's in each case. Even if the person from your country who remained here was able to learn them it would be of no use since your country has its own customs and regulations, and you would certainly not copy Chinese ones.

'The Celestial Empire, ruling all within the four seas,† simply concentrates on carrying out the affairs of Government properly, and does not value rare and precious things. Now you, O King, have presented various objects to the throne, and mindful of your loyalty in presenting offerings from afar, we have specially ordered the Yamen‡ to receive them. In fact, the virtue and power of the celestial Dynasty has penetrated afar to the myriad kingdoms, which have come to render homage, and so all kinds of precious things from "over mountain and sea" have been collected here, things which your chief envoy and others have seen for themselves. Nevertheless we have never valued ingenious articles, nor do we have the slightest need of your country's manufactures. Therefore, O King, as regards your request to send someone to remain at the capital, while it is not in harmony with the regulations of the Celestial Empire we also feel very much that it is of no advantage to your country. Hence we have issued these detailed instructions and have commanded your tribute envoys to return safely home. You, O King, should simply act in conformity with our wishes by strengthening your loyalty and swearing perpetual obedience so as to ensure that your country may share the blessings of peace.

'Besides giving both the customary and extra gifts, as listed separately, to the chief and assistant envoys, and to the various officials under them as well as to the interpreters, soldiers and servants, now, because your envoy is returning home we have issued this special edict, and confer presents on you, O King—elaborate

---

* Since one *li* is equivalent to about one-third of an English mile, this statement is an exaggeration and probably means no more than 'a long way'. The actual distance as the courier went at that time may have been about one thousand five hundred miles. However, dispatches travelling at express rate were known to have reached Canton from the capital in about eighteen days.

† A classical phrase with a long history. It is synonymous with 'ruling the world'.

‡ I.e. the appropriate Department dealing with foreign tribute. This was probably the Li-fan Yuan which dealt with the affairs of the dependencies such as Mongolia and Tibet, and with Russian affairs.

and valuable things all, in accordance with the usual etiquette. In addition we have bestowed brocades, gauzes, and elaborate curios; all precious things. These are listed separately.

'Let the King reverently receive them and know our kind regard for him.

'This is a special edict.'
(Chang-ku ts'ung-pien, III, pp. 18a–19b).

This is perhaps the most important single Chinese document for the study of Sino-Western relations between 1700 and 1860. The ideas herein expressed proved that western-style diplomatic relations with China were impossible. This edict gives, in beautifully precise and balanced Chinese, a classical exposition of the relations between the Celestial Empire and the countries of the Western Ocean as seen from the Chinese point of view. Thus China is the centre of the world and the prototype of civilization. Any barbarian country may send a special envoy to the capital to present tribute and so partake briefly in the benefits of a superior civilization. As regards trade, this is a privilege which is granted to foreigners and must be kept under close supervision; it is not necessary to the Celestial Empire. It is permitted out of compassion to the barbarians who need tea and silks and porcelain with which to make their lives bearable. As for the idea of a regular ambassador residing at Peking, it is unheard of. How can barbarian states have permanent intercourse with the Celestial Empire itself? They have nothing to offer, they do not know the correct etiquette. Their only task is to remain at peace, and from time to time to show their submission and loyalty by presenting tribute to the Imperial throne. This classic theory of China as the centre of civilization is perfectly presented in this edict. Even after the first Anglo-Chinese War of 1839–42 and the opening up of Treaty Ports the ideas embalmed in this document did not materially change. There was still no question of permanent ambassadors from Western countries being allowed to reside at Peking. Trade was still regarded as a concession, something that must be regulated at the ports by the local officials. It took the Second Anglo-Chinese War and the Convention of Peking in 1860 to bring about any real change in the Chinese outlook. Even then it was not a whole-hearted one. The basic ideas expressed in this edict have never entirely lost their power.

APPENDIX D

Annotated List of Writings which Contain First-Hand Material Relating to the Macartney Embassy

Alexander, William. *Journal of a Voyage to Pekin in China on board the Hindostan E.I.M. which accompanied Lord Macartney on his Embassy to the Emperor* (MS in the British Museum).

Besides making a vast number of colour-wash sketches while in China, Alexander kept a journal, the manuscript of which is preserved in the British Museum.* It contains a mass of details which he observed, and which are useful as a supplement to the accounts by Macartney, Staunton and Barrow. It is far superior to the second-rate and often second-hand narratives put together by literary hacks from what Aeneas Anderson or Samuel Holmes remembered of the embassy.

As an example, Alexander tells us what he felt when he learned that he was not to accompany Macartney to Jehol.

> September 2. At 2 a.m. the heart-stirring drum and ear-piercing fife roused all from their beds to prepare for the journey to Tartary. It was determined that Mr. Hickey, artist, Mr. Maxwell, Secretary, Dr. Scott to have charge of the sick, Dr. Dinwiddie and Mr. Barrow still at the Yuan-min Yuan, and myself should remain at Pekin. This to me was a most severe decision, and to have been within fifty miles of the famous Great Wall, that stupendous monument of human labour, and not to have seen that which might have been the boast of a man's grandson as Dr. Johnson has said I have to regret for ever. That the artists should be dismissed to remain immured at Pekin during this most interesting journey of the embassy, is not easily to be accounted for—would I had respectfully remonstrated or memorialized his Lordship....

He gives us some of the few references that we get to Thomas Hickey during the two years the embassy lasted. As one would expect, his descriptions of buildings at Peking and at the Yuan-ming Yuan are good. Furthermore, he was one of the party that left Macartney and the main body at Hangchow and went to Chusan to rejoin the *Hindostan* instead of proceeding to Canton. Thus his account covers a journey not described by any other member of the embassy except in the fragments which survived from Dinwiddie's

* Add. MS. No. 35174.

journal. In Canton he records visiting the shops of two Chinese painters, 'Puqua' and 'Chamfou', and remarks '. . . they copy accurately and produce very highly finished pictures, indifferently coloured, from the prints of Bunbury, Kauffman, etc., and many prints of this style were seen there for that purpose.' It was at Canton that a Chinese sculptor told Alexander that he could 'sa-vy Mis-sa Banks velly well'. Presumably by this the sculptor meant that he knew what Sir Joseph Banks looked like. Both he and the painters were employed to copy from European prints.

At the end of his journal Alexander records that when the embassy was off Folkestone, after an absence from England of two years, the unfortunate crew of the *Hindostan* were pressed into the Navy without a chance to set foot on shore. He wrote: 'Captain Mackintosh slept at Walmer Castle. Being on a visit to Mr. Pitt and Mr. Dundas, he made application that his men might be spared, but his entreaties, though backed by Lord Macartney, could not with good policy be complied with.'

This is an intelligent account of the embassy, though somewhat brief, and the handwriting is difficult to decipher in places. It contains a number of small colour-wash drawings.*

Anderson, Aeneas. *A Narrative of the British Embassy to China, in the years* 1792, 1793 *and* 1794 . . . (London, J. Debrett, 1795).

Anderson was Macartney's personal servant during the embassy, and there is some indication that Macartney may have known that he was likely to publish an account of the embassy. In his Journal for 15 December, when discussing the different accounts of the same event written by different people, he wrote: 'Even the memorandum of a *valet de chambre* might be of some value.' In fact the book is of little value. John Barrow, in his own account of the embassy,† dismissed Anderson's account as '. . . a book that was published in the name of one Aeneas Anderson, who was a livery servant of Lord Macartney, but which, in fact was a work vamped up by a London bookseller as a speculation that could not fail, so greatly excited was public curiosity at the return of the Embassy.' Since Anderson was not 'in the know' he could only speculate on the reasons for the dismissal of the embassy, and his account contains

---

* For further extracts from his Journal, see Graham Reynolds, 'Alexander and Chinnery in China', *The Geographical Magazine*, Vol. XX, no. 5 (September 1947), pp. 203–8.

† *Travels in China*, pp. 579–80.

nothing of value. The only contribution he makes is by giving fuller descriptions of buildings, especially of the palace which the embassy occupied in Peking. Thus he fills in a few details about food and lodging which the other accounts may have missed. At the beginning of his book is printed a fairly full 'list of the gentlemen who composed the retinue of Earl Macartney'.

Barrow, John. *A Voyage to Cochin China, in the Years* 1792 *and* 1793 ... (London, T. Cadell, 1806).

This gives an account of the outwards voyage as far as Cochin China, but not of the embassy in China. It thus covers the same ground as the first part of Macartney's Journal now preserved in the Wellcome Historical Medical Library in London. Barrow, while seeking to impress by his knowledge and literary style, and to correct others, was not particularly accurate himself, and his writings should be checked before assuming that the facts and dates which he gives are necessarily correct. The style of this work is discursive, and contains as many opinions as facts.

Barrow, John. *Travels in China* ... (London, T. Cadell, 1804, 2nd edn., 1806).

A hotch-potch consisting of some first-hand narrative of the embassy, some descriptions already given by Macartney and Staunton, and scraps of information on Chinese history and culture taken from earlier books. The contents of this book are not arranged in strict chronological sequence, and therefore Barrow's account of any particular event cannot easily be compared with other accounts of the embassy. On the other hand the work was first published in 1804, several years after the return of the embassy to England, and it sometimes contains information not in Macartney or Staunton. It has a rudimentary index and a number of illustrations. It was severely criticized by W. J. Proudfoot in his book *Barrow's Travels in China. An Investigation into the Origin and Authenticity of the 'Facts and Observations'* ... (London, 1861). Proudfoot was a grandson of Dr. Dinwiddie and edited his grandfather's notes and papers concerning the China embassy. It seems likely that Proudfoot inherited an antipathy to Barrow from Dr. Dinwiddie. Certainly Barrow was opinionated, but he had an enquiring, magpie-type of mind.

Barrow, John. *Some Account of the Public Life and a Selection from the Unpublished Writings of the Earl of Macartney.* 2 vols. (London, T. Cadell, 1807).

The important thing to remember is that this work only contains a 'selection' from Macartney's writings. It does not contain the complete China Journal but only parts of it, although the author gives the reader no indication where omissions have been made. In the Journal itself the number of passages omitted is considerable, perhaps as much as half, but Barrow has given almost the full text of the Observations on Government, etc. However, here, the wording differs continually from the Tokyo manuscript of the Observations, not with any obvious intention of altering the sense but rather with the object of 'improving' and polishing the style. Already by this time Barrow had literary ambitions and fancied himself as a writer. In using Macartney's manuscript material he clearly felt himself at liberty to alter Macartney's style and all his changes are towards pompous circumlocutions and elegant variations.

Barrow, John. *An Autobiographical Memoir of Sir John Barrow, Bart.* (London, John Murray, 1847.)

Written towards the end of his life this autobiography contains numerous references to the China embassy by which Barrow first came into public notice. These should be interpreted with caution since they may contain afterthoughts on the embassy, rather than immediate impressions. He makes some short and sharp observations on his fellow members of the embassy, which contain a few crumbs of useful information (pp. 46–52).

Dr. James Dinwiddie. See under Proudfoot.

Gower, Captain Sir Erasmus. *A Journal of His Majesty's Ship Lion beginning the 1st of October 1792 and ending the 7th September 1794* (British Museum, Add. MS. 21106).

As Captain of the *Lion* Gower kept a Journal, but it is mostly confined to nautical matters; wind, weather and the daily tasks of the crew. Thus it adds little to our knowledge of the embassy, and even the extensive sickness among the *Lion*'s crew in the Yellow Sea is only mentioned by Gower, and not in detail, which is a great pity, especially since a hospital was set up on land (when the *Lion* anchored at Chusan for six weeks) in order to tend the sick. The journal is illustrated by numerous colour-wash sketches.

There appear to be two versions of it, one in the British Museum, which runs from 1 October 1792 until 7 September 1794, and a similar version, but running from 5 August 1793 until 9 January 1794 only, in the Wason Collection at Cornell. In the National Maritime Museum at Greenwich there is another manuscript Journal kept by Gower entitled *Nautical Observations on a Voyage from England to China in His Majesty's Ship Lion* . . . This runs from the beginning of October 1792 until 7 September 1794, and as the title implies is devoted almost entirely to recording nautical information which Gower must have considered as an important part of his duties. It is illustrated by a number of charts and coastal panoramas.

Holmes, Samuel. *The Journal of Mr. Samuel Holmes . . . as one of the Guard on Lord Macartney's Embassy to China and Tartary* . . . (London, W. Bulmer, 1798).

Holmes was a private in the Light Dragoons. His account contains nothing of value about the business of the embassy, and is of even less interest than is Anderson's. It is very short and perfunctory.

Hüttner, J. C. *Nachricht von der Brittischen Gesandtschaftsreise durch China und einen Theil der Tartarei* (Berlin, 1797). Translated into French: *Voyage à la Chine* (Paris, 1800).

Hüttner was tutor to young George Staunton, but, once the embassy reached China, Macartney used Hüttner for various tasks. Since he was the best Latin scholar on Macartney's staff he did most of the translating from Latin. In this way he came to know more about the diplomatic side of the embassy than most of the other members of Macartney's suite, since documents for presentation to the Emperor had to be translated into Latin for the benefit of the missionaries at the capital, who also translated Chinese documents into Latin before these were handed to Macartney.

Macartney, George. See Helen H. Robbins.

Proudfoot, William Jardine. *Biographical Memoir of James Dinwiddie LL.D., Astronomer in the British Embassy to China, 1792, '3, '4 . . . compiled from his notes and correspondence . . .* (Liverpool, 1868).

This biography was put together by his grandson from Dinwiddie's papers, which included the manuscript of a 'journal through China', reported by Proudfoot as being effaced or mutilated, and thus difficult to read. The few extracts he gives from this journal are enough to make us wish that it had survived intact and had been printed. Being a trained scientist, Dinwiddie's observations may well have been of more interest than those of the valet Anderson and the self-taught Barrow. That Dinwiddie could write forcefully on occasion can be seen from this passage, quoted in Proudfoot's book, where Dinwiddie is stressing the need to be able to speak Chinese when in China.

> To travel through a fine country—to see pagodas, canals, and manufacturing towns without being able to ask a single question is extremely mortifying. To be conducted to the bottom of the Lin-ho by a Colao of the Empire—to receive a present from the Emperor at parting, and the Colao's farewell speech without knowing a word he said, and consequently to fall into numberless blunders in our attempt to reply—what information could we derive respecting the arts and sciences in a country where we could not converse with the inhabitants? With what countenance will Lord Macartney return to Europe after his shameful treatment? No apology will satisfy. We go home—are asked what we have done. Our answer—we could not speak to the people (p. 87).

Robbins, Helen H. *Our First Ambassador to China*; An Account of the Life of George, Earl of Macartney. . . . (London, John Murray, 1908).

The subtitle of this book reads 'An Account of the Life of George, Earl of Macartney, with extracts from his letters, and the narrative of his experiences in China, as told by himself, 1737–1806.' As a short biography it is of some value, and as a source of material for a fuller life of Macartney still to be written it is most valuable. But as an edition of Macartney's China Journal it is misleading and unsatisfactory. Having given a short account of the preparations of the embassy Mrs. Robbins then writes: 'The Embassy sailed from Spithead on September 26, 1792, and the account of their adventures on the voyage out and their doings in China will be given in Lord Macartney's own words in the succeeding chapters.' She then prints, without editorial comment or explanation, what the reader would suppose to be the full text of Macartney's two Journals, namely the Journal of the outward voyage as far as Tourane Bay in Cochin China, the last entry of which is dated 15 June 1793, and the actual Journal of the embassy in China which starts on 15 June. Nowhere does Mrs. Robbins hint that she has omitted whole sections of the Journal, cut out paragraphs, and altered or 'improved' the wording. Most of her footnotes consist of quotations from the accounts of other members of the embassy, and are often irrelevant and of little use. She makes no attempt to identify the various Chinese officials mentioned throughout the Journal.

Unfortunately Mrs. Robbins was not a frank editor. In the Preface to her book she gave no clear indication of the whereabouts of the text she used; she simply stated: 'I have had before me the original copies of the Chinese journals, and rough notes upon them, and the numerous letters and papers in the possession of my brother, Mr. C. G. Macartney, as well as the "Proceedings of the Select Committee of Fort St. George" and the manuscripts which are to be found in the British Museum.' This statement is somewhat ambiguous. At the date when her book was being written, about 1906–7, the China Journals were still in the possession of the heirs of Sir Thomas Phillipps (see p. 332). If Mrs. Robbins took her text from these Journals it is strange that she did not acknowledge that they were in the possession of the Phillipps family; unless, of course, she paid a fee for their use and no acknowledgement was considered necessary.

The fact remains that her version of the Journal is about one-third shorter than the manuscript Journal preserved in Tokyo. She omits many of the descriptions of places and scenery, while she shortens others, or runs together the dates of several entries. For example, if one compares the entries for 21 to 25 July as printed in the present version with the Robbins version for the same period, the kind of details she omits will become clear. Thus Helen Robbins gives no entries for 22 and 24 July at all. Macartney nearly always makes an entry for each day or else lumps together several dates under one entry. Furthermore, in her copying from the manuscript text she was not always exact. Thus under the entry for 3 October she has: 'At last we were conducted through several spacious courts, and over several magnificent bridges, to the foot of the great stairs of the Imperial Hall, where I found a line of yellow silk arm-chairs, representing the majesty of China and containing the Emperor's letter to the King.' The Tokyo text reads: '... where I found a fine yellow silk arm-chair, representing the majesty of China and containing the Emperor's letter to the King.' This makes sense, because only *one* chair covered with yellow silk was used as a symbol of the Emperor in such ceremonies. A more serious error in copying, due to ignorance of proper names in the story, is in the entry for 23 August. Here Helen Robbins has: 'This day the Tartar Legate sent to announce his intention of visiting me, and of bringing several of the European missionaries with him. He accordingly arrived at 10 a.m. with Bernando Almeyda Rodriguez and other Portuguese...'. She even gives a footnote to explain who this missionary is. In fact there is a comma in the text after Almeyda, and Macartney is writing about two different missionaries, viz., Joseph-Bernard d'Almeida and André Rodrigues.

As another example of her method of editing the text, this time by skilful omissions, I would cite the entry for 15 November. The version printed on page 80 can be compared with the one Mrs. Robbins gives. She omits the following sentences: 'The country on each side is full of mountains with fertile valleys between them. Near the banks grow a great variety of trees, among which were particularly pointed out to me the tallow tree and the camphor tree which I had not remarked before.' In the Tokyo text these sentences end the entry for 15 November, while the entry for 16 November begins: 'The country is beautiful and romantic somewhat resembling the scenes on the river Conway between Lanroost and the sea. I made a visit to the Viceroy...' It will be seen that not only does Mrs. Robbins omit three complete sentences without indicating the fact, but she also fails to state that she has omitted the date of 16 November, and has joined up the sentence about the visit to the Viceroy with the entry for 15 November. Thus by cutting out all reference to 16 November, and by omitting three sentences she has made the two entries for 15 and 16 November appear as a single one dated 15 November. As another example of this kind of editing, she gives only truncated versions for the entries for the period 14 to 21 October. In any case the entry for 14 October, as given by Mrs. Robbins, is dated 15 October in the Tokyo manuscript. The entry for 14 October is omitted altogether by her, perhaps because it contains descriptions of scenery only. She likewise omits the entries for 16, 18, 19 and 20 October. Presumably she was under pressure from her publisher to conserve space and therefore left out whatever seemed to her to be incidental to the main story. But sometimes I imagine that the omissions were made for other reasons. For instance, in transcribing the account of a day in the life of the Emperor Ch'ien-lung she gives the full text except for the last line, which she omits. It reads: 'A principal eunuch is always in waiting during the night in order to conduct to him any of the ladies whom he chooses to call for.'

As regards the Observations which Macartney wrote on 'Manners and Customs', and other subjects, Helen Robbins here gives the briefest selections, but without indicating where she omitted material. In her version these extracts are too short to be of any value and make Macartney's observations appear incredibly feeble. She also omitted to print the short summary of the voyage from England to Cochin China with which Macartney prefaces his China Journal proper. Thus she runs together the two Journals, making them appear as one organic journal by merely stating at 15 June 'End of First Part of Diary' when in fact the two Journals are quite separate and there is very clear evidence to show that the Journal of the outward voyage was kept merely as a way of passing the time.* The China Journal proper is quite separate and has its own brief introduction as printed here.

Perhaps it is unfair to be too harsh on Helen Robbins. Some blame should certainly fall on those historians who have assumed, incorrectly, that she has given us the full text of the Journal, when in fact she claimed no such thing, but merely stated that she was giving an account of the embassy to China in Macartney's own words. This she does, more or less, but as an editor she acted in a high-handed way and where she tampered with the text she covered up her traces cleverly.

Staunton, Sir George Leonard. *An Authentic Account of an Embassy from the King of Great Britain to the Emperor of China . . .* 2 vols., with atlas and engravings in a folio vol. (44 plates). (London, G. Nicol, 1797.) A Second Edition was published in 1798. There was also an abridged edition entitled *An Historical Account of the Embassy to the Emperor of China . . .* (John Stockdale, 1797).

Although this is the 'authentic' or official account of the embassy, in fact the amount of official information is rather meagre. At least one contemporary writer declared that Staunton gave the reader

* See 'Note on the transmission of the manuscript of Macartney's Journal', Appendix B.

more of the outward voyage than of the actual embassy. This criticism is fair since it is only at the end of the first bulky tome that the reader disembarks on Chinese soil. In the writing of these volumes Staunton had access to Macartney's manuscript Journal together with the 'Observations', as well as his dispatches and other papers, and he was assisted in the task by John Barrow who was his librarian from 1795 until 1797. By and large Staunton's version of the embassy is competent, worthy and dull. The style rolls the narrative along with a ponderous eighteenth-century rhythm which eventually dulls the reader's awareness. Staunton's account lacks the human touch, the sense of being immediately and personally involved which makes Macartney's Journal alive. It is good enough as an official 'blue book', but cannot compare with Macartney's own account of the complexities of the diplomacy involved. Nevertheless, it is more complete and reliable than any of the other eye-witness accounts, and in default of the full printed text of Macartney's own Journal it has been the next best thing for the last one hundred and sixty-five years.

Staunton, George Thomas. *Journal of a Voyage to China* (MS. in Duke University Library, North Carolina).

This is a manuscript journal of 179 pages covering the period 30 August 1793 to 1 February 1794, and is the second part of a longer journal, the first part of which has not come to light. At the time he kept this Journal young Staunton was twelve years old, and was officially described in the embassy as page to the ambassador. In this capacity he was presented to the Emperor at the audience at Jehol on 14 September 1793, his description of which is considerably shorter than Macartney's but agrees with it pretty closely. He describes how Macartney went to the edge of the platform on which the Emperor sat on his throne, and presented the King's letter. 'The Ambassador then came down and my Papa and I then went up and made the proper ceremony. The Emperor gave my Papa such a stone as he gave the Ambassador, and took one of the little yellow purses hanging by his side and gave it to me. He wished I should speak some Chinese words to him which I did, thanking him for his present.' His descriptions of the events at Jehol are quite full and add a few details not found in Macartney's Journal. On 16 September young Staunton noted 'Today as the Emperor wished it I drew for him the purse he gave me'.

FIRST-HAND ACCOUNTS

Most of his Journal, however, is rather like a schoolboy's holiday diary in which notes about the weather, the scenery, crops and natural phenomena play the main part. However, every now and then he supplies a useful piece of information not found elsewhere. He corroborates the statement made by Macartney that young Staunton copied out some of his letters in Chinese characters. Thus on 19 September he noted: 'Today Mr. Plumb went to the Colao with a note from the Ambassador copied by me in Chinese.' And on 12 November: 'This morning copied a Chinese letter for the Emperor which Lord Macartney soon after gave to Sung ta-gin.' His description of the temple of Pusa (15 December) is detailed and matter-of-fact. While staying at Canton and later Macao he recorded a number of details not found in any of the other accounts. He seems to have enjoyed looking at the clockwork automata which the English merchants had for sale there and describes several of them (28 and 30 December). Finally his Journal is perhaps of greatest value in helping to identify Macartney's 'Van' and 'Chou', the two conductors of the embassy.*

The handwriting is quite legible except in the first few pages.

Note. For a full bibliography of the printed editions of these works see Henri Cordier, *Bibliotheca Sinica*, Vol. IV (Paris, 1907–8), columns 2382–93.

* See Appendix A, pp. 326–9.

APPENDIX E

List of Embassies to China*

The first embassy of the Dutch from Batavia by De Goyer and Keyser.
91 days.	They arrived at Pekin	17 July 1656
	They departed from Pekin	16 October 1656

The second Dutch embassy from Batavia by Van Hoorn.
46 days	He arrived at Pekin	20 June 1667
	He departed from Pekin	5 August 1667

The first Russian embassy by Isbrant Ides.
106 days	He arrived at Pekin	5 November 1692
	He departed from Pekin	19 February 1693

The second Russian embassy by Ismailoff.
114 days	He arrived at Pekin	18 November 1720
	He departed from Pekin	2 March 1721

The Pope's embassy by Mezzabarba.
99 days	He arrived at Pekin	15 December 1720
	He departed from Pekin	24 March 1721

The Portuguese embassy of Senhor Pacheco.
39 days	He arrived at Pekin	1 May 1753
	He departed from Pekin	8 June 1753

The British embassy by Lord Macartney.
47 days	He arrived at Pekin	21 August 1793
	He departed from Pekin	7 October 1793

[The Dutch embassy under Isaac Titsingh arrived at Peking on 9 January 1795 and departed on 15 February 1795, having spent a total of 37 days at the capital.—Ed.]

*[This is one of the documents attached to Macartney's Journal now preserved in Tokyo. It shows the importance which Macartney attached to the length of time foreign embassies were permitted to remain at Peking, and is also his way of showing that the English embassy was dismissed from the capital no quicker than several other Western embassies.—Ed.)

LIST OF WORKS FREQUENTLY CITED IN THE NOTES

Barrow, J. *Travels in China*, 2nd edn. (London, 1806).
Cranmer-Byng, J. L. 'Lord Macartney's Embassy to Peking in 1793 from Official Chinese Documents', *Journal of Oriental Studies* (Hong Kong University), Vol. IV, 1–2 (1957–8).
Duyvendak, J. J. L. 'The Last Dutch Embassy to the Chinese Court, 1794–1795', *T'oung Pao*, XXXIV (1938).
Fairbank, J. K. and Teng, S. Y. *Ch'ing Administration: Three Studies* (Harvard University Press, 1960).
Hummel, A. W., ed. *Eminent Chinese of the Ch'ing Period*, 2 vols. (Washington, 1943–4).
Lettres édifiantes et curieuses écrites des Missions étrangères, 26 vols. (Paris, 1780–3).
Mémoires concernant l'Histoire, les Sciences, les Arts, les Moeurs, les Usages, etc., des Chinois: Par les Missionaires de Pekin, 15 vols. (Paris, 1776–91).
Needham, J. *Science and Civilization in China*, 4 vols. (3 more to come). (Cambridge University Press, 1954–   ).
Pfister, L. *Notices biographiques et bibliographiques sur les Jésuites de l'ancienne mission de Chine*, 1552–1773, 2 vols., (Shanghai, 1934).
Pritchard, E. H. 'Letters from Missionaries at Peking relating to the Macartney Embassy (1793–1803)', *T'oung Pao*, XXXI (1935).
Pritchard, E. H. 'The Instructions of the East India Company to Lord Macartney on his Embassy to China and his Reports to the Company, 1792–4', *Journal of the Royal Asiatic Society*, 1938, Parts II, III and IV.
Staunton, Sir George Leonard. *An Authentic Account of an Embassy from the King of Great Britain to the Emperor of China*, 2 vols. 2nd. edn. (London, 1798).

ABBREVIATIONS USED

J. Needham, *Science and Civilization in China*: SCC.
Macartney Documents in the Wason Collection on China and the Chinese at Cornell University: MDWC.

NOTES

1. The Ellicotts were a famous family of clockmakers who carried on their business under the Royal Exchange in London for nearly one hundred and fifty years. The most distinguished member of the family was John Ellicott II, inventor, and member of the Royal Society. He took his son Edward into partnership in 1757, and when Edward died in 1791 he was succeeded by his son Edward II. Among the presents which Macartney took to China were 'two plain gold seconds watches with gold hands—£86–2.' Also 'eight large size plain gold horizontal watches—£277–4.' These are listed as having been bought from Edward Ellicott. (Macartney Documents, Wason Collection, Cornell University, document no. 343. Hereafter abbreviated to MDWC). While in China Macartney distributed Ellicott watches as follows: one gold watch and one pocket watch each to Wang and Chou. One gold watch each to the missionaries Adeodato, Raux, de Poirot and Grammont (MDWC, 347). See R. K. Foulkes, 'The Ellicotts, a Family of Clockmakers', *Antiquarian Horology*, Vol. III, No. 4 (September 1960).

During the reign of Ch'ien-lung a large number of European clocks and watches were brought into China through the Canton trade. The Emperor and members of his Court seemed to have delighted in possessing them, and elaborate clocks and automata ('sing-songs') which played tunes were sent by the officials at Canton as gifts in order to obtain favour at Court. The Emperor had several fine collections of clocks and watches in his various palaces. Macartney saw one such clock in the throne room at the Yuan-ming Yuan, and states in his Journal that it was made by George Clarke (p. 95). It played twelve tunes, including airs from *The Beggar's Opera*, first produced in 1728. George Clarke was in business in Leadenhall Street during the period 1725–40. He is known for his fine table clocks as well as ornate ones with Turkish figures. Macartney also took with him to China as presents at least two watches by Josiah Emery (d. 1797), a distinguished watchmaker who had come to London from Geneva. He made many watches with lever escapements and also submitted four timekeepers to the Board of Longitude between 1792 and 1796. The official presents for the Emperor included clocks by Vulliamy. (See note 12.)

I am greatly indebted to Mr. H. Alan Lloyd for supplying me with ample references on this subject. He has written on this subject himself in 'English Clocks for the Chinese Market', *The Antique Collector*, Jan.–Feb. 1951. See also Georges Bonnant, 'The Introduction of Western Horology in China', *La Suisse Horlogère*, International edition, I (1960) pp. 28–38.

2. 'Cotton, myrrh, hot pepper, sugar it yields; other things, if you seek them, it will give obligingly.' Padre Jao Loureiro (1715–94), a Portuguese missionary who worked in Cochin China for nearly forty years. Having been trained in medicine and natural history he studied the plants of Cochin China and made a collection of nearly a thousand. In 1779 he went to Canton and while there collected plants from that region in order to complete his herbarium. He returned to Portugal by 1784 and in 1790 the results of his botanic studies were published in his *Flora Cochinchinensis* in two volumes. The material was classified according to the system recently devised by the Swedish botanist Linnaeus. In this work Loureiro noted 539 Chinese plants. See L. Pfister, *Notices biographiques . . .*, pp. 979–80, and E. Bretschneider, *History of European Botanical Discoveries in China* (London, 1898), Vol. I, p. 116.

3. William Parker was established in business at No. 69 Fleet Street from 1762. His son Samuel went into partnership with him in 1784 and ran the business from 1798 until his death in 1817. William Parker made 'great lenses' of 12- and 16-inch diameter, and lenses of this kind made by him were used by Joseph Priestley as burning glasses. Parker and Son continued to supply apparatus even after Priestley had settled in Pennsylvania. (I am grateful to Mr. G. H. Adams, Research Assistant at the Science Museum, South Kensington, for this information.)

Barrow, in his *Travels in China*, recorded that 'the great burning lens made by Mr. Parker of Fleet-Street, and carried out among the presents for the Emperor, was an object that excited no admiration in the minds of the Chinese' (p. 342). In fact, as Macartney shows, it was carried out on the *Hindostan* by Captain Mackintosh as part of his private trade. However, the East India Company did purchase an official present from William Parker and Son. This is listed as 'Two 18-light lustres richley cut and ornamented, mounted in metal, chased in gilt with argand lamps and shades', and the price paid was £840. (MDWC, 225.)

Henry Browne was the senior member of the Secret and Superintending Committee at Canton. The telescope Macartney purchased from him had been made by Sir William Herschel (MDWC, 345).

4. The Governor-General of Chihli at this time was Liang K'en-t'ang. He was born in the province of Chekiang, and became a *chü-jen* (i.e. obtained his first important degree under the examination system) in Ch'ien-lung's twenty-first year (1756–7). He received regular promotion in the bureaucracy, serving as a district magistrate, a Prefect, as Provincial Judicial Commissioner (*An-ch'a-shih*) of Shantung, and later as acting Governor of Honan. In the fifty-fifth year of Ch'ien-lung's reign (1790–1) he was appointed Governor-General of Chihli, and awarded the peacock feather and yellow jacket. In the first year of Chia-ch'ing's reign (1796–7), he took part in the banquet given to the one thousand grand old men. By now he was over eighty and he was presented with a tablet bearing four characters in the Imperial handwriting, the meaning of which was 'grand old man still serving diligently'. In the third year of Chia-ch'ing an edict stated that he was too old for active administration. However, he was made Governor-General of the Grand Canal, and warden of the Yü Mausoleum, with the title of Minister. He retired to his native district in Chia-ch'ing's sixth year (1801–2) and died in the same year, by which time he was more than eighty-five years old.

In other words his career was a copy-book example of the successive stages of promotion in the life of a successful scholar-official of the Ch'ing dynasty. In addition to his official biography in the *Ch'ing-shih lieh-chuan*, chüan 27, 33b–35b, we have Macartney's pen portrait of him given here, and also Barrow's endorsement that his politeness and dignity 'could not be exceeded by the most practised courtier in modern Europe'.

5. Robert Hanna, an Irish Lazarist, who arrived at Macao in 1788, and Louis-François Lamiot (1767–1831), who came to Macao in 1791. They were both still at Macao, waiting to enter the Emperor's service as mathematicians and astronomers, when Sir George Staunton landed there on 22 June 1793. At the earnest request of the Macao missionaries Hanna and Lamiot were given a passage to Tientsin with the embassy. However, this was contrary to Imperial regulations and they had to return in the *Hindostan* to Chusan. While at Jehol Macartney had written to Ho-shen recommending that a missionary be sent to Chusan to escort them back to the capital (p. 141). The reply which Ho-shen gave amounted to a rebuke to Macartney, who recorded the gist of it in his Journal for 19 September: '... that the two European mathematicians should be allowed to come to Pekin, and enter into the Emperor's service, and that the Minister would give proper directions for the purpose without our interference.' They had to go to Canton and finally in 1794 were allowed to proceed to Peking by the normal overland route.

Father Nicholas Raux, writing to Macartney in October 1794, mentioned that Hanna had arrived at Peking and was taking astronomical observations which he would gladly send to the Royal Society in London if they would be of use. See E. H. Pritchard, 'Letters from Missionaries', op. cit., pp. 43–5.

Hanna wrote two letters to Sir George Staunton from Canton in March 1794 and Lamiot wrote to him from Peking in February 1803. These are reproduced in E. H. Pritchard, ibid., pp. 31–9, 45–55.

6. Jean Joseph de Grammont (1736–?1812) was a French Jesuit who entered the Emperor's service as a musician and mathematician, arriving in Peking about 1770. Here he studied the Manchu language and also taught Latin to selected young Chinese. He was a competent musician, his favourite instrument being the violin. In 1785 he was granted Imperial permission to go to Canton for health reasons. While there he played an active part as interpreter in the negotiations of 1787 between the French, represented by a naval officer, the Chevalier d'Entrecasteaux, and the Canton officials. Grammont wanted to return to Europe, but in 1790 he was summoned by the Emperor to return to Peking. At the time of the Macartney embassy he appears to have held no official rank of any importance. Altogether at this time Grammont addressed four letters to Macartney which contain some useful information, as for instance when he observes 'Les affaires se traitent ici tout autrement qu'ailleurs, et ce qui seroit chez nous raison et justice, n'est souvent ici que deraison et mauvais humeur.' The full text of these letters is printed in Pritchard, 'Letters from Missionaries at Peking', op. cit., pp. 8–24. However, many of Grammont's other observations seem actuated more by malice than by sound judgment. Macartney summed up his character aptly in his Journal for 31 August: 'He is certainly a very clever fellow and seems to know this country well, but as he is said to be of a restless, intriguing turn it is necessary to be a good deal on one's guard with him.' See L. Pfister, op. cit., pp. 958–62.

7. Throughout the Journal Macartney wrote Fo-hi (and Fohi). The usual Chinese character for Buddha is *Fo*, though various appellations are also used, such as *Fo-yeh*, 'Lord Buddha', and *Fo-shih*, 'Buddha the teacher'. This character *shih* when pronounced by a Chinese from the south of China would sound more like '*shi*' or even '*hi*'. The term *Fo-shih* was frequently applied to Buddhist images in general. The main point is that Macartney is clearly referring to Buddha throughout. In his Observations, under the heading 'Religion', he states: 'The mass of the people in China are gross idolaters, and also worship a deity by the name of Fo or Fo-hi; but he is understood to be a different deity from Fo of the Court' (p. 233). Thus Macartney shows that he realized there was a difference between the Lama form of Buddhism which was brought into China by the Mongols of the Yuan dynasty, and the popular form of Chinese Buddhism which by this date had been thoroughly mixed with current superstitions.

Macartney makes further references to Fo-hi in his Journal for 17 September, and also in the Observations on p. 232. I have not taken up these references in separate notes since Macartney's information is somewhat vague and it would need more than a note to clarify these further references. It is worth remembering, however, that the serious study of Buddhism by western scholars did not take place until the early nineteenth century and of Chinese Buddhism even later, and thus at the time of Macartney's visit to China very little was known about this subject in the West. For further information the reader is referred to the following works: Albert Grünwedel, *Mythologie du Buddhisme au Tibet et en Mongolie* ... (Ernest Leroux, Paris, 1900). Alfred Foucher, *Etude sur l'Iconographie Bouddhique de l'Inde* (Ernest Leroux, Paris, 1900).

I wish to acknowledge the help I have received from Dr. G. E. Sargent in writing this note.

8. During the Ming dynasty the Grand Secretaries (*Ta Hsüeh Shih*) were

NOTES 9–10

familiarly called *Ko-lao*, 'Elders of the Grand Secretariat' (*Nei-Ko*). The Grand Secretariat acted as a kind of Imperial Chancery. This familiar title 'Ko-lao' was written by the Jesuit missionaries as Colao. However, during the Ch'ing dynasty the colloquial designation for Grand Secretary was *Chung-t'ang*, which is the term Macartney used, though he wrote it 'Chang-tong' or variants of this spelling. The missionaries seem to have continued to use the word Colao. The titles Colao and 'Chang-tong', however, should not be used together as Macartney and other members of his embassy sometimes did, since they both signify Grand Secretary. Since the term *Ko-lao* was obsolete by this time I have substituted 'Grand Secretary' throughout where Macartney writes Colao. It is important to remember, however, that Macartney uses the term Colao loosely, and it does not mean that every official whom he calls a Colao was, in fact, a Grand Secretary. At this period there were normally six Grand Secretaries. Their names in the year 1793 are given in note 20.

9. Joseph-Bernard d'Almeida (1728–1805). Called by Macartney Bernardo Almeyda or sometimes simply Bernardo. He was a Portuguese Jesuit who had been trained in astronomy. He entered the Emperor's service at Peking in 1759, and at the time of the embassy was a Vice-President of the Board of Mathematics, in which capacity he was ordered to Jehol to interpret and usher. See J. L. Cranmer-Byng, op. cit., pp. 150–1.

Helen Robbins, in the truncated version of Macartney's Journal which she published in *Our First Ambassador to China*, missed a comma which exists in the text and thus ran two names together, printing Bernando Almeyda Rodriguez, which is nonsense (p. 275). He died in Peking in 1805. See L. Pfister, op. cit., pp. 886–7.

André Rodrigues (1729–96). He arrived in Peking together with d'Almeida in 1759, and like him was a member of the Board of Mathematics, being its president at the time of the Macartney embassy (according to the *Chang-ku ts'ung-pien*, VII, 42a.) See L. Pfister, op. cit., pp. 888–9.

Louis de Poirot (1735–1814). A French Jesuit who entered the Emperor's service in 1771 as a painter. He became a good linguist and was called on to interpret both from Chinese and Manchu. In 1793 he was summoned to Jehol along with Joseph Panzi as a portrait painter. (The letter from the Grand Council containing these instructions is translated in part in my article on pp. 150–1.) For his biography see L. Pfister, op. cit., pp. 965–70.

Joseph Panzi (1733–1812). An Italian Jesuit who reached Peking in 1773 and entered the Emperor's service as a painter. He was often summoned to the palace to paint before the Emperor, and such episodes were described by Fr. Benoist in *Lettres édifiantes*. In 1789 he painted a Korean noble who had come to Peking as a tribute envoy, and while there had been converted and baptized by the missionaries. He was summoned to Jehol during the stay of the Macartney embassy in his capacity as a portrait painter. See L. Pfister, op. cit., pp. 971–4, and A. Hummel, *Eminent Chinese of the Ch'ing Period*, p. 372.

Joseph Paris (1738–1804). A French Lazarist who entered the Emperor's service in 1785 as a watchmaker and mechanist.

Peter Adeodato (d. ? 1822). An Italian Augustine who entered the Emperor's service in 1784 as a watchmaker and mechanist. Macartney and Staunton called him Deodati. He was sent to the Yuan-ming Yuan to act as interpreter to Barrow and Dinwiddie while they supervised the setting up of the presents. Towards the end of 1811 he was dismissed from the Emperor's service during one of the persecutions of Christians. When he arrived at Canton he was hospitably entertained at the East India Company's factory until he was able to get a passage to Manila.

10. I have been unable to identify this official positively, but I think Macartney was referring to Chin Chien, the President of the Board of Works at the time of the embassy. Whoever 'Chun' was he was certainly not a Grand Secretary, since the

names of the six Grand Secretaries in 1793 do not correspond in any way to 'Chun'. (For their names see note 20.) Towards the end of his entry for 23 August (p. 96) Macartney has a reference to an official whose name he spells Kun-san, and there is a further reference to him on 1 September (p. 105). I consider Chun and Kun to refer to the same person. Macartney implies that he was appointed to manage the affairs of the embassy together with Wang and Chou. From the Chinese documents concerning the embassy we know that two officials, Chin Chien, President of the Board of Works, and I-ling-a, a Junior Vice-President of the Board of Works, had been appointed to act conjointly with Cheng-jui in taking charge of Macartney once he arrived at Peking, and to arrange for him to go sight-seeing there. See J. L. Cranmer-Byng, op. cit., pp. 146–8.

Macartney also stated that 'Chun' was 'a cousin of the Emperor'. Allowing for a loose interpretation of the term, this would be possible, because Chin Chien's younger sister was a concubine of the Emperor Ch'ien-lung and between 1739 and 1752 gave birth to four of the Emperor's sons. Thus Macartney might have called him a 'cousin' of the Emperor. Chin Chien came of a Korean family which had originally lived near the Yalu river. He was Vice-President of the Board of Revenue from 1774–83, President of the Board of Works from 1783, and President of the Board of Civil Appointments from 1792 until his death in 1795. He was an efficient administrator with considerable experience in building enterprises. For his biography see A. Hummel, op. cit., pp. 159–60.

11. The name literally means 'round bright garden', and has the connotation 'garden of perfect brightness', or 'the garden *par excellence*'. This is the old Summer Palace which stood a few miles to the north-west of Peking. Originally it was a country villa which K'ang-hsi gave to his son, who ruled as the Emperor Yung-cheng from 1723 until 1736. However, it was not until Ch'ien-lung inherited it that the Yuan-ming Yuan became a fine series of palaces set in beautiful gardens. Early in his reign Ch'ien-lung started to enlarge the gardens and to build pavilions, until these assumed the proportions of a palace. To design some of these buildings and to lay out some of the gardens and to construct a fountain Ch'ien-lung employed several Jesuit missionaries. These worthy Fathers, without formal training as architects or engineers, succeeded in building attractive houses and gardens in the Italian style. Ch'ien-lung now made it one of his three main residences along with the Imperial Palace in Peking and the hunting lodge and park at Jehol. Luckily there is a contemporary description of the Yuan-ming Yuan by Father Attiret (d. 1768), who served the Emperor as artist. This was contained in a long letter from Peking sent in 1743, which was published in *Lettres édifiantes*, and was soon being read in Europe where it created a great interest in China and Chinese gardens. Yet even Attiret, who described the Yuan-ming Yuan so eloquently, despaired of doing it justice. 'Only the eye can grasp its true content', he wrote. Macartney was not alone in feeling unable to describe it.

It is one of the ironies of history that these lovely pavilions and gardens, some of them in an eighteenth-century European style, were partially destroyed by British troops acting on the orders of Lord Elgin in October 1860. Unfortunately this aberration of judgment in the career of an otherwise level-headed statesman has denied successive generations of Chinese and foreigners the opportunity to marvel at the splendours of the 'Gardens of perfect brightness'. Instead they have had to be content with the I Ho Yuan (also known as the Wan Shou Shan) which the Empress T'zu-hsi developed from an old imperial garden in the years 1886–91. But this 'New Summer Palace' fails to compensate the visitor for the disappearance of the Yuan-ming Yuan. Luckily a number of prints made by the Jesuits and a series of forty pictures painted by two Chinese artists have survived which show something of its past magnificence.

There is an English translation of Attiret's letter in Osvald Sirén, *Gardens of China*

NOTE 12

(Ronald Press, New York, 1949), pp. 117–30. Chapter 9 of this book describes both the old and the new summer palaces. See also Hope Danby, *The Garden of Perfect Brightness* (Williams and Norgate, London, 1950).

12. The Vulliamys were a distinguished family of clockmakers of Swiss origin, their founder François-Justin, settling in England about 1730. He went into partnership with Benjamin Grey and married his daughter. Their son, Benjamin, carried on the family business, though his interests were those of an English gentleman, and he was much engrossed in improving his house at Notting Hill Gate. He is chiefly known for excellent regulators and ornate clock cases. There is a description of one of the Vulliamy clocks taken as a present to the Emperor which shows that by 1792 the Vulliamys were clearly being influenced by Sheraton and Chippendale in making ornate cases, and in using the plaques and medallions made by Josiah Wedgwood. This description reads in part: 'From Vulliamy and Son. Delivered a pair of very fine inlaid satin-wood tables with three white statuary marble slabs with gilt mouldings round them . . . Upon the top slab of one is fixed a very good eight-day spring clock, name, Vulliamy, London (No. 253) which strikes the hours and quarters as it goes. . .' (MDWC, 225). In his Observations on the Arts and Sciences Macartney stated that most of the great officials who came to see the presents at the Yuan-ming Yuan 'affected to view them with careless indifference', but he added: 'They could not however conceal their sense of the beauty and elegance of our Derby porcelain, when they saw the ornamental vases belonging to Vulliamy's clocks' (p. 310).

François-Justin died in 1797 at an advanced age. His son Benjamin died in 1811, and the business was then conducted by the best known member of the family, Benjamin Lewis (1780–1854), who carried on the tradition of ornate cases in which his knowledge of the classics and of the fine arts was given wide scope. At his death the family had enjoyed royal patronage for 112 years continuously Their business was situated in old Pall Mall. The information in this note is based on three biographical articles by S. Benson-Beevers in *Antiquarian Horology*, viz.: Justin Vulliamy, Vol. I, 10 (March 1956); Benjamin, Vol. II, 2 (March 1957); Benjamin Lewis, Vol. I, 2 (March, 1954).

Derby porcelain. In the Macartney documents preserved at Cornell University a number of Wedgwood articles are listed. Among the items noted are 'a pair of ornamental vases in blue jasper with white foliage, a pair of tripod candelabra, a dejeune for two persons, a pair of ornamental vases in blue jasper with white figures and placed on pedestals, a copy of the Barberine, now Portland vase executed in the highest style, a pair of toothpick cases in ivory and gold beads with a medallion'. Together with these various articles went 'A catalogue of the manufactory of Josiah Wedgwood suitably bound' and also 'A description of the Barberine or Portland Vase, also suitably bound.' The total cost of all the Wedgwood articles together with their boxes was set down as £169 17s. (MDWC, 225).

Sir George Staunton in his *Authentic Account of an Embassy from the King of Great Britain to the Emperor of China*, when describing the presents displayed at the Yuanming Yuan, wrote: 'All eyes were, however, fixed on the vases, which were among the finest productions of the late Mr. Wedgwood's art. Of porcelain every Chinese is a judge. These specimens of the beauty of European manufacture were universally acknowledged and extolled' (Vol. II, p. 163). It seems likely that Macartney used the term Derby porcelain in a loose sense when it would have been more accurate to say Staffordshire pottery.

Wedgwood's use of ambassadors to introduce his wares to foreign courts and so obtain foreign trade was a new technique in the sale of English pottery. 'When the Portland vase was first successfully copied it was introduced to the courts of Europe in the finest possible style through Wedgwood's ambassadorial connections.' See N. McKendrick, 'Josiah Wedgwood: An Eighteenth-century Entrepreneur in

Salesmanship and Marketing Techniques', *Economic History Review*, Second Series, Vol. XII, No. 3 (1960), pp. 426–8.

The Planetarium formed the principal item among the presents from the King to the Emperor. It had been purchased by the Chairman and Deputy Chairman of the East India Company from Baron de Meylius for £600. It was sent to Vulliamy and Son for repairs, alterations and embellishments which had cost £656 13s. (MDWC, 225). According to Dinwiddie it had been invented and made under the direction of 'the late P. M. Hahn', and had taken thirty years to complete. See W. J. Proudfoot, op. cit., p. 26. Barrow in his Life of Lord Macartney states that it was made by 'a poor German mechanic'. As soon as Wang and Chou met Macartney they asked for a list of presents, and in order to explain these various scientific inventions it was thought necessary to give a general description of them 'somewhat in the oriental style'. See Sir G. L. Staunton, op. cit., 490–8. These descriptions make comic reading in English, but when translated in Chinese were almost incomprehensible. The Chinese version is printed in the *Chang-ku ts'ung-pien*, III, 22a–22b.

Fraser's Orrery. William Fraser of 3 New Bond Street was a mathematical instrument maker to King George III. His business was established by 1777 and continued until 1812. Fraser supplied 'a large Orrery' for the sum of £52 10s., together with a selection of mathematical instruments (MDWC, 225).

13. Victor Thibault or Thiébaud, was described as 'a mathematical instrument maker'. He was a mechanic employed to take care of the clocks and various instruments taken as presents for the Emperor.

Charles-Henri Petitpierre (b. 1769). A Swiss watchmaker who came to London and was known to Macartney through his mechanical skill. When the embassy returned to Macao he remained behind and was later employed by the Dutch embassy which went to Peking under Titsingh and van Braam in 1794–5. On the completion of this mission he worked for a short while as watchmaker to the firm of Beale and Co. in Canton before settling in Manila, and later in Batavia, where he married a Javanese wife. Some time later while on a voyage in the East Indies his ship was seized by Malay pirates and he was murdered. See A. Chapuis, *La Montre Chinoise* (Neuchâtel, 1919), p. 46.

14. Nicholas-Joseph Raux (1754–1801). A French Lazarist who entered the Emperor's service as a mathematician in 1785. Isaac Titsingh met him during the stay of the Dutch embassy in Peking early in 1795 and wrote this pleasant description of him:

> Rarely have I seen a man of better appearance, he was a picture of health, and the Chinese clothes suited him admirably. He spoke Chinese with a melodious fluency which made it sound pleasant, though in the mouths of the natives it sounds harsh and sharp. He seemed a past master in all the small compliments that in their intercourse with superiors they have to observe *ad nauseam*; when a servant of the mandarins entered he rose and bowed.' (Translated in J. J. L. Duyvendak, 'The Last Dutch Embassy to the Chinese Court', *T'oung Pao*, XXXIV, p. 84).

His biography is in J. van der Brandt, *Les Lazaristes en Chine, 1697–1935*. (Peiping, Imprimerie des Lazaristes, 1936), no. 13.

15. Jean-Joseph-Marie Amiot (1718–93). A French Jesuit who arrived at Peking in 1751. Perhaps the most learned of the missionaries at the Court of Ch'ien-lung, he studied widely with the help of a Chinese scholar and during his long residence at Peking wrote extensively about China. Among his works were: A Grammar of the Manchu Language, a Manchu-French dictionary, a translation of a poem by Ch'ien-lung in praise of Mukden, and a monograph on Chinese music. Many of his writings were printed in the *Mémoires concernant l'histoire* . . . and in *Lettres édifiantes* . . . His life of Confucius forms the twelfth volume of that collection. In addition to

his scholarly work he sometimes played the flute and the harpsichord at Court. He died in Peking on 8 October 1793, just after Macartney and his suite had left the capital. Amiot, perhaps more than any of the other missionaries at that time, helped to make China known to the West by his writings. See Pfister, op. cit., pp. 837–60.

16. Macartney obtained this information in a latter from Grammont dated 30 August 1793. These were not personal names but simply referred to Ch'ien-lung's surviving sons in the order in which they were born. Thus *pa* means eight and *yeh* means master. The list can be best understood if written as follows:

Pa-ye = Pa-yeh = 8th son = Yung-hsüan (1746–1832).
Che-y-ye = Shih-i-yeh = 11th son = Yung-hsing (1752–1823).
Che-ou-ye = Shih-wu-yeh = 15th son = Yung-yen (1760–1820).
Chet-si = Shih-ch'i-yeh = 17th son = Yung-lin (1766–1820).

Macartney's footnote on p. 101 is therefore wrong. Although Ch'ien-lung had seventeen sons, ten of whom reached maturity, only these four survived him. He was succeeded by his fifteenth son, Yung-yen, whose reign title was Chia-ch'ing.

Naturally Ch'ien-lung had numerous grandsons. They were named in series; thus sixteen having the character *mien* as part of their names survived him. Macartney writing about the Emperor's sons on 16 December (p. 201) stated that 'Mien-cul-ye, his eldest grandson, is a man of capacity, has been employed in affairs, and is supposed to be much in his favour.' Grammont wrote the name 'Mien-eul-ye', and I think that by this he means *erh*, i.e. second. Thus he was 'Second-master-*mien*'. Now the second in the '*mien*' series was Mien-en, who was also the eldest surviving grandson at that time. He died in the second year of the Emperor Tao-kuang (1822–3). But this identification is not really proved.

For the various great officials mentioned here see subsequent notes.

17. Macartney gave his name as Fou-liou. This version he got from Grammont's letter of 28 August 1793 where he wrote 'le *Fou liou* autre ministre favori'. Van Braam, who met him in 1795 wrote 'le Fok-lio-tayen' in his Journal, while de Guignes wrote Fo-lieou. All these men are referring to Fu-ch'ang-an, younger brother of the famous official and general Fu-k'ang-an (for whom see note 18). Although comparatively young he was made a member of the Grand Council, though he appears to have been a mere favourite rather than a man of ability. He owed his position to his elder brother's successful career, and to his own friendship with Ho-shen. The Emperor Chia-ch'ing regarded him as Ho-shen's closest accomplice, and as a result he was arrested. In fact one of the charges against both Ho-shen and Fu-ch'ang-an was that their offices, which were usually together, were located improperly close to Imperial residences. (See D. S. Nivison, 'Ho-shen and his Accusers' in *Confucianism in Action*, ed. D. S. Nivison and A. F. Wright (Stanford University Press, California, 1959), pp. 214, 239, 241.) Eventually his death sentence was commuted but only after a decree had been issued ordering him to be taken to Ho-shen's room and there witness the enforced suicide of his former colleague. The edict is translated in G. T. Staunton, *Ta Tsing Leu Lee* ... (T. Cadell, London, 1810), pp. 498–502. See Hummel, op. cit., I, 249.

18. This was the famous general Fu-k'ang-an, a Manchu of the Bordered Yellow Banner. He began his military career under A-kuei (see note 19) in 1773. He was sent with A-kuei in 1784 to quell a Muslim rebellion in Kansu and in 1787 to Formosa to put down a rebellion there. As a reward for his success in this campaign he was raised to the rank of *kung* (Duke). Shortly afterwards he was appointed Governor-General of Kwangtung and Kwangsi, but in 1791 was sent in command of a Chinese force to Tibet to drive out the Gurkhas of Nepal who had invaded that country. The campaign was well planned under the direction of A-kuei in Peking, and the army was well supplied from its base in Szechwan. The Chinese army was even

equipped with leather cannon which could be transported over mountains. Fu-k'ang-an and his forces reached Tibet early in 1792, yet in spite of snow and the mountainous countryside, by the autumn of that year the Gurkhas had been driven out of Tibet and suffered a final defeat inside Nepal, close to their capital Kathmandu. It was a remarkable campaign, well planned and executed, which brought a Chinese army to the borders of northern India. Among the terms of the treaty arranged by Fu-k'ang-an it was agreed that the Gurkhas should send tribute to Peking every five years, and this continued until 1908. Fu-k'ang-an remained in Tibet for several months strengthening the Chinese position there, but by the end of the summer of 1793 he was back at the capital. The Emperor thereupon made him a Grand Secretary. He was present at Jehol during Macartney's audience and showed a strong dislike of the English. Reading between the lines in Macartney's Journal it seems that he was thoroughly suspicious of British motives in showing interest in Tibet and sending emissaries to Lhasa from Bengal. In 1795 Fu-k'ang-an was sent against the Miao tribes which had rebelled in the Szechwan region but died in camp the following year. Although he was a very successful general he appears to have used his various terms as a provincial official to feather his own nest most efficiently, and posthumously he was accused by the Emperor Chia-ch'ing of extravagance in military matters. The cost of the campaign against the Gurkhas was very great and it seems that no complete statement of the expense was ever made known.

For his biography by Knight Biggerstaff see Hummel, op. cit., I, 253–5. For the campaign in Tibet see Alistair Lamb, 'Tibet in Anglo-Chinese Relations, 1767–1842', *Journal of the Royal Asiatic Society*, 1957, Parts III and IV; 1958, Parts I and II. The Gurkha side of the campaign is given in Mayura Jang Kunwar, 'China and War in the Himalayas, 1792–3', *English Historical Review*, vol. lxxvii (April 1962) pp. 283–297.

19. A-kuei (1717–1797), a Manchu of the Plain Blue Banner, was at this time an elder stateman, who had won a distinguished reputation as an official and as a commander of troops. Macartney's reference to 'Mémoires sur la Chine' is presumably to *Mémoires concernant l'histoire . . . des chinois par les Missionaires de Pekin*. During the period from 1789 until his retirement from office in 1796 he was usually entrusted with the direction of affairs at Peking while the Emperor was at Jehol. Although Ho-shen was the Emperor's favourite minister, and took the leading part in dealing with the Macartney embassy, yet in some important matters he was not averse from seeking A-kuei's advice formally, perhaps in order to share responsibility. For instance, in a Court Dispatch to 'the Princes and Ministers remaining at the Capital', Ho-shen set down the instructions he had received from the Emperor concerning Macartney's refusal to practice the kotow. The letter ends:

'If, when the barbarians come for an audience with the Emperor, they are sincere and reverential, we grant them our favour, so as to display our "cherishing by kindness". If they tend to be in the least haughty then they are not destined to receive our favour. Also we should immediately cut down the ceremony of their reception in order to demonstrate our system. This is the way to restrain foreign dependencies. A-kuei usually is far-sighted, what does he think about it?'
(See Cranmer-Byng, op. cit., p. 159.)

A-kuei died, full of honours, in 1796. His biography can be found in Hummel, op. cit., I, 6–8.

20. By the term 'first tribunal of state' I am not certain whether Macartney is referring to the Grand Secretariat or to the Grand Council. To some extent the same officials served on both bodies. Thus, according to the 'lists of great Officials of Departments' given in the *Ch'ing-shih kao* ('Draft history of the Ch'ing dynasty'), the Grand Secretariat had six members in the fifty-eighth year of Ch'ien-lung's reign (1793–4), viz.: A-kuei, Chi Huang, Ho-shen, Wang Chieh, Fu-k'ang-an and

Sun Shih-i. The three Manchu members I have already written about, but the three Chinese members are less well known.

Chi Huang (1711–94) achieved distinction as an administrator in river conservancy. He was also a famous calligrapher of that period, of whom it was said that he could write with a brush on a sesame seed. Since Ch'ien-lung's own artistic abilities were best displayed in his calligraphy it would be interesting to know whether Chi Huang's prominence as a calligrapher had anything to do with his promotion to Grand Secretary.

Wang Chieh (1725–1805). He was a Grand Secretary from 1787 until 1802.

Sun Shih-i (1720–96). One of the compilers of the great *Ssu-k'u ch'üan-shu*, a vast Imperial manuscript collection, which represents an attempt to bring together all works known at that time which the compilers (working under the scrutiny of the Emperor) considered worthy of preservation. It was completed in 1782. In 1788 Sun was sent in command of a Chinese army to intervene in a civil war in Annam but was repulsed. As the official in charge of the supplies for Fu-k'ang-an's army in the campaign against the Gurkhas he was in Lhasa in 1792, and later wrote an account of this campaign. See Hummel, op. cit., II, 680–2.

However, it is possible that Macartney was referring not to the Grand Secretariat but to the Grand Council. In the year 1793–4 the Grand Council consisted of seven members, viz.: A-kuei, Ho-shen, Wang Chieh, Fu-ch'ang-an, Ch'ing-kuei, Tung Kao and Sung-yun. The first three were concurrently members of the Grand Secretariat. Five out of the seven were Manchus.

Ch'ing-kuei (1735–1816) was a Manchu who held the post of Grand Councillor, 1771–3, 1784–93, 1799–1812. He was also a Grand Secretary, 1799–1813. See Hummel, op. cit., p. 921.

Tung Kao (1740–1818) was a Chinese scholar who was well known as a painter and calligrapher. He was appointed to the Grand Council in 1778. There is some evidence to show that when Ch'ien-lung became too old to write easily some of the calligraphy attributed to him was actually the work of Tung Kao. See Hummel, op. cit., 791–2.

Sung-yun (1752–1835). A Mongol who was appointed Grand Councillor in 1793. See note 38.

21. Alexandro Gouvea or Govea (1751–1808). A Portuguese who had been consecrated Bishop of Peking by the Pope before he set out for China. He arrived in Peking in 1784 and entered the Emperor's service as an astronomer. He was made a member of the Board of Mathematics and created a Mandarin of the sixth order. In scholarship and knowledge of China he was eclipsed by several other missionaries in Peking at this time. Macartney's remarks on his knowledge of algebra are not very laudatory. (See Observations, p. 266.) Barrow, *Travels in China*, p. 111, spoke favourably of his character: 'The prelate, however, appeared to be a man of mild and placid temper, pleasing manners and of a modest and unassuming deportment.' See Pfister, op. cit., 942.

22. Macartney took with him to China a band consisting of five German musicians. (There should have been six, but one deserted at Portsmouth.) They were paid £60 a year each, but their leader, John Zapfal, got £70. Here follows a list of the instruments they took with them: 2 violins, 1 tenor (a viola), 1 violoncello, 1 hautbois, 1 bassoon, 2 basset horns (a clarinet in F), 1 clarinet, 1 German flute (a transverse flute with one key), 1 fife (a transverse keyless flute) (See MDWC, 442).

In an account book which Macartney kept during the preparations for the embassy there is an entry for 22 August 1792 which reads 'To Dr. Burney, balance for musical instruments—£76–1–4' (MDWC, 344). This is interesting in view of the statement in Burney's Will that he had refused all pecuniary reward for supplying Macartney with instruments. Dr. Burney and Lord Macartney were both members of The Club. On his return from China Macartney presented him with two Chinese instruments. See Percy A. Scholes, *The Great Doctor Burney* . . . 2 vols. (Oxford University Press, 1948), Vol. 2, pp. 115–16.

23. At this point in his Journal Macartney makes three rather misleading statements which need clarification.

(1). As a result of the musical activities of the Jesuits at the Chinese Court during the seventeenth and eighteenth centuries Western music was known to Ch'ien-lung and his courtiers. During K'ang-hsi's reign Thomas Pereira and Théodoric Pedrini published a treatise in Chinese on European music which contained specimens of Western musical notation (see the *Lü-lü cheng i*, block printed in 1713). During the early years of his reign Ch'ien-lung showed considerable interest in Western music, and two Jesuits, Jean Walter and Florian Bahr, were employed as musical instructors at Court. They trained Chinese pupils to put on a comic opera, *Cecchina*, then fashionable in Rome, which Ch'ien-lung enjoyed. As a result he ordered that a Western-style orchestra should be formed, and eighteen young Chinese pages were trained as musicians. Bahr, and later Grammont, were both competent violinists and so it is possible that a Chinese at Court might have been able to play a European-style violin. However, the Chinese had possessed their own version of the fiddle centuries before Macartney's visit to Peking. This was the *hu-chin*, a small fiddle with two strings, between which the bow passes. Grammont was also reputed to be a capable performer on another kind of Chinese fiddle, the *t'i-chin*.

(2). It is possible, in view of what has just been said, that some Chinese musicians at this date could transcribe a tune in staff notation. But it should be remembered that before the arrival of the Jesuits the Chinese had various methods of setting down music by the use of characters. (For details of these methods see L. Picken, 'The Music of Far Eastern Asia' in *Ancient and Oriental Music*, ed. Egon Wellesz, Oxford University Press, 1957, p. 100.) Western five-line notation is specially convenient for writing music in parts, but for writing a melody the Chinese method is typographically simpler and therefore less expensive to print.

(3). The subject of early Chinese punctuation is somewhat obscure, but it is not true to imply that the Chinese had never used any form of punctuation until they learnt it from the Jesuits. A rudimentary method of punctuation was sometimes used in texts intended for semi-popular use centuries before the arrival of the Jesuits in China. Thus among the manuscripts recovered from the Tunhuang caves, which date from early times, are a few showing brush marks which approximate in use to the Western comma and full stop. It might be truer to say that the Jesuits helped to make the use of punctuation more widespread but the subject is debatable.

24. In the margin of the Tokyo manuscript of the Journal, opposite the words 'Sir Joshua Reynolds' is written 'Query by Romney'. This is not a sensible correcrection since there is no evidence that Romney ever painted King George III and Queen Charlotte. However, if the query had read 'Ramsay' this would have been a possible correction, because the first and most successful portraits of the King and Queen were painted by Allan Ramsay sometime in 1760 or 1761. The King was pleased with the result, and subsequently a number of copies were made from the original. Sir Joshua Reynolds painted the royal pair in 1779 and the result was exhibited at the Academy (then housed in Somerset House) in 1780. Ramsay died in 1784 and Reynolds was appointed Principal Portrait Painter to the King in his place. The artist who held this appointment had the right to manufacture all the royal portraits required for British embassies and consulates abroad and for presents to foreign rulers. Thus, in 1789 Reynolds is known to have had completed, seven portraits of the King and five of the Queen. (See Derek Hudson, *Sir Joshua Reynolds*, Geoffrey Bles, London, 1958, p. 179.) Unfortunately, while examining the documents dealing with the preparations for the embassy preserved at Cornell, I have found no references to the royal portraits which Macartney took to Peking.

25. Thomas Gill (fl. 1770–1800). A Birmingham cutler. He started his career as a

NOTES 26–27

file cutter, progressed to become a sawmaker and by 1785 called himself, in a Birmingham directory of that date, 'sword cutler to Government, the Army, the Navy, etc.' His address was Jennens Row. In 1800 he took out a patent for rifling the bores of cannon, and also for rifling the barrels of muskets, carbines, guns and pistols. He died in 1801.

In a list of articles bought by the East India Company to send to China for distribution to the great officials whom Macartney would meet, the following items are recorded as being supplied by Thomas Gill: 'four state sword blades, twelve plain horsemen's blades, one Chinese, one Persian, one Roman, and one Turkish pattern scimitar, one Chinese two ways crooked and various other swords.' (MDWC, 225.) In another document at Cornell University there is a note of the presents delivered to various Chinese officials, and this shows that Wang received three sword blades and Chou two, which were for their sons as well as for themselves (MDWC, 354). Macartney records the delight of the soldier Wang in possessing these swords. However, in 1795, when the East India Company, in following up a suggestion by Macartney, sent out various goods as an experiment, including a case of sword blades, permission was refused for the swords to be landed at Canton.

I am grateful to the City Librarian of the Birmingham Public Libraries for kindly supplying information about Thomas Gill.

26. Kerseymeres and vigonias. It would be tempting to quote the definition given by the O.E.D. and leave it at that. Unfortunately definitions of cloth trade terms are not necessarily accurate for every period in the long history of the English woollen cloth trade, which was flourishing in the sixteenth century and only surpassed by the manufacture of cotton cloth early in the nineteenth century. For instance, elsewhere in the Journal and in the Observations Macartney uses the term broadcloth. Originally this was a 'fine plain wove, dressed and double width cloth', but later the term came to imply quality rather than width. Another term used by Macartney which defies accurate definition in relation to the late eighteenth century is long ells. Yet another term is camlet, a name originally applied to a costly eastern fabric and then later to substitutes for it made of various combinations of wool and silk. Thus the precise meanings of these terms changed from period to period. However, the use of these various cloth trade terms by Macartney helps to remind the reader of the importance of English woollen manufactures even as late as the end of the eighteenth century.

27. Long Acre in London, between Charing Cross Road and Drury Lane, near Covent Garden. It appears that three carriages were taken by Lord Macartney to China, and they are described in some detail as among the presents bought by the East India Company for the Emperor. They were made by John Hatchett of Long Acre. The first was listed as a Summer Chariot and described as follows: 'To a new elegant Town Chariot on Crane Necks made of the best materials seasoned timber and workmanship the body framed and grooved to receive sliding glasses and blinds', etc., etc. The second was listed as a Winter Chariot and described in detail: 'To an elegant Town Chariot on handsome Crane Neck carriage, finished in every respect like the summer chariot except the lining which is velvet instead of water tabby and only four glasses and four Venetian blinds instead of eight glasses and eight blinds and a set of bars complete', etc., etc. The third was a variation of the first. Altogether they cost £1,842 (MDWC, 225).

John Hatchett flourished in the last part of the eighteenth century. 'The principal improvements in carriages in London from 1770 to 1790 were the invention of Mr. John Hatchett, of Long-acre whose taste in building appears to have been prominent and other coachbuilders generally copied him' (G. A. Thrupp, *The History of Coaches*, London, 1877, p. 67). In 1815 the firm of Hatchett was still mentioned as leading coachbuilders. Washington Irving in a review of a travel book about Spain, which was published in *The Quarterly Review* of February 1831, after mentioning the dangers of travelling in Spain, added: 'Hence it is rare indeed, that the well hung, well peopled and well victualled production of Long-acre is seen rolling down the southern declivities of the Pyrenees.'

Macartney fully expected that the Emperor would be pleased to use the carriages (p. 145). Yet in spite of their elegance they were never used but were kept in one of the buildings of the Summer Palace near the K'un Ming Lake as though they were tribute trophies. When the Dutch embassy visited the Summer Palace at the beginning of 1795 van Braam noted in his Journal that in one of the Imperial audience halls 'our conductor pointed out to us the coach of which Lord Macartney made a present to the Emperor last year, standing against the wall on the left side of the throne. It is exquisitely painted, perfectly well varnished, and the whole of the carriage covered with gilding.' Quoted in Hope Danby, *The Garden of Perfect Brightness* (Williams and Norgate, Ltd., 1950), pp. 155–6. See also Barrow, *Travels in China*, p. 215.

But this was not the last of the carriages. In September 1860 British and French forces entered Peking after a short campaign. As a result of harsh treatment by the Chinese a few prisoners-of-war died. When Lord Elgin, the British Envoy, learned of this he gave orders that the Summer Palace should be burned. Robert Swinhoe, the British Consul at Amoy, happened to be attached to the Commander-in-Chief as interpreter, and while exploring the Summer Palace after it had been partially destroyed, made an interesting discovery.

> 'In an outhouse two carriages, presented by Lord Macartney to the Emperor Ch'ien-lung, were found intact and in good order. The Emperor appears never to have used them, preferring instead the springless native cart or the sedan. Two howitzer guns, with equipments complete, the gift also of Lord Macartney, were likewise found; and among astronomical and various other scientific instruments a double-barrelled English-made gun in case occurred. . . .' R. Swinhoe, *Narrative of the North China Campaign of 1860* . . . (London, 1861), p. 331.

I believe the two howitzers were sent to Woolwich.

28. Macartney gives a detailed itinerary of the route from Peking to Jehol, but from his spelling of names it is impossible to identify with certainty the places he mentions. I have thus been forced to retain his spelling but have suggested the most likely modern names. The only names which I have been able to identify positively are Ku-pei-k'ou and Miyun. For a more recent description of a journey from Peking to Jehol, by Ford car in the summer of 1930, see *Jehol, City of Emperors*, by the Swedish explorer Sven Hedin (Kegan Paul, London, 1932). It took Hedin two full days to cover the hundred odd miles, and he calls it the worst motor road in the world. It appears to have been in a better state in 1793. (See Journal, p. 117.)

The early Manchu Emperors used Jehol not only as a palace among the hills where they could avoid the summer heat of Peking, but also as a centre from which to go on hunting expeditions in order to keep up the warlike spirit of their Manchu subjects and to keep in touch with their homeland. It was also a convenient place to which the Mongol princes could come in order to pay their allegiance to the Emperor. For its religious importance see note 43.

29. Cheng-jui seems to have acted on his own initiative in this matter and in a high-handed way, for which he received an official rebuke. See Introduction, p. 29. Cheng-jui's idea of the importance of his commission seems to have gone to his head. As Ho-shen, in a letter of 31 August, was moved to remark: 'Since the tribute envoy set out on the overland route from Tientsin he has been in Cheng-jui's sole charge, and as a consequence Cheng-jui reckoned that there was no service more important. He actually thought that his merit was as great as Fu-k'ang-an's in suppressing the Gurkhas.' See J. L. Cranmer-Byng, op. cit., pp. 153–5. No wonder that Wang and Chou considered Cheng-jui as 'a sort of crazy and morose man' (Journal, p. 86).

NOTES 30–34

30. The Great Wall was started by the first Emperor of China, Ch'in Shih-huang (221–210 B.C.), but repaired and extended at various times, especially during the Ming dynasty. Starting from the sea at Shanhaikuan in the Gulf of Liaotung, near the frontier of China Proper with Manchuria, it runs westwards, passing quite close to the north of Peking. Then it goes south-west across Shansi to the Yellow River, and finally ends at Kiayukwan west of Suchow. This part lies near the Gobi desert and protects the main caravan route from Central Asia to China. A branch of the Wall then runs west and south to protect the Tibetan frontier. In some places there are inner and outer walls and various loops. Visitors to Peking today can see the Great Wall at the Pataling gate of the Nankow Pass where it is still in a fair state of repair. See William E. Geil, *The Great Wall of China* (John Murray, London, 1909). The text is puerile, but the book contains many excellent photographs which show how the wall looked at the beginning of this century. For a more recent account see Peter Lum, *The Purple Barrier: the Story of the Great Wall of China* (Robert Hale, 1960).

31. Tufa. A rock usually formed in terraces in rivers owing to deposits of calcium carbonate. It is true that the water from melted snow would lack iodine, which is useful in preventing goitres. But this is not a sufficient explanation alone. In fact goitres can be found anywhere in China, and most certainly in the south. They are apt to occur more frequently in mountainous country, simply because the people there cannot afford to buy salt owing to the high cost of transporting it. That tufa stone affects drinking water has not been proved, but locally lack of iodine and generally lack of salt can cause goitres. However, Gillan discounts the idea that snow water causes goitres. See Observations, pp. 286–7. On the subject of salt, see note 155.

32. During the Ch'ing dynasty there were Six Boards or Departments at the capital dealing with routine administration. These were, in order of importance: Civil Office, Revenue, Ceremonies (Rites), War, Punishments, and Works.

The Board of Rites (*Li Pu*) was responsible for supervising the whole code of rites and ceremonies binding on all people irrespective of their position in society. It also controlled the state sacrifices. A second very important function of the Board was the supervising of education in China and control of the all-powerful examination system. Thirdly, it was in charge of all dealings with the West, with the reception of tribute envoys, etc. Also under its control was a subsidiary Board dealing with ceremonial state music.

The Board of Revenue (*Hu Pu*) was a large and important Department which was responsible for the control of land, preserving records of boundaries, keeping a census of the population, collecting taxes and presenting accounts. Also it was responsible for currency and coinage, collection of customs, control of state granaries and treasuries, and keeping standard weights and measures.

Each Board had two Presidents and four Vice-Presidents, appointments being divided equally between Manchu and Chinese officials.

33. By this Macartney meant a *ju-i*, which was usually a piece of jade carved in the form of a sceptre. It was considered to be a symbol of good luck, the phrase *ju-i* meaning 'what you will'. As such it was often given by Chinese emperors to their great officials as a special mark of favour. The Dutch envoys were given the same present the following year and van Braam described it as 'a kind of Chinese sceptre, made out of a superb block of transparent green stone, like agate'. For an illustration of *jui-i* of the Ch'ien-lung period, see B. Laufer, *Jade* (South Pasadena, 1946), p. 335.

34. Macartney is presumably referring to an embassy sent by King Bodawpaya of Burma. The capital during his reign (1782–1819) was Amarapura and not Pegu, though Pegu had been the capital during the sixteenth century, and had become well known to European merchants. During Bodawpaya's reign Chinese missions

came to his capital on five occasions and he in turn sent four embassies to Peking. The one which Macartney met is recorded as having left Amarapura in October 1792, and consisted of five officials who brought valuable presents for the Emperor and also for the Governor-General of Yunnan and Kweichow. See G. E. Harvey, *History of Burma* (Longmans, Green and Co., 1925), pp. 278-9 and 362. For the Kalmucks see note 44.

35. Presumably Macartney is referring to Luton Hoo owned by his father-in-law, Lord Bute. Between 1764 and 1774 Lancelot Brown was employed to improve the landscape. Arthur Young, passing through Luton in 1770, has left a graphic description of the park while it was still being transformed. Macartney's description of the 'park of ten thousand trees' at Jehol makes it sound as if it, too, had been transformed by the genius of 'Capability' Brown.

36. Lancelot Brown (1716-83), nicknamed 'Capability' because of his ability quickly to size up the capabilities of an estate for improvement by landscape gardening. See Dorothy Stroud, *Capability Brown* (Country Life, 1950). This is an admirable book, beautifully illustrated, and also contains a thoughtful introduction by Christopher Hussey. Brown's niche in English history is well summarized by Miss Stroud: 'Brown was in fact a very remarkable man who deserves to be taken seriously for his achievement in transforming thousands of acres of English countryside from bog or heath or rough pasture into the magnificent parks which were one of the eighteenth century's most valuable contributions to our heritage' (p. 21). For Hamilton, see note 37.

37. Stowe, near Buckingham, the seat of Lord Cobham, one of the great English country houses of the eighteenth century. Brown was at work there between 1740 and 1750 softening and breaking up the lay-out of the grounds. See Dorothy Stroud, op. cit., pp. 28-32.

Woburn. Macartney uses the common eighteenth-century spelling 'Woodburn'. Woburn Abbey, near Dunstable in Bedfordshire, seat of the Duke of Bedford, lies in a fine park of undulating pastures and old trees.

Painshill in Surrey. The Hon. Charles Hamilton (1704-87), youngest son of the sixth Earl of Abercorn, began to lay out the landscape garden of Painshill in the 1740s and during the next twenty years he continued to improve the grounds until his private fortune was used up, and he was forced to sell it in 1775. During the eighteenth and nineteenth centuries it was widely known for its landscape garden, and during its heyday was praised by Horace Walpole and Uvedale Price among others. Hamilton was probably one of the first to introduce the use of rhododendrons and azaleas into England. See Gordon Nares, 'Painshill, Surrey', *Country Life*, 2nd and 9th January 1958.

38. Sung-yun (1752-1835) was a Mongol of the Plain Blue Banner. Having trained as an interpreter, he became a clerk in the Office of Colonial Affairs, and in 1776 was appointed a secretary to the Council of State. Owing to border troubles with Russia he was sent as Imperial agent on the frontier from 1786 to 1792. In that year he signed, together with the Russian representative, a new commercial treaty at Kiakhta, the previous treaty having been signed in 1727. On his return to Peking in 1793 Sung-yun was appointed a vice-president of several Boards as well as being made a Grand Councillor. He accompanied Lord Macartney as far as Hangchow during his journey from Peking to Canton. Since Macartney had spent three years in Russia as British ambassador and Sung-yun had recently negotiated with the Russians in Siberia, they had something in common and appear to have got on well together (see Journal, 9 November).

During his subsequent career he filled many posts, being Imperial resident in Tibet from 1794-9, and Governor-General in various provinces. He died in 1835, after a long career in which he was acknowledged as being incorruptible. See A. E. Hummel, op. cit., 961-2.

NOTES 39-43

39. It is as well that Macartney added his footnote of warning since his information is liable to be misleading. The Mongol term *Boydo ejen qan* means 'Holy lord emperor' and was used by the Mongols as a title for the Chinese emperor. The Kalmuks heard it from the Mongols and the Russians got it from the Kalmuks. As a result in the eighteenth century the Russians called the Manchus 'Bogdoi Tartars' and thus used the term to imply a race. See J. F. Baddeley, *Russia, Mongolia, China* . . ., 2 vols. (London, 1919). I have been unable to identify Macartney's informant Poo-ta-vang.

40. Macartney here states clearly that he and the members of his suite did not kotow. His page, young Staunton, also states quite definitely in his Journal that they did not do so. For a very detailed study of the whole kotow question, including its repercussions during the Amherst embassy in 1816, see E. H. Pritchard, 'The Kotow in the Macartney Embassy to China in 1793', *Far Eastern Quarterly*, II, no. 2 (1943). The evidence showing that Macartney did not kotow is overwhelming.

41. For Father Attiret's description of the Gardens of the Summer Palace a few miles outside Peking, see note 11.

Sir William Chambers (1726–96) was born at Gothenburg in Sweden where his father was a merchant. At the age of sixteen he entered the service of the Swedish East India Company, and made his first voyage to the East about 1740. A second voyage followed in 1743–5 and in 1748 he made a third voyage to India and China as a Supercargo. While at Canton he obtained some sketches of Chinese costume and architecture. In 1749 he left the service of the Swedish East India Company and went to Paris where he studied architecture. Later he continued his studies in Rome until 1755 when he went to England and started to practice as an architect. In 1757 he published *Designs of Chinese Buildings, Furniture, Dresses, Machines, and Utensils*. At this time he was employed by the Princess Dowager of Wales to lay out the grounds at Kew Palace, and here he designed the orangery, various temples, and the Chinese pagoda. In 1772 he published his *Dissertation on Oriental Gardening*, which was in substance an attack on Lancelot Brown and his style of natural gardening, though Chambers fathered this attack 'upon the Chinese who I thought lived far enough off to be out of reach of critical abuse'. In this essay of just over ninety pages Chambers made some shrewd comments on Chinese gardens but also gave some rather fanciful descriptions. His knowledge of the subject was slight, but his *Dissertation* did something to foster for a while in England an interest in what was imagined to be the Chinese style of gardening. For a study of this interesting subject see Osvald Sirén, *China and Gardens of Europe in the Eighteenth Century* (Ronald Press Company, New York, 1950). For Sir William Chambers, see H. M. Colvin, *A Biographical Dictionary of English Architects, 1660–1840* (John Murray, London, 1954), pp. 130–5.

42. Lowther Hall, near Penrith, the seat of the ambitious politician Sir James Lowther 1st Earl of Lonsdale (1736–1802). He was a great borough patron who by 1767 was said to control directly the votes of 800 freeholders; it seems that eventually he controlled nine seats in the House of Commons. Sir James was Macartney's brother-in-law, having married in 1761 Mary, daughter of the Earl of Bute, while Macartney married her sister Jane in 1768. In that year Macartney had been elected M.P. for Cockermouth, doubtless through the influence of Sir James, and he must have stayed at Lowther Hall at that time. Although Capability Brown went to Lowther in 1763 and later submitted a plan for alterations, nothing was done. Sir James Lowther died in 1802 and was succeeded by Sir William Lowther who erected a new building in 1809 and changed Lowther Hall into the fine seat which was henceforth styled Lowther Castle. Perhaps Macartney influenced Sir William in his decision to improve Lowther Hall.

43. The Temple itself is known as the Potala. It is an imposing Lama temple, built in the style of the Potala at Lhasa. It was completed in 1771, in time to

commemorate the eightieth birthday of Ch'ien-lung's mother, and his own sixtieth birthday. The Emperor himself wrote an explanation of why it was built, which is translated in part in Sven Hedin, *Jehol, City of Emperors* (Kegan Paul, 1932), pp. 17–18. He stated that it was as a sign of friendliness towards the loyal princes of Mongolia and Sinkiang and the chiefs of the Dzungar tribes, all of whom believed in the Lama form of Buddhism. Moreover, just at that time the Torguts had returned to the borders of the Chinese empire after living under Russian protection for some years (see note 44). Thus the Potala signified the religious and political solidarity of the Manchus and Mongolian tribes at that time. In the very centre of the temple was an inner square which contained the beautiful golden-roofed temple. A replica of this was erected in Chicago for the Exposition of 1933. There is a recent description of the palaces and temples at Jehol in *Wen-wu ts'an-k'ao tse-liao* ('Reference Materials for Antiquity'), Peking, 1956, no. 10, pp. 59–66; no. 11, pp. 29–35; no. 12, pp. 9–13.

44. The Torguts were a tribe of the Kalmuks or Western Mongols. At the beginning of the seventeenth century the Torguts had migrated to the Volga region, and had lived under Russian suzerainty. Eventually the Torguts came more and more under Russian control. This finally caused such unrest that they decided to make a mass migration from the lower Volga to the region of Ili in Sinkiang. In December 1770 nearly 200,000 Torguts set out with their belongings on the dangerous trek eastwards. They were pursued by Russian troops, and attacked by Kazaks and Buruts until they lost half their number and most of their cattle and goods before reaching Ili in July 1771. Ch'ien-lung ordered clothing, cattle and food supplies to be given them and summoned their chiefs to Jehol, where he created their leader Khan and some of his supporter princes. The Torgut were allotted pasture land in the Urumchi area. Their voluntary return to the Chinese Empire helped to reinforce the idea of China as the defender of Lamaism, and was considered by Ch'ien-lung as a particularly happy omen. Father Amiot wrote a contemporary account of their epic journey which was published in *Mémoires concernant l'histoire* ... (1776), Vol. I. De Quincey's spirited account in English was published in 1837 under the title *The Revolt of the Tartars*. The best modern account is by C. D. Barkman, 'The Return of the Torghuts from Russia to China', *Journal of Oriental Studies* (University of Hong Kong), Vol. II, no. 1, 1955.

45. Sadlers Wells. During Macartney's lifetime Covent Garden and Drury Lane held a monopoly for the presentation of drama under the Licensing Act of 1737. But a number of quasi-theatres flourished on the outskirts of London, mostly displaying burlesque and circus acts. Sadler's Wells, on the banks of the New River at Islington, was originally a chalybeate spring. From about 1700 it had a theatre, and later specialized in aquatic dramas. An advertisement of 1779 for Sadler's Wells mentions tumbling, rope-dancing, etc.

Astley's Amphitheatre. At this time Philip Astley ran the 'Amphitheatre of Arts' at Lambeth. Every winter the company went over to Dublin to perform in Astley's Amphitheatre there. Charles Dibdin the younger gives some excellent and intimate details of Astley's during the years 1797–8. He wrote a Harlequinade 'inventing all the mechanical changes and pantomine tricks' and offered it to Astley who employed him. Astley himself was an ex-cavalry sergeant-major who had originally opened an arena on the south side of the Thames near Westminster Bridge where he demonstrated horse training and gave riding lessons. Later he obtained a licence to operate a circus and gradually built up an elaborate business. See *Professional and Literary Memoirs of Charles Dibdin the Younger (1797–1830)*, ed. George Speaight (London, 1956), pp. 17–33.

Hughes. I have found a reference to an equestrian showman called Hughes who in 1788 brought his company from the Royal Circus in London to perform at Cambridge. This may be Richard Hughes who bought a quarter-share in Sadler's Wells in 1791. Subsequently he became the Managing Proprietor of that theatre until his death in 1815.

46. This is rather vague. A 'former Hoppo' might refer to one of a number of previous Superintendents of Maritime Customs at Canton. In his Observations, at the beginning of the section entitled 'Trade and Commerce', Macartney remarks that 'several of the Hoppos or treasurers on their return to Pekin have been called to a strict account. Some have suffered large confiscations and others a severer punishment....' Here follows a list of Superintendents of Maritime Customs at Canton for the period 1778-90. It is taken from the *Yueh hai-kuan chih, chuan* 7, the years but not the months being shown.

1777–8	Te K'uei
1778–81	T'u-ming-e
1781–4	Li Chih-yin
1785–6	Mu-sheng-e
1786–9	Fu Ning
1789–91	O-erh Teng-pu

47. The Grand Council had sent instructions to Cheng-jui dated 22 September which stated that after the envoy had welcomed the Emperor on his return to the capital from Jehol he should remain in the city a few days, 'and then having chosen an auspicious day let him receive the Imperial Decree and gifts at the T'ai-ho gate'. (See J. L. Cranmer-Byng, op. cit., pp. 166–7.) This is the gate of 'Supreme Harmony' in the Forbidden City, between the Wu-men ('Meridian gate') and the 'Palace of Supreme Harmony'. This is the first of the three great halls of ceremony. It was here that Manchu Emperors came to receive the congratulations of the Court on New Year's Day, on Imperial birthdays, and other great ceremonial occasions.

48. The first mild attack of King George III's illness (a kind of melancholia) occurred as far back as 1765. In November 1788 he fell into a state of violent depression which amounted to insanity. However, he had recovered by the beginning of 1789, and a thanksgiving service was held at St. Paul's Cathedral on 23 April which caused demonstrations of loyalty among his subjects who lined the route to see the King drive past.

49. Macartney is here referring to the Six Boards or Departments (*pu*) at the capital which formed the central administration of the Manchu government (see note 32). Two of them, the Board of Civil Office and the Board of Ceremonies are called in Chinese *Li-pu*, though the characters for *Li* are different. Macartney may have heard the words *Li-pu* used frequently and assumed that it was a generic term. These Boards were known collectively as the *Liu-pu*, 'the Six Departments'.

50. But Sung-yun's statement is directly contradicted by a letter from Father Poirot to Lord Macartney dated Peking, 29 September 1794, in which he explained how he and Father Raux had translated the Emperor's reply to King George's letter. Poirot's version was that a Mandarin read aloud one sentence at a time and the missionaries translated it. When they came to the clause concerning the churches which the English were alleged to want in China the missionaries were dumbfounded, and they suggested that the English had no wish to propagate their religious beliefs. The Mandarin, however, told the missionaries to translate the word 'churches'. In his letter Poirot then went on to explain that:

> 'Our practice is to modify certain expressions here and there, since we cannot delete a whole clause for fear that they would doubt the exactness of our translation and simply call in a third missionary to scrutinize it and so reassure themselves.... What we were able to do was to insert all the terms of respect for the King of England in the Imperial reply; for they treat our Kings just like their princelings who are nothing more than the Emperor's slaves.'

The French text of this letter is given in full in E. H. Pritchard, 'Letters from Missionaries at Peking', op. cit., pp. 40–3. The English translation is mine.

51. Macartney is correct in stating that Ch'ang-lin was allied to the Emperor; he was a Manchu of the Imperial clan, being a collateral descendant of Nurhachi's father. He held various high offices in which he showed himself to be a good administrator and a just official. But in 1792 he fell out with Ho-shen because he exposed the falseness of charges brought against various people accused of harbouring a rebel. At the beginning of 1793 he was appointed Governor of Chekiang and then in September promoted to the post of Governor-General of the two Kwangs. In August 1795 he was transferred to be Governor-General of Fukien and Chekiang. However, another official, Chu Kuei, who had been appointed Governor of Kwangtung in 1794, was temporarily in charge of the two Kwangs from March 1795. It thus looks as though Ch'ang-lin left Canton in March 1795 after being there for only one year and three months. His career seems to have received a setback at this time, possibly because of his brush with Ho-shen or because of his friendliness towards Macartney. However, after the death of Ho-shen he filled other great offices. He died in 1811.

52. The distance from Canton to Peking was about 5,500 *li*, which is equivalent to about 1,500 miles. Important official documents were carried by couriers riding horses in relays. During the Ch'ing dynasty the courier system was under the Remount Department of the Board of War. Radiating from Peking throughout the provinces were many postal stations where military officers were in charge of the transmission of official mail. If a document was considered urgent it was up to the sender to state that it must be sent 'express' and also to specify the degree of expressness by stating how many hundred *li* per day it must travel. If sent express the document had to be carried by night as well as by day. Documents concerning the Macartney embassy passing between Peking and the provinces were mostly sent 'express', and some of them were endorsed with the words 'at the rate of 600 *li* per day', which was the maximum rate laid down. Thus, Macartney's information was correct, though the highest express rate was sparingly used. Macartney made another reference to the efficiency of the courier service in his Journal for 19 November. For details of how the courier system worked at this period, see J. K. Fairbank and S. Y. Teng, 'On the Transmission of Ch'ing Documents' in *Ch'ing Administration*, op. cit., pp. 1–35.

53. This is not quite true; they sailed beside and not under it. In fact it was not so much a bridge as a long causeway of arches containing a central bridge, as Barrow's description makes clear:

> 'It was in this part of the canal where the bridge of ninety-one arches was thrown across the arm of a lake that joined the canal. I lament exceedingly that we passed this extraordinary fabric in the night. It happened to catch the attention of a Swiss servant, who, as the yacht glided along, began to count the arches, but finding them increase in number much beyond his expectation and, at the same time, in dimensions, he ran into the cabin, calling out with great eagerness, "For God's sake, gentlemen, come upon deck, for here is a bridge such as I never saw before; it has no end." Mr. Maxwell and I hastened upon deck, and, by the faint light, could sufficiently distinguish the arches of a bridge running parallel with the eastern bank of the canal, across the arm of a vast lake, with which the navigation thus communicated.' (*Travels in China*, pp. 520–1.)

From the Journal it is clear that they saw this bridge soon after leaving Soochow on their way to Hangchow. While sightseeing just outside Soochow in 1958 I noticed a similar causeway which had over fifty arches, the central one being large enough for a medium size junk to pass under with its mast lowered. This is called the 'Precious Belt Bridge' and it was originally built in the T'ang dynasty to span part of a lake which borders on the Grand Canal because frequent high winds disturbed

NOTES 54-57

the waters of the lake so much that small boats had difficulty passing along the Grand Canal. A description written in 1442 stated that it had fifty-three arches. It was this causeway or a similar one in the same vicinity which Macartney is referring to.

54. For an illustration of these purses see Sir G. L. Staunton, *An Authentic Account of an Embassy*; op. cit., Plate XVIII, Vol. II, p. 235. Chinese officials wore them hanging from the girdle of their robes; according to Staunton they carried areca nuts in them.

By 'paper of happiness' Macartney means the character *fu*, 'happiness, good-fortune', which would have a specially lucky significance if written in the Emperor's own calligraphy. In 1795 the Dutch embassy also received the character *fu* written by the Emperor as a gift for the non-existent King of Holland.

55. Catherine the Great, the daughter of a German princeling, was married to Peter, the heir to the throne of Russia, who became Tsar in 1761. He was an uncouth fellow of boorish manners who preferred military life and the habits of the barracks to married life, and was publicly hostile to his wife. While Peter III was alienating the loyalty of his subjects by his behaviour, Catherine was winning their support by her obvious devotion to Russia. In June 1762 the Orlov brothers carried out a successful *coup d'état* and the troops in St. Petersburg proclaimed Catherine empress. She gave orders that Peter should be held under arrest by the Orlov brothers on a country estate and there, four days later, he died mysteriously. No one was punished for the Tsar's death. On her ambition, see note 83.

56. This was a tactful way of warning Macartney not to create trouble on his return to Macao. In doing so Ch'ang-lin was echoing a Court letter from Ho-shen addressed to Ch'ang-lin and the Governor of Kwangtung, dated 23 September. However, the original document was almost brutal in its frankness, and Ch'ang-lin seems to have conveyed its implications in a courtier-like manner. A translation of the relevant part reads:

'Now, after the tribute envoy arrived he made many entreaties and repeatedly pestered us. It seems that these barbarians after all are ignorant. Moreover, we have not allowed them to leave a man at the Capital so that when the King of that country receives the Imperial edict, because he has not achieved what he wanted, he may be disgruntled, and relying on his distant and strategic position may find a pretext for making trouble.... Perhaps they may conspire to stir up trouble in Macao, and we must be prepared to guard against it. After Ch'ang-lin has arrived in Canton he must act circumspectly and must at all times be on the alert.'

See J. L. Cranmer-Byng, op. cit., pp. 167-8.

57. Robert Kyd (1746-93). Joined the E.I.C. as a cadet in 1764, served with the Bengal Infantry and reached the rank of Lieut.-Colonel. He was fond of botany and horticulture and built up a private botanical garden at Sibpur, outside Calcutta. It was this garden which formed the nucleus of the present Botanic Garden, founded by the Company in 1787, with Col. Kyd as its first Honorary Superintendent. It seems that in 1780 some seeds of the China tea plant were brought to Calcutta by captains of East India Company ships and that Kyd managed to grow some plants from this seed in his garden. In 1788 Sir Joseph Banks sent the Directors of the East India Company a memorandum on the cultivation of tea in India, recommending certain areas where it would be most likely to grow well. (See H. C. Cameron, *Sir Joseph Banks*, Batchworth Press, 1952, pp. 72-3.) Also A. Lamb, 'Lord Macartney in Batavia, March 1793', *Journal of the South Seas Society*, Vol. XIV, 1 and 2, 1958, pp. 57-68.) Banks' ideas were endorsed by Col. Kyd, and Macartney was instructed by the E.I.C. to obtain tea plants from China during his embassy. To help him in his task he was given some written advice from Sir Joseph Banks on how best to transplant the seeds and plants (MDWC, nos. 177 and 429) and also a paper by Col.

NOTES 58–59

Kyd. Reporting to the East India Company from Canton on 23 December 1793, Macartney mentioned that 'among your instructions you mention how extremely desirable it would be that tea could be produced within the territories of the Company in India, and you recommend the circumstance in the strongest manner to my attention, and among the papers delivered to me for my information by Mr. Dundas, is one written by Colonel Kyd, a gentleman conversant in natural history and agriculture, who has a public garden in Bengal for the purpose of making useful experiments relative to the introduction of new plants.' This report is printed in full in E. H. Pritchard, 'The Instructions of the East India Company to Lord Macartney', op. cit., 1938, Pt. III, pp. 388–9.

With the permission of Ch'ang-lin, the new Governor-General of the two Kwangs, Macartney was able to 'take up several young plants of the best kind, which I ordered to be put in proper boxes, with earth, in which they continue still to thrive.' These plants, together with several seeds 'fit for growth' were entrusted to Dr. Dinwiddie who was leaving the embassy at Canton and proceeding to Calcutta. (See Macartney to Sir John Shore, 3 February 1794, printed in Pritchard, op. cit., 1938, Pt. IV, pp. 500–1.) Dinwiddie reached Calcutta on 27 September 1794 and handed over the tea plants to Dr. William Roxborough, who had been appointed superintendent of the Botanic Garden on the death of Colonel Kyd in 1793.

The plants and seeds thus reached their destination, but unfortunately I have been unable to discover whether they survived or not. However, there seems no reason why they should not have flourished at Calcutta, since in 1835–6 a large number of seedlings of the China tea plant raised in the Botanic Gardens at Calcutta were sent to various Government tea nurseries in India.

From 1823 onwards there were reports of indigenous tea plants growing in Assam, and a great controversy eventually arose as to whether efforts should be concentrated on cultivating China tea plants or the native ones of Assam. See William H. Ukers, *All about Tea* (Tea and Coffee Trade Journal Company, New York, 1935), Vol. I, pp. 134–52.

58. The Liuchiu (Luchu) or Ryuku isles lie strung out between Formosa and southern Japan in a chain of fifty-five islands. From the late fourteenth century onwards the ruler of this island kingdom paid tribute to China, the port of entry being Foochow, where a limited trade was allowed. In the seventeenth century the Lord of Satsuma in southern Kyushu conquered the northern group of these islands, and thus at the time of Macartney's embassy the ruler of the Liuchius owed a double allegiance—to the Emperor of China and the Shogun of Japan. Finally in 1879 the last King of the Liuchius was taken to Tokyo and the islands were incorporated into Japan as the prefecture of Okinawa.

The people of these islands are closely related to the Japanese ethnically and speak a variant form of the Japanese language. It is not possible to say with certainty when the first European ship visited the Liuchiu islands, but certainly the Englishman Captain Broughton was shipwrecked there in 1797 and left a description which can be found in John M'Leod, *Voyage of His Majesty's Ship Alceste, along the Coast of Corea, to the Island of Lewchew* (John Murray, 2nd edn., 1818, pp. 136–41). H.M.S. *Alceste* had disembarked Lord Amherst and his embassy at the mouth of the Peiho in July 1816 and then spent the next three months exploring and surveying the coasts of that part of the China Sea.

59. Barrow is more explicit. Describing the descent from the top of the Meiling pass he says that there was an almost continuous line of houses by the side of the road.

> 'Half of the buildings consisted, however, of places of convenience, to which passengers might retire to obey the calls of nature; and the doors, or rather openings into such erections, were always invitingly fronting the street. To each single

dwelling, whether alone or joined with others, was annexed a fabric of this description. Each was constructed upon a large terrace cistern, lined with such materials that no absorption could take place; and straw and other dry rubbish are thrown in by the owners, from time to time, to prevent evaporation. In one of the streets of Canton is a row of buildings of this kind, which, in so warm a climate is a dreadful nuisance, but the consideration of preserving that kind of manure, which by the Chinese is considered as superior for forcing vegetation to all others, has got the better of both decency and prudence.' (Barrow, *Travels in China*, London, 1806, p. 544.)

60. The word 'kaolin' comes from the Chinese *kao-ling*, meaning 'a high ridge', the name given to a hill east of Ching-te-chen, which was famous for its deposits of 'kaolin' clay.

Petuntse is another name for feldspar, and is derived from the Chinese *pai tun-tz'u*, or 'white bricks', which is the form in which the material reaches the factories. For technical information on this subject see William Willets, *Chinese Art* (Penguin Books, 1958), Vol. II, pp. 402–3. The porcelain manufacturing town of Ching-te-chen is the subject of note 62.

61. Thomas Pennant (1726–98). Zoologist and antiquary. Fellow of the Royal Society (1767). He was a close friend of Sir Joseph Banks, whose own account of Staffa and its rock pillars was published in Pennant's *Tour in Scotland*. He was a regular correspondent of the naturalist Gilbert White and they used to exchange information on natural history. White relates that Pennant 'had a toad that lived under his doorstep for thirty-six years and every evening came forth to be picked up and placed on the table where it was given its supper'. The following books by Pennant were in Macartney's Library at the time of its sale in 1854: *British Zoology*, 4 vols. (1776–7); *History of Quadrupeds* (1781); *Tour of Wales*; *Tour in Scotland and Voyage to the Hebrides*, 3 vols.; *Journal from Chester to London*. It is typical of Pennant that he should have sent a zoological question to a traveller in such a distant and little-known land as China. But as far as I have been able to ascertain there is nothing noteworthy about the fish of lake Poyang.

62. It is a pity that Macartney and his 'natural philosophers' were unable to visit this famous centre of porcelain manufacture. A description, especially by someone trained in chemistry, might have been valuable. Dr. Gillan does make a few perfunctory remarks on Chinese porcelain among his observations on chemistry in China, but he obviously lacked the necessary information. Fortunately an excellent description exists of the potteries there by the Jesuit priest, d'Entrecolles, in a letter written in 1712. 'The sight with which one is greeted on entering through one of the gorges consists of volumes of smoke and flame rising in different places, so as to define all the outlines of the town; approaching at nightfall, the scene reminds one of a burning city in flames . . .' Quoted in John Goldsmith Phillips, *China Trade Porcelain* (Harvard University Press, 1956). This book contains a good account of Ching-te-chen, together with further extracts from Father d'Entrecolles (pp. 2–11).

63. In his Journal of the outward voyage, under the entry for 1 February 1793, Macartney observed: 'The art of flying in a balloon is now becoming almost as easy as that of driving a whiskey, and Dr. Hawes and the Humane Society raise the dead without difficulty by a mechanical operation.' William Hawes (1736–1808) became prominent in 1773 when he started a campaign to persuade people in England that it was possible to revive those who had been drowned or asphyxiated. As a result of the interest aroused, Hawes and some friends met in the following year and this led to the founding of the Humane Society. Experiments in artificial respiration in Europe go back to the sixteenth century, when Vesalius discovered that he could keep an animal alive by blowing air into its lungs with a bellows. In the following century Robert Hook also experimented on animals by supplying the lungs with fresh air,

and reported his findings to the Royal Society. I am not certain, however, to what exact 'mechanical operation' Macartney is referring. It is known that the celebrated surgeon John Hunter was interested in the work of the Humane Society and wrote in 1776, for the Royal Society, his 'Proposals for the Recovery of People apparently Drowned', and later invented an apparatus for forced respiration.

Macartney's statement about the 'extraction or depression of the glaucoma' is somewhat vague. European eye surgery in the eighteenth century owed much to Jacques Daviel, who cured cataract on the eye by the extraction of the crystalline lens. The Austrian opthalmologist, George Joseph Beer, cured glaucoma during the last decade of the eighteenth century by removing the iris of the eye. Perhaps Macartney was referring to Beer's operation. 'Depression' would refer to the reduction of the pressure on the eye, one method of attempting to cure this condition.

64. A form of 'balloon mania' hit Europe from 1783 onwards. It started in France in that year when the Montgolfier brothers rose to a height of 6,000 feet in a balloon lifted by hot air. A hydrogen balloon was successfully tested in Paris a few months later. As a result of these experiments numerous balloon flights were undertaken in Europe. The first human ascent made in Britain was by James Tytler of Edinburgh in August 1784, in a hot air balloon. In September of that year the handsome young Italian, Vincenzo Lunardi, made an ascent in a hydrogen balloon from Moorfields in London watched by the Prince of Wales. At the end of this flight Lunardi landed near Ware in Hertfordshire. In 1785 George Biggin and Mrs. Letitia Anne Sage made an ascent in Lunardi's balloon from St. George's Fields and descended near Harrow-on-the-Hill. A lively painting of this event was made by Julius Ceasar Ibbetson.

The climax to this mania came in 1785 when a Frenchman, J. P. Blanchard, and an American physician, John Jeffries, crossed the channel in a balloon. See A. Wolf, *A History of Science, Technology and Philosophy in the Eighteenth Century* (2nd edn., revised, London, 1952), pp. 576–82.

65. In his Observations, under the heading 'Government', Macartney returns to the same theme: 'There are certain mysterious societies in every province who are known to be disaffected, and although narrowly watched by the government, they find means to elude its vigilance and often to hold secret assemblies, where they revive the memory of ancient glory and independence, brood over recent injuries and meditate revenge' (p. 239). Between 1770 and Ch'ien-lung's death in 1799 the following major insurrections broke out:

1771–6 Revolt in west Szechwan among the mountain aborigines (Chin-ch'uan rebels).
1784 Muslim uprising in Kansu.
1787–8 Revolt in Formosa among Chinese settlers (organized by a secret society).
1795–1804 Rebellion of the White Lotus Sect in Hupeh.
1795–7 Revolt of Miao tribesmen in the Kweichow-Szechwan-Hunan border region. It required a large number of troops under Fu-k'ang-an to crush the revolt.

In Honan a secret religious society known as Pai-lien chiao ('White Lotus Sect') was active. By 1793 it had become strong enough in Honan, Hupeh, Szechwan and Shensi to start an armed uprising and the Government ordered the arrest of its leaders. In 1795 the people of western Hupeh were so oppressed by the local officials that they began armed resistance under the slogan 'The officials have forced the people to rebel'. They joined the White Lotus Sect, which now embarked on a rebellion which lasted for nine more years. It was probably in operations against these rebels in Shensi that Wang was killed on 12 September 1800. Macartney mentions on p. 250 that Fu-k'ang-an had recently been appointed to command an expedition against the rebels in Szechwan. (See Hummel, op. cit., 222–4.)

Finally, pirates were very active along the southern coasts of China at this time and it took over twenty years (c. 1787–1810) before they were brought under control. The exciting story of this long battle between the pirate chiefs and the commanders of naval forces on the coasts of Chekiang, Fukien, Kwangtung and Kwangsi provinces is told in outline in Hummel, op. cit., 446–8.

66. This is the Mei-ling Pass in the province of Kiangsi, which rises to a height of about 1,000 feet. The distance between the two rivers is about twenty-five miles. It forms part of a well-travelled route from central China by waterways to Canton. The traveller going southwards to Canton left his boat at Nan-an, where the river Kan is no longer navigable and re-embarked at Nan-yung on the upper reaches of the North River. For a description of crossing this pass in 1710 see the *Memoirs of Father Ripa*, trans. Fortunato Prandi (John Murray, London, 1855), pp. 38–9. This can be compared with the descriptions given by Macartney and Barrow. In Father Ripa's time vehicles and animals of every kind were excluded. He says that this route was covered with people along its whole length and had the appearance of a fair.

67. Nurhaci, the founder of the Ch'ing dynasty, organized his followers into eight companies or 'banners' during the period 1601–15. Each of these companies was distinguished by the colour of its banner, which was yellow, white, blue or red, and either had a border or was plain. This military and civil organization comprised all the people of Manchuria, and the banners were given land. The Manchus also included a large number of Chinese and Mongols in their banners and they took part in the overthrow of the Ming dynasty in 1644. After the conquest of China, units of the eight banners were stationed in Peking and in various strategic places throughout the country. These garrisons were under Manchu ('Tartar') generals and were disposed so as to control the Chinese soldiers scattered in smaller garrisons. The Manchu policy was to keep the bannermen separate from the Chinese people, and they were forbidden to take part in employment, but were supported by income from banner lands. By the end of Ch'ien-liung's reign the bannermen had declined and instead of being formidable warriors had become demoralized. (See Hsieh Pao-chao, *The Government of China (1644–1911)*, Baltimore, 1925, pp. 55–67.) The Chinese militia, known as Green Standard troops, formed a separate force organized on a provincial basis (see note 103).

68. The Sanskrit word *bodhisattva* was transliterated into Chinese by characters pronounced *p'u-t'i-sa-t'o*. Pusa is a contraction of these characters.

The Chinese name for this temple was the 'cliff of Kuan-yin', since the temple was built into a rock-formation which resembled an image of the Goddess of Mercy, Kuan-yin. It is situated about sixty miles south of Shao-chou, on a tributary of the Pei-kiang (North River). It is in Ying-te District, about twelve miles from the town of Ying-te. It is mentioned very briefly in the *Kuang-tung t'ung-chih* ('Gazetteer of Kwangtung Province') which also quotes an attractive poem on this cliff by Wang Shih-chen (Commercial Press, Shanghai, photostat edition, *chüan* 102, page 1977). I am indebted to my colleague, Mr. V. T. Yang, for kindly informing me of this reference. Barrow also described this temple in the same strain as Macartney, with bated breath. The Stauntons, both father and son, give a more matter-of-fact account. It is interesting to know that the famous Commissioner Lin Tse-hsü of the so-called 'Opium War', when journeying southwards towards Canton early in 1839, stopped at this temple and prostrated himself in front of the image. (See Arthur Waley, *The Opium War through Chinese Eyes*, Allen and Unwin, 1958, p. 20.) There is a drawing of the rock in Sir G. L. Staunton's *An Authentic Account*... op. cit., folio volume of plates, no. 43.

69. Situated in the mountains above Sintra in Portugal. Also called *Convento dos Capuchos* after the Franciscans who founded it. It was visited by William Beckford on 27 July 1787, and he wrote the following description of it:

NOTES 70–72

'We followed a winding goat's path which leads over the brow of the eminences to the Cork Convent, which looked at a distance like the settlement of Robinson Crusoe. Before the entrance, which is formed by two ledges of ponderous rock, is a little smooth spot of greensward browsed by cattle. Their tinkling filled me with rural ideas. The hermitage is lined with cork; its cells, chapel and refectory are all scooped out of the rock. Several of the little passages which lead about are not only roofed but paved with cork, soft and pleasant to the feet.'

The Journal of William Beckford in Portugal and Spain, 1787–1788. Ed. Boyd Alexander (London, 1954), pp. 147–8. No part of this Journal, however, was published during Macartney's lifetime.

70. The island to which Macartney refers is Honam island, on which stands Honam temple. The East India Company was not allowed to buy a piece of land and put up their own factory but had to rent an existing one, outside the city walls, from the Hong merchants. The foreign factories were at the south-west corner of the city and on the banks of the Pearl river, i.e. between the city wall and what later became the Shameen.

For plans of Canton and of the foreign factories see H. B. Morse, *The Chronicles of the East India Company trading to China*, Vol. II, p. 320, and III, p. 1. For a picture of the factories as they appeared to the artist William Daniell in 1785 see Morse, II, p. 144.

71. Thomas Harris (d. 1820). In 1767, together with George Colman and others, he purchased the patent of Covent Garden Theatre. Harris became stage-manager, and later proprietor and manager of Covent Garden Theatre, a position he held until his death in 1820. See D.N.B.

Richard Brinsley Sheridan (1751–1816). His first successful play, *The Rivals*, was produced at Covent Garden in 1775. In 1776 he became manager and chief proprietor of Drury Lane Theatre. The second Drury Lane Theatre was pulled down in 1791 and, while it was being rebuilt by Henry Holland, Sheridan transferred to the Haymarket. In 1794 the third Drury Lane Theatre was completed and Sheridan returned there for another long period as chief proprietor.

William Thomas Lewis (1748?–1811). His father was an actor-manager in Ireland, and the son became a popular actor in Dublin in the period 1770–2. He first appeared in London at Covent Garden in 1773, where he remained until the end of his career. His biography in the D.N.B. gives an enthusiastic appraisal of his talent as an actor.

John Philip Kemble (1757–1823). Son of a theatre manager, he started his adult acting career in 1776. His first London appearance was at Drury Lane in 1783. He became manager of the Theatre Royal, Drury Lane, from 1788 until it was rebuilt in 1791–4, when he was at the Haymarket Opera House.

Sarah Siddons (1775–1831). Sister of John Philip Kemble, and wife of William Siddons, an actor. She first came to prominence through her performances at Bath. In 1782 she came to London and played at Drury Lane, where she soon became famous in a number of outstanding roles, especially that of Lady Macbeth. Reynolds made a famous painting of her as the Tragic Muse.

Elizabeth Farren (1759–1829). Born of a family of strolling players. Performed at Drury Lane, where her father William Farren was also engaged, from 1776–84. She was recognized as an outstanding player of fine ladies. She had a tall, slim figure and a beautiful voice. Horace Walpole considered her the best actress he had ever seen. She had a keen wit and was received on an equal footing with women of noble birth. The Earl of Derby had been in love with her for many years and on the death of his wife in 1797 he married her. Elizabeth Farren made her last stage appearance in that year in the role of Lady Teazle.

72. The Licensing Act of 1737 had placed theatres under the Crown, with control exercised by the Lord Chamberlain. Playhouses could only be established under

NOTES 73-75

Royal Patent, and this was made exclusive to Drury Lane and Covent Garden. In 1793 Harris had the royal licence for Covent Garden while Sheridan held it for Drury Lane. The Haymarket was a smaller theatre, used chiefly as an opera house.

73. Botany Bay, near where Sydney now stands, was discovered in 1770 by James Cook during the voyage of the *Endeavour*, and so named by him. 'The great quantity of plants Mr. Banks and Dr. Solander found in this place occasioned my giving it the name of Botany Bay.' In 1779 Sir Joseph Banks, in evidence before a Committee of the House of Commons which was to report on the state of the gaols in Britain, suggested that Botany Bay might be a suitable place for convicts serving a long sentence. In 1786, when Pitt was Head of the Ministry, the Admiralty was ordered to fit out a fleet of convict ships for dispatch to New South Wales. Captain Arthur Phillip, R.N., was appointed the first Governor of the new Colony. In order to cut down the expense of the venture, the Admiralty secured a cargo of tea to be shipped from Canton to England in the empty convict ships. Hence the term Botany Bay ship. (See Hector Charles Cameron, *Sir Joseph Banks*, Batchworth Press, London, 1952, pp. 31 and 179–83.) The *Bellona* was built at London in 1782. She was sent out to Botany Bay as a storeship, and also carried seventeen women convicts aboard. She sailed from Gravesend in August 1792 and took 163 days days for the voyage, arriving at Port Jackson on 16 January 1793. (See Charles Bateson, *The Convict Ships, 1787–1868*, Brown, Son and Ferguson, Glasgow, 1959, pp. 129–30.)

74. The official Chinese title of a provincial governor was *Hsun-fu*, and his courtesy title was *Fu-yuan*. The anglicized version of *Fu-yuan* was spelt in various ways but I have adhered to the version 'Fuyuen' which seems to be the one used most consistently in the documents of the East India Company for this period.

The *Tsung-ping* was the commander of the Green Standard troops (i.e. Chinese provincial forces) within a district. His common title was *Ch'en-t'ai*, hence Europeans at Canton sometimes called him the 'Chentai', while they corrupted *Tsung-ping* into 'Chumpien'. He was not strictly a governor but rather commander of the local forces stationed at Shao-chou-fu, which had been made the headquarters of a *Tsung-ping* in 1683. (See *Ch'u-kiang hsien-chih, chüan* 11, p. 5.) Macartney mentioned meeting this official again on 8 January 1794.

75. The instructions issued to Lord Macartney dated 8 September 1792 and signed by Henry Dundas contained the following paragraphs relating to Japan:

'It is possible that you may find it either necessary or expedient to touch upon the coast of Japan. That country produces tea as good as, and probably cheaper, than that of China. The difficulties of trading there, which have so long deterred other nations from attempting it, are now said to have almost ceased.

'It is [not] impossible that the competition of the Japan market with that of China might render the commodities of both places cheaper to the purchaser. The probability of such a resource might at least operate in some degree to facilitate the negotiations at Pekin.' (Printed in Morse, *Chronicles*, Vol. II, p. 241.)

On 10 July 1793 Macartney wrote a letter addressed to 'the great and puissant Prince the Cubo or Temporal Sovereign of Japan.' (MDWC, 260.) Sir Erasmus Gower was to take the letter to Yedo and if possible to bring back a reply. In his instructions to Gower, Macartney stated, among other points: 'As soon as you shall have received an answer from the Japanese Sovereign at Jeddo, or after waiting about a fortnight, if you should happen to find that no answer either written or verbal is likely to be given to the letter delivered by you, you will proceed to Manila ...' (MDWC, 263).

After disembarking the embassy at the mouth of the Peiho, Gower sailed in the *Lion* to Chusan where he spent six weeks while the sick members of his crew were put into an improvised hospital on land. Early in October the *Lion* ran out of drugs and Gower was forced to go to Macao for more. At the beginning of November he made more than one attempt to sail to Japan, but the weak state of his crew and the violence of storms prevented him, and he was forced to return to Macao.

From the beginning of the seventeenth century the Tokugawa Shoguns had ruled Japan from their castle city of Yedo, while the Emperor and his court were virtually prisoners at Kyoto. Even if Gower had succeeded in reaching Yedo Bay and had delivered Macartney's letter to the Shogun the answer would have been unfavourable. A Russian expedition under Lieutenant Laxman had been despatched from Siberia in 1792, and when he reached Japan he was informed that according to Japanese law no dealings with foreigners were permitted, and that he and his crew were liable to be arrested. Eventually he was allowed to depart, and was informed that the Russians *might* be permitted to trade but only if they came to Nagasaki. (See G. A. Lensen, *The Russian Push toward Japan*, Princeton, 1959, pp. 96–120.)

76. The word 'qua' here stands for the character *kuan*, 'an official'. I take Macartney's version 'Pan-ke' to refer to P'an Chen-ch'eng (1714–88), known to foreigners at Canton as Puan Khequa. His son P'an Yu-ti inherited the firm and was also usually referred to by foreign merchants as Puan Khequa. He died in 1821, having been chief of the Co-hong from 1796 to 1808. He was one of the two senior Hong merchants sent by the Governor of Kwangtung to the Commissioners of the East India Company in March 1792 to make preliminary enquiries about the projected English embassy.

The name Chi-chin most probably refers to the merchant called by westerners Shy Kinqua, which was a corruption of Shih Ch'ing-kuan, his business name. His proper name was Shih Chung-ho, and he was the head of the *Erh-i hong*. Shy Kinqua I had died in 1790 and had been succeeded by his son Shy Kinqua II, sometimes known as Gonqua. There is no comprehensive study of the individual Hong merchants. Meanwhile see Morse, *Chronicles*, II, pp. 197 and 261–4.

77. Macartney is referring to the fact that the East India Company had traded at Chusan from 1700–10, and again in 1755. Attempts were made to trade at Ningpo in 1736, while in the years 1755–7 a determined effort was made to be allowed to trade permanently at Ningpo, but this ended in failure. (See Morse, *Chronicles*, Vol. V, pp. 49–63.) Macartney was not on very firm ground when he implied that the Company had been allowed to trade at these two places freely.

78. Bankshall: a warehouse. Probably derived from a Bengali word. William Hickey, visiting Canton in 1769, gave a fuller description:

> 'Whampoa is pleasantly situated, having two islands close to the ships, one called Deans, upon which each ship erects what is called a "bankshall", being a lightly constructed wooden building from sixty to one hundred feet in length, into which the upper masts, yards, spars, sails, rigging and stores are deposited, and, previous to being re-embarked, are all repaired and put into order. The other is called French Island, where the officers and sailors walk or amuse themselves at different games for exercise and pastime. Upon French Island all the Europeans who die are buried.' (See *Memoirs of William Hickey*, ed. Peter Quennell, Hutchinson, 1960, p. 133.)

79. In 1773 a revolt broke out in the Tay-son district of Annam which marked the beginning of a long civil war. It was led by the brothers Nguyen, who occupied Hanoi, the capital of Annam, and overthrew the last king of the Li dynasty. A member of the old ruling family, Nguyen Anh, escaped and for many years was helped by the French. Meanwhile, since the rulers of Annam had paid tribute to the Emperor of China, Ch'ien-lung ordered an army to be sent in support of the deposed King of Annam, but the Tay-son rebels routed this Chinese force in 1789. However, one of the rebel brothers, Nguyen Van-Hué, asked the Chinese to recognize him as a tributary ruler, and in 1790 he actually went to Peking to congratulate Ch'ien-lung on his eightieth birthday. In 1792 Nguyen Anh, the survivor of the Li family, who

NOTES 80–83

was being helped by the French, was strong enough to attack Nguyen Van-Hué in the north of Annam and it is this attack to which Macartney is referring. For an account of this civil war and the part played by the French in finally restoring Nguyen Anh to power in Annam, see D. G. E. Hall, *A History of South-East Asia* (Macmillan and Co., 1955), pp, 355–71. For Chinese relations with Annam at this period, see Hummel, op. cit., pp. 680–1.

80. In fact they had very little effect. I have discussed this question in the Introduction, p. 31.

81. There had been spasmodic attempts on the part of individual Supercargoes to learn Chinese, but it was a difficult undertaking since the Chinese themselves were forbidden to teach foreigners the language. For instance in 1734 we know from the Company records that Andrew Reid, who had learnt some Chinese, accompanied the Supercargoes to the city gate at Canton in order to explain their grievances to the Governor-General's secretary (Morse, *Chronicles*, I, 227). In 1736 a young man called James Flint was left at Canton to learn the language. By 1746 he was acting as interpreter to the Supercargoes, and in 1750 he was being paid an allowance as interpreter. For his subsequent adventures see note 84. In 1753 the Company sent out Thomas Bevan and — Barton to Canton to learn the language, but in 1755 the master who taught them was warned by the local magistrate not to teach them any longer (Morse, op. cit., V, pp. 27–8). When a memorial of grievances was submitted to the Governor-General at the end of 1758 the reply received stated among other things: 'Our language is different and you are allowed Linguists to make representations. However, the Supercargoes persevered, and in 1759 Francis Wood was trying to learn Chinese, though by 1761 he was reported to be prostrate with illness and out of his mind. In 1793 three young men, John Travers, Thomas Pattle and John Roberts, were studying under a Chinese tutor at Macao, under circumstances of some secrecy. (See Susan Reed Stifler, 'The Language Students of the East India Company's Canton Factory', *Journal of the North China Branch of the Royal Asiatic Society*, Vol. LXIX, 1938, pp. 46–82.) The Chinese 'Linguists', so-called, spoke a pidgin English which may have been adequate for business transactions but was quite unsatisfactory when more complicated matters, such as the grievances of the Supercargoes, were at stake.

82. Lantao is a large island near Hong Kong; its western extremity points towards Macao. In February 1794 Lieutenant Parish was sent in the *Jackall* to survey Lantao and other islands between Macao and Hong Kong. He wrote a report for Lord Macartney which runs to eight pages, including information on an island he calls Cowhee. From a sketch map he made it appears that this is in fact Ma Wan island off the tip of Lantao and near the mainland. Parish's map is preserved in the British Museum (Add. MS. 19, 822). In the course of his report he discussed the possibility of making a settlement on this island and wrote: 'The establishment might at first be small and at very little expense, and the island of Lantao would at all times admit of its being extended at pleasure' (MDWC, 371). This is most interesting in the light of subsequent events. As it turned out, the island of Hong Kong was chosen in preference to Lantao, but already by 1794 Lantao and the adjacent islands had been considered in case a settlement was required in the future. As Macartney predicted, as soon as Britain made a settlement elsewhere (in the event at Hong Kong from 1841 onwards) the trade of Macao quickly declined to nothing. In the so-called Opium War of 1839–42 the forts of the Bocca Tigris were, in fact, demolished by a few broadsides (see note 85). Lantao eventually became part of the Colony of Hong Kong in 1898 when Britain leased the so-called New Territories from China for a period of ninety-nine years.

83. In the middle of the seventeenth century the Cossacks reached the sea of Okhotsk on the Pacific coast north of Manchuria, and also the Amur river. The Amur served as their boundary with the Chinese empire, then recently conquered by

NOTES 84–86

the Manchus. Albazin was a fort on the Amur where the Cossacks tried to establish themselves permanently, but were twice forced to withdraw by Chinese troops. The position was finally regularized by the Treaties of Nerchinsk (1689) and Kiakhta (1727); which set a temporary limit to Russia's drive across central Asia. In their search for furs in the eighteenth century Russian adventurers had crossed the Bering Strait and hunted seals on the coast of Alaska. (See George Alexander Lensen, *The Russian Push toward Japan*, Princeton University Press, 1959, pp. 14–22.)

84. James Flint came to Canton in 1736 and studied the Chinese language, being employed later by the East India Company as an interpreter. In 1757 the Governor-Generals of the two Kwangs and of Fukien-Chekiang issued orders prohibiting foreign trade at any port other than Canton. This was aimed at English ships attempting to trade at Ningpo and Chusan. The Supercargoes of the Company protested, but in vain, and as a last resort they purchased a seventy-ton ship, and sent her to Ningpo under Flint. Here Flint presented a memorial setting out the grievances of the Supercargoes at Canton and requesting that these be made known to the authorities at Peking. The Ningpo officials refused to receive this petition so Flint took the bold step of sailing northwards to Tientsin. Here he succeeded in delivering a copy of the memorial to an official who forwarded it to Peking. Flint was later informed that the Emperor was sending an Imperial Commissioner to Canton to investigate the complaints. Flint was then escorted back to Canton by the overland route. He was subsequently imprisoned by the Chinese for three years at Macao for violating Imperial orders by going to places outside Canton. In 1762 he was released from prison and deported. He returned to England, but was never allowed to go to China again. As a result of an enquiry conducted at Canton many of the complaints were found to be true and the Hoppo was recalled to Peking in disgrace. For a detailed account of this episode see Morse, *Chronicles*, Vol. I, pp. 301–5; Vol. V, pp. 75–84; and Vol. IV, pp. 317–20.

85. Macartney was wrong in calling it the Pe-kiang river. He was referring to the Pearl river (Chu-kiang). The Pei-kiang is the 'North River' which carries the important waterway route northwards towards the Yangtze valley in the centre of China.

The entrance to the Pearl river from the sea was called by the Chinese the *Hu-men*, 'the tiger-gate'. Hence the Portuguese name Bocca Tigris, and the English version, 'Bogue'. On both sides of the river at the narrowest point there were hills, thus making it a natural gateway, easily defended. Here the Chinese had built forts on three islands. To the south of the entrance was the island and fort of Taikoktow, to the north Anunghoi and Chuenpi. During the Anglo-Chinese war of 1839–42 these forts were captured in February 1841. For the English side of this story see W. D. Bernard, *Narrative of the Voyages and Services of the Nemesis from 1840 to 1843 . . . in China*, 2 vols., 2nd edn. (Colburn, London, 1844). Vol. I, pp. 256–67; and for the Chinese side see Arthur Waley, *The Opium War through Chinese Eyes* (Allen and Unwin, 1958), pp. 139–40.

86. Luiz de Camões was born about 1524 and studied at Coimbra University. Exiled for killing a court official in a brawl, he sailed for India in 1553. A few years later he appears to have been appointed Trustee for the Dead and Absent at Macao, where China had recently permitted the Portuguese to form a settlement. It was here that he is said to have written part of his epic poem about the great Portuguese explorers which he called *Os Lusiádas*. He returned to Lisbon in 1572 and his poem was published two years later. He died in 1580, poor and little honoured. The house lent to Macartney by one of the Supercargoes was known as the 'Casa da Quinta de Camões', and was in fact rented by the Company from a prominent citizen of Macao. It can still be seen today, though the top floor was removed earlier this century. It stands in the public gardens now known as 'Camoens Gardens', where the poet is traditionally said to have written part of his epic. The headquarters of the Company at Macao was on the Praya Grande, at a point near to the present Riviera Hotel.

See C. R. Boxer, 'Was Camoens ever in Macau?', *T'ien Hsia*, Vol. X, no. 4 (1940), pp. 324–33.

87. Livonia was the old name for the Baltic Duchy, later known as Latvia. It is possible that Macartney is here referring to 'house servants' in Livonia only. He could have obtained this information while British Ambassador in St. Petersburg. However, if he really means 'house servants and house negroes of a great landlord in Livonia' this can be explained in the following way. In the seventeenth century Jacobus, Duke of Courland, claimed to rule both Courland and Livonia. In 1654 the first regular colony of Courland, in Tobago in the West Indies, was established. From this time onwards the Duchy of Courland, and by extension the Duchy of Livonia, had a strong connection with the West Indies. Macartney knew all about negro servants, having himself been Governor of Grenada and Tobago from 1776 until 1779. (See Edgar Anderson, 'The Couronians and the West Indies; the first Settlement', *Caribbean Quarterly*, Vol. 5, no. 4, 1957.)

88. The Colony was founded in 1786 on the island of Penang off the north-west coast of Malaya. The island had been ceded by the Sultan of Kedah to the East India Company in that year as a result of the negotiations of Captain Francis Light, an ex-naval officer in the service of a Madras firm which traded with ports in the Straits of Malacca. Light became the new Colony's first Governor. By 1788 Chinese settlers formed about two-fifths of the population of the Colony and played an enterprising part in its development. Macartney's observations are borne out by Francis Light himself, in a dispatch to the Governor-General of Bengal, dated January 1794. Describing the Chinese of the Colony, he wrote: 'They are excessively fond of gaming—there is no restraining them from it. This leads them into many distresses, and frequently ends in their ruin.' This dispatch is quoted in H. P. Clodd, *Malaya's First British Pioneer, the Life of Francis Light* (Luzac and Co., London, 1948), pp. 98–9. Writing of the Chinese in the same dispatch, Light said, 'They are the only people in the East from whom revenue can be raised without expense and extraordinary effort.'

89. Shortly after the end of the Seven Years' War, for a number of reasons, both geographical and naval, England sent several expeditions to the South Seas under the direction of the Admiralty. In 1768 Captain Cook sailed in the *Endeavour* for the Pacific to observe the transit of the planet Venus. Cook recorded in his *Journal*: 'I was ordered, therefore, to proceed directly to Otaheite, and after the astronomical observations should be completed, to prosecute the design of making discoveries in the South Pacific Ocean...' He remained at Tahiti from 12 April until 15 July 1769, and he and his party, including Joseph Banks and Dr. Solander, the Swedish botanist, observed all they could about the life of the inhabitants. As a result of Cook's second voyage in the *Resolution* her consort ship *Adventurer* brought back to England an inhabitant of an island near to Tahiti. This was the gentle Omai who was presented to King George III, stayed at Hinchinbrooke with Lord Sandwich, at that time First Lord of the Admiralty, and had his portrait painted by Sir Joshua Reynolds. Otaheite was the name used by the inhabitants of Tahiti themselves, and is the form most frequently used in eighteenth-century England.

90. Matthew Prior (1664–1721), Poet and diplomat. A collected edition of his poems was published in 1718 which achieved some popularity. Prior wrote urbane *vers de société* which contained many topical allusions. He excelled at narrative verse containing much broad humour. His poems were frequently about women who not only had neat figures but were frolicsome as well.

In the next paragraph Macartney mentions 'eking out a skeleton figure by a cork rump'. This is a reference to a fashion in England which lasted from about 1775 to 1785 when fashionable women took the trouble to increase the width of their hips by adding side panniers and even back panniers, vulgarly called 'cork rumps'.

91. Father Matteo Ripa, an Italian secular priest, entered the Emperor's service in

1710. After many interesting experiences at the Court he managed to obtain the Emperor's permission to return to Europe in 1724. He also managed to take with him five Chinese converts, and after much difficulty obtained permission from the Pope in 1732 to establish a college at Naples for training missionaries who were to be sent to China. Ripa's history of this College was published in Naples in 1832, and a selection of those parts dealing with his residence in China was translated into English by Fortunato Prandi under the title *Memoirs of Father Ripa* (John Murray, London, 1855). For information about the College, see pp. 147–50, 157–60.

92. *Lettres édifiantes et curieuses écrites des Missions étrangères par quelques Missionnaires de la Compagnie de Jesus.* This work was issued in Paris at intervals between 1702 and 1776, by which time 34 volumes had been printed. A new edition in 26 volumes entitled *Lettres édifiantes et curieuses écrites des Missions étrangères*, was published in Paris between 1780–3. In this edition volumes 16–26 contain all the material relating to China. There were several other editions of this work and in Cordier's *Bibliotheca Sinica* it occupies the whole of columns 926–40.

By 'other Jesuitical publications' Macartney is probably referring to *Mémoires concernant l'Histoire, les Sciences, les Arts, les Moeurs, les Usages, etc., des Chinois: Par les Missionaries de Pekin*, 15 vols. (Paris, 1776–91). A sixteenth and final volume was added in 1814. Contributions to this important work were made by missionary scholars such as Amiot, Gaubil and Prémare, as well as two Chinese scholars, Ko and Yang, who spent a year at Paris studying under the direction of Turgot. Much of this work consists of translations of Chinese texts into French. Volume I contains as frontispiece an engraving of Ch'ien-lung made from a portrait of him painted by Father Panzi, and volume XV an engraving of Amiot from a portrait by the same artist.

Macartney may also be referring to *Description Geographique, Historique, Chronologique, Politique, et Physique de l'Empire de la Chine et de la Tartarie Chinoise*, by Jean-Baptiste du Halde, 4 vols. (Paris, 1735). This was really an encyclopedia of China, and was the first comprehensive account available to the west. A valuable feature of this work is the series of maps of China engraved in Europe and based on surveys made in China by command of the Emperor between 1708 and 1721 by a group of missionaries and their Chinese collaborators (see note 100). It was translated into English in 1736, and went through several revised editions. It was probably the most influential work on China available in Europe in the eighteenth century.

There is much bibliographical information of interest on this subject in *East and West; Europe's Discovery of China and China's Response to Europe, 1511–1839* (Princeton University, 1957). This is a check list of an exhibition held at Princeton in 1957.

93. Methodists. This term was first given to a group of students at Oxford because of the regularity of their lives. In 1729 John and Charles Wesley together with other members of the University established a religious society in order to promote piety. Later the term was applied to all those who took part in the evangelistic movement led by the Wesleys and George Whitefield.

Seceders. A group of Presbyterians who seceded from the Church of Scotland in the middle of the eighteenth century. They formed the Secession Church.

Swedenburghers. Emanuel Swedenborg (1688–1772) was a Swedish scientific and religious writer. In 1788 a body of followers of his mystical religious teaching styled themselves the 'New Jerusalem Church'. William Blake was strongly influenced by the writings of Swedenborg.

Moravians. Members of the 'Unity of Moravian Brethren', a Protestant sect founded in Saxony early in the eighteenth century by emigrants from Moravia, which was part of the Austro-Hungarian Empire. They continued the traditions of the United Brethren, founded in Moravia in the fifteenth century to propagate the doctrines of John Huss.

NOTES 94-95

Muggletonians. Members of a sect founded in England in the middle of the seventeenth century by John Reeve and Lodowicke Muggleton, who claimed to be the two witnesses mentioned in Revelation xi, 3, 6: 'And I will give power unto my two witnesses, and they shall prophesy a thousand two hundred and three score days, clothed in sack cloth . . . .' Members of this sect believed in the personal inspiration of its founders. In external organization it had some resemblance to the Quaker sect. There were four meeting-houses used by Muggletonians in London in 1796.

All these sects mentioned by Macartney were prominent for one reason or another during his own lifetime.

94. The four Emperors referred to were:
(1) Fu-lin, the founder of the Manchu dynasty who ruled under the reign title of Shun-chih from 1644–61.
(2) Hsüan-yeh, reign title K'ang-hsi (1661–1722).
(3) Yin-chen, reign title Yung-cheng (1723–36).
(4) Hung-li, reign title Ch'ien-lung (1736–96).

The Emperor Shun-chih was religiously inclined towards Buddhism, had a violent temper and suffered from ill-health. He can hardly be classed with the other three Emperors. K'ang-hsi defeated the Eleuths and established suzerainty over Tibet by an expedition in 1720. By his military skill he stabilized the position in China's northern and western borders. During Yung-cheng's reign the power of the Emperor over the Manchu princes was consolidated, and in 1729 the Grand Council was established to deal in secret with military strategy, especially the campaigns at that time in the north-west. The great conquests of Ch'ien-lung's reign have already been outlined (Introduction, pp. 25–6).

A few pages further on (p. 238) Macartney remarks 'who is the Atlas destined by him to bear this load of empire when he dies is yet unknown . . .' In fact his successor was Yung-yen, reign title Chia-ch'ing (1796–1820), who came to the throne when Ch'ien-lung abdicated. But he inherited a troubled Empire and was himself without the initiative and ability to effect the necessary remedies. Although he quickly got rid of Ho-shen he failed to weed out corruption at Court, and revolts inside China increased during his reign.

95. It would be interesting to make a comparison between the use of capital punishment in England and China in the last decade of the eighteenth century. In both countries the law laid down the death penalty in a large variety of cases, though often this was a maximum sentence, and was not necessarily imposed. It has been reckoned that by the end of George III's reign (1820) there were some 160 offences which carried the penalty of death by hanging. Certainly at the time of Macartney's embassy the law in England was savage where theft was concerned. For instance, in 1784 Boswell witnessed the execution of fifteen people at Newgate: twelve burglars, two street robbers, and one man for impersonating another in order to get his wages. Among other offences punishable by death at this time were arson, burglary, house-breaking, highway robbery, horse stealing, and stealing from the person more than one shilling. Transportation to the penal settlement at Botany Bay had begun in 1788 and many cases of petty thieving were dealt with by transportation.

In China at the same time the clauses of the criminal law dealing with robbery and theft also provided harsh penalties, though in China considerable use was made of beating with the bamboo. Anything from 50 to 150 strokes might be given. Transportation was paralleled by exile, especially to the newly acquired frontier province of Sinkiang (Turkestan). However, it is dangerous to generalize from the actual clauses of the law since certain classes of people were exempt from capital punishment and the maximum penalty was not necessarily awarded. Whereas in England the death penalty was carried out by hanging, in China there were three forms of capital punishment at this time: strangling, beheading, and slow death by slicing. To say whether the penal system of England was harsher than that of China is a matter of conjecture and opinion; the point is that at this time both systems were savage. For the Chinese system see G. T. Staunton, *Ta Tsing Leu Lee, being the Fundamental Laws, and a Selection of Supplementary Statutes of the Penal Code of China* (T. Cadell, London, 1810). For stealing in general, see pp. 284–5.

96. Macartney is correct in stating that the only Chinese coin in circulation was the copper coin known to foreigners at that time as a 'cash'. These were made of an alloy of copper and lead with a square hole in the middle, and were usually strung together in rolls of 100. However, among foreign merchants in Canton at this time the basic circulating coin was the Spanish dollar with an intrinsic value of 4s. 2d. The Chinese *liang* (tael) was a hypothetical coin of pure silver. However, the same character *liang* was also used to specify a measure of weight. This was the so-called Chinese ounce, which in fact was equal to $1\frac{1}{3}$ oz. avoirdupois. The whole question of Chinese currency and also Chinese weights and measures is a complicated one, and it is often difficult to give suitable modern European equivalents. The picture is further complicated because Europeans trading under the old Canton system used measures with names derived from Indian or Malay words such as catty, mace, candareen, tael and so forth. For a detailed study of the subject, see H. B. Morse, *The Trade and Administration of China*, 3rd edn. (Kelly and Walsh, Shanghai, 1921), pp. 141–94.

Note.—Macartney writes 'takel' throughout the Observations when he is referring to the tael. Since the word 'takel' is not usually found in the documents of the period I have substituted for it the common word tael.

97. Abbé Grosier (1743–1823). *Description Générale de la Chine* (Paris, 1785). This book formed a thirteenth and supplementary volume to Joseph de Mialla's *Histoire Générale de la Chine . . .*, 12 vols. (Paris, 1777–83). The orientalist Abel Rémusat, who reviewed Grosier's book, praised it as a useful résumé of the *Lettres édifiantes*, Du Halde's *Histoire* and the *Mémoires* of the missionaries in China, put into a convenient order and enriched with some useful additions. It was translated into English and published in 1788 under the title *A General Description of China; Containing the Topography of the Fifteen Provinces which compose this vast Empire; that of Tartary, the Isles, and other Tributary Countries . . .*, 2 vols. (G. and J. Robinson, London).

98. Cornelius de Pauw (1739–99). A learned Dutch scholar and cleric who was private reader to Frederick the Great of Prussia. He held controversial and dogmatic opinions which he set forth in a work called *Recherches philosophiques sur les Egyptiens et les Chinois* (1774). Frederick II, writing to Voltaire in 1776 said: 'I leave the Chinese to you and to the Abbé Pauw along with the Indians and the Tartars. The European nations keep my mind sufficiently occupied, so that it has no inclination to desert this most attractive portion of the earth's surface.' (Quoted in A. Reichwein, *China and Europe, Intellectual and Artistic Contacts in the Eighteenth Century* (Kegan Paul, London, 1925), p. 93). Barrow, writing rather sharply about William Scott, the surgeon of the embassy, stated: 'Doctor Scott had been a surgeon in the Navy, had read a great deal and talked much more. He had fortified himself for the present occasion . . . by getting almost by heart the production of Mr. Pauw, a philosopher of Berlin, who compiled a work of considerable ability but in many respects of not much authority.' *An Auto-biographical Memoir of Sir John Barrow, Bart.* (John Murray, London, 1847), p. 48.

Selections from M. Pauw, by Daniel Webb, was published in England in 1795, and in the same year a translation by Captain Thomson of his 'philosophical dissertations' on the Egyptians and Chinese was published.

99. A recent work on the controversial subject of China's population sheds some useful light on the size of the population at the time of Macartney's embassy.

'A continuous rapid growth of population was reflected in the official [census] figures for the years 1779–94, the first years of improved *pao-chia* population registration without noticeable regional omissions.... The population of China, which was presumably in the neighbourhood of 150,000,000 around 1700 or shortly after, probably increased to 275,000,000 in 1779 and 313,000,000 in 1794.'—Ping-ti Ho, *Studies on the Population of China, 1368–1953* (Harvard, 1959), p. 270.

In appendix I Dr. Ho prints the official yearly population figures for the period 1741–1850. For 1793 it was given as 310,497,210. The figures given by Chou may, therefore, be a little high, but not so inaccurate as might be expected. According to Dr. Ho, the official figures were usually underestimated, even after 1776 when the improved system of registration came into effect (pp. 45–6).

100. The Jesuit missionary Jean-François Gerbillon (1654–1707) obtained permission from the Emperor K'ang-hsi to collect geographical information from various parts of China. Finally the Emperor decided to undertake a complete survey of the Empire. This task lasted from 1707 until 1717 and covered China proper together with Manchuria and Mongolia. It was carried out by several Jesuits working in conjunction with several Chinese scholars. This Jesuit Atlas was engraved on 44 copper plates by Matteo Ripa in 1718. It was the best map that had ever been made in Asia. It was reproduced in Paris (1730–4) and at The Hague (1737). See Needham, op. cit., III, pp. 585–6.

101. Macartney's list of buttons agrees pretty closely with the lists of later authorities with the exception that the seventh grade is generally called 'plain gold'. However, the authorities do not always agree on the exact details. A ninth grade of 'figured gilt' was added later in the dynasty.

The grades of official rank, as Macartney states, were also denoted by badges (*p'u tzu*) about twelve inches square, worn on the front and back of the surcoat. For the civil officials these were: 1st grade, White crane; 2nd grade, Golden pheasant; 3rd grade, Peacock; 4th grade, Wild goose; 5th grade, Silver pheasant; 6th grade Egret; 7th grade, Mandarin duck; 8th grade, Quail.

The peacock feather was a distinction given as a reward for outstanding public service or as a mark of Imperial favour. It was not automatically awarded to every official. It was divided into three grades. For information on Ch'ing Dynasty dress, see A. C, Scott, *Chinese Costume in Transition* (Donald Moore, Singapore, 1958), especially pp. 20–4.

102. I have left the titles of the provincial officials in Macartney's own method of romanization since I cannot be certain of the exact identification of these ranks. However, Macartney's list can be compared with the following list of the chief civil officials in a province at this period.

Tsung-tu. Governor-General (Viceroy) of two provinces, except for Chihli, the metropolitan province, which had a Governor-General to itself. At this time the Governor-General of Kwangtung and Kiangsi had his official residence at Shiuhing (Chao-ch'ing) near the West River, and only maintained a 'flying office' at Canton.

Hsun-fu (official designation *Fu-yuan*). Governor of a province, being a colleague rather than a subordinate of the Governor-General. They often memorialized the throne jointly.

Hai-kuan-pu ('Hoppo'). Superintendent of Maritime Customs. The rank varied according to the place and amount of work entailed. Sometimes the position was filled by a Taotai in addition to his other duties. At Canton the post was filled by a great official sent from Peking as Imperial representative.

An-ch'a-shih. Provincial Judicial Commissioner.

Tao-t'ai. Intendant of a circuit. He was placed in administrative control of two or more Prefectures (*Fu*). He also had control over the military forces within his circuit.

N.B. All officials of the above ranks were addressed as *Ta-jen* ('great man', excellency).

Chih-fu. Prefect. He governed the largest of the provincial subdivisions, a *Fu*, of which most provinces had several.
Chih-chou. Magistrate of a Department (*Chou*).
Chih-hsien. Magistrate of a District (*Hsien*).
   Towards the end of his list Macartney's romanization becomes rather obscure. When he writes *quen* he clearly means *kuan* (an official), and I think that by *Tao* he means *Tao-t'ai*, so that his *Tao-quen* is really *Tao-t'ai*. Likewise I think that by *Foo-quen* he intends *Chih-fu*, and by *Kiou-quen* he probably intends *Chih-chou* and by *Sieu-quen* probably *Chih-hsien*. However, I am not certain to which official he is referring when he writes *Siou-jou*, though he may be referring to Commissioners for education (*t'i-tu hsueh-cheng*), who were sent from the capital to each province to make two tours each year in the various Districts of a province and to examine candidates for admission to the District Colleges. The Inspectors-General whom he mentions at the foot of his list may refer to the Censors who toured the provinces as commissioners of enquiry to assist in the examination of officials once every three years, and to supervise the duties and the personal conduct of all provincial officials. (See H. S. Brunnert and V. V. Hagelstrom, *Present Day Political Organization of China*, Shanghai, 1912. Also Hsieh Pao-chao, *The Government of China, 1644–1911*, Baltimore, 1925.)

103. I have left these military titles in Macartney's own spelling although in fact they correspond reasonably closely to the standard list of ranks in the Chinese ('Green Banner') army during the Ch'ing dynasty. The following list shows Macartney's own version of each title, the Wade-Giles romanization of it, followed by the number of the paragraph in which the title (in Chinese) is given in W. F. Mayers, *The Chinese Government*, 2nd edn. (Shanghai, 1886). Lastly I have given an approximate description of the function of each officer rather than an English title such as 'Major' or 'Brigadier' which is merely misleading.

Macartney	Wade-Giles	Mayers paras.	Function
Tou-ton	T'i-tu	440	Commander of the Chinese troops (Green Banner) in a Province.
Zun-ping	Tsung-ping	441	Ditto in a Prefecture.
Foo-zien	Fu-chiang	442	Ditto in a District.
Tchoo-zien	Ts'an-chiang	443	
Giou-zi	Yu-chi	444	Officers, in descending order of seniority, serving under the commander of a District.
Tou-tze	Tu-szu	445	
Sciou-foo	Shou-fu (Shou-pei)	446	
Zien-zun	Ch'ien-tsung	447	
Pa-zun	Pa-tsung	448	

104. The first American ship reached Canton in 1784. The Americans were introduced to the Chinese by the French and were allowed to trade as individual merchants, though the Canton officials always tried to make one American merchant responsible for the good behaviour of all the others. The principal American exports to China at this early period were furs and Turkish opium, but much of their purchases from the Chinese had to be paid for in silver. Gradually American trade expanded and by 1817 American merchants were shipping English goods to Canton in competition with English merchants. (See S. E. Morison, *The Maritime History of Massachusetts*, Houghton, Mifflin Co., Boston, 1921.)

105. The Dutch East India Company was founded in 1602. Throughout the seventeenth century its trade prospered and its trading posts in the Far East multiplied. By 1775 the Dutch were complete masters of Java, and were the only Europeans trading with Japan, where they had a factory in Nagasaki bay. They also had a settlement at Chinsura in Bengal, where they took part in the growing trade in

Patna opium. The Dutch Company was also the controlling power in Ceylon. But for a variety of reasons, one being the self-enrichment of its servants, the Company was already at this time in financial difficulties. The growing power of the British Company in India weakened Dutch trade there, while Dutch participation in the war between England and the American colonists was disastrous for Holland's trading stations and colonies in the East, and her trade was at a standstill. From now onwards Britain challenged Dutch trade even in the Malay archipelago, and the founding of Penang in 1786 stimulated a process already taking place. By now the Dutch Company carried a rapidly mounting deficit in its accounts, with the result that it could no longer raise loans on credit. In 1795, just when it seemed that some measures of reform might be adopted, the forces of Revolutionary France overran Holland and the King fled to England. In 1797 the Dutch Company was finally declared bankrupt and in 1799 the Company was wound up and its possessions were taken over by the State, together with its debts, which then stood at 134 million guilders.

106. William Coxe (1747–1828). Scholar and Fellow of King's College, Cambridge. While acting as tutor to Lord Herbert, later eleventh Earl of Pembroke, during a tour of the continent, he made a short visit to Russia. As a result he wrote *An Account of the Russian Discoveries between Asia and America. To which are added, the Conquest of Siberia, and the History of the Transactions and Commerce between Russia and China* (T. Cadell, London, 1780). He later became Canon of Salisbury and in 1805 Archdeacon of Wiltshire. Although he had given up his Fellowship at King's he never gave up his historical research and it is as Archdeacon Coxe, the historian, that he is best known. His works include *Memoirs of Sir Robert Walpole* (1798), *History of the House of Austria* (1807), and *Memoirs of John, Duke of Marlborough* (1818). As an historian his writings are marked by careful research based on original documents, and as such are still of value to historians. There is a portrait of him by Sir William Beechey in the dining hall of King's College.

107. Catherine the Great was preoccupied during much of her reign with expanding Russia's frontiers at the expense both of Poland and of Turkey. It was left to Alexander I actually to do what Macartney hinted at. Following Russian colonization in Alaska the Russian-American Company had been founded in 1797. In order to find a profitable outlet for the furs of the Russian trading posts both at Sitka in Alaska and at Kamchatka on the Pacific coast of Siberia a Captain Krusenstern had proposed that supplies for these trading posts should be sent by ship from Kronstadt first to the Aleutian islands then to Alaska, then to Kamchatka, and finally that the ship, laden with furs, should call at Canton and trade them for Chinese goods then in demand in Russia. In other words, he proposed a round-the-world expedition in order to supply Russia's new northern Pacific colonies. Eventually an important official, Count Rezanov, was appointed, and was given instructions to go to Japan in order to follow up the visit made there by Lieutenant Laxman in 1793 (see note 75). After completing his embassy to Japan he was to proceed to Canton to conduct commercial negotiations with the Chinese officials there. However, Rezanov died soon after the expedition left Japan. Finally, in December 1805, Captain Krusenstern in the Russian ship *Nadezhda* reached Canton and tried to negotiate. The Governor-General of the two Kwangs at this time, Na-yen-ch'eng, referred the matter to the Emperor. In February 1806 the Imperial reply was received prohibiting the Russians from trading at Canton on the ground that facilities for trade already existed at Kiakhta. (See G. A. Lensen, *The Russian Push toward Japan*, Princeton, 1959, pp. 121–8.)

108. This was No. 21 Hanover Square. It was occupied in 1720 (when the square was first built) by George Carpenter, whose son was created Viscount Tyrconnel in 1761. Lord Tyrconnel's first wife was divorced in 1777, and his second wife 'famed for Disdain of Virtue', appears to have left him in 1791. Lord Fife, writing at that

time said, 'I hear at Court yesterday that Lady Tyrconnel had gone off with Lord Strathmore. This Lord will never keep a wife: he must tie his next to the bed-post.' In 1792 No. 21 Hanover Square was bought by Henry Pelham, Lord Palmerston, the father of the statesman. The house then became well known for its 'social and political assemblies', though I imagine that by this time the name Tyrconnel House was too firmly established to be displaced. Dr. Burney attended the Palmerstons' assemblies there in 1799 and described the house as an 'elegant mansion'.

Lambert in his *History of London* (1806) stated: 'The house in the south-west corner [of Hanover Square] is considered the finest piece of brick-work in the metropolis.' It was pulled down as recently as the 1930s, and the site is now occupied by No. 23 Hanover Square. I am much indebted to Mr. Nicholas Cooper of the National Building Record for kindly giving me this information.

109. This is what Macartney and the other members of his suite thought as a result of the very limited information which they were able to obtain during their six months in China. Being unable to speak or to read Chinese they were in no position to make an accurate assessment of Chinese science. Since they were forced to rely mainly on the evidence of their eyes they misjudged the nature of Chinese scientific ideas and achievements. Their opinions were strongly influenced by the apparent lack of technological skill in China as compared with England at the end of the eighteenth century. They judged everything by the position in 1793. What they did not know was that in medieval times China was ahead of Europe both in scientific theory and in technology. It was only from the time of the Renaissance that Europe outdistanced China. Thus they were particularly unlucky in the date at which they visited China, for it is true that neither Ch'ien-lung nor his great officials showed any interest in scientific ideas and inventions; but this did not mean that the Chinese people had never been interested in science. They had, in fact, achieved much both in theory and practice. For a fuller development of this point see Joseph Needham, with the collaboration of Wang Ling, *Science and Civilization in China* (Cambridge University Press, 1954—), Vol. III, pp. 448 ff. Hereafter abbreviated to *SCC*.

I wish here to state my debt to Dr. Needham for the great help which he has given me in preparing the notes which I have included on all scientific matters from this point onwards.

110. This statement is refuted by the facts given in Needham, *SCC*, Vol. III, passim.

111. Gothic arches were of course unknown in Asia. But the earliest segmental arch bridge in any civilization was Chinese, and its construction is attributed to Li Ch'un, who flourished c. A.D. 610 (See D. G. Mirams, *A Brief History of Chinese Architecture*, Shanghai, Kelly and Walsh, 1940.) It thus preceded the Italian examples such as the Ponte Vecchio in Florence by some seven centuries.

112. James Brindley (1716–72). Apprenticed to a millwright. In 1742 he started to repair old machinery at Leek in Staffordshire, and began to make important improvements in machinery. His name is always linked with that of his great patron, the Duke of Bridgewater. In 1761 Brindley completed a canal to bring coal from the Duke's mines at Worsley to Manchester. His subsequent works included the construction of the Bridgewater Canal from Manchester to Liverpool as well as the Trent and Mersey Canal. Macartney is correct when he implies that Brindley had no formal education, since at the end of his apprenticeship he could neither read nor write. Later he could make notes after a fashion. Though he had no training as an engineer he developed into an engineer of genius.

Richard Arkwright (1732–92). Started his career as a barber at Bolton, in Lancashire, but about 1767 gave up this work and turned all his attention to mechanical inventions. In 1769 he invented a spinning mill, in 1771 erected machinery at Cromford in Derbyshire for the manufacture of ribbed stockings, and in 1775 patented a series of inventions and adaptations for performing on one machine the whole process of yarn manufacture. In 1784 he was in Scotland helping to erect the New Lanark Mills, and in 1790 he introduced Boulton and Watt's steam engine into his own mill at Nottingham. He was knighted in 1786.

113. There seems to be no evidence for such a policy in Chinese history. J. Needham and his collaborators have not come across any instance of the discouragement of an invention for fear of causing unemployment. Cf. Needham's contribution to the Oxford Symposium, *The Structure of Scientific Change* (1961) entitled 'Poverties and Triumphs of the Chinese Scientific Tradition'.

114. The Grand Canal (Yun-ho) is the longest artificial waterway in the world. It starts near Hangchow and ends at Tungchow near Peking. The first Grand Canal was built in the Sui dynasty (581–617), but the complete canal as it exists today was constructed during the Yuan (Mongol) dynasty, and was begun during the reign of the Emperor Kublai. It was a great feat of engineering which posed many difficult problems, especially in the section between the Yangtze and the Yellow River. Here, the land to the west of the canal is somewhat higher than the land to the east. Also to the west lie several large lakes which supply most of the water for this section of the canal and the regulating of the flow of water in this part was a difficult engineering problem. Furthermore, to the east lies the low and fertile plain of the River Huai, which had to be protected by a system of dykes.

The original reason for constructing such a long and costly canal was strategic—in order to carry the imperial grain junks from central China to the capital. When Kublai made Peking his capital he had to feed the large staff of officials and the garrison of soldiers settled there, and since rice does not grow in northern China almost all the food needed for Peking had to be brought from the south. Traffic on the canal, however, was not confined to imperial grain junks and it was extensively used for private trade and travel. So important was the canal that each succeeding dynasty had to spend a great deal of money and labour on its maintenance. (See Needham, op. cit., Vol. IV, Sect. 28(f). Also Harold C. Hinton, *The Grain Tribute System of China, 1845–1911*, Harvard University Press, 1956.)

115. Block printing began in ninth-century China and movable type was invented by Pi Sheng about A.D. 1060. Kublai opened a government printing press in Cambaluc (Peking) in 1236. The rulers of Korea, at least fifty years before Gutenberg, had books printed from type made of bronze, which was now, for the first time, cast from moulds.

The latest information is given in T. F. Carter, *The Invention of Printing in China, and its spread Westward*, 2nd edn., revised by L. Carrington Goodrich (New York, Ronald Press, 1955).

116. See Needham, *SCC*, Vol. IV, Pt. 2, Sect. 27, under '*fan che*', noria, etc.

117. See Needham, *SCC*, Vol. IV, Pt. 2, Sect. 29.

118. This is not true. There were abundant charts of the coast of China. (See Needham, *SCC*, Vol. III, Sect. 22.)

119. The Chinese certainly used armillary spheres, and probably quadrants. (See Needham, *SCC*, Vol. III, Sect. 20.) The evidence concerning the cross-staff ('Jacob's Staff') presented in Needham, Vol. III, p. 574, suggests that it originated in China in or before the eleventh century A.D., i.e. three centuries or so earlier than its first mention in Europe, and well prior to its use in the fifteenth century by the Arab, Indian and Chinese navigators of the China seas and Indian Ocean for taking star altitudes.

120. The magnetic compass was fully described in China about two centuries before its first mention in Europe. It had a background history of gradual development from the Han time onwards. (See Needham, *SCC*, Vol. IV, Pt. I, Sect. 26, and Li Shu-hua, 'Origine de la Boussole', *Isis*, Vol. 45, Pt. 1, 1954, pp. 78–94. For the

development of the compass in the West see E. G. R. Taylor, *The Haven-finding art, a history of navigation from Odysseus to Captain Cook*, Hollis and Carter, 1956. For an illustration of a Chinese compass at the time of the embassy, see Sir G. L. Staunton, *An Authentic Account...*, op. cit., Vol. I, p. 443.)

121. But not all nations had agreed. From ancient times China used $365\frac{1}{4}$ degrees. Below this the degree was divided decimally: a very sensible arrangement. The sexagesimal division was imposed by the influence of the seventeenth-century Jesuit Mission. (See Needham, *SCC*, Vol. III, pp. 82, 186, 374.)

122. Sir William Jones (1746–94). An oriental scholar with the reputation for a prodigious memory. Called to the Bar in 1774 he came out to India in 1783 to be a judge of the Supreme Court at Calcutta. Already by that time he had a good knowledge of Arabic and Persian. He now started to learn Sanskrit. In 1784 he was a founder of the Asiatic Society of Bengal, started for the purpose of 'enquiry into the history and antiquities, arts, sciences and literature of Asia'. He wrote good French and was able to translate from Italian, Greek, Latin, Arabic, Persian, Turkish and Sanskrit. He once classified the languages he had studied into three groups: (1) Eight languages which he had 'studied critically'. (2) Eight which he had studied less perfectly but were intelligible to him with the use of a dictionary. Hebrew was included in this group. (3) Twelve languages which he had started to study. This group included Welsh, Tibetan and Chinese. His interest in the Chinese language had started in England in 1767 when he copied out 'the keys of the Chinese language' (the radicals). In the 1770s there were two Chinese in London whom he met, and while in India he corresponded with one of them, Wang A-tong, then in Canton. In 1790 he delivered the seventh anniversary lecture to the Asiatic Society of Bengal on the subject of China, and this address shows how muddled his knowledge of China was. But this was inevitable, derived as it was at second or third hand from unreliable sources. Shortly before his premature death in 1794 he was proposing to make a voyage to Canton in order to study Chinese at first hand. It seems from all this that Macartney's claim, that Sir William Jones could have mastered Chinese if he could have applied himself solely to it, was well founded. (See A. J. Arberry, *Asiatic Jones. The Life and Influence of Sir William Jones*, London, 1946. Also Fan Tsen-chung, 'Sir William Jones' Chinese Studies', *The Review of English Studies*, Vol. XXII, 1946, pp. 304–14.)

123. Compare Macartney's attitude as he voyaged towards China reading and making notes from 'all the books that had been written upon that country in all the languages I could understand' with the attitude of Lord Macaulay on his outward voyage to India in 1834. Macaulay had been appointed a member of the Supreme Council of India and recorded for posterity how he spent his time on board ship. 'During the whole voyage I read with keen and increasing enjoyment. I devoured Greek, Latin, Spanish, Italian, French and English; folios, quartos, octavos, and duodecimos.' (Quoted by Sir George Otto Trevelyan in *The Life and Works of Lord Macaulay*, vol. ix, p. 365.) Not a word here about India, her history, literature or civilization. No wonder that Macaulay's famous Minute on Education which he wrote shortly after his arrival in Calcutta, contained the fantastic claim that 'I have never found one among the orientalists who could deny that a single shelf of a good European library was worth the whole native literature of India and Arabia.' Yet only fifty years before this, Sir William Jones was studying Sanskrit and translating from Persian and Arabic and Sanskrit into English. The reasons for this change in attitude are clearly explained in Eric Stokes, *The English Utilitarians and India* (Oxford University Press, 1959), Chapter I.

124. Gillan was not in a position to judge it properly. It may have appeared so to him in 1793 from his personal observations and from the very limited information available to him through the Chinese interpreter, speaking to him in Italian or Latin. However, he does not appear to have been in touch with educated physicians but

to have obtained his knowledge at second or third hand from low-grade people (see note 141). Had Gillan been able to study a translation of the *I-tsung Chin-chien* ('Golden Mirror of Medicine', 1740) he would have been reasonably well informed on the knowledge of medicine in China at the time of the embassy. For a wider view of the subject, see Wang Chi-min, 'Status of the Medical Profession in China', *Chinese Medical Journal*, Vol. 38 (1924), p. 674. Also numerous articles by Li T'ao contributed to the *Chinese Medical Journal* between 1934 and 1958.

125. While it is quite true that there were never any medical schools in the post-Renaissance sense of the West, nevertheless there was organized medical training in China, and medicine formed part of the examination system at various times, for example as a result of the reforms of Wang An-shih during the Sung dynasty (eleventh century). A medical academy existed near Hangchow in Sung times with four professors and over two hundred students. (See Li T'ao, 'Achievements of Chinese Medicine in the Northern Sung Dynasty', *Chinese Medical Journal*, Vol. 72, 1954, p. 65, and on the achievements under the Southern Sung, in the same Journal, Vol. 72, p. 225.)

126. It is true that dissection was rarely practised in China. But from the Han to the Sung dynasty Chinese knowledge of anatomy almost kept pace with European knowledge of the subject. It was only after the Renaissance that the gap became wide. (See E. T. Hsieh, 'Review of Ancient Chinese Anatomy', *Anatomical Record*, Vol. 20, 1921, p. 123. Also E. V. Cowdry, 'Ancient Chinese Anatomical Charts and the *funfbilder seri*', *Anatomical Record*, Vol. 22, 1921, p. 1.)

127. Gillan clearly knew nothing of the tradition of systematic pathology in China, the greatest repository of which is the *Ch'ao Shih Ping Yuan* by Ch'ao Yuan-fang, who lived about A.D. 610. This Chinese tradition had affinities with the ideas of Sydenham and the system of exhaustive classification of disease syndromes in vogue in seventeenth-century Europe.

128. This is a staggering statement. One wonders what Gillan meant by the qualification 'as sciences'. Even a slight acquaintance with the *Pen T'sao* books, an enormous series of works devoted to Chinese materia medica, written from the second century B.C. through to the eighteenth century A.D., would have prevented Gillan from making such wild pronouncements. (See E. Bretschneider. *On the Study and Value of Chinese Botanical Works*, Foochow, 1870. Also E. D. Merrill and E. H. Walker, *Bibliography of Eastern Asiatic Botany*, Arnold Arboretum, Harvard University, 1938.)

129. This is not only not correct, it is rather the inverse of the truth. Chinese medicine was never herbal only, but from earliest times included many mineral drugs, and still does today.

130. What work was referred to here we shall probably never know, but perhaps there was some confusion between the pharmaceutical and the agricultural literature, equally voluminous. Apart from the specialist books, the great Ch'ing dynasty encyclopedia of 1725, the *T'u-shu Chi-ch'eng*, is full of information on medicinal herbs. This vast encyclopedia is in fact a florilegium containing passages taken from many thousands of books.

131. In fact it was divided into thirteen highly specialized branches.

132. The pulse was only one of four means of diagnosis employed by Chinese physicians. The treatise on the pulse here referred to was one of the versions of the *Mo Ching*, the first of which was written in the tenth century A.D. Du Halde translated it rather literally without understanding the medical ideas which it contains, and hence his version does not always make sense. It was included in his famous book *Description géographique, historique, chronologique, politique et physique de l'empire de la Chine et de la Tartarie Chinoise*. First published in 1735, this book was soon available in English. It was widely read in eighteenth-century Europe and was the main source of information on China until the end of the century.

133. It should be remembered that Ho-shen was a Manchu and that if he consulted Manchu physicians at Jehol the medical practice there was of a rudimentary kind. It is unlikely that Chinese physicians would have used acupuncture on such a swelling. In this connection it is ironical that at the very time Gillan was examining Ho-shen's hernia in Manchuria, in London the historian Edward Gibbon was suffering from a huge hernial protrusion of long standing which was shortly to cause his death early in 1794. 'Under the mistaken belief that the swelling was due to a hydrocele, it had been punctured on three occasions at short intervals. The third time proved fatal. Inevitably infection was conveyed to the peritoneum and Gibbon died on January 16th.' H. C. Cameron, *Sir Joseph Banks* (London, Batchworth Press, 1952), p. 173.

In the event Ho-shen was luckier than Gibbon.

134. The earliest known use of a model for medical teaching comes from China, where figures of the human body were used from Sung times onwards, with places marked on them to show where the needles should be inserted. Pictures of such models can be seen in George Soulié de Mourant, *L'acuponcture Chinoise* (Jacques Lafitte, Paris, 1957). The value of acupuncture is still very much under debate and efforts are being made in China today to study its rationale. It is still widely used. (See T. Nakayama, *Acupuncture et Medicine Chinoises Vérifiées au Japon.* Trans. from the Japanese by G. Soulié de Mourant, Paris, 1934.)

135. Here Gillan was confusing medical practice with the work of barbers and masseurs. But apart from that, the better products of Chinese scissor-makers have always been excellent and are still coveted today.

136. Since there was no value in bleeding anyway, Chinese physicians cannot be blamed for not adopting the practice.

137. This, again, is the opposite of the truth, for ancient and medieval Chinese prescriptions have been criticized as too complex. Synergic action of the many plant drugs in the Chinese pharmacopoeias was recognized from the Han onwards. Gillan could have seen these plant drugs in the shops, though his lack of the language would have made it impossible for him to understand what he was being shown. Moreover, to accuse the Chinese of 'their ignorance in general of chemical compositions' was a travesty of the facts; one has only to think of the metallurgical and ceramics industries, the lacquer and mirror makers, or the very elaborate pickling and fermentation techniques.

138. This elementary hygienic precaution was still a century away from justification in the minds of Europeans. Moreover, the writer does not seem to have known that it was a common practice to use alum in the water in order to precipitate the salts and various impurities.

139. For some information about foundling hospitals, medical dispensaries, etc., in the first half of the nineteenth century, see W. C. Milne, *Life in China* (Routledge, London, 1857; new edn., 1861), pp. 40–60. Such institutions were mostly the result of Buddhist influence.

140. But so did physicians in eighteenth-century Europe. The whole history of venereal disease, both in the East and the West, is still very much under discussion. It is important here to distinguish between syphilis and gonorrhoea. Gonorrhoea was recognized in the ancient world, and the Chinese certainly knew and described it. Chancres were mentioned in China as early as the seventh century A.D. The origins of syphilis in the West are still under dispute, but it does not appear to have been known in China until it was brought into the country from abroad sometime in the Ming dynasty. Wang and Chou may have had gonorrhoea, but it is difficult to be certain, since knowledge of this disease at that time even in Europe was muddled. (See Chimin Wong and Wu Lien-teh, *History of Chinese Medicine*, Shanghai, 1936.) For a general summary of recent ideas on the subject, see C. C. Mettler, *History of Medicine* (Blakiston, Phil., 1947), pp. 601 ff.

141. I asked two Chinese professors of medicine about these terms. They confirmed that no educated person would ever refer to the disease in these words, which are crude in the extreme. This rather bears out my argument that Gillan obtained his meagre information on Chinese medicine at secondhand from men who were not sufficiently educated to be able to give him accurate information.

142. The root of the peony (Chinese: *mu-tan*) is used by the Chinese as a drug. *Pung-fu-lin* is the name of a prescription, but is here used as a synonym for *mu-tan*. As a drug it is used for treating stomach aches, dysentery, etc., and also for diseases of the ovaries.

143. It is important to distinguish between variolation (the introduction of variolus material from one human being into another) and vaccination. The modern view of the subject is that variolation was a process which originated in China and spread westwards via Russia and Turkey. One of the people concerned in this transmission from Asia to western Europe was Lady Mary Wortley Montagu. She noticed the practice of variolation against smallpox while in Turkey, and described it in a letter from Adrianople written in April 1717. (See R. Halsband, 'New Light on Lady Mary Wortley Montagu and Inoculation', *Journal of the History of Medicine*, Vol. VIII, 1953, p. 390.)

There is some evidence to suggest that variolation first started in China during the late Sung period; certainly by the late Ming (end of the sixteenth century) its practice was prevalent. It was first used in Europe in the early eighteenth century. Lady Mary Wortley Montagu had her small son inoculated on her return from Turkey. There is a good description of how the process was carried out in England at that time by William Hickey who, as a boy, was inoculated in 1756. (See *Memoirs of William Hickey*, ed. Peter Quennell, Hutchinson, London, 1960, p. 23.)

The difficulty of variolation was that the patient ran the risk of smallpox itself, and even an epidemic might be started. Since Edward Jenner was familiar with variolation it occurred to him that inoculation with cowpox, a related form of the disease always mild in man, might give protection against it. Thus in 1796 he successfully inoculated a boy with cowpox and subsequently with smallpox. The boy had the former but not the latter. In 1798 Jenner published an account of his experiments with cowpox. In 1805 Alexander Pearson, a surgeon in the service of the East India Company in Canton, wrote a pamphlet on Jenner's smallpox vaccine which was translated into Chinese by Sir G. T. Staunton with the help of a Chinese physician. Copies of this pamphlet were sent to the great officials at Canton and also distributed free of charge among the people. In 1817, a Chinese physician, Chiu Hao-chuan, published a book on the history and practice of Jenner's vaccination. Finally the famous scholar and administrator Juan Yuan, who was Governor-General of the two Kwangs between 1817 and 1826, wrote a pamphlet commenting on the success of vaccination, which gave it the seal of official approval. The wheel had thus come full circle, and a process which originated in China was reintroduced into that country centuries later in an improved modern form. (See Hou Pao-chang, 'Notes on the History of Smallpox in China', *The Elixir*, Hong Kong University Medical Society Magazine, 1951, pp. 75–9. Also Chimin Wong and Wu Lien-teh, *History of Chinese Medicine*, Shanghai, 1936, pp. 215–16, 273–81.)

144. The Muslim physician al-Razi (860–925) wrote a treatise 'On Smallpox and Measles' which gave what is generally considered the first clear differentiation of the symptoms and treatment of these diseases. However, current research in Chinese medical history shows that he may have been preceded. Even by the end of the eighteenth century physicians in Europe did not properly understand the nature of measles, since the role of viruses in the causation of disease had not yet been discovered.

145. Here Gillan makes no distinction between modern and medieval science. In general Chinese science and technology was considerably more advanced than in

Europe until the fifteenth century. After that time, however, Renaissance Europe began to take the lead. The fact that this break-through from medieval to modern science took place only in Europe does not mean that China had not already achieved outstanding advances in the field of science and technology before the Renaissance. What Gillan is emphasizing is really the modern meaning of the word 'science'. He simply implies that eighteenth-century China was not so scientifically minded and technically advanced as eighteenth-century Europe, which was true. But this is a short-term view. Gillan visited China at the worst possible time for the study of her medicine and science. For information on Chinese chemistry see Li Ch'iao-p'ing, *The Chemical Arts of Old China* (Journal of Chemical Education, Pennsylvania, 1948). Also J. Needham, *SCC*, Vol. V.

146. This statement is absurd if considered in the light of China's whole previous history. There was a continual development of technique. Gillan was clearly surprised to find that the Chinese, having developed their science and technology to a certain point, had failed to keep up with Europe. But his attempt to explain the reason for this was far too simple.

147. See, however, *T'ien Kung K'ai Wu*, an encyclopedia of technology and industrial processes compiled by Sung Ying-hsing and printed in 1637.

148. This is a traditional idea with a long history and is connected with attempts to make gold by alchemy. See O. S. Johnson, *A Study of Chinese Alchemy* (Commercial Press, Shanghai, 1928), p. 71, where he discusses life-prolonging medicines and the special efficacy of artificially made gold. For the art of making gold see Masumi Chikashige, *Alchemy and other Chemical Achievements of the Ancient Orient* (Rokakuho Uchida, Tokyo, 1936). Also J. Needham, *SCC*, Vol. V, Sect. 33.

149. In eighteenth-century Europe the word was written 'paktong', and this was the name of an alloy of copper, zinc and nickel which was exported from China. It was a kind of pewter. As a metal it is still in widespread use for hotel cutlery, though it is now known as electro-plate nickel-silver, or German silver. Under the heading of copper Gillan also mentions tutenag and then gives, from the technical point of view, a good description of how the Chinese extracted zinc from calamine. For both paktong and tutenag, see A. Bonnin, *Tutenag and Paktong* (Oxford, 1924), and Needham, *SCC*, Vol. V, Sect. 36.

150. On this subject see J. Needham, *The Development of Iron and Steel Technology in China* (Newcomen Society, London, 1958).

151. The use of coal for industrial purposes in China long antedates its use in Europe. (See T. T. Read, 'The Earliest Industrial Use of Coal', *Transactions of the Newcomen Society*, Vol. XX, 1939, pp. 119 ff.)

152. Whitehaven on the coast of Cumberland was virtually the creation of Sir John Lowther of Whitehaven towards the end of the seventeenth century. Here he opened up new coal mines and improved the harbour in order to supply the profitable Dublin coal trade. Macartney probably visited Whiteheaven in 1768 when he was elected M.P. for nearby Cockermouth, a safe seat under the control of Macartney's brother-in-law Sir James Lowther. At one election Sir James threatened that unless his instructions were carried out, the coal business, Whitehaven's main source of prosperity, would immediately be suspended. (See Brian Bonsall, *Sir James Lowther and Cumberland and Westmorland Elections, 1754–75*, Manchester University Press, 1960.)

153. The English East India Company started to import Chinese porcelain in small quantities at the beginning of the eighteenth century. The amount increased steadily, the heyday of the trade being from about 1740 until 1785, with peak sales round about 1760–75. Finally in 1791 the Company decided that it was no longer worth its while to import porcelain from China. There was now less demand for it in England since the expanding production of good European ware could supply cheaply and well the need for artistic porcelain. Josiah Wedgwood's *First Pattern*

Book had already been published. However, a fair amount of porcelain was still dispatched from Canton to America during the first half of the nineteenth century. For an excellent survey of this whole subject, beautifully illustrated, see John Goldsmith Phillips, *China-Trade Porcelain* (Harvard University Press, 1956).

154. An account of glass technology and the manufacture of spectacles in China is given in Needham, *SCC*, Vol. IV, Pt. 1, Sect. 26.

155. Not all were on the coast. Lake salt was produced mostly in Kansu and Shansi, from wells constructed around the salt lakes. There was a brine field in Szechwan centred on Tzu-liu-ching. Here the brine was obtained from bore-holes which had been drilled as much as two thousand feet. (See Li Ch'iao-p'ing, *The Chemical Arts of Old China*, Journal of Chemical Education, Easton, Penn., 1948, pp. 55–65, which contains some good illustrations.) In Kwangtung there were considerable salt fields near the coast, one being where present-day Kowloon stands. The method of evaporation used is described in Ch'ü Ta-chün, *Kuang-tung Hsin-yü* (edn. of 1700), *chüan* 7, pp. 12–14. A partial translation of this is given by Peter Y. L. Ng in *The 1819 Edition of the Hsin-An Hsien-chih: A Critical Examination with Translation and Notes. Hong Kong, Kowloon and the New Territories (1644–1842)*. (Unpublished Master's Thesis, University of Hong Kong, 1961), pp. 111–14.

156. Patently untrue; see *A Compendium of Minerals and Stones used in Chinese Medicine from the Pen-ts'ao kang mu, A.D.1596*, compiled by B. E. Read and C. Pak (2nd edn. Peking, 1936).

157. Fatty acid soaps were not used in traditional China, but there was a large production of detergents from plants which Gillan noted. (See J. Needham and Lu Gwei-Djen, 'Hygiene and Preventive Medicine in Ancient China', *Medical History* 1961, abridged in *Health Education Journal*, Sept. 1959.)

158. Gunpowder was used in warfare in China from the tenth century onwards. The oldest formula for the mixture of gunpowder in any civilization was written down in A.D. 1044 (See Li Ch'iao-p'ing, *The Chemical Arts of Old China*, pp. 113–18. For the invention and use of gunpowder in general see J. R. Partington, *A History of Greek Fire and Gunpowder*, Heffer, Cambridge, 1960, pp. 237–97.)

159. Highly doubtful, though it may possibly have been true at the time of the Macartney embassy only. Details have survived of arsenals in China from most dynasties.

160. By 'tcha-wha' Gillan is referring to the *ch'a-hua* ('tea-flower') which is the *Camellia japonica*, L, and is closely related to the tea plant. The species of *Camellia* from which the oil is obtained is the *sasanqua*. (See B. E. Read, *Chinese Medicinal Plants from the Pen-ts'ao kang mu, A.D. 1596*, Peking Natural History Bulletin, 1936, no. 226. Also *Plantae Wilsonianae* (Plants collected in western China for the Arnold Arboretum by E. H. Wilson), ed. C. S. Sargent, Harvard University Press, 3 vols. 1913–17, Vol. II, pp. 391–4.)

161. Gillan's remarks leave the reader little wiser on the subject. By son-tchou he may have meant *san-shao* ('thrice fired') but more probably *shao-chiu* ('burnt wine'). The usual spelling adopted in western writings of this period was samsu or samshu.

There were many kinds of liquors made in China, each province having its own speciality. The Chinese had plenty of fermented wines, i.e. rice wine, and the *Pen-ts'ao kang mu* lists sixty-four kinds of wine. They also distilled a spirit from *kao-liang* (*Sorghum vulgare*), but according to the *Pen-ts'ao kang mu* this was a foreign process introduced during the Yuan dynasty. This distilled spirit is usually known as *shao-chiu*, which is probably what Gillan had in mind. It is somewhat like the *arrack* of the Arabs. For a description of wine-making see Li Ch'iao-p'ing, *The Chemical Arts of Old China*, pp. 184–210.

INDEX

1 徵瑞
2 梁肯堂
3 長麟
4 王文雄
5 喬人傑
6 如意
7 貢收
8 送禮
9 掌故叢編
10 國朝耆獻類徵
11 通州志,卷六,官師志
12 天津府志,卷十二,職官志;卷四十,宦績傳
13 續天津縣志,卷九,職官志;卷十一,名宦傳

INDEX

Notes

(1) The numbers 1–13 shown beside entries in the Index refer to the Chinese characters printed on the page opposite.

(2) The words printed in square brackets after entries represent Macartney's own versions of proper names, titles, etc.

(3) References to my own notes have been given in the form n24, etc., whereas the footnotes are indicated by 24n, etc. The notes are printed between pages 355 and 398, and at the top of each page, for easy reference, the numbers are given of the notes printed on that particular page.

(4) No attempt has been made to include all the place names mentioned by Macartney in his Journal, nor have references been given for all the provinces which he mentions by name.

Acupuncture, 281, 283, n134
Adeodato [Deodati], Fr. Peter, missionary, 54n, 93, n1, n9
Administration, of provinces. *See* Provincial administration
Agoti, Spanish agent at Macao, 32, 63, 64
A-kuei [A-cou-i, A-Chong-tong], Grand Councillor, 101, 102, n19, n20
Alaska [Onalaska], 211, n83, n107
Albazin, fort on frontier between Manchuria and Siberia, 211, n83
Alchemy, in China, n148
Alexander, William, artist, 54; painting of Ch'ien-lung, 26; sketch of temple of Pusa, 39; brief biography of, 314–16; drawing of Wang, 314; drawing of Ch'ien-lung, 316; Barrow on, 316; MS. Journal of, 342; did not go to Jehol, 342
Algebra, in China, 266, n110
Alkalis, Chinese; fossil and vegetable, 300
d'Almeida [Bernardo Almeyda], Fr. Joseph-Bernard, missionary, 89, 93, 94, n9
American(s), in China; called 'second chop Englishmen', 208; trade at Canton, 215, 261–3, n104

Amherst, William Pitt, Earl Amherst; embassy to Peking, 308, n40
Amiot [Amyot, Amyott], Fr. Jean-Joseph-Marie, missionary, n92; on reasons for failure of embassy, 32; on embassies to China, 34, 151; letter to Macartney, 100, 334; admirer of Chinese, 245; his works, n15
Amoy (Emoy, Emoi), 5; junk trade to Tientsin from, 81; port for Luichiu envoys, 182
Amputation, not practised in China, 190. *See also* Castration
Amur (Amour), river between Manchuria and Siberia, 4, 211, n83
Anatomy, in China, 283, n126
Anderson, Aeneas, valet to Macartney, 24; on Jacobus Li, 320; his *Narrative* of the embassy, 343; Barrow's opinion of, 343
Annam, 5, 25, n79. *See also* Cochin China
Antonio, Padre, Portuguese missionary, 265
Anunchoi (Anunghoi), fort at Bocca Tigris, 218, n85
Architecture, Chinese, style of, 75, 272, n111. *See also* Jehol, Yuanming Yuan

2D 401

INDEX

Arkwright, Sir Richard, 267, n112
Arms, in China, 70; weapons of Manchus, 130; of soldiers, 174, 254; permission to import, 257, n25
Artificial respiration, 190, n63
Astley, Philip, circus master, 139, 238, n45
Astronomy, Chinese, nature of, 264-5
Astronomy, Imperial Board of [College of Mathematics], called by Pfister and others 'Board of Mathematics', 93, n9, n21
Attiret, Fr. Jean-Denis, missionary, 26, 133, n11

Balloon(s), air, 54, 191, 310, n63; mania in Europe over, n64
Balzas, rafts of wood, 189
Bamboo, used for: sails, 81; carrying loads, 88, 270; punishment, 113, 227, n95; water-wheels, 192, 272-4; making paper, 303
Banka [Banca], island off Sumatra, 16; tin from, 25n, 296
Band, Macartney's German. *See* Musicians
Banks, Sir Joseph; President of the Royal Society, 56; plants from China for, 318; his instructions for cultivating tea plants, 318, n57; dispersal of his MSS., 334; and a sculptor at Canton, 343; and Botany Bay, n73; at Tahiti, n89
Bankshalls, at Whampoa, 208, n78
Banners, the eight Manchu, 130, 196, 253, n67
Baring, Francis, Chairman of Court of Directors, E.I.C., 310, 318
Barrow, John, XI, 66, 145, 206; description of temple of Pusa by, 39, 41; account of the embassy by, 43, 344; at Yuan-Ming Yuan, 97, 99; brief biography of, 308-9; on Scott, 311, n98; on Parish, 314; on Hickey, 315; on Alexander, 316; on Li, 319; on Wang, 326-7; his *Life* of Macartney, 333-4, 345; not at Jehol, 342; on Anderson, 343; his *Voyage to Cochin China*, 344; his

Autobiographical Memoir, 345; librarian to Sir G. L. Staunton, 351; description of a long bridge by, n53; on Chinese manure, n59
Batavia, 139, 205; Macartney's stay at, 38, 61, 333; Chinese sailing to, 274
Beckford, William, 39, 41, n69
Bellona, Botany Bay ship, 205, 206, n73
Bengal, 20, 21, 51; British possessions in, 86, 87; tea plants sent to, 186; imports to Canton from, 260
Benoist, Fr. Michel, missionary, 26
Benson, Lt-Col. George, 24, 66, 115, 218
Blindness, in China; curing of, 190; many suffer from, 285, n63
Blood, circulation of, 282
Board(s) (Ministries), at Peking; six in charge of administration, 28, n32; Manchus 'managers' of, 237-8; of Rites, n32; of Revenue, n32; Chinese title for, n49
Bocca Tigris, 211, n82; forts at, 218; Parish's report on, 313; location of, n85
Bogdoi Khans, 130, n39
Bombay; Marine service, 68; imports to Canton from, 260, 263
Boswell, James; and Macartney, 19; his *Life* of Johnson annotated by Macartney, 19, 42
Botanist(s); with Macartney's embassy, 24, 317-18. *See also* Haxton, Stronach
Botany Bay; naming of, 56; ships, n73; penal settlement at, n95
Bound feet, 74, 192; Chou on the custom of, 228; erotic appeal of, 229
Braam, Houckgeest, A. E. van, Dutch envoy to Peking, 34, 312, n17, n27, n33
Bribery, in China; presents given in law suits, 240, 241; presents given to Ho-Shen, 322, 323-4
Bridge(s), in China; of boats at Tientsin, 86; of white marble, 92; on caissons, 108; of three arches, 175; of 100 arches, 175, n53; on stone piers, 194; construction of, 267, n111

402

INDEX

Brindley, James, 267, n112
Brown, Lancelot, 'Capability', 126, n35, n36, n37, n41, n42
Browne, Henry, senior E.I.C. Commissioner at Canton, 178, 202, 206, 217; sells a telescope, 69, n3; and the *Hindostan*'s dues, 261
Buddhism. See Fo-hi
Bunbury, Henry William, artist; Chinese at Canton copy from, 343
Burke, Edmund; a friend of Macartney, 17, 41, 307
Burke, William, 17
Burma [Tatze or Pegu], 3, 25; envoys at Jehol from, 124, n34
Burney, Dr. Charles, n108; and Macartney's band, n22
Bute, John Stuart, 3rd Earl of; Macartney married his daughter, 18, n42; letter from Dr. Johnson to, 19; and Luton Hoo, n35
Buttons, worn on a Chinese official's hat as sign of rank; sold at Canton, 207; eight grades of, 252, n101; imported from Venice, 299

Calcutta; possible communication to Peking from, via Tibet, 16; Macartney at, 21; botanic garden at, 311, n57; Fort William College at, 311
Camoens [Camões, Luiz de], 219; gardens, in Macao, n86
Campbell, 1st Lieut. of H.M.S. *Lion*, 24, 67, 68, 218
Camphor, in China, 302; preparation of, 298
Canals, Chinese; sluices of, 269. See also Grand Canal
Cannon, taken to China by Macartney, six light brass, 36, 90; field-pieces and howitzers, 84, n27
Canton, 5, 28, 29, 35, 193, n143; conditions of foreign merchants at, 7 ff., system of trade at, 12–13; junk trade with Tientsin, 81; duties levied at, 150, 162–3, 250–1; prejudice against foreigners at, 181; route from Peking to, 183; Ch'ang-lin suspects corruption at, 190; Macartney arrives at, 203; Governor of, 205; description of, 208–10; attitude of British at, 210; need for a permanent minister at, 214; American trade at, 215, 261–3, n104; the only port for European trade, 256; imports from Bombay and Bengal to, 260; extortions at, 261; venereal disease prevalent at, 287; Chinese craftsmen at, 291, 295, 299; use of tin at, 296; sing-songs sold at, 312, n1; courier service to Peking, n52; location of foreign factories at, n70; James Flint at, n84; Russians at, n107
Castiglione, Fr. Giuseppe, missionary and artist, 26
Castration, 228, 284
Cathcart, Lt.-Col. Charles Allen; mission to China of, 16, 17, 309, 314
Catherine the Great, Empress of Russia; Macartney as envoy to, 17; her manner of obtaining the throne, 179, n55; her ambitions in the East, 211, n83; and trade to Canton, 262, n107
Chambers, Sir William, 10, 133, n41
Chang-ku ts'ung-pien[9]; Chinese documents of Macartney's embassy printed in, 6, 24, 28; Ch'ien-lung's edict to George III in, 336
Ch'ang-lin[3] [Chan-ta-gin], 31, 172, 174, 203, 228; appointed Viceroy of Canton, 168; first meeting with Macartney, 176; on difficulties of trade at Chusan, 177; conversations with Macartney, 180–1, 184, 190; Macartney's good opinion of, 185; sends for kaolin, 187; explains an edict from Emperor, 193; writes to Emperor about the embassy, 195; argues with the Hoppo, 205; issues two proclamations at Canton, 31, 29; takes leave of Macartney, 215–216; his connection with the Imperial family, 217, n51; has gonorrhoea, 288; Court Letter to him about Macartney, n56
Chao-chou-fou, 195, 196; Governor of, 205, 216, n74

403

INDEX

Charcoal, in China; uses of, 197, 301

Carriage(s) (*also* chariot, coach); English design of, 45, 85, 116, 145, n27; Chinese design of, 91, 145, 225. *See also* Post-chaise

Charts, of Chinese coast, 275, n118

Chemistry, in China; Dr. Gillan's remarks on, 291

Cheng-jui[1] (Chin-ta-gin, the Legate, the Tartar), 121, 142, 146, 163; Court Letter to, 29; instructions to, 32, 33; meets embassy at Tientsin, 78; explains the kotow, 84, 119; prejudiced against embassy, 85, 144; Wang and Chou's opinion of, 86; his action over Macartney's letter to Gower, 110, n29; degraded by Emperor, 118; religious beliefs of, 232; brief biography of, 322–5

Chia-ch'ing, Emperor (1796–1820); his hatred of Ho-shen, 322; admonished Cheng-jui, 323–5; troubles in his reign, n94

Ch'iao Jen-chieh[5], 328–31

Chi-chin-qua, Hong merchant, promised to try out new articles of trade, 207, n76

Ch'ien-lung [Kien-lung, Tchien-lung] *See* Emperor

Chihli [Pe-che-li, Pecheli], gulf of, 68, 76, 193, 211; advantages of sailing to, 35, 193; shallowness of, 65; weather in, 67; tides in, 70; bar of, 73

Chihli, province of; Viceroy of, 74; plants growing in, 83; population of, 246; revenue of, 248; saltpetre found in, 300

Children, Chinese, 74; status of, 224; selling of, 244–5

China, size and population of, 245–7. *See also* Chinese characteristics, children, language, trade, etc.

Chin Chien [?Chun ta-gin, Kun-san, Keen-san], 94, 96, 105, n10

Chinese, characteristics of; exaggeration, 46, 114; lack of interest in science, 53–4, 190, 264–6; willingness to work hard, 72, *passim*; inquisitiveness, 80; behaviour of Mandarins, 87; ideas on truth, 90, 223; attitude towards Tartars, 108, 113; attitude towards foreigners, 129, 226; vainness, 215; attitude to merchants, 216; manners and characteristics, 221–30; differences between Chinese and Tartars, 221; love of gambling, 223, n88; treatment of children, 224; of the common people, 226; attitude to morality, 227; religious tolerance, 234; ignorance of foreign trade, 262; skill as craftsman, 264

Ch'ing dynasty, collected Statutes of, 7, 9n, 308

Ching-te-chen [Kin-chin-fou], porcelain manufacturing town, 188, n60, n62

Cho, Paolo, interpreter and missionary, 24, 308, 319; leaves the embassy at Macao, 64; comes to Peking, 148

Chou (Chou-ta-gin), 73, 78, 94, 97, 100, 109, 113, 121, 131, 141, 154, 190, 228, 289, n1, n25; conversations with Macartney, 84–7, 161, 200–2; takes leave of Macartney, 45, 216; his rank, 71; explains kotow, 84, 90, 119; favours embassy, 85; his opinion of Cheng-jui, 86; shows respect to Cheng-jui, 96; richness of, 98; accompanies Macartney to audience, 122; friendliness of, 144; appears dejected, 148; explains the Grand Canal, 171; known to Ch'ang-lin, 180, 195; his work as an official, 195, 240; Macartney's estimate of, 217; on foot-binding, 228; religious beliefs of, 232; on the population of China, 245, n99; 'Governor of Tientsin', 246; on revenue, 248; catches gonorrhoea, 288; brief biography of, 328–31

Christians, in China, 102, 230–1

Chun [?Kun-san, Keen-san], a great official, 94, 96, 105, n10

Chung-t'ang (Chong-tong, Chang-tong), Grand Secretary (Colao), 226, n 8, n20

INDEX

Chusan [*also* Cheusan], 5, 261; Staunton obtains pilots at, 65; Macartney asks for a depot at, 150; difficulties of trading at, 177; desirability of trading at, 208; *Hindostan* remains at, 342; hospital for crew of *Lion* at, 346; E.I.C. formerly trading at, n77, n84

Clarence, small brig as tender, 64 ff., 73, 218

Clarke, George, clockmaker, 95, n1

Clive, Robert, 213

Clock(s), foreign, in China, 79, 97; by Clarke at Yuan-ming Yuan, 95; Vulliamy's, 96, 99; Emperor's collection of, 125, 261, n1

Cloth, English woollen, 12, 16, 30; E.I.C.'s exports to China of, 105, 212, 256; kerseymere, 105; vigonia 105, 258; broad-cloth, 257, 275; superfine imported through Russia, 262; problem of definition, n26

Club, the, of Dr. Johnson's friends; Marcartney a member of, 19

Coal, in China, 200, n151; pit in Kwangtung of, 297; coke, 297

Cochin China, 30, 206, 208, n2; possibility of English trade to, 16; Macartney's arrival in, 61; Chinese trade with, 256, 274; Chinese language understood in, 276; revolt in, 206, 208, n79

Co-hong, at Canton, 15, 172; formation of, 12

Colao (Grand Secretary), 89, 347, n8

Coleridge, Samuel Taylor, 41

Commissioners, of E.I.C. at Canton (officially called the Secret and Superintending Committee), 202, 205, 216, 217. *See also* Henry Browne, Eyles Irwin, William Jackson

Commonplace book, kept by Macartney in China, 44, 54

Commutation Act, 1784, 15, 256

Compass, Chinese, 275, n120

Concubine(s), of Ch'ien-lung, 201, n10

Congregation *de Propaganda Fide*, 24n, 235, 319, 338n

Conway, river, 180

Cook, Captain James, 42, 56, n73, n89

Cookery, Chinese, 302

Coote, General Sir Eyre, 20

Copper, in China; composition of white, 259; red copper sold by Hong merchants, 259; used for coinage, 259, n96; Gillan's remarks on, 292–5; tutenag, 293–5

Cordier, Henri, sinologist, XI

Cork Convent, Portugal, 199, n69

Cotton, raw from India, 14, 52, 212; amount imported into China, 260, 263; Chinese need of, 275

Country trade, 190; definition of, 13–16; country merchants smuggling, 52; extent of, 259, 260, 263

Courier system, in China; speed of, 169, 184, n52

Covent Garden Theatre, 204, n71, n72

Cow-hee (Ma Wan), island off Lantao, 211, 318, n82

Coxe, Archdeacon William, historian, 262, n106

Crewe, Lieut. John, 24, 115

Crystal, rock; spectacles made of, 299

Dalai Lama [Delai-Lama], 232

Danes, the; decline in trade of, 261, 263

Danish island (also known as Danes), 208, n78

Derbyshire porcelain; admired by Chinese, 96, 99, 266, n12

Diamond, used in cutting glass at Canton, 295

Dibdin, Charles, the younger; on Astley's amphitheatre, n45

Dinwiddle, Dr. James, 24, 53, 57; reports Emperor's comment on air pump, 54; at Yuan-ming Yuan, 97; lectures at Canton, 266; on Chinese canals, 269; brief biography of, 310; duties during embassy, 310; takes tea plants to Calcutta, 311, n57; lectures in India, 311; not at Jehol, 342; travels to Chusan, 342; *Biographical Memoir* of, 347; on not knowing the Chinese language, 347; MS. of his Journal, 347

405

INDEX

Diseases, in China; the main ones, 285–90; ophthalmia, 285; goitre, 286; venereal disease, 287; smallpox, 290; measles, 290
Diving bell (Smeaton's), 54, 310
Dress, Chinese; of men, 224–5; of women, 229; distinction of rank by, n101
Drummond (? James), 219, n86
Drury Lane Theatre, 204, n71, n72
Dundas, Henry, 23, 309; Home Secretary in Pitt's administration, 15–16; instructions to Macartney of, 30; Macartney's dispatches to, 34, 177, 207 (of 9 Nov. 1793), 141n ff. (of 23 Dec. 1793), 185 ff. (of 7 Jan. 1794), 209 ff.; received copy of Macartney's Journal, 46; Mackintosh dines with, 343; instructions to Macartney concerning Japan from, n75
Du Halde, Fr. Jean-Baptiste, author; on moveable type in China, 270; his translation of a work on the pulse, 280, n132; his *Description Geographique*, n92
Dutch, the, 4, 5, 13, 63; embassy to Peking in 1794 of, 34, 313, 361, n27, n54; decline of trade at Canton of, 215, 261; East India Company, 262, n105; importing tin to China, 296; previous embassies of, 353
Duties, on goods at Canton, 9, 31, 150, 251

Eades, Henry, metallurgist, 24, 91
East India Company (E.I.C.), English, 3, 22, 62, 263; Macartney's relations with when Governor of Madras, 20–1; instructions to Macartney concerning China embassy from, 30; cost of embassy to, 35; requests copy of Macartney's Journal, 46; and opium, 51; Commissions of, at Canton, 202, 216; its trade to Canton, 256, 257, 258, 263; private trade by ships' officers of, 311–12, 257; queries to Macartney about silk manufacture, 271; ceased to export porcelain from China to England, 298, n153; awarded Sir G. L. Staunton a pension, 307; Botanic Gardens at Calcutta of, 311, n57; site of Factory at Canton, n70; trading to Chusan and Ningpo, n77; language students at Canton of, n81
East Indiamen; at Canton, *Abergavenny, Bombay Castle, Brunswick, Ceres, Chesterfield, Exeter, Glatton, Hawke, Henry Dundas, Minerva, Osterley, Princess Royal, Royal Charlotte, Thurlow, Triton, Walsingham, Warley*, 204–6; *Princess Royal* taken by the French, 257; *Woodcot*, 257; *Bombay Castle* carries plants to England, 319. See also *Hindostan*
Edinburgh; importance of, 57; University of, 57, 310, 311
Ellicot, watchmaker, 62, n1
Embassies to China; Chinese attitude to, 3, 88, 159; ceremony expected of, 32–3; length of stay of, 146, 353; Fr. Amiot's opinion on, 151
Embassy from China; hypothetical, to England, 147
Embassy, Lord Macartney's; the Emperor's poem on, x; Chinese documents concerning, 6, 24, 28; as a reconnaissance, 22; Gillray's cartoon of, 23; members of suite of, 23–4; aims of, 30–1; reasons for failure of, 31–4; cost to E.I.C. of, 35; results of, 35, 55; Dutch and Portuguese in Macao jealous of, 63; junks carrying fly flags with words 'the English ambassador bringing tribute to the Emperor', 88; Macartney's disappointment at lack of success, 152; cost to Emperor of, 161; Emperor's opinion of, 172; eye-witness accounts of, 342–52
Emery, Josiah, watchmaker, n1
Emperor, the (Ch'ien-lung, 1736–96), 16, 27, 28, 30, 36, 63, 65, 299, n94; poem of to celebrate the embassy by, x; position towards barbarians of, 6; his reign, 25–6; created the

INDEX

Yuan-ming Yuan, 26, n11; reactions towards embassy of, 35; his remark on scientific apparatus, 54; partiality towards Tartars, 85, 227, 238; sons and grandsons of, 101, 238, n16; orchestra of, 104; gives Macartney an audience, 122-4; appearance of, 123; collection of clocks belonging to, 125, 261, n1; favourite weapon of, 130; birthday celebrations of, 131, 136-40; religious beliefs of, 136, 232; book written by, 137; grandeur of, 140; presents to George III from, 142, 149, 176; return to Peking of, 145; edict to George III from, 148, 149, 336-41; his answer to Macartney's requests, 155, 166-8; goodwill of towards embassy, 170, 172; his method of conducting government, 173; daily routine of, 201; good health of, 202; a true Tartar, 237; all authority derived from, 238; wisdom of, 239; instituted buttons of rank, 252; uninterested in scientific experiments, 266, n109; his physicians, 280; drawings by Alexander of, 315-16; his interest in western music, n23; has the Potola built at Jehol, n43; rebellions at the end of his reign, n65; an engraving of, n92

Endeavour, brig, of Bombay Marine, 64, 68, 70, 77

Entertainments, Chinese; a puppet show at Jehol, 134; theatricals on Emperor's birthday, 137-40; a Nanking troupe perform, 203-4

d'Estaing, Count, 18-19

Eunuchs, 121; as Emperor's attendants, 201, 280; castration of, 284

Factory, English, at Canton, 5, 206, 209; site of, 204, n70

Famines, in China, 244

Farren, Elizabeth, actress, 204, n71

Flint, James, supercargo; sent to Tientsin, 214, n84; learning Chinese at Canton, n81

Fo-hi, 197, 238; temple of at Tung-chow, 89; statue of at Jehol, 135-6; Emperor's worship of, 201, 232; Tartars' belief in, 232; common peoples' belief in, 233; Macartney's ideas about, n7

Foot-binding. *See* Bound feet

Forbidden City, in Peking. *See* Imperial Palaces

Formosa, 5, 102, 211, n65

Fraser, William, mathematical instrument maker; orrery of, 96, n112

French, the, 13; decline of French trade to Canton, 215, 261, 263

French island, near Whampoa, 208, n78

Fu-ch'ang-an [the Fou-liou], 120, 127, 131, 134, 146, 155, 156; Emperor's second favourite minister, 102, n17

Fu-k'ang-an [Fou-chang-tong, Foo-chan-tong], 29, 126, 131, 134, 142, 146, 155, 156; his campaign against the Gurkhas, 36, n118; obtained imperial favour through his brother's influence, 102; his dislike of the English, 127, 181; in Szechwan to quell disturbances, 250, n65

Fukien [Fo-kien], 5, n65; salt on coast of, 299; population of, 246; revenue of, 248

Furs, 302; Capt. Mackintosh has for sale, 45; trade to Canton in, 256, 259-60; Russian trade in, 262; preparation of skins, 302

Gardens, Chinese; style of, 116, 271-2, n41; at Jehol, 124-7, 132-3

Garrison(s), Chinese; arms of, 174, 203; guns of, 179; Macartney saluted by, 192; at Bocca Tigris, 218; in each walled town, 255; Parish's report on, 313. *See also* Soldiers

Gazettes, the Tientsin, 114; printed in main towns weekly, 270

George III, King of England; painting of by Reynolds displayed, 99, 104, n24; Emperor's presents to, 142, 147, 149, 176; Emperor's letters to, 148, 149, 166-8; illness of, 156, n48;

407

INDEX

wanted to have an ambassador resident in Peking, 184; edict from Ch'ien-lung to, 337–41

Gerbillon, Fr. Jean-François, missionary; his map of China, n100

Gibbon, Edward, 56; his hernia, n133

Gill, Thomas, Birmingham cutler; sword blades made by, 105, 257, n25

Gillan, Dr. Hugh, 24, 53, 57, 111n, 335; at Jehol, 121, 145; consulted by Ho-shen on medical grounds, 129, 281–3; his observations on Chinese medicine and surgery, 279–90, n124; observations on Chinese chemistry, 291–303, n145; brief biography of, 311, n145; letter to Macartney from, 318

Gillray, James; cartoon of Macartney by, 23

Glass; uses of, in China, 299, n154; imported from Venice, 299; manufactory for, at Peking, 299

Goitres, in China, 114, 286, n31

Gold, in China; made into charms, 291, n148

Gonorrhoea; Wang and Chou catch, 288; Chinese treatment of, 289, n142

Gouvea, Alexandro, Bishop of Peking, 103, 265–6, n21

Government, of China; working of the, 27–8; Macartney's observations on, 50, 236–40; power of, 77; attitude to foreigners, 129, 164; much discretion left to the Viceroys, 168; 'a tyranny of a handful of Tartars', 236–8; all authority from Emperor, 238; attitude of self-sufficiency of, 275; members of the Grand Secretariat and Grand Council, n20; the Six Boards, n32. *See also* Provincial administration

Governor; of Kwangtung, 8, 205; of a province, 252, n74, n102

Gower, Captain Sir Erasmus, 24, 66, 70, 76, 98, 110, 147, 154, 160, 172; journal kept by, 35, 345–6; establishes a hospital at Chusan, 105;

letter to Macartney from, 177; arrival at Macao, 184; at Whampoa, 208; brief biography of, 309—10; attempted to sail to Japan, n75

Grammont, Fr. Jean Joseph de, missionary; his reasons for failure of embassy, 32; offers his services, 80; Macartney's estimate of, 103; receives present of a watch, n1; career of, n6; letter from, n16; as a musician, n23

Grand Canal [Eu-ho], 164, 169, 170, 173; description of, 171; account of construction of, 268–9, n114

Grand Council; working of, 27–8; instructions to Cheng-jui from, 33; note concerning edicts to George III from, 337; members of in 1793, n20

Grand Secretariat; working of, 27; terms for, n8; members of in 1793, n20

Grand Secretary [Colao, Chong-tong] *See Chung-t'ang*

Gray, Thomas, 41

Great Wall, of China; Dr. Johnson concerning, 40–1; Macartney's description of, 111–13, 143, n30; Parish's plan of, 112n

Green Standard, Chinese Army of, n74, n103

Grenada, Macartney Governor of, 18

Grosier, Abbé, author, 245, 270, n97

Gum, for lanterns, 303

Gunpowder, in China; ingredients of, 301, n158

Gurkhas, of Nepal; driven out of Tibet by Chinese, 25–6, 36, n18. *See also* Tibet

Haidar Ali, ruler of Mysore, 20

Hainan [Hai-nan] island, 211

Hall, —, Secretary to Commissioners at Canton, 202, 217

Halls, the, four Christian Churches in Peking, 338

Hamilton, Hon. Charles, of Painshill; as a landscape gardener, 126, n37

INDEX

Hangchowfu [Han-chou-fou], 176, 177; description of, 178; ladies of, 288; camphor prepared at, 298; Imperial silk factory at, 323; journey to Chusan from, 342–3

Hanna, Robert, missionary, 64, 78, 141, 142, n5

Harris, Thomas, theatre manager, 204, n71

Hastings, Warren, Govenor-General of Bengal; relations with Macartney, 20–1

Hatchett, John, coach-builder of London, n27

Hawes, Dr. William; his method of artificial respiration, n63

Haxton, John, botanist taken on embassy by Sir G. L. Staunton, 317

Herbal medicine, in China, 284, n130, n137

Hernia; Ho-shen suffers from, 283, n133

Herschel, Sir William, astronomer, 56, n3

Hickey, Thomas, artist, 24; accompanied embassy as painter, 314; produced little work, 314–15; drawing of Wang by, 314, 327; Barrow's opinion of, 315; did not go to Jehol, 342

Hickey, William, diarist; at Canton, n78, n143

Hindostan [*also Indostan*], East Indiaman, 23, 24, 62, 66; sailed from England, 61; Macartney buys presents from ship's officers, 62, 70; arrival on China coast, 64; hoping to obtain cargo at Chusan for, 73, 143, 147, 176–7; to carry baggage from Chusan to Macao, 171–2; to be exempt from duties at Canton, 177, 261; voyages of, 312; Alexander and Hickey travel home on, 314, 343; crew press-ganged at end of voyage, 343

Holland, 15. *See also* Dutch

Holland, Henry Fox, 1st Baron, 17

Holmes, Samuel, 346

Honam island, Canton, 204, n70

Hong merchants; their function at Canton, 9–15; garden house of, 202; Macartney's estimate of, 207, n76; 'squeezed' by Mandarins, 207, 261; sell red copper, 259; unaware of value of silver, 263; some interest in scientific experiments, 266

Hoppo(s) [Hou-poo, Hou-pou], 11, 12, 216, n84; functions of, 8; power of, 31, n102; house in Peking of former, 158; Ch'ang-lin argues with, 205; extortion at Canton of, 261; forbids building of English-type ship, 275; list of, n46

Ho-shen (the Minister, Cho-chang-tong), 25, 26, 131, 133, 145, 154, 181; courtesy of, 29, 127; his instructions to Cheng-jui on kotow, 32, 33; Macartney's note on kotow to, 33, 99, 118; various ailments of, 93, 118, 129, 282, 283, n133; Emperor's favourite Minister, 101; Macartney's description of, 120; his questions on Russia, Italy and Portugal, 120; conducts Macartney through gardens at Jehol, 125–9, 131–4; difficulty of discussing business with, 128, 134, 148; Macartney sends note about *Hindostan* to, 146; Macartney calls on him at Yuan-ming Yuan, 146–8; receives Macartney in the Imperial Palace, 149; Macartney's note of six requests to, 150; bids farewell to Macartney, 155; discourages experiments, 191; brief biography of, 320–2; Macartney's estimate of, 321; 'patronage' of, 322; relations with Cheng-jui, 323–4, n29; Court Letter to Ch'ang-lin about Macartney, n56

Hospitals, in China, 286, n139

Houses, in China, 224. *See also* Architecture

Hsü Tientsin hsien-chih[13] ('Supplementary local history of Tientsin'), 329n

Hughes, ?Richard, showman, 139, n45

Hunter, John, Surgeon, 57, n63

409

INDEX

Hüttner, J. C., German tutor to young Staunton, 24; sent to meet Mandarins near Taku, 68, 69, 70; served as 'Latin secretary', 346; account of embassy by, 346

Hwang Ho [Hoang-ho], Yellow River, 171, 173; junction of Grand Canal with the, 268–9, n114

Hydraulics, Chinese; bamboo water wheel, 192, 272–4; *illustr.*, 273

Ibbetson, Julius Caesar, painter; accompanies Cathcart's embassy, 314; declines to accompany Macartney's embassy, 314

Ides, Isbrant, Russian envoy, 4, 352

Imperial Palace, Peking; Macartney at, 149, n47; right to ride a horse in, 325

d'Incarville, Fr. Pierre, missionary, 26

India; trade with China, 13–17, 212, 260. *See also* Bengal, Bombay, Calcutta, Madras

Inoculation, against smallpox, 290, n143

Interpreter(s), Chinese, 24, 32, 49, 54, 118, 121, 141, 148, 206, 276, 288; refuses to practise the kotow, 90; at setting up of presents, 97, 144; teaching young Staunton Chinese, 99–100; Macartney's opinion of, 221. *See also* Li and Cho

Iron, abundant in China, 295, n150

Irwin, Eyles, E.I.C. Commissioner at Canton, 202, 207, 217; letter to Macartney from, 149, 152, 334

Italy, 120

Iwasaki, Baron; bought MS. of Macartney's Journal, 332

Izmailov, Leon V., Russian envoy, 4, 353

Jackall, brig; as tender, 61; arrives on China coast, 63 ff.; explores gulf of Chihli, 67; at Macao, 218; sails to Calcutta, 310; attempts to survey coast of Lantao island, 313, n82

Jackson, William, E.I.C., Commissioner at Canton, 202, 207, 217

Jamaica, 222, n87

Japan, 5, 16, 30, 206; hope of bringing English trade to, 16, n75; seclusion of, 183; Macartney's reasons for not visiting, 206; Chinese trade with, 256, 274; camphor from, 298

Jehol [Gehol], 28, 33, 39n, 75, 79, 261, 262, 281, 287; Macartney's journey to, 106–14; Macartney at, 115–42; description of gardens at, 124–36; temples at, 134–6, 233; artists not taken to, 314; as a hunting lodge, n28; religious significance of, n43

Jesuits, in China, 231, 235, 247, n23, n92, n100. *See also* under individual names of missionaries

Johnson, Samuel, 55, 57; and Macartney, 19, 41, 42; his thoughts about the Great Wall, 40, 342; and Sir G. L. Staunton, 307

Jones, Sir William, orientalist; as a linguist, 277, n122, n123

Journal, Macartney's, 23, 35; of voyage to Cochin China, 38; of embassy to China; scope of, 38–55; style of, 41–2; historical background to, 42, 55–57; method of compilation, 43–48; copies of required by Government and E.I.C., 46n; Macartney's Conclusions to, 219–20; transmission of MS. of, 332–4

Jui-i[6] [*ju-eu-jou* or *giou-giou*], Chinese 'sceptre', 122, 126, n33

Junks (*also* junkas); description of, 81; trade carried on by, 81; armed men-of-war, 175, 218; large sea-going, 268; Macartney's opinion of, 274, n117; and foreign models, 275; on the Peiho, 296

Justice, in China, 11; Macartney's observations on, 240–2; use of torture, 242; capital punishment, n95

Kalmucks [Calmuks], Western Mongols, n39; envoys at Jehol from, 124; their envoys spoke to Macartney, 138; return of from Russian to Chinese protection, n43, n44

INDEX

K'ang-hsi [Cam-hi], Emperor (1662–1723), 26, 238, n11, n23; interest in science of, 191; map of China made with his encouragement, 247, n100; his prowess, n94

Kaolin [ca-o-lin]; clay for porcelain, 187, 298, n60

Kauffman, Angelica, artist; Chinese at Canton copy from works of, 343

Kemble, John Philip, actor, 204, n71

Kiakhta [Kiachta], Treaty of, n83; Sung-yun signed supplementary treaty of, 127, n38

Kiangsi [Kiang-si, Kian-si], 185, 188; the women of, 193n; population of, 246; revenue of, 248

Korea [Corea], 3, 5, 211, n10, n115; possibility of English trade to, 16; Chinese trade with, 256

Kosielski, Fr. Romoaldo, missionary, 146

Kotow, the, ceremony of, 29; how performed, 6; effects of Macartney's refusal to perform, 32–4; instructions to Cheng-jui concerning, 33; Macartney's written statement on, 33, 99, 118; performed by Dutch embassy, 34; explained to Macartney, 84; demonstrated by Wang and Chou, 90; mentioned by Cheng-jui, 98; Macartney urged to practice, 119; Macartney did not perform, 120, 154, n40

Krusenstern, Adam Johann von, Russian naval captain; at Canton, n107

Kublai Khan [Cublai], 130, 222, n114

Kung-shou[7] (*Cong-so*), 97n

Kuo-ch'ao ch'i-hsien lei-cheng[10] ('historical records of famous people of the reigning dynasty', 1890), 324, 326

Ku-pei-k'ou [Cou-pe-kiou], town near the Great Wall, 110, 113, 143, n28

Kwangtung (Quan-tong), 7, 8, 52; Macartney travels through province of, 193–203; population of, 246; revenue of, 249; pirates along coast of, n65; salt made on coast of, n155. *See also* Canton, sometimes used as synonymous with Kwangtung

Kyd, Lt-Colonel Robert, horticulturalist, 182, n57

Lamiot, Louis-François, missionary, 78, 141, 142, n5; at Macao, wanting to enter Emperor's service, 64

Language, the Chinese, 35, 50, 267; Chinese forbidden to teach foreigners, 9; as a barrier between China and Europe, 53–4; English ignorance of, 210, 251, 347; as the state language, 236; Macartney's remarks on, 270, 276–7, attempts of Super-cargoes to learn, n81; Sir William Jones attempted to learn, n122

Lanroost, on river Conway, 180

Lantao, island, near Hong Kong, 211; Parish's observations on, 313, 318, n82

Law, Chinese; on homicide, 11; on borrowing money, 15; Macartney's observations on, 240–2; G. T. Staunton's translation of Ch'ing statutes, 308; as regards capital punishment, n95. *See also* Statutes

Laxman, Lieut. Adam, n75, n107

Lazarists [Congregation of St. Lazarus], at Peking, 98, 235. *See also* under individual missionaries

Lead; English trade to Canton in, 256; little used by the Chinese, 296

Leather; tanning of, 302

Legate, the Emperor's. *See* Cheng-jui

Lens, great, burning; made by William Parker, 69, 79, n3. *See also* Presents

Leprosy, 289

Lettres édifiantes, 231, n9, n11, n92, n97

Lewis, William Thomas, actor, 204, n71

Li, Jacobus ['my interpreter'], 24, 148, 206, 288, 308; as Macartney's interpreter, 54; refuses to practise the kotow, 90; and setting up the

411

INDEX

presents, 97, 144; take note to Ho-Shen, 141; Macartney's opinion of, 221; brief biography of, 319–20; left embassy at Macao, 320; letters to Macartney from Shansi, 320

Liang K'en-t'ang² [Viceroy of Pe-che-li], his dealings with Macartney, 74–80; Macartney's impression of, 76; his career, n4

Linguists, Chinese, at Canton, 8; pidgin English of, 210, n81. *See also* Language

Linnaeus, Carl; system of classification of plants, 56, n2

Linnean Society, the, of London, 308

Lion, man-of-war, 23, 65, 76, 147, 203, 206, 309; Gower's journal of voyage of, 35, 345–6; sails from England with Macartney, 61; arrived on China coast, 64; size and force of, 69; sickness of crew of at Chusan, 73, 105, 178, 345, n75; Emperor's picture in cabin of, 118; sailed from Chusan, 171; at Whampoa, 208; Macartney returns to, 216; to act as convoy to East Indiamen, 219

Lisbon, English merchants at, 215

Literary Inquisition, the; under Ch'ien lung, 26

Liuchui islands [Lequeses islands], 3; envoys from, 182, n58

Livonia, Baltic Duchy of, 222, n87

Long-acre, London, 106, n27

Louis XVIII, exiled King of France; Macartney's mission to Court of, 43

Loureiro [Loreiro], Fr. Jao, missionary and botanist, 62, n2

Lowther Hall, near Penrith, 133; seat of Sir James Lowther, politician, 42, n42

Lowther, Sir James, 1st Earl of Lonsdale, Macartney's brother-in-law, n42, n152

Lustres; chandeliers taken by Macartney as presents for the Emperor, 79, 95, 97; made by William Parker, 99, n3

Luton (Hoo), seat of Lord Bute, 125, n35

Macao, 29, n84; Staunton sent to, 63; transit duties between Canton and, 150; weakness of Portuguese at, 211; arrival of embassy at, 218; Governor of, 219; Chief Judge of, 219; report by Parish on defences of, 313; foreign merchants forced to reside at, 339n; Macartney's residence while at, n86

Macartney, George, Earl Macartney, in the county of Antrim, Ireland (Cr. 1, March 1794); career of, 17–23, n42; painted by Reynolds, 17; ambassador to Russia, 17–18, 43; married daughter of Lord Bute, 18; Governor of Grenada, 18; met Dr. Johnson, 19; his annotated copy of Boswell's *Life* of Johnson, 19; Governor of Madras, 20–1; declined Governor-Generalship of Bengal, 21; wounded in a duel, 21; appointed ambassador to the Emperor of China, 21; character of, 22; Governor of Cape Colony, 23; Gillray's cartoon of, 23; death of, 23; embassy to China of: instructions from Government and E.I.C. concerning embassy, 30–1; refuses to practise the kotow, 33; his two journals, 38, 332–4; scope of his China Journal, 38–55; his style, 41; catalogue of his library, 42; method of compiling Journal, 43–8; commonplace-book kept in China by, 44, 54; relations with Mackintosh, 44; on Chinese exaggeration, 46; on relations between China and England, 48; Observations on China of, 49–55, 221–78; wide interests of, 57; on Chinese architecture, 75, 272; his account of audience with Ch'ien-lung, 122–4; description of celebrations on Emperor's birthday, 136–40; leaves Jehol, 142; ill with rheumatism, 144; greets Emperor at Peking, 145;

412

INDEX

sends note to Ho-shen, 146; interview with Ho-shen, 146–8; hoped to reside at Emperor's Court, 147, 184; illness of, 149, 151, 170; receives Emperor's letter to George III, 149–50; sends six requests to Ho-shen, 150, 155; disappointment at failure of embassy, 152; his explanation of failure of embassy, 153–4; sends note to Ho-shen, 154; leaves Peking for Canton, 155; explains grievances of English merchants, 162; discusses Emperor's letters to George III, 166–8; gives Ch'ang-lin list of English grievances, 185; sends a personal note to the Emperor, 187; on the inevitability of progress, 191; description of the temple of Pusa, 197–9; thoughts on relations between England and China, 209–15; on the status of China, 212; on the future of China, 239; his study of China before starting on the embassy, 278; audience with George III, 309; his estimate of Ho-shen, 320–1; his relations with Wang and Chou, 325–30; *Life* of, by Barrow, 343; biography of, by Robbins, 347–50; warned not to create trouble at Macao, n56; secures tea plants, n57; his attitude to the East compared with Macaulay's, n123; elected M.P. for Cockermouth, n152

Macaulay, Thomas Babington, Lord; his attitude to the East compared with Macartney's, n123

Mackintosh, Captain William, 23, 128, 141, 145, 146, 147; his relations with Macartney, 44–5; wanting to trade at Peking, 45; at Macao, 63; sells Parker's lens to Macartney, 69, 356; goes to Peking, 73; sells watches to Macartney, 101; permission to trade at Chusan, 142; his ship exempt from duties, 176; difficulties to trade at Chusan facing, 177; extortion of Hoppo at Canton, 261; brief biography of, 311–13; value of his private trade, 312; his Factory at Canton, 312; dined with Pitt and Dundas, 343

Madras; Macartney Governor of, 20; Dinwiddie at, 311

Maggs Bros., antiquarian booksellers; sold MS. of Macartney's journal of voyage to Cochin China, 333

Malacca, tin from, 296

Malaya, trade from India to, 212

Manchu(s) [Mantchoo, Mant-chou, Mantchoux], 35, 36, 37, 50, 51, 129, 158, 196, 222, n20, n28; appointed Grand Secretaries, 27; on the six Boards, 28; naval weakness of, 52, 170; and the Mongols, 130, 228, n43; marriage of 228; education of princes, 267; Banners, n67; medicine, n133. *See also* Tartars, the name by which Macartney usually referred to them. *See also* under names of the great officials, most of whom were Manchus.

Manchu language, the, 27, 99, 227; preserved in China, 227; Ch'ien-lung's sons study, 267; edict to George III translated from Chinese into, 337; Fr. Amiot's grammar of, n15

Mandarins (western term used loosely for a Chinese official); wanting to buy watches, 70; inquisitiveness of at Tientsin, 80; politeness of, 87; visit Macartney in Peking, 104; at the audience, 123; conversation with Macartney at Jehol, 138; difficult position of, 226–7; responsibilities of, 244; various ranks of, 252–3, n102; of Canton, giving presents to officials at Court, 261; not interested in science, 266; dress of, n101. *See also* Government

Mangalore, Treaty of; between Macartney and Tipu Sultan, 20

Manila [*also* Manilla], n9, n13; cotton growing near, 262; Chinese sailing to, 274; instructions to Gower to sail to, n75

Manure, in China, 186, n59

413

INDEX

Map, of China; made by Jesuits and Chinese, 247, n100. *See also* Charts
Marco Polo, 222, 270, 275
Marriage; women of Kiangsi and, 193n; between Chinese and Tartars, 228
Mathematics, Board [College] of, official title 'Imperial Board of Astronomy', 93, n9, n21
Mathematics, Chinese; Macartney's remarks on, 264–6
Maxwell, Acheson, a Secretary to Macartney, 23, 46, 63, 94, 342
Measles, 290, n144
Medicine, Chinese; Gillan's observations on, 279–90; *materia medica* of, 279; no authorized pharmacopoeia of, 279; composition of medicines, 284; notes and references, n124–n144
Mei-ling pass, 193–4, n66
Mémoires Concernant l'Histoire, etc., 102, n15, n19, n44, n92, n97
Mercury, in China; used in cure of venereal disease, 284, 289, 297; formula for mercurial pills, 289; other uses of, 297
Metals, in China; Gillan on the uses of, 291–6. *See also* Copper, Gold, etc.
Methodists, 235, n93
Mien-cul-ye, grandson of Emperor, 101, 201, n16
Milton, John, 42; Macartney's quotations from, 125, 131
Missionaries, Christian, in China, 64, 144; Macartney wants the assistance of, 80; Macartney visited by seven, 93; grown own grapes, 101, 302; the Bishop of Peking, 103; enmity between Portuguese and other, 103; introduced western music and punctuation, 104, n23; translation of Emperor's letter by, 167, n50; indiscretion of, at Peking, 230; entering the Emperor's service, 234, 339; position of, in Peking, 235; as astronomers at Peking, 265; not proficient in science, 266; formula for mercurial pills of, 289; mistaken ideas about copper, 293; established glass manufactory at Peking, 299; their Churches at Peking, 338. *See also* Adeodato, d'Almeida, Amiot, Antonio, Attiret, Benoist, Castiglione, Cho, Gerbillon, Gouvea, Grammont, Hanna, d'Incarville, Kosielski, Lamiot, Li, Loureiro, Panzi, Paris, Poirot, Raux, Ripa, Rodrigues
Money, Chinese; values of, 243, n96; prices of goods at Peking, 244
Mongols [*also* Monguls], 25, 222, n7, n28, n38, n39, n43, n44
Montgomery, Captain of *Bombay Castle*, 206
Moravians, sect of, 235, n93
Morrison, Dr. G. E., *The Times* Correspondent in China; MS. of Macartney's Journal in his library at Peking, 332; catalogue of his books, 332
Mukden [Moukden, Moakden]; Emperor's Tartar capital, 130; imperial treasure at, 249
Music, Chinese; Emperor's orchestra, 104; played on Emperor's birthday, 131; and western music in Ch'ien-lung's reign, n23
Musicians, five taken on embassy by Macartney, 24; concerts given by the band, 104; instruments of, n22

Nankeen [Nankin], Chinese cotton cloth, 188; amount exported in 1792, 260; how made, 262–3
Nanking [Nankin]; advantages over Peking as capital, 175; actors from, 203–4; Hong merchants trade no further than, 207; merchants of, in strong position, 208; silk from, 271
Naples; Chinese missionary College at, 24n, 231, 319, n91
Navigation, Chinese; Macartney's observations on, 274–6; lack of instruments, 275; use of mariner's compass, 275–6
Nepal [Napual], 250. *See also* Gurkhas
Nerchinsk, Treaty of (1689), n83

INDEX

Ningpo [Ning-po, Limpo]; junk trade between Tientsin and, 81; Macartney requests permission for English to trade to, 150; difficulties of trading at, 177; desirability of trade to, 208, n77; Flint at, n84
Nitre, 301, 302

Observations, made by Macartney on Chinese government, etc., 44, 46; method of compiling, 48; range of, 49–55; text of, 221–78
Officials, Chinese; list of civil, 252, n102; list of military, 255, n103. *See also* Mandarins, Grand Secretaries
Oil, in China; used for cooking, 302, n160
Onalaska (Alaska), 211, n83, n107
Opium, 14, 212, 223; from India imported into China, 51–2; amount imported in 1792, 260; Chinese need of, 261, 275; brought in American ships, n104
Ostend Company; sailing under foreign colours, 208, 257
Otaheite (Tahiti), 228, n89

Painshill, Surrey; compared with gardens at Jehol, 126, n37
Paktong [*pe-tung*], 292–5, n149
Pan-ke-qua, Hong merchant, 207, n76
Panzi [Pansi], Fr. Joseph, missionary, n92; visits Macartney, 93, n9;
Paotingfu [Pao-ting-fou]; residence of Viceroy of Chihli, 74
Paper, Chinese; method of making, 303
'Paper of happiness'; written by the Emperor, 176, n54
Paris, Joseph, missionary, visits Macartney, 93, n9
Parish, Lieut. Henry William, 24, 115n; his plan of the Great Wall, 112n; his drawing of the Potala, 135n; brief biography of, 313–14; sketches made at Jehol by, 313, 315, 316; various reports written by, 313; death of 314; visit to Lantao island by, n82

Parker, William; great lens made by, 69, n3; lustres (chandeliers) made by, 79, 95, 97, 99, 145, 264
Pauw, Cornelius de, 245, n98
Pearl river, 8, n85
Pearson, Alexander; pamphlet on Jenner's smallpox vaccine, by, n143
Pegu; envoys at Jehol with Macartney from, 124, n34
Pei-chihli. *See* Chihli
Peiho [Pay-ho], river in Chihli, 73, 164, 296; description of, 82
Peking [Pekin], 30, 79, 100, 104, 148, 175, 314, 317; Macartney arrives at, 92; his residence at, 98; Christians in, 102, 235; Bishop of, 103; Macartney's returns from Jehol to, 144; Imperial Palace at, 149, n47; Macartney requests warehouse at, 150; Macartney's description of, 156–8; route from Canton to, 183; articles which might be in demand at, 257; list of embassies to, 353
Penang [Prince of Wales Island]; the Chinese in, 223, n88
Pennant, Thomas, zoologist, 42; query about fish in Poyang lake from, 188, n61
Peony, root of, 289, n142
Petitpierre, Charles-Henry, watchmaker, 24, 97, n13
Petuntse [Pe-tun-tse], for making porcelain, 186, 298, n60
Petworth House, 17
Phillipps, Sir Thomas, bibliophile, 332, 333n, 348
Philippines; Indian trade to, 212; Chinese trade to, 256
Pigou, Frederick, supercargo, 11–12
Pigtail, Chinese, 72
Pott, William, the younger, 15–16, 309, 343
Planetarium, the, taken by Macartney as present to Ch'ien-lung from George III; set up at the Yuan-ming Yuan, 79, 99, 144, 146; a Chinese workman cuts a plate of glass from, 264; origin of, n12

415

INDEX

Plants, in China; noted in Chihli, 83; en route to Jehol, 106; varnish, tallow and tea plants secured, 182, 310, n57; Staunton's lists of, 317–18; Stronach's list of, in Camoens garden, 318; arrival in England of, 319. *See also*, Botanists, Loureiro

Poirot, Fr. Louis de, missionary, n1; visits Macartney, 93, n9; letter about translating reply to Macartney's six requests from, n50

Population of China; vast size of, 74, 86, 156; Macartney's observations on, 245–7; various calculations of, 245, 246, n99

Porcelain, Chinese; 264; manufactured at Ching-te-chen, 188, n60, n62; Gillan's reasons for quality of, 298; imported into England, n153

Portugal; Ho-shen's question on, 120–1; embassy to China from, 151, 353

Portuguese, 4, 80; in Macao, 63, 211; Jesuits, 235; names for money, 243

Post-chaise, taken by Macartney to China, 36, 42, 225; Macartney sets out for Jehol in, 105; Wang and Chou ride in, 109; Macartney's carriages, n27

Potala [Pou-ta-la], Lama temple at Jehol; Macartney's description of, 134–6, n43; roof of great temple of, 292; drawn by Alexander, 316; drawn by Parish, 135n

Poyang lake, 188, n61

Presents, the giving of by Chinese officials. *See* Bribes.

Presents, taken on Macartney's embassy; completion of the, 69; list requested by Wang and Chou, 72; difficulty of transport of, 75; to be left at Peking, 79; chariot for the Emperor, 85; displayed at Yuan-ming Yuan, 96, n12; Chinese title for, 97; fanciful Chinese account of, 114; at Jehol, 121; instructing missionaries left in charge of, 144

Priestley, Dr. Joseph, 57, n3

Prince of Wales Island (Penang); the Chinese in 223, n88

Printing, in China, 270, n115

Prior, Matthew, poet, 229, n90

Proctor' —, Captain in the Bombay Marine, 64, 68, 77

Property, in China; Macartney's remarks on, 242–5

Proudfoot, W. J., grandson of Dinwiddie; his *memoir* of Dinwiddie, 310n, 347; his criticism of Barrow's *Travels in China*, 344

Provincial administration, 8, 28, 31, n74, n102; temptations for corruption in, 261; as carried out by Ch'iao Jen-chieh, 329–30. *See also* Viceroy, Governor, etc.

Puan Khequa, Hong merchant, n76

Pulley; use of in China, 267

Pulo Condore, island off Mekong delta, Cochin China, 61; written Chinese understood in, 276

Pulse, the; importance of in Chinese medicine, 280, n132

Pump, chain, 186

Punishment, in China, 11; bamboo used as, 227; various methods of, 241; of debtors, 242; capital, n95

Purses, Chinese; as a present for George III, 176, n54; presented to young Staunton, 351

Pusa [Puso], rock temple of, in Kwangtung; three different accounts of, 39, 41; Alexander's sketch of, 39; Macartney's description of, 197–9, n68; poem by Wang Shih-chen about, n68; visited by Lin Tse-hsu in 1839, n68

Puttick and Simpson, book auctioneers, 332

Quadrant, Chinese, 275, n119

Quesnay, François, 55n

Raux, Fr. Nicholas-Joseph, missionary; n1, n5, 101; descriptions of, 98, n14; translated a note for Macartney, 99; on Christians in China, 102; how he and Fr. Poirot

416

translated the Emperor's reply to George III, n50
Rebellions, in China; in the provinces, 191, 238, n65; in 1794, 249; mentioned by Li in 1801, 320; Wang involved against, 327
Religion, in China; Macartney's remarks on, 89, 230–5; of Tartars, 232; Lama, 233; of common people, 233; of Taoists, 235. *See also* Fo-hi
Revenue, Board of [Tribunal of Finance], 8, 120, n32
Reynolds, Sir Joshua, 19, 55; painted Macartney, 17; painting of George III and Queen Charlotte by, 104, n24
Ripa, Fr. Matteo, missionary; founder of Chinese College at Naples, 319, n91; *Memoirs* of, n66; engraved map of China, n100
Rites, Board of [Court of Rites], 28, 101, 120, n32, n49
Robbins, Helen H, xi, 333–4; the biography of Macartney by, 347–50
Rodrigues, [Rodriguez], Fr. André, missionary, 93, n9
Roxborough, Dr., 311, n57
Royal Asiatic Society (London), the; Sir G. T. Staunton presented Chinese books to, 308
Royal Society, the, 56; Sir G. L. Staunton a Fellow of, 307; Dr. Gillan a Fellow of, 311; offered astronomical observations from Peking, n5
Russia, 211, n55; relations between China and, 4, 30; Macartney signs treaty with, 17; Macartney's account of, 18; Macartney's embassy to, 43, 133; Ho-shen's question on, 120; Sung-yun's conversations with Macartney concerning, 127, 160, 178; Kalmucks' discontent with, 138, n44; a grand canal in, 170; fierceness of the people of, 226; a passport needed for leaving, 234; extent of, 247; trade between China and, 262; embassies to China from, 353; and Japan, n75; expansion in Siberia of, n83; attempt to trade at Canton by, n107

Sadlers Wells [Sadler's wells], Islington, 139, n45
St. Petersburg [*also* St. Petersbourgh), 17, 18, 215, 247, 262
Salisbury, 1st Marquis of; Lord Chamberlain, 204
Salt, in China; price of, 244; making and storing, 299–300, n155; Chengjui as salt administrator of Tientsin, 322–3; results of lack of, n31
Saltpetre, 300–1
Sandwich, James Montague, 4th Earl; as Secretary of State, 17; as First Lord of the Admiralty, n89
Science, in China; attitude towards, 53–4; neglect of, 190; Macartney's observations on, 264–7; Mandarins' lacks of interest in, 266; Macartney's limited information on, n109; compared with Europe, n145;
Scott, William, surgeon to the embassy; 24, 342; Barrow's opinion of, 311, n98
Seceders, sect of, 235, n93
Secret Societies, in China, 239, n65
Select Committee, of E.I.C. at Canton; requests made by in 1796, 31
Shao-chou-fou [Chao-chou-fou], in northern Kwangtung, 195, 196; Commander of forces at, 205, 216, n74
Sheridan, Richard Brinsley; manager of Drury Lane Theatre, 204, n71
Shy Kinqua, Hong merchant, n76
Siberia; Russian expansion across, n83, n107
Siddons, Sarah, 204, n71
Silk, Chinese, 14, 175, 260; at Hangchow, 177, 323; Macartney obtains eggs of silkworms, 182, 310; high quality of, 271
Silver; as currency in China, 243, 263, n96; uses of in China, 292
Sing-songs (clockwork automata), 12; Emperor's collections at Jehol and Yuan-ming Yuan of, 125–6; as

INDEX

articles of private trade, 260, n1; imported by Mackintosh at Canton, 312; described by G. T. Staunton, 312, 352

Smallpox, in China, 239; inoculation against, 290, n143

Snuff; some used in China, 225

Snyders, Captain of an Ostend Company ship, 208

Soap, in China, 225, 300, n157

Solander, Daniel, Swedish botanist, 56n, n73, n89

Soldiers, in China; Macartney's observations on military matters, 253–6; the number of, 253; pay of, 254; arms of, 254; ranks of officers, 255; Manchu, n67; Chinese, n74, n103. *See also* Garrisons

Soochow [Sou-chou-fou]; Macartney passes by, 175; Imperial silk factory at, 323; long bridge near, n53

Sotheby and Co., book auctioneers; Macartney's MSS. sold by, 332

Spirits, Chinese, 225; '*samsu*' 10; '*son-tchou*', 302, n161

'Squeeze', in China; 12, 31, 34, 52; Mandarins squeeze presents from Hong merchants, 207

Statutes, of Ch'ing dynasty (*Ta Ch'ing Hui-tien*), 7, 9n, 308, n17

Staunton, Sir George Leonard, 23, 129; negotiates with Tipu Sultan, 20, 307; his *Authentic Account* of the embassy, 38, 43, 350–1; description of temple of Pusa by, 39, 41; at Macao, 63; obtains pilots at Chusan, 65; at Yuan-ming Yuan, 97; sets out for Jehol, 106; visits Ho-shen, 118; has audience with Ch'ien-lung, 122–3, 351; at the Emperor's birthday entertainments, 136–40; brief biography of, 307; as an amateur botanist, 317–18; description of English presents by, n12

Staunton, George Thomas, 'young Staunton', Lord Macartney's page, 24, 226; studies Chinese, 35, 99–100; copies out a letter in Chinese, 99, 352; rides in post-chaise to Jehol, 105; visits Ho-shen, 118; writes Chinese characters, 187; his ability to speak Chinese, 210, 277; brief biography of, 308; translation of Ch'ing laws by, 308; visits Mackintosh's factory at Canton, 312, 352, n95; his spelling of Wang and Chou's names, 326–9; MS. of journal of embassy by, 351–2; at audience with the Emperor, 351; translated a pamphlet on smallpox vaccine into Chinese, n143

Steel; instruments of in China, 295

Stowe, seat of Lord Cobham; compared to gardens at Jehol, 126, n37

Stronach, David, botanist with the embassy, 24, 317; makes list of plants in the Camoens garden, 318

Stuart, Major-General James, 20; fights duel with Macartney, 21; his description of Macartney, 22

Stuart, Lady Jane, 2nd daughter of Lord Bute; married to Macartney, 18, n42

Sulphur, in China, 301

Sunda, Straits of, 205; Chinese trade with isles of, 256

Sung-li[8] [*sung-lo*], 97n

Sung-yun [Sun-ta-gin], Mongol, Grand Councillor, 132, 134, 171, 175, 181, 228; on the Russians, 127, 160, 178, n38; appointed to conduct Macartney to Chusan, 154–5; on the Chinese idea of embassies, 159; conversations between Macartney and, 162–3, 166–9, 170; accompanies Mackintosh and Dinwiddie to Ningpo, 176, 347; Macartney's estimate of, 178; on taxes in China, 250

Supercargoes, of E.I.C. at Canton, 3, 8, 9, 11, 13, 15, 31, 49, n81

Surat, India, English merchants at, 263

Surgery, in China; Gillan's remarks on, 283–4

Swendenburghers, 235, n93

Swedes, at Canton; decline in trade of, 261, 263

INDEX

Szechuen [Sechuen, Se-chuen]; disturbances in, 250, 320, n65; population of, 246; revenue of, 248; gold in, 291; salt from, n155

Tael [*also* takel], Chinese coin and weight; cost to Emperor of the embassy calculated in, 161; Hong merchant buys rank for 10,000, 207; definition of a, 243–4, n96

Taku [Ta-cou], at mouth of Peiho, 72, 73, 267; *map*, 107

Tartar(s), 28, 96, 108, 127, 225, 249, 250; Emperor's partiality towards, 86; jealousy between Chinese and, 113–14; Princes, at audience at Jehol, 123, 130; troops, 196, 253–4, n67; different from Chinese, 221–3, 227, 249; do not bind feet of their women, 228; religion of, 232–3; Macartney's remarks on, 236–9; predominance over Chinese of, 237; attain high rank at early age, 252. *See also* Manchus

Tartar Banners, 196, 253, n67

Taxes, in China; on crops, 243; Macartney's remarks on, 250–1

Tea, 5, 14, 52, 296, 302, n160; E.I.C. trade in, 14–15; Macartney obtains plants of, 182, 186; the constant drink of the Chinese, 285–6; Dinwiddie takes plants to India, 310; memo by Banks on tea plants, 318; Lady Mendip's plant, 319; introduction of Chinese plants into India, n57; Japanese, n75

Technology, in China; limitations of, 53–4; Macartney's descriptions of some technical inventions, 267–70, n109, n146, n147. *See also* Science

Telescope(s), presented to Ch'ienlung; made by Herschel, 69, n3; taken to Jehol, 121

Tengchowfu [Ten-chou-fou], Shantung province, 256; arrival at 66; description of, 67; junk trade to Tientsin from, 81

Theatrical performances; at Jehol, 137–8; at Canton, 203–4

Thibault [Tiebault], Victor, mathematical instrument maker, 24, 97, n13

Tibet [Thibet], 163, 211, 243, 250; possible route through, 16; Chinese campaign in, 36, 102, n118; England accused of helping insurgents in, 86; weapons of Chinese troops in, 254; Sung-yun Imperial resident in, n38

Tientsin [Tien-sing, Teen-sing], 28, 29, 68, 80, 156, 163, 164, 214, n84; arrival of embassy at, 78; description of, 80–1; junk trade from, 81; bridge of boats at, 86; gazettes of, 114; Macartney requests permission to trade at, 150; story of a widow of, 243; salt stored at, 300; report by Parish on troops at, 313; Cheng-jui salt administrator of, 323; the Taotai of, 328–9; floods near, in 1792, 329

Tientsin fu-chih[12] ('local history of Tientsin prefecture'), 329

Timber, in China; lack of in north, 83; floats of, on river, 189; fir trees planted, 189n

Tin, 12n; English trade to China in, 256, 258; imported from Banca, 258n; amount imported in 1792; 260; Chinese need of, 275; uses of, in China, 296

Tipu, ruler of Mysore, 20

Titsingh [Titzingh], Isaac, Dutch envoy to Peking in 1794, 34, 205n, 335n, n13, n14

Tobacco, in China, 225

Tongking [Tonquin]; war in, 163, 208, 250, n79

Torguts, tribe of Mongols. *See* Kalmuks

Tourane Bay [Turon, Thuron], in Cochin China, 38; Macartney's stay at, 61–2; ruler of tributary to China, 120; possibility of an English settlement at, 208–9; Parish's report on, 313

Tōyō Bunko, the, Oriental Library, Tokyo; MS. of Macartney's Journal in, 332

INDEX

Trackers, Chinese boatmen; hauling the embassy junks, 82, 164, 171; hard work of, 194; pay of, 244; drawn by, 314

Trade, Chinese, 5; system at Canton of, 7–15; carried on by junks, 81; Nanking merchants and, 207–8; with England, 212; Macartney's observations on, 256–63; export of copper, 258–9; with Russia, 262, n107; export of nankeen cloth, 262; and balance of payments, 263

Trade, English, in the East; to China, 4–5; system of, at Canton, 7–15; growth of the Country Trade, 13–14, 52, 259; hopes of extending it to Japan and Cochin China, 16, n75; objects of Macartney's embassy concerning, 30–1; Macartney's remarks on English trade with China, 51–2, 212, 256–63; to Chusan and Ningpo, 208, n77; articles of private trade, 256–7

Translation, of documents concerning the embassy, 337; from English into Chinese, 99; from Chinese into Latin, 167, n50

Treasury, Imperial; Secret, 249; State, 249

Tribute; tributary princes, 3; foreign trade with China under guise of, 5; envoys, 7; 'English ambassador bringing tribute to Emperor of China,' 88

Trinity College, Dublin; Macartney at, 17

Tufa, rock, 114, n31

T'ung-chou chih[11], ('local history of Tungchow'), 326–8

Tungchow [Tong-siou], near Peking, 72, 73, 79, 88; arrival at, 86; departure from, 159; military commander at, 326–7

Tutenag [tutanag, tu-te-nag], Chinese zinc, n149; amount exported in 1792, 260; Gillan's remarks on, 293–4

Typa, island off Macao; anchorage at, 218

Tyrconnel House, Hanover Square, 264, n108

Van [ta-gin]. *See* Wang

Vegetables, Chinese, 71, 83, 302

Venereal disease; Gillan's observations on, 287–9, n140; more prevalent at Canton, 287; Wang, Chou and Ch'ang-lin contract gonorrhoea at Hang-chow, 288

Viceroy (Governor-General), usually of two provinces; of the two Kwangs, 8, 31, n192. *See also* Ch'ang-lin, Liang K'en-t'ang

Voltaire, 17, 42

Vulliamy, family of clockmakers; clocks displayed at Yuan-ming Yuan by, 96, 99, 266–7; presents made by, n12; planetarium repaired by, n12

Wang Wen-hsiung[4], 326–7

Wang [Van-ta-gin], 73, 76, 78, 94, 97, 100, 109, 113, 114, 121, 131, 141, 154, 190, 228, n65; Macartney's description of parting from, 45, 216; first meeting with Macartney, 71; explains the kotow, 84, 90, 119; conversations between Macartney and, 84–7, 161, 200–2; in favour of embassy, 85; his opinion of Chengjui, 86; shows deference to Chengjui, 96; duties of, 98; receives swords from Macartney, 105, n25; respect for Tartars of, 108; accompanies Macartney to the audience, 122; friendliness of, 144; appears dejected, 148; as Military Commander at Tungchow, 158; on regimental equipment, 174; known to Ch'ang-lin, 180, 195; military career of, 195, 253; religious beliefs of, 232; on firearms, 254n; contracts gonorrhoea at Hangchow, 288; drawing by Hickey of, 314, 327; drawing by Alexander of, 314; brief biography of, 325–8; receives a watch, n1

Wan-shu-Yuan [Van-shou-yen], gardens at Jehol; Wordsworth read

420

Macartney's description of, 41n; Macartney's description of eastern part, 124–6; description of western part, 132–6

Watches; made by Ellicott and Emery, 62, n1; Mandarins wanting to buy, 70; Macartney buys from Mackintosh, 101; Macartney presents a pair to the Emperor, 123; presented to Governor of Kiangsi, 188; Emperor's collection of, 261; Chinese desire for, 275

Water-closets, lack of in China, 225, n59

Water-wheel, bamboo; description of working of, 192, 272–4; *illustr.*, 273

Wayqua (Wu Chao-p'ing), Hong merchant, 339

Weapons. *See* arms

Wedgwood, Josiah, 55, n153; specimens of his pottery taken by Macartney, n12

Wellcome Historical Medical Library; MS. of Macartney's Journal of the voyage to Cochin China in, 333, 344

Whampoa [Wampo], anchorage for foreign ships in river near Canton, 208; description of, n78

Whitehaven, Cumberland, 297, n152

White Lotus sect; rebellion of, n65

Winder, Edward, a Secretary to Macartney, 23, 46

Wine, in China, 225; made by missionaries from grapes, 101, 302; made by the Chinese, 302, n161

Woburn [Woodburn] Abbey, Bedfordshire, compared to gardens at Jehol, 126, n37

Woollens, English trade to China in. *See* Cloth

Women, in China, 44; country-women, 74, 165, 192; at Court, 137; of Kiangsi especially hard-working, 193; Macartney's remarks on, 228–30

Wordsworth, William; read Macartney's description of gardens at Jehol, 41

Wu Chao-p'ing (Wayqua), Hong merchant, 339

Yangtze [Yang-tse], 174, n114

Yuan-ming Yuan [Yuen-min-yuen], 'the Summer Palace', 28, 84, 89, 261, 317, 322, 343; European style of part of, 26; distance from Peking, 88; first impression of, 92; great hall of, 95; presents displayed at, 96, 144–5; *map*, 107; European automata at, 126; Macartney visits Ho-shen at, 146; excellent brick work at, 264; brief history of, n11; Macartney's carriages found at, in 1860, n27

Yu-ho [Eu-ho], river, 164. *See also* Grand Canal

Yung-cheng [Yong-chin], Emperor (1723–1736), 238, n11, n94

Yunnan [Yu-nan], n34; population of, 246; revenue of, 249; gold found in, 291; *pe-tung* found in, 294

Zinc, in China, 293, 302, n149

Zapfal, John; leader of Macartney's band, 24, n22